02

FULLMETAL EDITION
FULLMETAL ALCHEMIST

by HIROMU ARAKAWA

02

FULLMETAL EDITION

FULLMETAL
ALCHEMIST

by HIROMU ARAKAWA

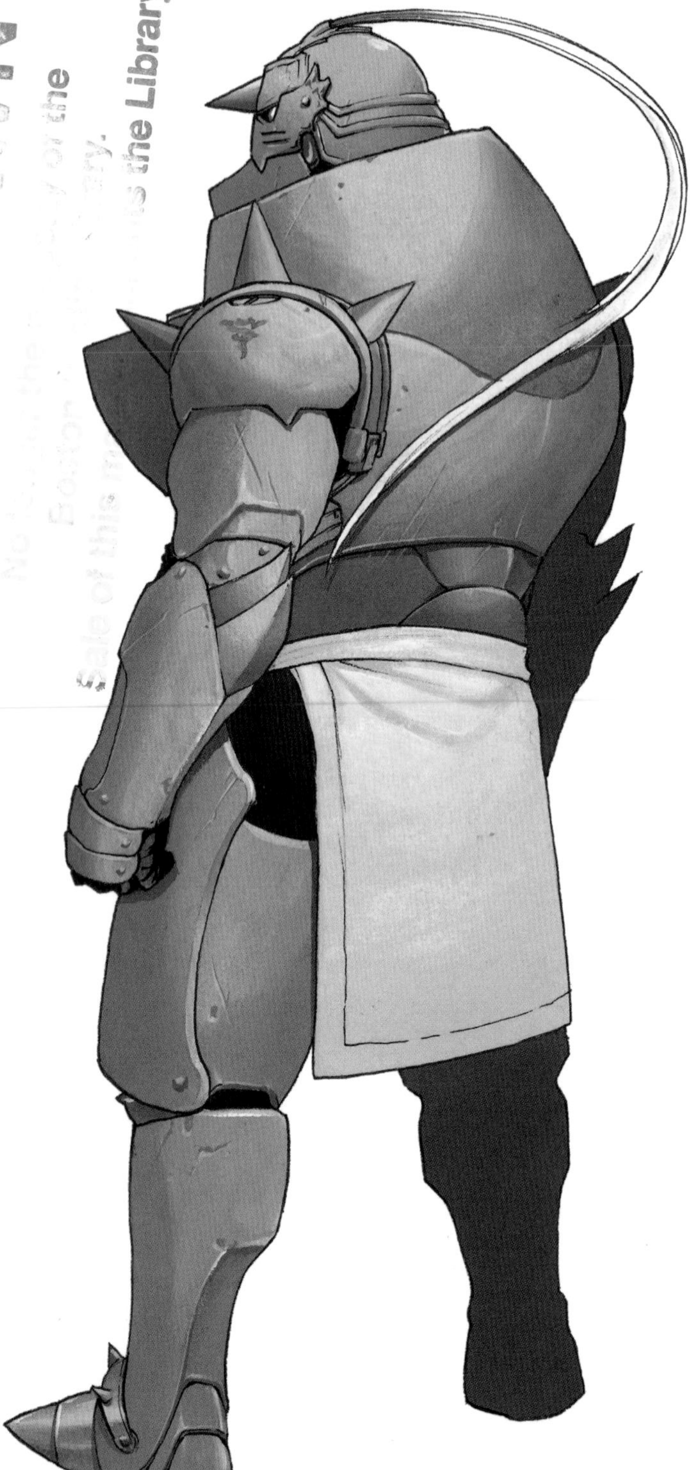

FULLMETAL EDITION

FULLMETAL ALCHEMIST

02

CONTENTS

CHAPTER 7 AFTER THE RAIN — 003

CHAPTER 8 THE ROAD OF HOPE — 043

CHAPTER 9 A HOME WITH A FAMILY WAITING — 089

CHAPTER 10 THE PHILOSOPHER'S STONE — 133

CHAPTER 11 THE TWO GUARDIANS — 171

CHAPTER 12 THE DEFINITION OF HUMAN — 215

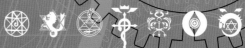

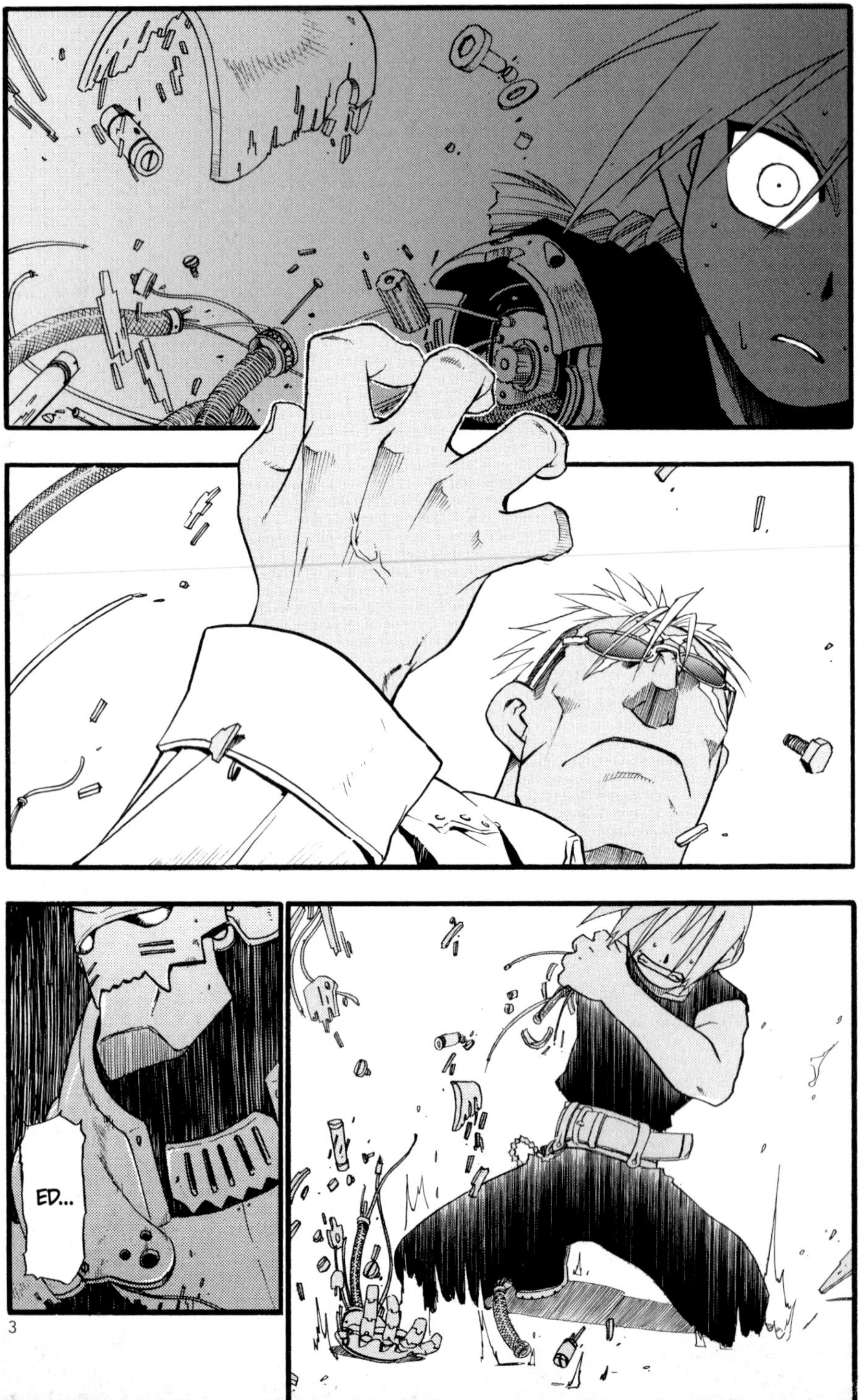
ED...

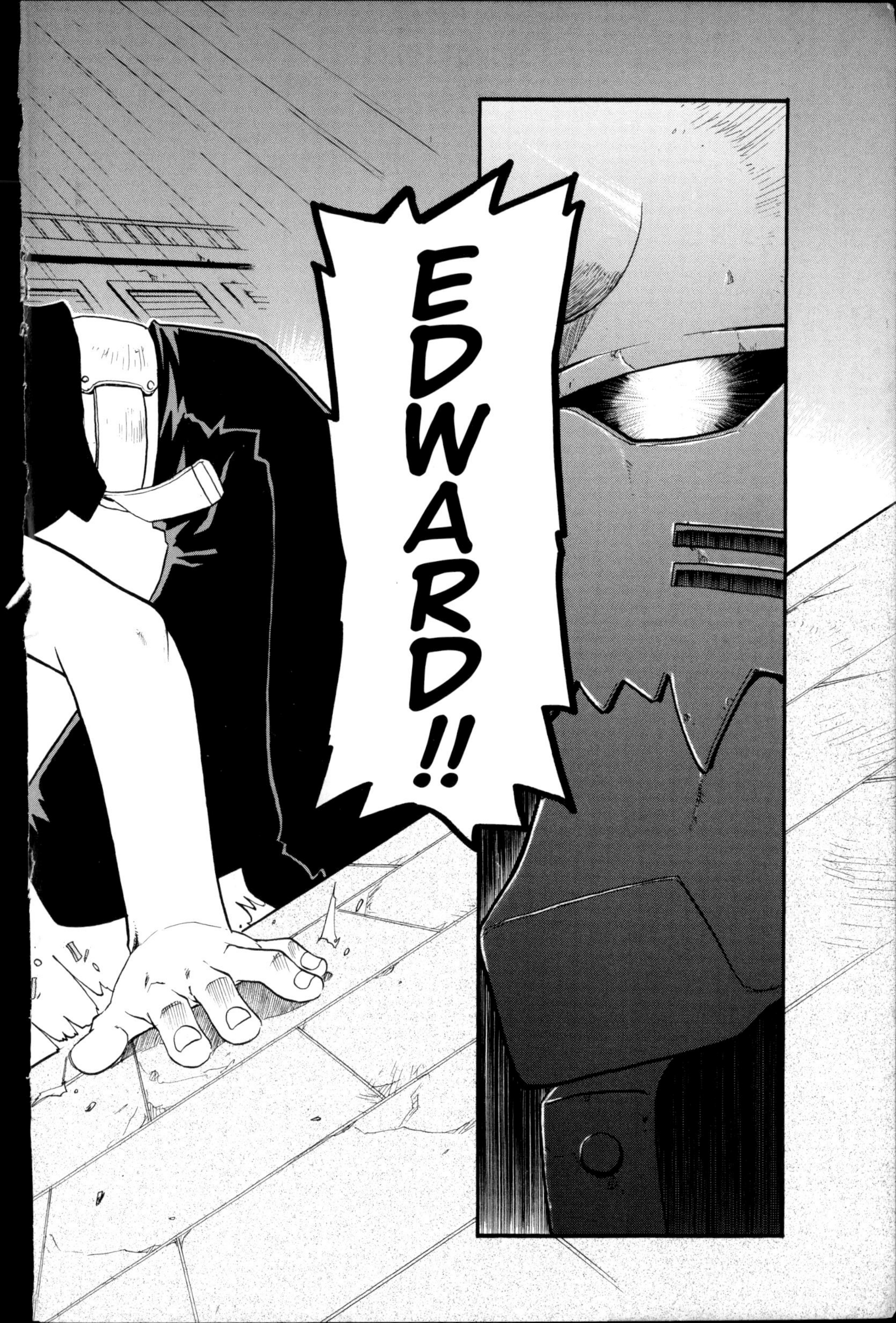
EDWARD!!

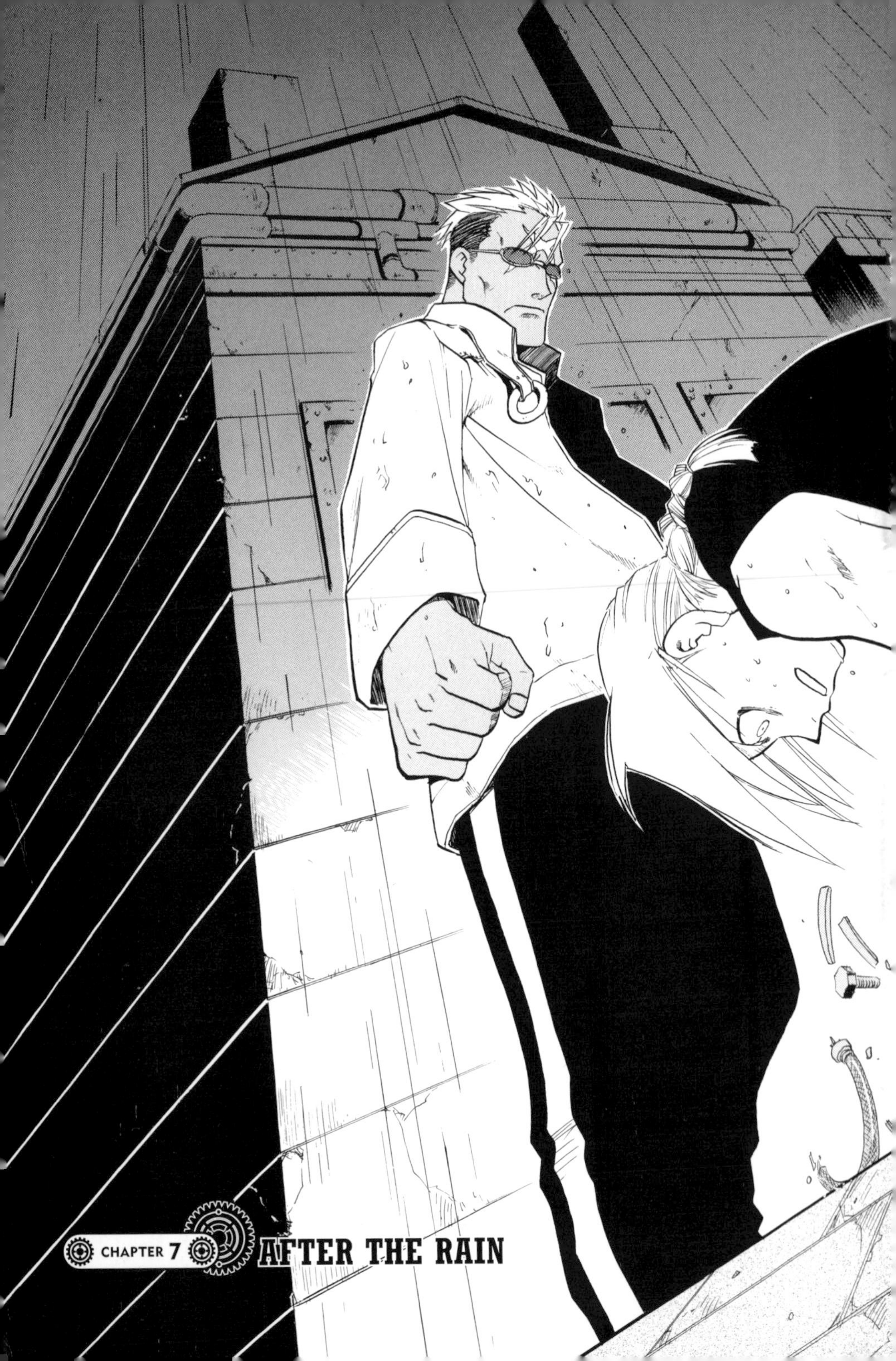

CHAPTER 7 AFTER THE RAIN

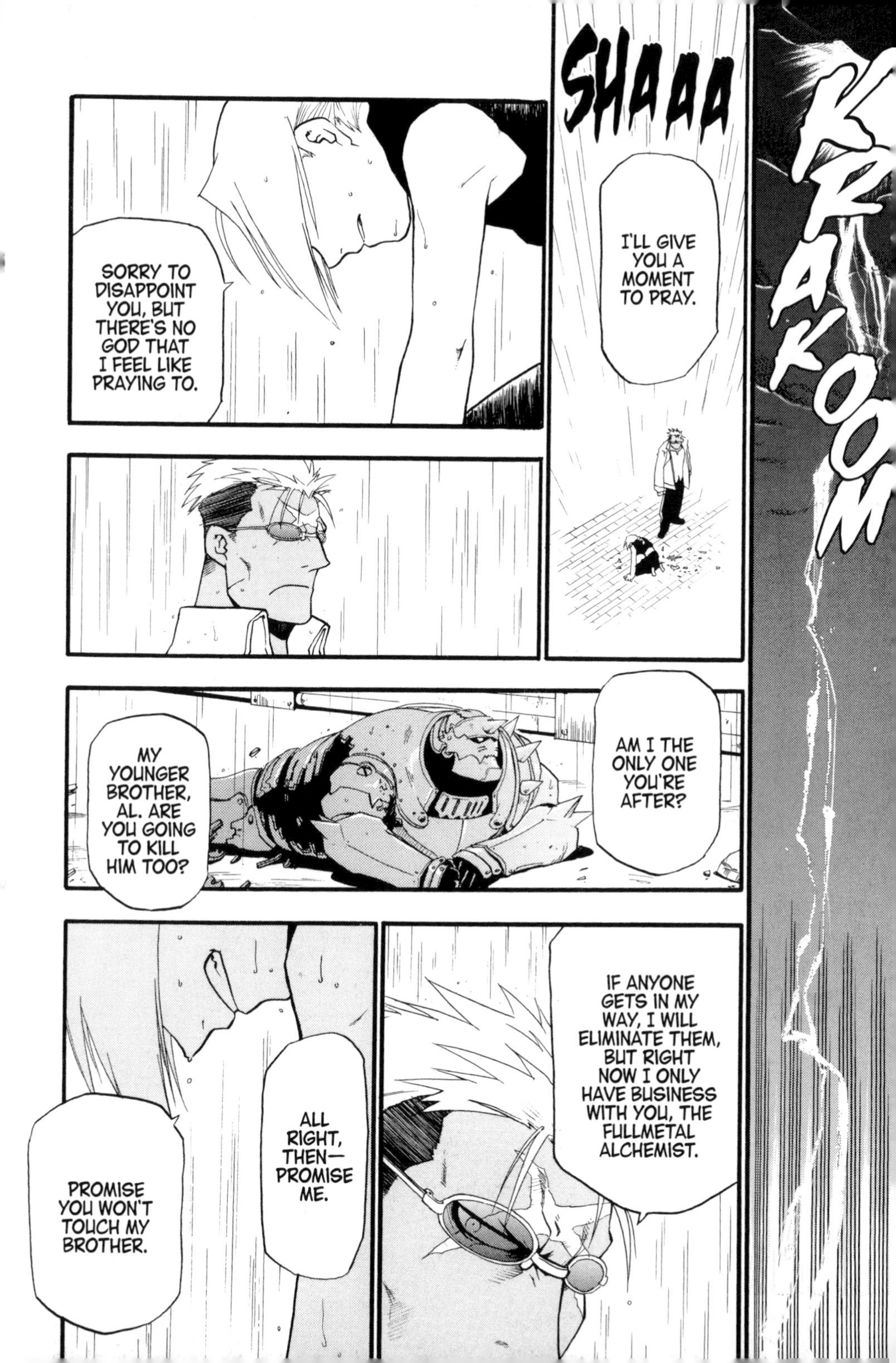

KRAKOOM
SHAAA
I'LL GIVE YOU A MOMENT TO PRAY.
SORRY TO DISAPPOINT YOU, BUT THERE'S NO GOD THAT I FEEL LIKE PRAYING TO.
AM I THE ONLY ONE YOU'RE AFTER?
MY YOUNGER BROTHER, AL. ARE YOU GOING TO KILL HIM TOO?
IF ANYONE GETS IN MY WAY, I WILL ELIMINATE THEM, BUT RIGHT NOW I ONLY HAVE BUSINESS WITH YOU, THE FULLMETAL ALCHEMIST.
ALL RIGHT, THEN—PROMISE ME.
PROMISE YOU WON'T TOUCH MY BROTHER.

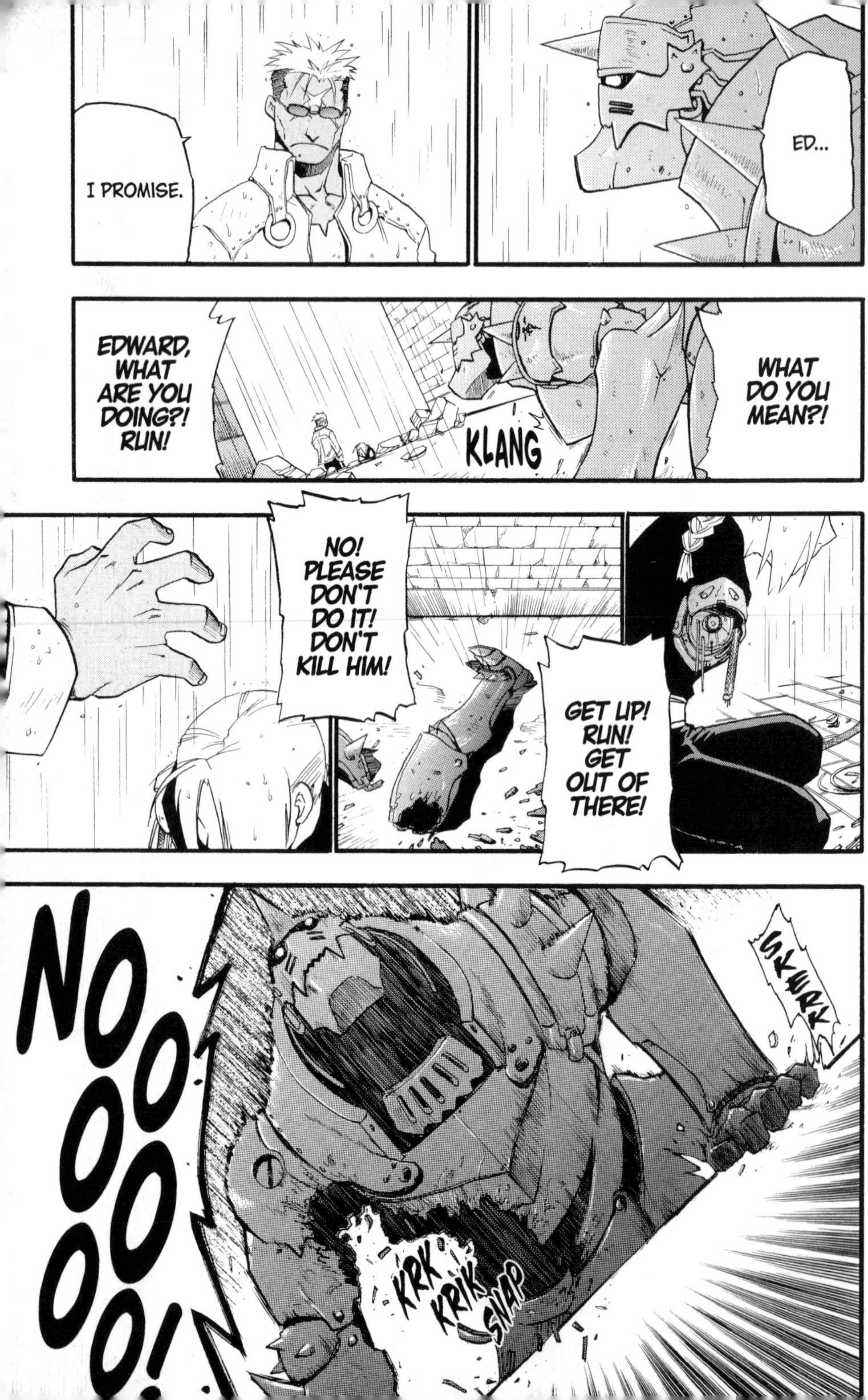
ED...
I PROMISE.
WHAT DO YOU MEAN?!
EDWARD, WHAT ARE YOU DOING?! RUN!
KLANG
GET UP! RUN! GET OUT OF THERE!
NO! PLEASE DON'T DO IT! DON'T KILL HIM!
SKERK
NOOOOOO!
KRK KRIK SNAP

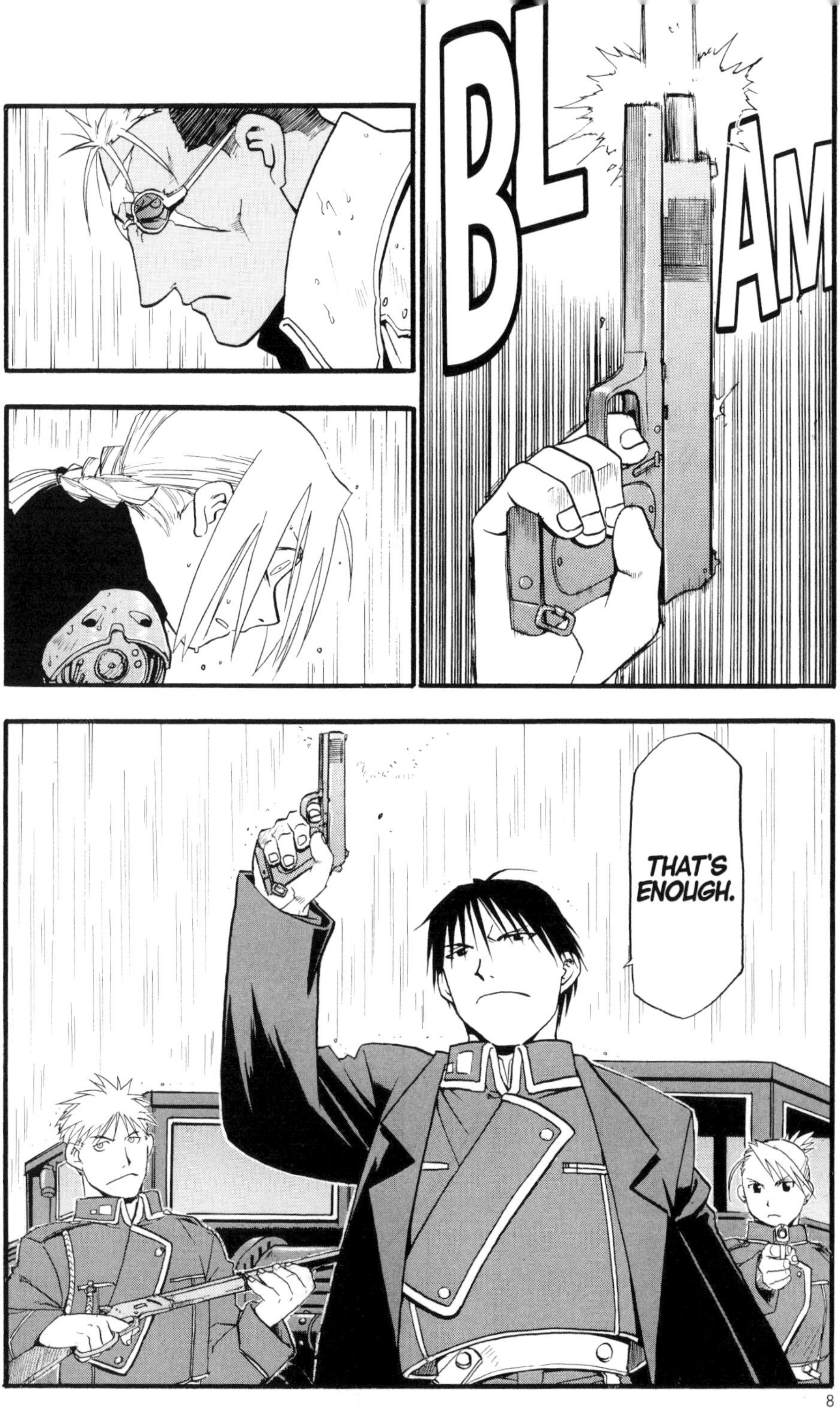
BLAM
THAT'S ENOUGH.

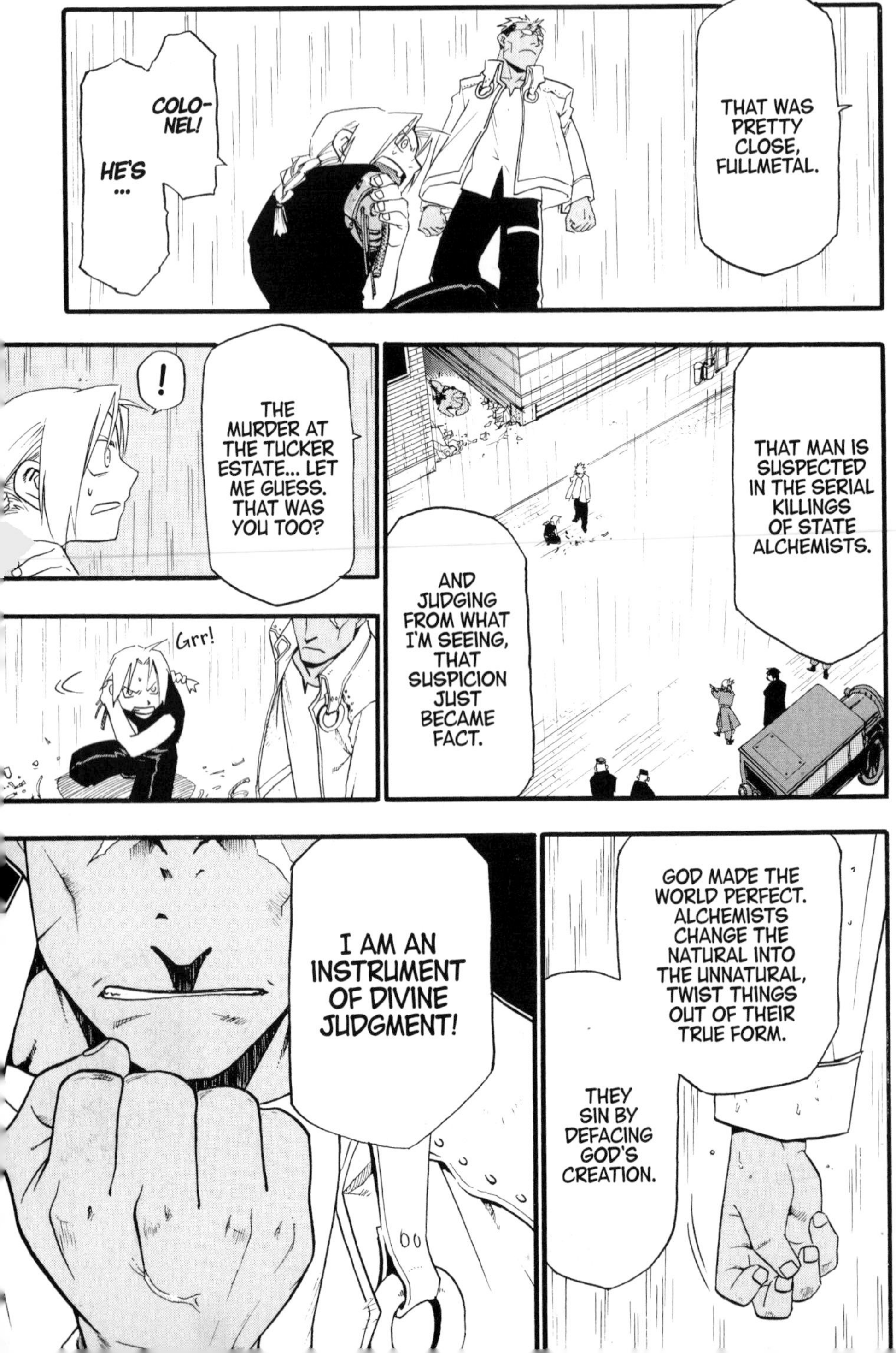
THAT WAS PRETTY CLOSE, FULLMETAL.
COLO-NEL!
HE'S ...
THAT MAN IS SUSPECTED IN THE SERIAL KILLINGS OF STATE ALCHEMISTS.
AND JUDGING FROM WHAT I'M SEEING, THAT SUSPICION JUST BECAME FACT.
THE MURDER AT THE TUCKER ESTATE... LET ME GUESS. THAT WAS YOU TOO?
!
Grr!
GOD MADE THE WORLD PERFECT. ALCHEMISTS CHANGE THE NATURAL INTO THE UNNATURAL, TWIST THINGS OUT OF THEIR TRUE FORM.
THEY SIN BY DEFACING GOD'S CREATION.
I AM AN INSTRUMENT OF DIVINE JUDGMENT!

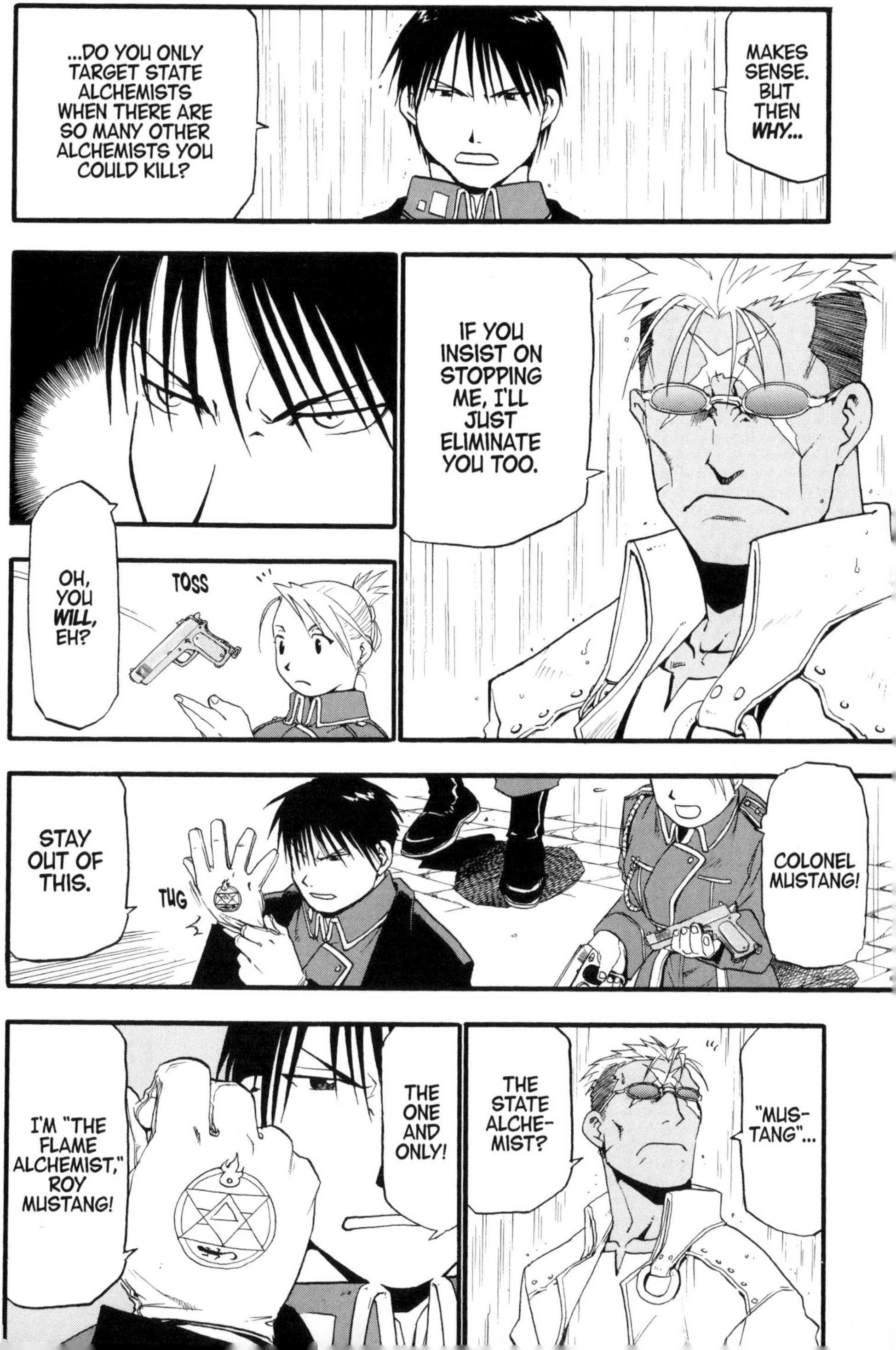
MAKES SENSE. BUT THEN WHY...
...DO YOU ONLY TARGET STATE ALCHEMISTS WHEN THERE ARE SO MANY OTHER ALCHEMISTS YOU COULD KILL?
IF YOU INSIST ON STOPPING ME, I'LL JUST ELIMINATE YOU TOO.
OH, YOU WILL, EH?
TOSS
COLONEL MUSTANG!
TUG
STAY OUT OF THIS.
"MUS-TANG"...
THE STATE ALCHE-MIST?
THE ONE AND ONLY!
I'M "THE FLAME ALCHEMIST," ROY MUSTANG!

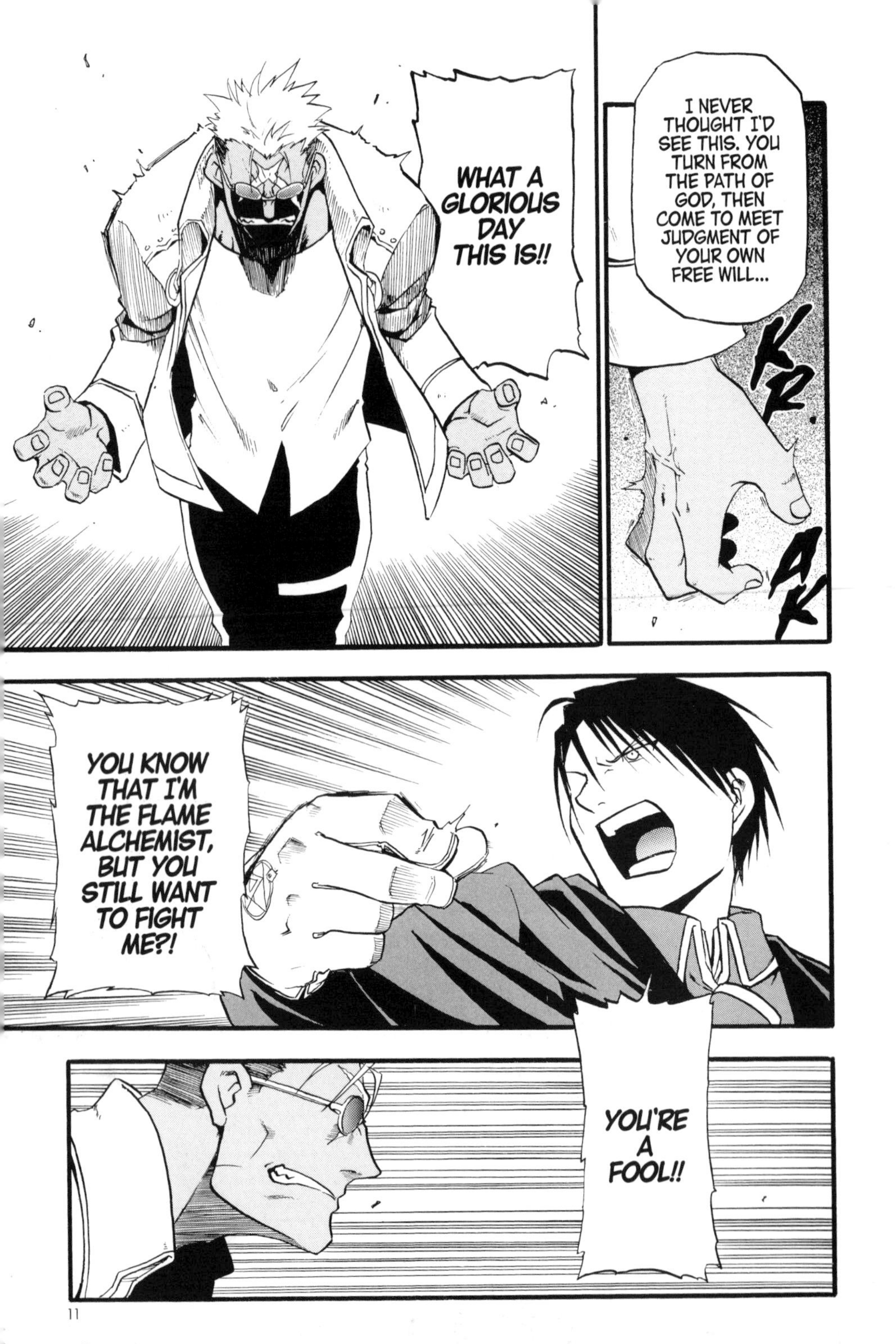
I NEVER THOUGHT I'D SEE THIS. YOU TURN FROM THE PATH OF GOD, THEN COME TO MEET JUDGMENT OF YOUR OWN FREE WILL...
KRAK
WHAT A GLORIOUS DAY THIS IS!!
YOU KNOW THAT I'M THE FLAME ALCHEMIST, BUT YOU STILL WANT TO FIGHT ME?!
YOU'RE A FOOL!!

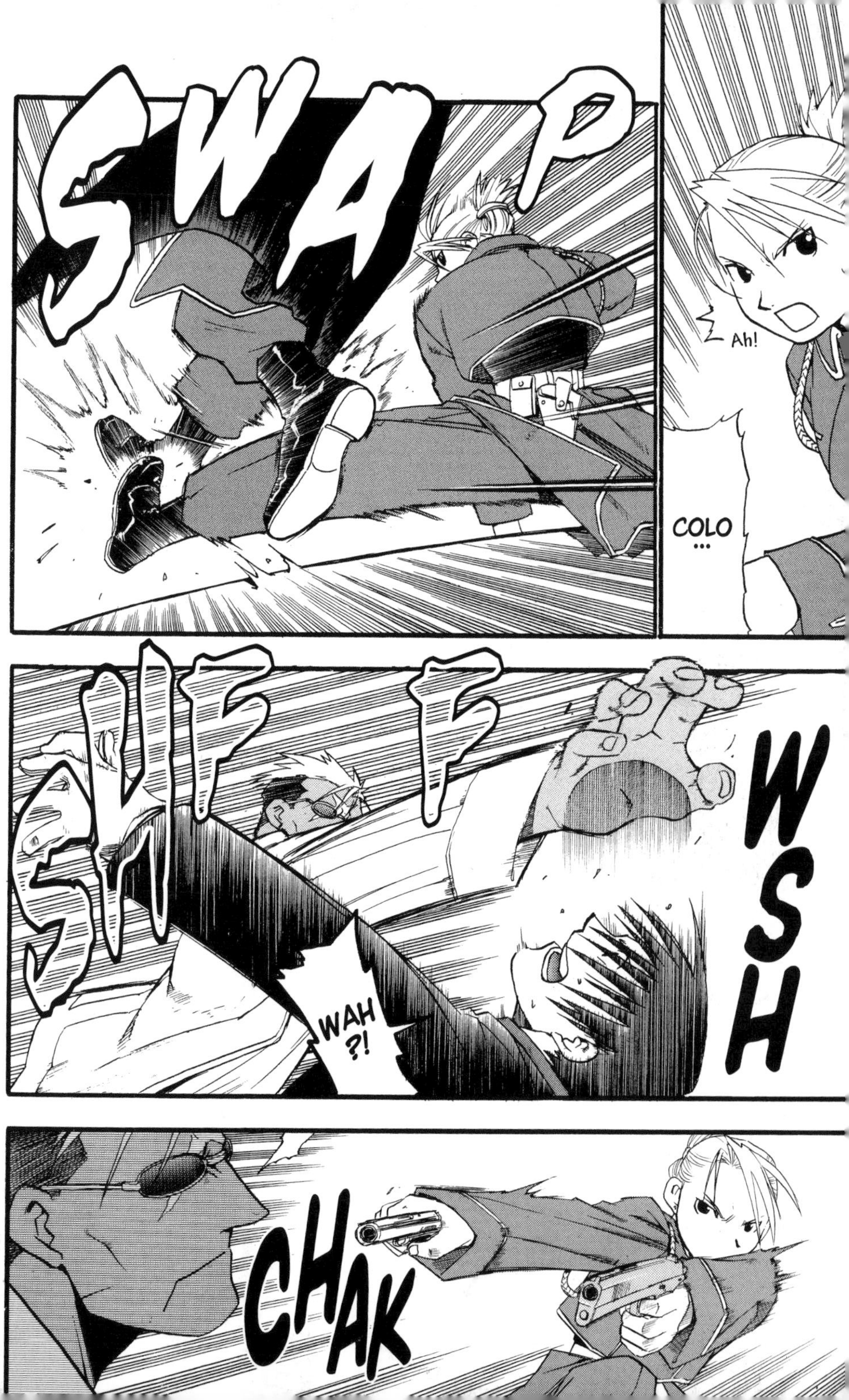
Ah!
COLO...
SWAP
WSH
WAH?!
SHFF
CHAK

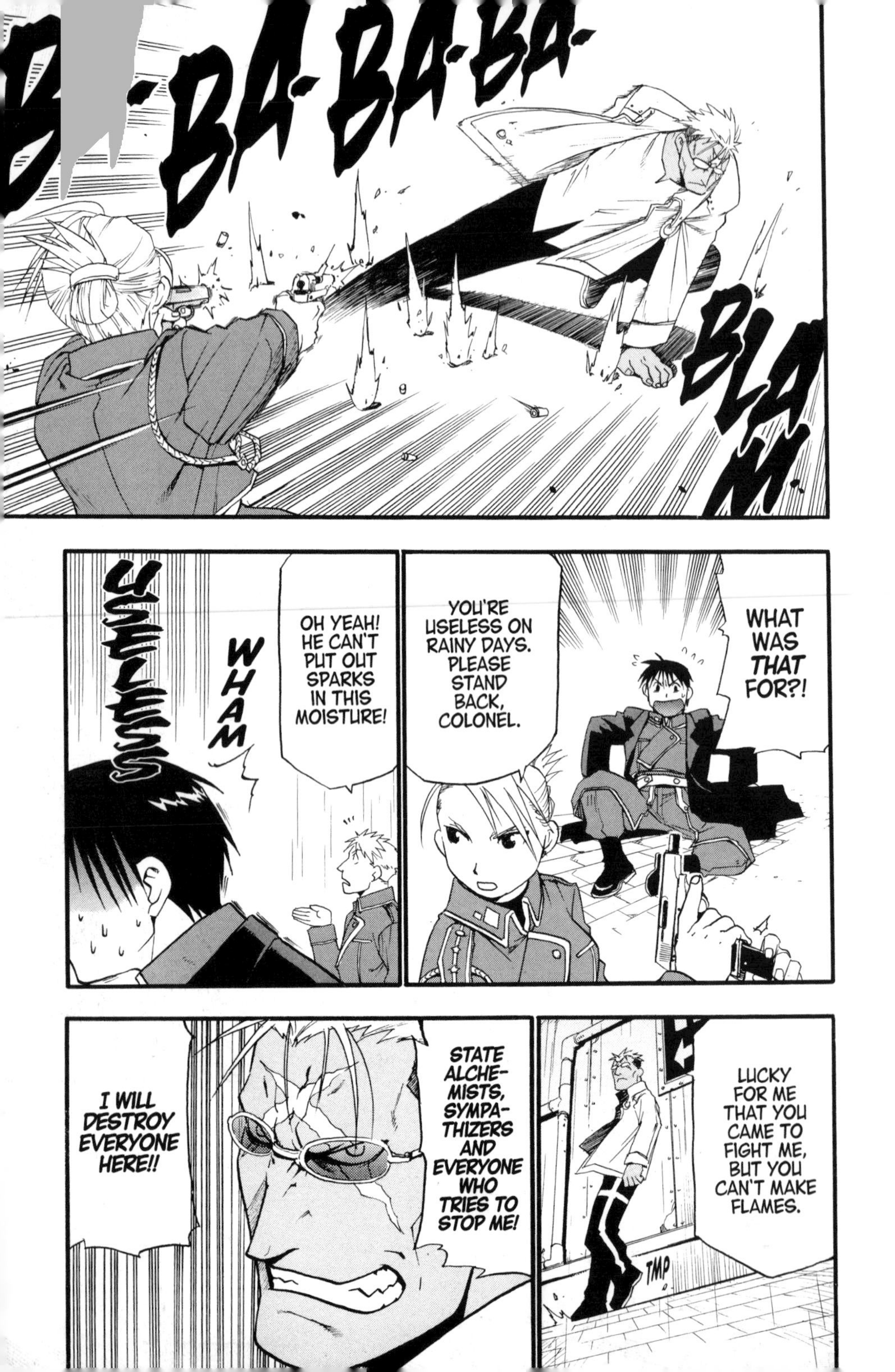
BA-BA-BA-BA-
BLAM...
WHAT WAS THAT FOR?!
YOU'RE USELESS ON RAINY DAYS. PLEASE STAND BACK, COLONEL.
OH YEAH! HE CAN'T PUT OUT SPARKS IN THIS MOISTURE!
WHAM
USELESS
LUCKY FOR ME THAT YOU CAME TO FIGHT ME, BUT YOU CAN'T MAKE FLAMES.
TMP
STATE ALCHEMISTS, SYMPATHIZERS AND EVERYONE WHO TRIES TO STOP ME!
I WILL DESTROY EVERYONE HERE!!

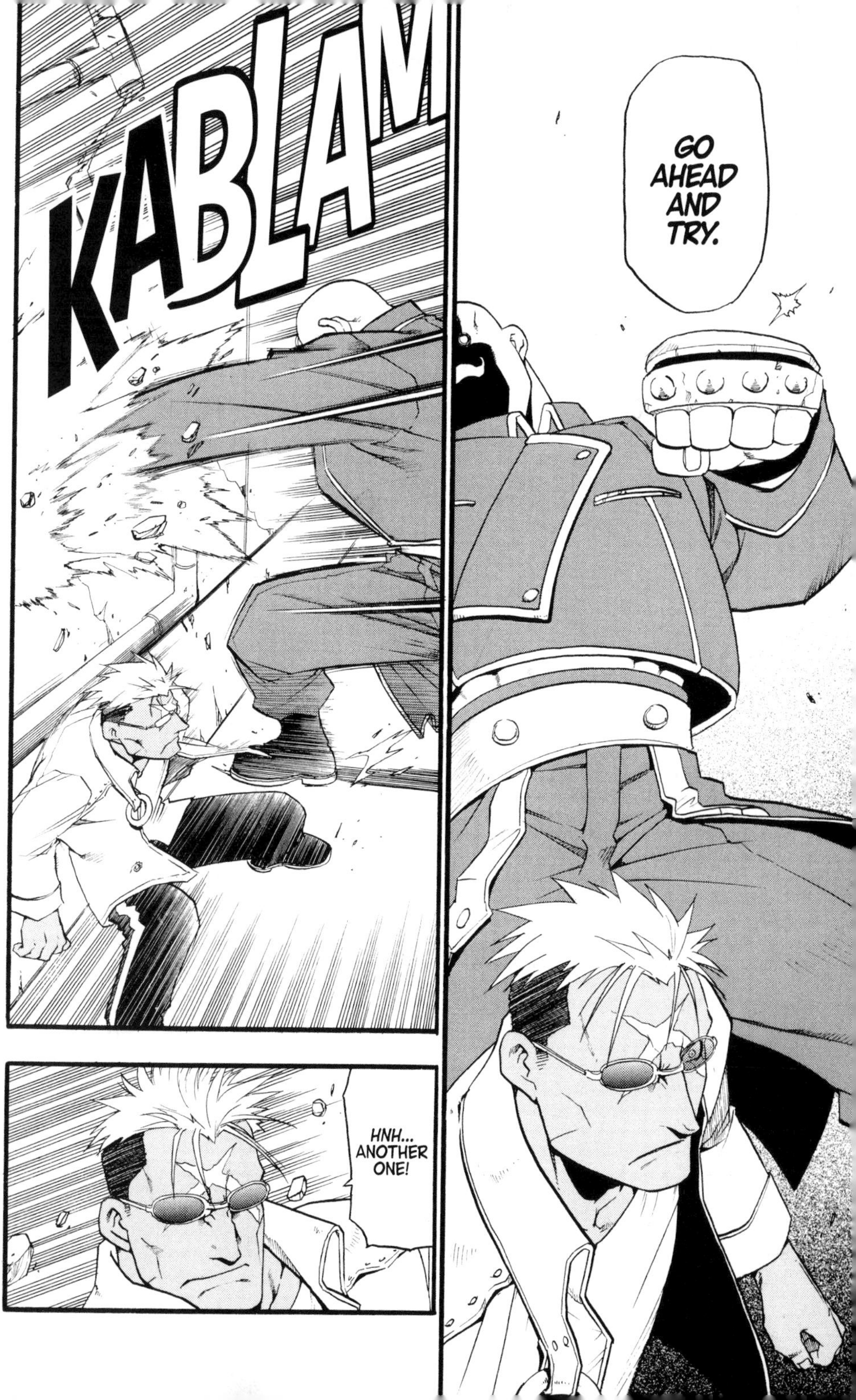
GO AHEAD AND TRY.
KABLAM
HNH... ANOTHER ONE!

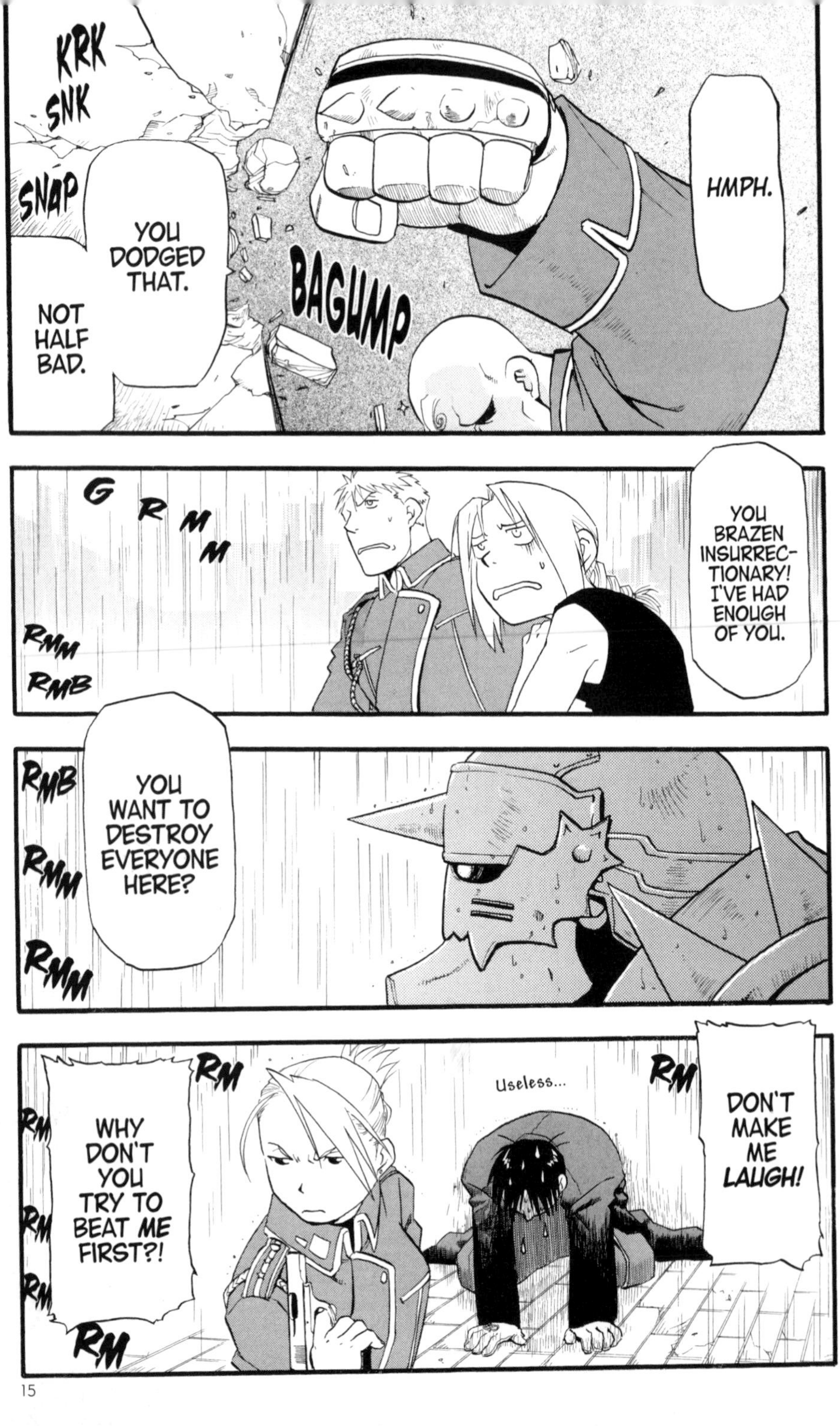
KRK
SNK
SNAP
HMPH.
BAGUMP
YOU DODGED THAT.
NOT HALF BAD.
YOU BRAZEN INSURRECTIONARY! I'VE HAD ENOUGH OF YOU.
G R M M
RMM
RMB
YOU WANT TO DESTROY EVERYONE HERE?
RMB
RMM
RMM
DON'T MAKE ME LAUGH!
Useless...
WHY DON'T YOU TRY TO BEAT ME FIRST?!
RM
RM
RM
RM
RM
RM

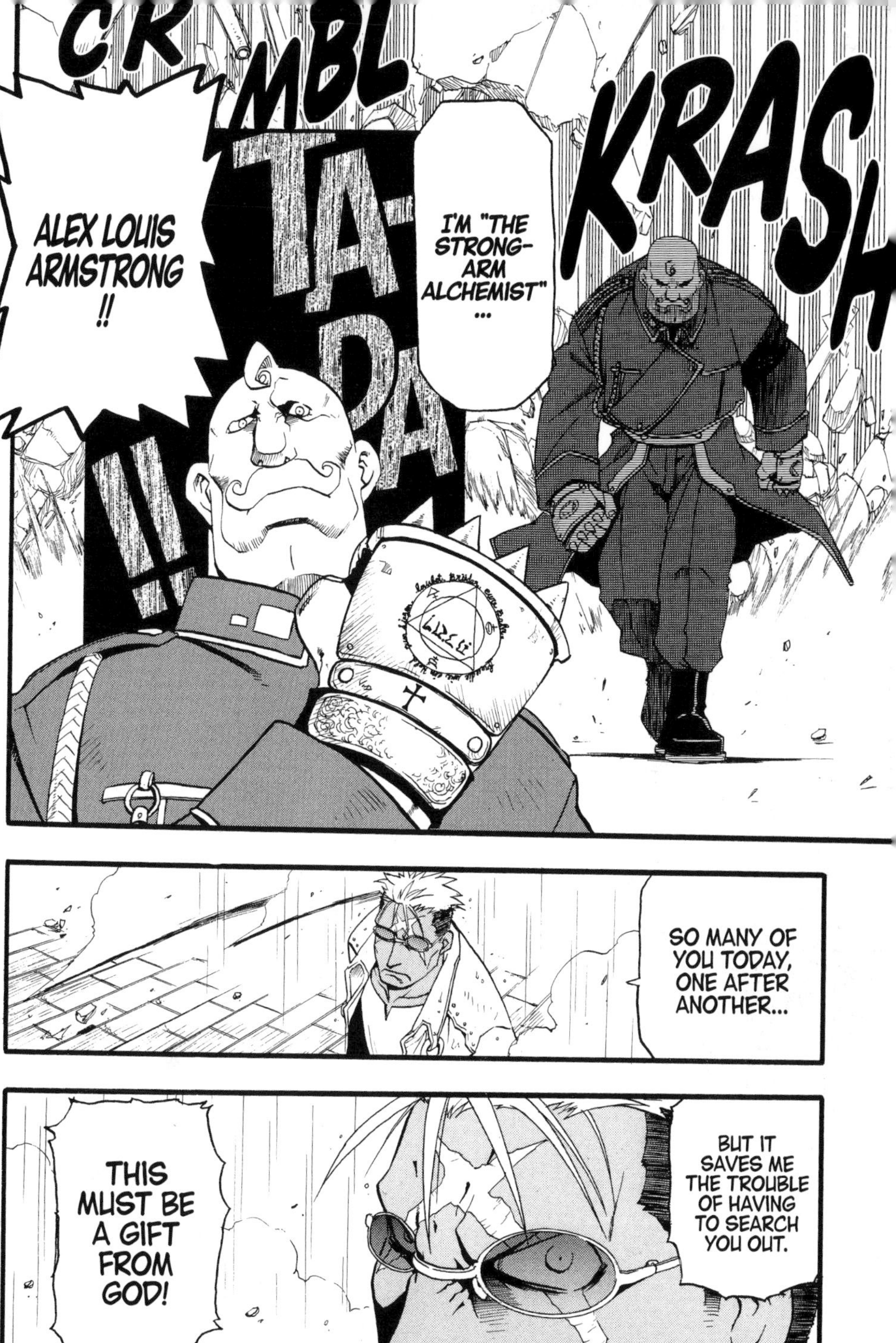
KRASH
I'M "THE STRONG-ARM ALCHEMIST" ...
ALEX LOUIS ARMSTRONG !!
TA-DA !!
CR MBL
SO MANY OF YOU TODAY, ONE AFTER ANOTHER...
BUT IT SAVES ME THE TROUBLE OF HAVING TO SEARCH YOU OUT.
THIS MUST BE A GIFT FROM GOD!

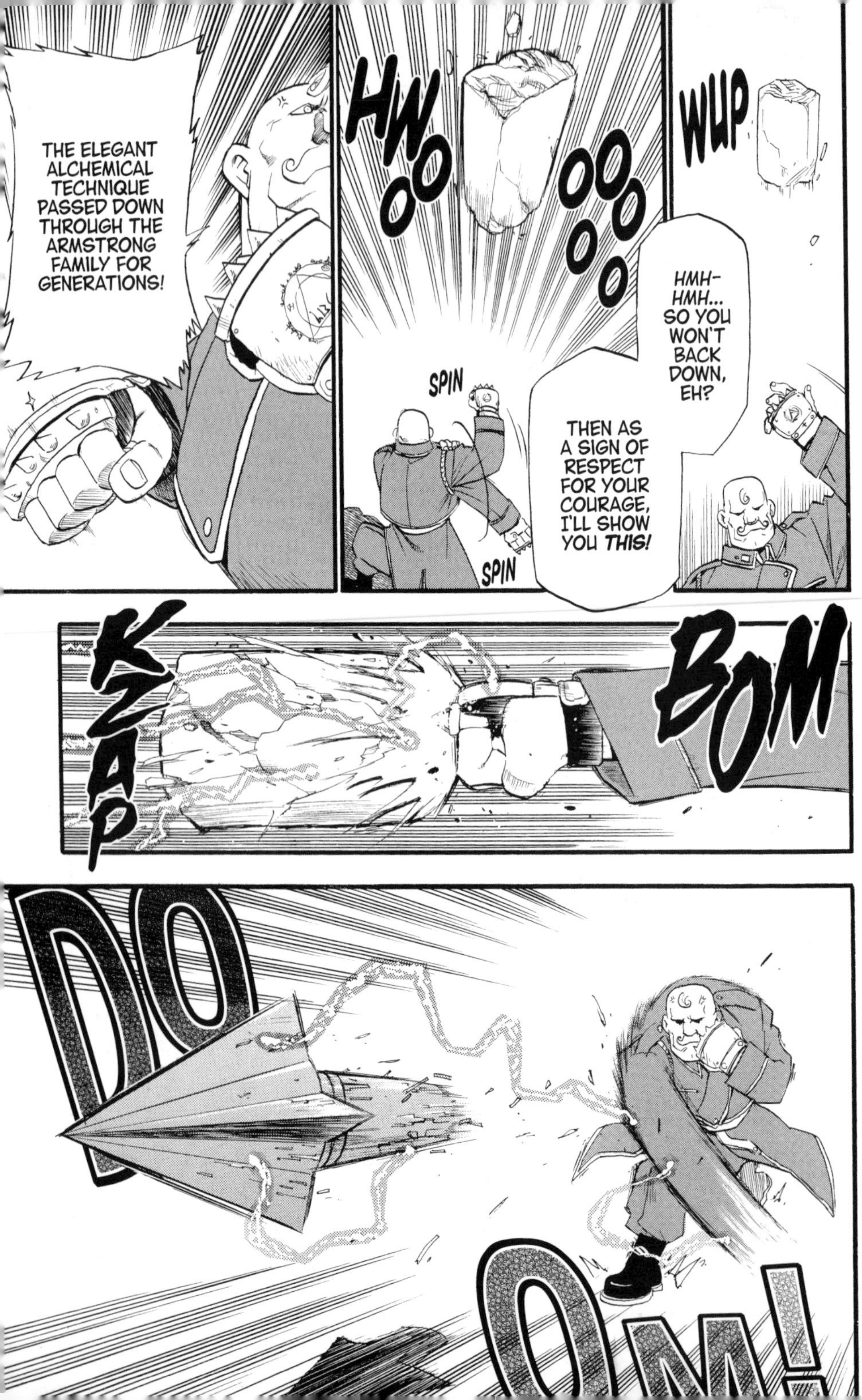
WUP
HMH-HMH... SO YOU WON'T BACK DOWN, EH?
HWOOOOOOOOOOO
SPIN
SPIN
THEN AS A SIGN OF RESPECT FOR YOUR COURAGE, I'LL SHOW YOU **THIS!**
THE ELEGANT ALCHEMICAL TECHNIQUE PASSED DOWN THROUGH THE ARMSTRONG FAMILY FOR GENERATIONS!
BOM
KZAP
DOOM!

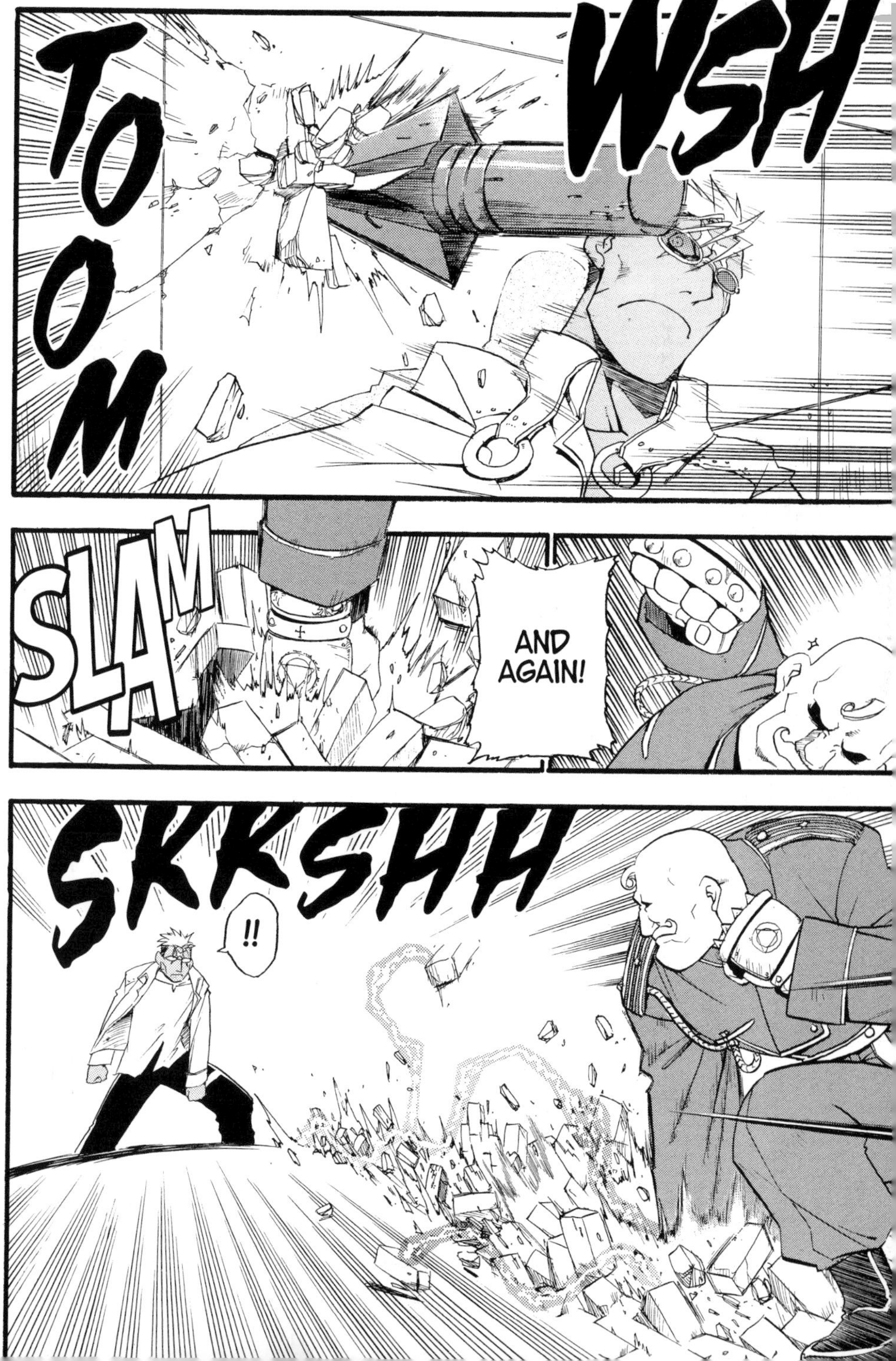
WSH
TOOM
AND AGAIN!
SLAM
SKKSHH
!!

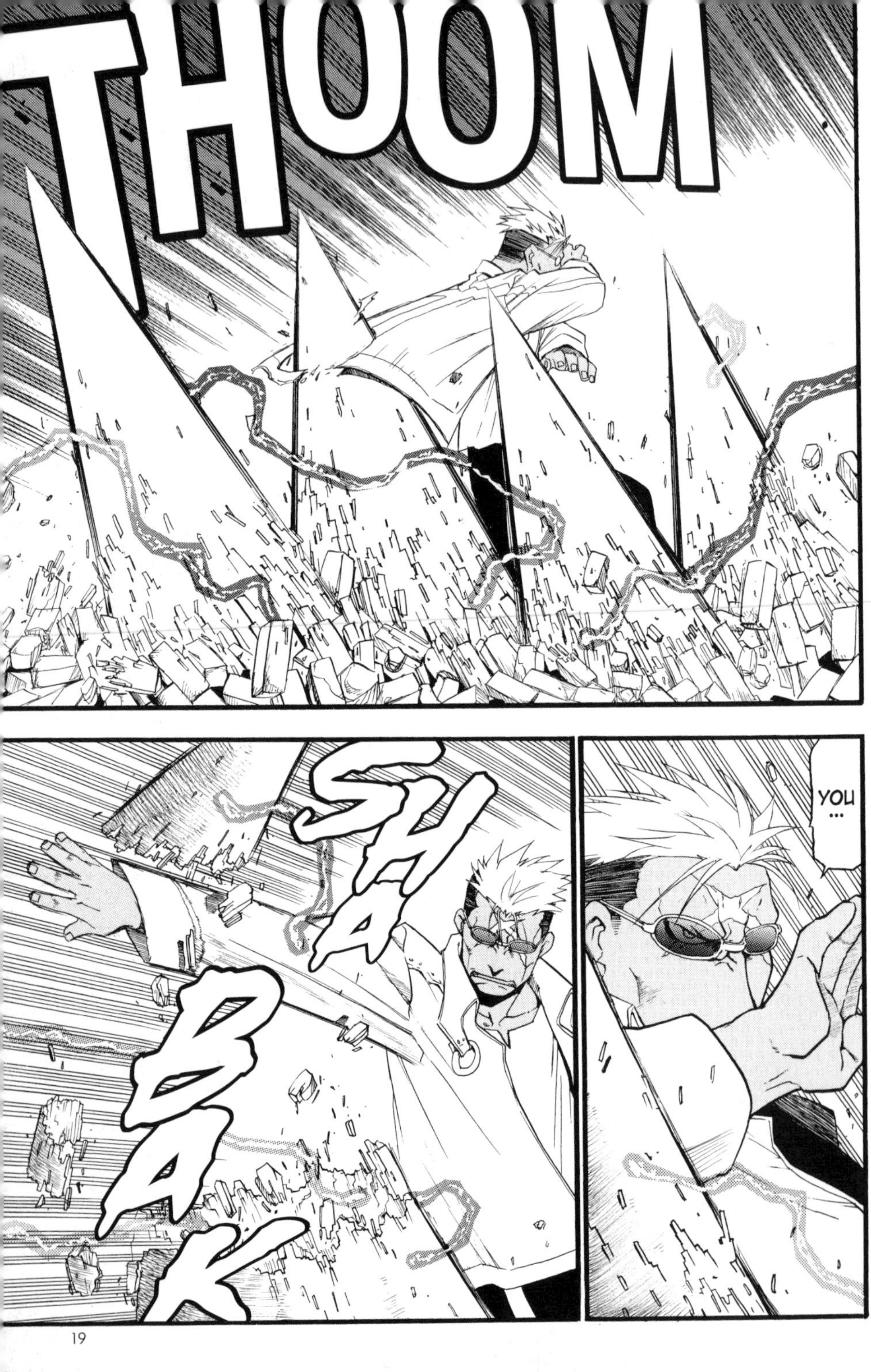
THOOM
YOU ...
SHA
BAK

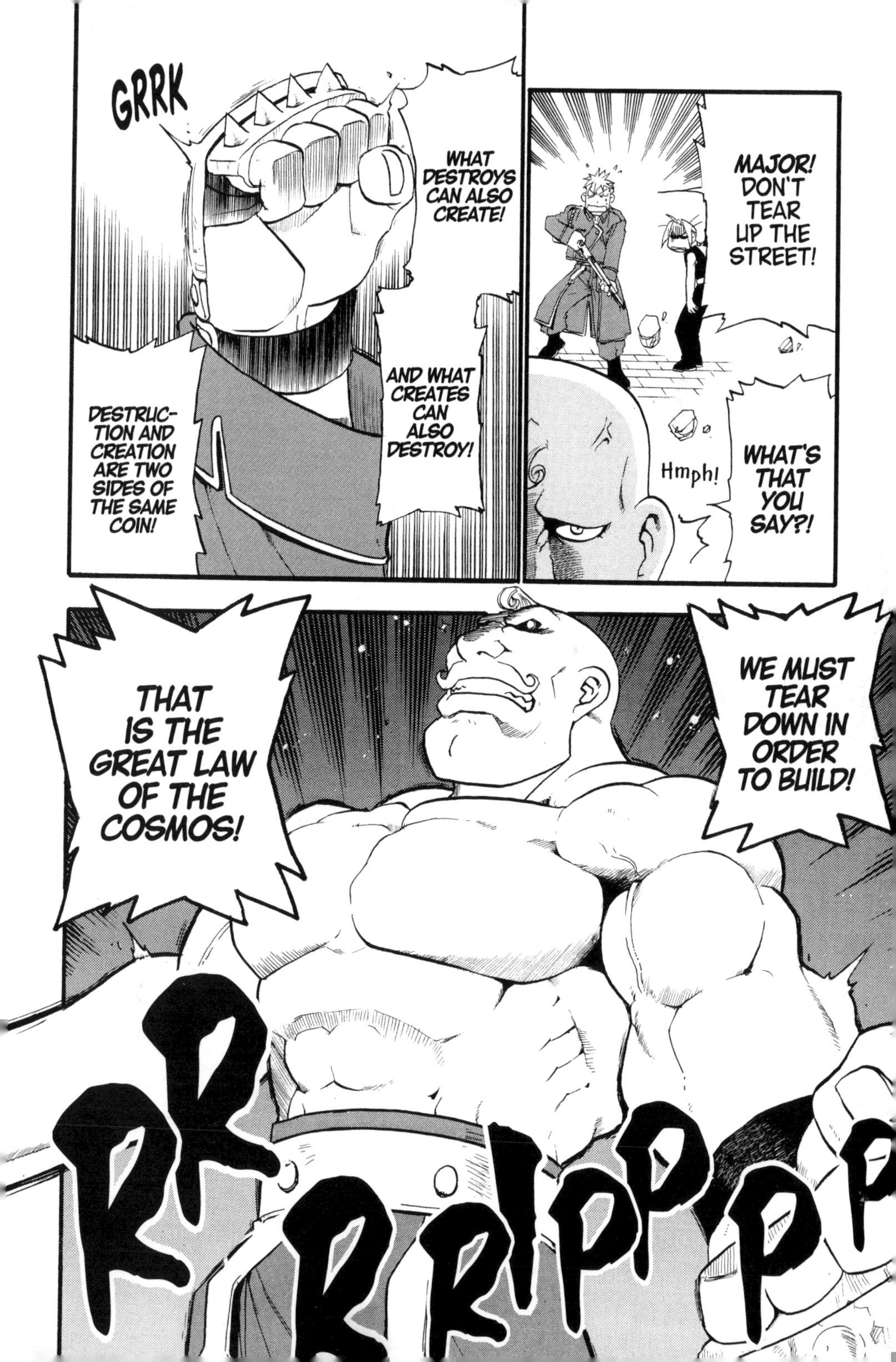
MAJOR! DON'T TEAR UP THE STREET!
WHAT'S THAT YOU SAY?!
Hmph!
GRRK
WHAT DESTROYS CAN ALSO CREATE!
AND WHAT CREATES CAN ALSO DESTROY!
DESTRUCTION AND CREATION ARE TWO SIDES OF THE SAME COIN!
WE MUST TEAR DOWN IN ORDER TO BUILD!
THAT IS THE GREAT LAW OF THE COSMOS!
RRRIPPPPP

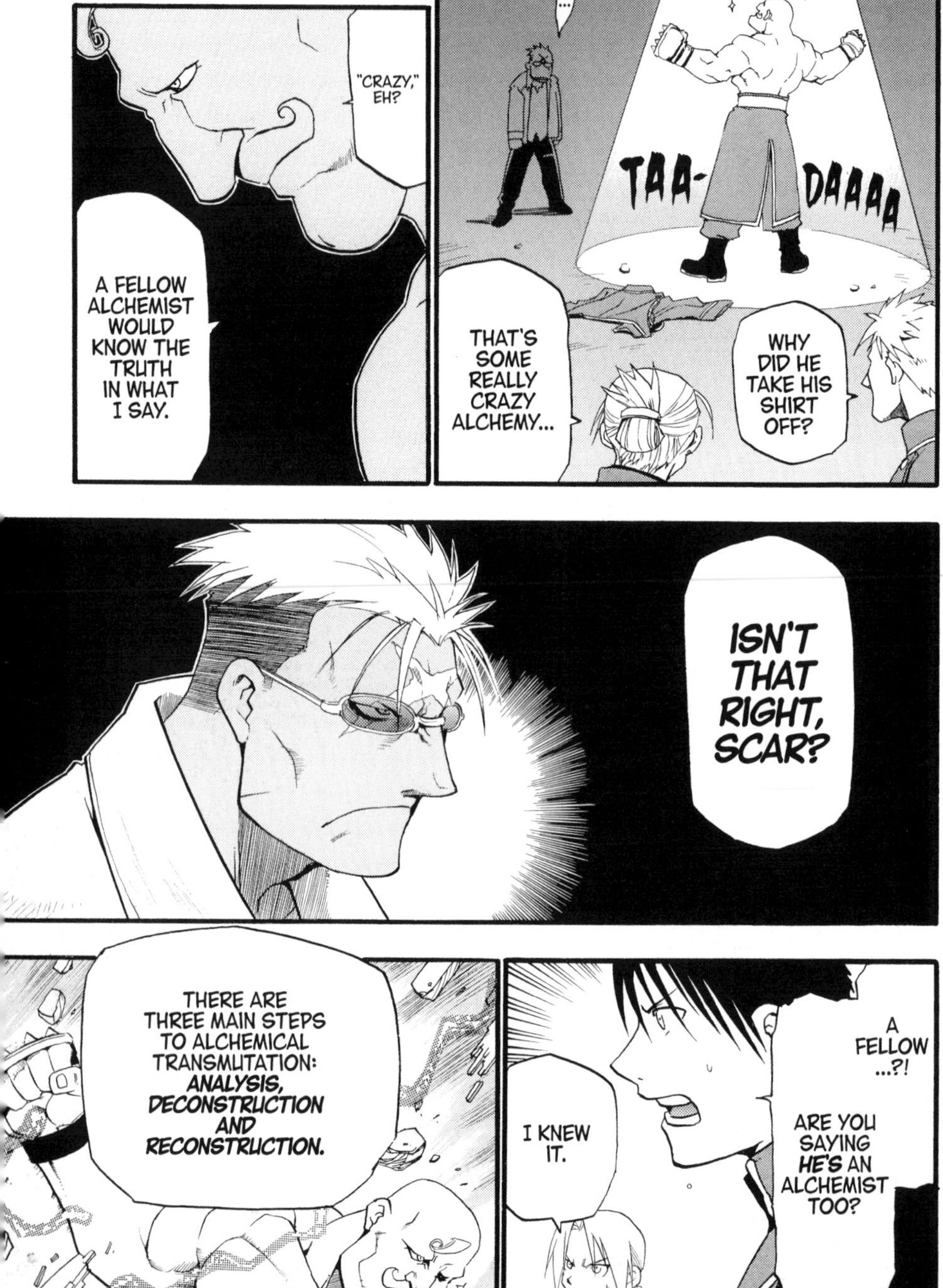
...
TAA-DAAAA
WHY DID HE TAKE HIS SHIRT OFF?
THAT'S SOME REALLY CRAZY ALCHEMY...
"CRAZY," EH?
A FELLOW ALCHEMIST WOULD KNOW THE TRUTH IN WHAT I SAY.
ISN'T THAT RIGHT, SCAR?
A FELLOW ...?!
ARE YOU SAYING HE'S AN ALCHEMIST TOO?
I KNEW IT.
THERE ARE THREE MAIN STEPS TO ALCHEMICAL TRANSMUTATION: ANALYSIS, DECONSTRUCTION AND RECONSTRUCTION.

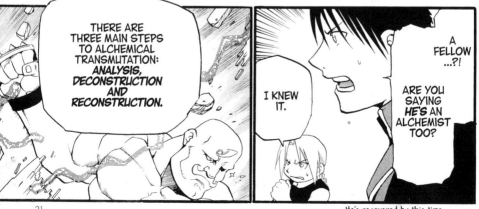

He's recovered by this time...

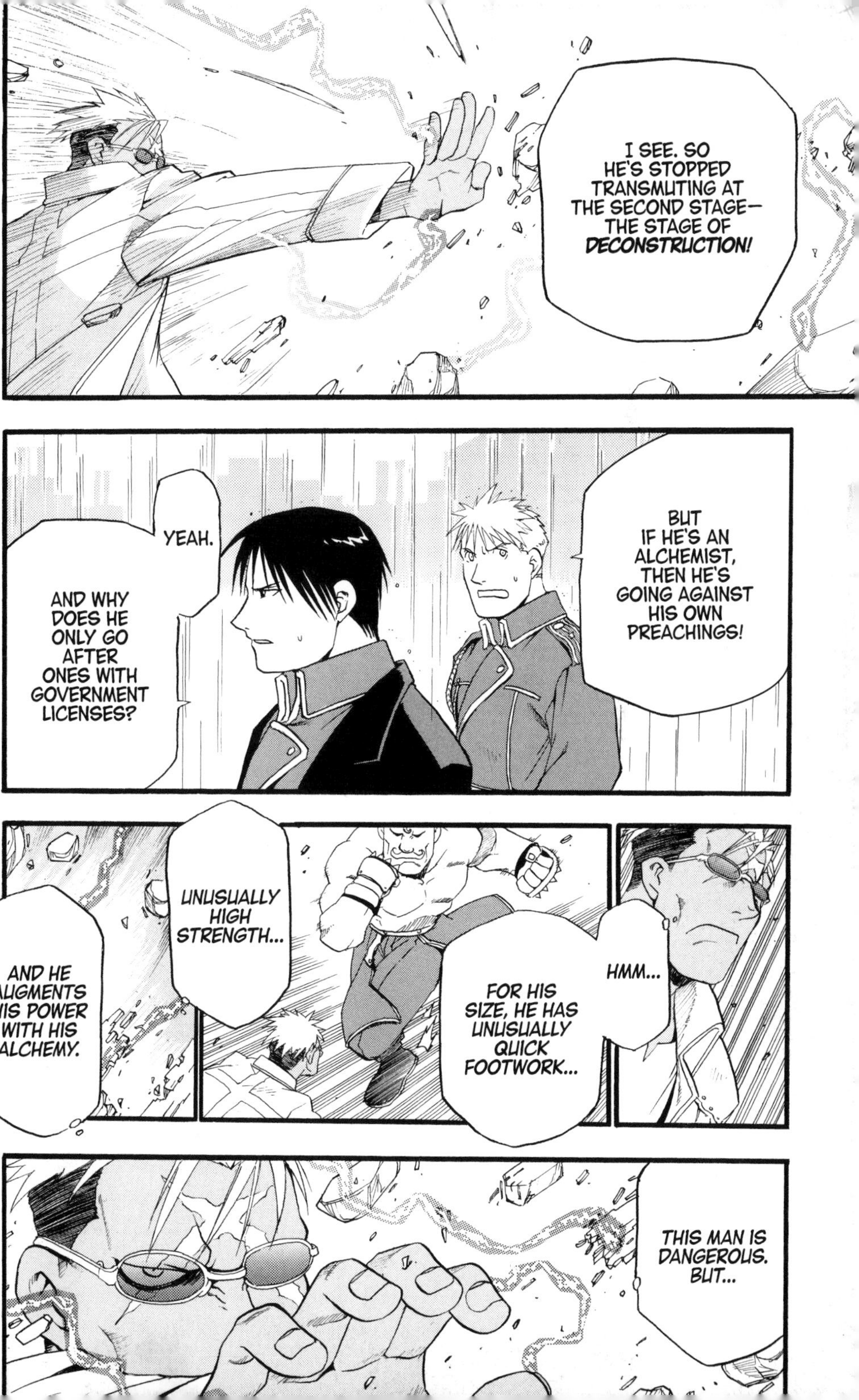
I SEE. SO HE'S STOPPED TRANSMUTING AT THE SECOND STAGE—THE STAGE OF **DECONSTRUCTION!**
BUT IF HE'S AN ALCHEMIST, THEN HE'S GOING AGAINST HIS OWN PREACHINGS!
YEAH.
AND WHY DOES HE ONLY GO AFTER ONES WITH GOVERNMENT LICENSES?
HMM...
FOR HIS SIZE, HE HAS UNUSUALLY QUICK FOOTWORK...
UNUSUALLY HIGH STRENGTH...
AND HE AUGMENTS HIS POWER WITH HIS ALCHEMY.
THIS MAN IS DANGEROUS. BUT...

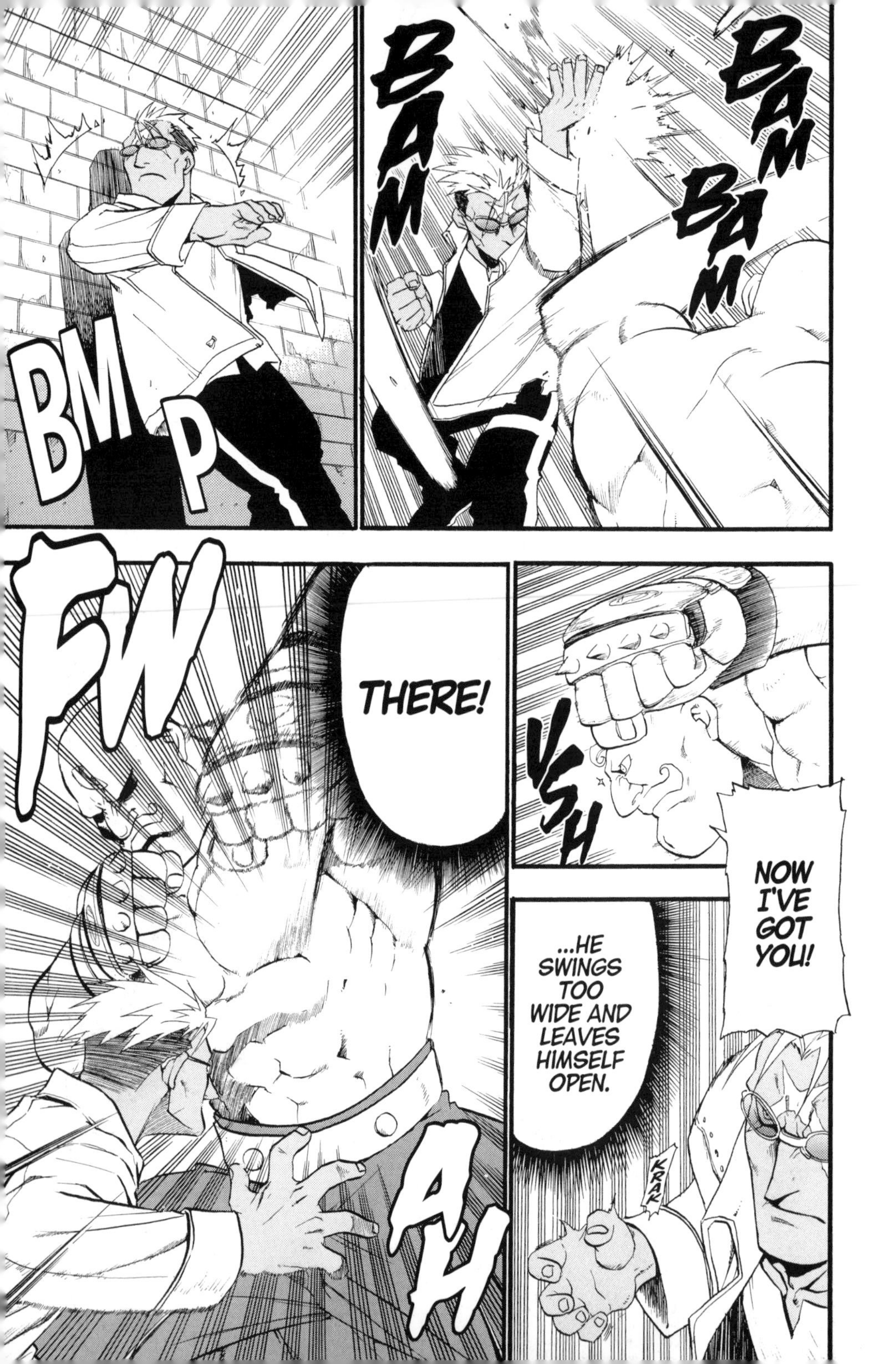
BAM
BAM
BAM
BMP
VSH
NOW I'VE GOT YOU!
...HE SWINGS TOO WIDE AND LEAVES HIMSELF OPEN.
KRAK
FW
THERE!
AH

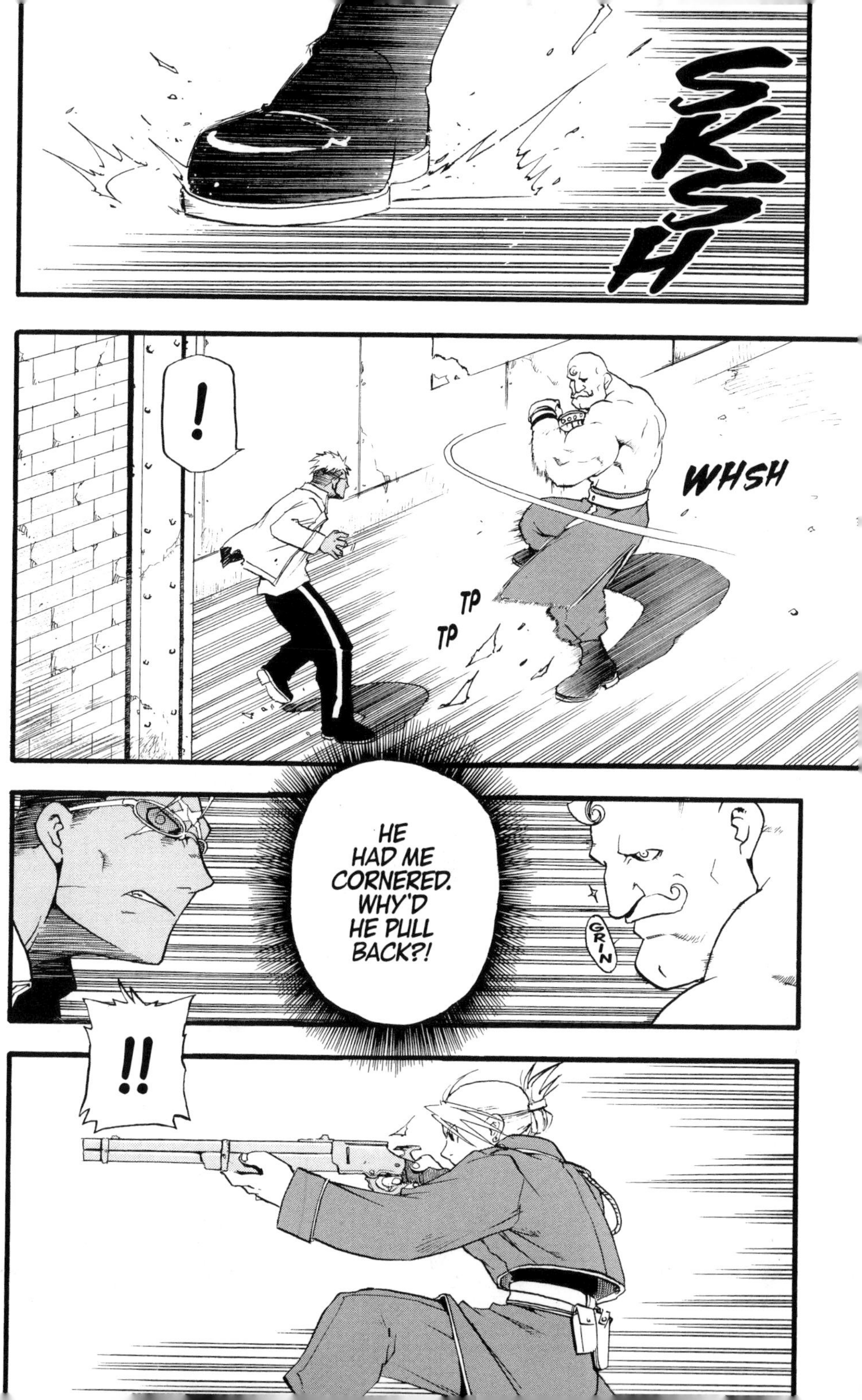
SKSH
WHSH
TP TP
!
GRIN
HE HAD ME CORNERED. WHY'D HE PULL BACK?!
!!

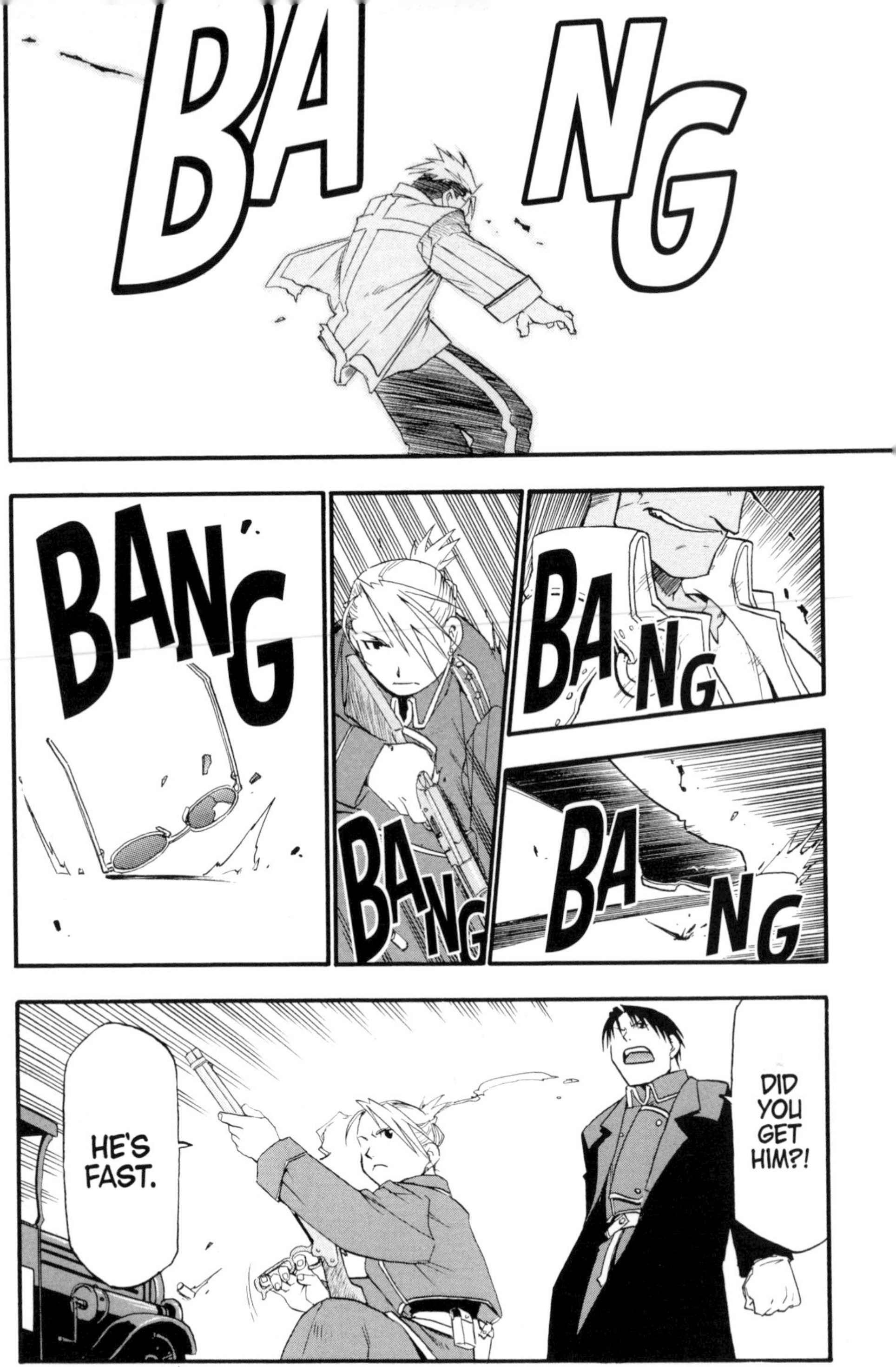
BANG
BANG
BANG
BANG
BANG
DID YOU GET HIM?!
HE'S FAST.

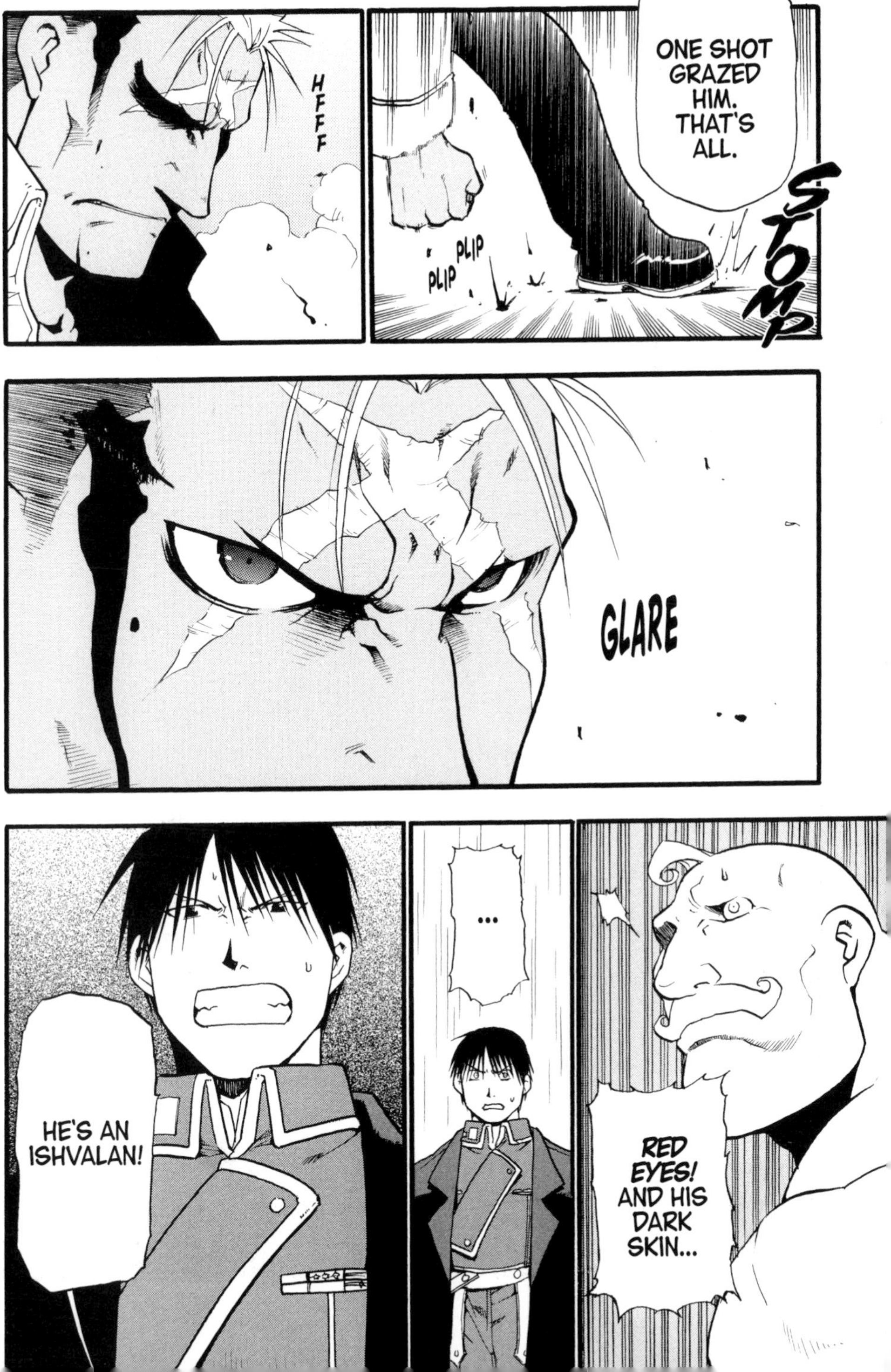
ONE SHOT GRAZED HIM. THAT'S ALL.
STOMP
PLIP PLIP
HFFF
GLARE
RED EYES! AND HIS DARK SKIN...
...
HE'S AN ISHVALAN!

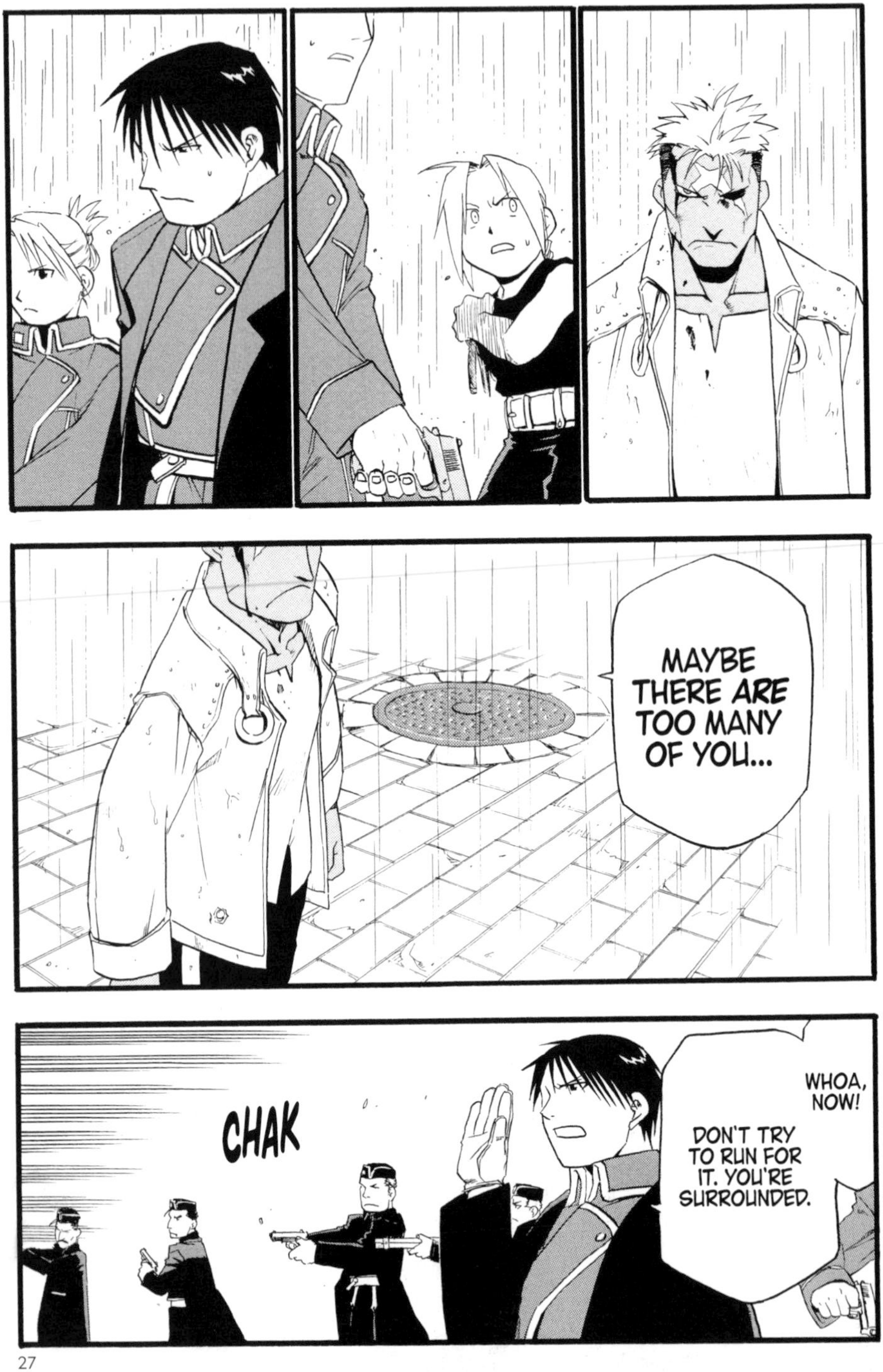
MAYBE THERE ARE TOO MANY OF YOU...
WHOA, NOW!
DON'T TRY TO RUN FOR IT. YOU'RE SURROUNDED.
CHAK

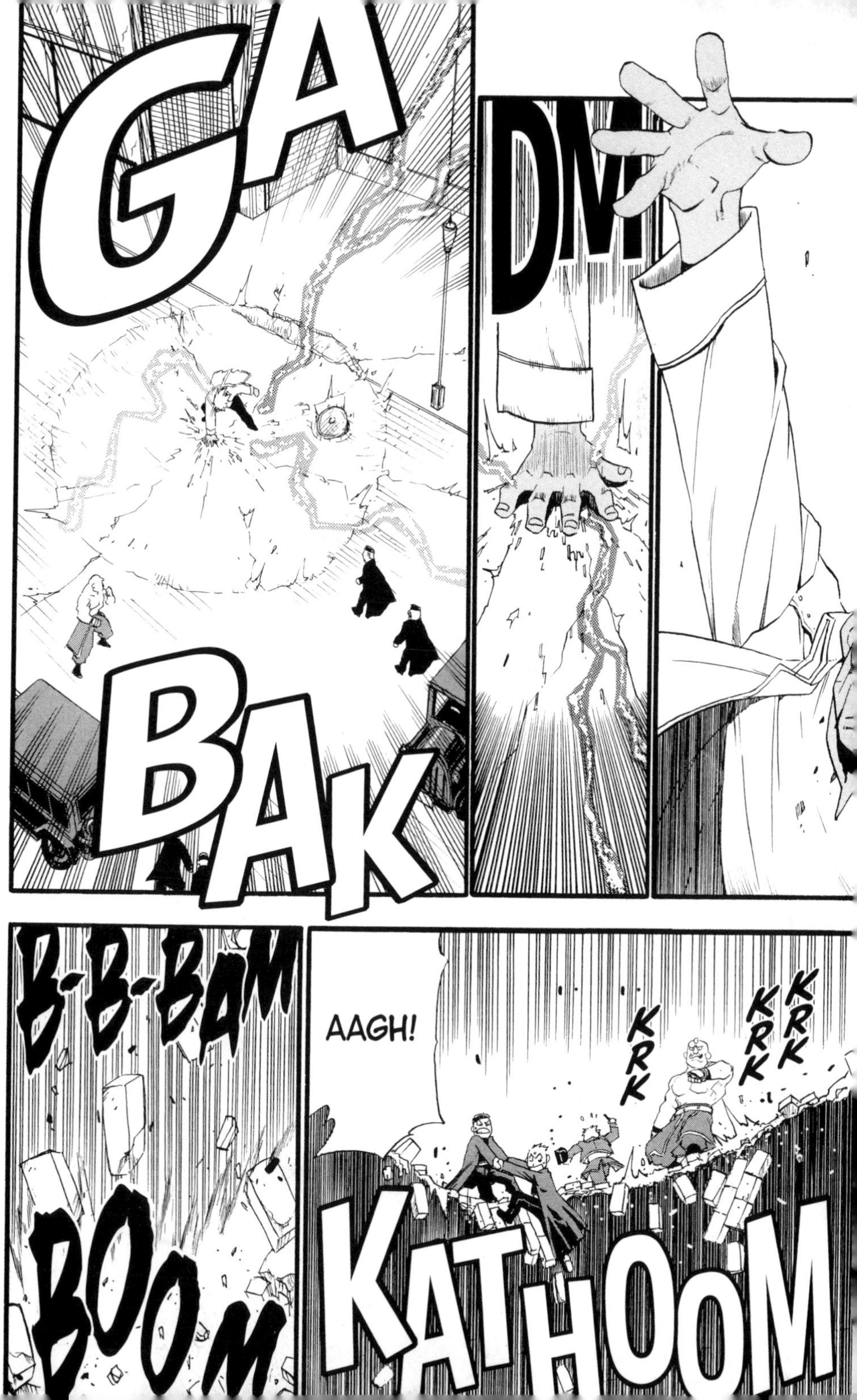
DM
GA
BAK
AAGH!
KRK
KRK
KRK
KATHOOM
B-B-BAM
BOOM

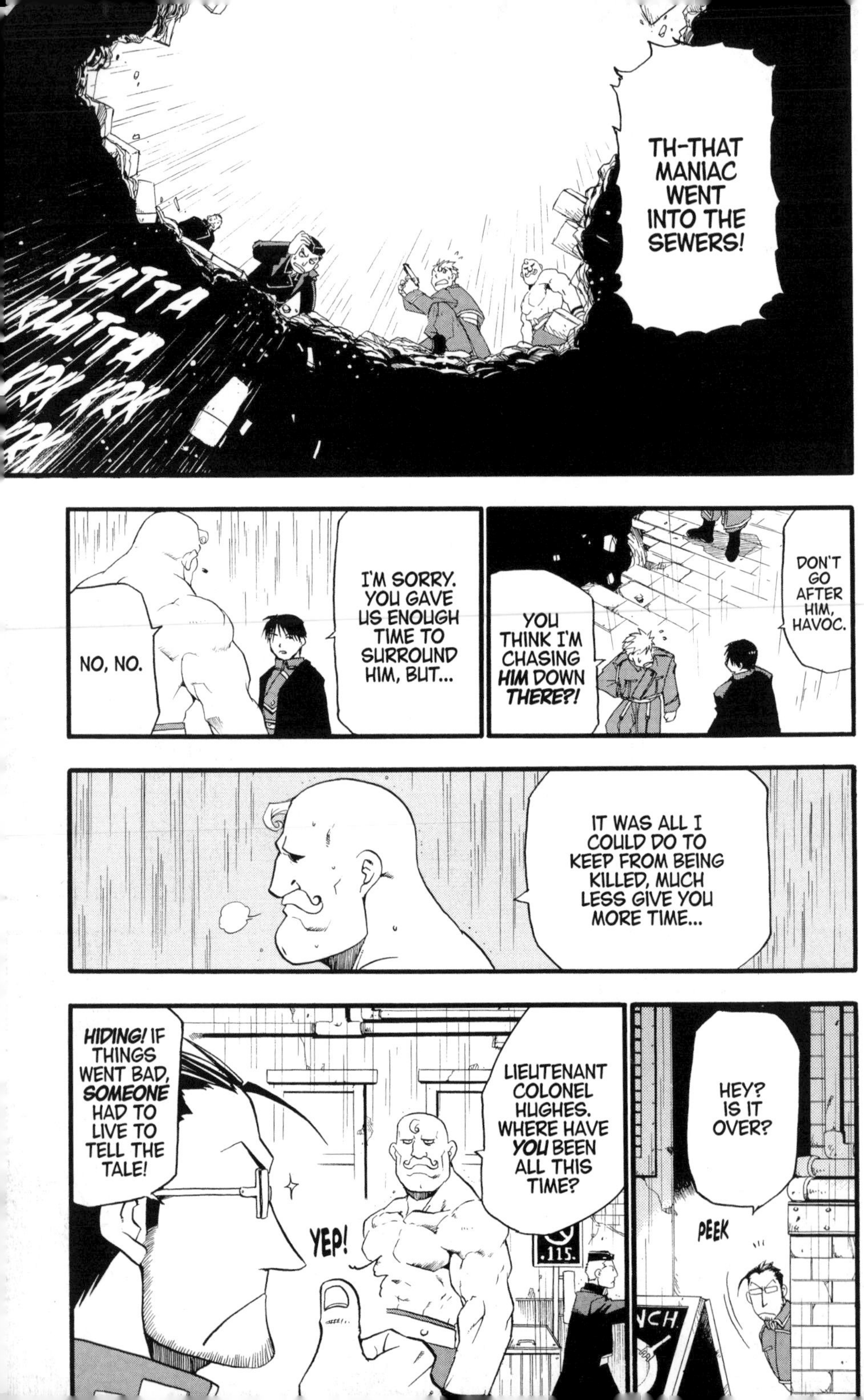
TH-THAT MANIAC WENT INTO THE SEWERS!
KLATTA KLATTA KRK KRK KRK
DON'T GO AFTER HIM, HAVOC.
YOU THINK I'M CHASING *HIM* DOWN *THERE?!*
I'M SORRY. YOU GAVE US ENOUGH TIME TO SURROUND HIM, BUT...
NO, NO.
IT WAS ALL I COULD DO TO KEEP FROM BEING KILLED, MUCH LESS GIVE YOU MORE TIME...
HEY? IS IT OVER?
PEEK
LIEUTENANT COLONEL HUGHES. WHERE HAVE *YOU* BEEN ALL THIS TIME?
.115.
HIDING! IF THINGS WENT BAD, *SOMEONE* HAD TO LIVE TO TELL THE TALE!
YEP!

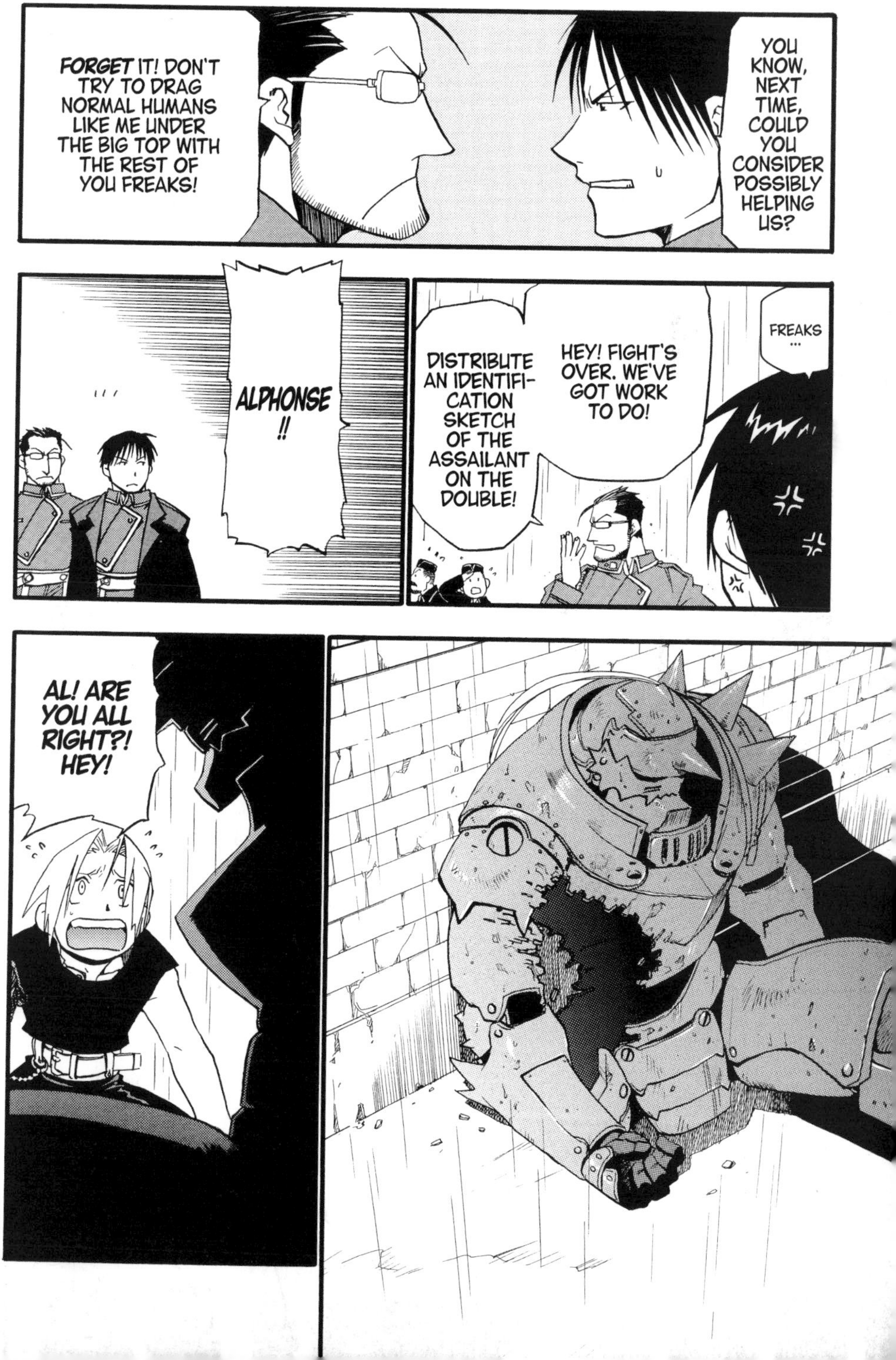
YOU KNOW, NEXT TIME, COULD YOU CONSIDER POSSIBLY HELPING US?
FORGET IT! DON'T TRY TO DRAG NORMAL HUMANS LIKE ME UNDER THE BIG TOP WITH THE REST OF YOU FREAKS!
FREAKS ...
HEY! FIGHT'S OVER. WE'VE GOT WORK TO DO!
DISTRIBUTE AN IDENTIFICATION SKETCH OF THE ASSAILANT ON THE DOUBLE!
ALPHONSE !!
AL! ARE YOU ALL RIGHT?! HEY!

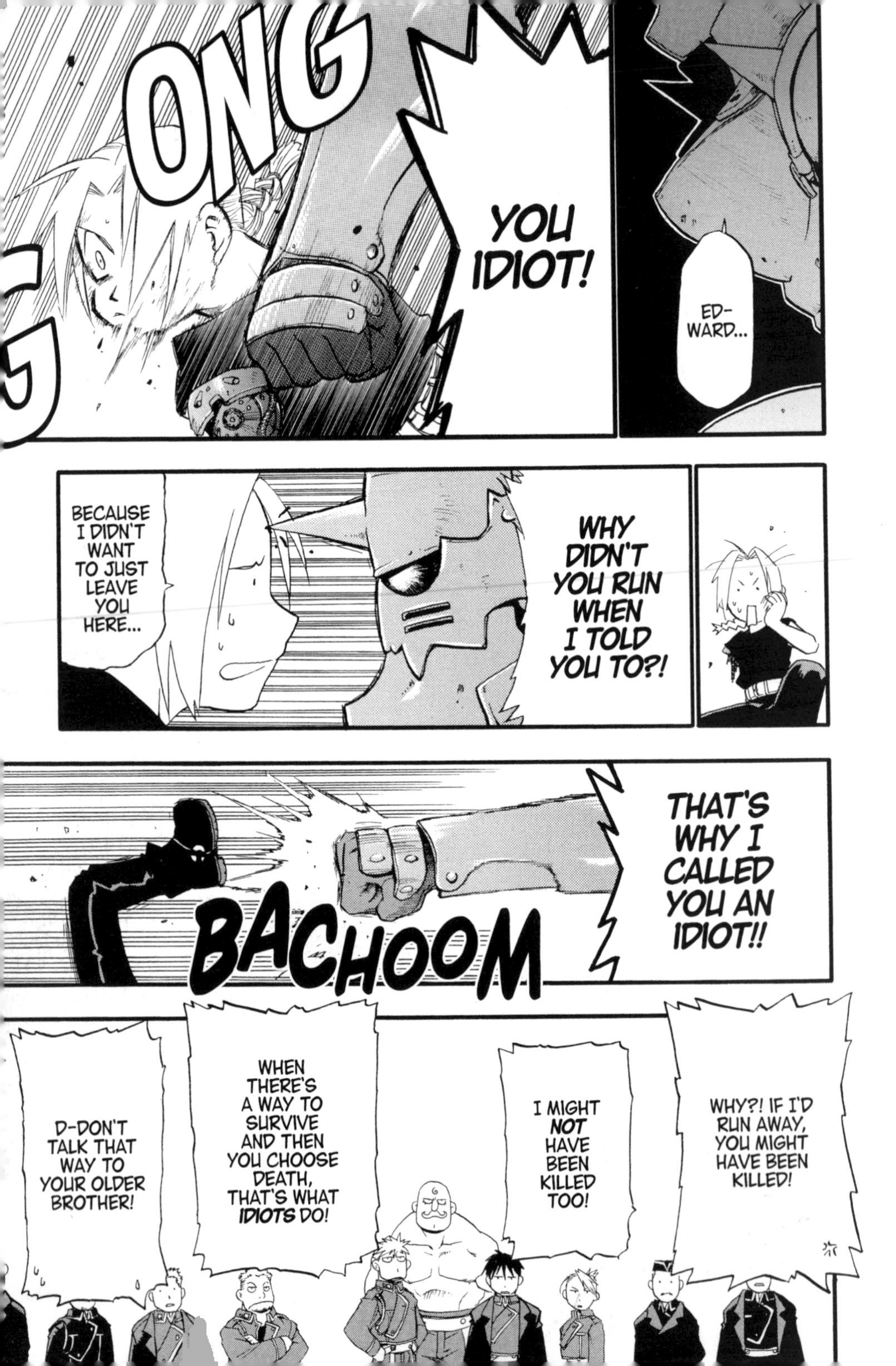
ED-WARD...
YOU IDIOT!
GONG
WHY DIDN'T YOU RUN WHEN I TOLD YOU TO?!
BECAUSE I DIDN'T WANT TO JUST LEAVE YOU HERE...
THAT'S WHY I CALLED YOU AN IDIOT!!
BACHOOM
WHY?! IF I'D RUN AWAY, YOU MIGHT HAVE BEEN KILLED!
I MIGHT NOT HAVE BEEN KILLED TOO!
WHEN THERE'S A WAY TO SURVIVE AND THEN YOU CHOOSE DEATH, THAT'S WHAT IDIOTS DO!
D-DON'T TALK THAT WAY TO YOUR OLDER BROTHER!

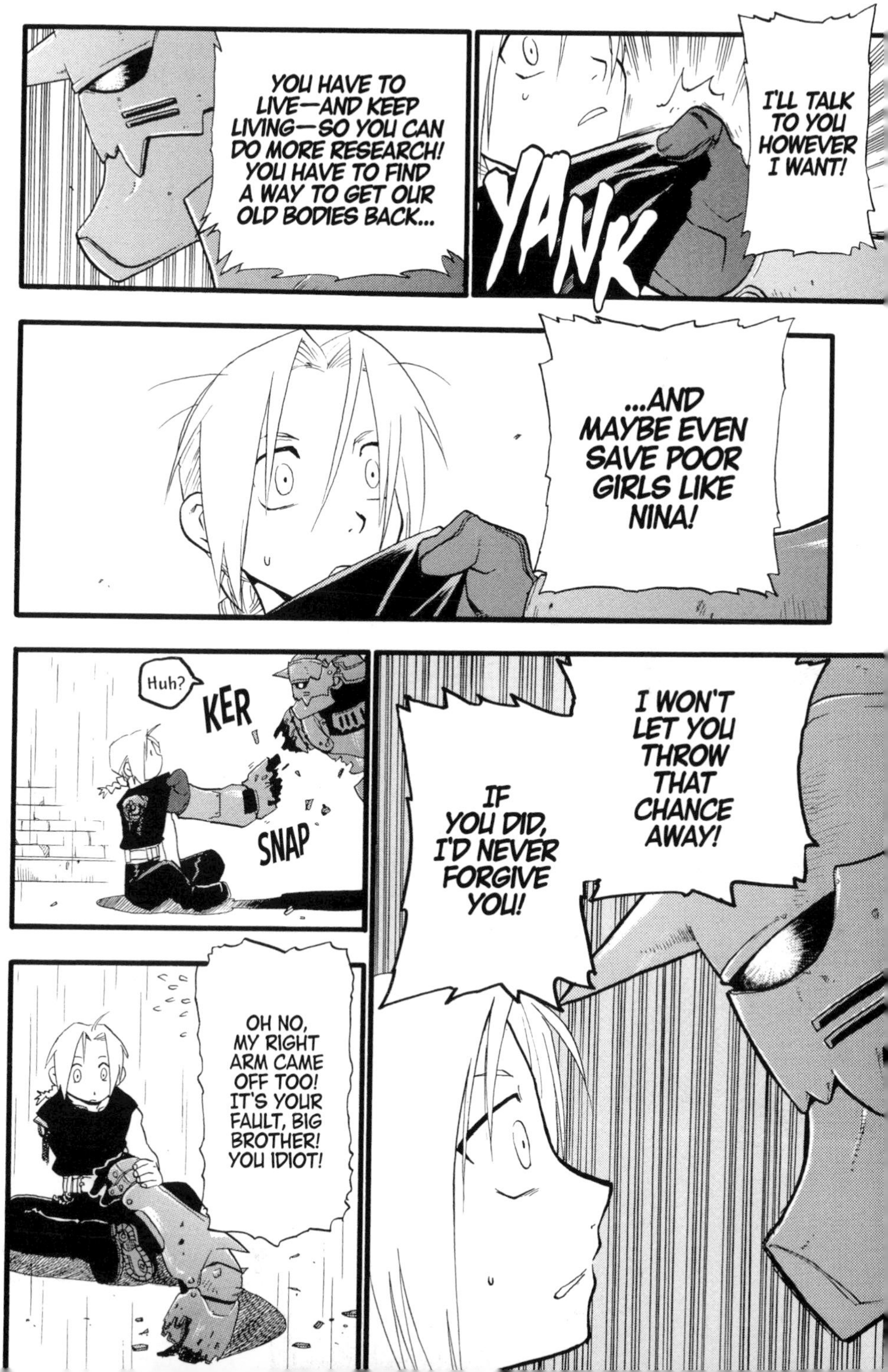
I'LL TALK TO YOU HOWEVER I WANT!
YANK
YOU HAVE TO LIVE—AND KEEP LIVING—SO YOU CAN DO MORE RESEARCH! YOU HAVE TO FIND A WAY TO GET OUR OLD BODIES BACK...
...AND MAYBE EVEN SAVE POOR GIRLS LIKE NINA!
I WON'T LET YOU THROW THAT CHANCE AWAY!
IF YOU DID, I'D NEVER FORGIVE YOU!
Huh?
KER
SNAP
OH NO, MY RIGHT ARM CAME OFF TOO! IT'S YOUR FAULT, BIG BROTHER! YOU IDIOT!

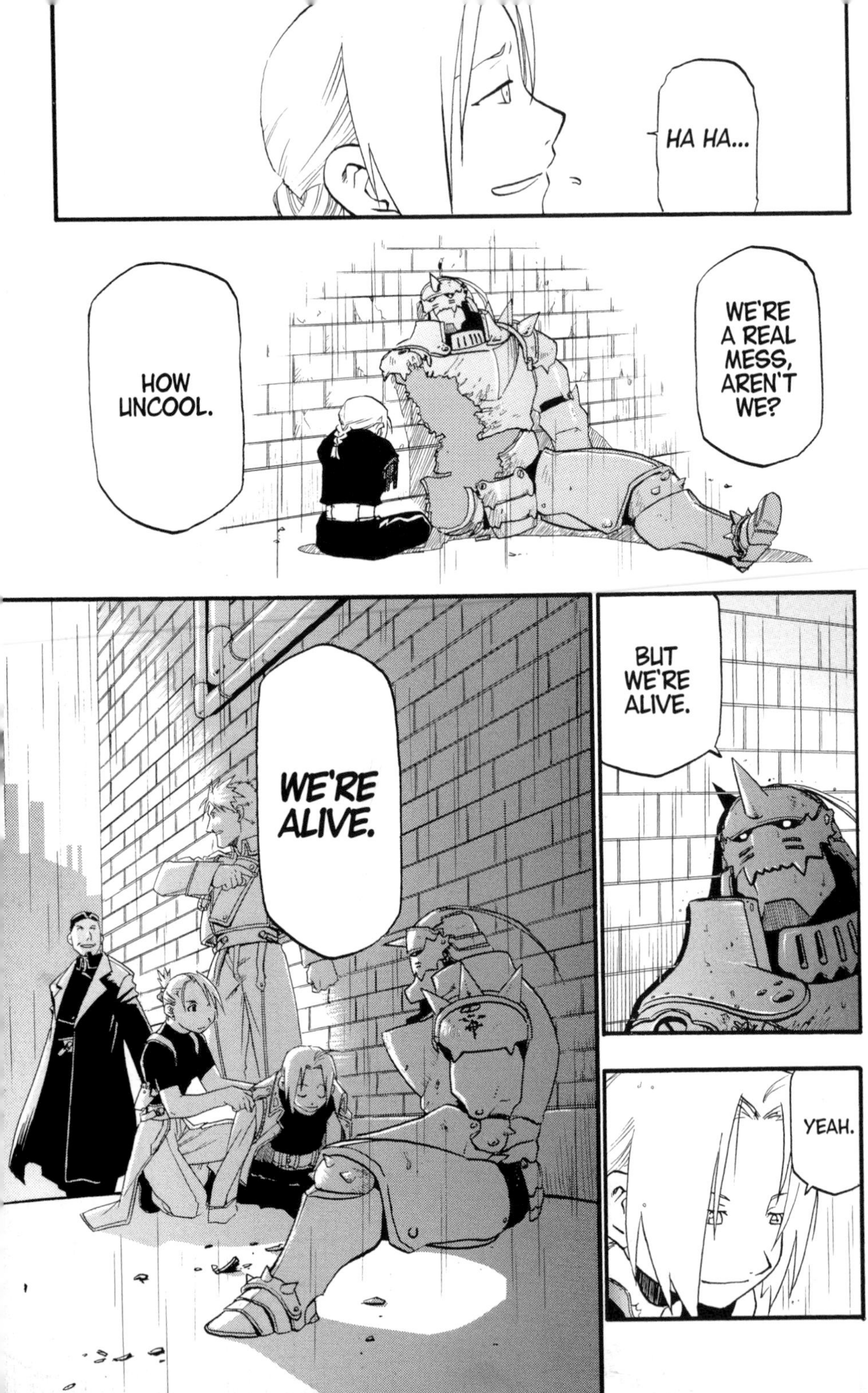
HA HA...
WE'RE A REAL MESS, AREN'T WE?
HOW UNCOOL.
BUT WE'RE ALIVE.
YEAH.
WE'RE ALIVE.

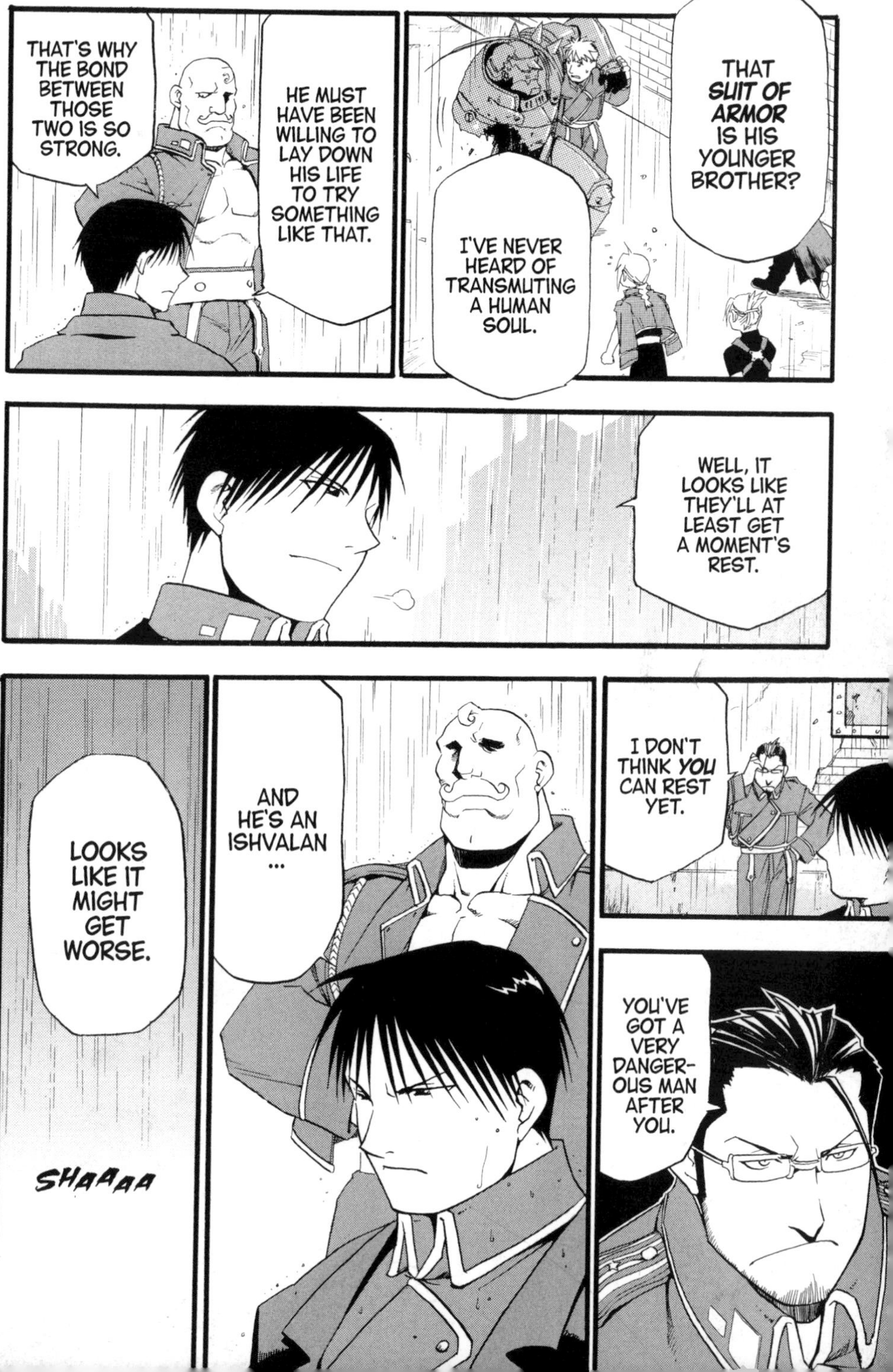
THAT SUIT OF ARMOR IS HIS YOUNGER BROTHER?
I'VE NEVER HEARD OF TRANSMUTING A HUMAN SOUL.
HE MUST HAVE BEEN WILLING TO LAY DOWN HIS LIFE TO TRY SOMETHING LIKE THAT.
THAT'S WHY THE BOND BETWEEN THOSE TWO IS SO STRONG.
WELL, IT LOOKS LIKE THEY'LL AT LEAST GET A MOMENT'S REST.
I DON'T THINK YOU CAN REST YET.
YOU'VE GOT A VERY DANGER-OUS MAN AFTER YOU.
AND HE'S AN ISHVALAN ...
LOOKS LIKE IT MIGHT GET WORSE.
SHAAAA

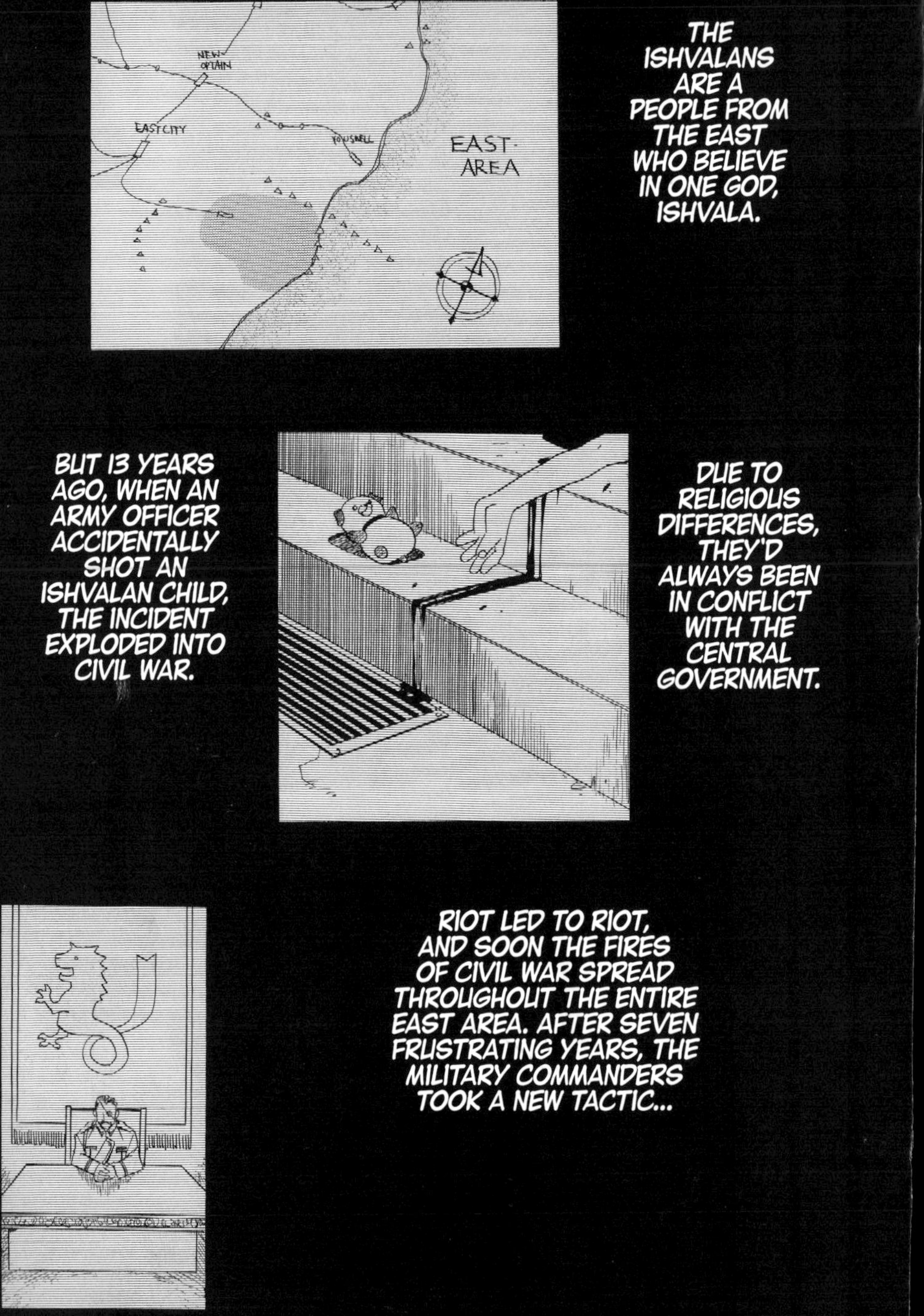
THE ISHVALANS ARE A PEOPLE FROM THE EAST WHO BELIEVE IN ONE GOD, ISHVALA.
NEW OPTAIN
EASTCITY
YOUSWELL
EAST AREA
DUE TO RELIGIOUS DIFFERENCES, THEY'D ALWAYS BEEN IN CONFLICT WITH THE CENTRAL GOVERNMENT.
BUT 13 YEARS AGO, WHEN AN ARMY OFFICER ACCIDENTALLY SHOT AN ISHVALAN CHILD, THE INCIDENT EXPLODED INTO CIVIL WAR.
RIOT LED TO RIOT, AND SOON THE FIRES OF CIVIL WAR SPREAD THROUGHOUT THE ENTIRE EAST AREA. AFTER SEVEN FRUSTRATING YEARS, THE MILITARY COMMANDERS TOOK A NEW TACTIC...

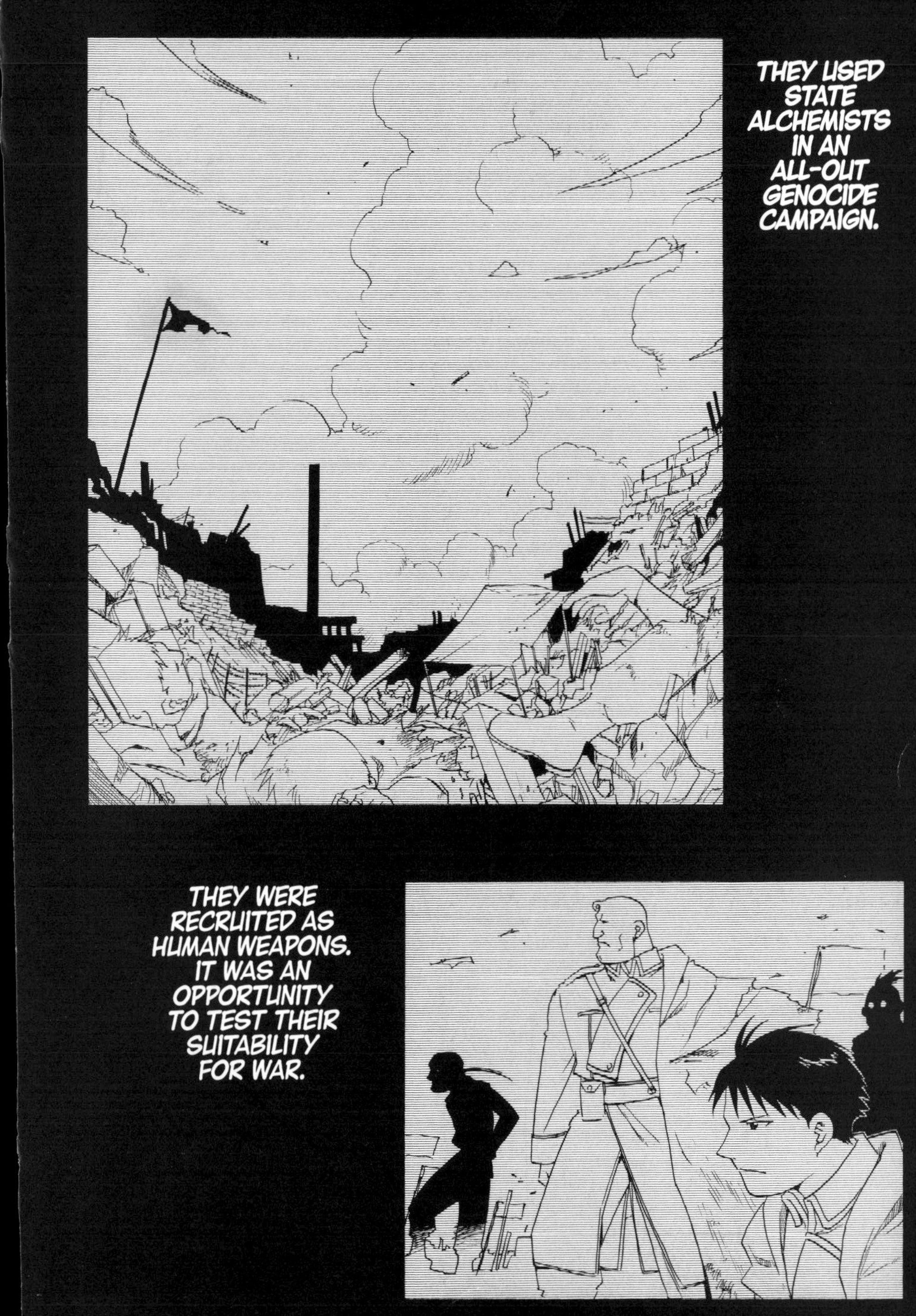
THEY USED STATE ALCHEMISTS IN AN ALL-OUT GENOCIDE CAMPAIGN.
THEY WERE RECRUITED AS HUMAN WEAPONS. IT WAS AN OPPORTUNITY TO TEST THEIR SUITABILITY FOR WAR.

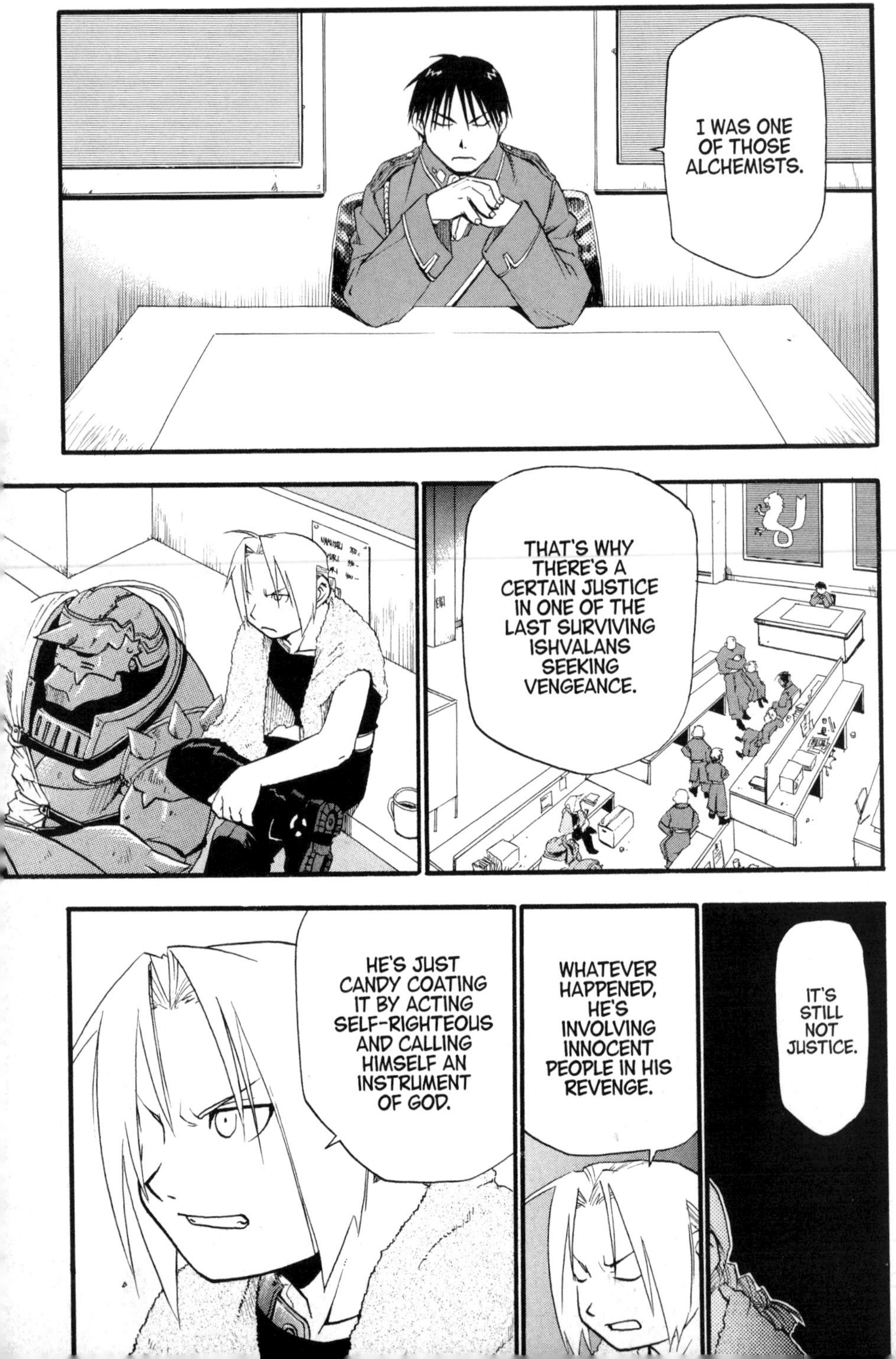
I WAS ONE OF THOSE ALCHEMISTS.
THAT'S WHY THERE'S A CERTAIN JUSTICE IN ONE OF THE LAST SURVIVING ISHVALANS SEEKING VENGEANCE.
IT'S STILL NOT JUSTICE.
WHATEVER HAPPENED, HE'S INVOLVING INNOCENT PEOPLE IN HIS REVENGE.
HE'S JUST CANDY COATING IT BY ACTING SELF-RIGHTEOUS AND CALLING HIMSELF AN INSTRUMENT OF GOD.

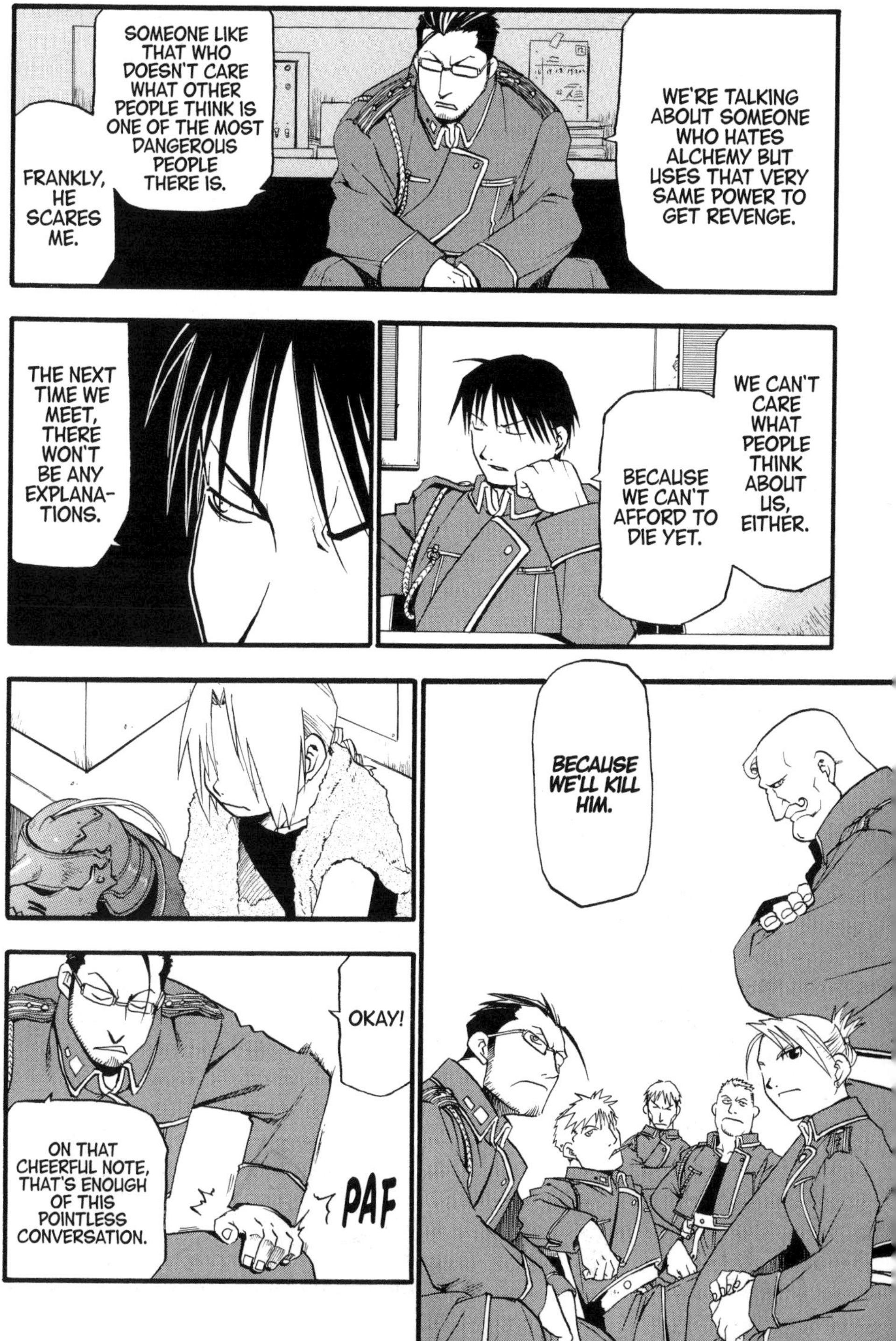
WE'RE TALKING ABOUT SOMEONE WHO HATES ALCHEMY BUT USES THAT VERY SAME POWER TO GET REVENGE.
SOMEONE LIKE THAT WHO DOESN'T CARE WHAT OTHER PEOPLE THINK IS ONE OF THE MOST DANGEROUS PEOPLE THERE IS.
FRANKLY, HE SCARES ME.
WE CAN'T CARE WHAT PEOPLE THINK ABOUT US, EITHER.
BECAUSE WE CAN'T AFFORD TO DIE YET.
THE NEXT TIME WE MEET, THERE WON'T BE ANY EXPLANA-TIONS.
BECAUSE WE'LL KILL HIM.
OKAY!
ON THAT CHEERFUL NOTE, THAT'S ENOUGH OF THIS POINTLESS CONVERSATION.
PAF

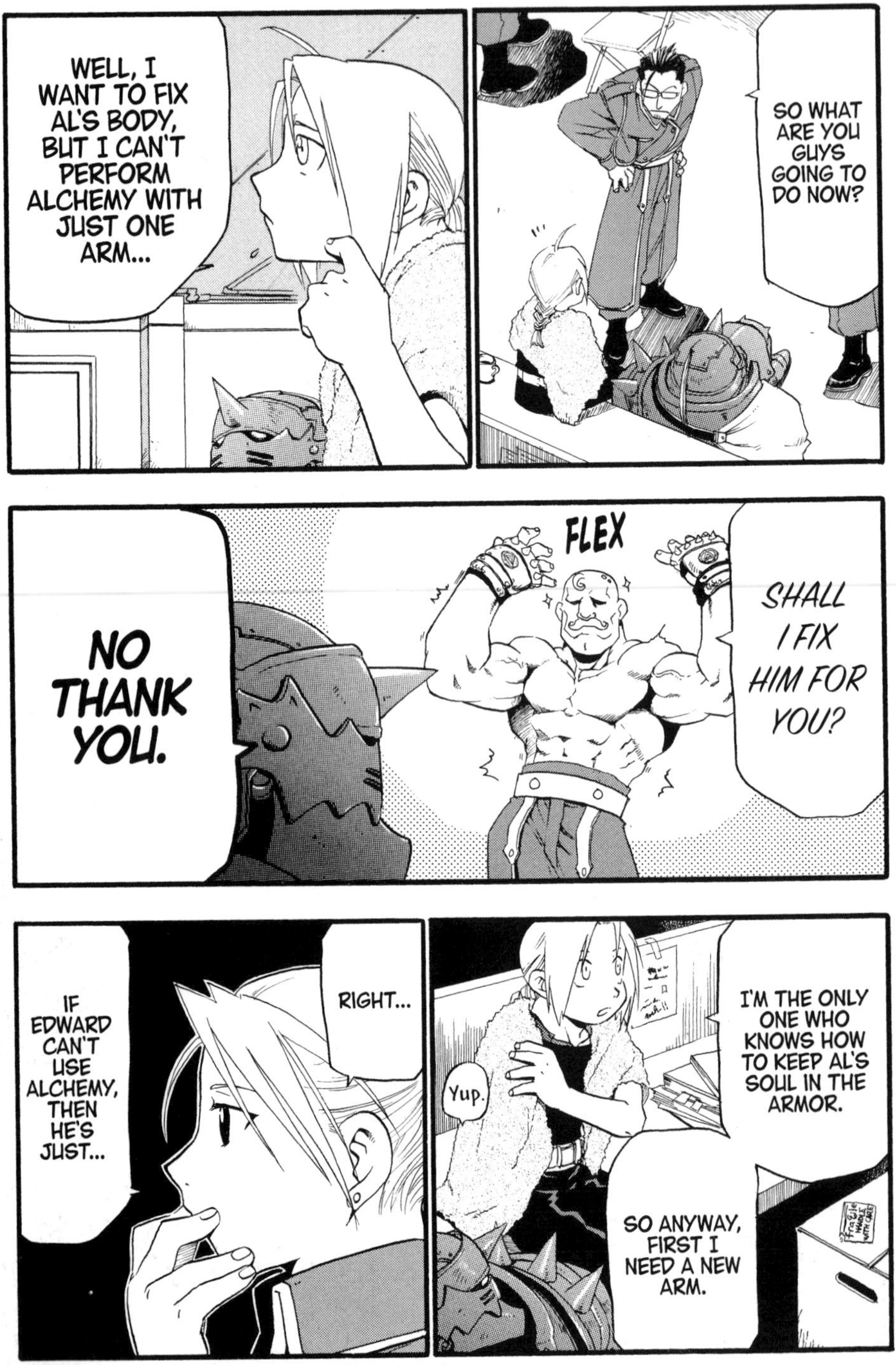
SO WHAT ARE YOU GUYS GOING TO DO NOW?
WELL, I WANT TO FIX AL'S BODY, BUT I CAN'T PERFORM ALCHEMY WITH JUST ONE ARM...
FLEX
SHALL I FIX HIM FOR YOU?
NO THANK YOU.
I'M THE ONLY ONE WHO KNOWS HOW TO KEEP AL'S SOUL IN THE ARMOR.
Yup.
SO ANYWAY, FIRST I NEED A NEW ARM.
RIGHT...
IF EDWARD CAN'T USE ALCHEMY, THEN HE'S JUST...

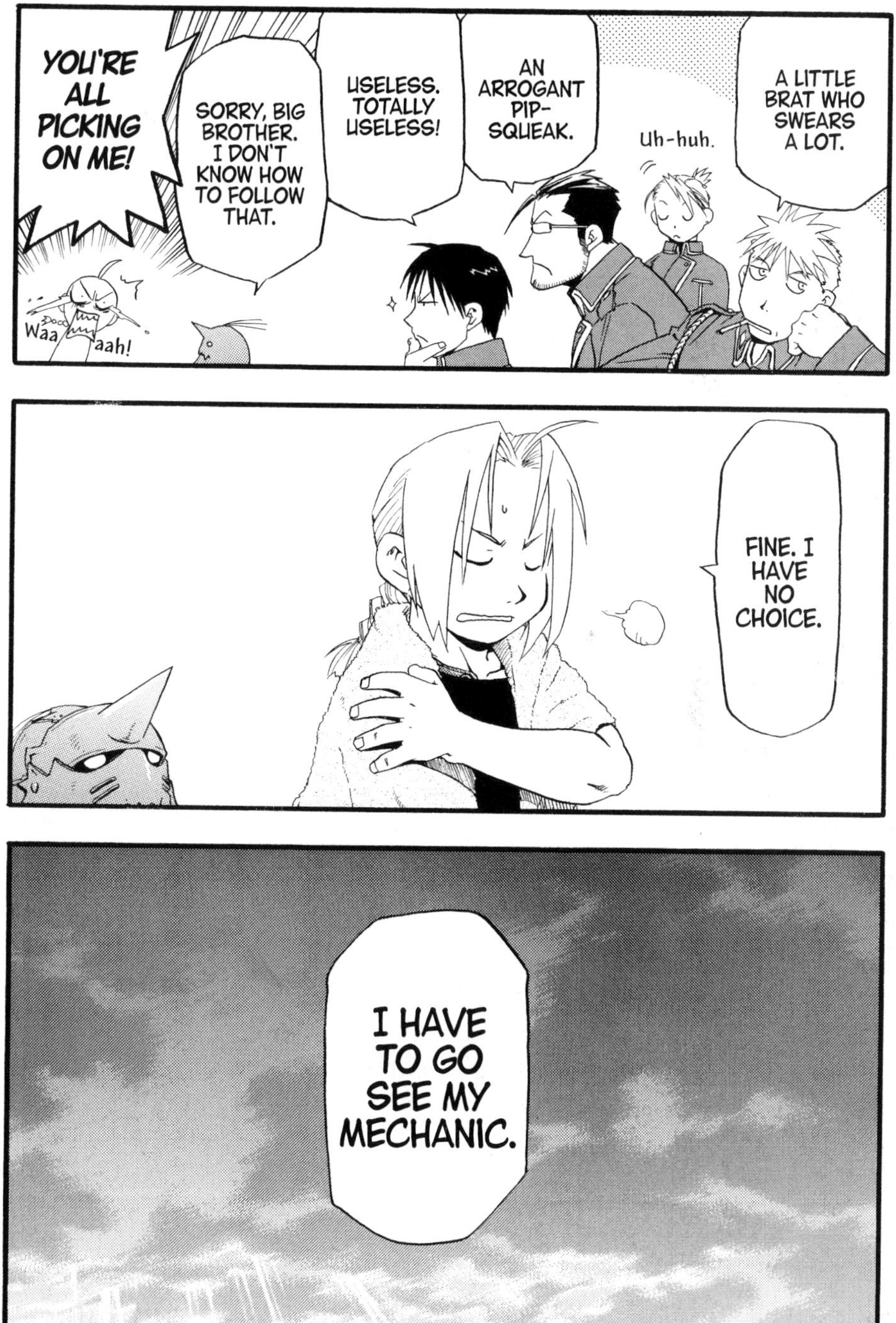
A LITTLE BRAT WHO SWEARS A LOT.
Uh-huh.
AN ARROGANT PIP-SQUEAK.
USELESS. TOTALLY USELESS!
SORRY, BIG BROTHER. I DON'T KNOW HOW TO FOLLOW THAT.
YOU'RE ALL PICKING ON ME!
Waa aah!
FINE. I HAVE NO CHOICE.
I HAVE TO GO SEE MY MECHANIC.

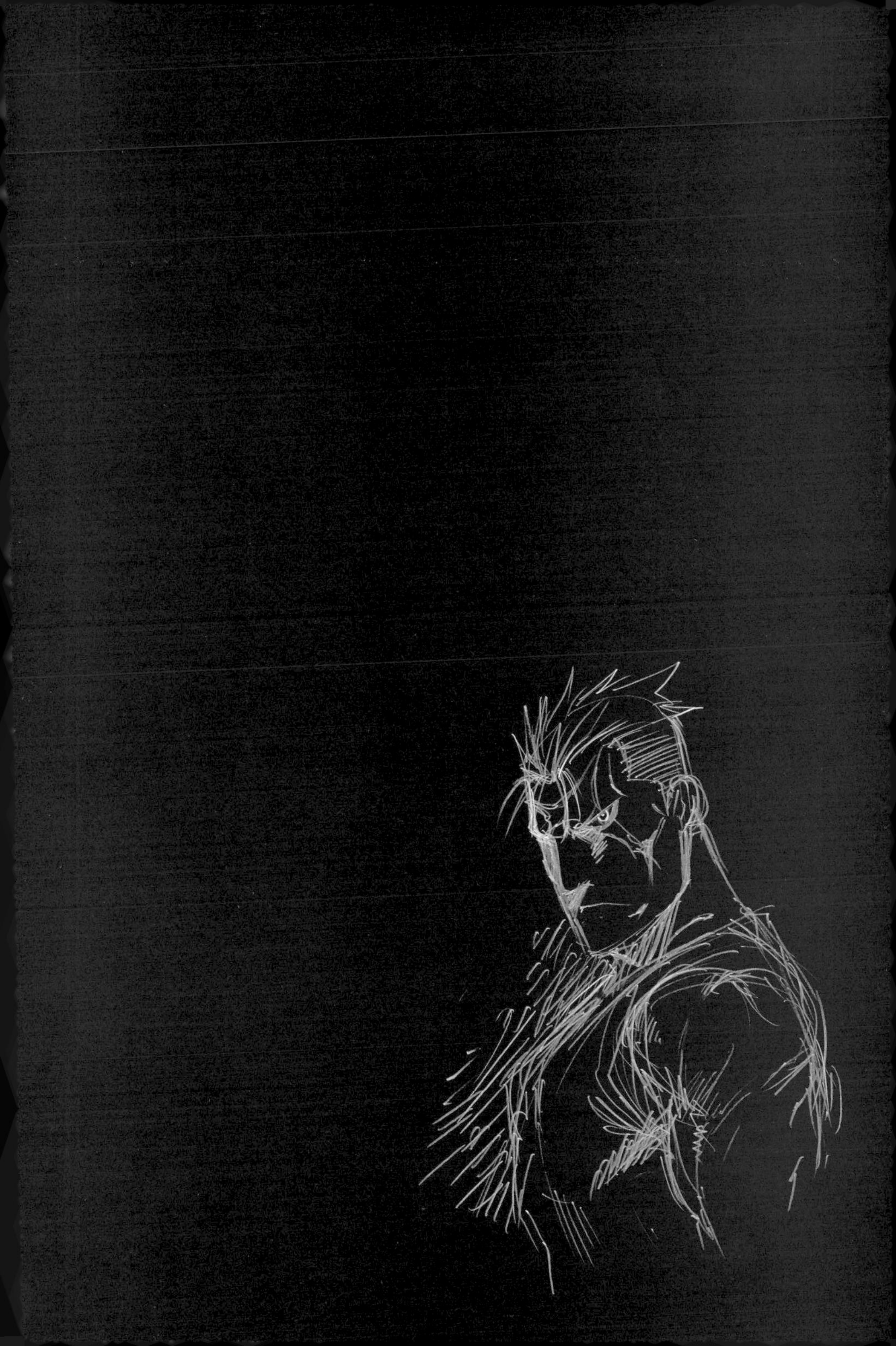

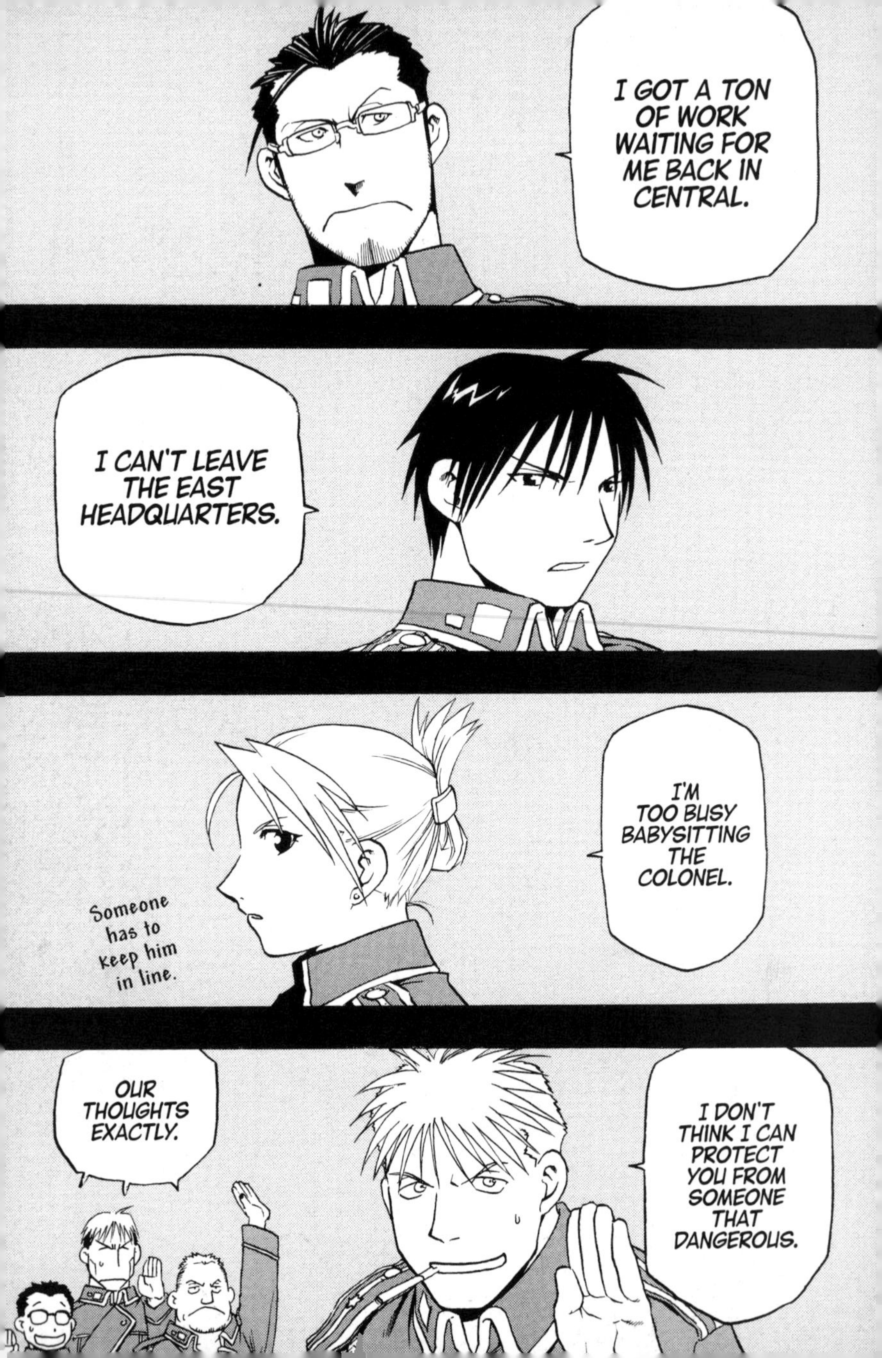
I GOT A TON OF WORK WAITING FOR ME BACK IN CENTRAL.
I CAN'T LEAVE THE EAST HEADQUARTERS.
I'M TOO BUSY BABYSITTING THE COLONEL.
Someone has to keep him in line.
I DON'T THINK I CAN PROTECT YOU FROM SOMEONE THAT DANGEROUS.
OUR THOUGHTS EXACTLY.

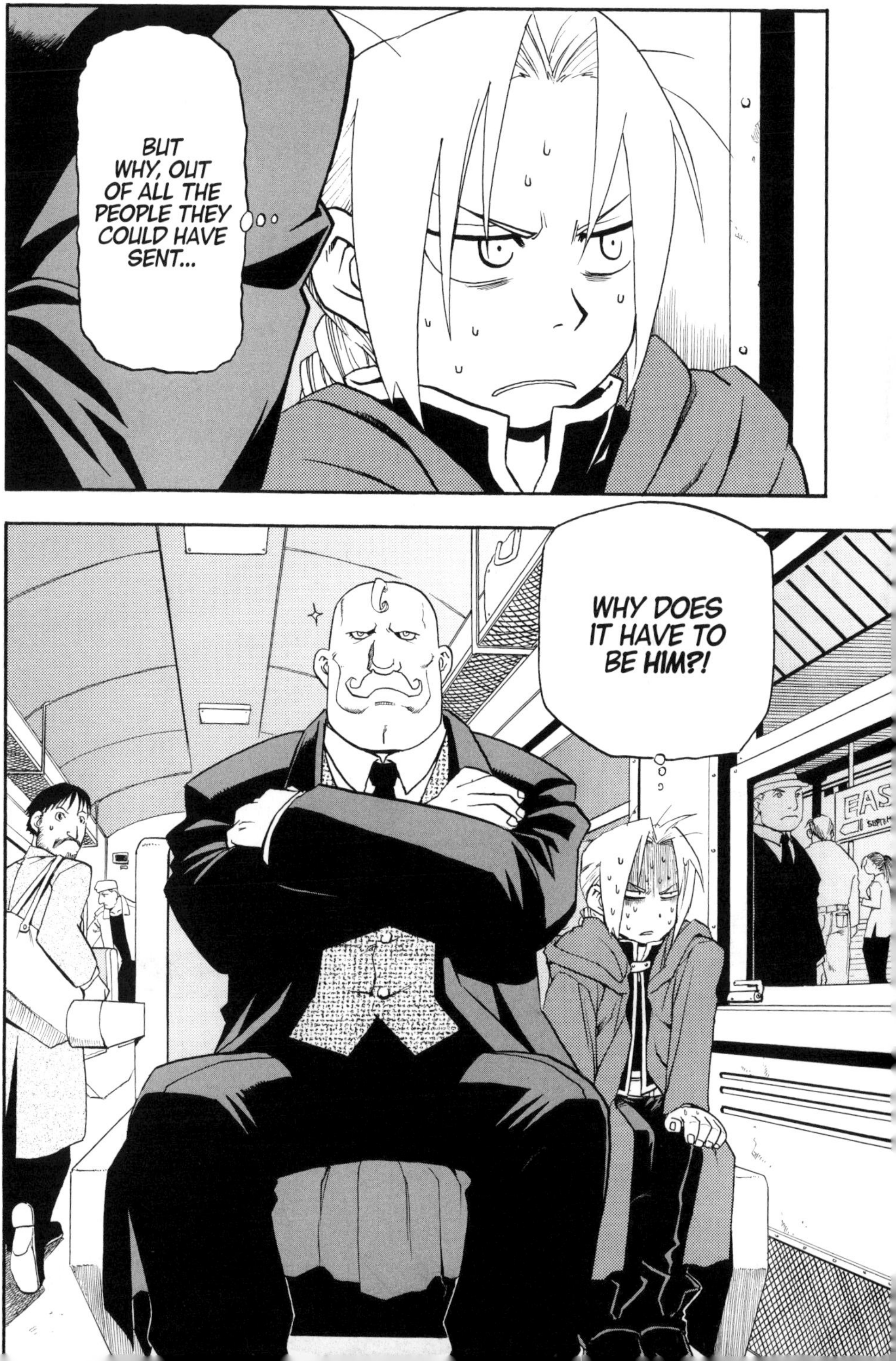
BUT WHY, OUT OF ALL THE PEOPLE THEY COULD HAVE SENT...
WHY DOES IT HAVE TO BE HIM?!

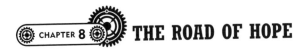

CHAPTER 8 THE ROAD OF HOPE

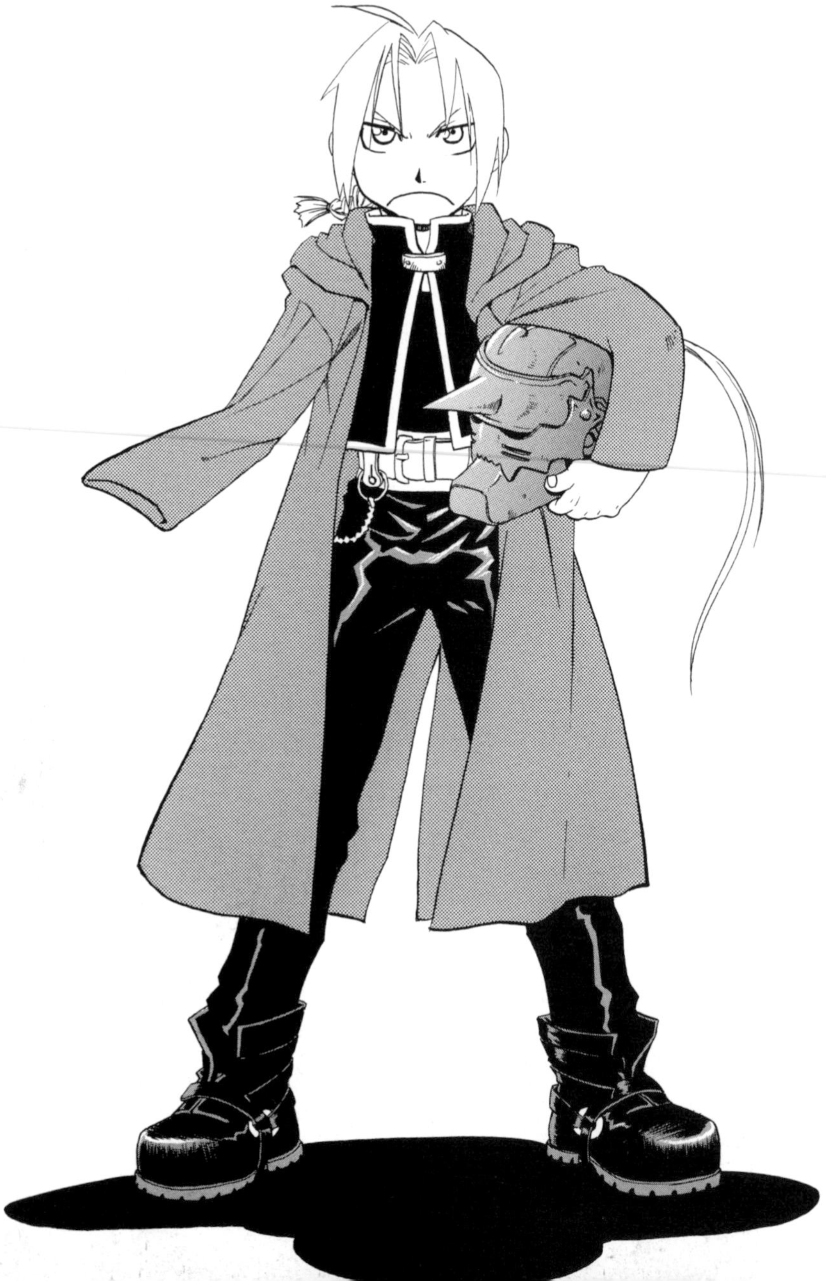

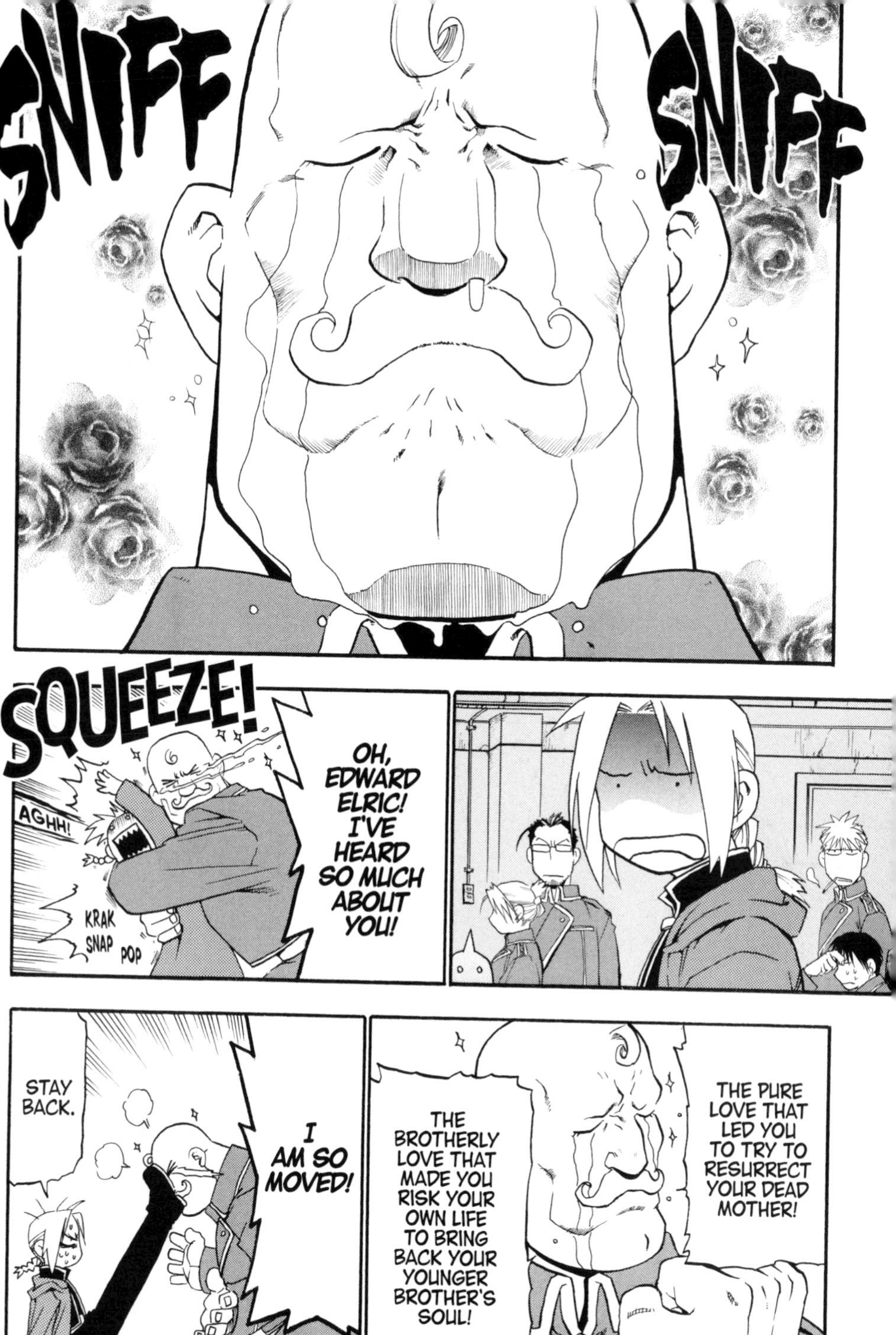
SNIFF
SNIFF
OH, EDWARD ELRIC! I'VE HEARD SO MUCH ABOUT YOU!
SQUEEZE!
AGHH!
KRAK
SNAP
POP
THE PURE LOVE THAT LED YOU TO TRY TO RESURRECT YOUR DEAD MOTHER!
THE BROTHERLY LOVE THAT MADE YOU RISK YOUR OWN LIFE TO BRING BACK YOUR YOUNGER BROTHER'S SOUL!
I AM SO MOVED!
STAY BACK.

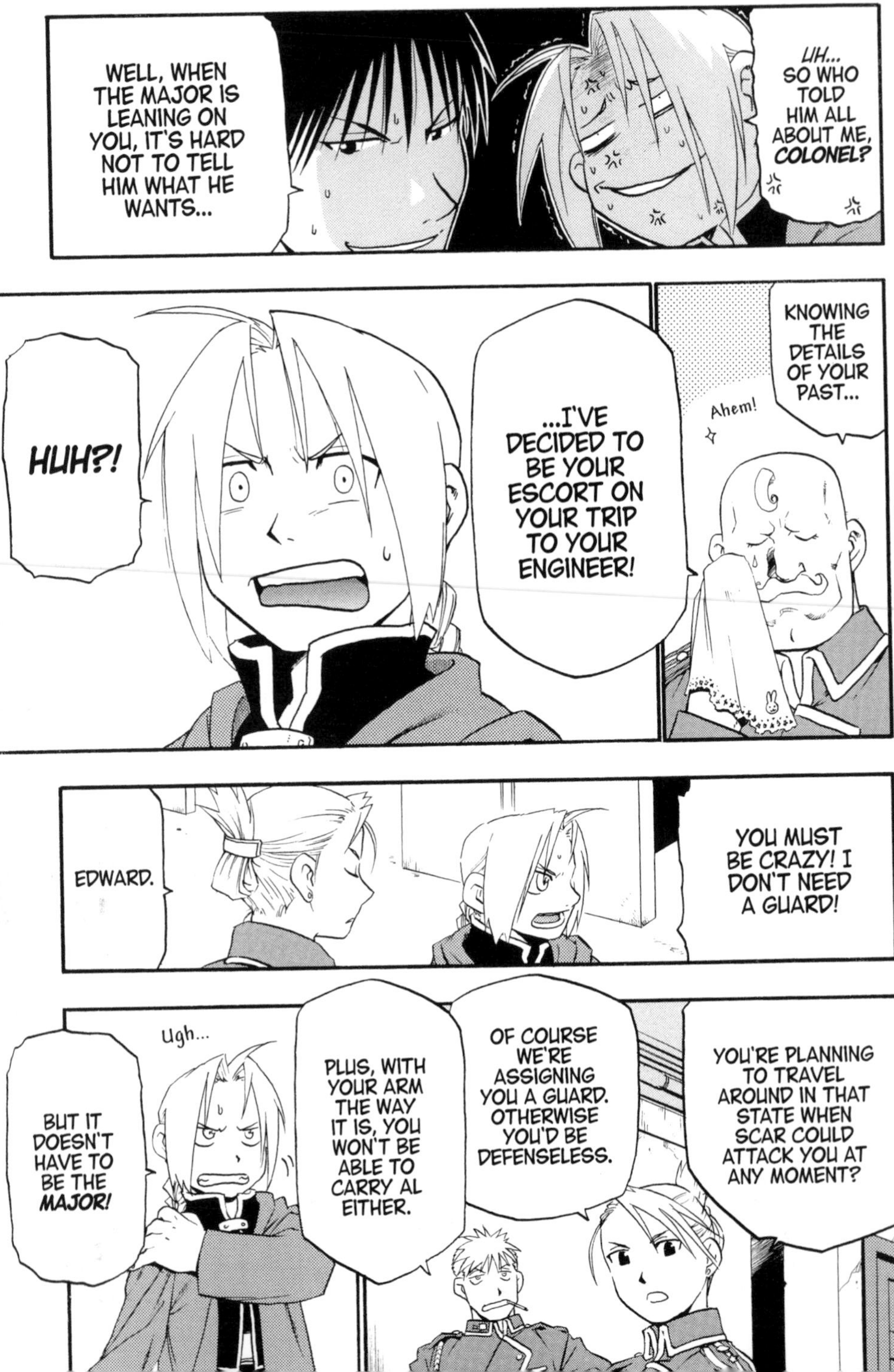
UH... SO WHO TOLD HIM ALL ABOUT ME, *COLONEL?*
WELL, WHEN THE MAJOR IS LEANING ON YOU, IT'S HARD NOT TO TELL HIM WHAT HE WANTS...
KNOWING THE DETAILS OF YOUR PAST...
Ahem!
...I'VE DECIDED TO BE YOUR ESCORT ON YOUR TRIP TO YOUR ENGINEER!
HUH?!
YOU MUST BE CRAZY! I DON'T NEED A GUARD!
EDWARD.
YOU'RE PLANNING TO TRAVEL AROUND IN THAT STATE WHEN SCAR COULD ATTACK YOU AT ANY MOMENT?
OF COURSE WE'RE ASSIGNING YOU A GUARD. OTHERWISE YOU'D BE DEFENSELESS.
PLUS, WITH YOUR ARM THE WAY IT IS, YOU WON'T BE ABLE TO CARRY AL EITHER.
Ugh...
BUT IT DOESN'T HAVE TO BE THE *MAJOR!*

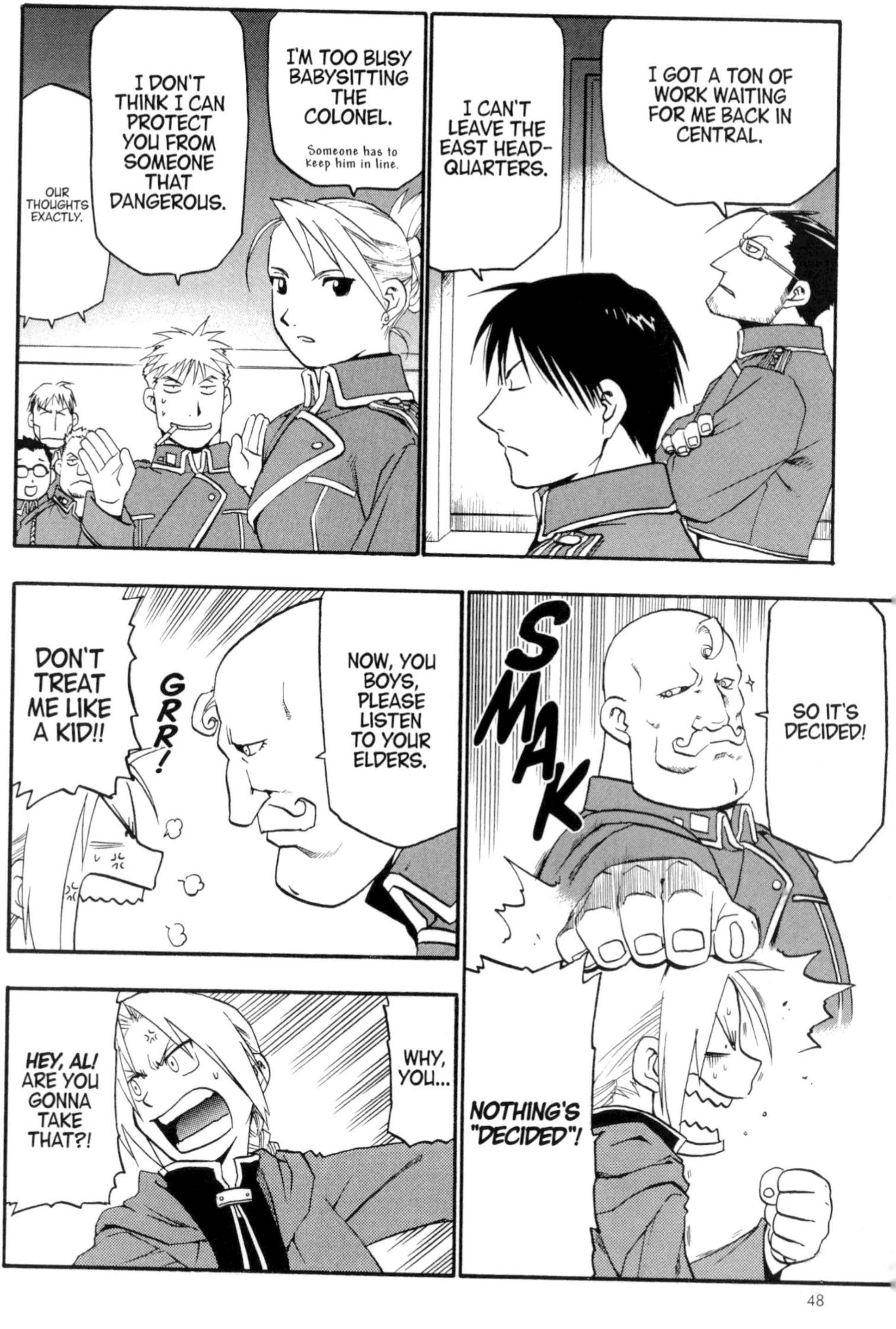
I GOT A TON OF WORK WAITING FOR ME BACK IN CENTRAL.
I CAN'T LEAVE THE EAST HEAD-QUARTERS.
I'M TOO BUSY BABYSITTING THE COLONEL.
Someone has to keep him in line.
I DON'T THINK I CAN PROTECT YOU FROM SOMEONE THAT DANGEROUS.
OUR THOUGHTS EXACTLY.
SO IT'S DECIDED!
SMAK
NOTHING'S "DECIDED"!
NOW, YOU BOYS, PLEASE LISTEN TO YOUR ELDERS.
GRR!
DON'T TREAT ME LIKE A KID!!
WHY, YOU...
HEY, AL! ARE YOU GONNA TAKE THAT?!

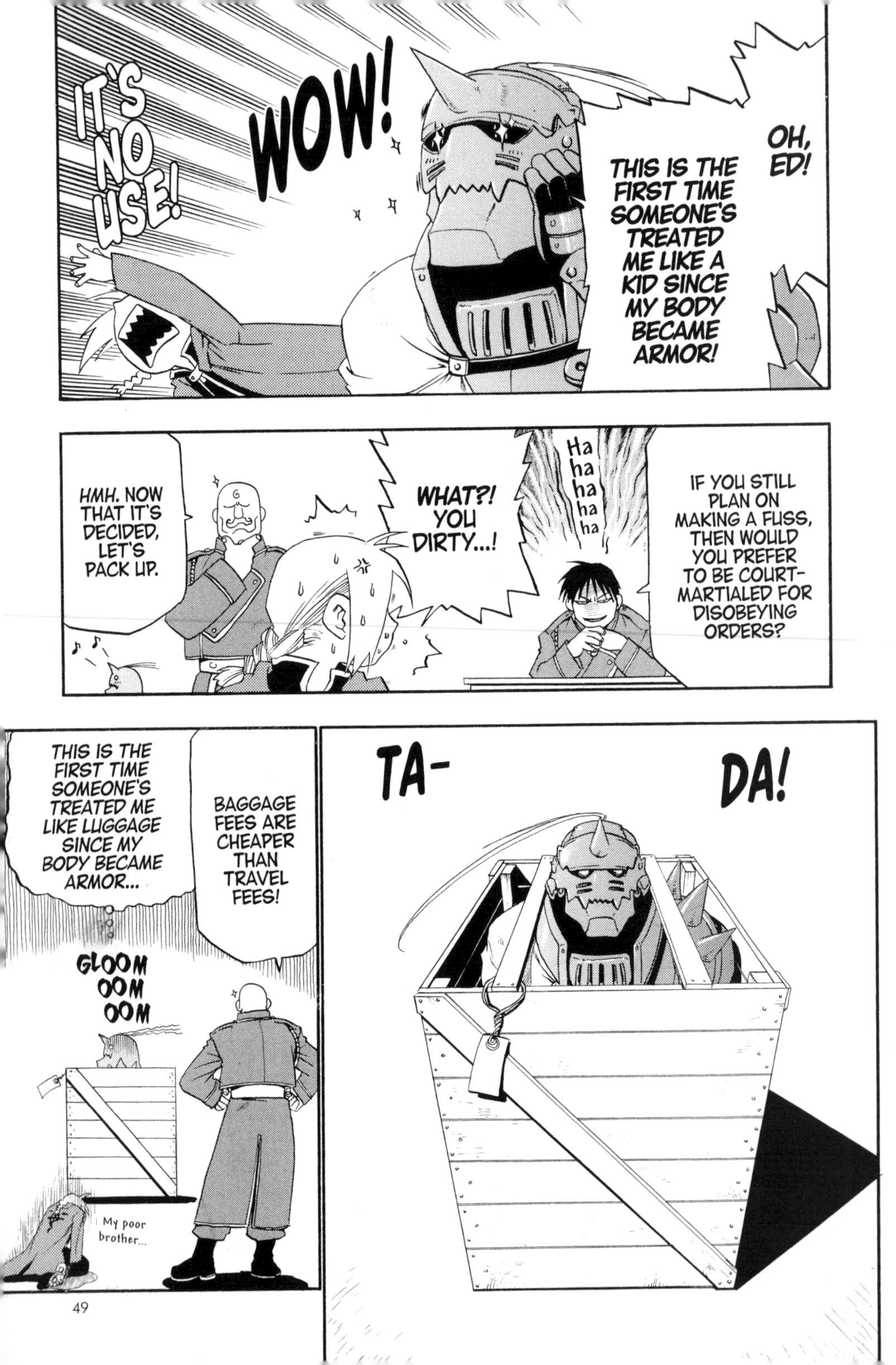
OH, ED!
THIS IS THE FIRST TIME SOMEONE'S TREATED ME LIKE A KID SINCE MY BODY BECAME ARMOR!
WOW!
IT'S NO USE!
IF YOU STILL PLAN ON MAKING A FUSS, THEN WOULD YOU PREFER TO BE COURT-MARTIALED FOR DISOBEYING ORDERS?
Ha ha ha ha ha
WHAT?! YOU DIRTY...!
HMH. NOW THAT IT'S DECIDED, LET'S PACK UP.
TA-DA!
BAGGAGE FEES ARE CHEAPER THAN TRAVEL FEES!
THIS IS THE FIRST TIME SOMEONE'S TREATED ME LIKE LUGGAGE SINCE MY BODY BECAME ARMOR...
GLOOM OOM OOM
My poor brother...

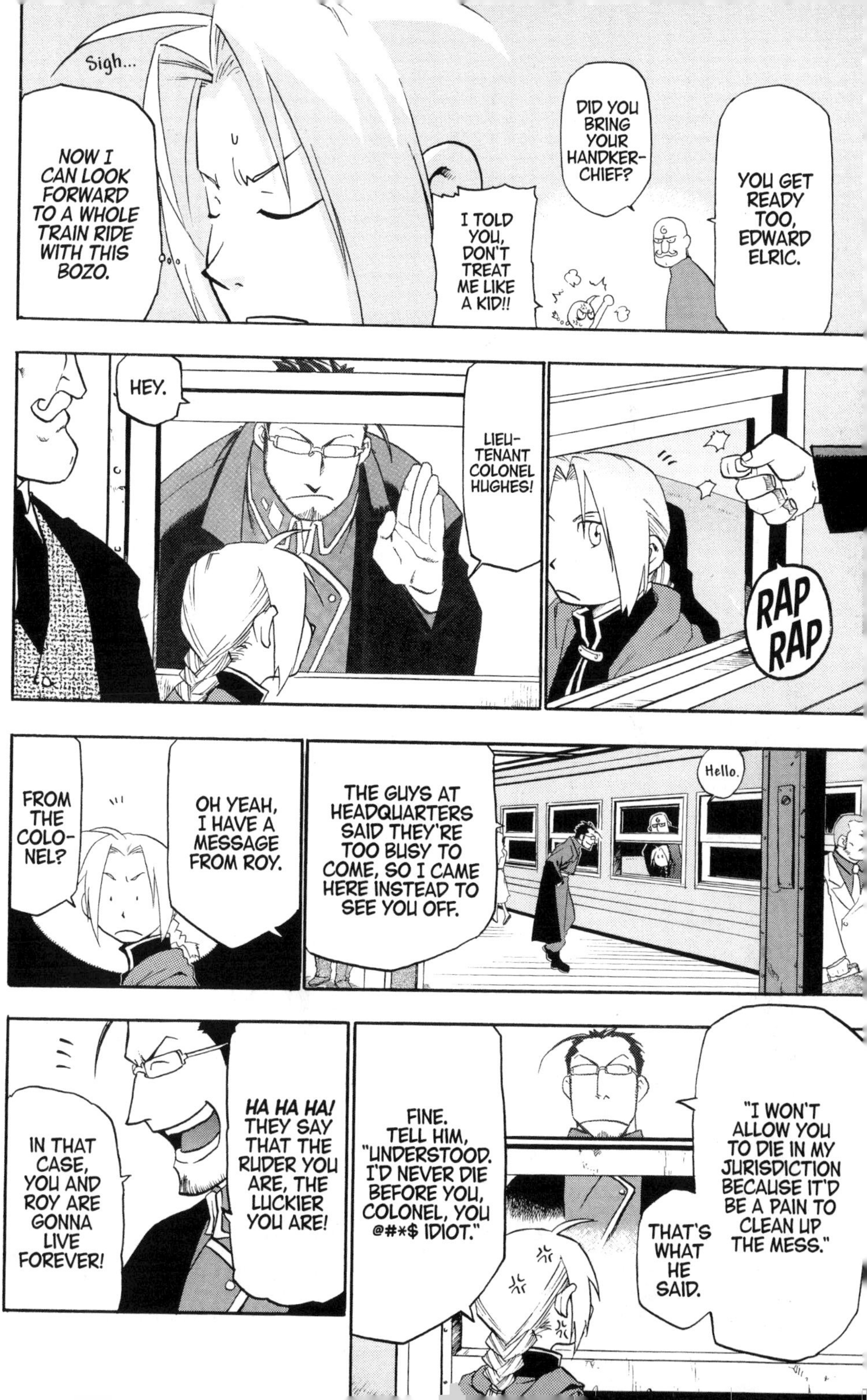
YOU GET READY TOO, EDWARD ELRIC.
DID YOU BRING YOUR HANDKER-CHIEF?
I TOLD YOU, DON'T TREAT ME LIKE A KID!!
Sigh...
NOW I CAN LOOK FORWARD TO A WHOLE TRAIN RIDE WITH THIS BOZO.
RAP RAP
LIEU-TENANT COLONEL HUGHES!
HEY.
Hello.
THE GUYS AT HEADQUARTERS SAID THEY'RE TOO BUSY TO COME, SO I CAME HERE INSTEAD TO SEE YOU OFF.
OH YEAH, I HAVE A MESSAGE FROM ROY.
FROM THE COLO-NEL?
"I WON'T ALLOW YOU TO DIE IN MY JURISDICTION BECAUSE IT'D BE A PAIN TO CLEAN UP THE MESS."
THAT'S WHAT HE SAID.
FINE. TELL HIM, "UNDERSTOOD. I'D NEVER DIE BEFORE YOU, COLONEL, YOU @#*$ IDIOT."
HA HA HA! THEY SAY THAT THE RUDER YOU ARE, THE LUCKIER YOU ARE!
IN THAT CASE, YOU AND ROY ARE GONNA LIVE FOREVER!

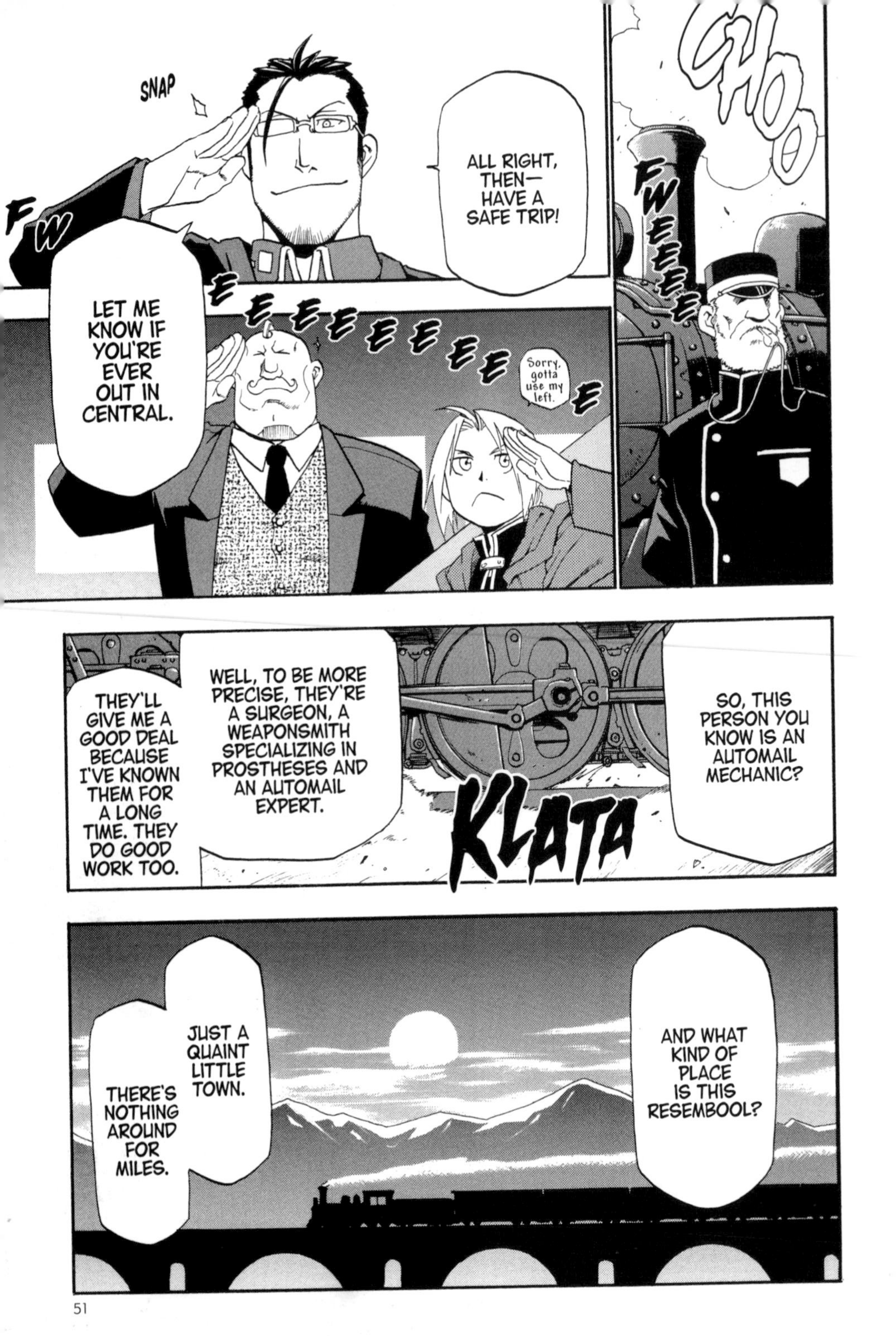
CHOO
FWEEEEE
SNAP
FW
ALL RIGHT, THEN—HAVE A SAFE TRIP!
EEEEEEEEEE
LET ME KNOW IF YOU'RE EVER OUT IN CENTRAL.
Sorry, gotta use my left.
SO, THIS PERSON YOU KNOW IS AN AUTOMAIL MECHANIC?
KLATA
WELL, TO BE MORE PRECISE, THEY'RE A SURGEON, A WEAPONSMITH SPECIALIZING IN PROSTHESES AND AN AUTOMAIL EXPERT.
THEY'LL GIVE ME A GOOD DEAL BECAUSE I'VE KNOWN THEM FOR A LONG TIME. THEY DO GOOD WORK TOO.
AND WHAT KIND OF PLACE IS THIS RESEMBOOL?
JUST A QUAINT LITTLE TOWN.
THERE'S NOTHING AROUND FOR MILES.

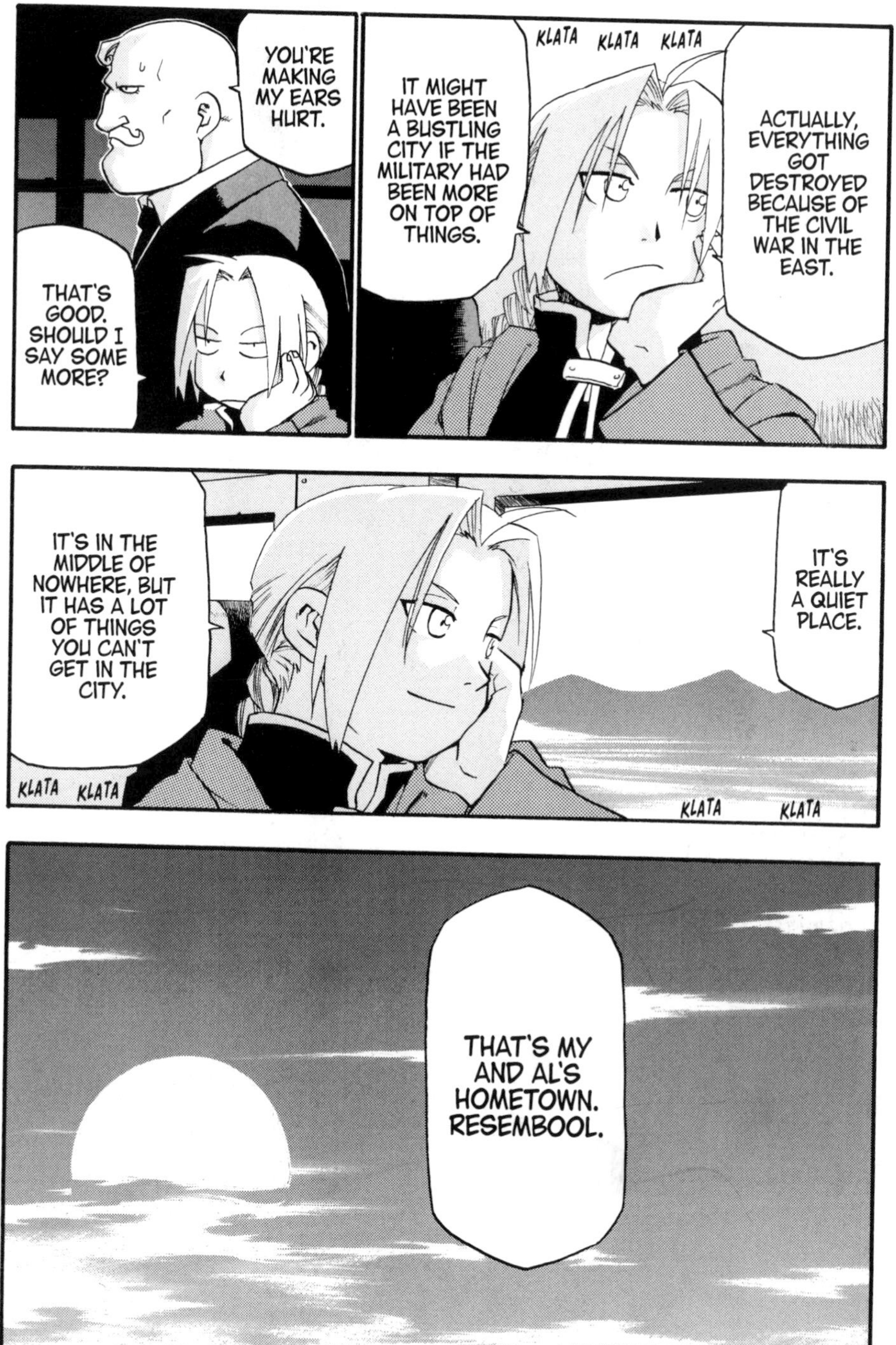
KLATA KLATA KLATA
ACTUALLY, EVERYTHING GOT DESTROYED BECAUSE OF THE CIVIL WAR IN THE EAST.
IT MIGHT HAVE BEEN A BUSTLING CITY IF THE MILITARY HAD BEEN MORE ON TOP OF THINGS.
YOU'RE MAKING MY EARS HURT.
THAT'S GOOD. SHOULD I SAY SOME MORE?
IT'S REALLY A QUIET PLACE.
IT'S IN THE MIDDLE OF NOWHERE, BUT IT HAS A LOT OF THINGS YOU CAN'T GET IN THE CITY.
KLATA KLATA
KLATA KLATA
THAT'S MY AND AL'S HOMETOWN. RESEMBOOL.

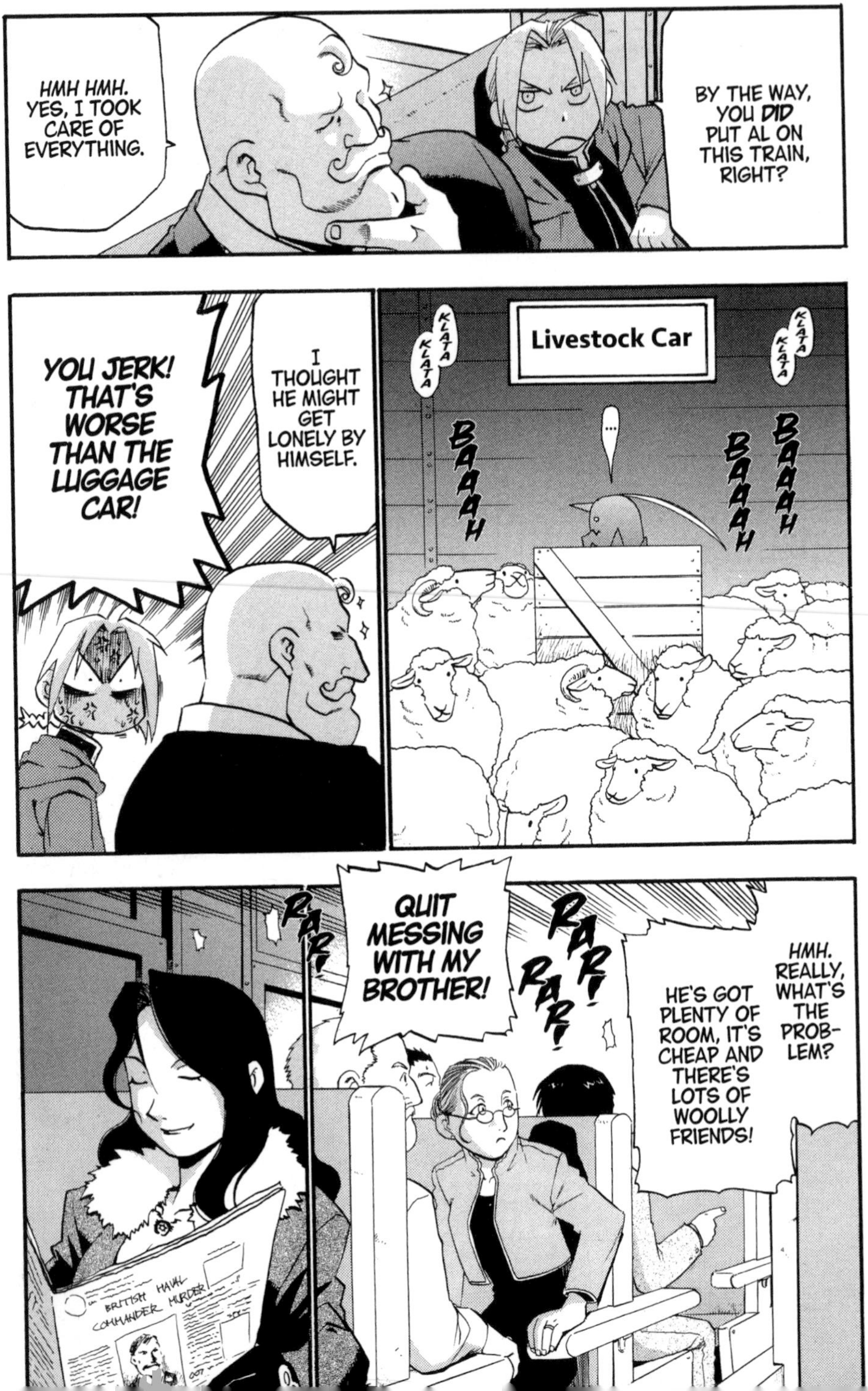

BY THE WAY, YOU **DID** PUT AL ON THIS TRAIN, RIGHT?
HMH HMH. YES, I TOOK CARE OF EVERYTHING.
Livestock Car
KLATA KLATA
KLATA KLATA
BAAAAH
BAAAAH
...
BAAAAH
I THOUGHT HE MIGHT GET LONELY BY HIMSELF.
YOU JERK! THAT'S WORSE THAN THE LUGGAGE CAR!
HMH. REALLY, WHAT'S THE PROB-LEM?
HE'S GOT PLENTY OF ROOM, IT'S CHEAP AND THERE'S LOTS OF WOOLLY FRIENDS!
RAR! RAR!
QUIT MESSING WITH MY BROTHER!
RAR!

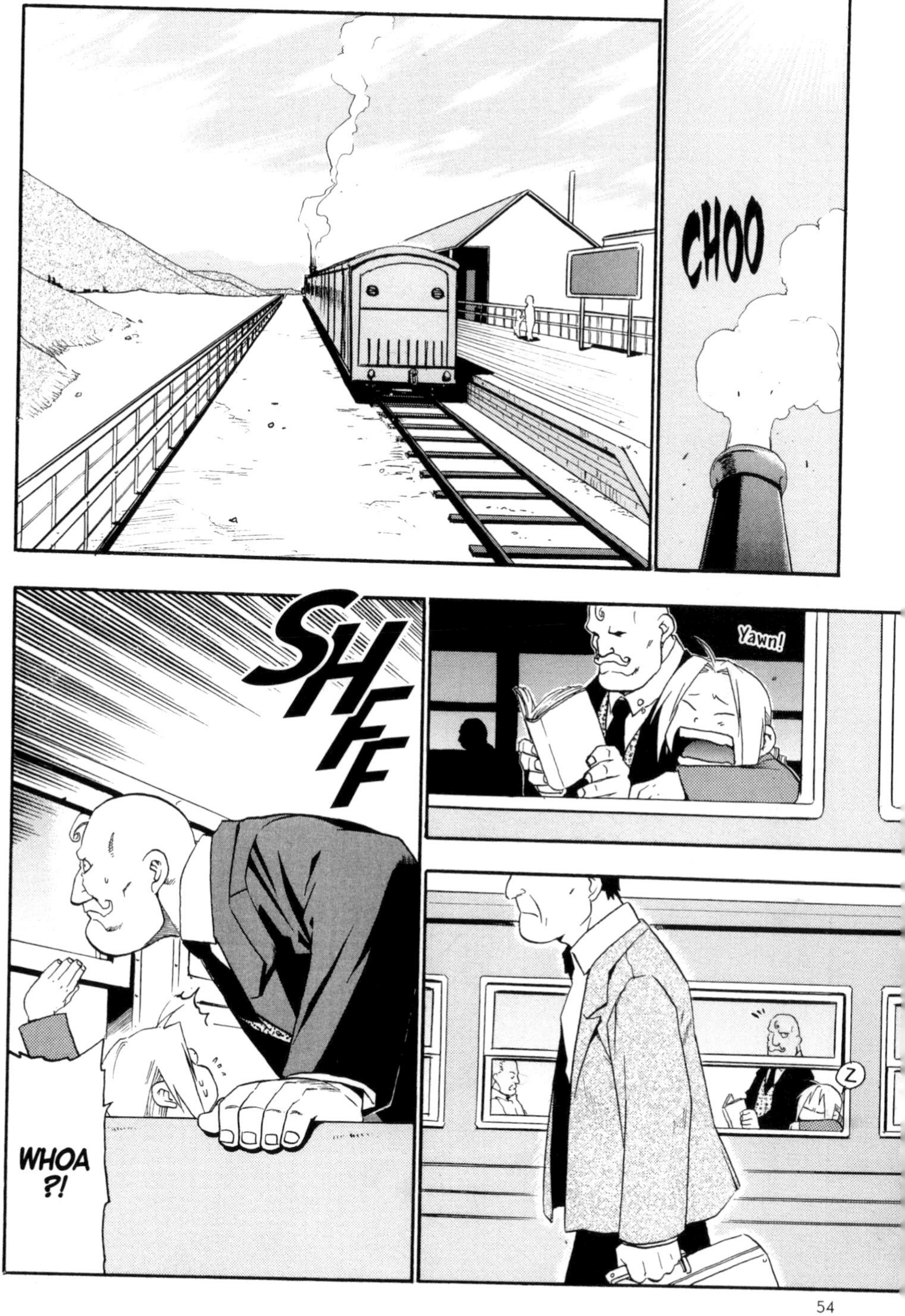
CHOO
Yawn!
Z
SHFF
WHOA?!

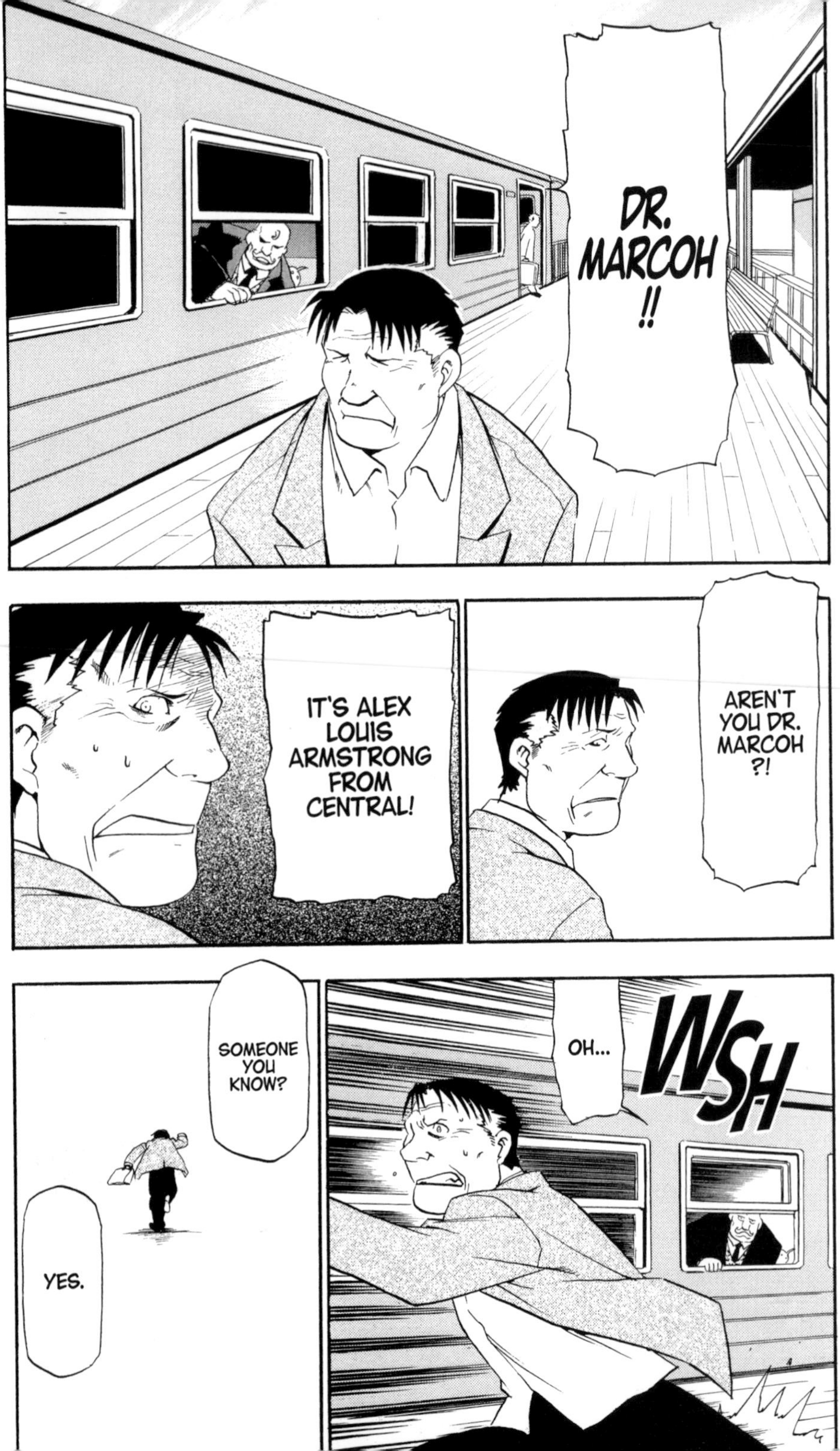
DR. MARCOH !!
AREN'T YOU DR. MARCOH ?!
IT'S ALEX LOUIS ARMSTRONG FROM CENTRAL!
OH...
WSH
SOMEONE YOU KNOW?
YES.

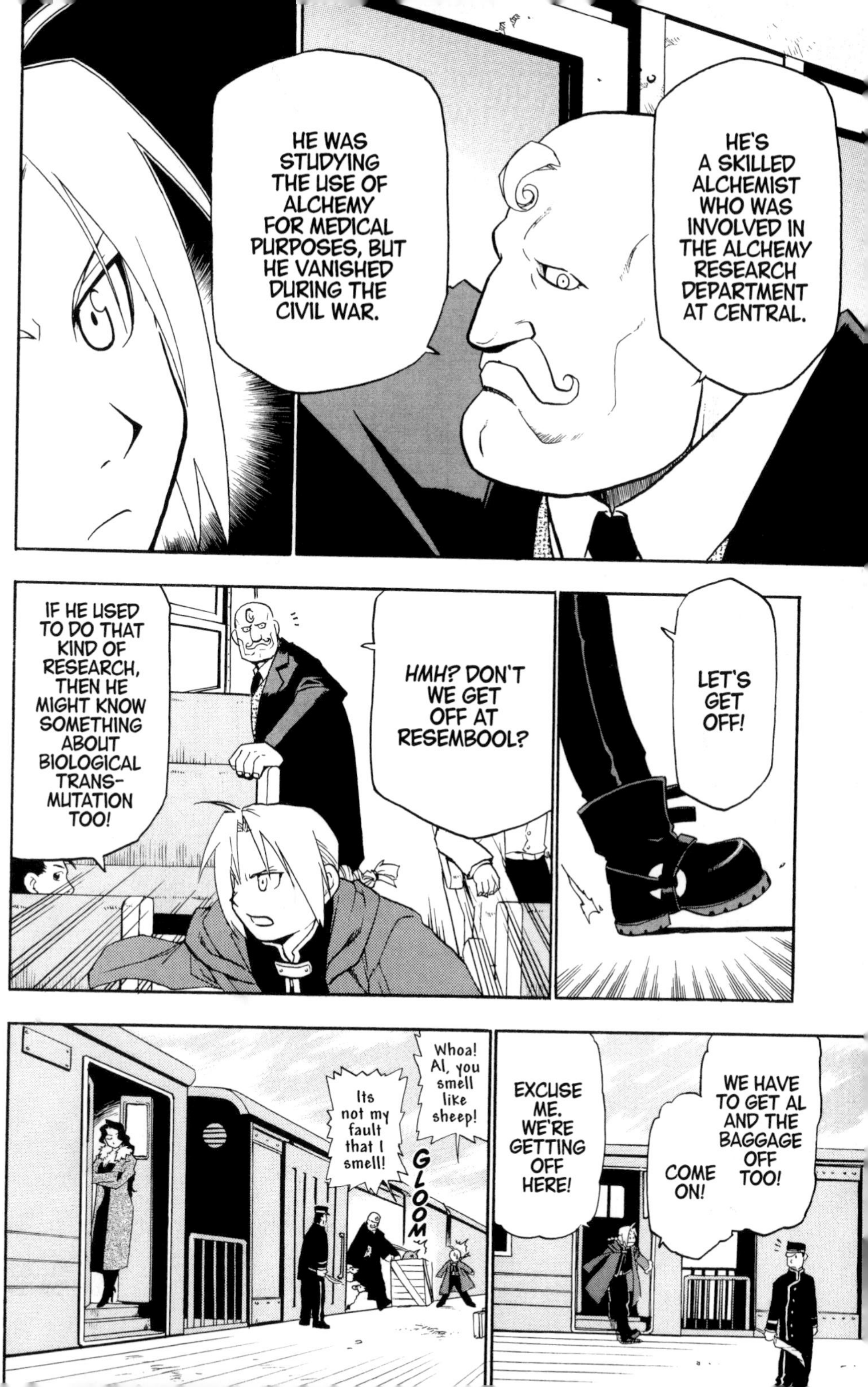
HE'S A SKILLED ALCHEMIST WHO WAS INVOLVED IN THE ALCHEMY RESEARCH DEPARTMENT AT CENTRAL.
HE WAS STUDYING THE USE OF ALCHEMY FOR MEDICAL PURPOSES, BUT HE VANISHED DURING THE CIVIL WAR.
LET'S GET OFF!
HMH? DON'T WE GET OFF AT RESEMBOOL?
IF HE USED TO DO THAT KIND OF RESEARCH, THEN HE MIGHT KNOW SOMETHING ABOUT BIOLOGICAL TRANS-MUTATION TOO!
WE HAVE TO GET AL AND THE BAGGAGE OFF TOO!
COME ON!
EXCUSE ME. WE'RE GETTING OFF HERE!
Whoa! Al, you smell like sheep!
Its not my fault that I smell!
GLOOM

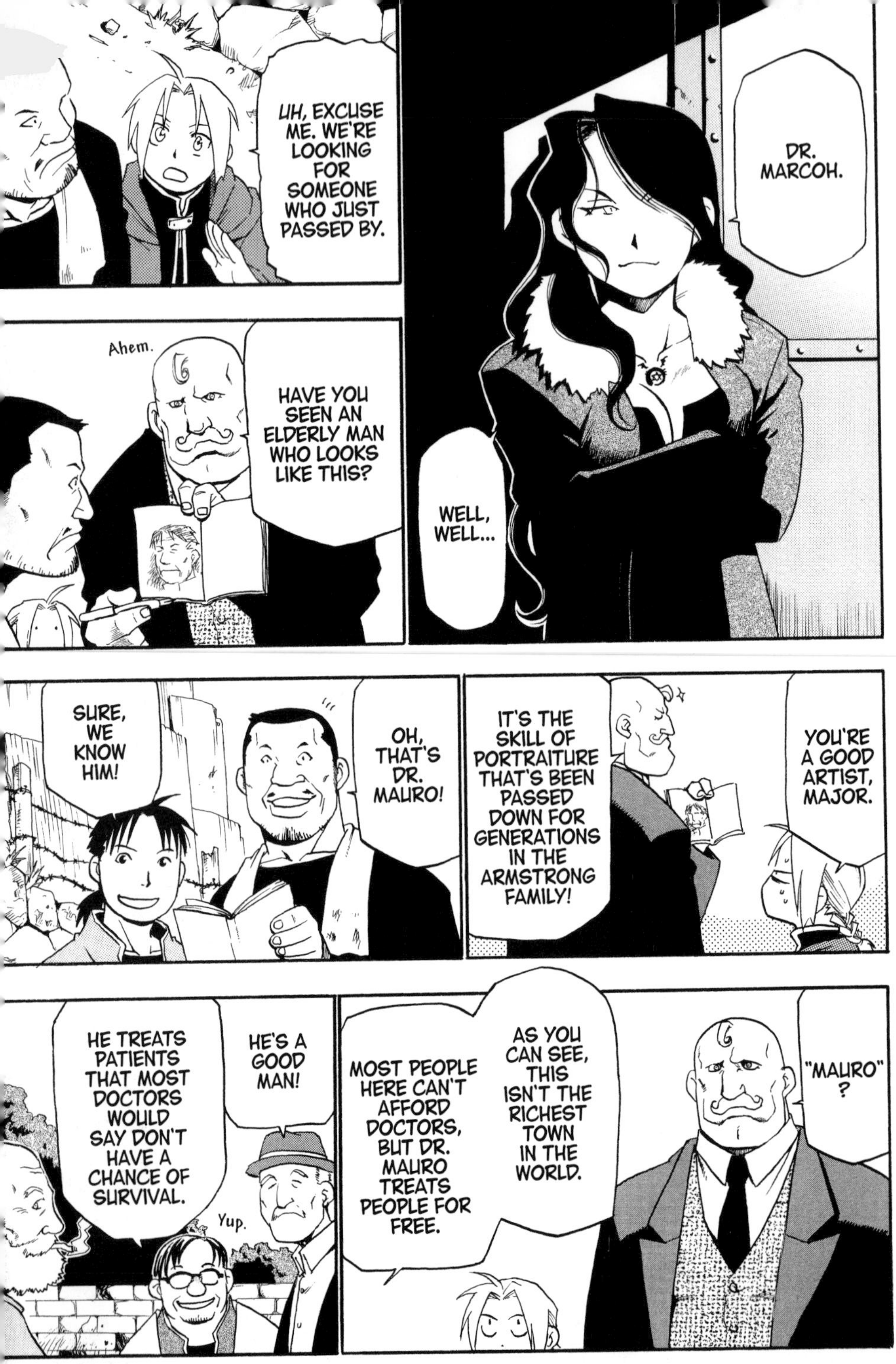
DR. MARCOH.
WELL, WELL...
UH, EXCUSE ME. WE'RE LOOKING FOR SOMEONE WHO JUST PASSED BY.
Ahem.
HAVE YOU SEEN AN ELDERLY MAN WHO LOOKS LIKE THIS?
YOU'RE A GOOD ARTIST, MAJOR.
IT'S THE SKILL OF PORTRAITURE THAT'S BEEN PASSED DOWN FOR GENERATIONS IN THE ARMSTRONG FAMILY!
OH, THAT'S DR. MAURO!
SURE, WE KNOW HIM!
"MAURO"?
AS YOU CAN SEE, THIS ISN'T THE RICHEST TOWN IN THE WORLD.
MOST PEOPLE HERE CAN'T AFFORD DOCTORS, BUT DR. MAURO TREATS PEOPLE FOR FREE.
HE'S A GOOD MAN!
HE TREATS PATIENTS THAT MOST DOCTORS WOULD SAY DON'T HAVE A CHANCE OF SURVIVAL.
Yup.

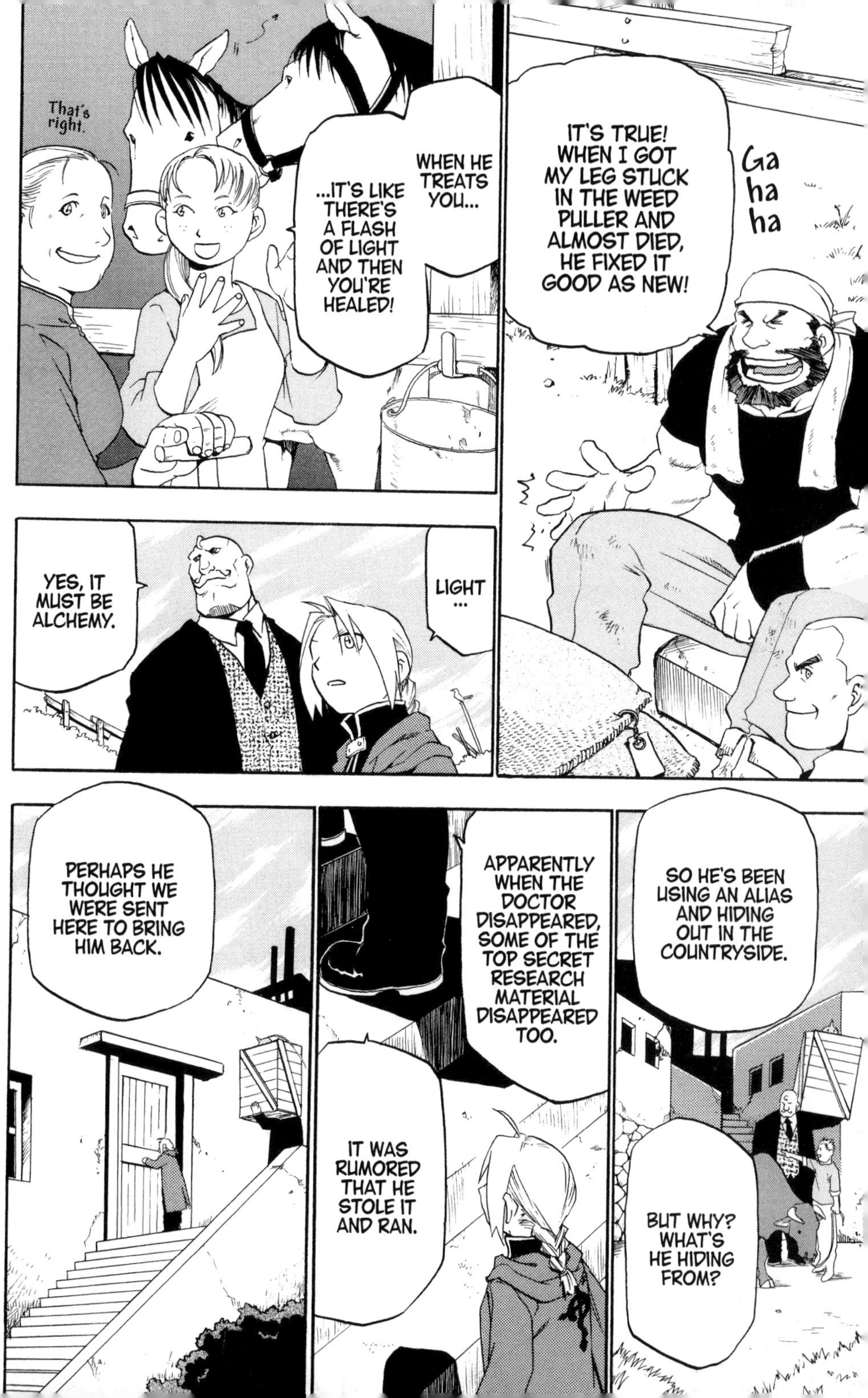
IT'S TRUE! WHEN I GOT MY LEG STUCK IN THE WEED PULLER AND ALMOST DIED, HE FIXED IT GOOD AS NEW!
Ga ha ha
That's right.
WHEN HE TREATS YOU...
...IT'S LIKE THERE'S A FLASH OF LIGHT AND THEN YOU'RE HEALED!
LIGHT...
YES, IT MUST BE ALCHEMY.
SO HE'S BEEN USING AN ALIAS AND HIDING OUT IN THE COUNTRYSIDE.
BUT WHY? WHAT'S HE HIDING FROM?
APPARENTLY WHEN THE DOCTOR DISAPPEARED, SOME OF THE TOP SECRET RESEARCH MATERIAL DISAPPEARED TOO.
IT WAS RUMORED THAT HE STOLE IT AND RAN.
PERHAPS HE THOUGHT WE WERE SENT HERE TO BRING HIM BACK.

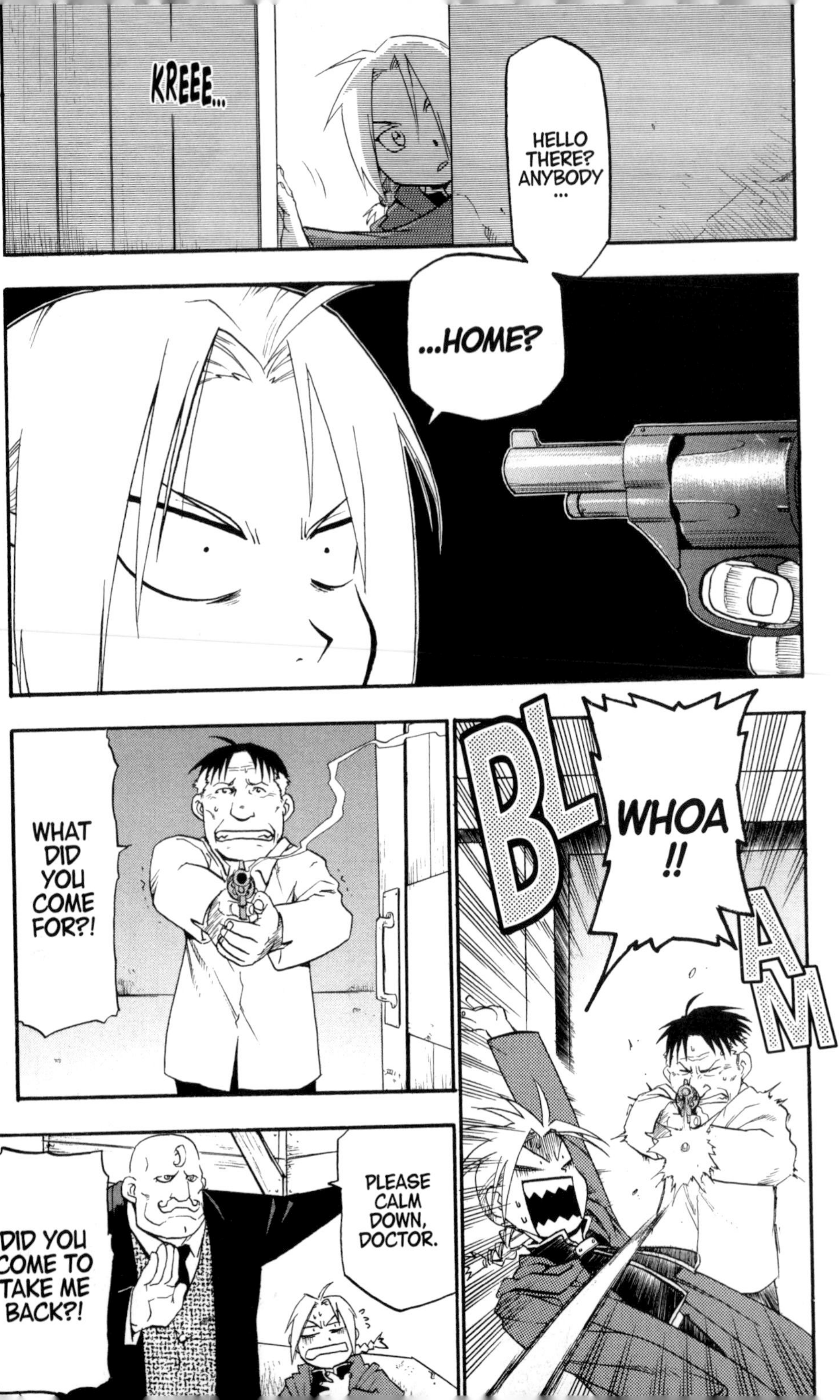
HELLO THERE? ANYBODY ...
KREEE...
...HOME?
BLAM
WHOA !!
WHAT DID YOU COME FOR?!
PLEASE CALM DOWN, DOCTOR.
DID YOU COME TO TAKE ME BACK?!

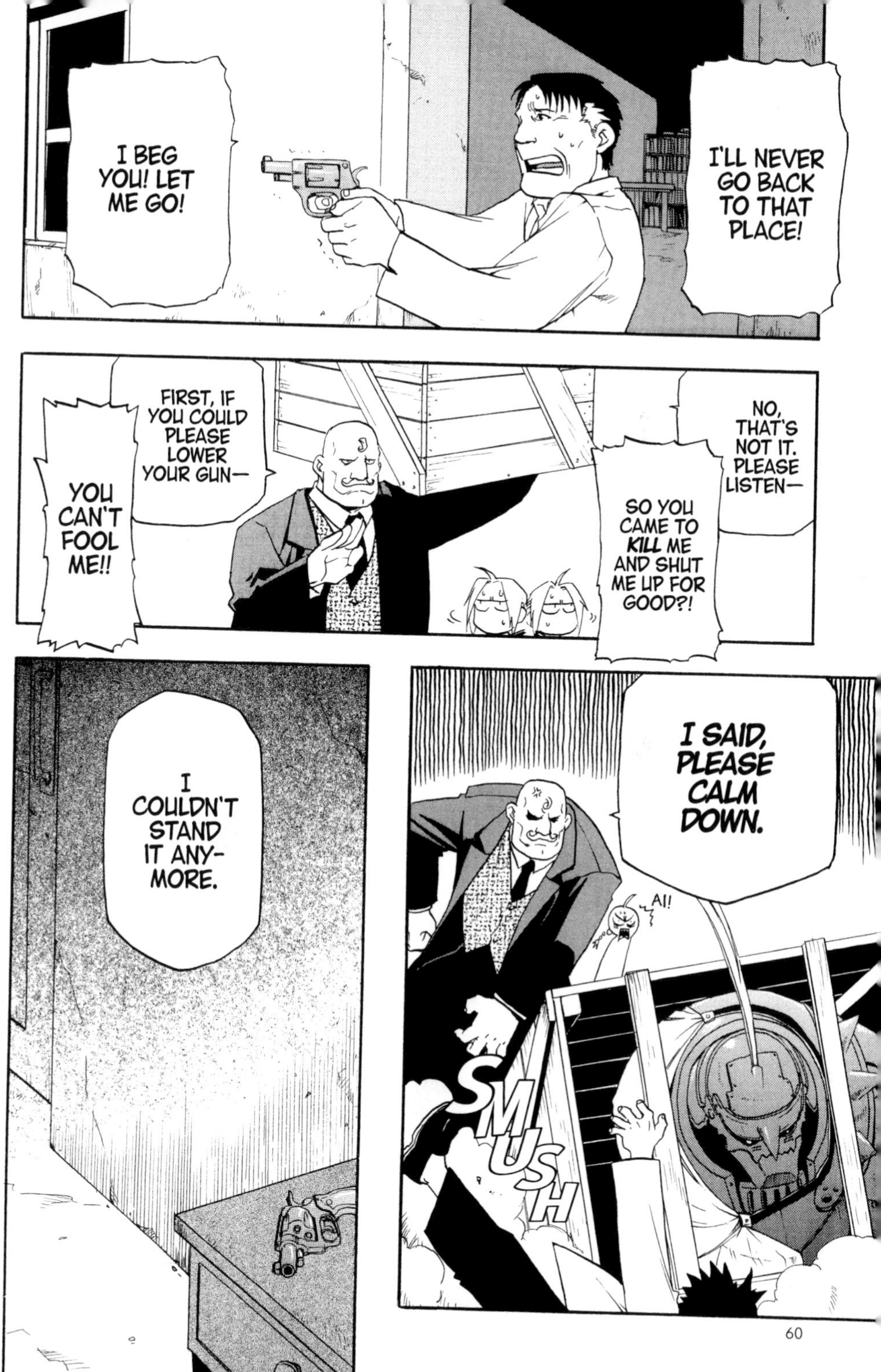
I'LL NEVER GO BACK TO THAT PLACE!
I BEG YOU! LET ME GO!
NO, THAT'S NOT IT. PLEASE LISTEN—
SO YOU CAME TO KILL ME AND SHUT ME UP FOR GOOD?!
FIRST, IF YOU COULD PLEASE LOWER YOUR GUN—
YOU CAN'T FOOL ME!!
I SAID, PLEASE CALM DOWN.
AI!
SMUSH
I COULDN'T STAND IT ANY-MORE.

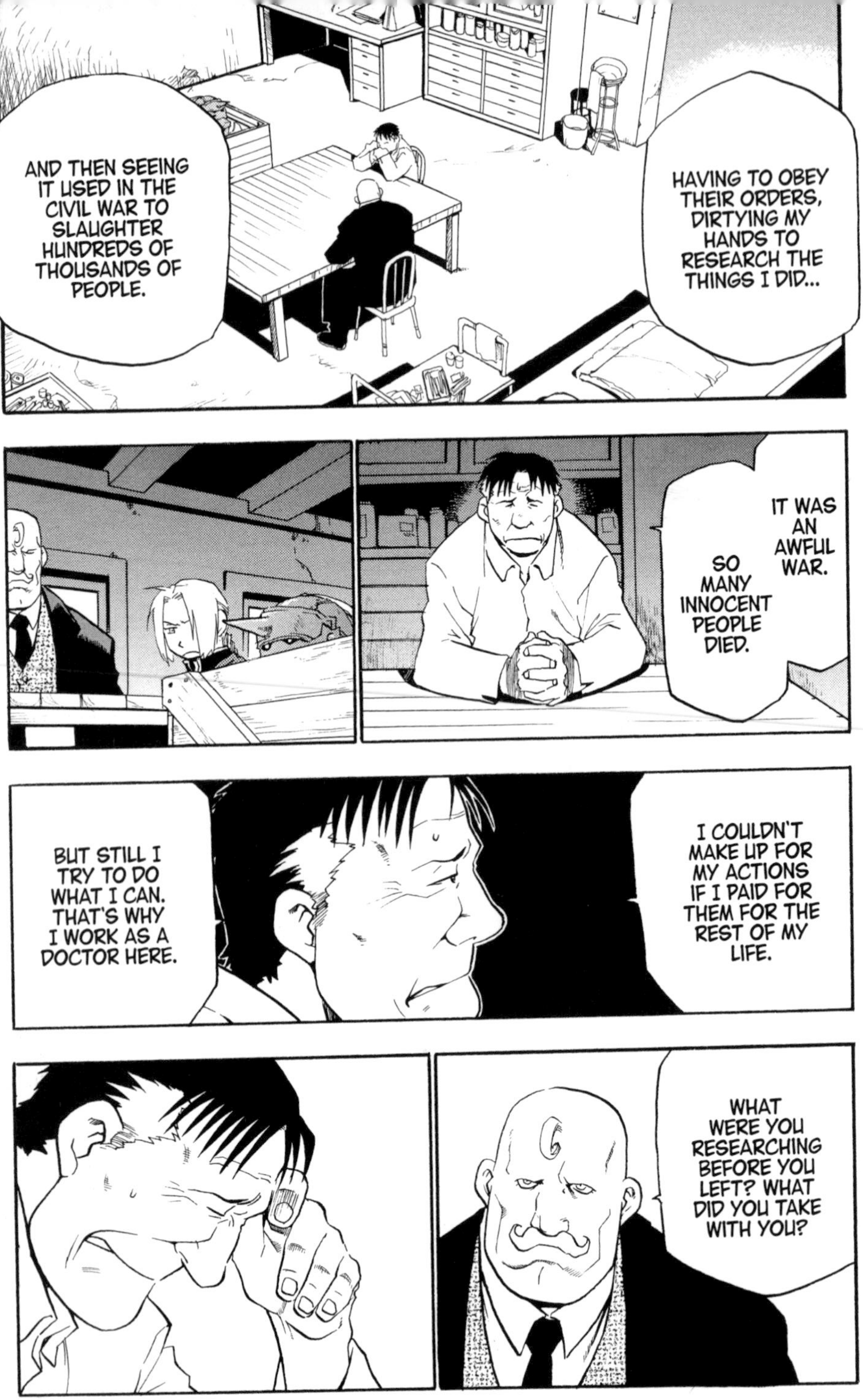
HAVING TO OBEY THEIR ORDERS, DIRTYING MY HANDS TO RESEARCH THE THINGS I DID...
AND THEN SEEING IT USED IN THE CIVIL WAR TO SLAUGHTER HUNDREDS OF THOUSANDS OF PEOPLE.
IT WAS AN AWFUL WAR.
SO MANY INNOCENT PEOPLE DIED.
I COULDN'T MAKE UP FOR MY ACTIONS IF I PAID FOR THEM FOR THE REST OF MY LIFE.
BUT STILL I TRY TO DO WHAT I CAN. THAT'S WHY I WORK AS A DOCTOR HERE.
WHAT WERE YOU RESEARCHING BEFORE YOU LEFT? WHAT DID YOU TAKE WITH YOU?

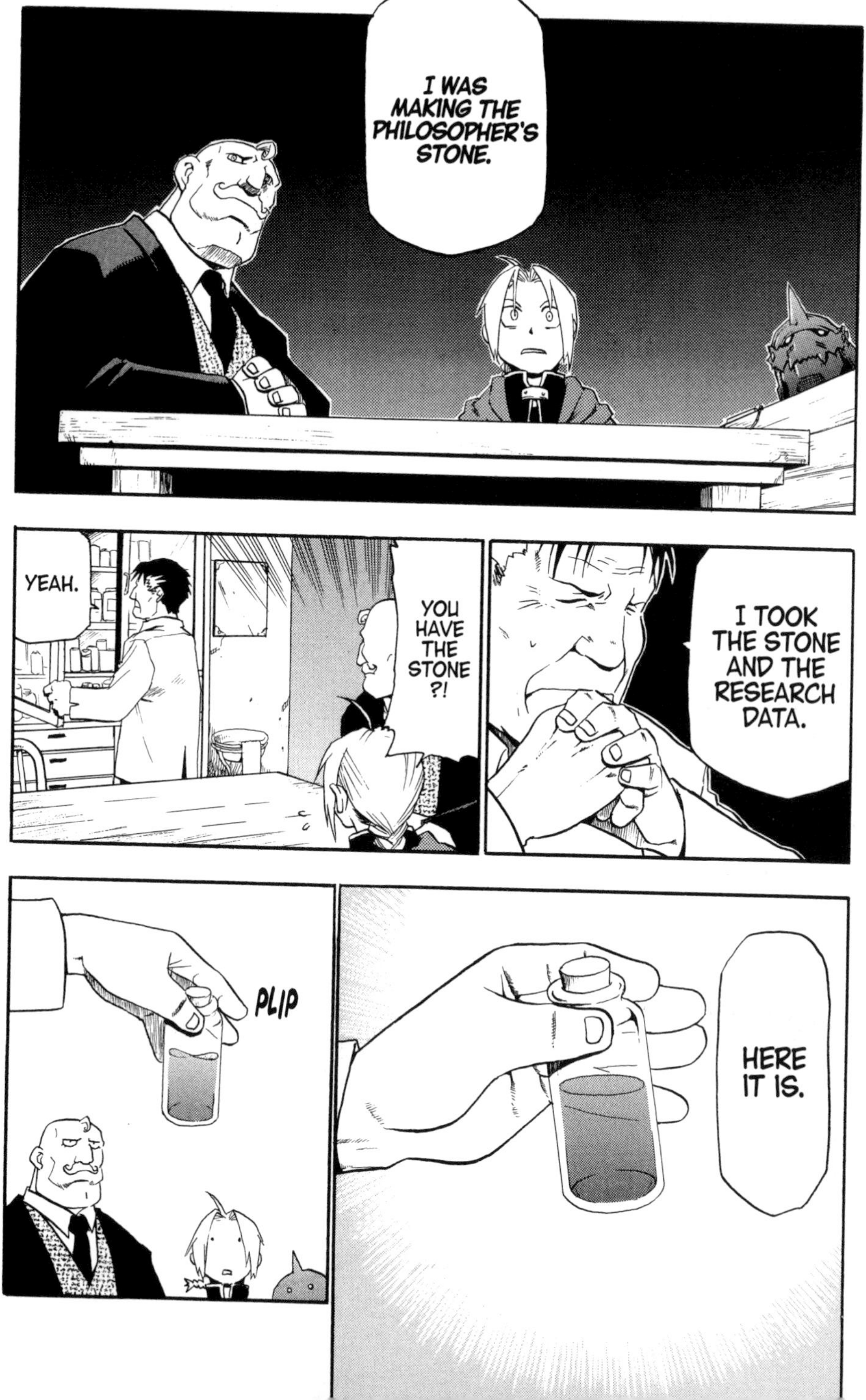
I WAS MAKING THE PHILOSOPHER'S STONE.
I TOOK THE STONE AND THE RESEARCH DATA.
YOU HAVE THE STONE ?!
YEAH.
HERE IT IS.
PLIP

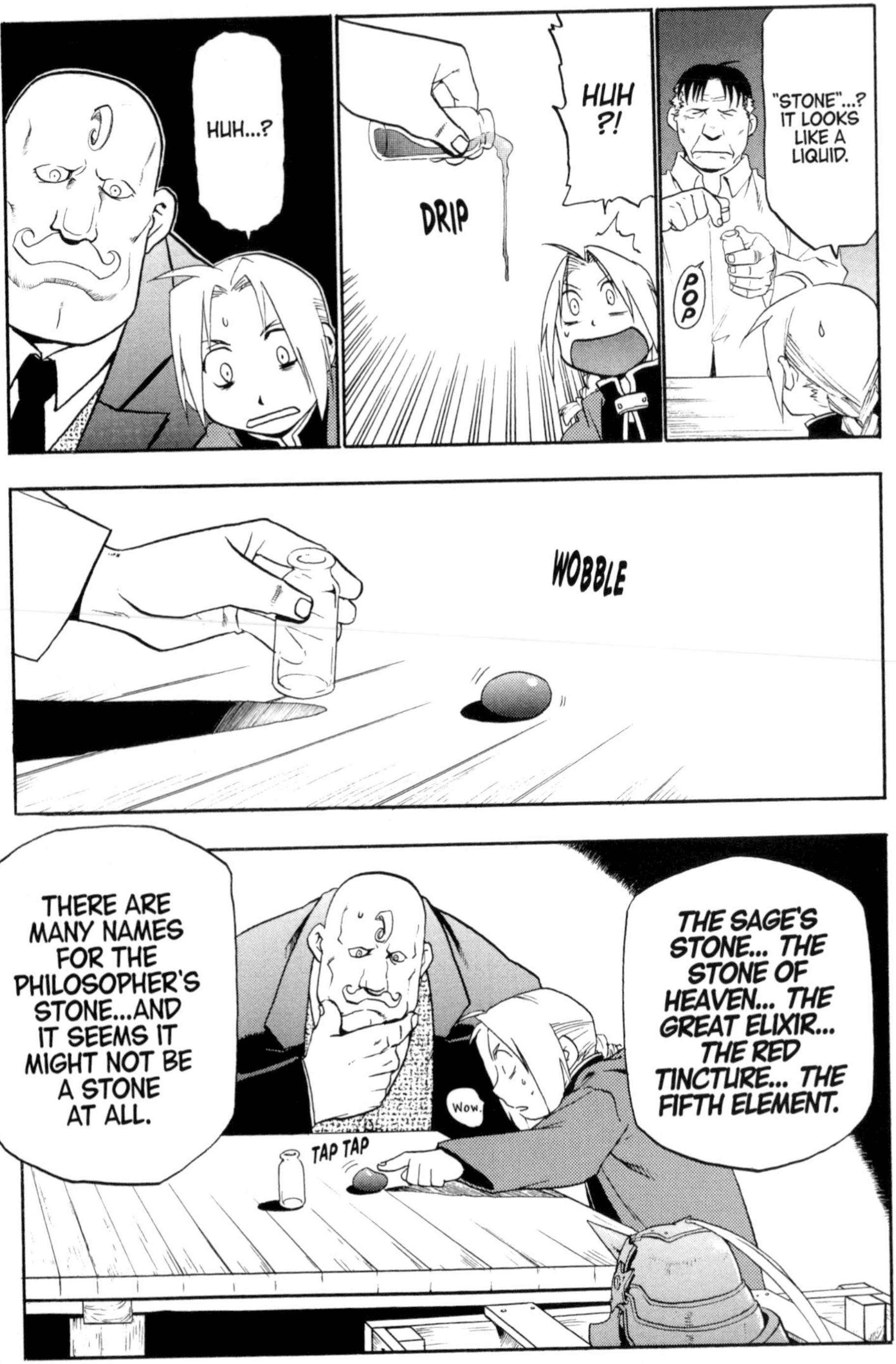

"STONE"...? IT LOOKS LIKE A LIQUID.
POP
HUH ?!
DRIP
HUH...?
WOBBLE
THE SAGE'S STONE... THE STONE OF HEAVEN... THE GREAT ELIXIR... THE RED TINCTURE... THE FIFTH ELEMENT.
THERE ARE MANY NAMES FOR THE PHILOSOPHER'S STONE...AND IT SEEMS IT MIGHT NOT BE A STONE AT ALL.
Wow.
TAP TAP

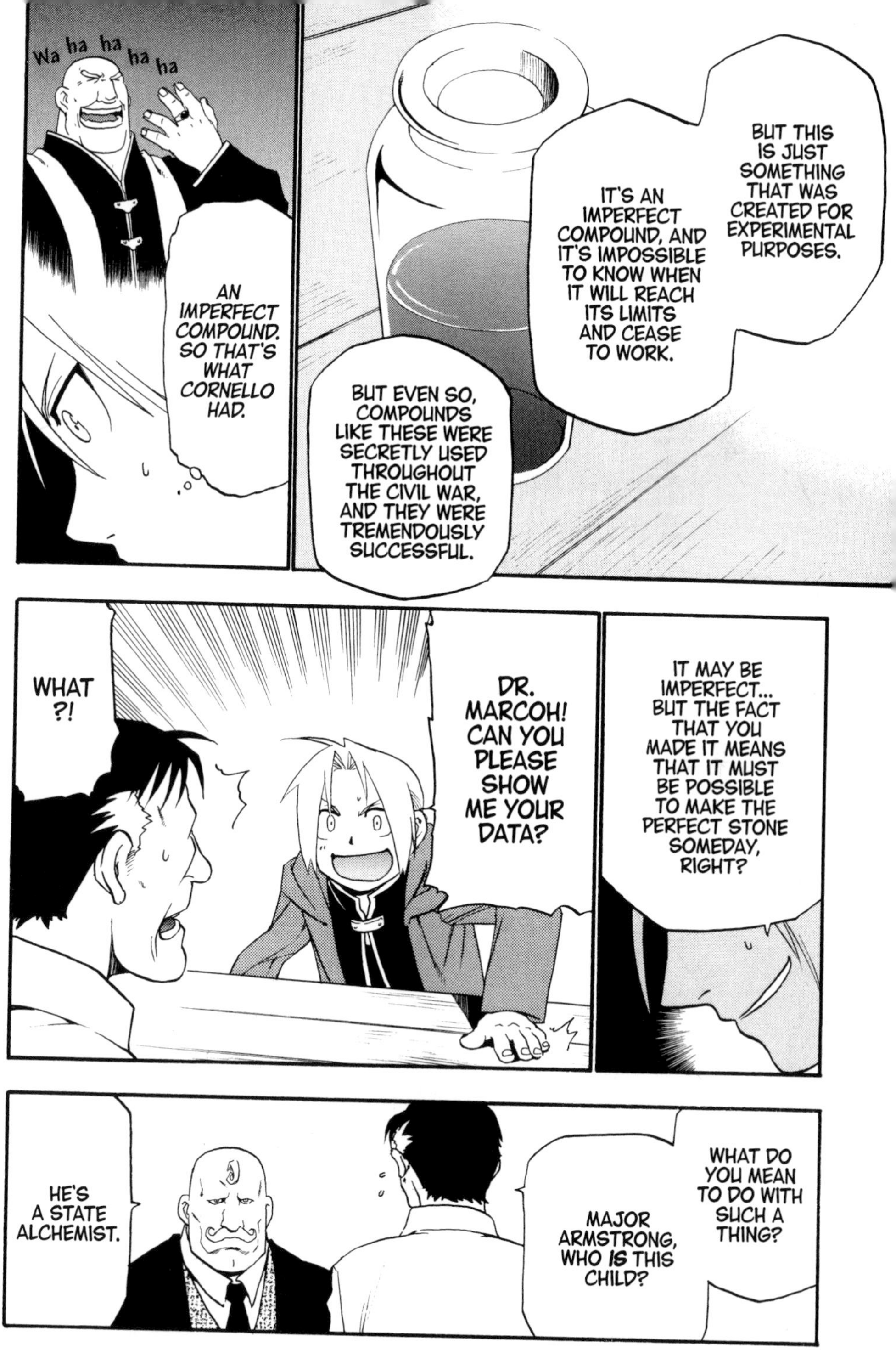
BUT THIS IS JUST SOMETHING THAT WAS CREATED FOR EXPERIMENTAL PURPOSES.
IT'S AN IMPERFECT COMPOUND, AND IT'S IMPOSSIBLE TO KNOW WHEN IT WILL REACH ITS LIMITS AND CEASE TO WORK.
BUT EVEN SO, COMPOUNDS LIKE THESE WERE SECRETLY USED THROUGHOUT THE CIVIL WAR, AND THEY WERE TREMENDOUSLY SUCCESSFUL.
Wa ha ha ha ha
AN IMPERFECT COMPOUND. SO THAT'S WHAT CORNELLO HAD.
IT MAY BE IMPERFECT... BUT THE FACT THAT YOU MADE IT MEANS THAT IT MUST BE POSSIBLE TO MAKE THE PERFECT STONE SOMEDAY, RIGHT?
DR. MARCOH! CAN YOU PLEASE SHOW ME YOUR DATA?
WHAT ?!
WHAT DO YOU MEAN TO DO WITH SUCH A THING?
MAJOR ARMSTRONG, WHO **IS** THIS CHILD?
HE'S A STATE ALCHEMIST.

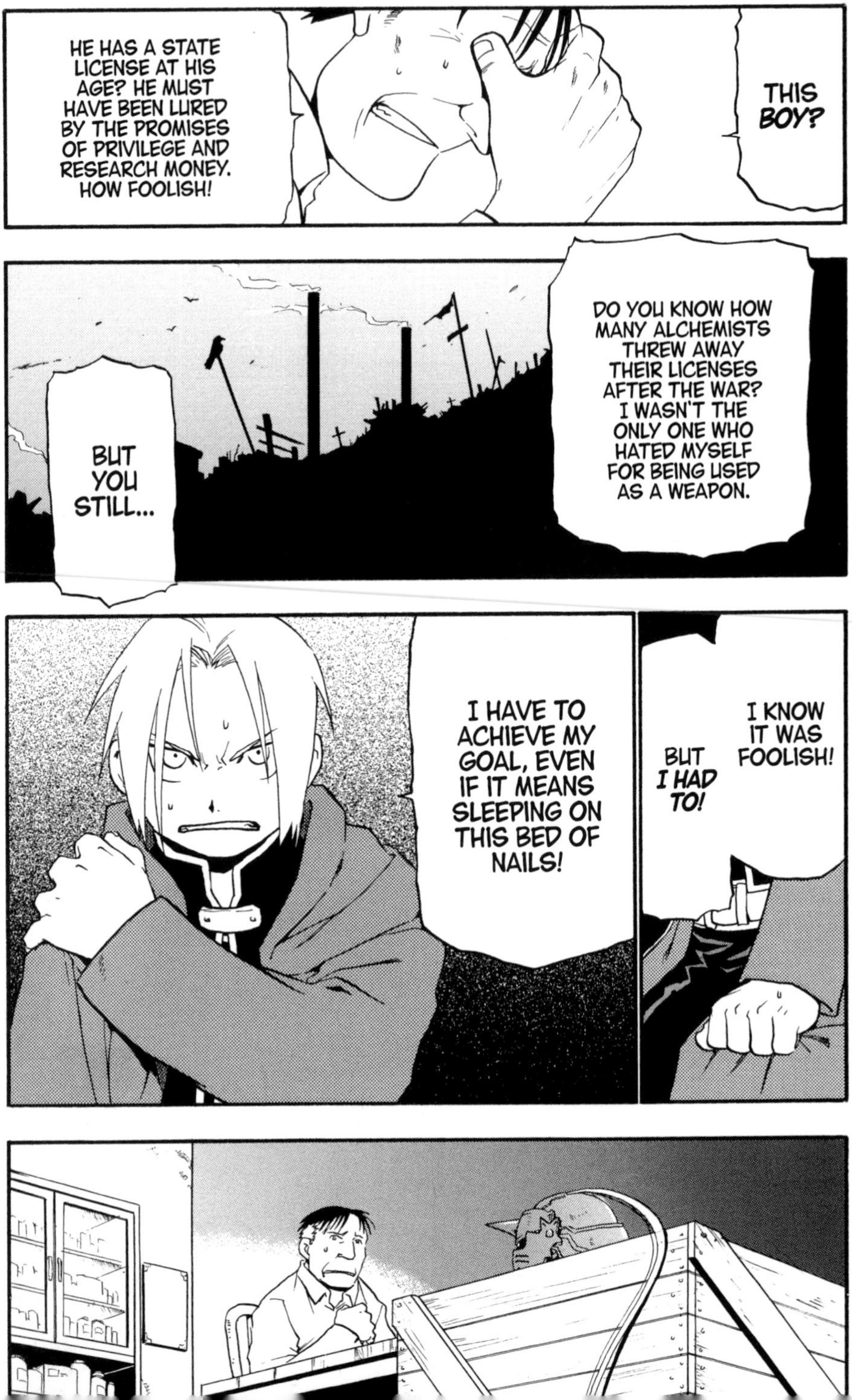
THIS *BOY?*
HE HAS A STATE LICENSE AT HIS AGE? HE MUST HAVE BEEN LURED BY THE PROMISES OF PRIVILEGE AND RESEARCH MONEY. HOW FOOLISH!
DO YOU KNOW HOW MANY ALCHEMISTS THREW AWAY THEIR LICENSES AFTER THE WAR? I WASN'T THE ONLY ONE WHO HATED MYSELF FOR BEING USED AS A WEAPON.
BUT YOU STILL...
I KNOW IT WAS FOOLISH!
BUT *I HAD TO!*
I HAVE TO ACHIEVE MY GOAL, EVEN IF IT MEANS SLEEPING ON THIS BED OF NAILS!

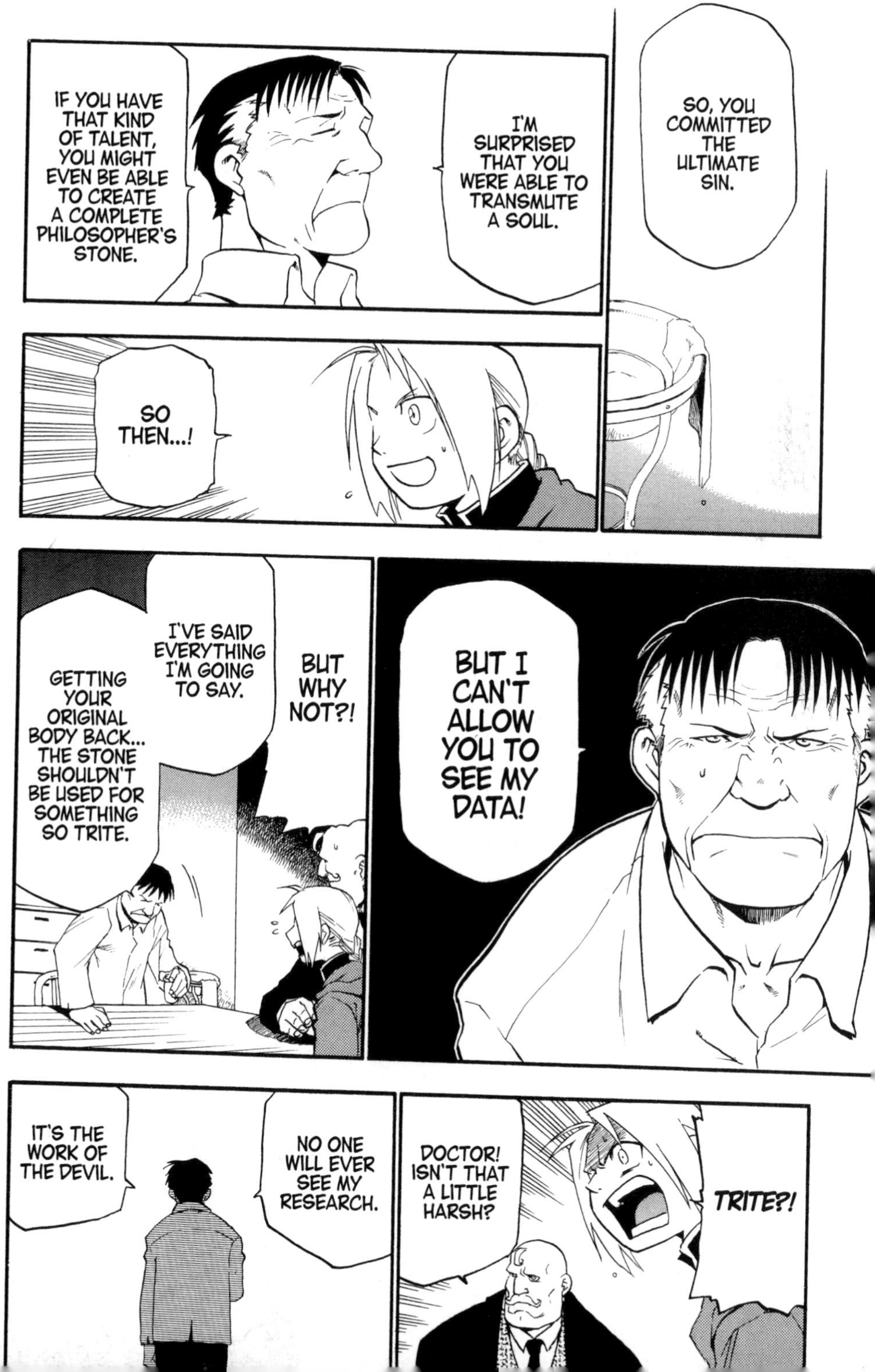
SO, YOU COMMITTED THE ULTIMATE SIN.
I'M SURPRISED THAT YOU WERE ABLE TO TRANSMUTE A SOUL.
IF YOU HAVE THAT KIND OF TALENT, YOU MIGHT EVEN BE ABLE TO CREATE A COMPLETE PHILOSOPHER'S STONE.
SO THEN...!
BUT I CAN'T ALLOW YOU TO SEE MY DATA!
BUT WHY NOT?!
I'VE SAID EVERYTHING I'M GOING TO SAY.
GETTING YOUR ORIGINAL BODY BACK... THE STONE SHOULDN'T BE USED FOR SOMETHING SO TRITE.
TRITE?!
DOCTOR! ISN'T THAT A LITTLE HARSH?
NO ONE WILL EVER SEE MY RESEARCH.
IT'S THE WORK OF THE DEVIL.

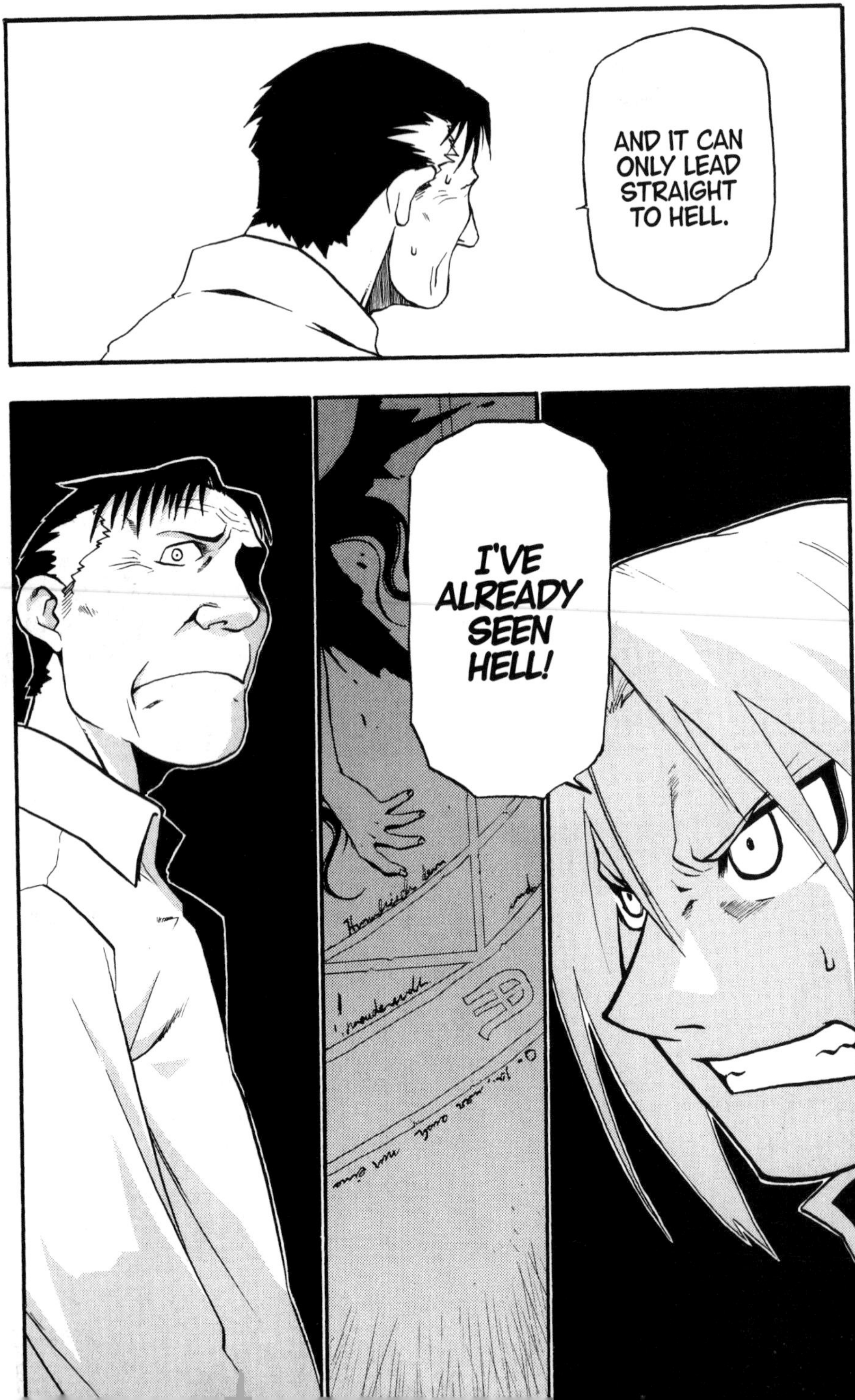
AND IT CAN ONLY LEAD STRAIGHT TO HELL.
I'VE ALREADY SEEN HELL!

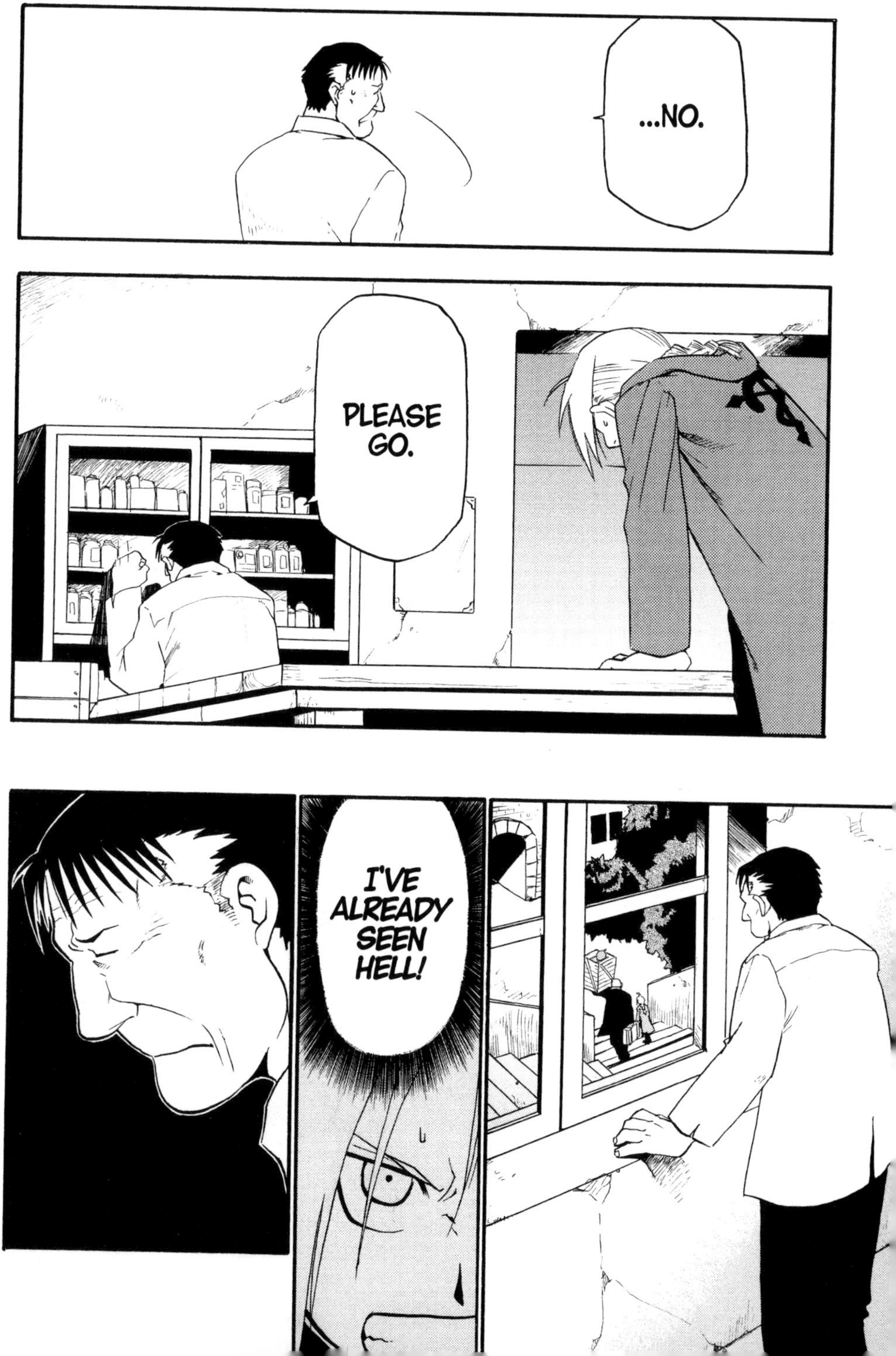
...NO.
PLEASE GO.
I'VE ALREADY SEEN HELL!

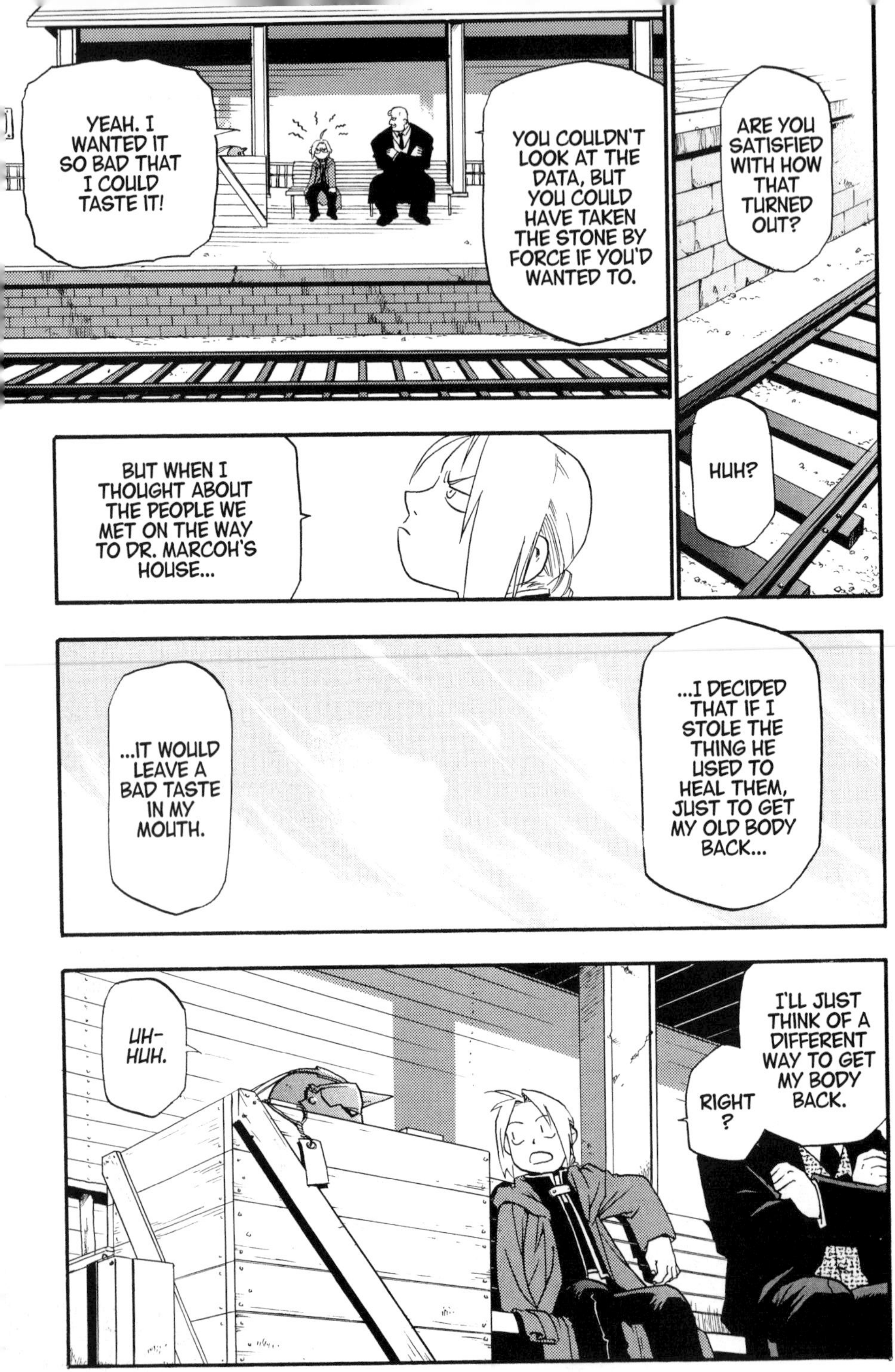
ARE YOU SATISFIED WITH HOW THAT TURNED OUT?
HUH?
YOU COULDN'T LOOK AT THE DATA, BUT YOU COULD HAVE TAKEN THE STONE BY FORCE IF YOU'D WANTED TO.
YEAH. I WANTED IT SO BAD THAT I COULD TASTE IT!
BUT WHEN I THOUGHT ABOUT THE PEOPLE WE MET ON THE WAY TO DR. MARCOH'S HOUSE...
...I DECIDED THAT IF I STOLE THE THING HE USED TO HEAL THEM, JUST TO GET MY OLD BODY BACK...
...IT WOULD LEAVE A BAD TASTE IN MY MOUTH.
I'LL JUST THINK OF A DIFFERENT WAY TO GET MY BODY BACK.
RIGHT?
UH-HUH.

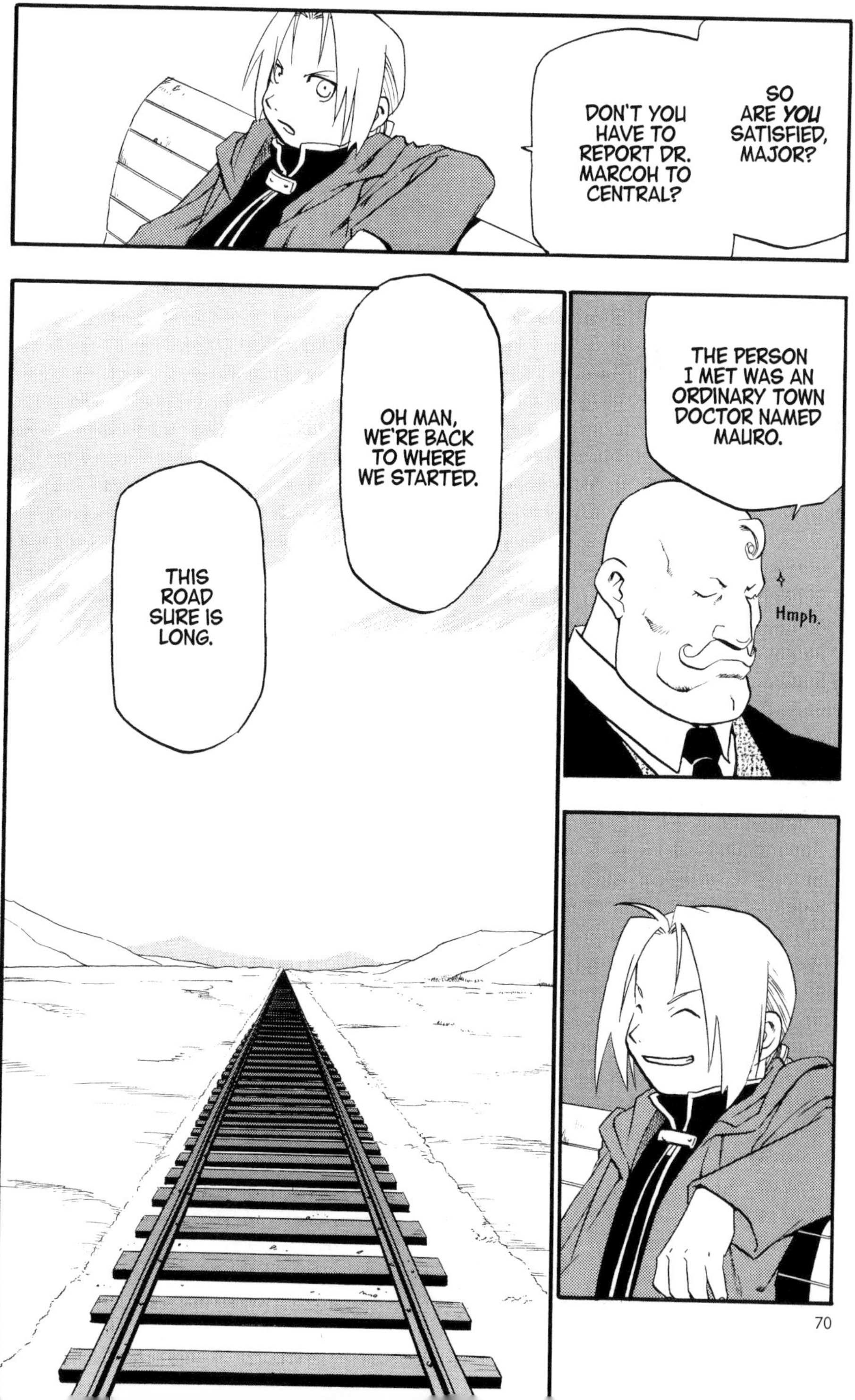
SO ARE *YOU* SATISFIED, MAJOR?
DON'T YOU HAVE TO REPORT DR. MARCOH TO CENTRAL?
THE PERSON I MET WAS AN ORDINARY TOWN DOCTOR NAMED MAURO.
Hmph.
OH MAN, WE'RE BACK TO WHERE WE STARTED.
THIS ROAD SURE IS LONG.

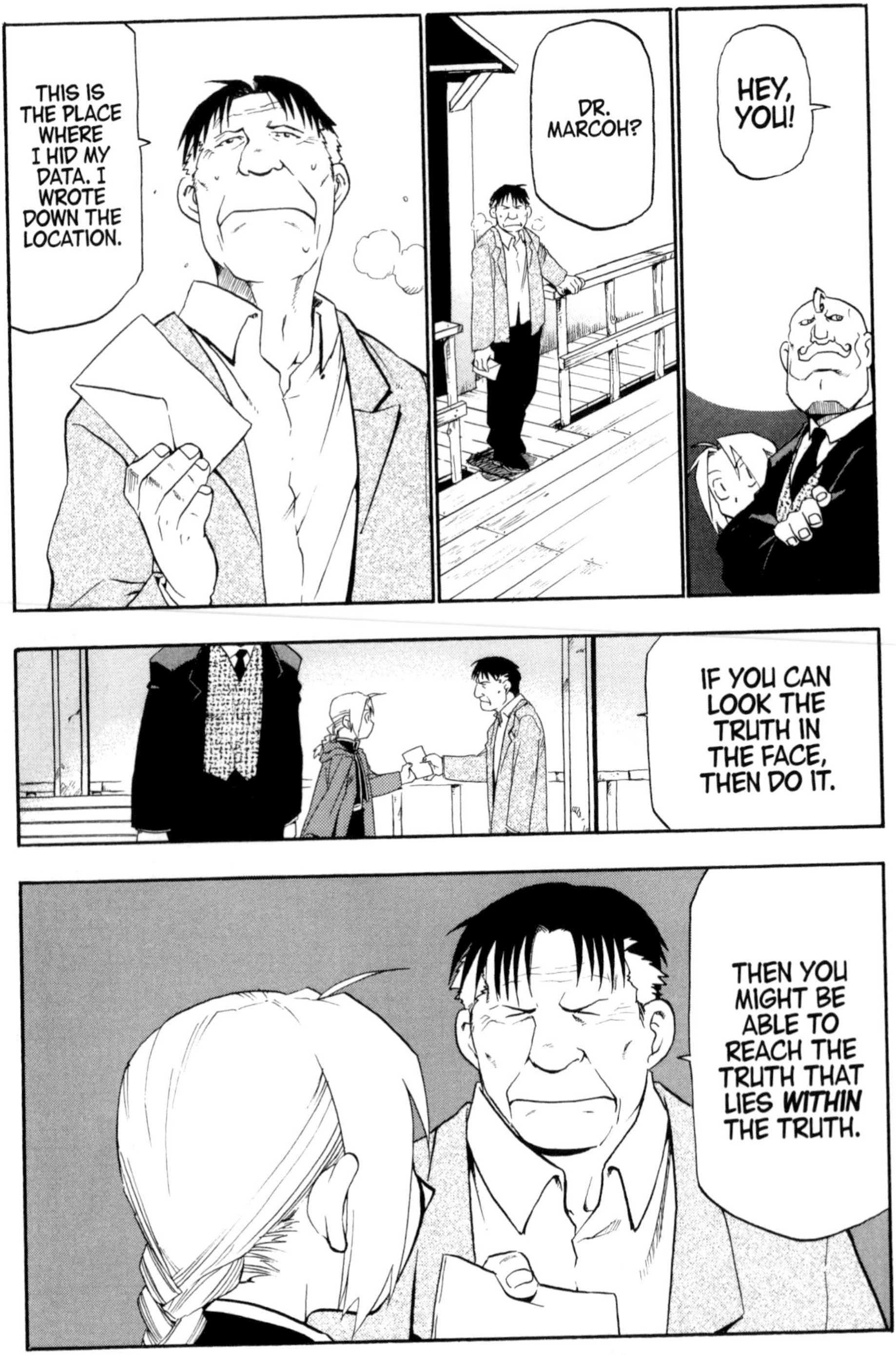
HEY, YOU!
DR. MARCOH?
THIS IS THE PLACE WHERE I HID MY DATA. I WROTE DOWN THE LOCATION.
IF YOU CAN LOOK THE TRUTH IN THE FACE, THEN DO IT.
THEN YOU MIGHT BE ABLE TO REACH THE TRUTH THAT LIES *WITHIN* THE TRUTH.

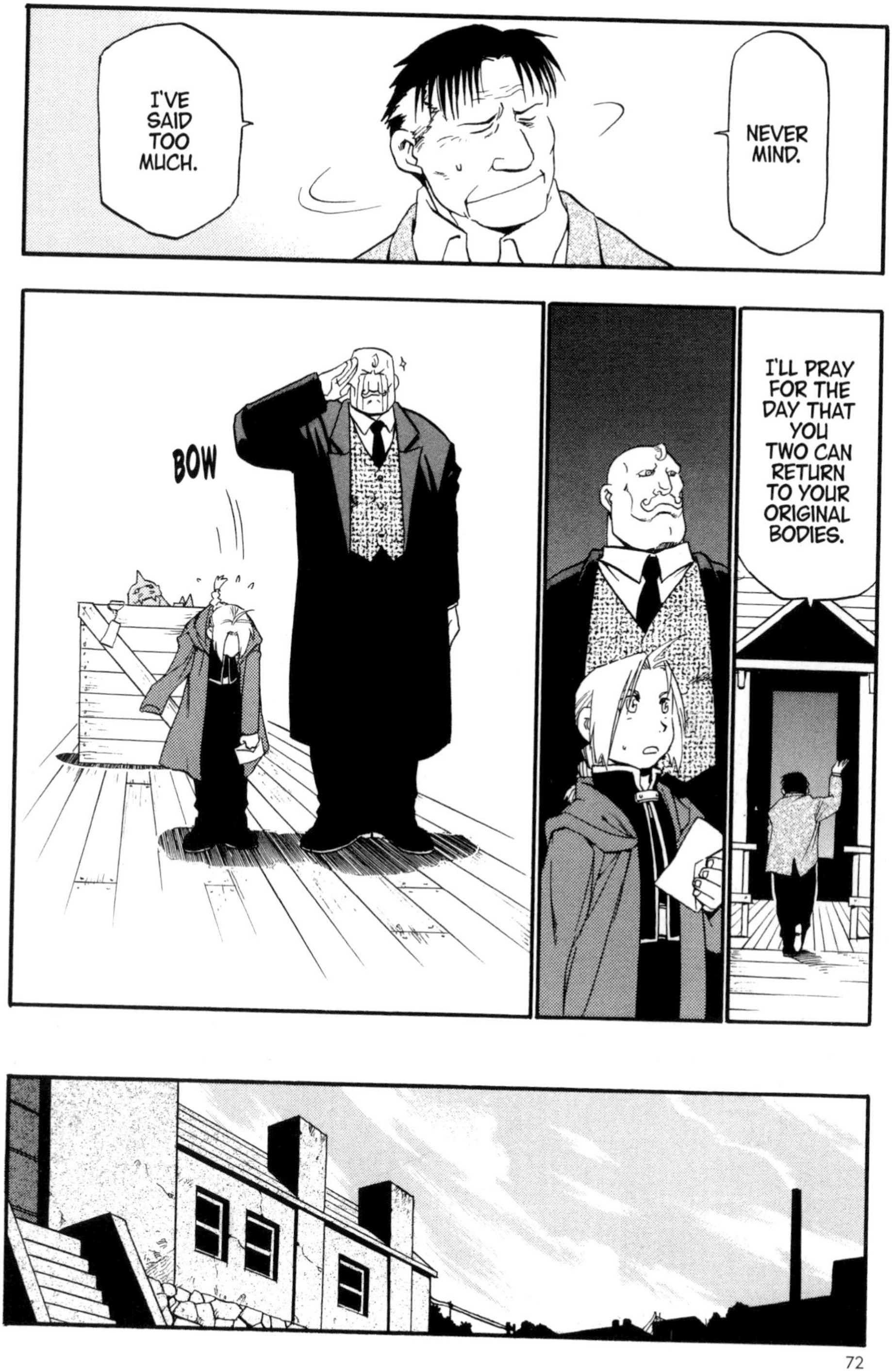
NEVER MIND.
I'VE SAID TOO MUCH.
I'LL PRAY FOR THE DAY THAT YOU TWO CAN RETURN TO YOUR ORIGINAL BODIES.
BOW

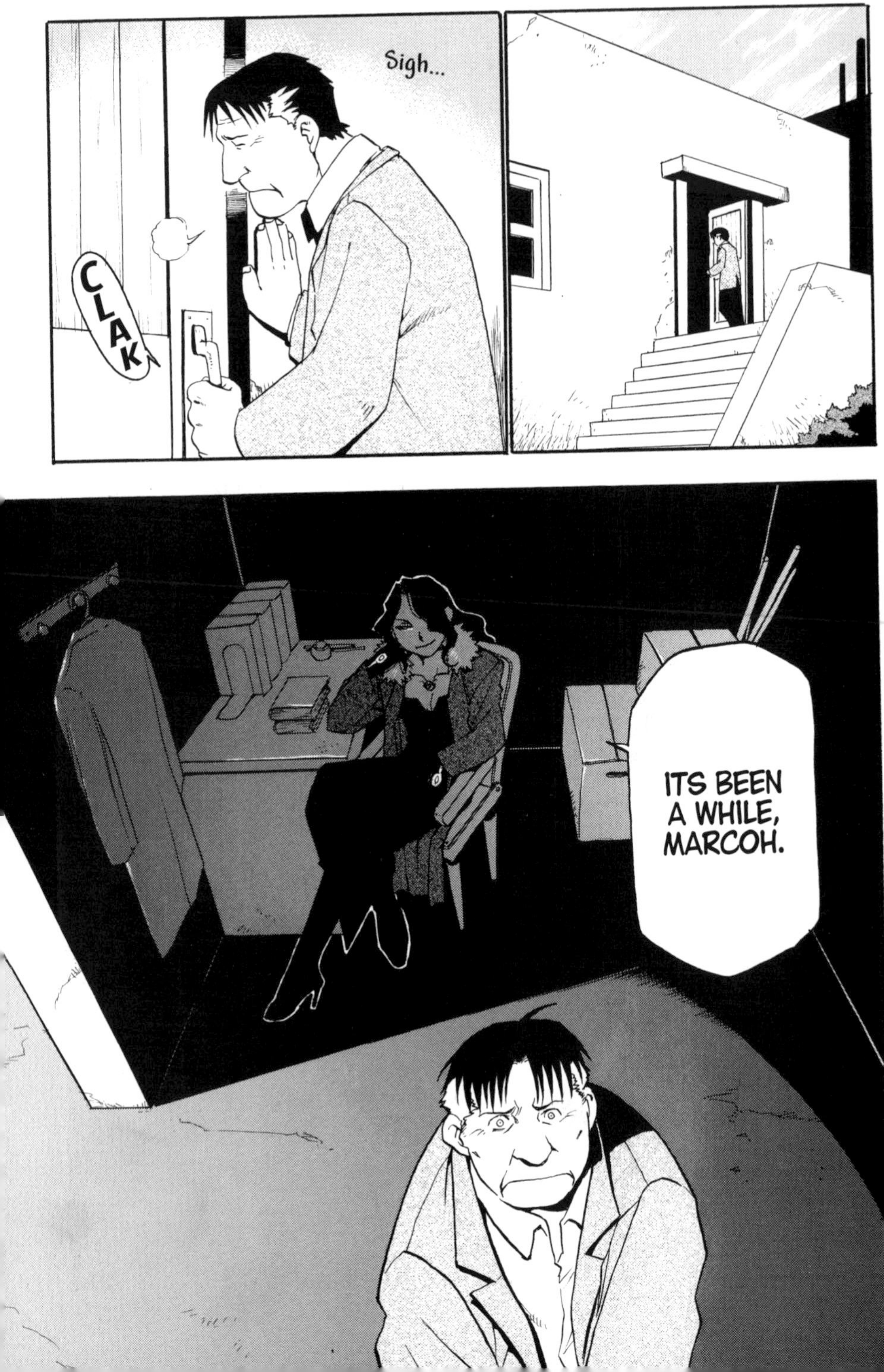
Sigh...
CLAK
ITS BEEN A WHILE, MARCOH.

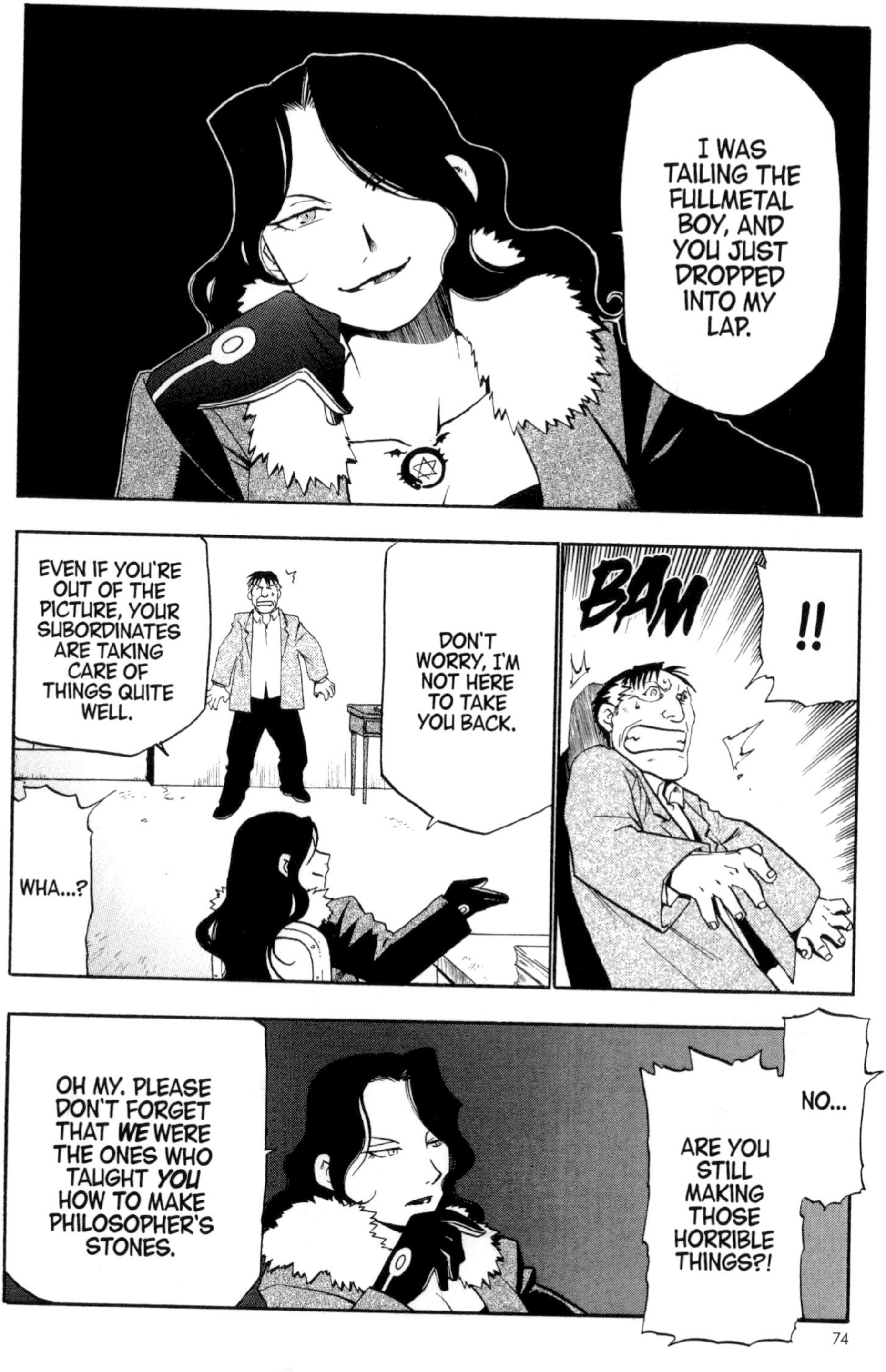
I WAS TAILING THE FULLMETAL BOY, AND YOU JUST DROPPED INTO MY LAP.
BAM
!!
DON'T WORRY, I'M NOT HERE TO TAKE YOU BACK.
EVEN IF YOU'RE OUT OF THE PICTURE, YOUR SUBORDINATES ARE TAKING CARE OF THINGS QUITE WELL.
WHA...?
NO...
ARE YOU STILL MAKING THOSE HORRIBLE THINGS?!
OH MY. PLEASE DON'T FORGET THAT *WE* WERE THE ONES WHO TAUGHT *YOU* HOW TO MAKE PHILOSOPHER'S STONES.

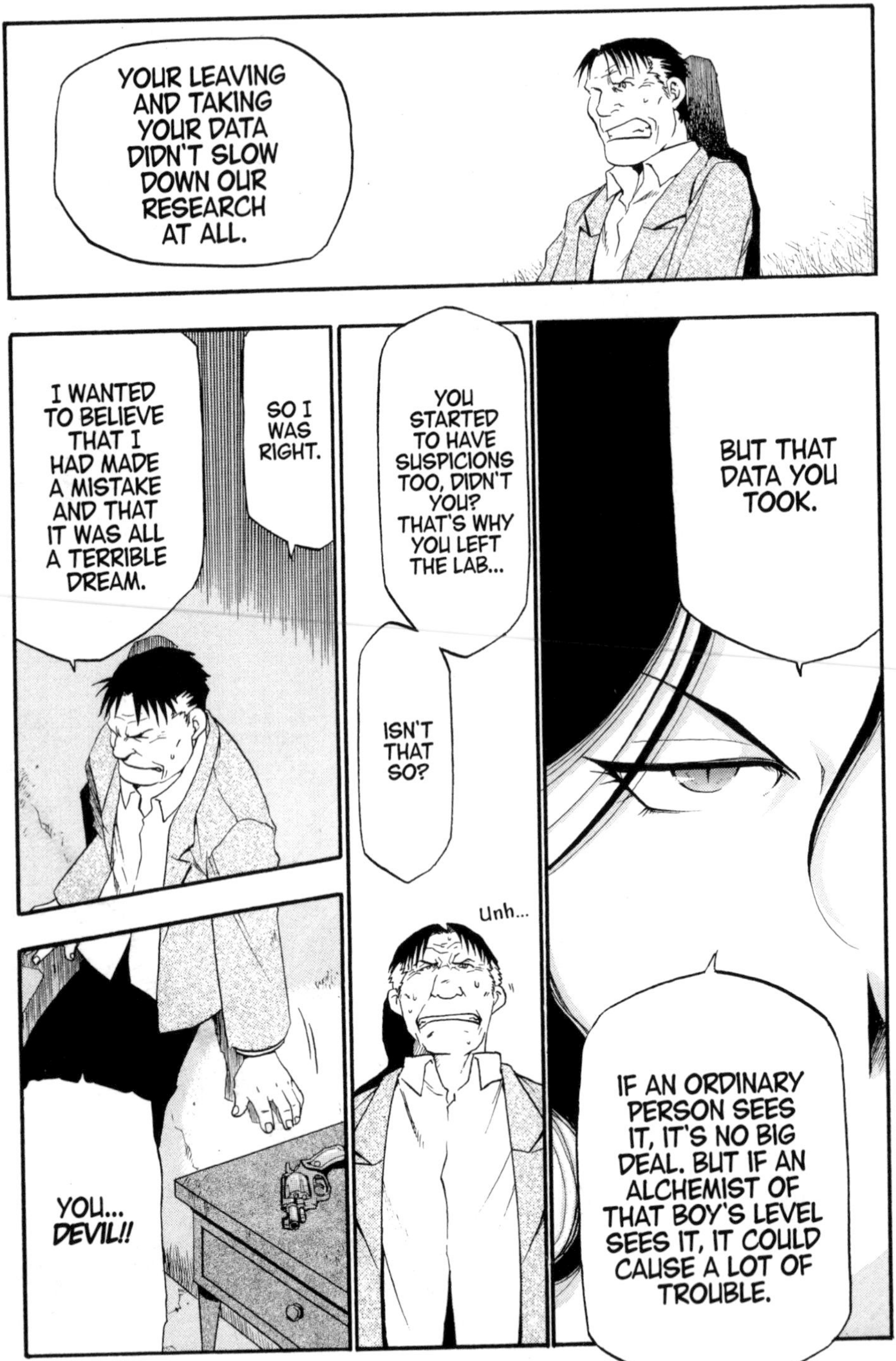

YOUR LEAVING AND TAKING YOUR DATA DIDN'T SLOW DOWN OUR RESEARCH AT ALL.
BUT THAT DATA YOU TOOK.
IF AN ORDINARY PERSON SEES IT, IT'S NO BIG DEAL. BUT IF AN ALCHEMIST OF THAT BOY'S LEVEL SEES IT, IT COULD CAUSE A LOT OF TROUBLE.
YOU STARTED TO HAVE SUSPICIONS TOO, DIDN'T YOU? THAT'S WHY YOU LEFT THE LAB...
ISN'T THAT SO?
Unh...
SO I WAS RIGHT.
I WANTED TO BELIEVE THAT I HAD MADE A MISTAKE AND THAT IT WAS ALL A TERRIBLE DREAM.
YOU... DEVIL!!

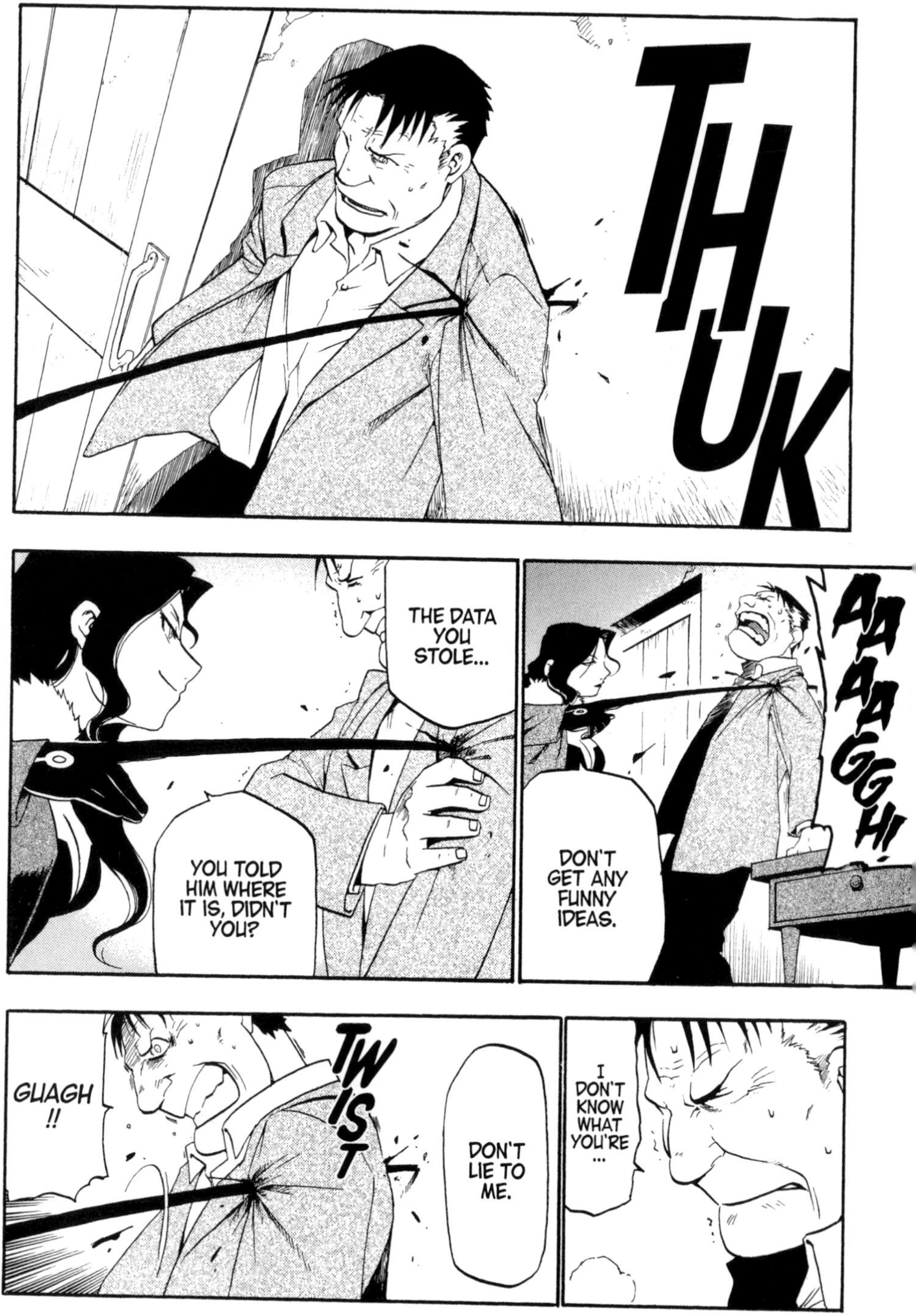
THUK
AAAAAGGH!
DON'T GET ANY FUNNY IDEAS.
THE DATA YOU STOLE...
YOU TOLD HIM WHERE IT IS, DIDN'T YOU?
I DON'T KNOW WHAT YOU'RE ...
TWIST
DON'T LIE TO ME.
GUAGH !!

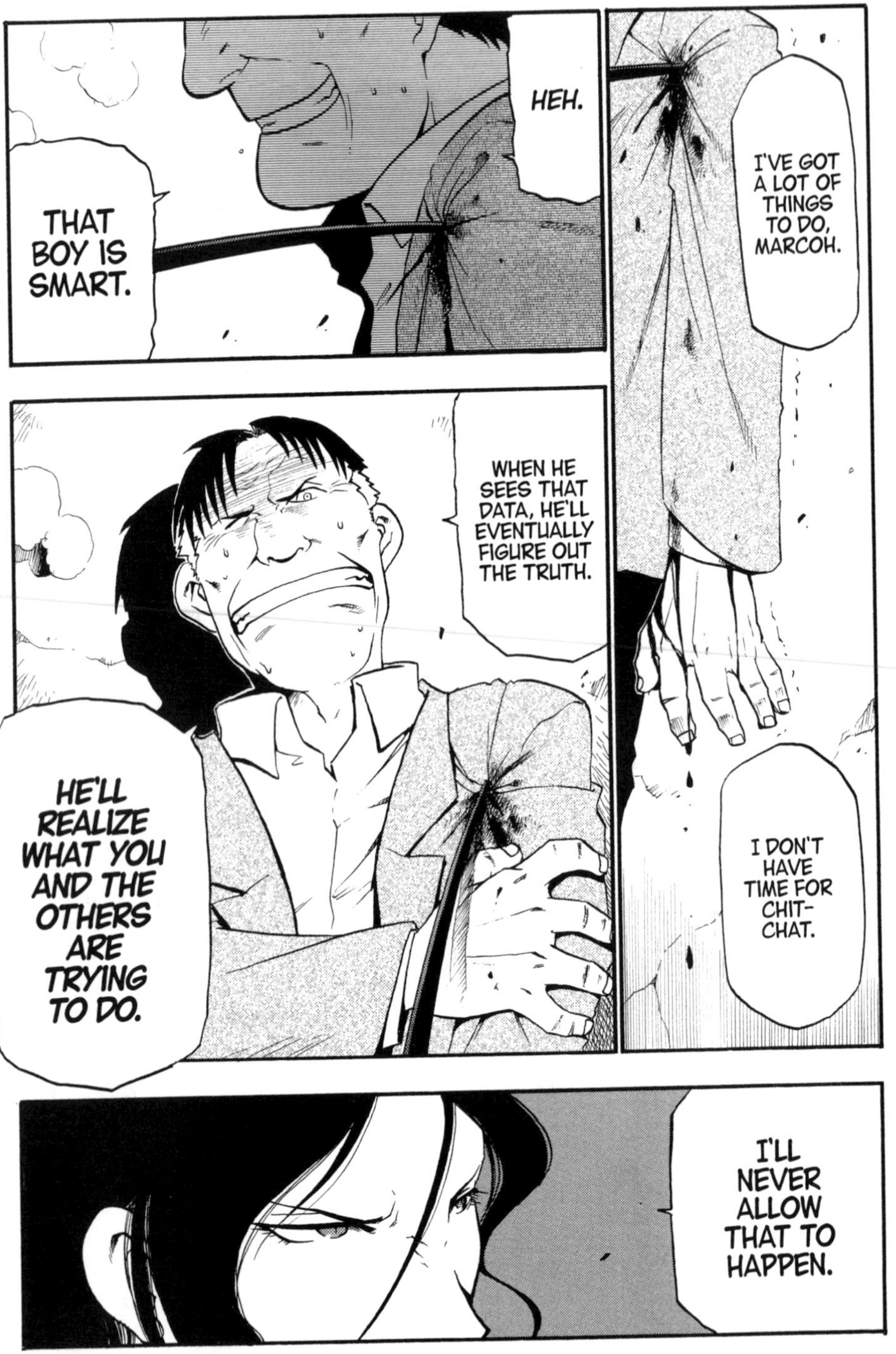
I'VE GOT A LOT OF THINGS TO DO, MARCOH.
I DON'T HAVE TIME FOR CHIT-CHAT.
HEH.
THAT BOY IS SMART.
WHEN HE SEES THAT DATA, HE'LL EVENTUALLY FIGURE OUT THE TRUTH.
HE'LL REALIZE WHAT YOU AND THE OTHERS ARE TRYING TO DO.
I'LL NEVER ALLOW THAT TO HAPPEN.

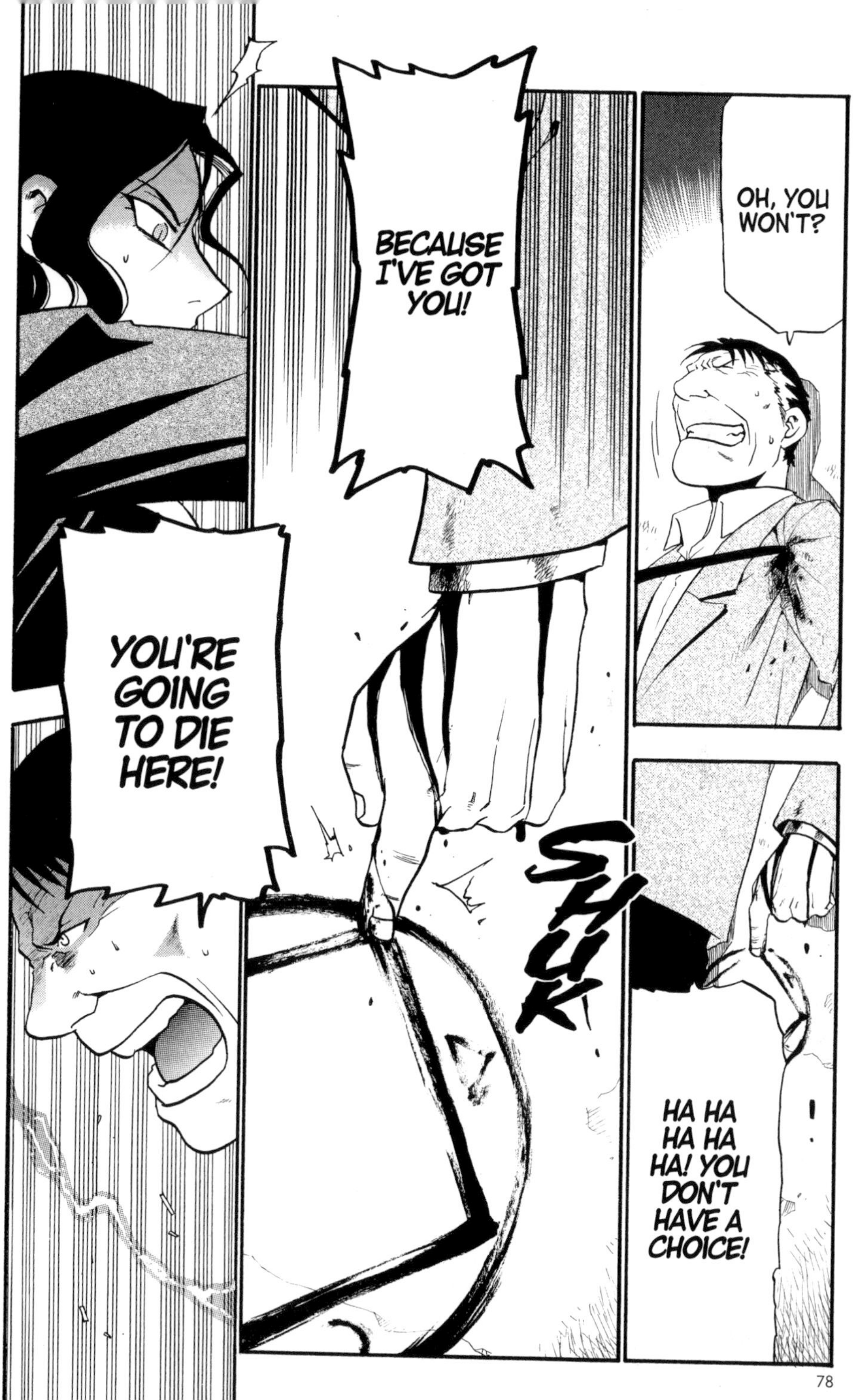
OH, YOU WON'T?
HA HA HA HA HA! YOU DON'T HAVE A CHOICE!
BECAUSE I'VE GOT YOU!
SHUK
YOU'RE GOING TO DIE HERE!

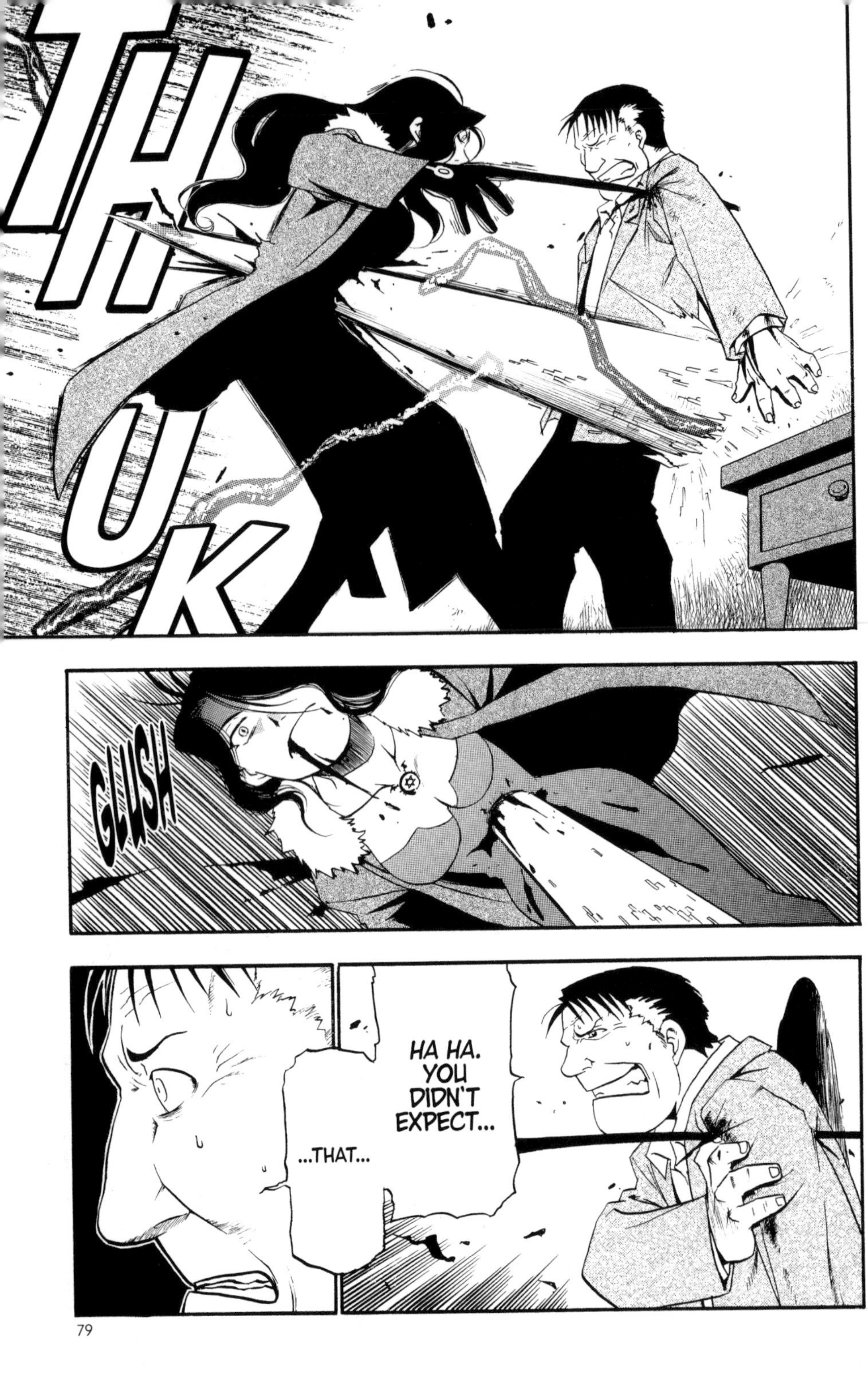
THUK
GLUSH
HA HA. YOU DIDN'T EXPECT...
...THAT...

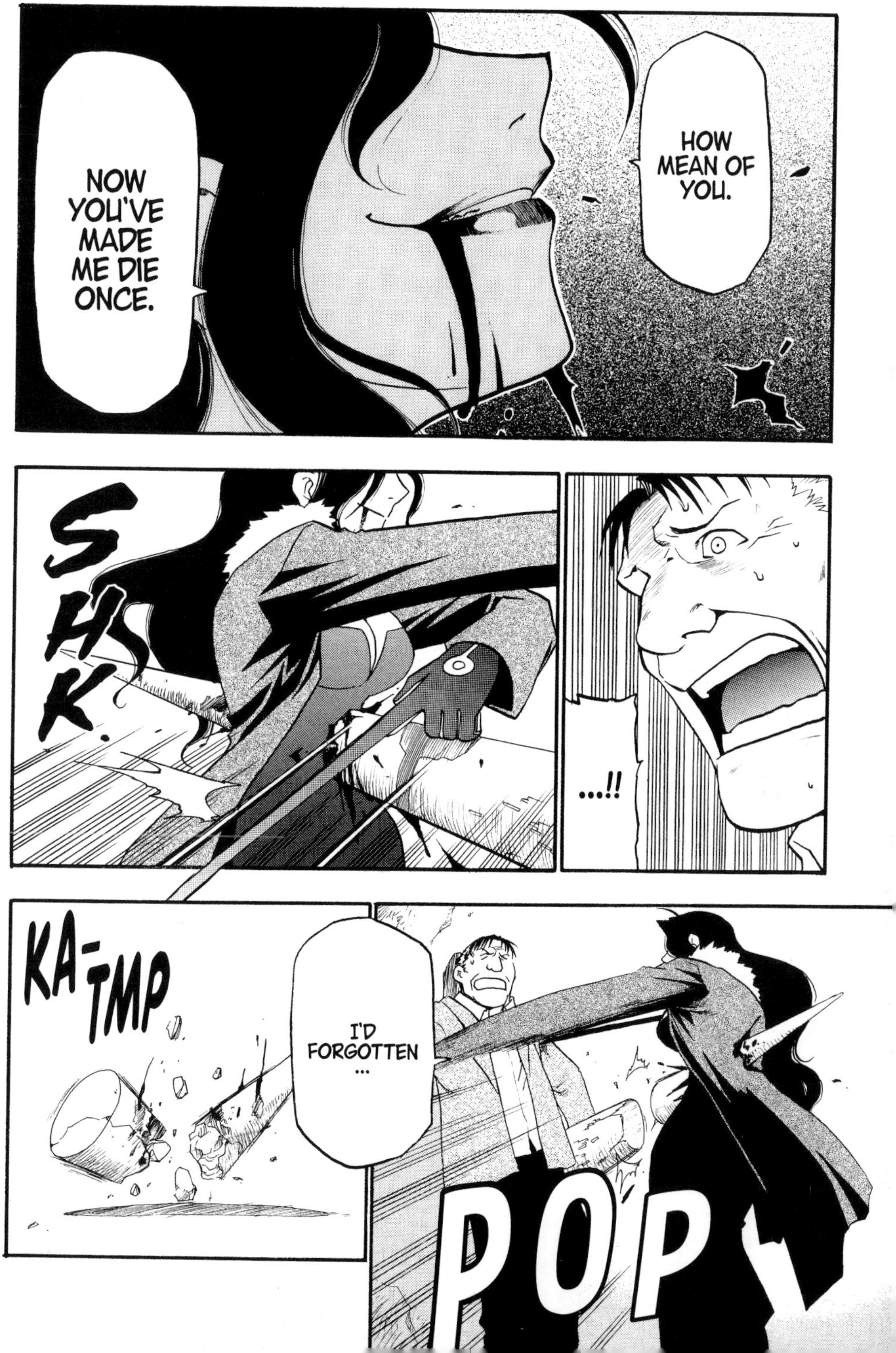
HOW MEAN OF YOU.
NOW YOU'VE MADE ME DIE ONCE.
...!!
SHK.
I'D FORGOTTEN ...
POP
KA-TMP

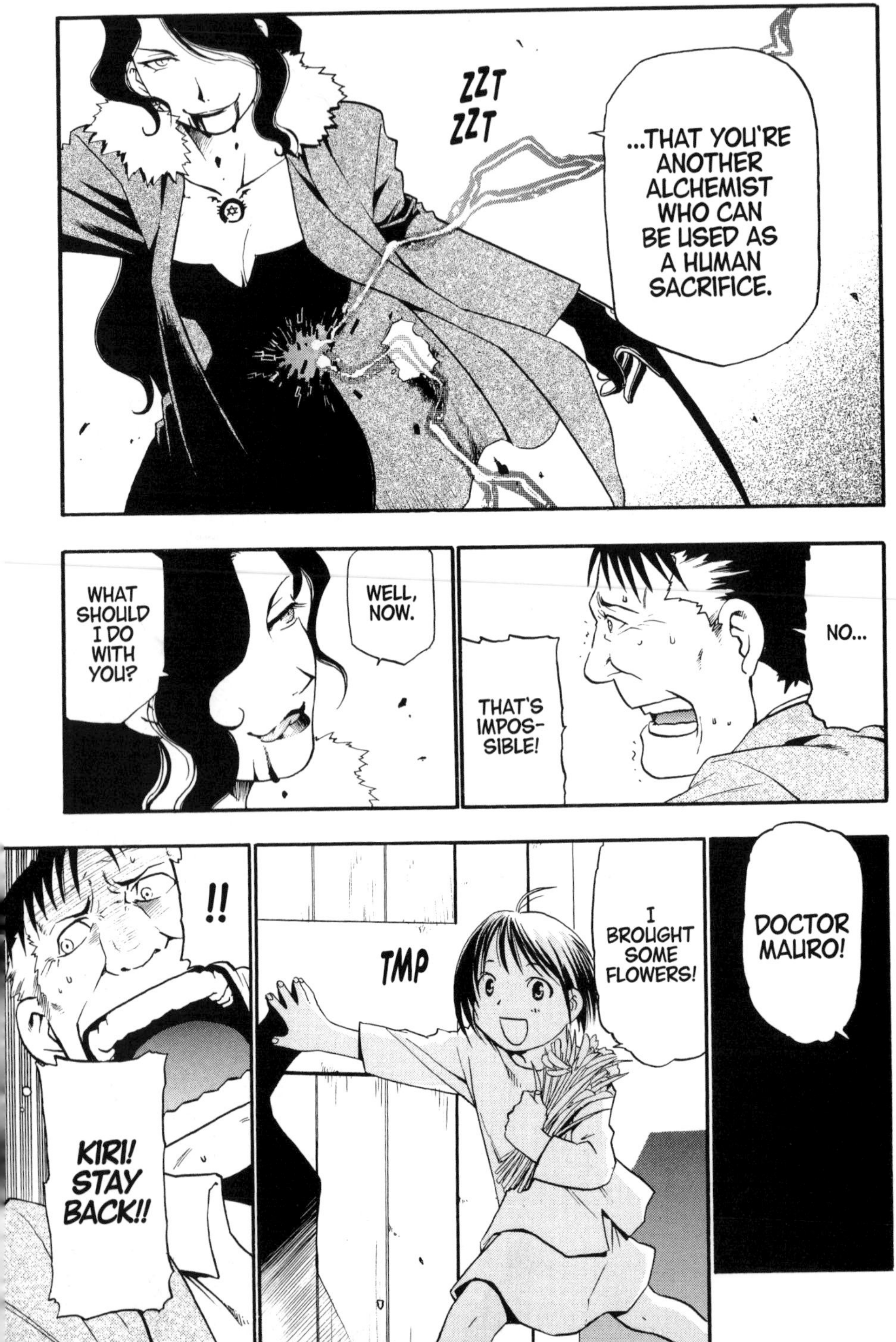
...THAT YOU'RE ANOTHER ALCHEMIST WHO CAN BE USED AS A HUMAN SACRIFICE.
ZZT ZZT
NO...
THAT'S IMPOSSIBLE!
WELL, NOW.
WHAT SHOULD I DO WITH YOU?
DOCTOR MAURO!
I BROUGHT SOME FLOWERS!
TMP
!!
KIRI! STAY BACK!!

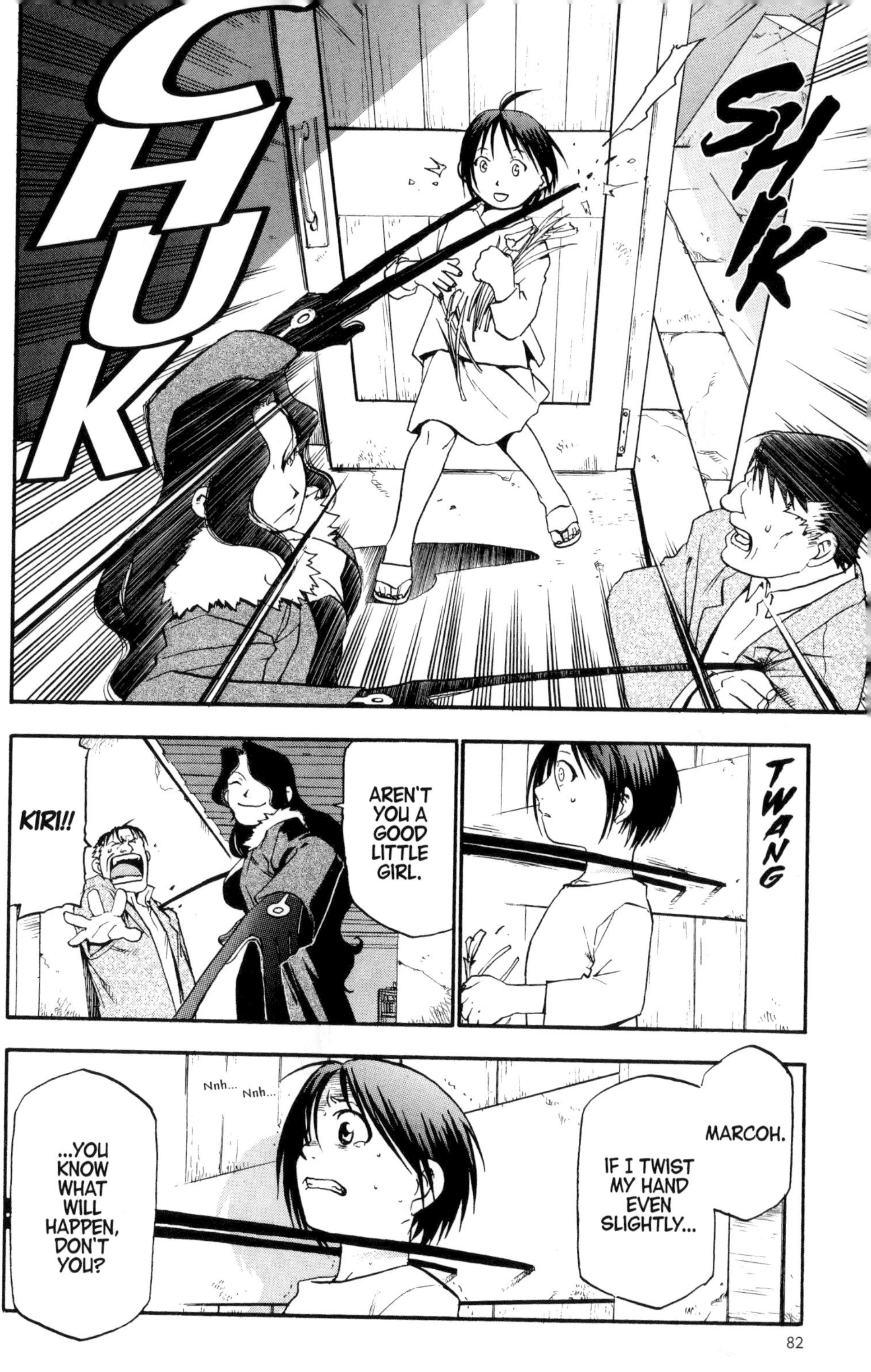
SHIK
CHUK
TWANG
AREN'T YOU A GOOD LITTLE GIRL.
KIRI!!
MARCOH.
IF I TWIST MY HAND EVEN SLIGHTLY...
Nnh... Nnh...
...YOU KNOW WHAT WILL HAPPEN, DON'T YOU?

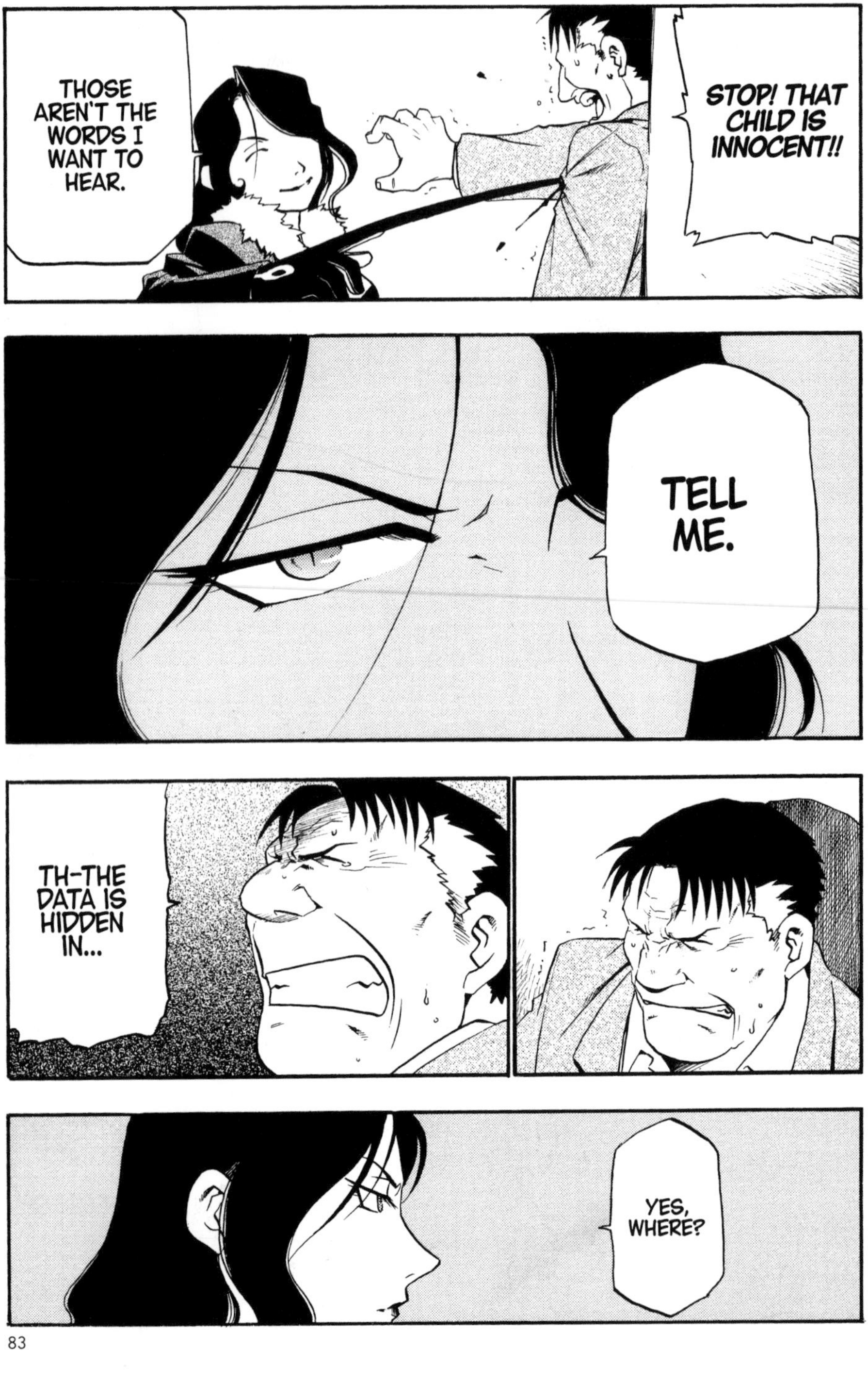
STOP! THAT CHILD IS INNOCENT!!
THOSE AREN'T THE WORDS I WANT TO HEAR.
TELL ME.
TH-THE DATA IS HIDDEN IN...
YES, WHERE?

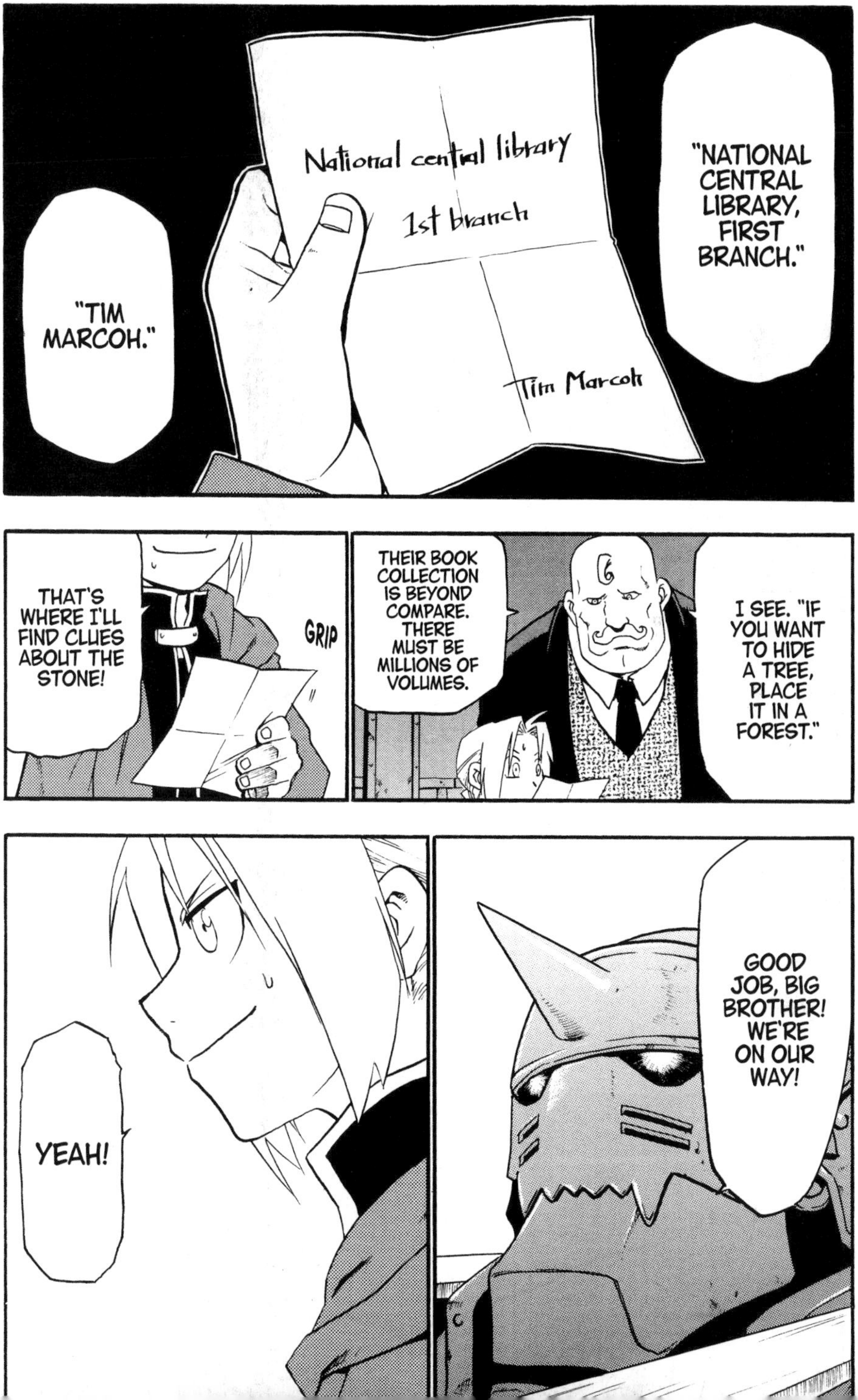
"NATIONAL CENTRAL LIBRARY, FIRST BRANCH."
National central library
1st branch
Tim Marcoh
"TIM MARCOH."
I SEE. "IF YOU WANT TO HIDE A TREE, PLACE IT IN A FOREST."
THEIR BOOK COLLECTION IS BEYOND COMPARE. THERE MUST BE MILLIONS OF VOLUMES.
GRIP
THAT'S WHERE I'LL FIND CLUES ABOUT THE STONE!
GOOD JOB, BIG BROTHER! WE'RE ON OUR WAY!
YEAH!

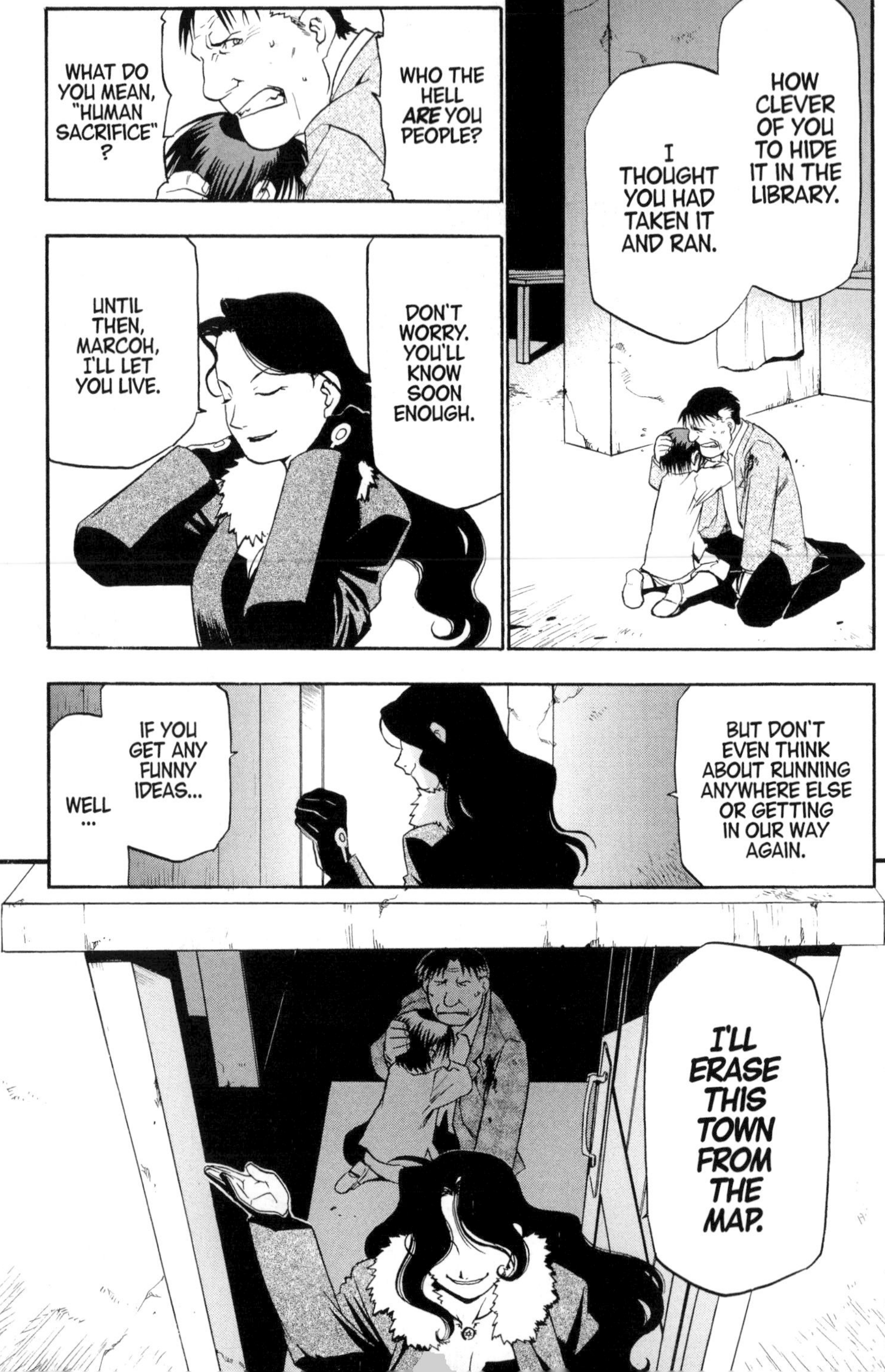
HOW CLEVER OF YOU TO HIDE IT IN THE LIBRARY.
I THOUGHT YOU HAD TAKEN IT AND RAN.
WHO THE HELL ARE YOU PEOPLE?
WHAT DO YOU MEAN, "HUMAN SACRIFICE"?
DON'T WORRY. YOU'LL KNOW SOON ENOUGH.
UNTIL THEN, MARCOH, I'LL LET YOU LIVE.
BUT DON'T EVEN THINK ABOUT RUNNING ANYWHERE ELSE OR GETTING IN OUR WAY AGAIN.
IF YOU GET ANY FUNNY IDEAS...
WELL...
I'LL ERASE THIS TOWN FROM THE MAP.

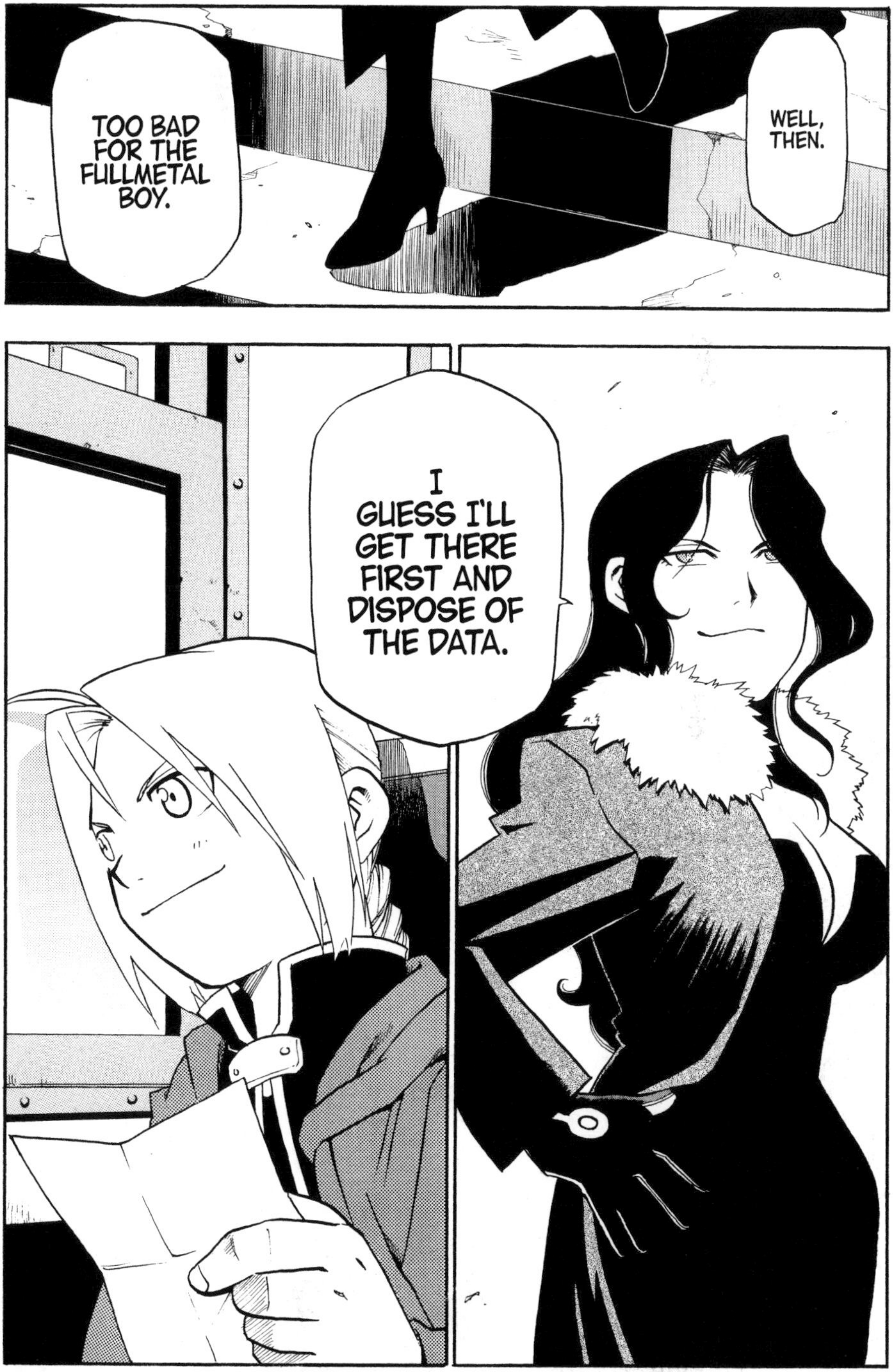
WELL, THEN.
TOO BAD FOR THE FULLMETAL BOY.
I GUESS I'LL GET THERE FIRST AND DISPOSE OF THE DATA.

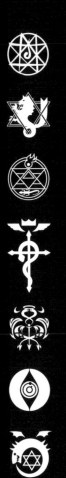

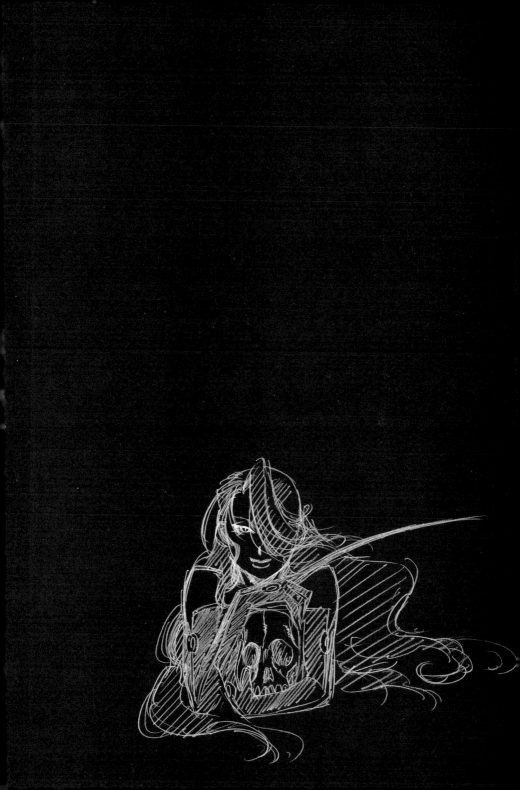

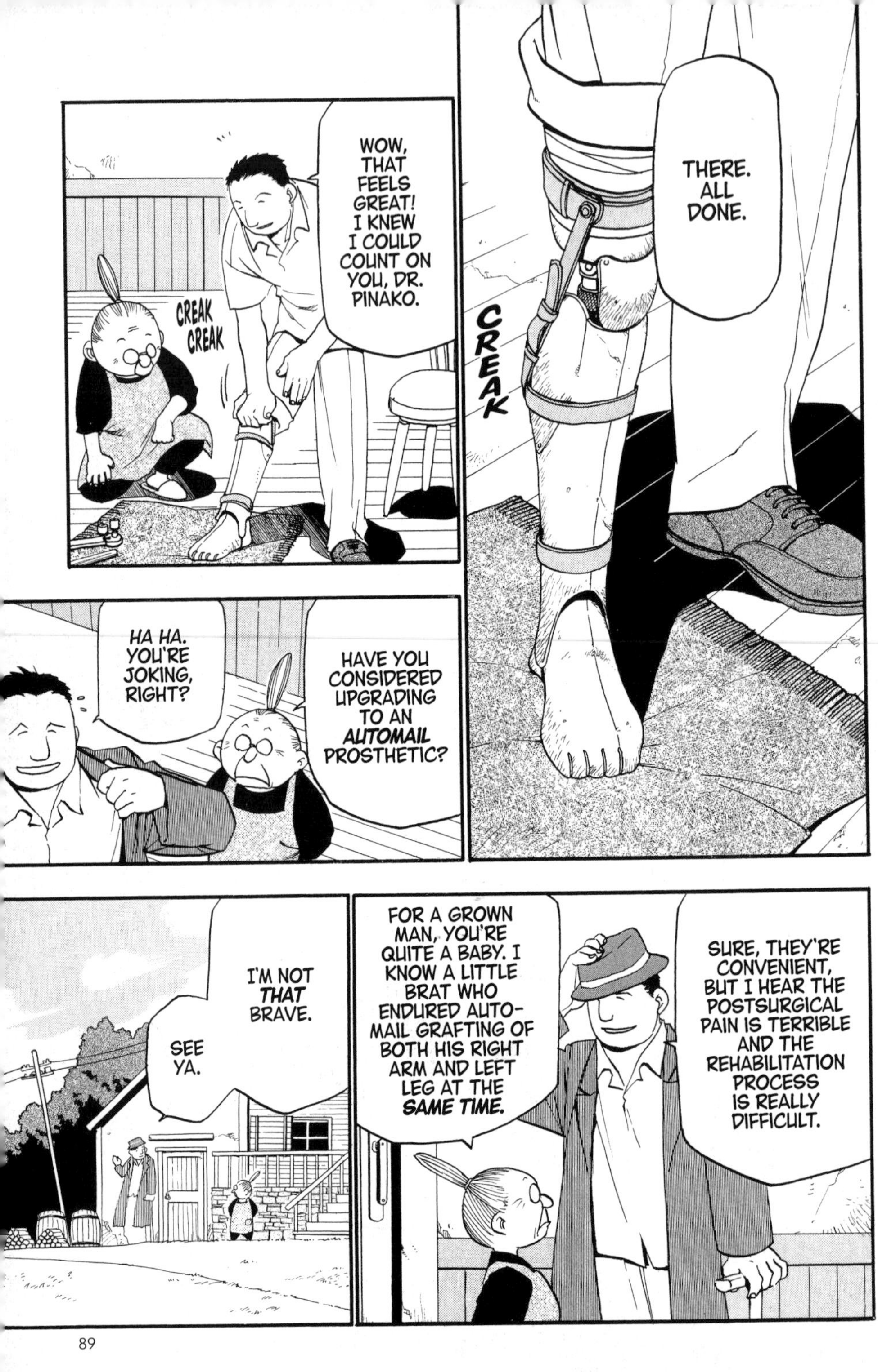
THERE. ALL DONE.
CREAK
WOW, THAT FEELS GREAT! I KNEW I COULD COUNT ON YOU, DR. PINAKO.
CREAK CREAK
HAVE YOU CONSIDERED UPGRADING TO AN AUTOMAIL PROSTHETIC?
HA HA. YOU'RE JOKING, RIGHT?
SURE, THEY'RE CONVENIENT, BUT I HEAR THE POSTSURGICAL PAIN IS TERRIBLE AND THE REHABILITATION PROCESS IS REALLY DIFFICULT.
FOR A GROWN MAN, YOU'RE QUITE A BABY. I KNOW A LITTLE BRAT WHO ENDURED AUTO-MAIL GRAFTING OF BOTH HIS RIGHT ARM AND LEFT LEG AT THE SAME TIME.
I'M NOT THAT BRAVE.
SEE YA.

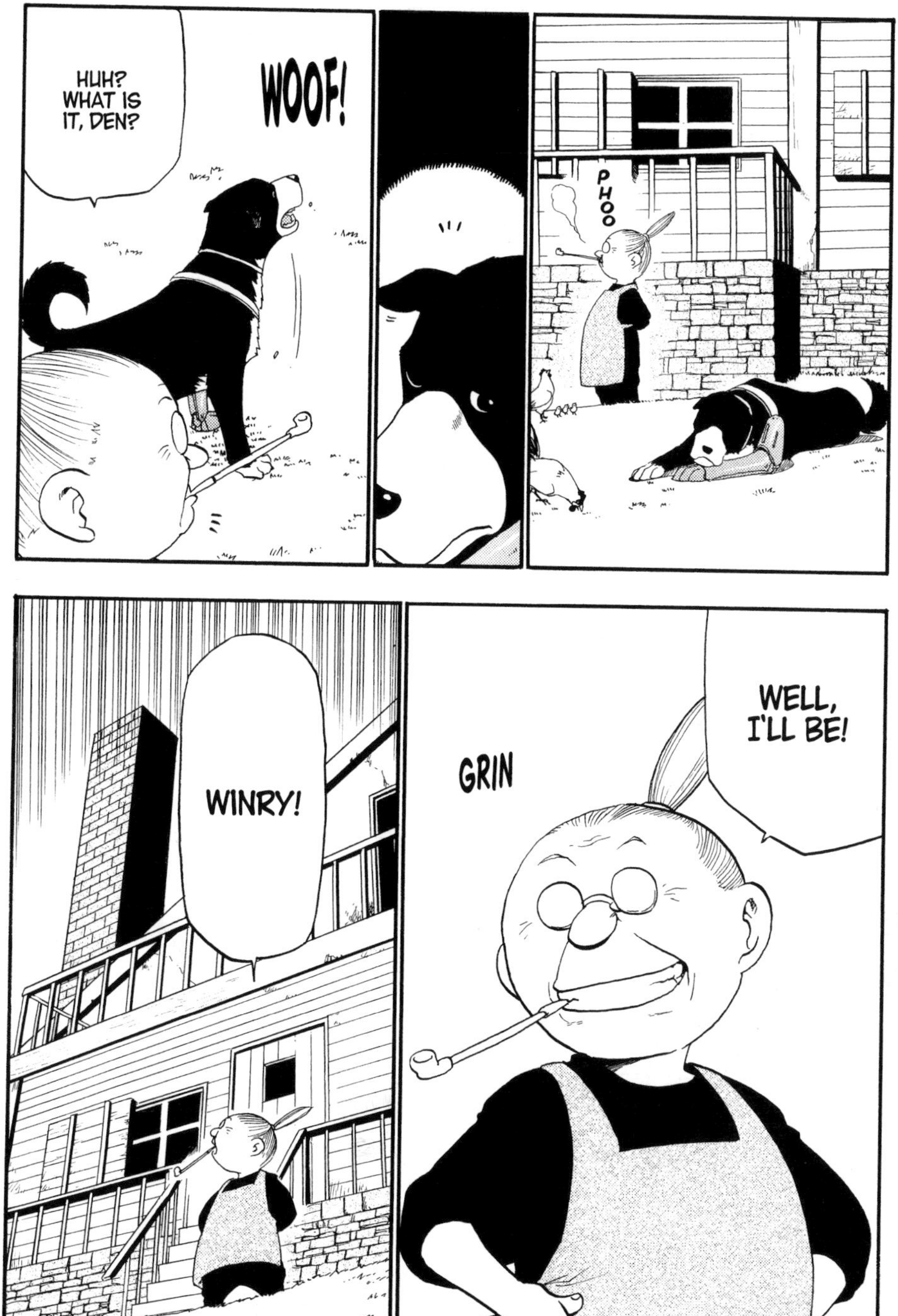
PHOO
WOOF!
HUH? WHAT IS IT, DEN?
WELL, I'LL BE!
GRIN
WINRY!

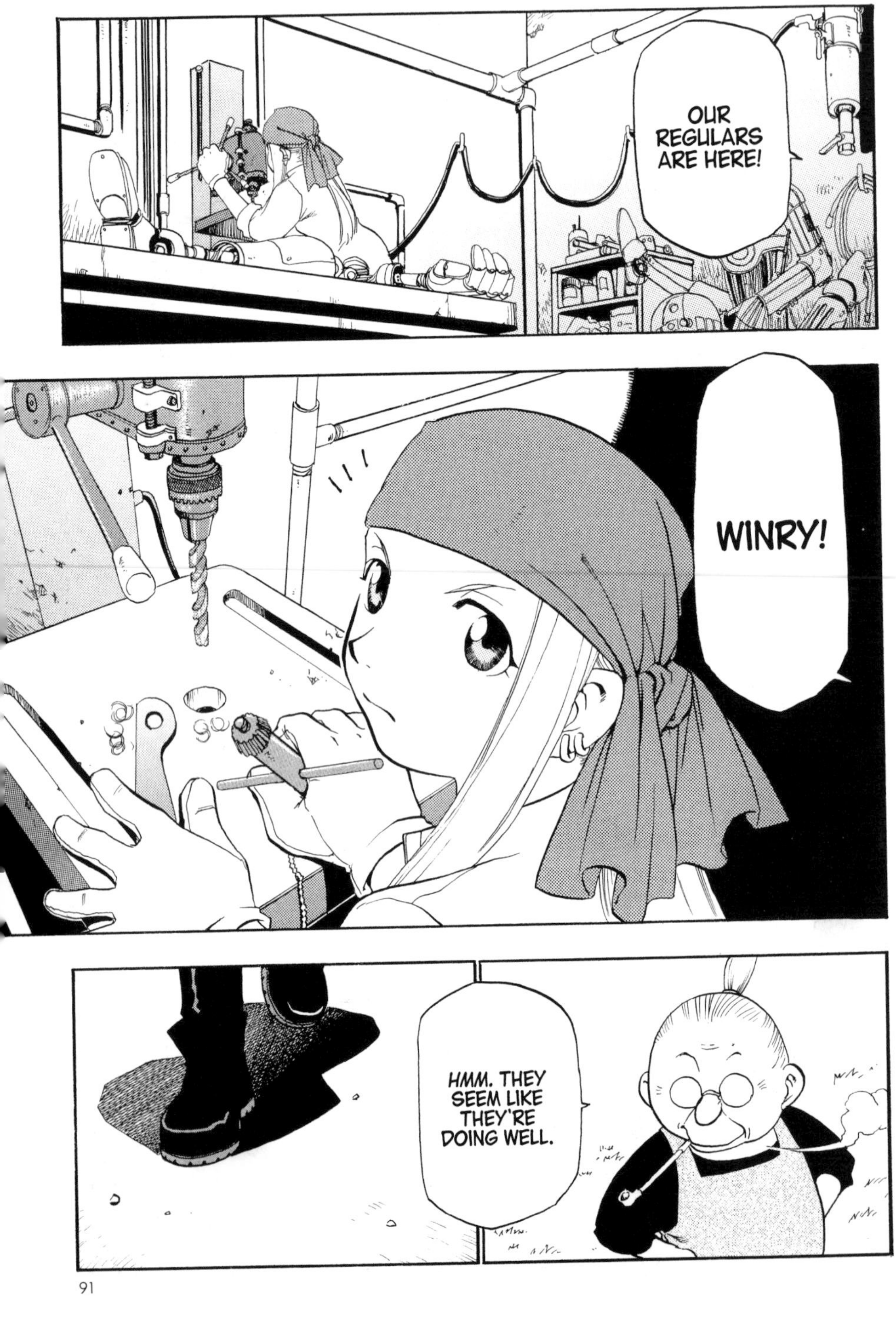
OUR REGULARS ARE HERE!
WINRY!
HMM. THEY SEEM LIKE THEY'RE DOING WELL.

A HOME WITH A FAMILY WAITING
CHAPTER 9

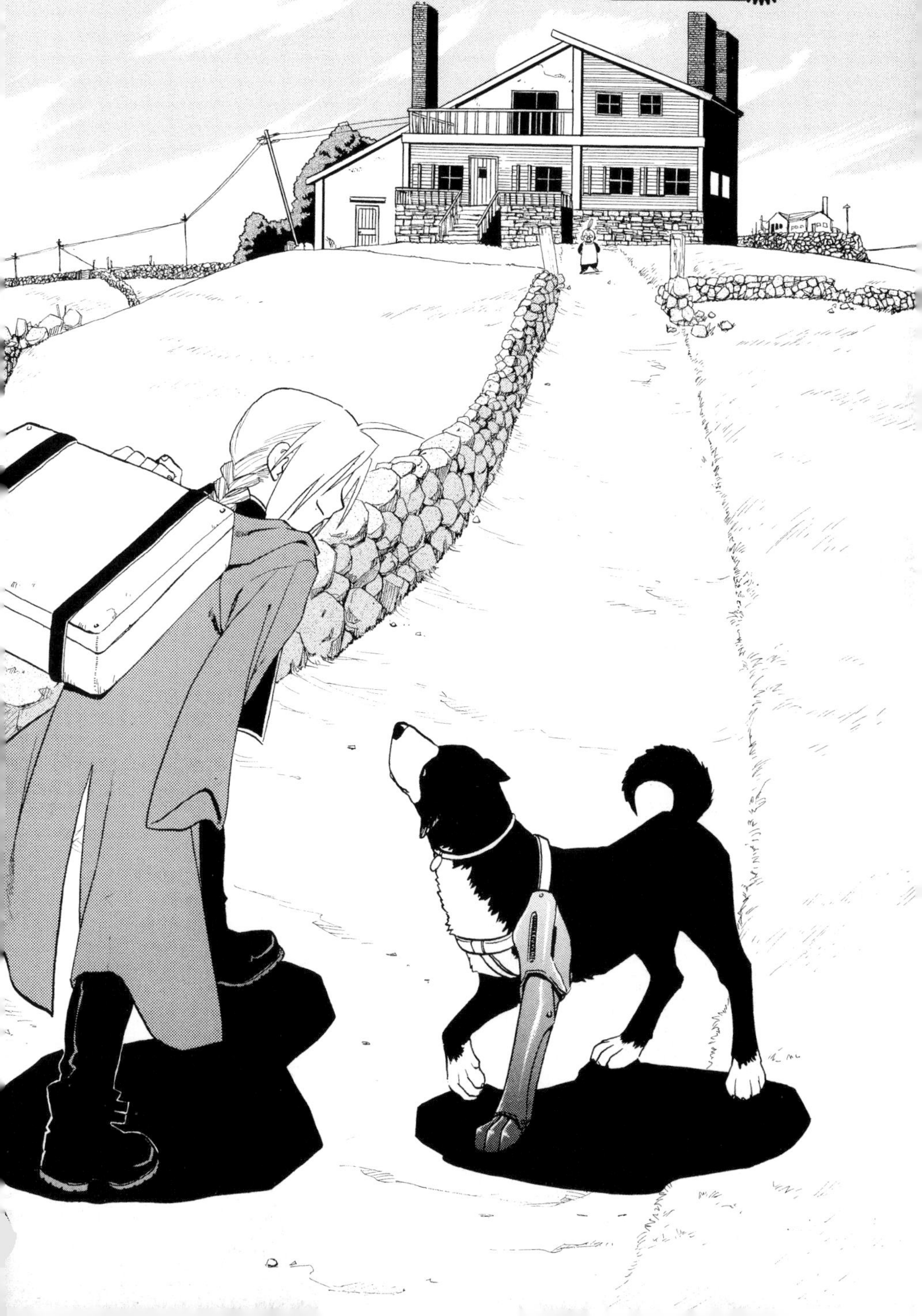

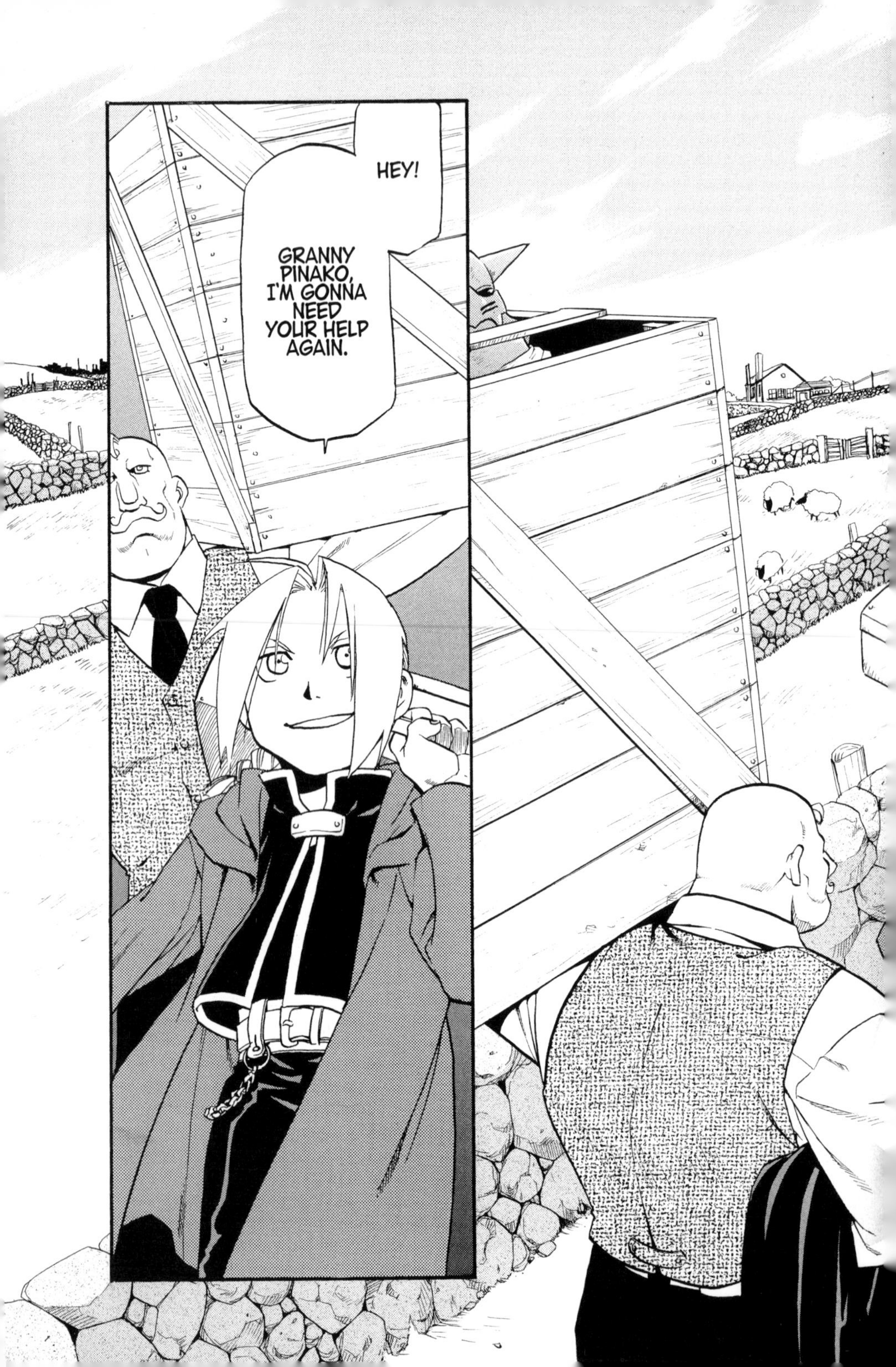
HEY!
GRANNY PINAKO, I'M GONNA NEED YOUR HELP AGAIN.

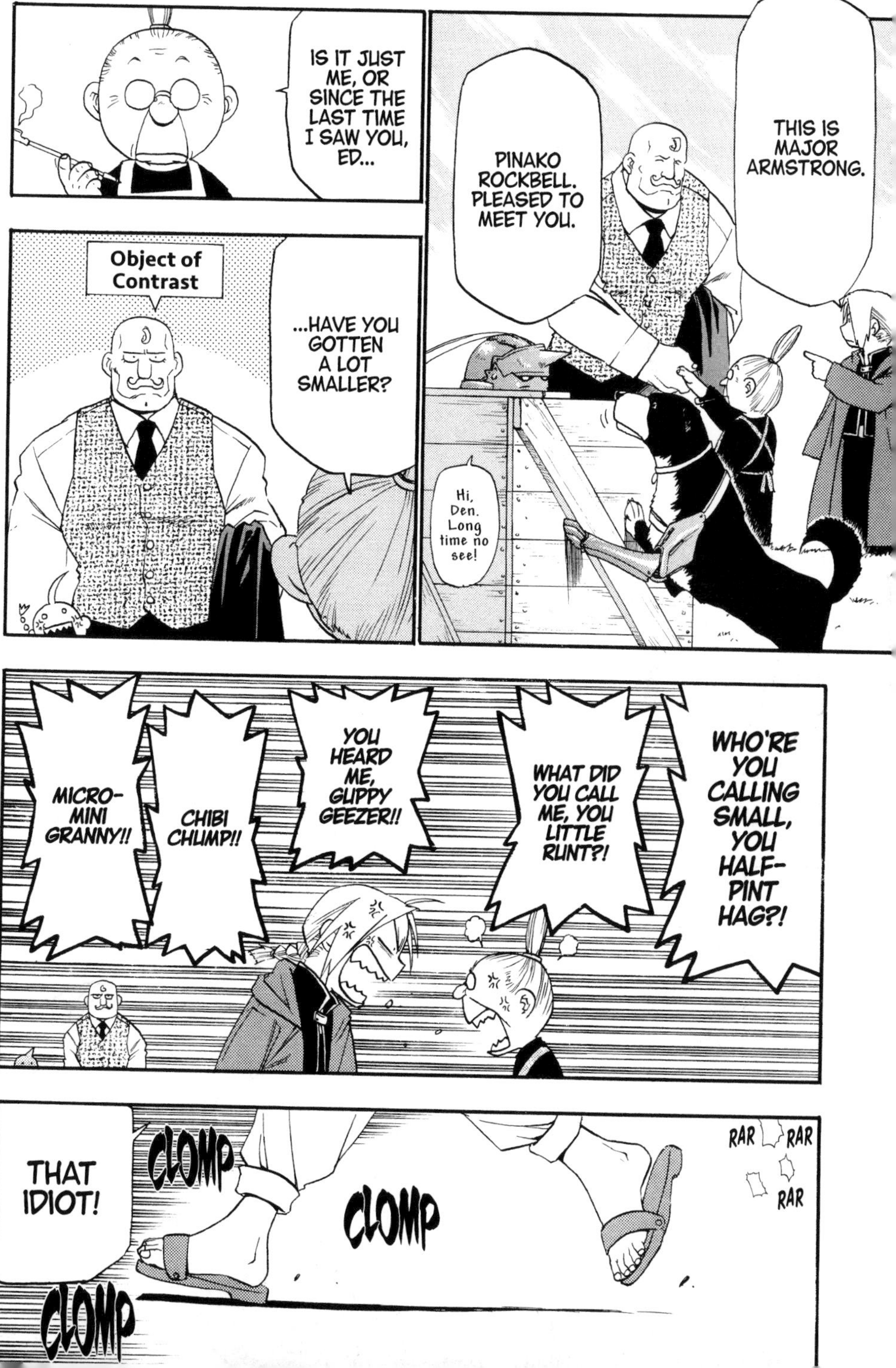
THIS IS MAJOR ARMSTRONG.
PINAKO ROCKBELL. PLEASED TO MEET YOU.
Hi, Den. Long time no see!
IS IT JUST ME, OR SINCE THE LAST TIME I SAW YOU, ED...
Object of Contrast
...HAVE YOU GOTTEN A LOT SMALLER?
WHO'RE YOU CALLING SMALL, YOU HALF-PINT HAG?!
WHAT DID YOU CALL ME, YOU LITTLE RUNT?!
YOU HEARD ME, GUPPY GEEZER!!
CHIBI CHUMP!!
MICRO-MINI GRANNY!!
RAR RAR RAR
CLOMP
CLOMP
CLOMP
THAT IDIOT!

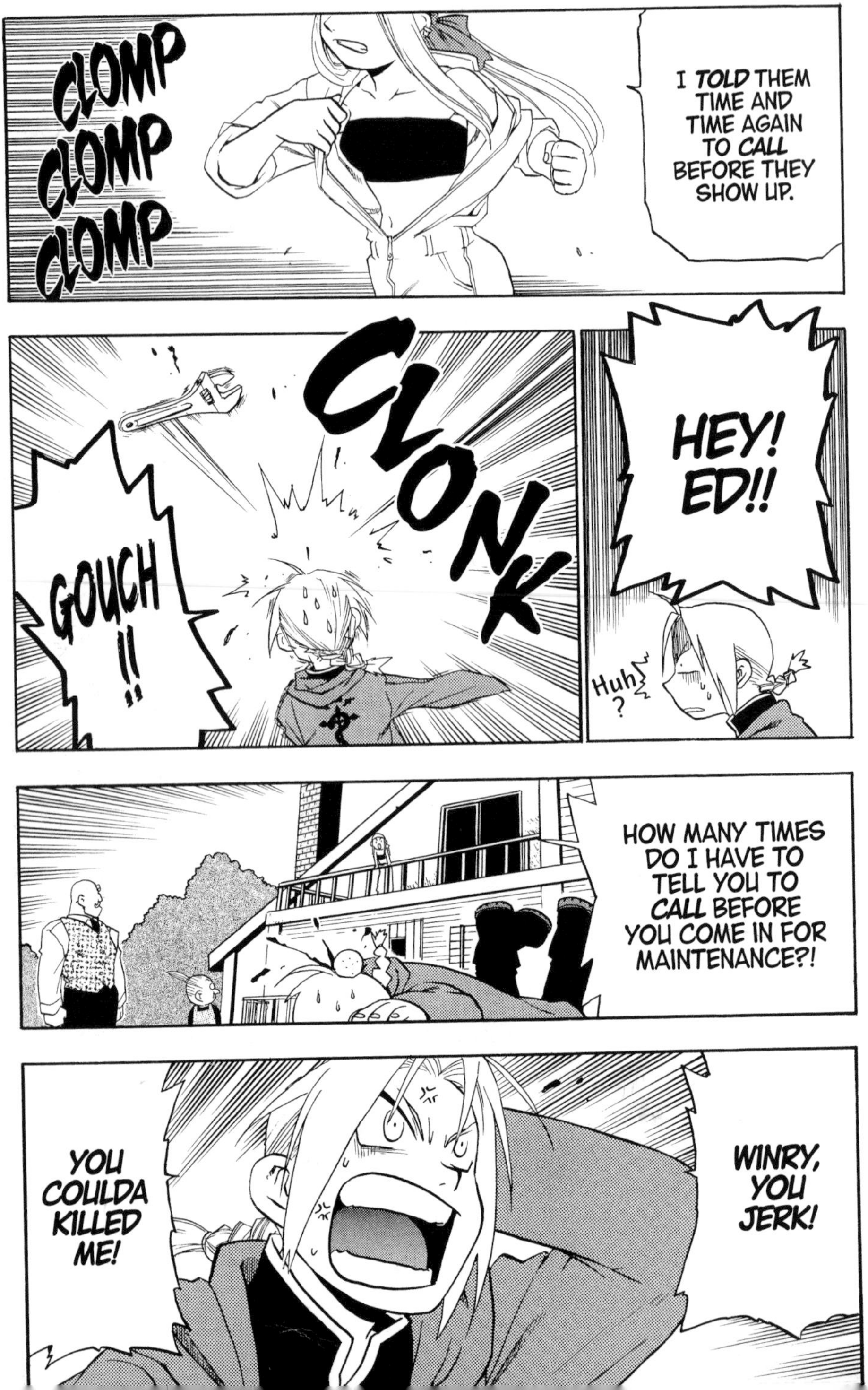
I TOLD THEM TIME AND TIME AGAIN TO CALL BEFORE THEY SHOW UP.
CLOMP CLOMP CLOMP
HEY! ED!!
Huh?
CLONK
GOUCH!!
HOW MANY TIMES DO I HAVE TO TELL YOU TO CALL BEFORE YOU COME IN FOR MAINTENANCE?!
WINRY, YOU JERK!
YOU COULDA KILLED ME!

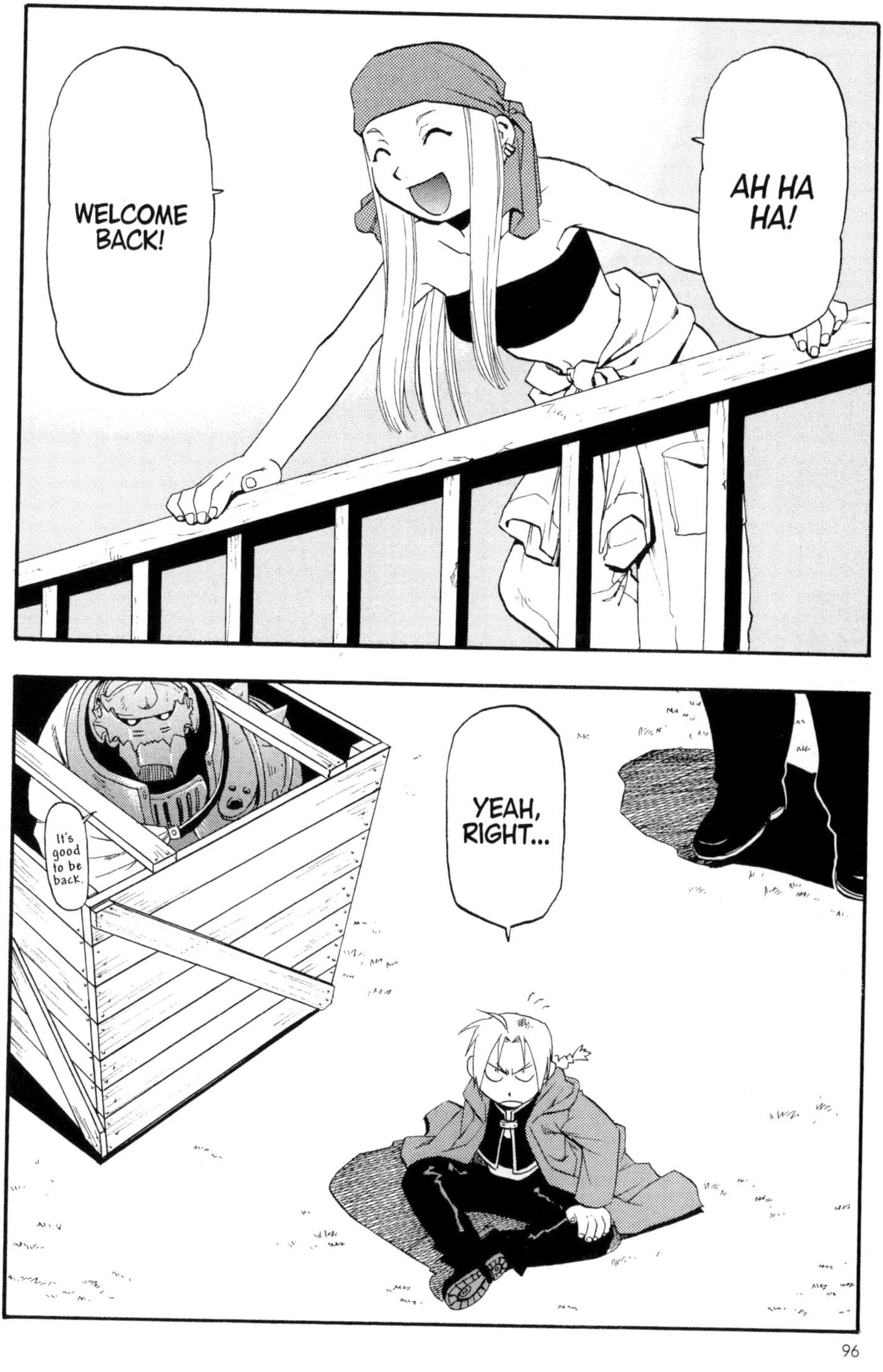
AH HA HA!
WELCOME BACK!
YEAH, RIGHT...
It's good to be back.

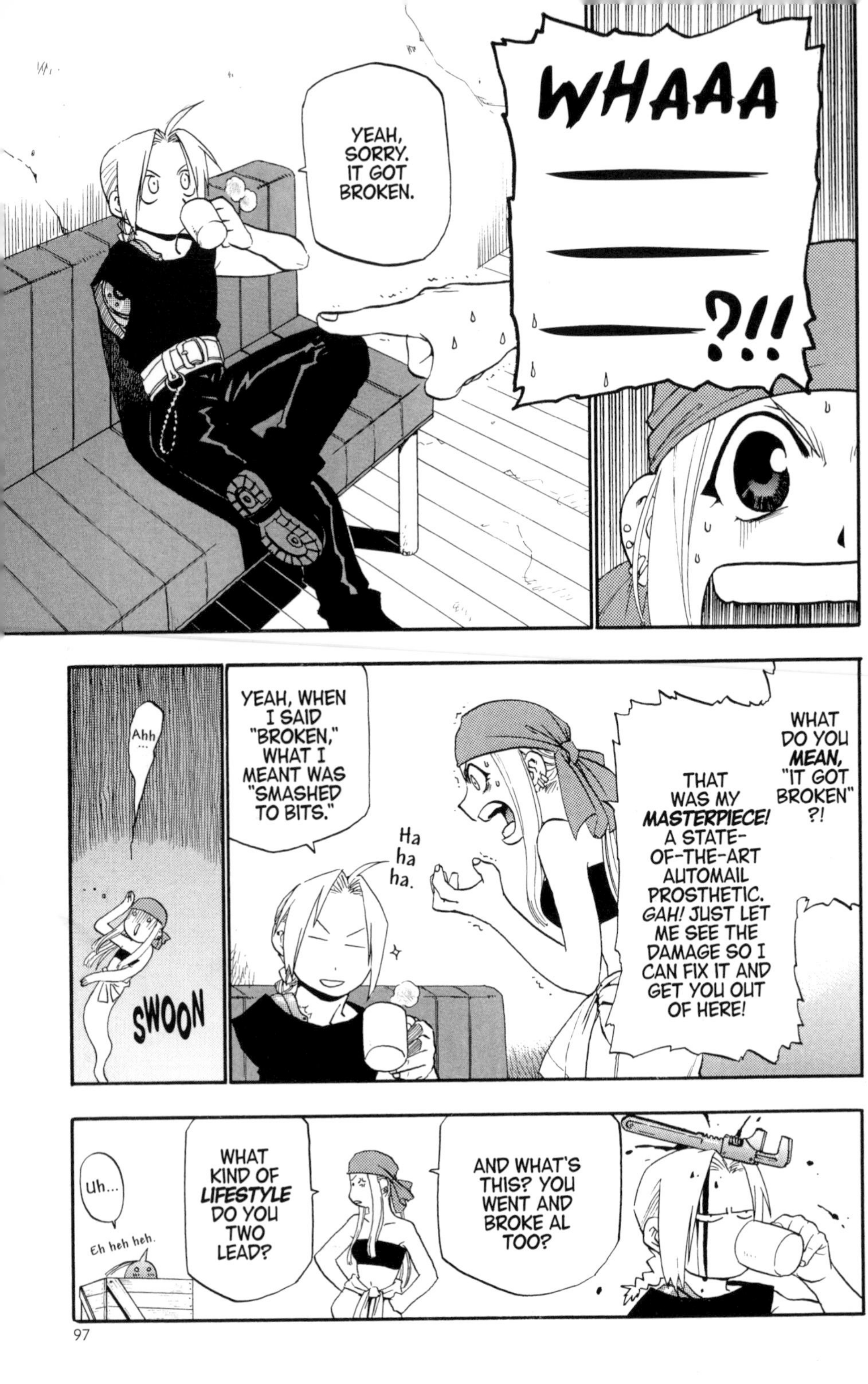
WHAAA———?!!
YEAH, SORRY. IT GOT BROKEN.
WHAT DO YOU MEAN, "IT GOT BROKEN"?!
THAT WAS MY MASTERPIECE! A STATE-OF-THE-ART AUTOMAIL PROSTHETIC. GAH! JUST LET ME SEE THE DAMAGE SO I CAN FIX IT AND GET YOU OUT OF HERE!
YEAH, WHEN I SAID "BROKEN," WHAT I MEANT WAS "SMASHED TO BITS."
Ha ha ha.
Ahh...
SWOON
AND WHAT'S THIS? YOU WENT AND BROKE AL TOO?
WHAT KIND OF LIFESTYLE DO YOU TWO LEAD?
Uh...
Eh heh heh.

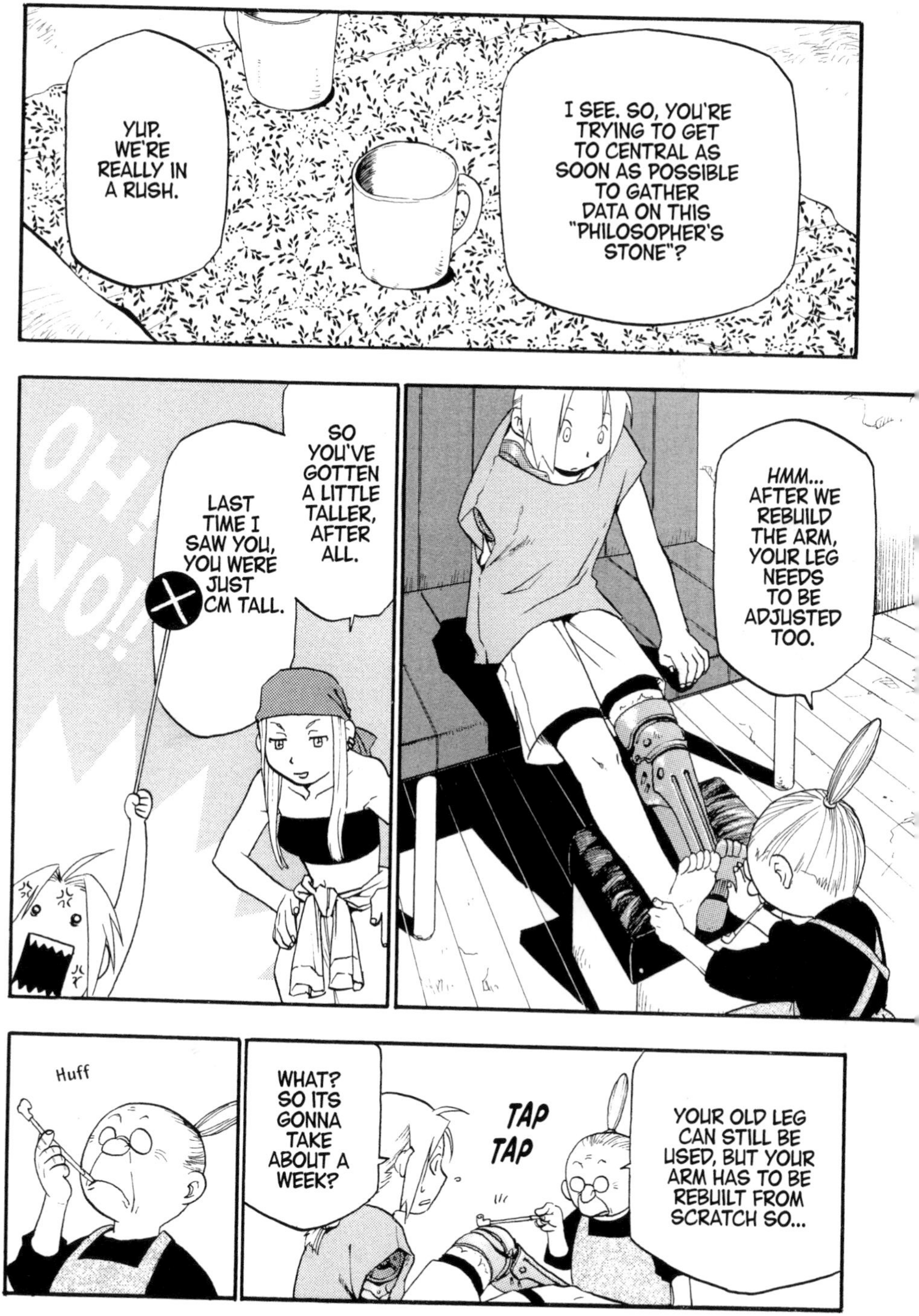
I SEE. SO, YOU'RE TRYING TO GET TO CENTRAL AS SOON AS POSSIBLE TO GATHER DATA ON THIS "PHILOSOPHER'S STONE"?
YUP. WE'RE REALLY IN A RUSH.
HMM... AFTER WE REBUILD THE ARM, YOUR LEG NEEDS TO BE ADJUSTED TOO.
SO YOU'VE GOTTEN A LITTLE TALLER, AFTER ALL.
LAST TIME I SAW YOU, YOU WERE JUST CM TALL.
OH! NO!!
YOUR OLD LEG CAN STILL BE USED, BUT YOUR ARM HAS TO BE REBUILT FROM SCRATCH SO...
TAP TAP
WHAT? SO ITS GONNA TAKE ABOUT A WEEK?
Huff

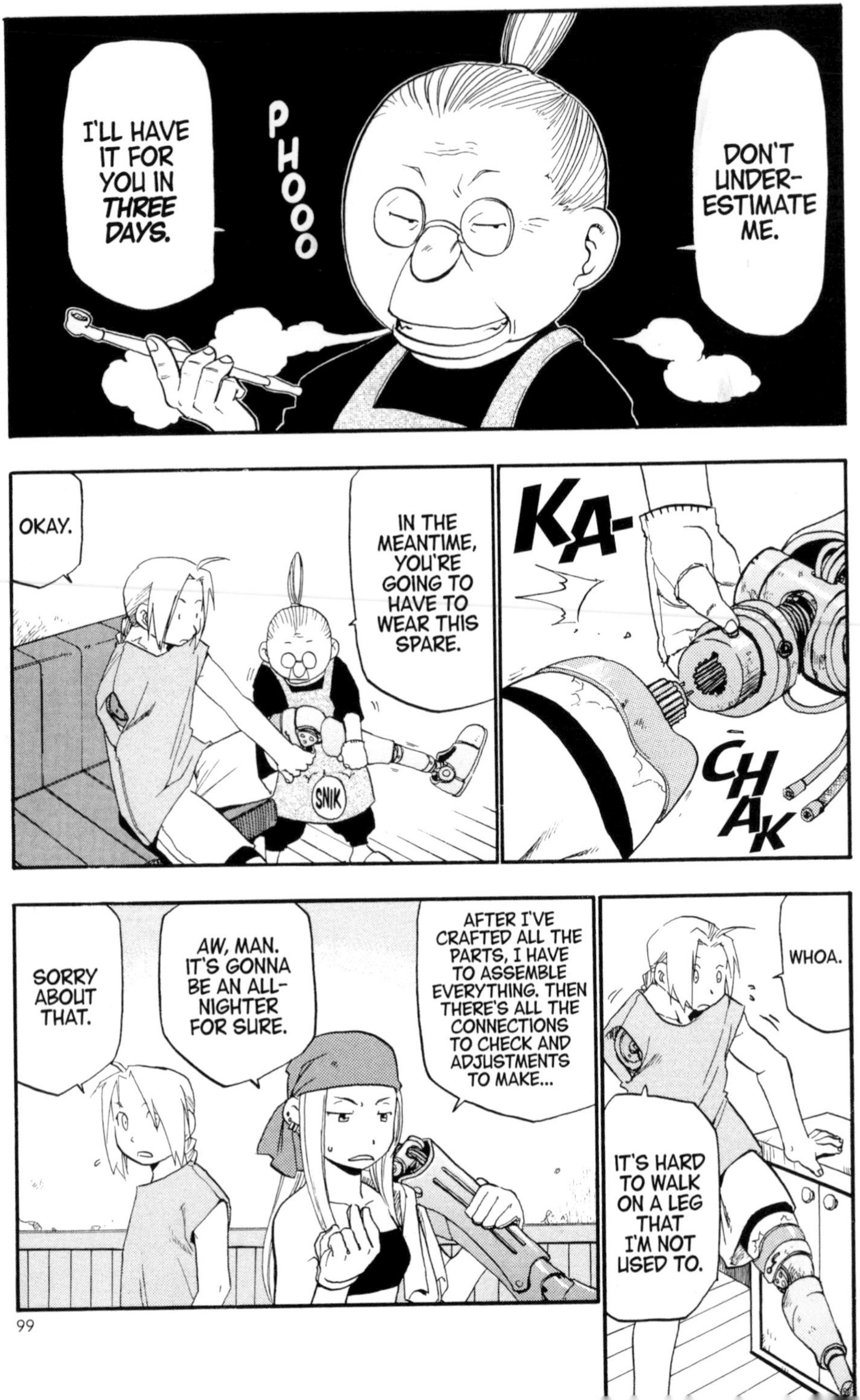
DON'T UNDER-ESTIMATE ME.
PHOOO
I'LL HAVE IT FOR YOU IN THREE DAYS.
KA-CHAK
IN THE MEANTIME, YOU'RE GOING TO HAVE TO WEAR THIS SPARE.
SNIK
OKAY.
WHOA.
IT'S HARD TO WALK ON A LEG THAT I'M NOT USED TO.
AFTER I'VE CRAFTED ALL THE PARTS, I HAVE TO ASSEMBLE EVERYTHING. THEN THERE'S ALL THE CONNECTIONS TO CHECK AND ADJUSTMENTS TO MAKE...
AW, MAN. IT'S GONNA BE AN ALL-NIGHTER FOR SURE.
SORRY ABOUT THAT.

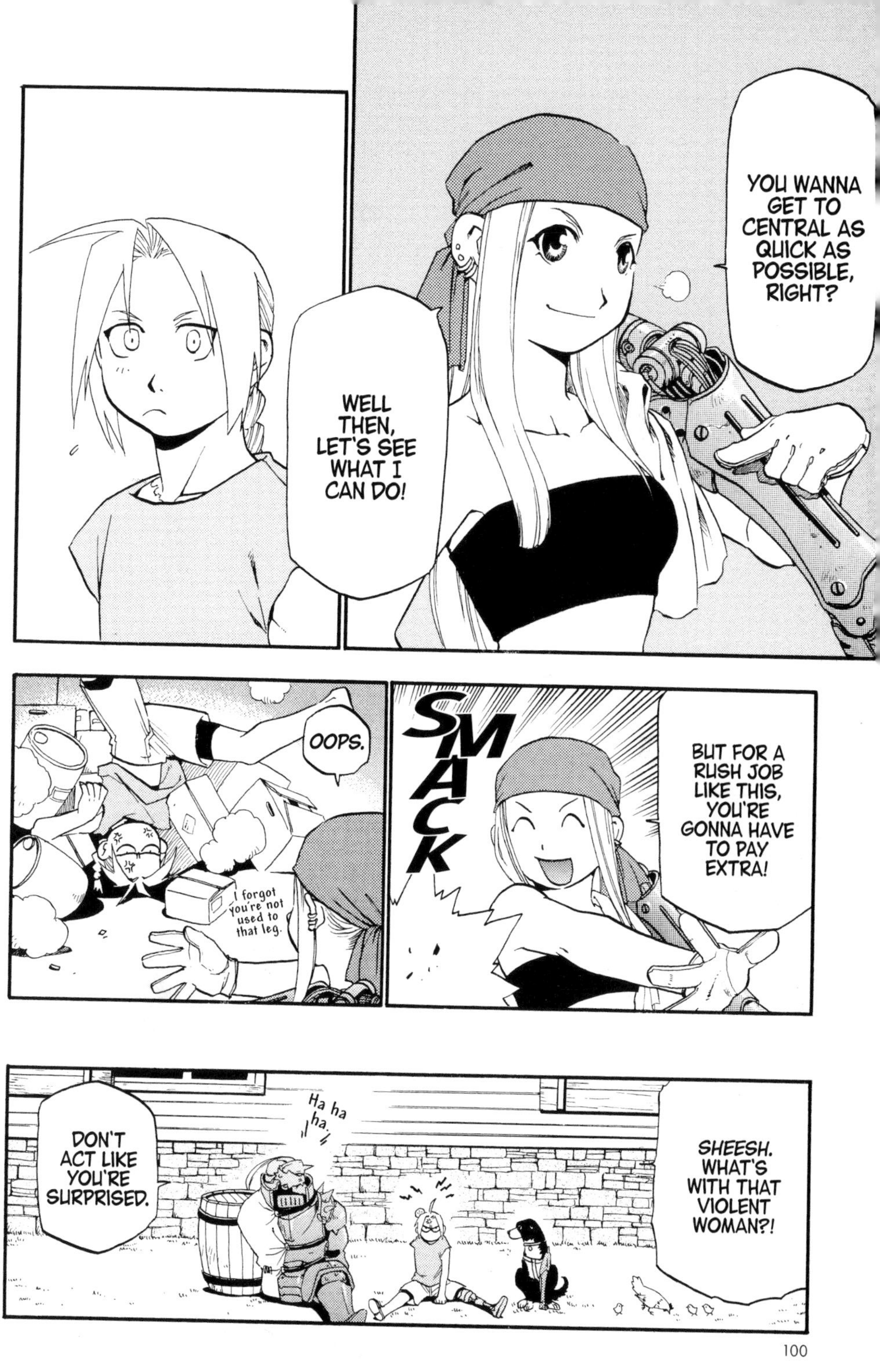
YOU WANNA GET TO CENTRAL AS QUICK AS POSSIBLE, RIGHT?
WELL THEN, LET'S SEE WHAT I CAN DO!
SMACK
BUT FOR A RUSH JOB LIKE THIS, YOU'RE GONNA HAVE TO PAY EXTRA!
OOPS.
I forgot you're not used to that leg.
SHEESH. WHAT'S WITH THAT VIOLENT WOMAN?!
Ha ha ha.
DON'T ACT LIKE YOU'RE SURPRISED.

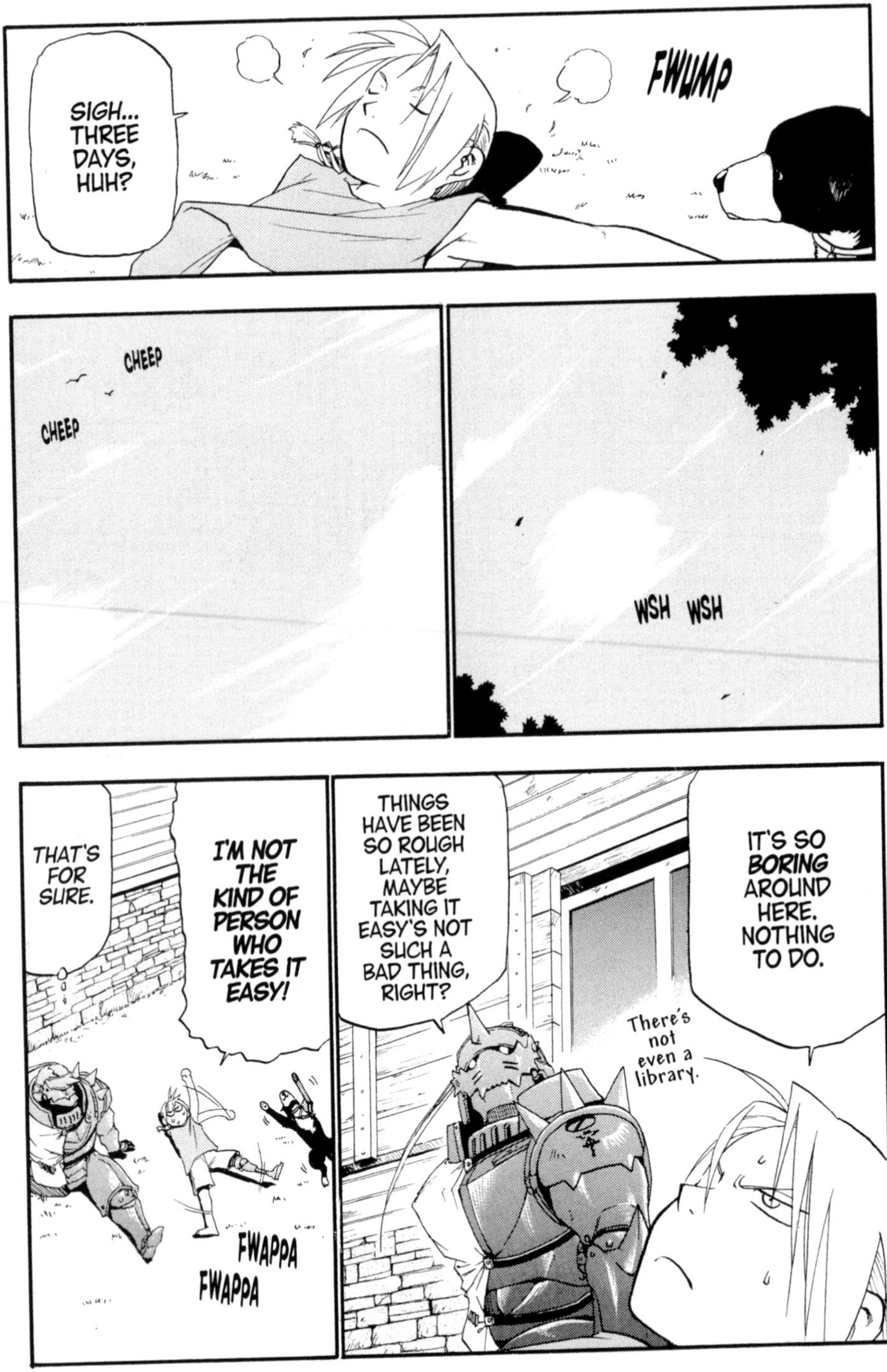
FWUMP
SIGH... THREE DAYS, HUH?
WSH WSH
CHEEP
CHEEP
IT'S SO BORING AROUND HERE. NOTHING TO DO.
There's not even a library.
THINGS HAVE BEEN SO ROUGH LATELY, MAYBE TAKING IT EASY'S NOT SUCH A BAD THING, RIGHT?
I'M NOT THE KIND OF PERSON WHO TAKES IT EASY!
THAT'S FOR SURE.
FWAPPA
FWAPPA

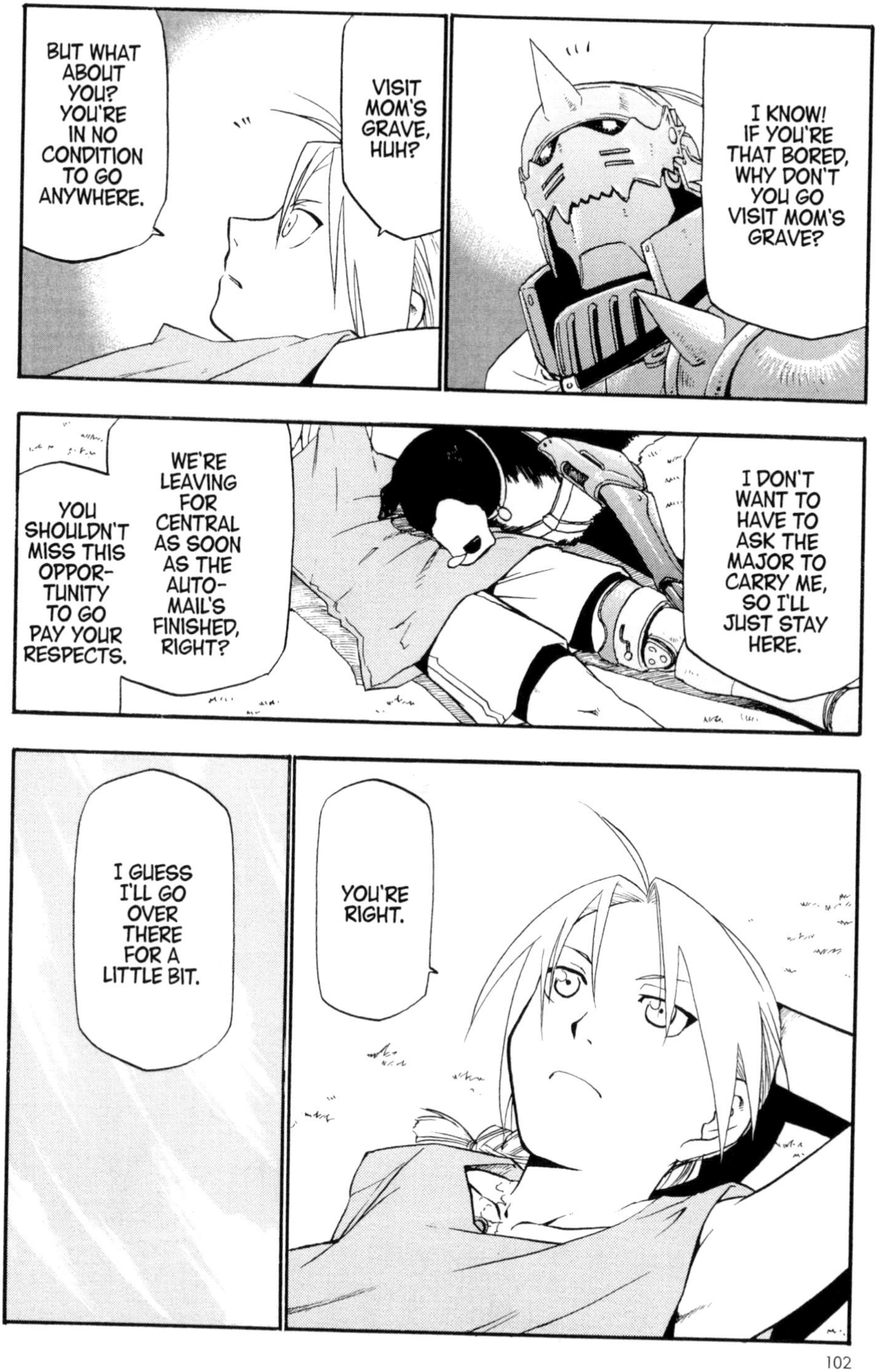
I KNOW! IF YOU'RE THAT BORED, WHY DON'T YOU GO VISIT MOM'S GRAVE?
VISIT MOM'S GRAVE, HUH?
BUT WHAT ABOUT YOU? YOU'RE IN NO CONDITION TO GO ANYWHERE.
I DON'T WANT TO HAVE TO ASK THE MAJOR TO CARRY ME, SO I'LL JUST STAY HERE.
WE'RE LEAVING FOR CENTRAL AS SOON AS THE AUTO-MAIL'S FINISHED, RIGHT?
YOU SHOULDN'T MISS THIS OPPOR-TUNITY TO GO PAY YOUR RESPECTS.
YOU'RE RIGHT.
I GUESS I'LL GO OVER THERE FOR A LITTLE BIT.

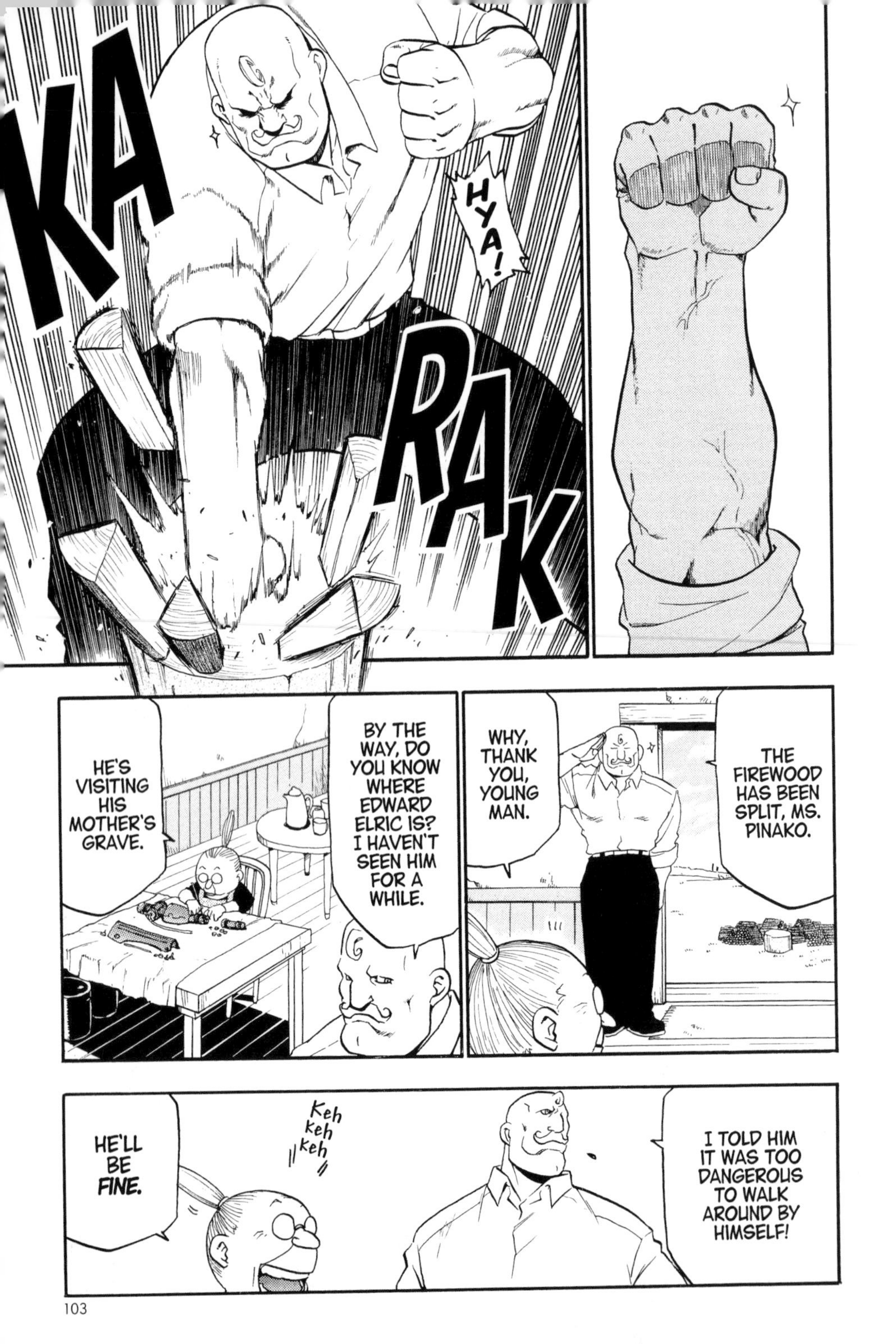
HYA!
KA
RAK
THE FIREWOOD HAS BEEN SPLIT, MS. PINAKO.
WHY, THANK YOU, YOUNG MAN.
BY THE WAY, DO YOU KNOW WHERE EDWARD ELRIC IS? I HAVEN'T SEEN HIM FOR A WHILE.
HE'S VISITING HIS MOTHER'S GRAVE.
I TOLD HIM IT WAS TOO DANGEROUS TO WALK AROUND BY HIMSELF!
Keh keh keh
HE'LL BE *FINE*.

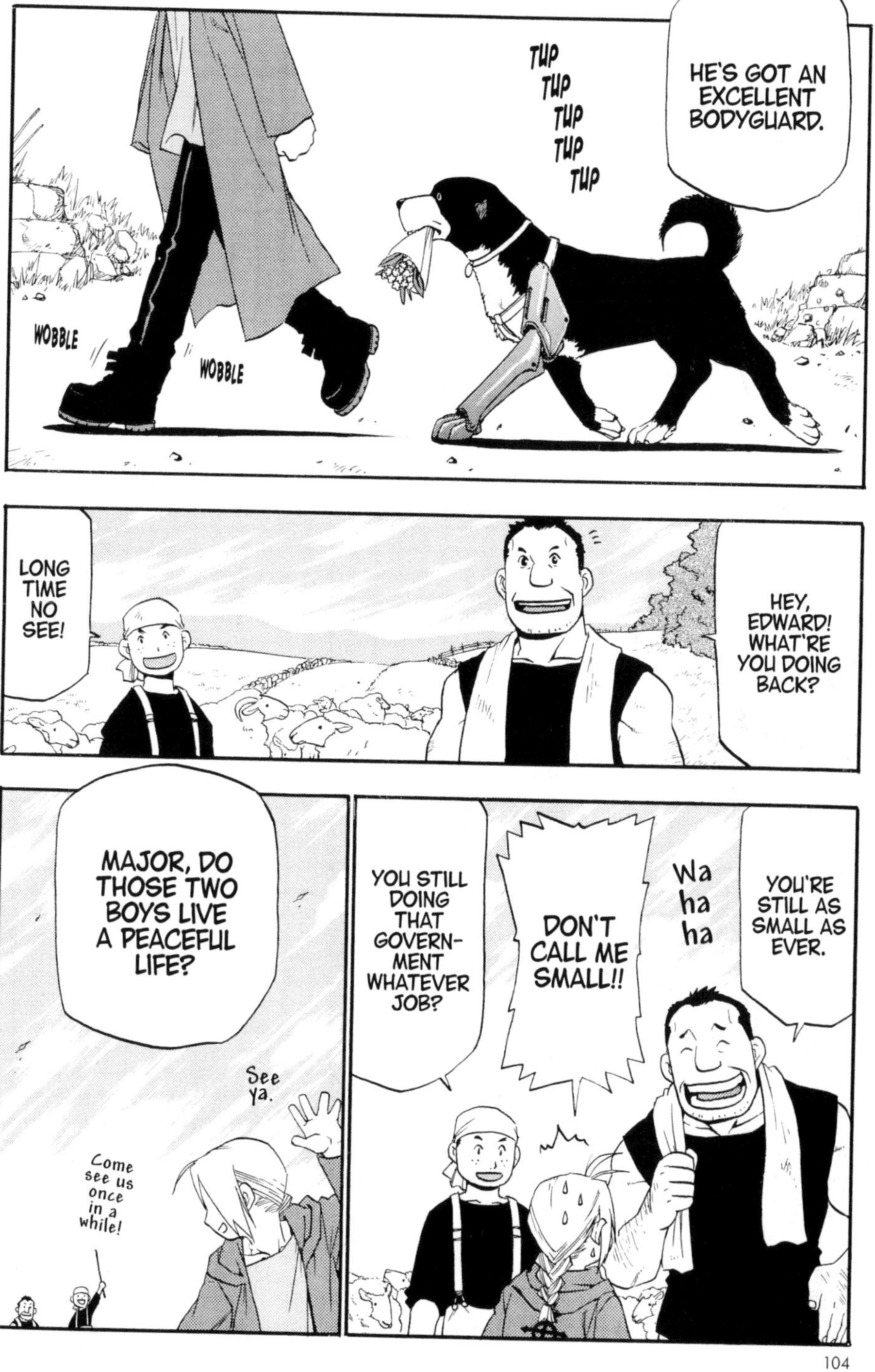
HE'S GOT AN EXCELLENT BODYGUARD.
TUP TUP TUP TUP TUP
WOBBLE WOBBLE
HEY, EDWARD! WHAT'RE YOU DOING BACK?
LONG TIME NO SEE!
YOU'RE STILL AS SMALL AS EVER.
Wa ha ha
DON'T CALL ME SMALL!!
YOU STILL DOING THAT GOVERN-MENT WHATEVER JOB?
MAJOR, DO THOSE TWO BOYS LIVE A PEACEFUL LIFE?
See ya.
Come see us once in a while!

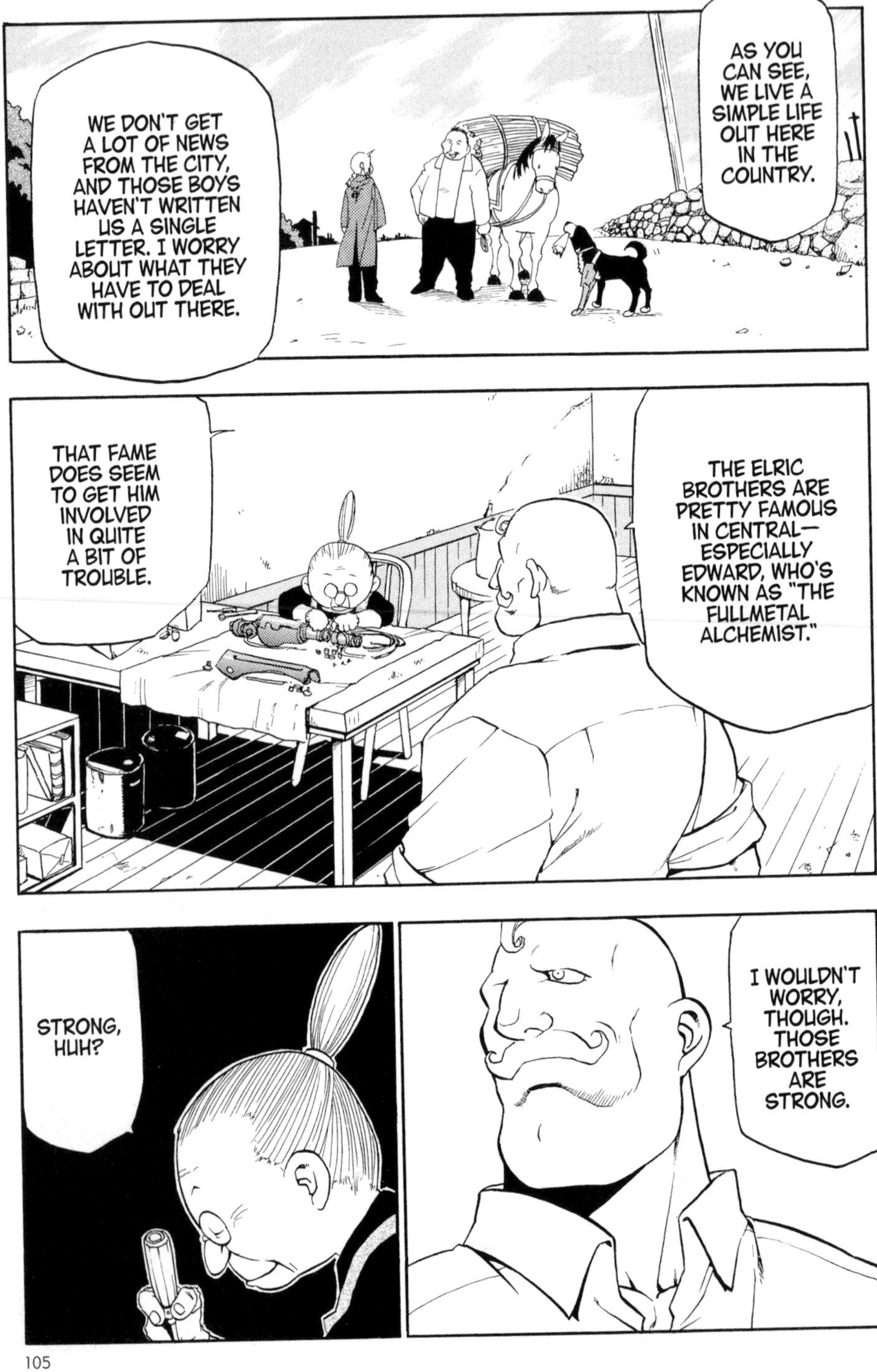
AS YOU CAN SEE, WE LIVE A SIMPLE LIFE OUT HERE IN THE COUNTRY.
WE DON'T GET A LOT OF NEWS FROM THE CITY, AND THOSE BOYS HAVEN'T WRITTEN US A SINGLE LETTER. I WORRY ABOUT WHAT THEY HAVE TO DEAL WITH OUT THERE.
THE ELRIC BROTHERS ARE PRETTY FAMOUS IN CENTRAL—ESPECIALLY EDWARD, WHO'S KNOWN AS "THE FULLMETAL ALCHEMIST."
THAT FAME DOES SEEM TO GET HIM INVOLVED IN QUITE A BIT OF TROUBLE.
I WOULDN'T WORRY, THOUGH. THOSE BROTHERS ARE STRONG.
STRONG, HUH?

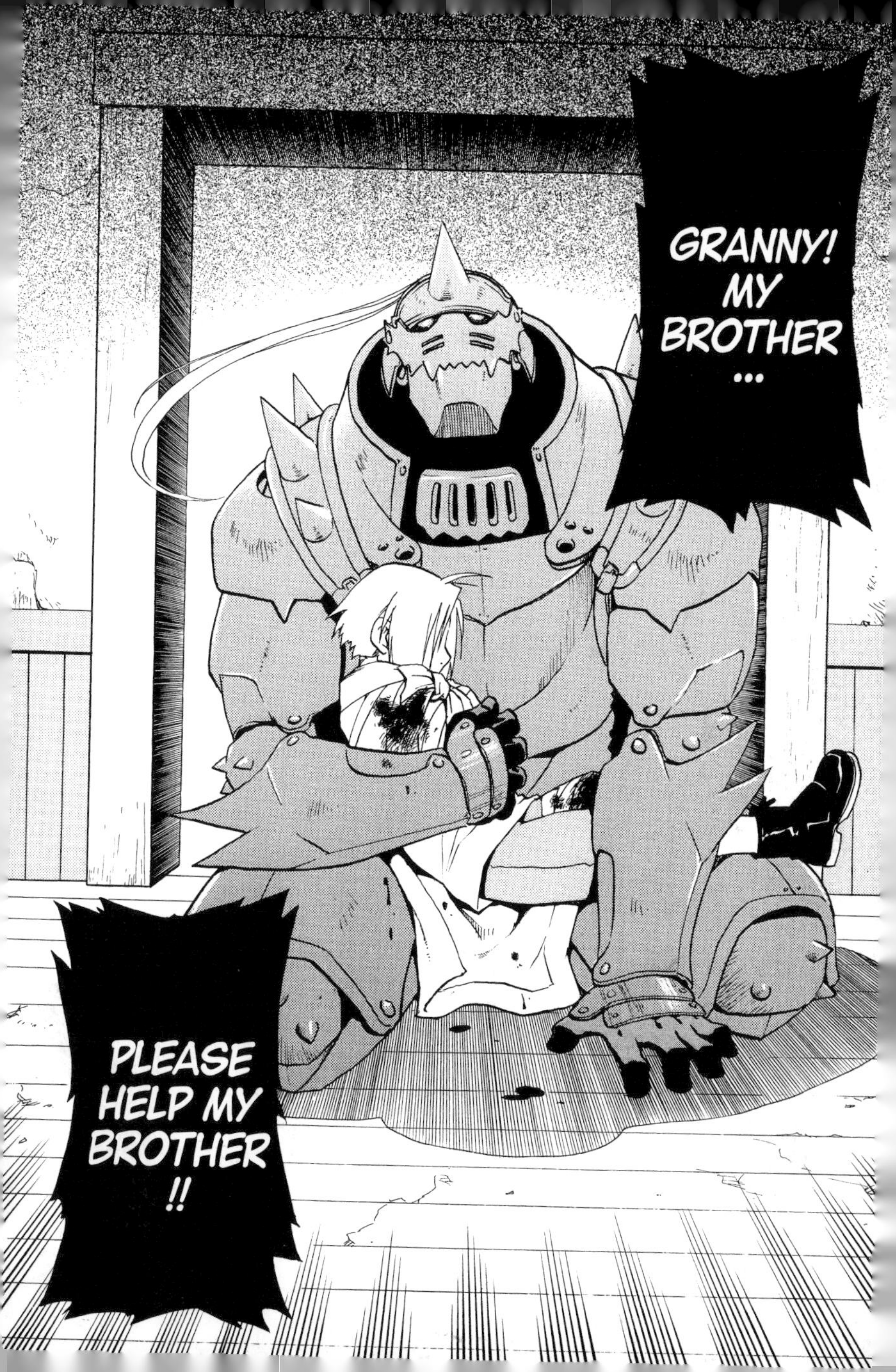
GRANNY! MY BROTHER ...
PLEASE HELP MY BROTHER !!

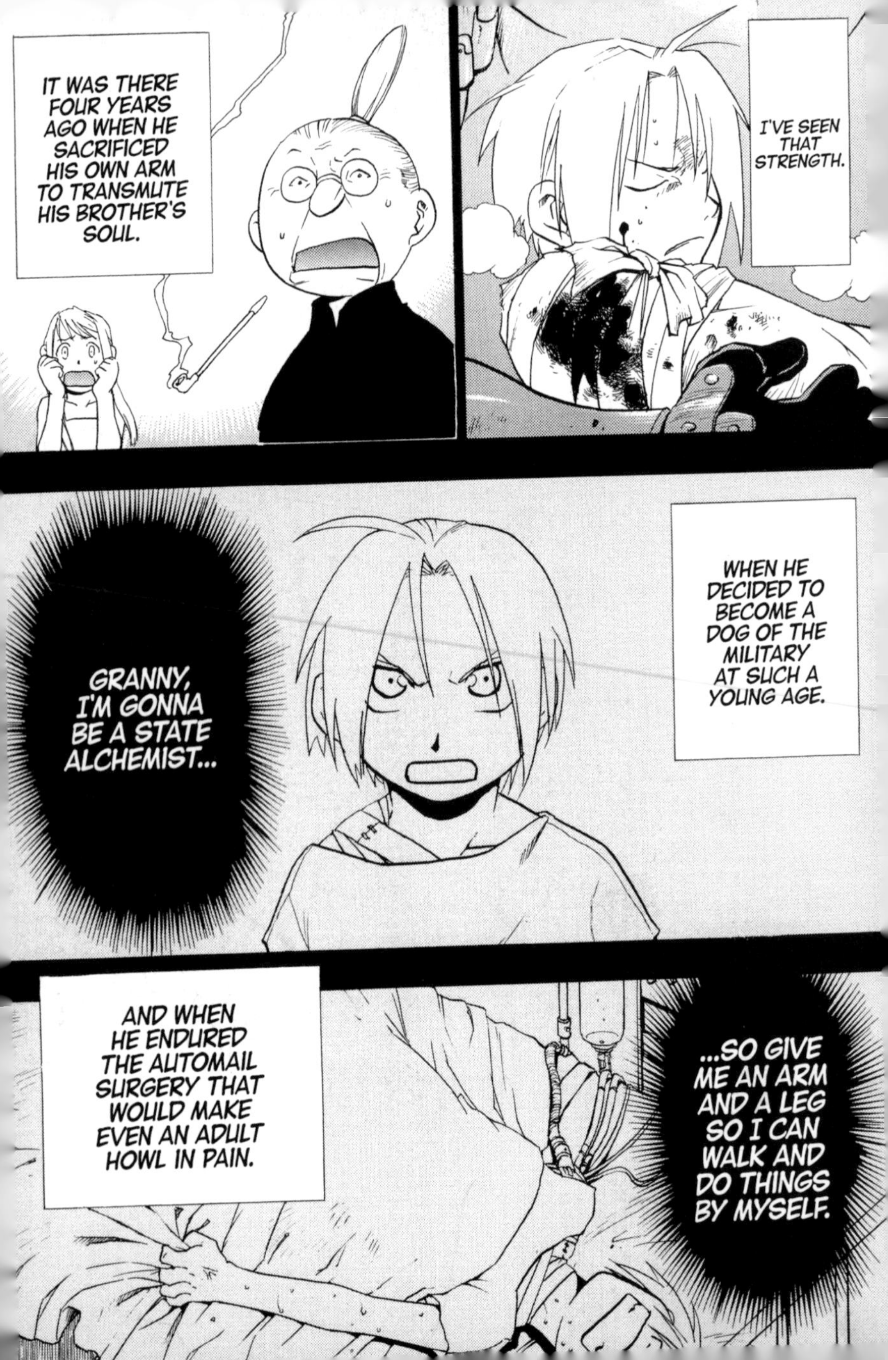
I'VE SEEN THAT STRENGTH.
IT WAS THERE FOUR YEARS AGO WHEN HE SACRIFICED HIS OWN ARM TO TRANSMUTE HIS BROTHER'S SOUL.
WHEN HE DECIDED TO BECOME A DOG OF THE MILITARY AT SUCH A YOUNG AGE.
GRANNY, I'M GONNA BE A STATE ALCHEMIST...
...SO GIVE ME AN ARM AND A LEG SO I CAN WALK AND DO THINGS BY MYSELF.
AND WHEN HE ENDURED THE AUTOMAIL SURGERY THAT WOULD MAKE EVEN AN ADULT HOWL IN PAIN.

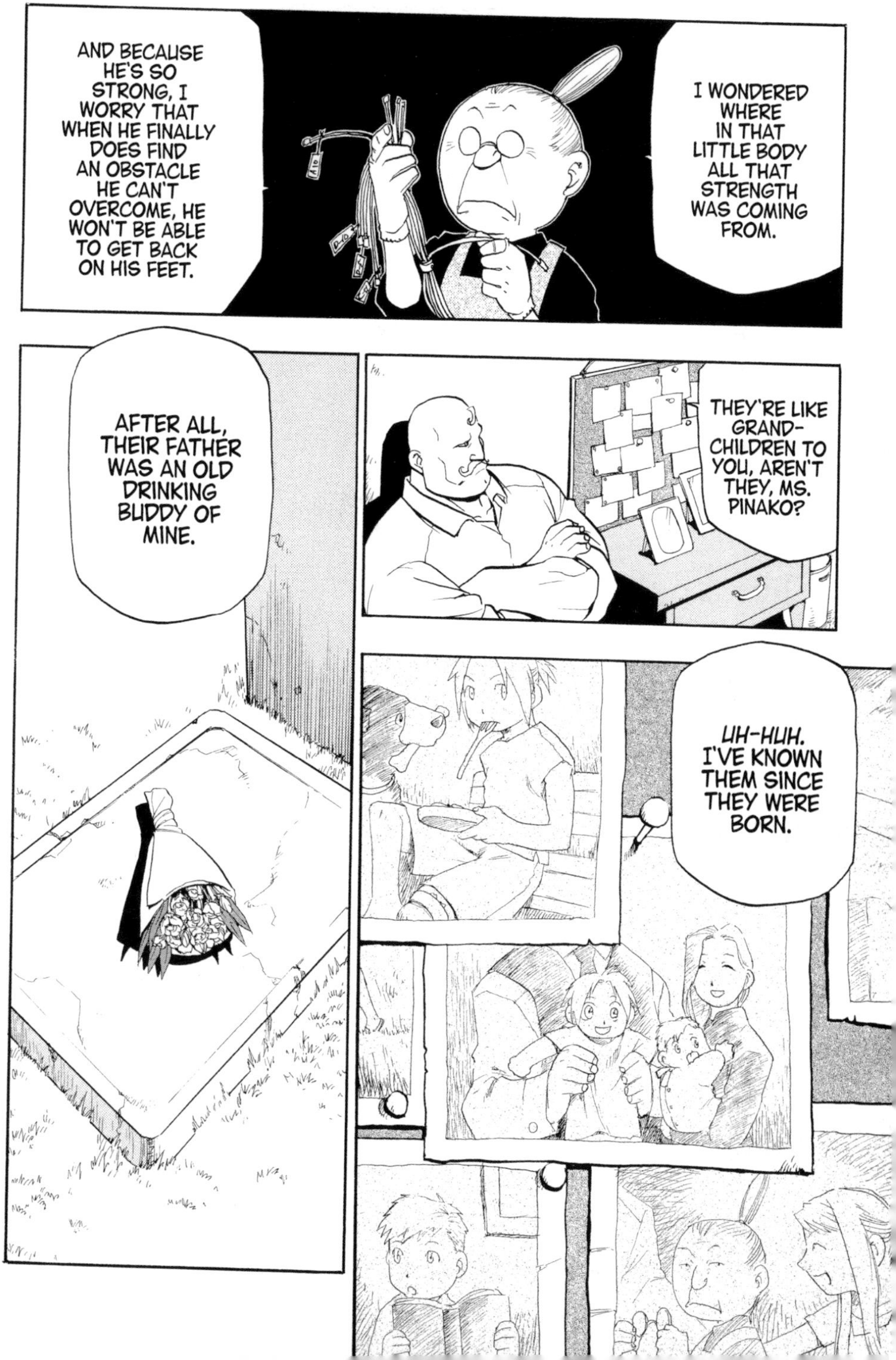
I WONDERED WHERE IN THAT LITTLE BODY ALL THAT STRENGTH WAS COMING FROM.
AND BECAUSE HE'S SO STRONG, I WORRY THAT WHEN HE FINALLY DOES FIND AN OBSTACLE HE CAN'T OVERCOME, HE WON'T BE ABLE TO GET BACK ON HIS FEET.
THEY'RE LIKE GRAND-CHILDREN TO YOU, AREN'T THEY, MS. PINAKO?
UH-HUH. I'VE KNOWN THEM SINCE THEY WERE BORN.
AFTER ALL, THEIR FATHER WAS AN OLD DRINKING BUDDY OF MINE.

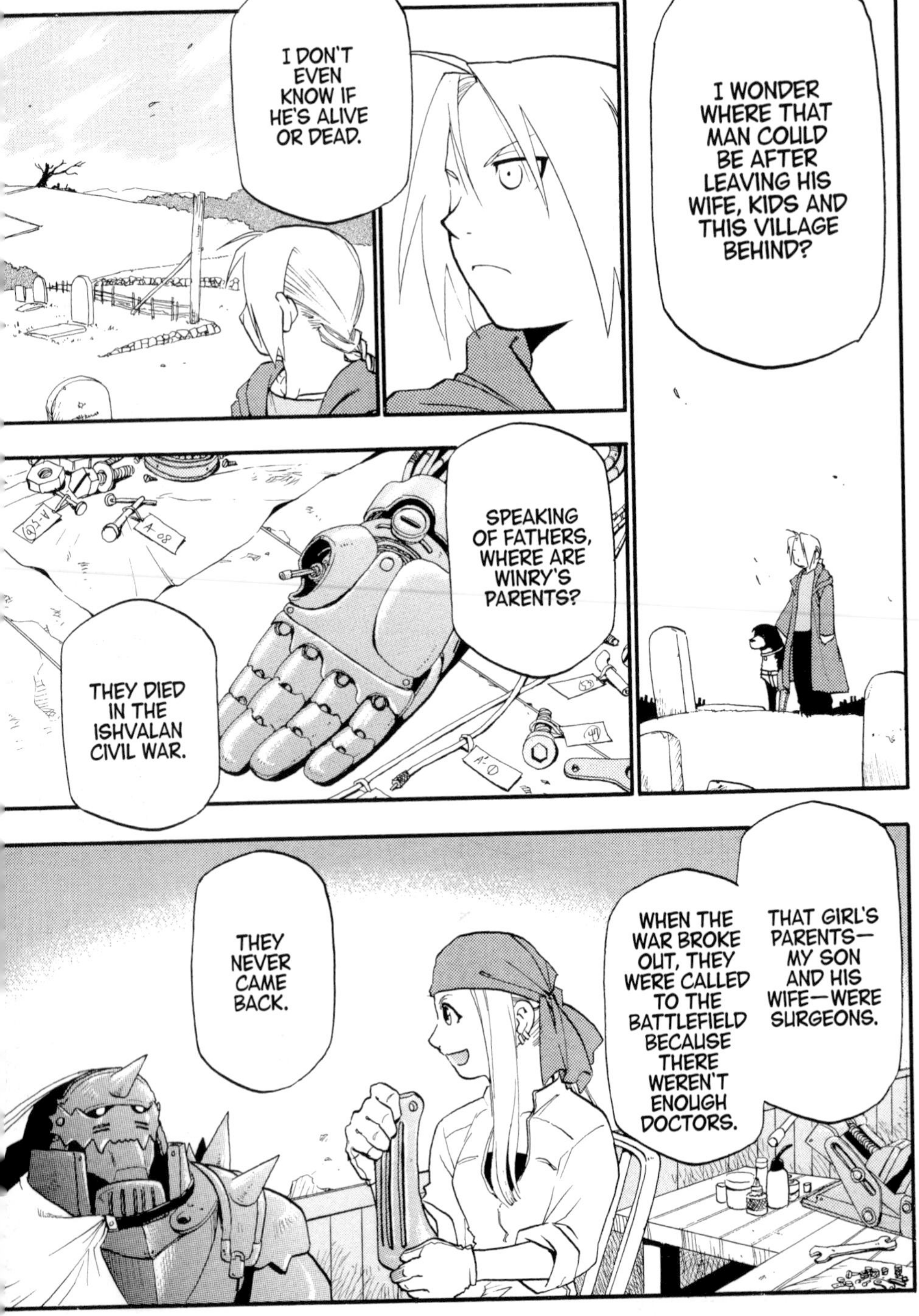
I WONDER WHERE THAT MAN COULD BE AFTER LEAVING HIS WIFE, KIDS AND THIS VILLAGE BEHIND?
I DON'T EVEN KNOW IF HE'S ALIVE OR DEAD.
SPEAKING OF FATHERS, WHERE ARE WINRY'S PARENTS?
THEY DIED IN THE ISHVALAN CIVIL WAR.
THAT GIRL'S PARENTS— MY SON AND HIS WIFE—WERE SURGEONS.
WHEN THE WAR BROKE OUT, THEY WERE CALLED TO THE BATTLEFIELD BECAUSE THERE WEREN'T ENOUGH DOCTORS.
THEY NEVER CAME BACK.

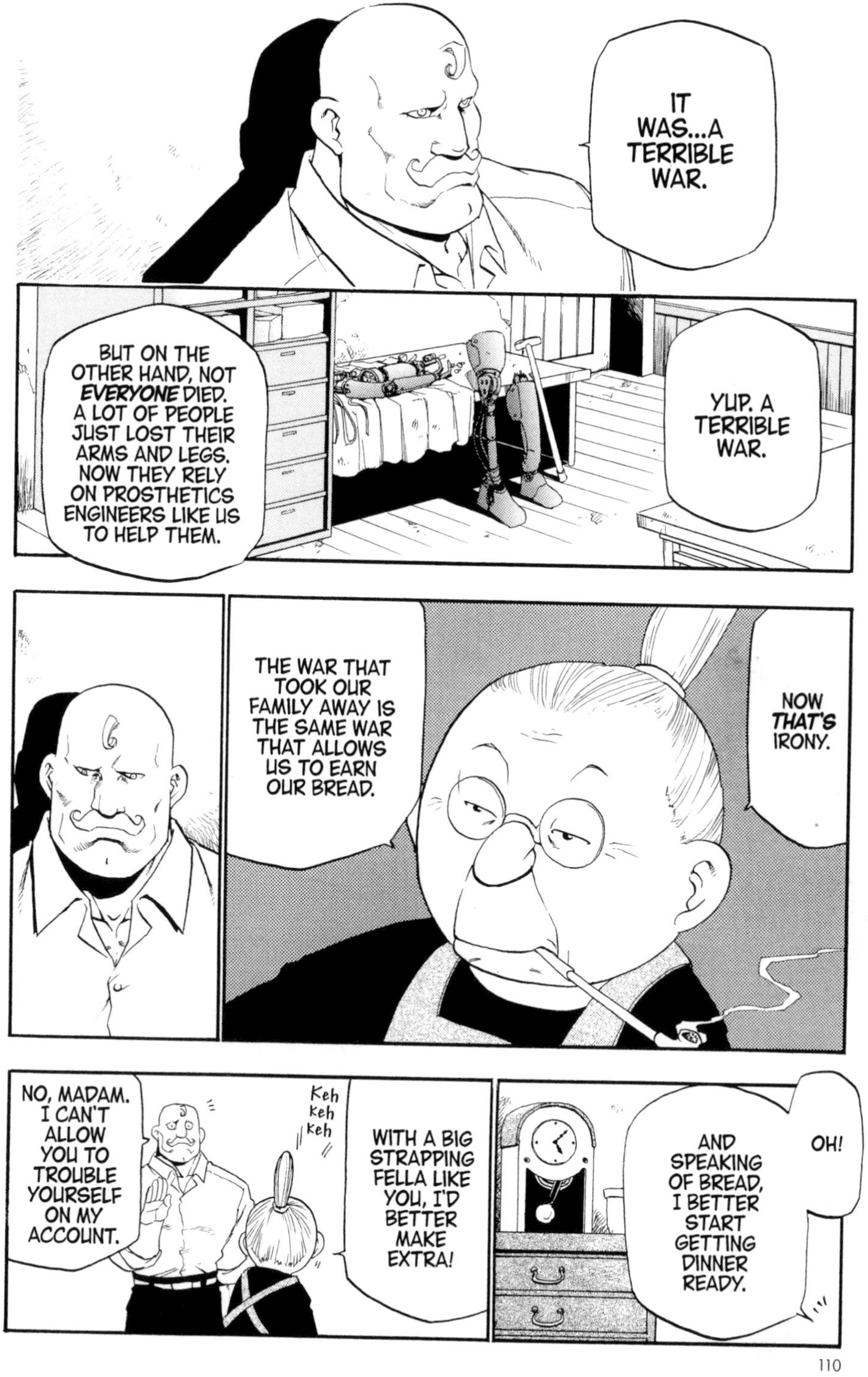
IT WAS...A TERRIBLE WAR.
YUP. A TERRIBLE WAR.
BUT ON THE OTHER HAND, NOT *EVERYONE* DIED. A LOT OF PEOPLE JUST LOST THEIR ARMS AND LEGS. NOW THEY RELY ON PROSTHETICS ENGINEERS LIKE US TO HELP THEM.
THE WAR THAT TOOK OUR FAMILY AWAY IS THE SAME WAR THAT ALLOWS US TO EARN OUR BREAD.
NOW *THAT'S* IRONY.
OH!
AND SPEAKING OF BREAD, I BETTER START GETTING DINNER READY.
WITH A BIG STRAPPING FELLA LIKE YOU, I'D BETTER MAKE EXTRA!
Keh keh keh
NO, MADAM. I CAN'T ALLOW YOU TO TROUBLE YOURSELF ON MY ACCOUNT.

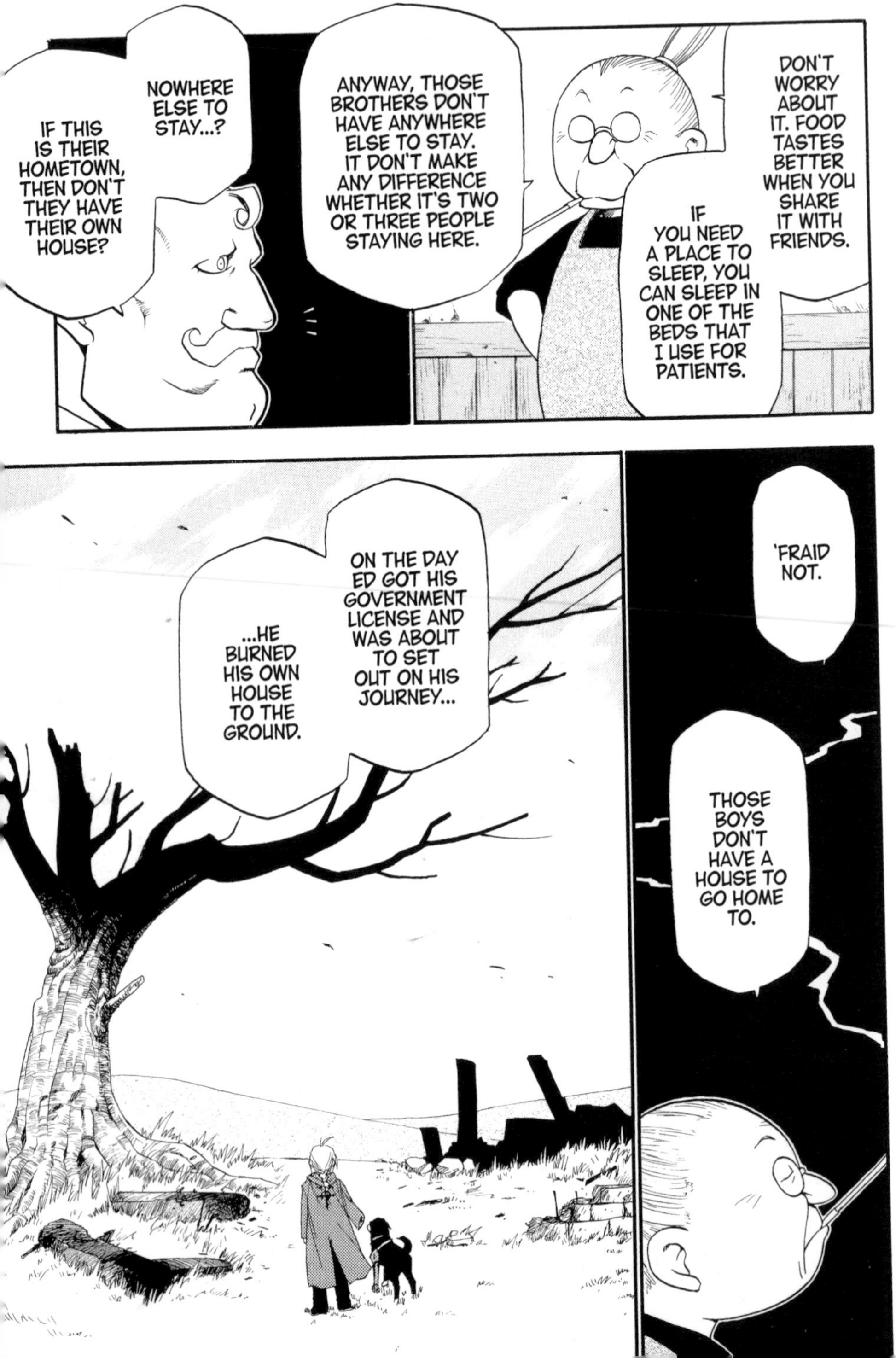
DON'T WORRY ABOUT IT. FOOD TASTES BETTER WHEN YOU SHARE IT WITH FRIENDS.
IF YOU NEED A PLACE TO SLEEP, YOU CAN SLEEP IN ONE OF THE BEDS THAT I USE FOR PATIENTS.
ANYWAY, THOSE BROTHERS DON'T HAVE ANYWHERE ELSE TO STAY. IT DON'T MAKE ANY DIFFERENCE WHETHER IT'S TWO OR THREE PEOPLE STAYING HERE.
NOWHERE ELSE TO STAY...?
IF THIS IS THEIR HOMETOWN, THEN DON'T THEY HAVE THEIR OWN HOUSE?
'FRAID NOT.
THOSE BOYS DON'T HAVE A HOUSE TO GO HOME TO.
ON THE DAY ED GOT HIS GOVERNMENT LICENSE AND WAS ABOUT TO SET OUT ON HIS JOURNEY...
...HE BURNED HIS OWN HOUSE TO THE GROUND.

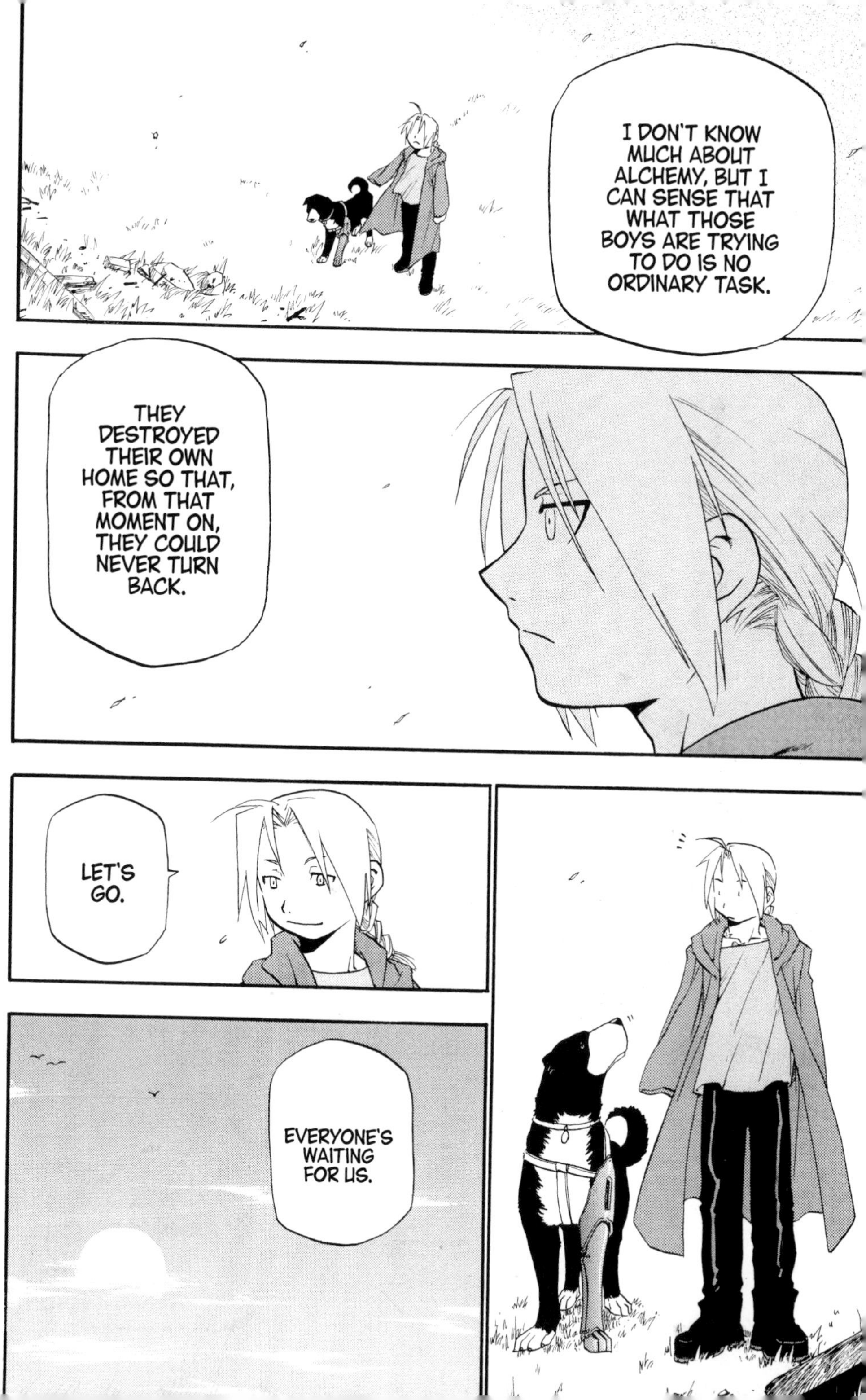
I DON'T KNOW MUCH ABOUT ALCHEMY, BUT I CAN SENSE THAT WHAT THOSE BOYS ARE TRYING TO DO IS NO ORDINARY TASK.
THEY DESTROYED THEIR OWN HOME SO THAT, FROM THAT MOMENT ON, THEY COULD NEVER TURN BACK.
LET'S GO.
EVERYONE'S WAITING FOR US.

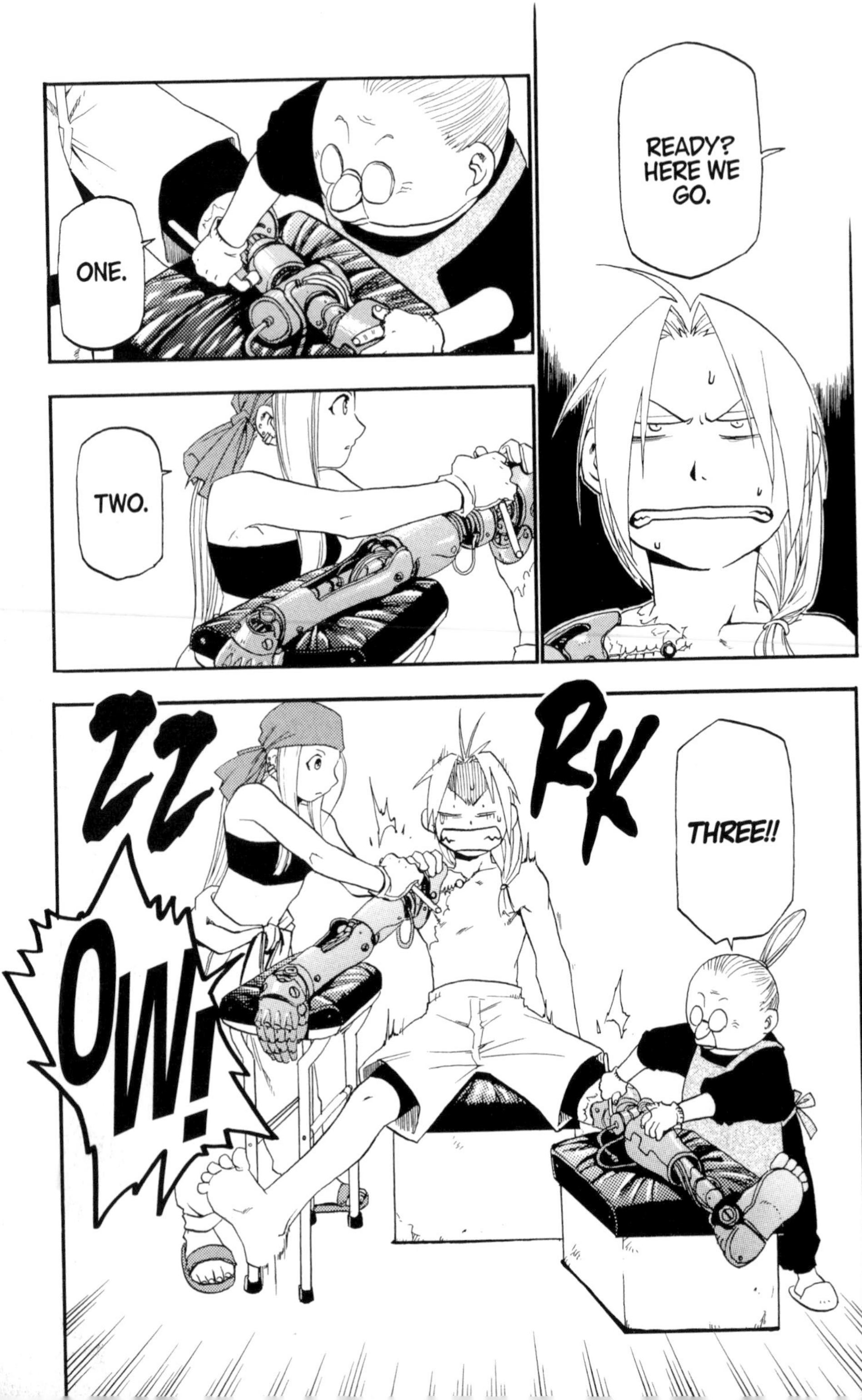
READY? HERE WE GO.
ONE.
TWO.
THREE!!
ZZRK
OW!

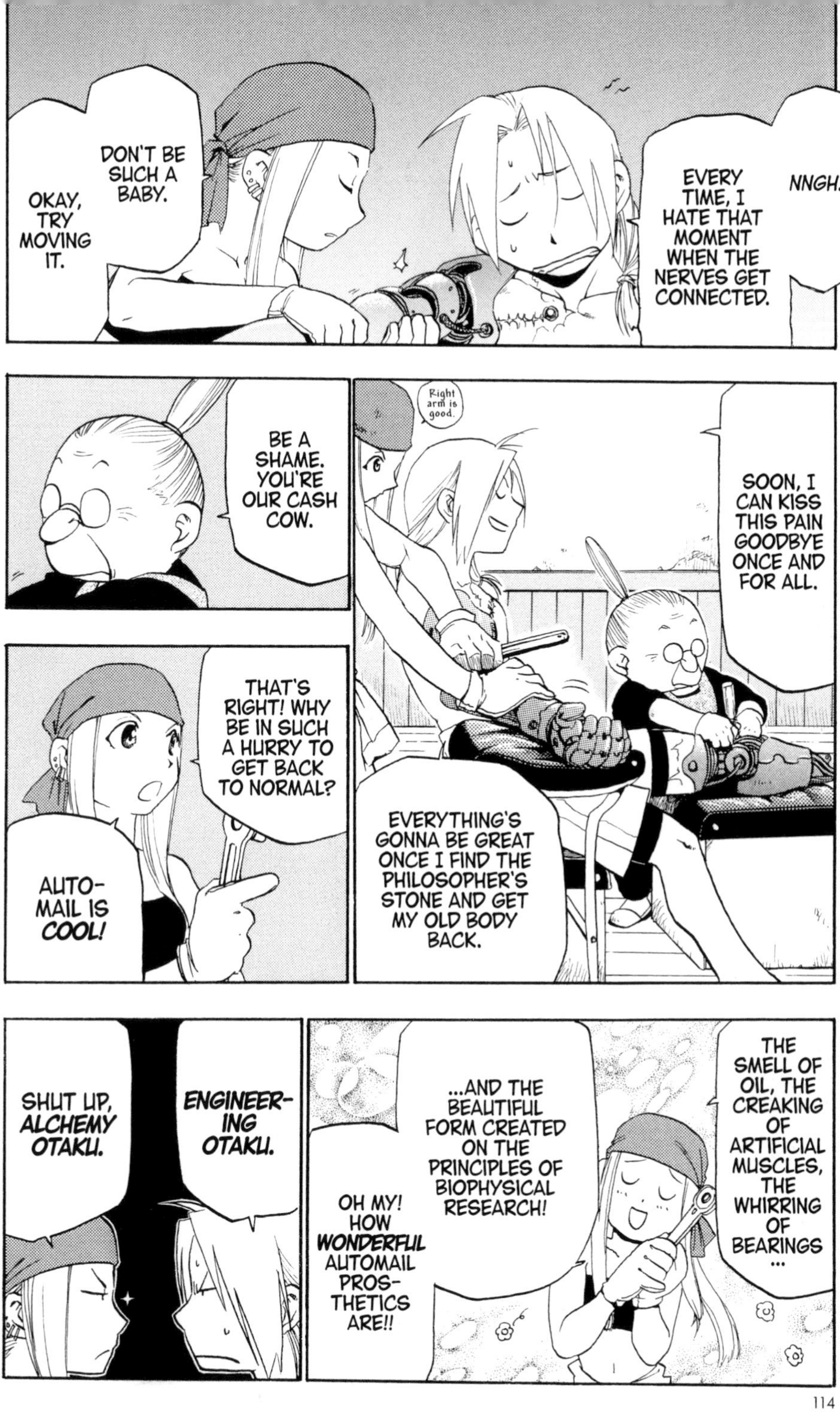
NNGH...
EVERY TIME, I HATE THAT MOMENT WHEN THE NERVES GET CONNECTED.
DON'T BE SUCH A BABY.
OKAY, TRY MOVING IT.
SOON, I CAN KISS THIS PAIN GOODBYE ONCE AND FOR ALL.
Right arm is good.
EVERYTHING'S GONNA BE GREAT ONCE I FIND THE PHILOSOPHER'S STONE AND GET MY OLD BODY BACK.
BE A SHAME. YOU'RE OUR CASH COW.
THAT'S RIGHT! WHY BE IN SUCH A HURRY TO GET BACK TO NORMAL?
AUTO-MAIL IS **COOL!**
THE SMELL OF OIL, THE CREAKING OF ARTIFICIAL MUSCLES, THE WHIRRING OF BEARINGS...
...AND THE BEAUTIFUL FORM CREATED ON THE PRINCIPLES OF BIOPHYSICAL RESEARCH!
OH MY! HOW **WONDERFUL** AUTOMAIL PROS-THETICS ARE!!
ENGINEER-ING OTAKU.
SHUT UP, **ALCHEMY OTAKU.**

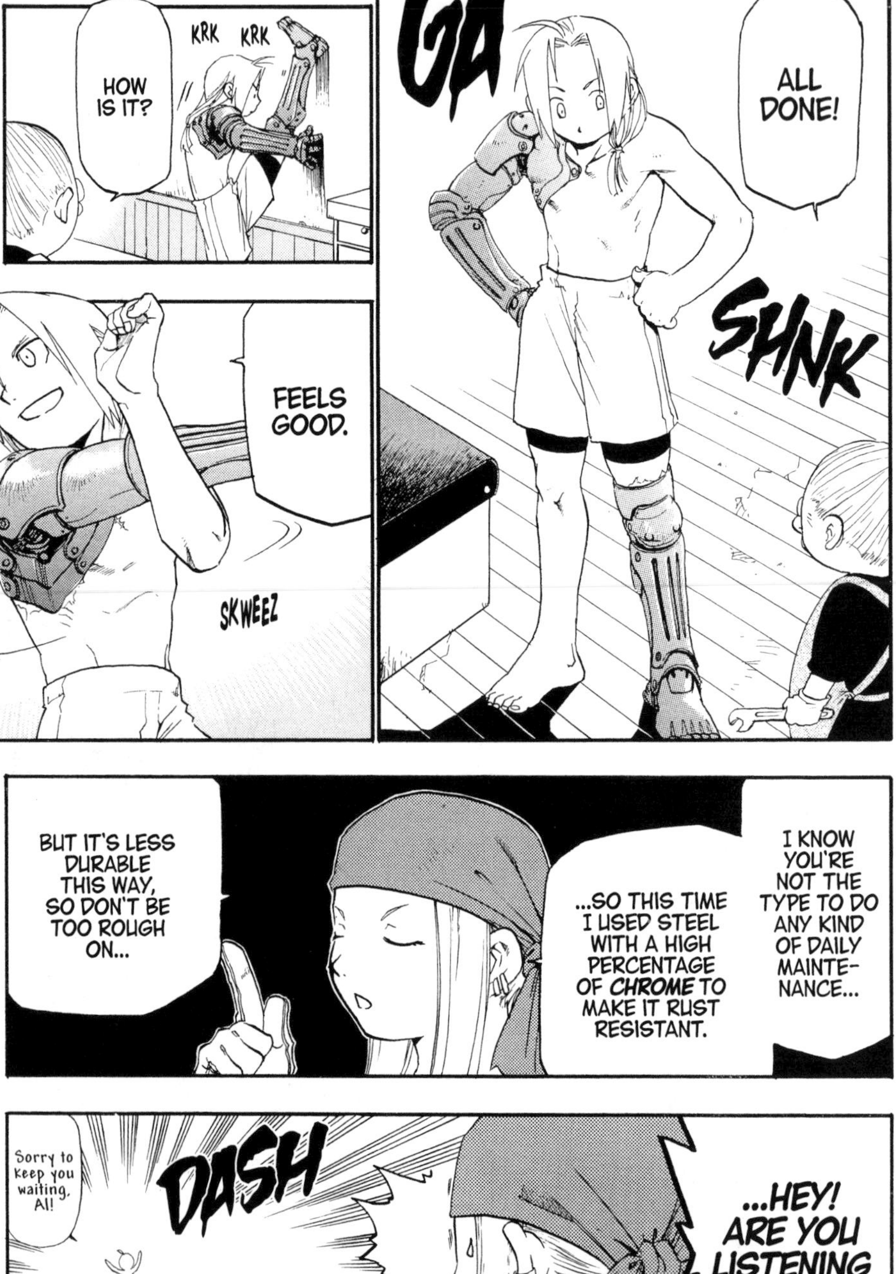
GA
ALL DONE!
SHNK
HOW IS IT?
KRK KRK
FEELS GOOD.
SKWEEZ
I KNOW YOU'RE NOT THE TYPE TO DO ANY KIND OF DAILY MAINTE-NANCE...
...SO THIS TIME I USED STEEL WITH A HIGH PERCENTAGE OF **CHROME** TO MAKE IT RUST RESISTANT.
BUT IT'S LESS DURABLE THIS WAY, SO DON'T BE TOO ROUGH ON...
...HEY! ARE YOU LISTENING ?!!
DASH
Sorry to keep you waiting, Al!

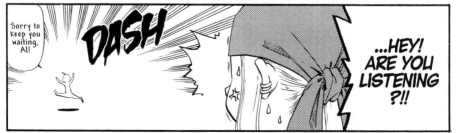

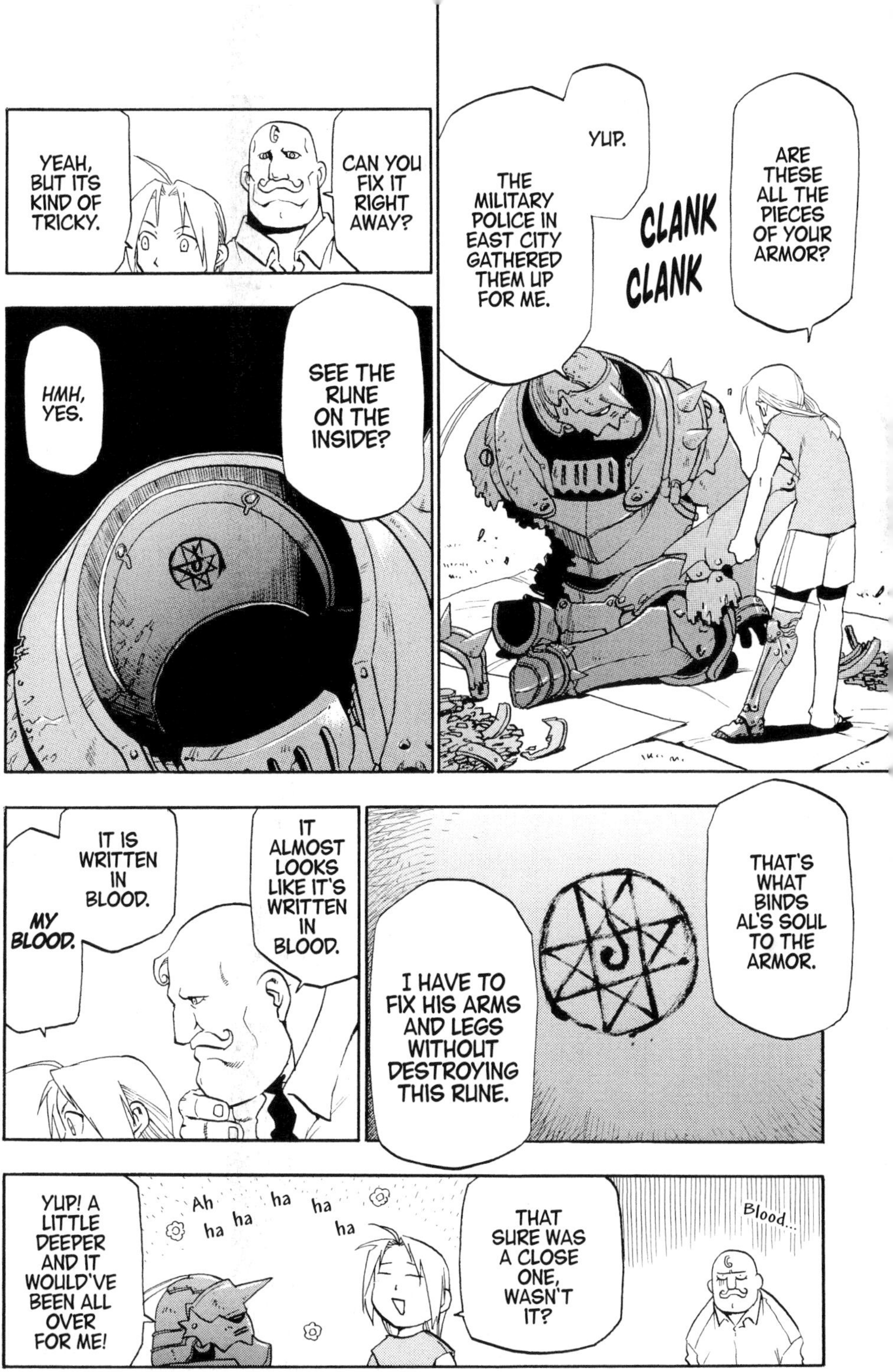
ARE THESE ALL THE PIECES OF YOUR ARMOR?
CLANK
CLANK
YUP.
THE MILITARY POLICE IN EAST CITY GATHERED THEM UP FOR ME.
CAN YOU FIX IT RIGHT AWAY?
YEAH, BUT ITS KIND OF TRICKY.
SEE THE RUNE ON THE INSIDE?
HMH, YES.
THAT'S WHAT BINDS AL'S SOUL TO THE ARMOR.
I HAVE TO FIX HIS ARMS AND LEGS WITHOUT DESTROYING THIS RUNE.
IT ALMOST LOOKS LIKE IT'S WRITTEN IN BLOOD.
IT IS WRITTEN IN BLOOD.
MY BLOOD.
Blood...
THAT SURE WAS A CLOSE ONE, WASN'T IT?
Ah ha ha ha ha ha
YUP! A LITTLE DEEPER AND IT WOULD'VE BEEN ALL OVER FOR ME!

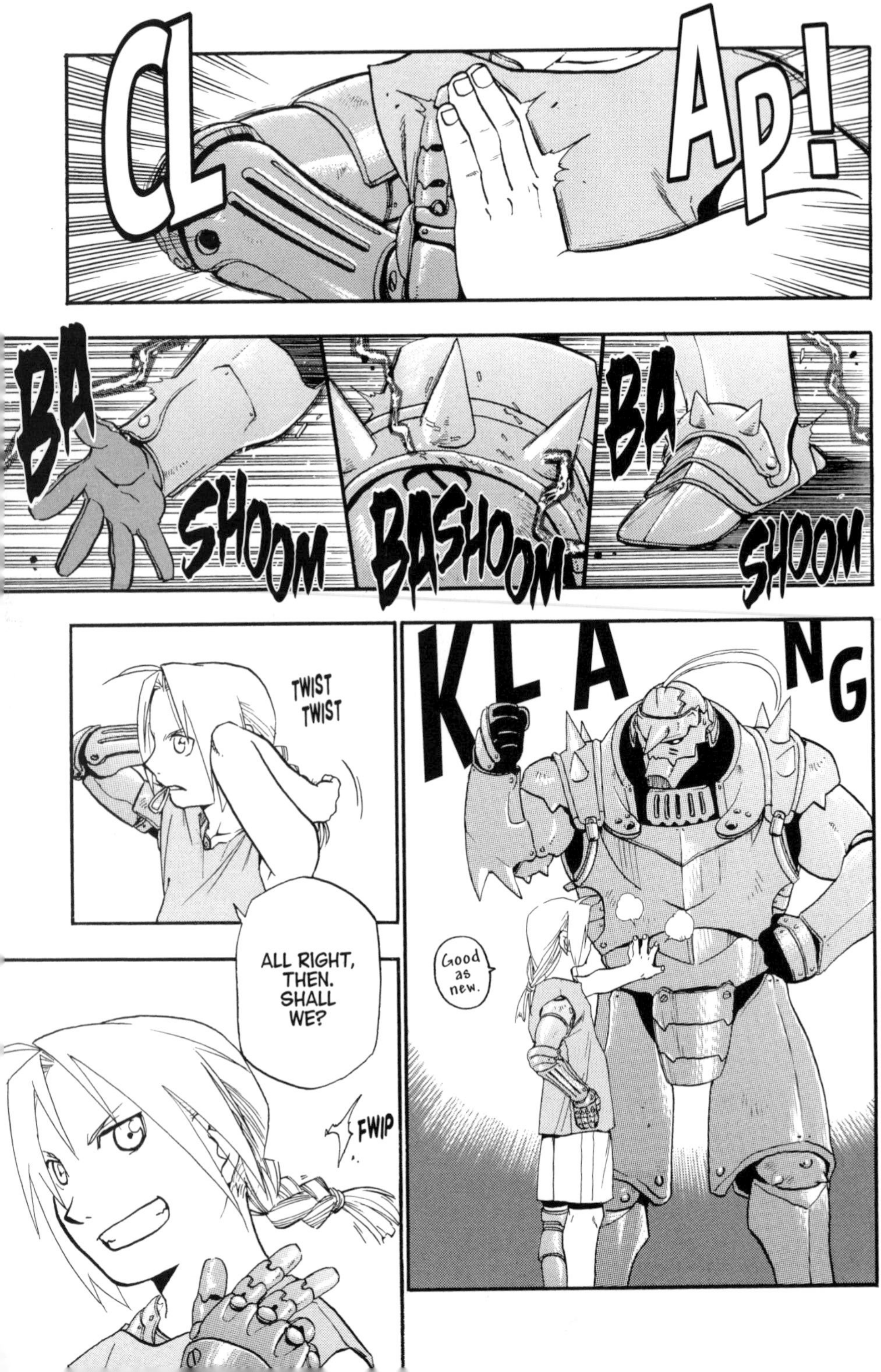
CLAP!
BA SHOOM
BASHOOM
BA SHOOM
KLANG
Good as new.
TWIST TWIST
ALL RIGHT, THEN. SHALL WE?
FWIP

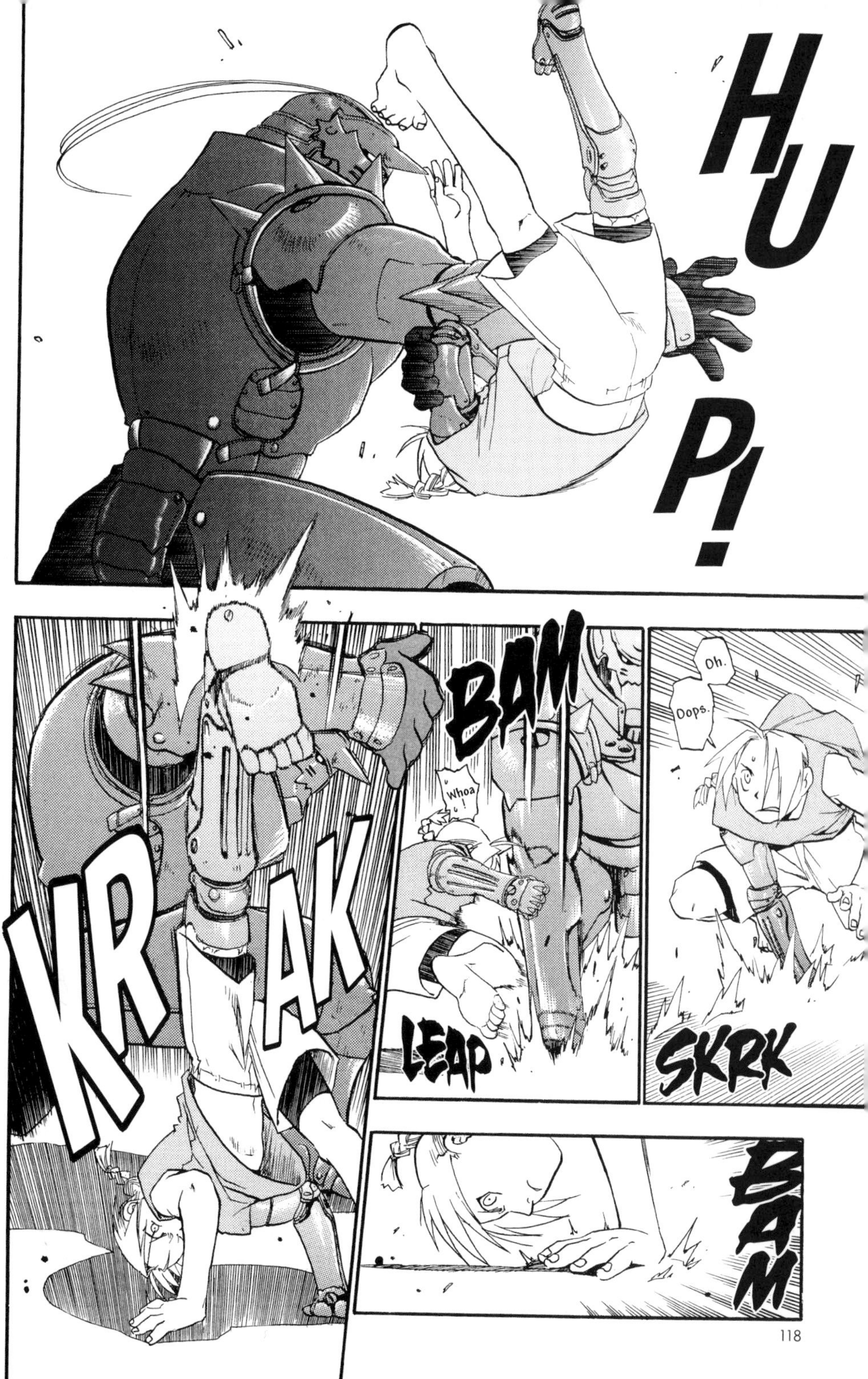
HUP!
Oh.
Oops.
SKRK
BAM
Whoa!
LEAP
BAM
KRAK

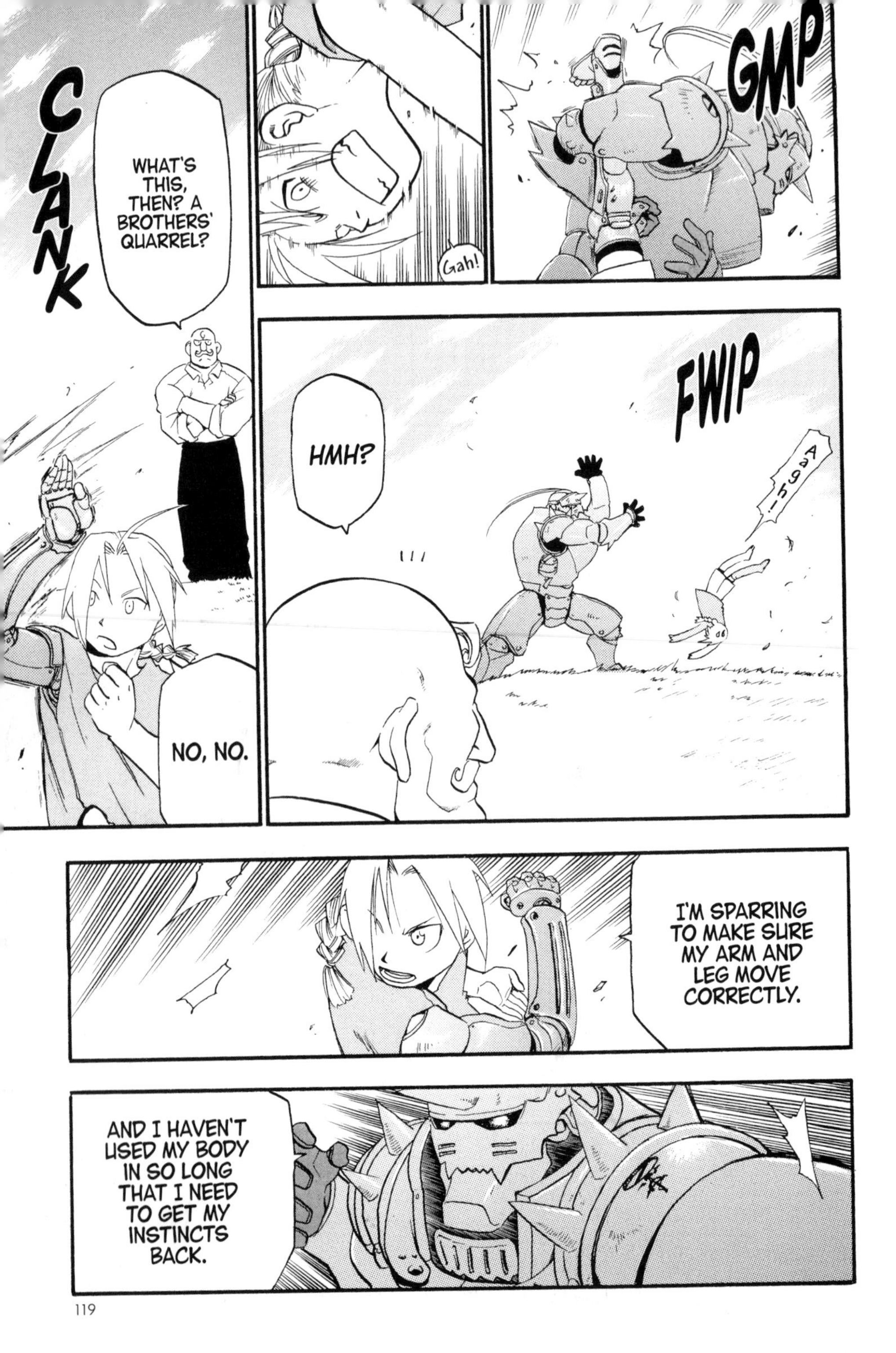
GMP
Gah!
FWIP
Aagh!
HMH?
CLANK
WHAT'S THIS, THEN? A BROTHERS' QUARREL?
NO, NO.
I'M SPARRING TO MAKE SURE MY ARM AND LEG MOVE CORRECTLY.
AND I HAVEN'T USED MY BODY IN SO LONG THAT I NEED TO GET MY INSTINCTS BACK.

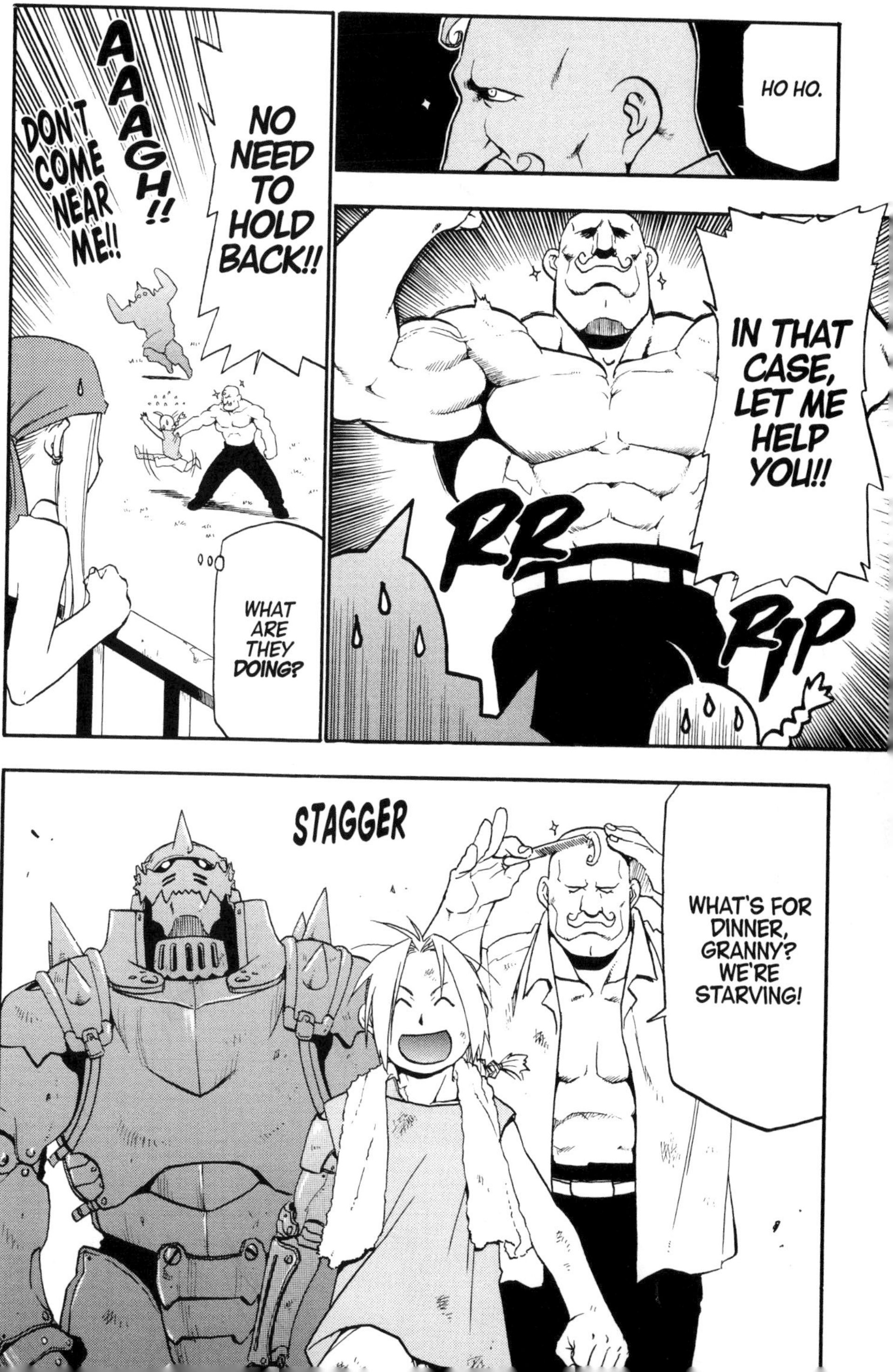
HO HO.
IN THAT CASE, LET ME HELP YOU!!
RR
RIP
NO NEED TO HOLD BACK!!
AAAAGH!!
DON'T COME NEAR ME!!
WHAT ARE THEY DOING?
WHAT'S FOR DINNER, GRANNY? WE'RE STARVING!
STAGGER

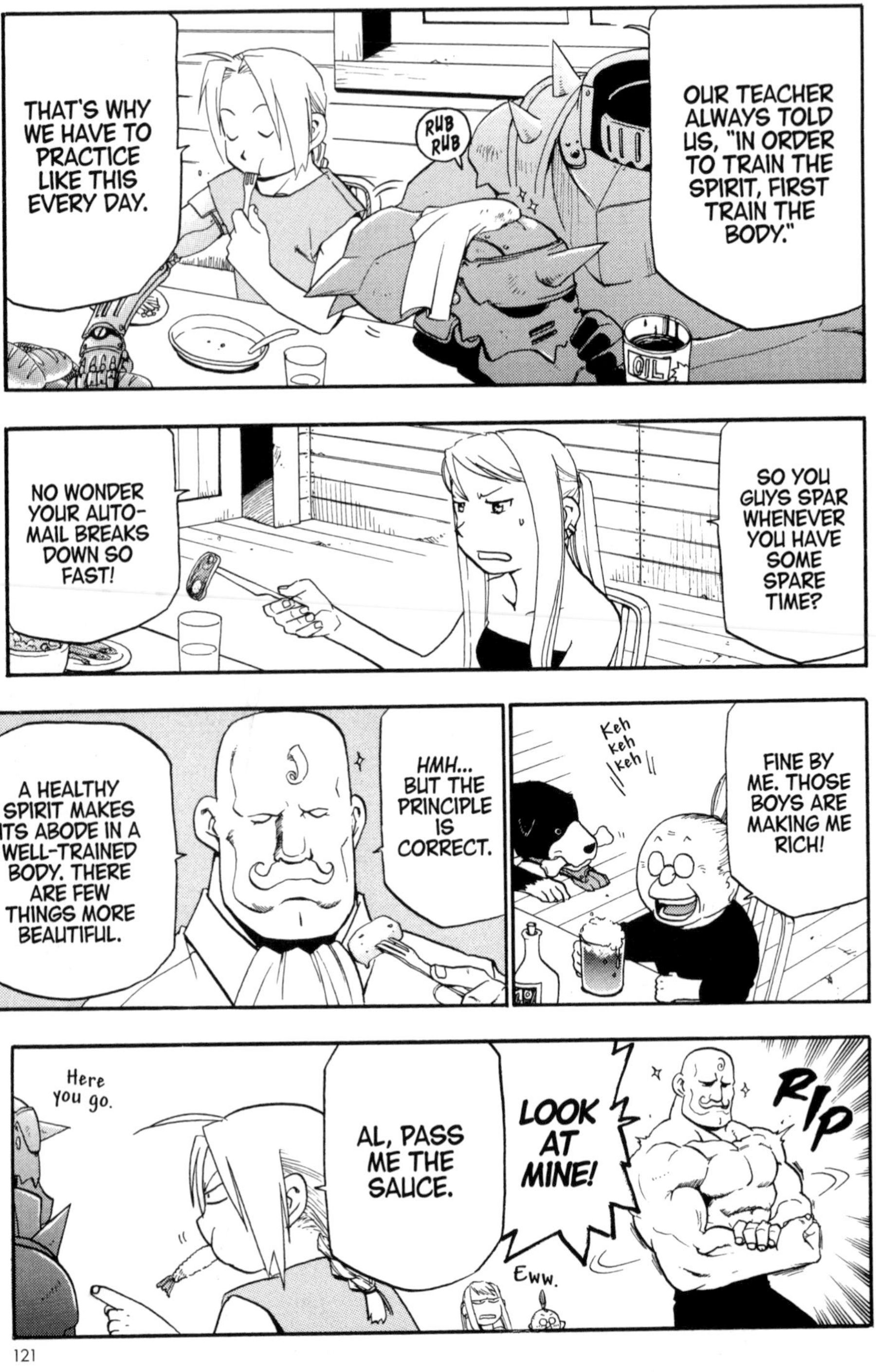
OUR TEACHER ALWAYS TOLD US, "IN ORDER TO TRAIN THE SPIRIT, FIRST TRAIN THE BODY."
RUB RUB
THAT'S WHY WE HAVE TO PRACTICE LIKE THIS EVERY DAY.
OIL
SO YOU GUYS SPAR WHENEVER YOU HAVE SOME SPARE TIME?
NO WONDER YOUR AUTO-MAIL BREAKS DOWN SO FAST!
FINE BY ME. THOSE BOYS ARE MAKING ME RICH!
Keh keh keh
HMH... BUT THE PRINCIPLE IS CORRECT.
A HEALTHY SPIRIT MAKES ITS ABODE IN A WELL-TRAINED BODY. THERE ARE FEW THINGS MORE BEAUTIFUL.
RIP
LOOK AT MINE!
Eww.
AL, PASS ME THE SAUCE.
Here you go.

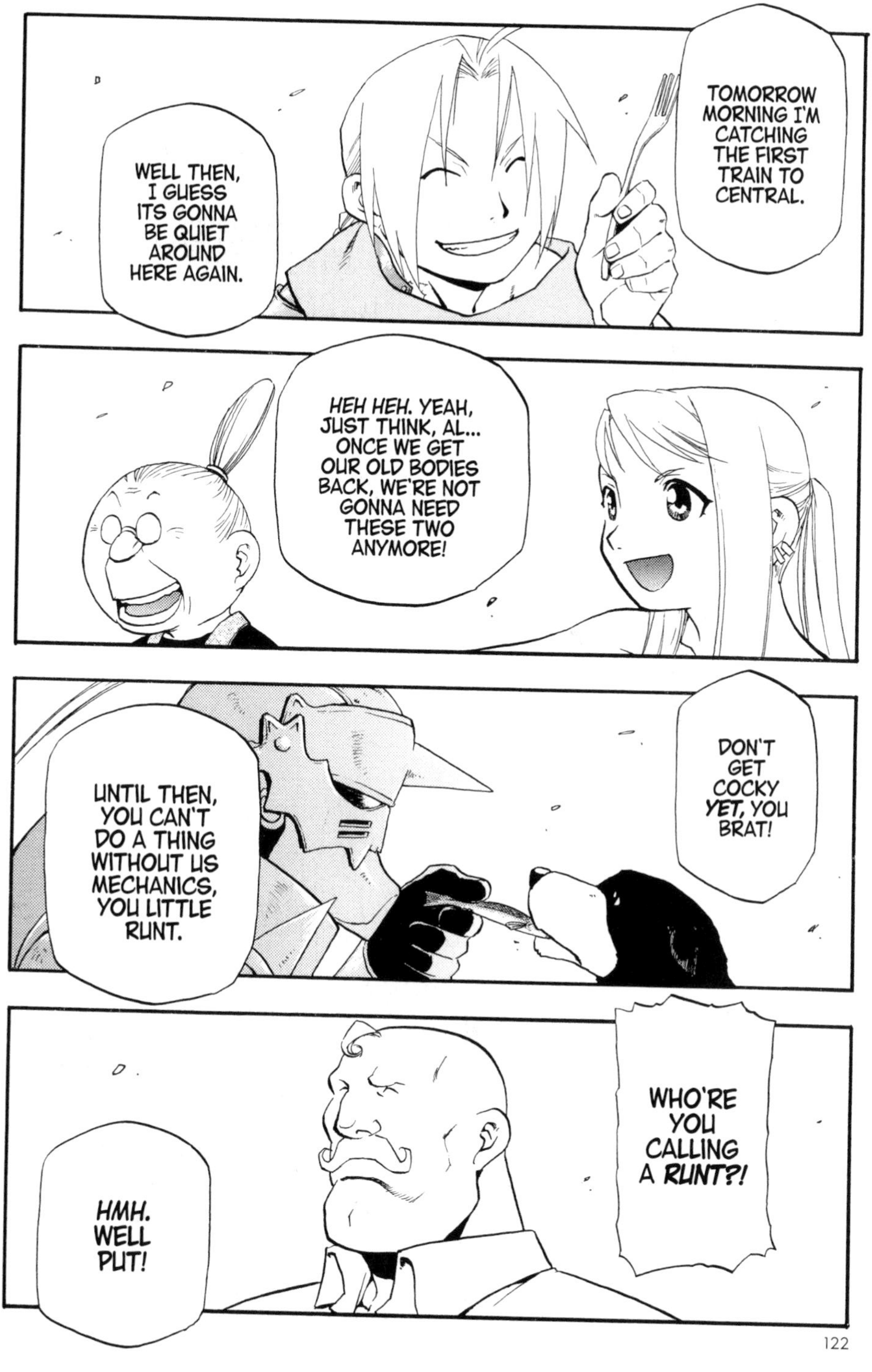
TOMORROW MORNING I'M CATCHING THE FIRST TRAIN TO CENTRAL.
WELL THEN, I GUESS ITS GONNA BE QUIET AROUND HERE AGAIN.
HEH HEH. YEAH, JUST THINK, AL... ONCE WE GET OUR OLD BODIES BACK, WE'RE NOT GONNA NEED THESE TWO ANYMORE!
DON'T GET COCKY YET, YOU BRAT!
UNTIL THEN, YOU CAN'T DO A THING WITHOUT US MECHANICS, YOU LITTLE RUNT.
WHO'RE YOU CALLING A RUNT?!
HMH. WELL PUT!

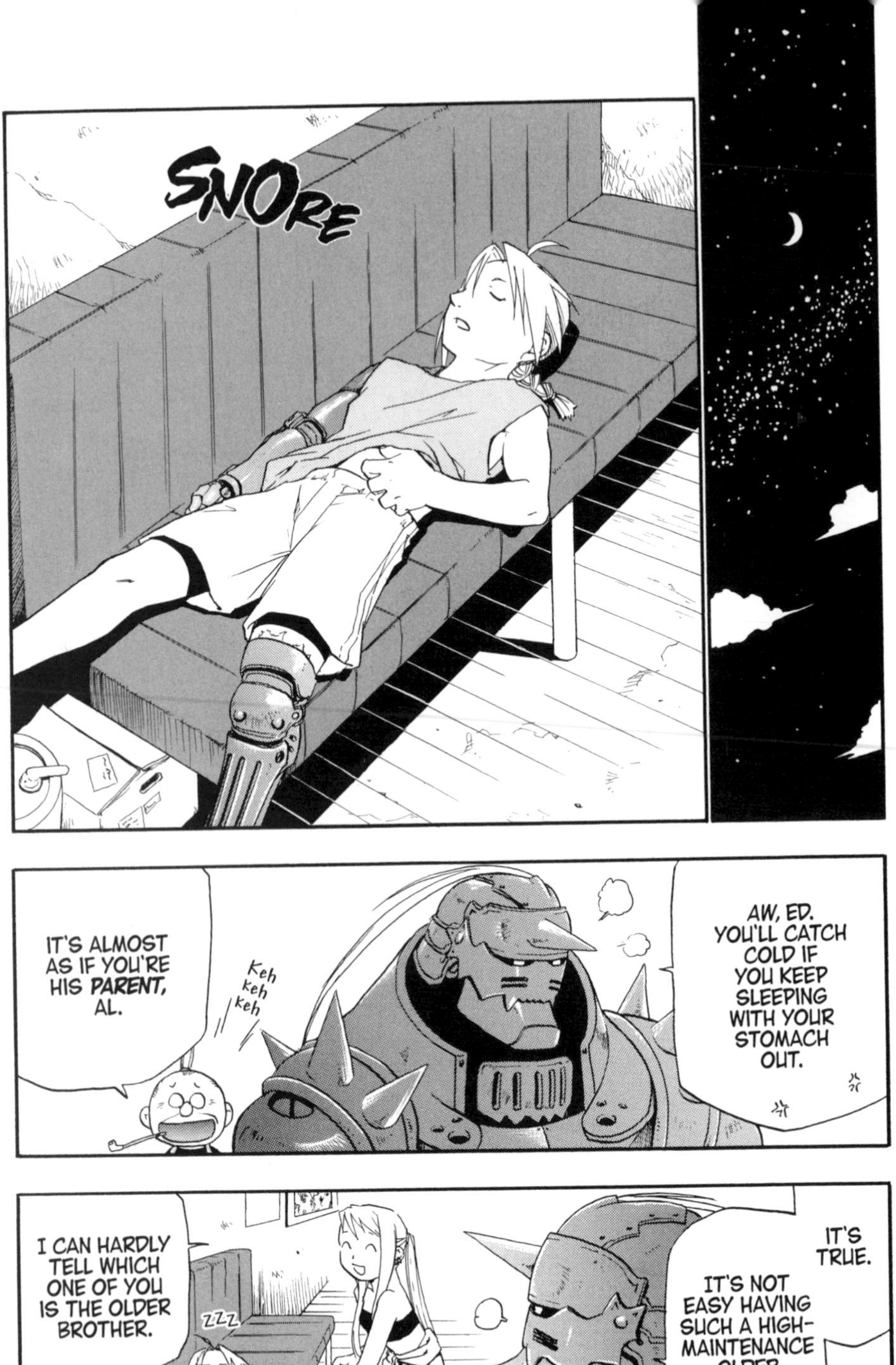
SNORE
AW, ED. YOU'LL CATCH COLD IF YOU KEEP SLEEPING WITH YOUR STOMACH OUT.
Keh keh keh
IT'S ALMOST AS IF YOU'RE HIS PARENT, AL.
IT'S TRUE.
IT'S NOT EASY HAVING SUCH A HIGH-MAINTENANCE OLDER BROTHER.
ZZZ
I CAN HARDLY TELL WHICH ONE OF YOU IS THE OLDER BROTHER.

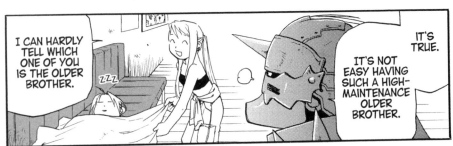

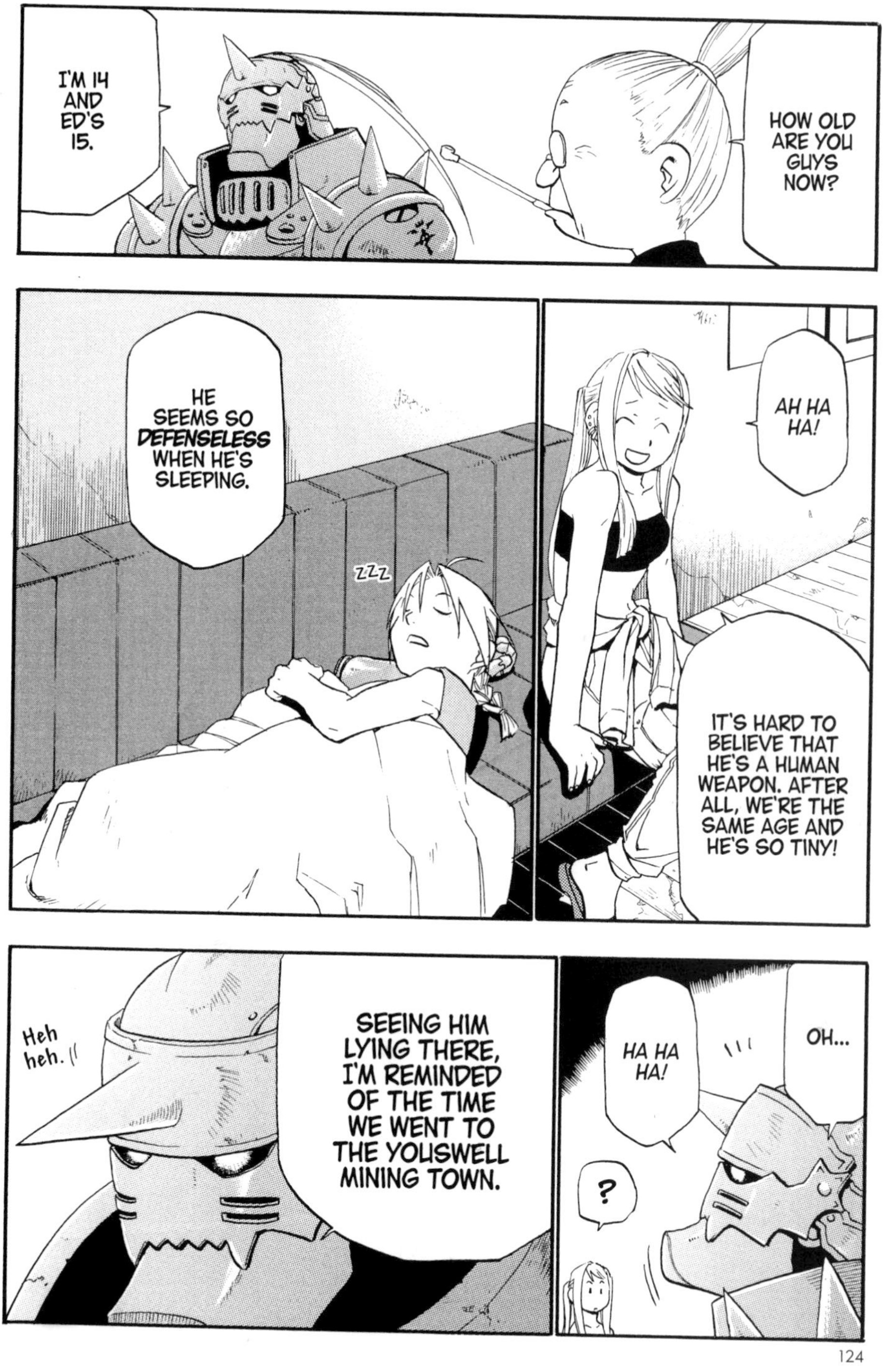
HOW OLD ARE YOU GUYS NOW?
I'M 14 AND ED'S 15.
AH HA HA!
IT'S HARD TO BELIEVE THAT HE'S A HUMAN WEAPON. AFTER ALL, WE'RE THE SAME AGE AND HE'S SO TINY!
HE SEEMS SO DEFENSELESS WHEN HE'S SLEEPING.
ZZZ
OH...
HA HA HA!
?
SEEING HIM LYING THERE, I'M REMINDED OF THE TIME WE WENT TO THE YOUSWELL MINING TOWN.
Heh heh.

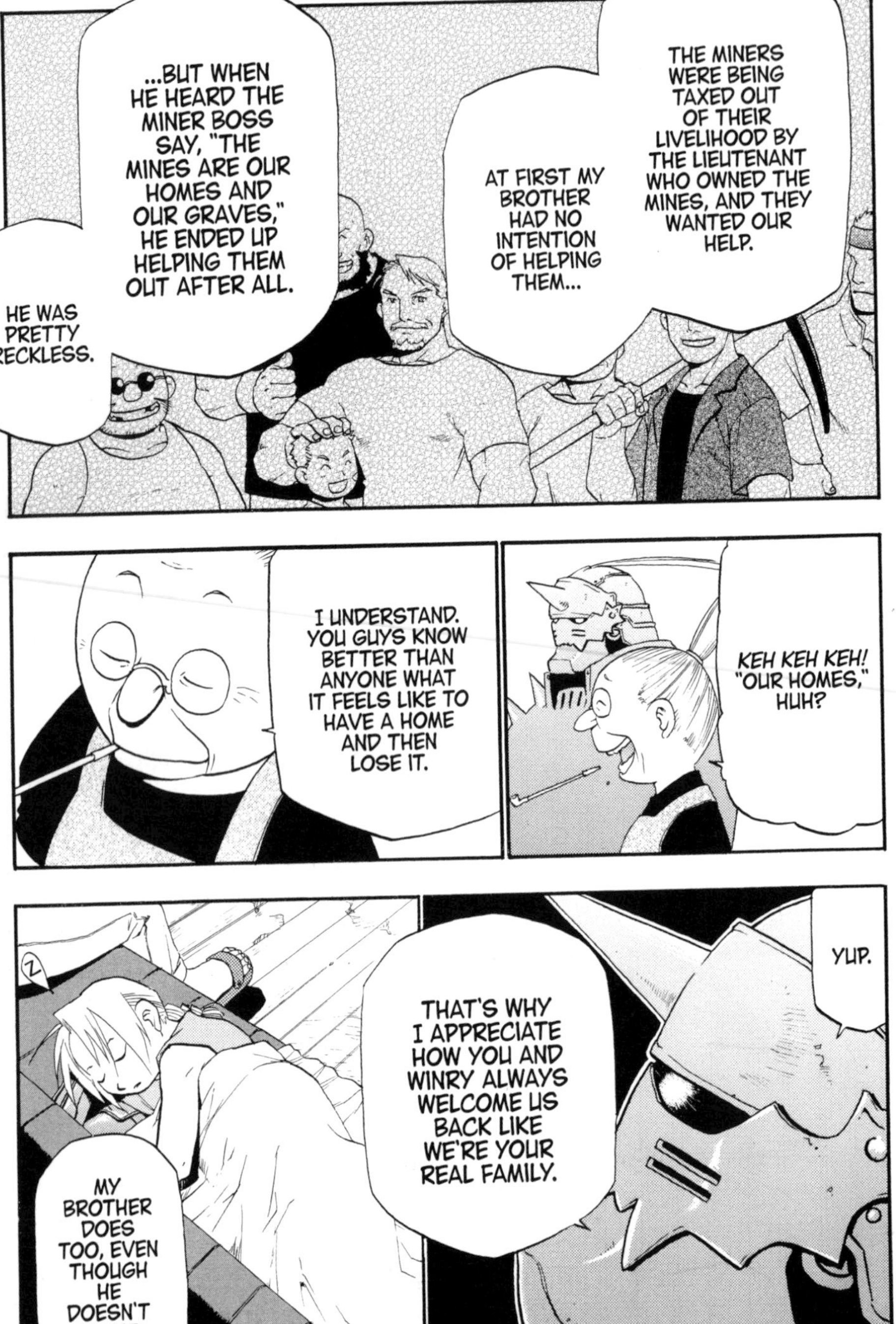
THE MINERS WERE BEING TAXED OUT OF THEIR LIVELIHOOD BY THE LIEUTENANT WHO OWNED THE MINES, AND THEY WANTED OUR HELP.
AT FIRST MY BROTHER HAD NO INTENTION OF HELPING THEM...
...BUT WHEN HE HEARD THE MINER BOSS SAY, "THE MINES ARE OUR HOMES AND OUR GRAVES," HE ENDED UP HELPING THEM OUT AFTER ALL.
HE WAS PRETTY RECKLESS.
KEH KEH KEH! "OUR HOMES," HUH?
I UNDERSTAND. YOU GUYS KNOW BETTER THAN ANYONE WHAT IT FEELS LIKE TO HAVE A HOME AND THEN LOSE IT.
YUP.
THAT'S WHY I APPRECIATE HOW YOU AND WINRY ALWAYS WELCOME US BACK LIKE WE'RE YOUR REAL FAMILY.
MY BROTHER DOES TOO, EVEN THOUGH HE DOESN'T SAY IT.

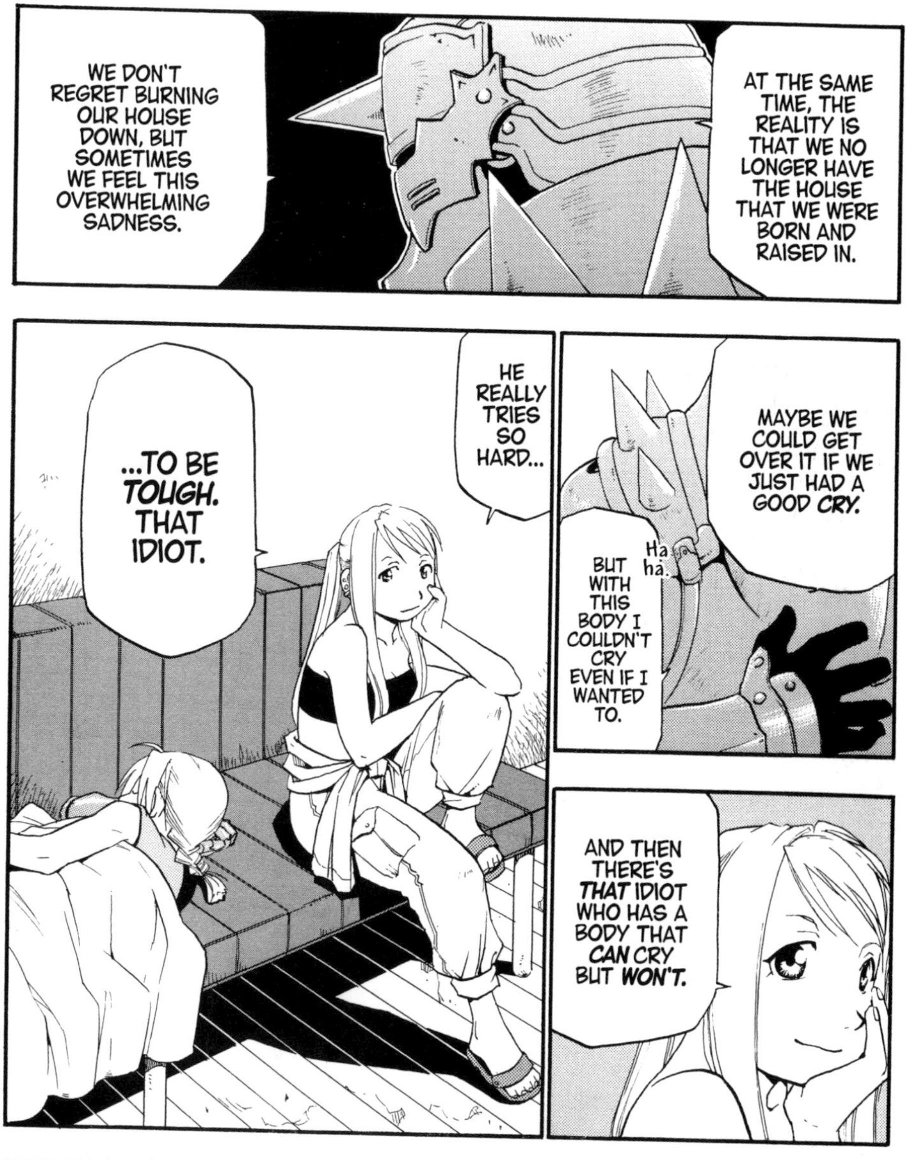
AT THE SAME TIME, THE REALITY IS THAT WE NO LONGER HAVE THE HOUSE THAT WE WERE BORN AND RAISED IN.
WE DON'T REGRET BURNING OUR HOUSE DOWN, BUT SOMETIMES WE FEEL THIS OVERWHELMING SADNESS.
MAYBE WE COULD GET OVER IT IF WE JUST HAD A GOOD *CRY.*
Ha ha.
BUT WITH THIS BODY I COULDN'T CRY EVEN IF I WANTED TO.
AND THEN THERE'S *THAT* IDIOT WHO HAS A BODY THAT *CAN* CRY BUT *WON'T.*
HE REALLY TRIES SO HARD...
...TO BE *TOUGH.* THAT IDIOT.

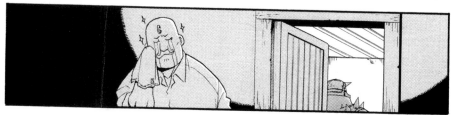

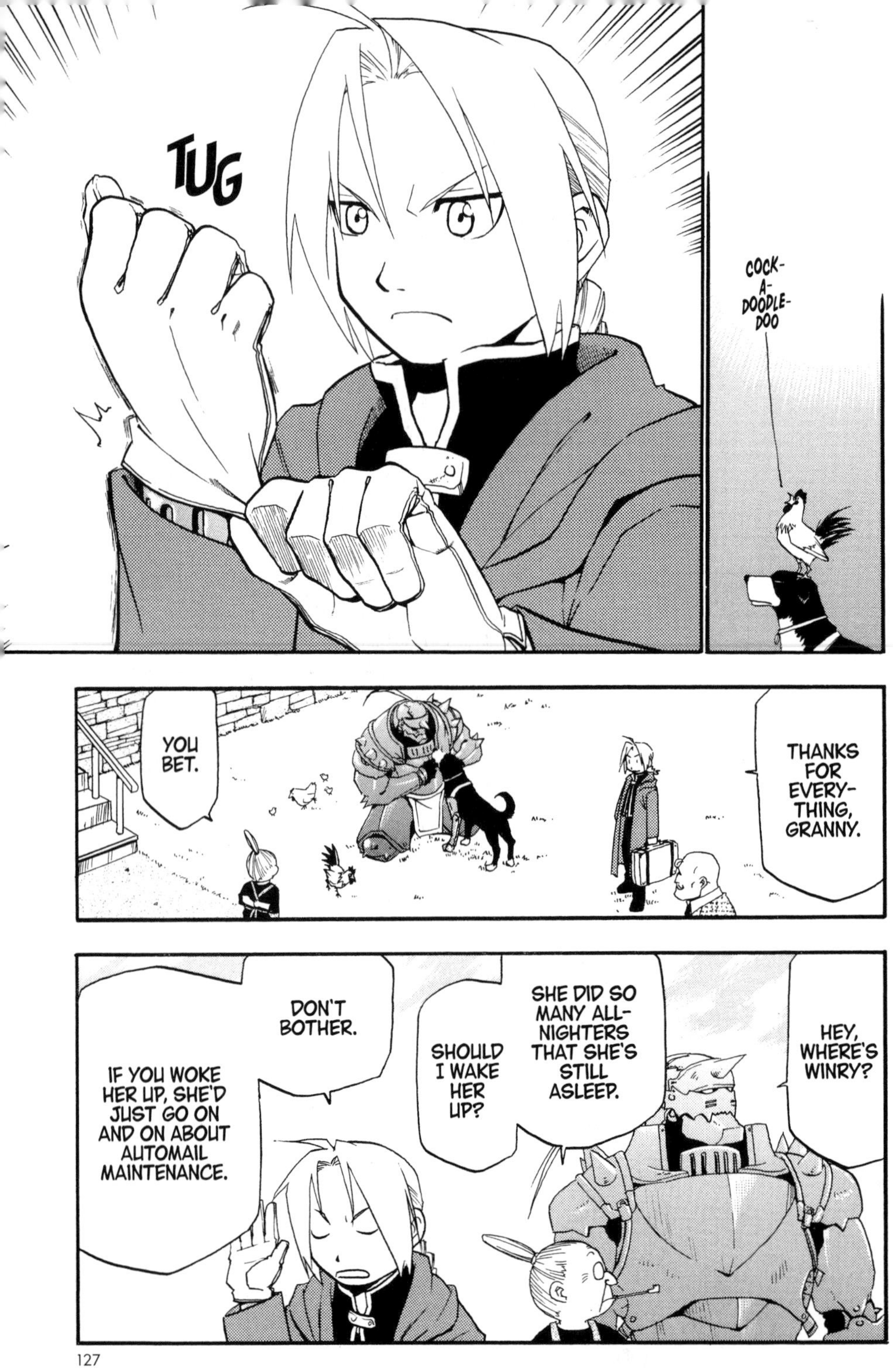
COCK-A-DOODLE-DOO
TUG
THANKS FOR EVERYTHING, GRANNY.
YOU BET.
HEY, WHERE'S WINRY?
SHE DID SO MANY ALL-NIGHTERS THAT SHE'S STILL ASLEEP.
SHOULD I WAKE HER UP?
DON'T BOTHER.
IF YOU WOKE HER UP, SHE'D JUST GO ON AND ON ABOUT AUTOMAIL MAINTENANCE.

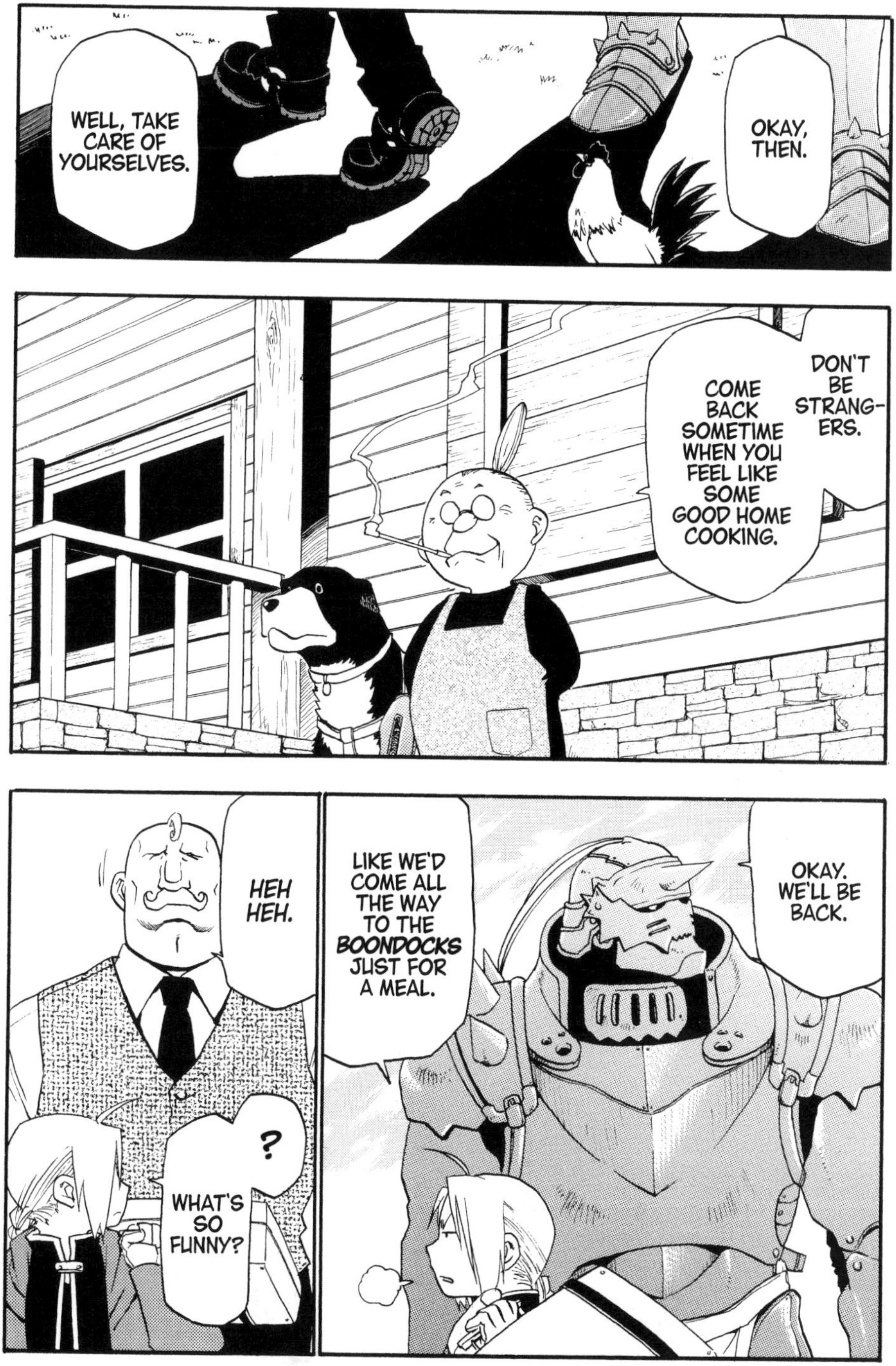
OKAY, THEN.
WELL, TAKE CARE OF YOURSELVES.
DON'T BE STRANGERS.
COME BACK SOMETIME WHEN YOU FEEL LIKE SOME GOOD HOME COOKING.
OKAY. WE'LL BE BACK.
LIKE WE'D COME ALL THE WAY TO THE *BOONDOCKS* JUST FOR A MEAL.
HEH HEH.
?
WHAT'S SO FUNNY?

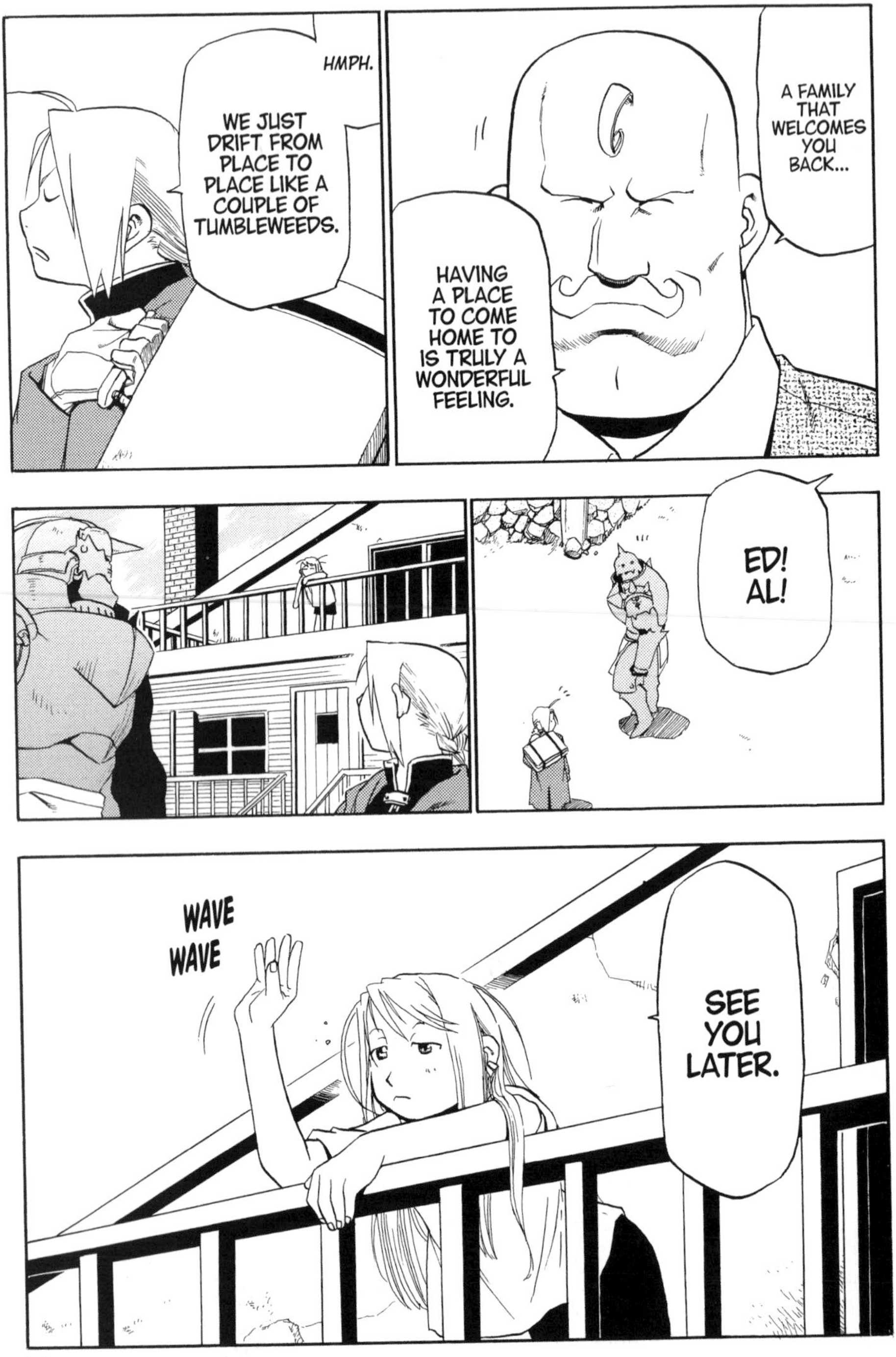
A FAMILY THAT WELCOMES YOU BACK...
HAVING A PLACE TO COME HOME TO IS TRULY A WONDERFUL FEELING.
HMPH.
WE JUST DRIFT FROM PLACE TO PLACE LIKE A COUPLE OF TUMBLEWEEDS.
ED! AL!
SEE YOU LATER.
WAVE WAVE

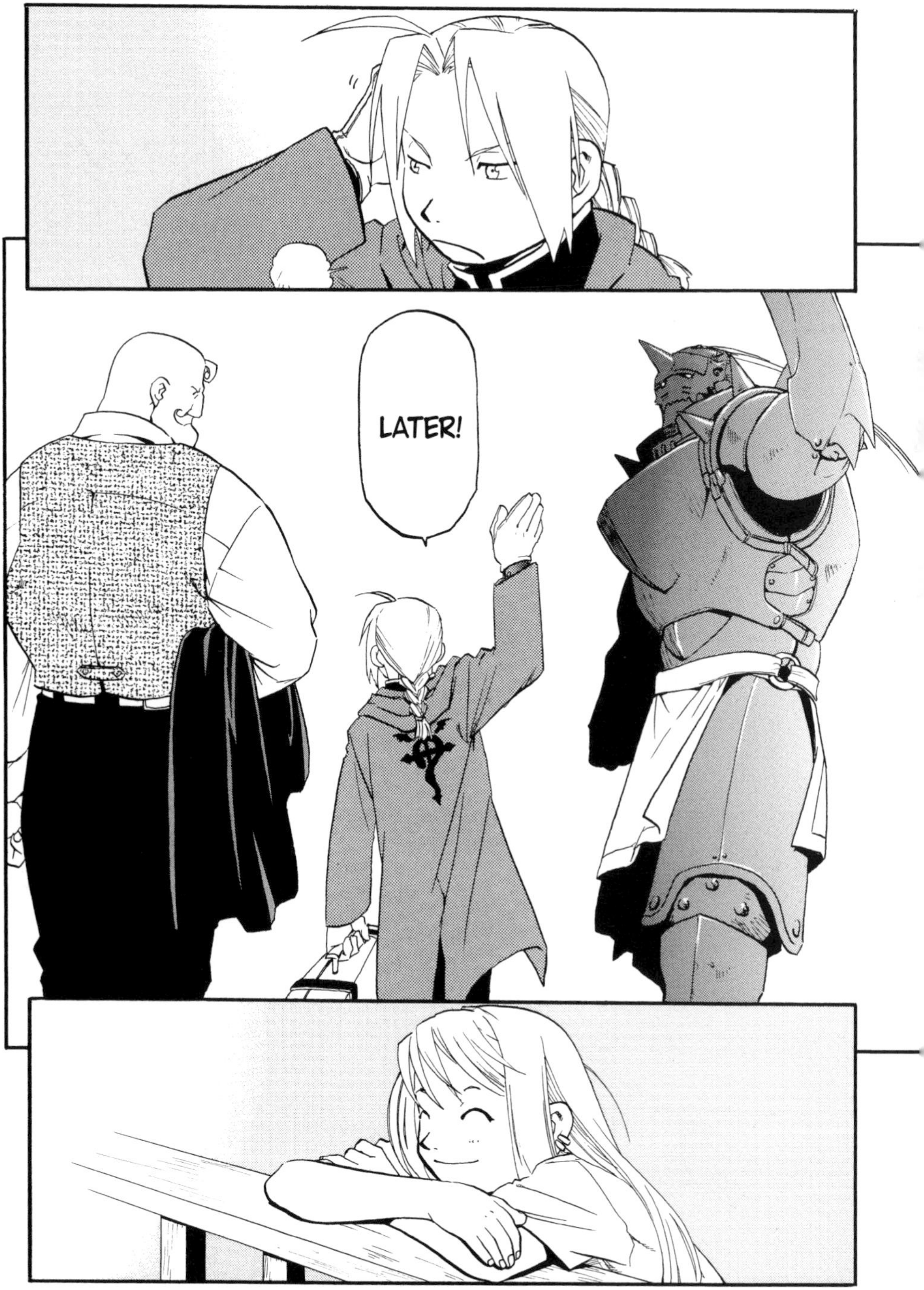
LATER!

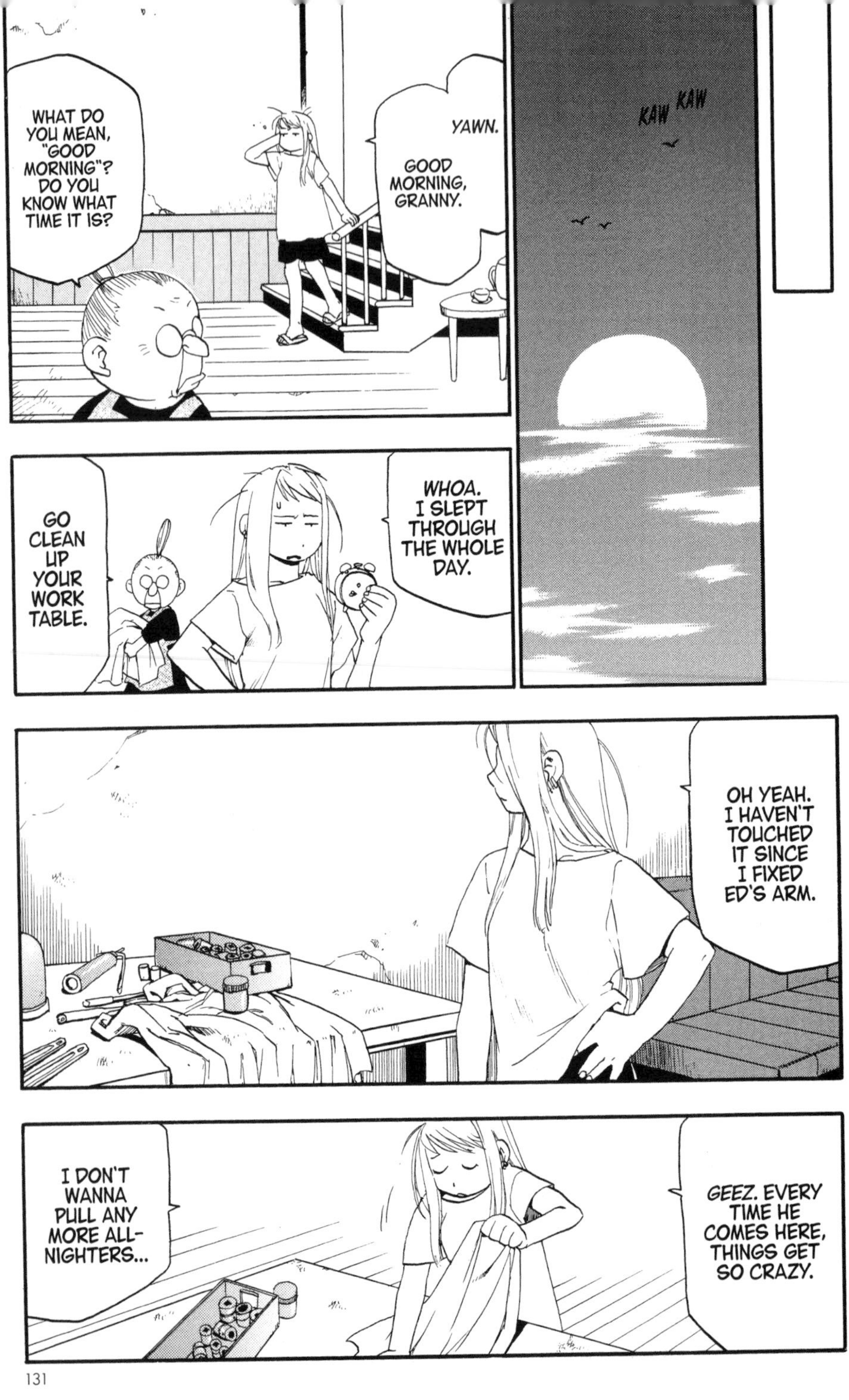
KAW KAW
YAWN.
GOOD MORNING, GRANNY.
WHAT DO YOU MEAN, "GOOD MORNING"? DO YOU KNOW WHAT TIME IT IS?
WHOA. I SLEPT THROUGH THE WHOLE DAY.
GO CLEAN UP YOUR WORK TABLE.
OH YEAH. I HAVEN'T TOUCHED IT SINCE I FIXED ED'S ARM.
GEEZ. EVERY TIME HE COMES HERE, THINGS GET SO CRAZY.
I DON'T WANNA PULL ANY MORE ALL-NIGHTERS...

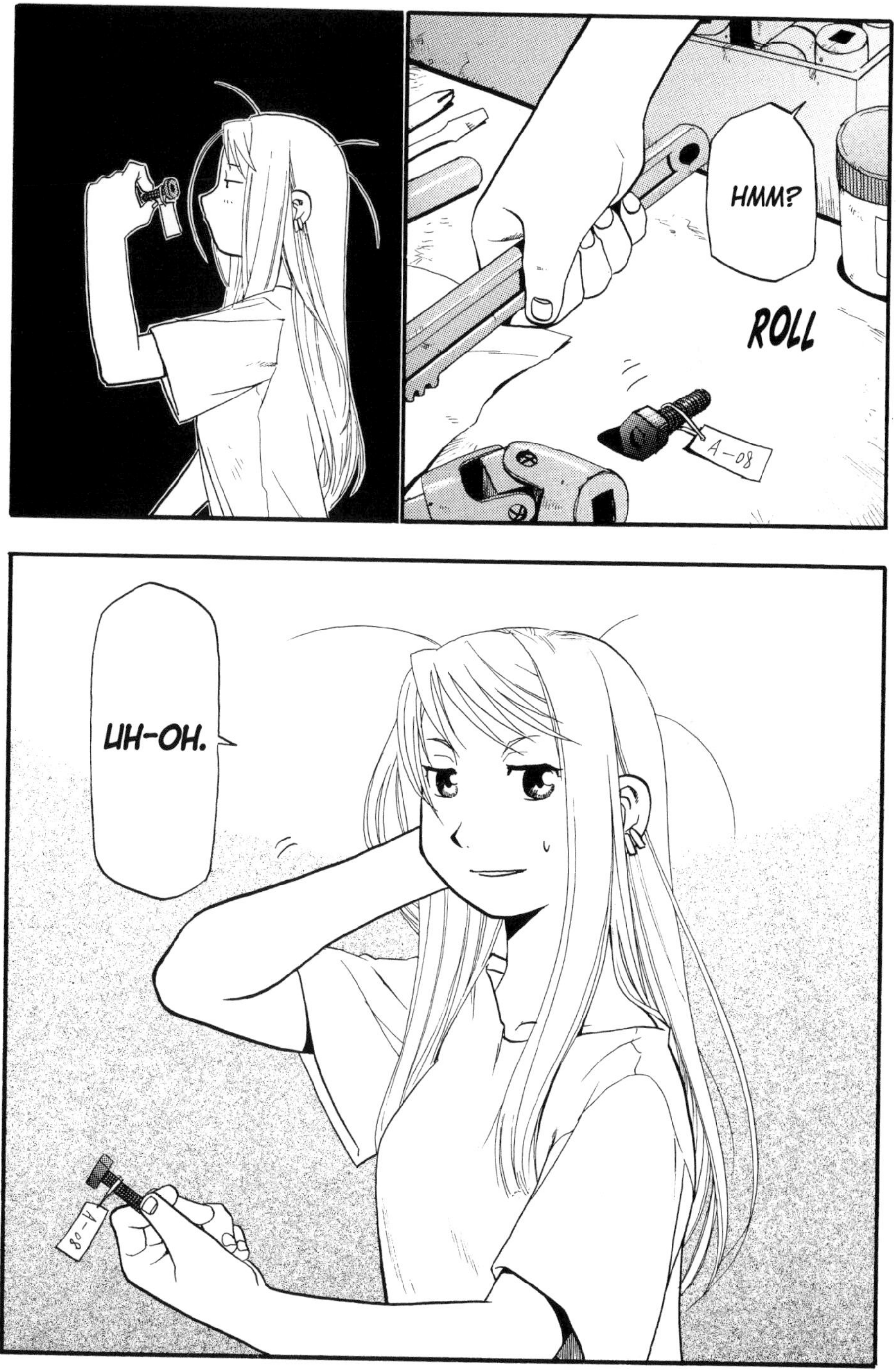
HMM?
ROLL
A-08
UH-OH.
A-08

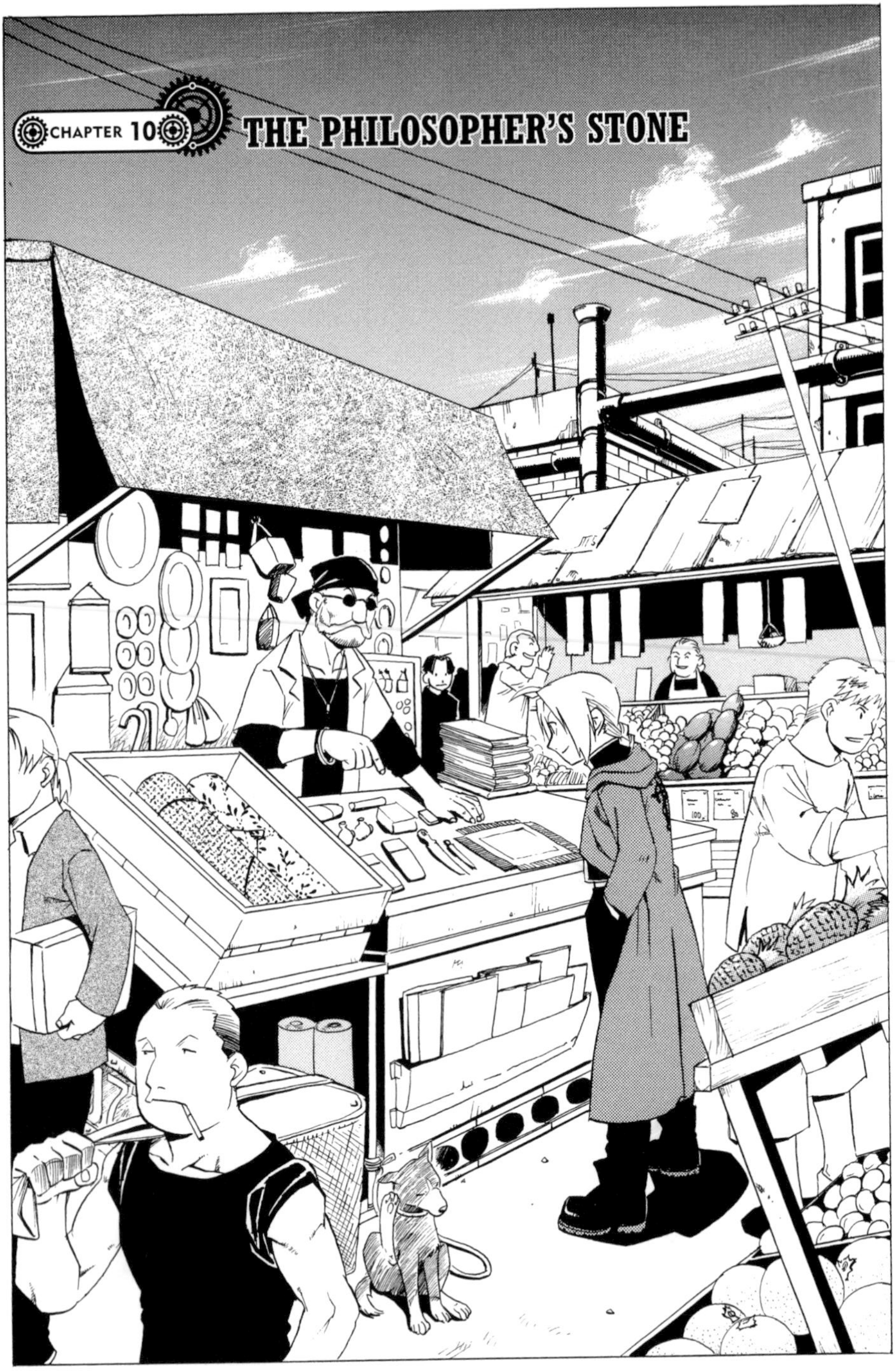
CHAPTER 10
THE PHILOSOPHER'S STONE

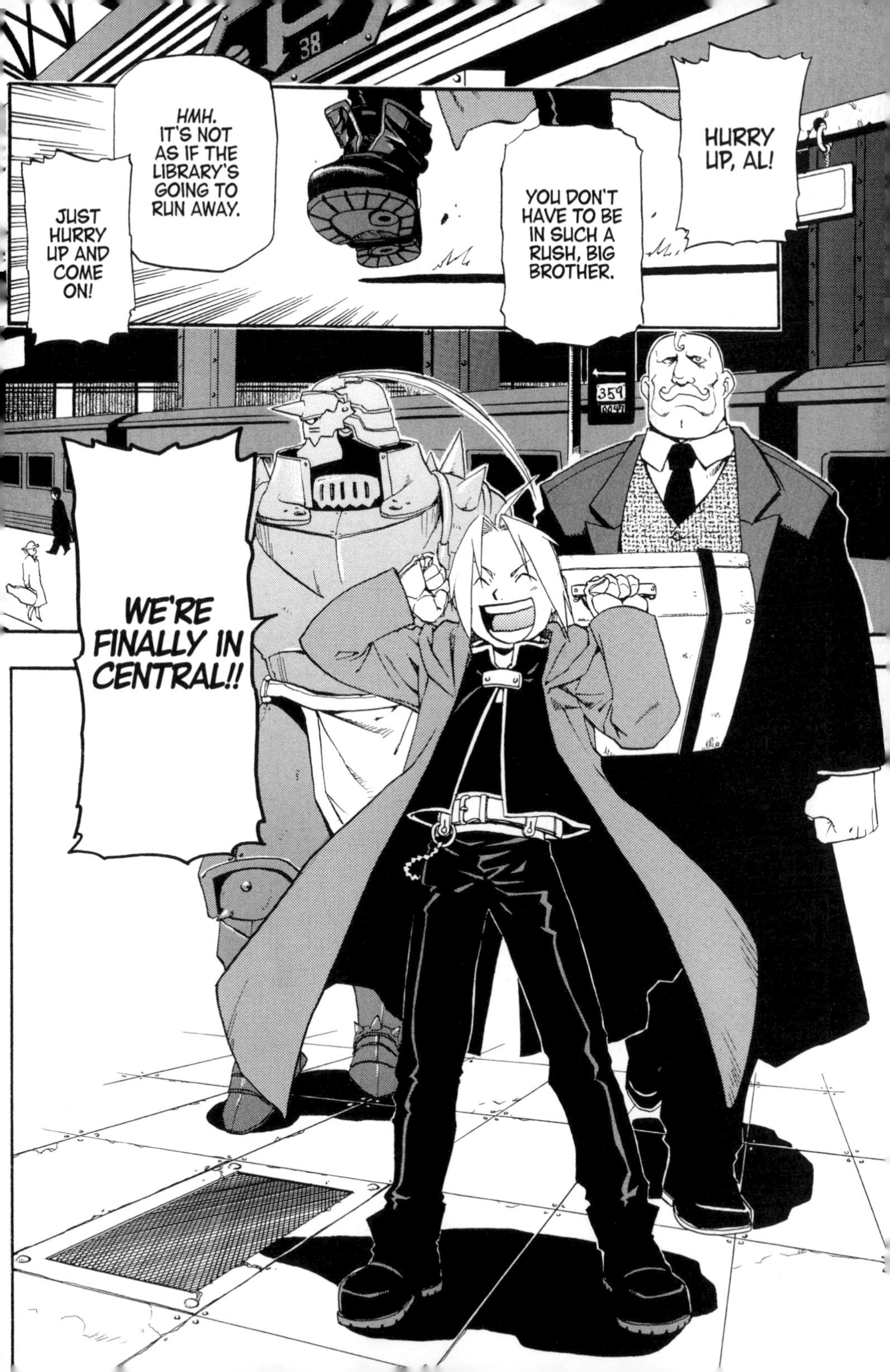
HURRY UP, AL!
YOU DON'T HAVE TO BE IN SUCH A RUSH, BIG BROTHER.
HMH. IT'S NOT AS IF THE LIBRARY'S GOING TO RUN AWAY.
JUST HURRY UP AND COME ON!
WE'RE FINALLY IN CENTRAL!!

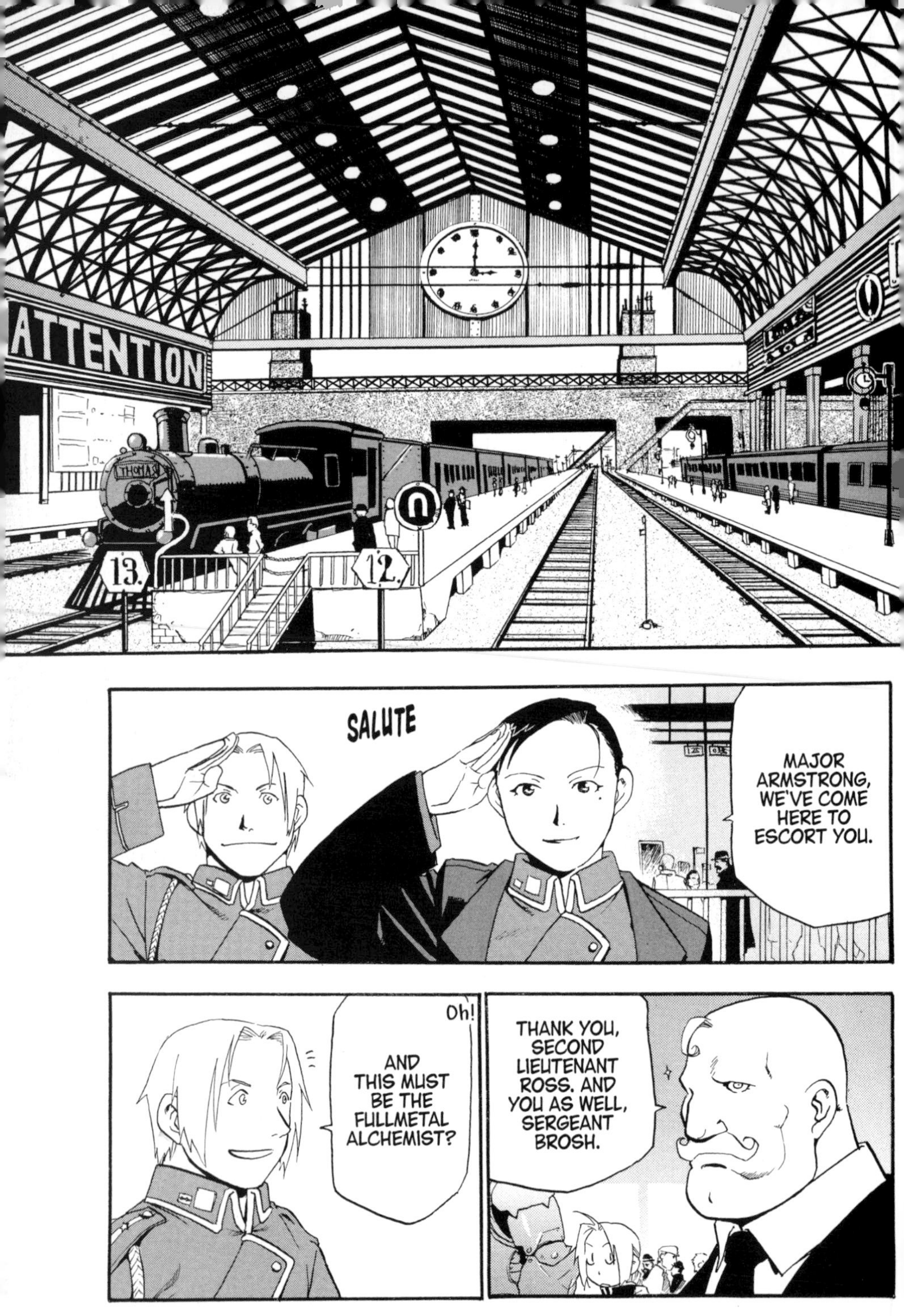
ATTENTION
13.
12.
MAJOR ARMSTRONG, WE'VE COME HERE TO ESCORT YOU.
SALUTE
THANK YOU, SECOND LIEUTENANT ROSS. AND YOU AS WELL, SERGEANT BROSH.
Oh!
AND THIS MUST BE THE FULLMETAL ALCHEMIST?

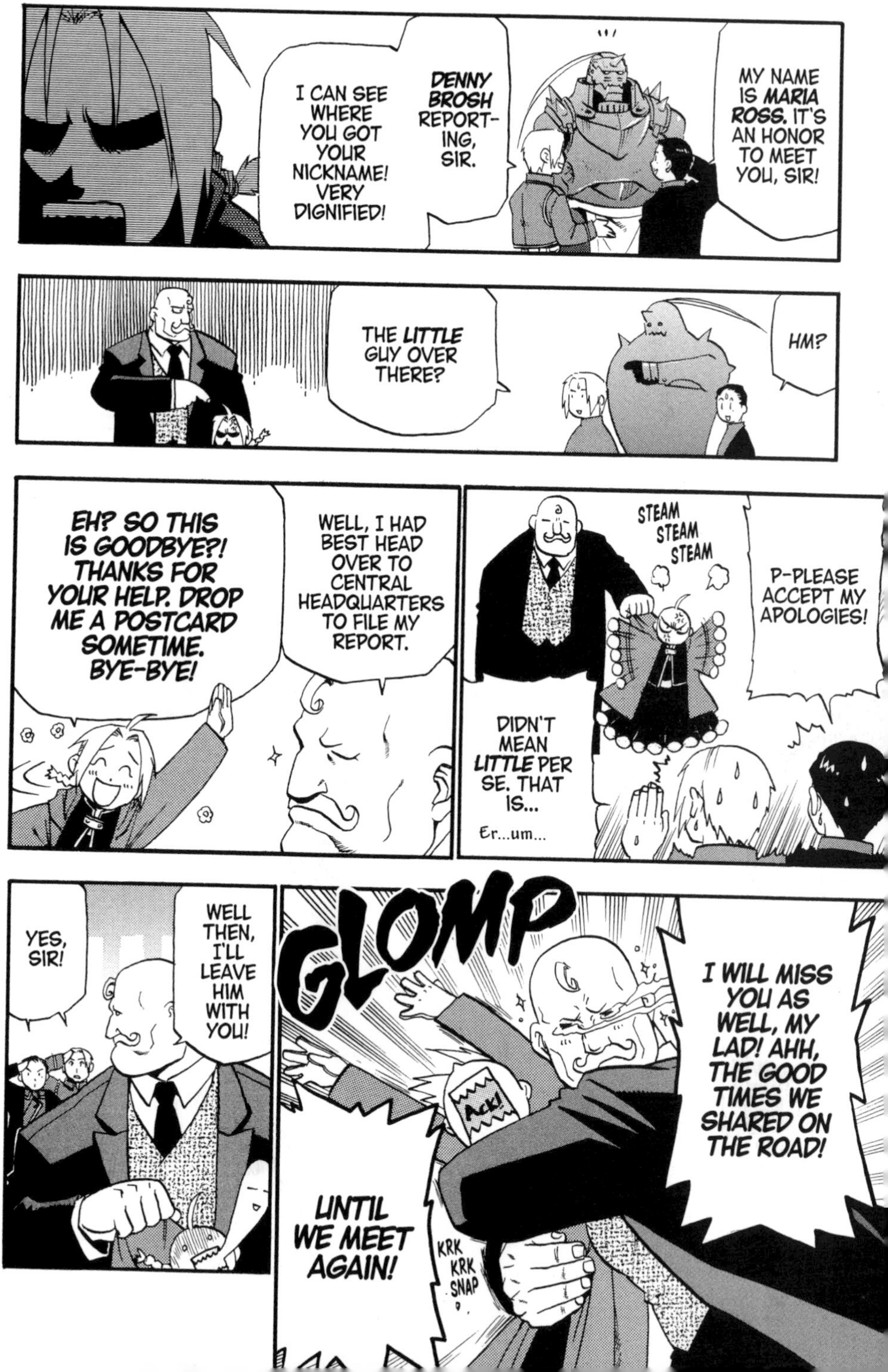

MY NAME IS MARIA ROSS. IT'S AN HONOR TO MEET YOU, SIR!
DENNY BROSH REPORTING, SIR.
I CAN SEE WHERE YOU GOT YOUR NICKNAME! VERY DIGNIFIED!
HM?
THE LITTLE GUY OVER THERE?
STEAM STEAM STEAM
P-PLEASE ACCEPT MY APOLOGIES!
DIDN'T MEAN LITTLE PER SE. THAT IS...
Er...um...
WELL, I HAD BEST HEAD OVER TO CENTRAL HEADQUARTERS TO FILE MY REPORT.
EH? SO THIS IS GOODBYE?! THANKS FOR YOUR HELP. DROP ME A POSTCARD SOMETIME. BYE-BYE!
GLOMP
I WILL MISS YOU AS WELL, MY LAD! AHH, THE GOOD TIMES WE SHARED ON THE ROAD!
ACK!
UNTIL WE MEET AGAIN!
KRK KRK SNAP
WELL THEN, I'LL LEAVE HIM WITH YOU!
YES, SIR!

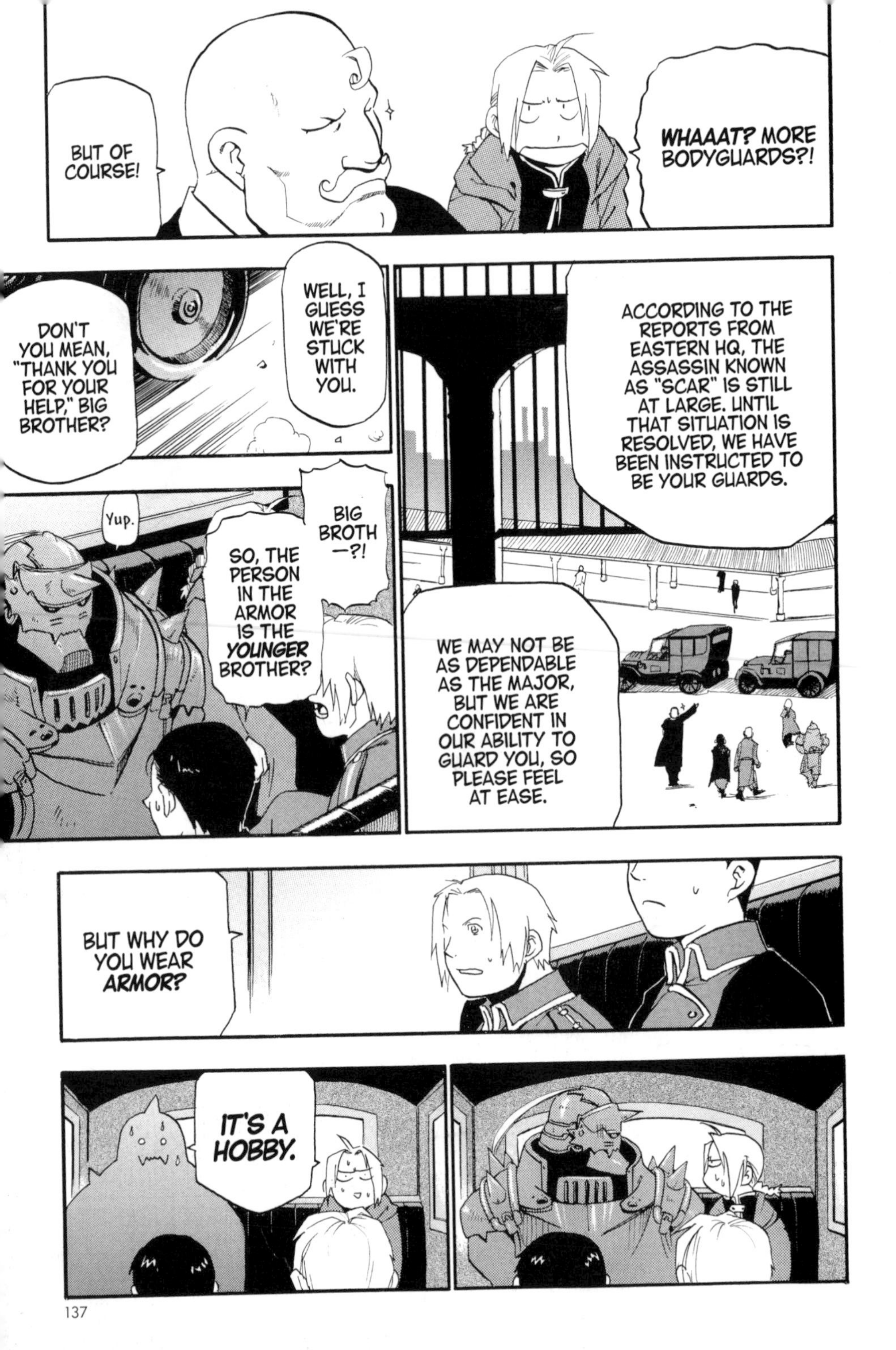
WHAAAT? MORE BODYGUARDS?!
BUT OF COURSE!
ACCORDING TO THE REPORTS FROM EASTERN HQ, THE ASSASSIN KNOWN AS "SCAR" IS STILL AT LARGE. UNTIL THAT SITUATION IS RESOLVED, WE HAVE BEEN INSTRUCTED TO BE YOUR GUARDS.
WE MAY NOT BE AS DEPENDABLE AS THE MAJOR, BUT WE ARE CONFIDENT IN OUR ABILITY TO GUARD YOU, SO PLEASE FEEL AT EASE.
WELL, I GUESS WE'RE STUCK WITH YOU.
DON'T YOU MEAN, "THANK YOU FOR YOUR HELP," BIG BROTHER?
BIG BROTH—?!
SO, THE PERSON IN THE ARMOR IS THE YOUNGER BROTHER?
Yup.
BUT WHY DO YOU WEAR ARMOR?
IT'S A HOBBY.

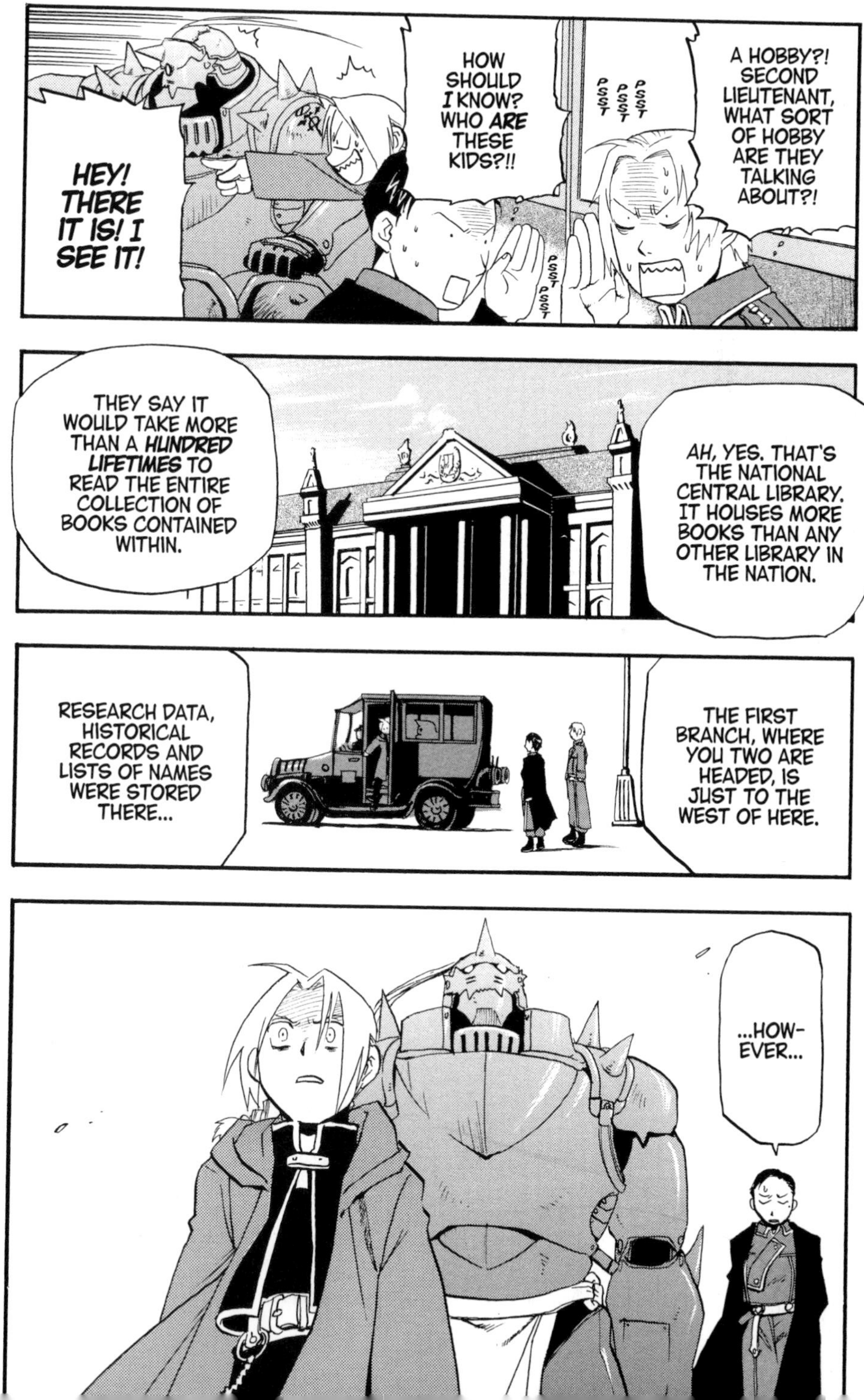
A HOBBY?! SECOND LIEUTENANT, WHAT SORT OF HOBBY ARE THEY TALKING ABOUT?!
PSST PSST PSST
HOW SHOULD I KNOW? WHO ARE THESE KIDS?!!
PSST PSST
HEY! THERE IT IS! I SEE IT!
AH, YES. THAT'S THE NATIONAL CENTRAL LIBRARY. IT HOUSES MORE BOOKS THAN ANY OTHER LIBRARY IN THE NATION.
THEY SAY IT WOULD TAKE MORE THAN A HUNDRED LIFETIMES TO READ THE ENTIRE COLLECTION OF BOOKS CONTAINED WITHIN.
THE FIRST BRANCH, WHERE YOU TWO ARE HEADED, IS JUST TO THE WEST OF HERE.
RESEARCH DATA, HISTORICAL RECORDS AND LISTS OF NAMES WERE STORED THERE...
...HOW-EVER...

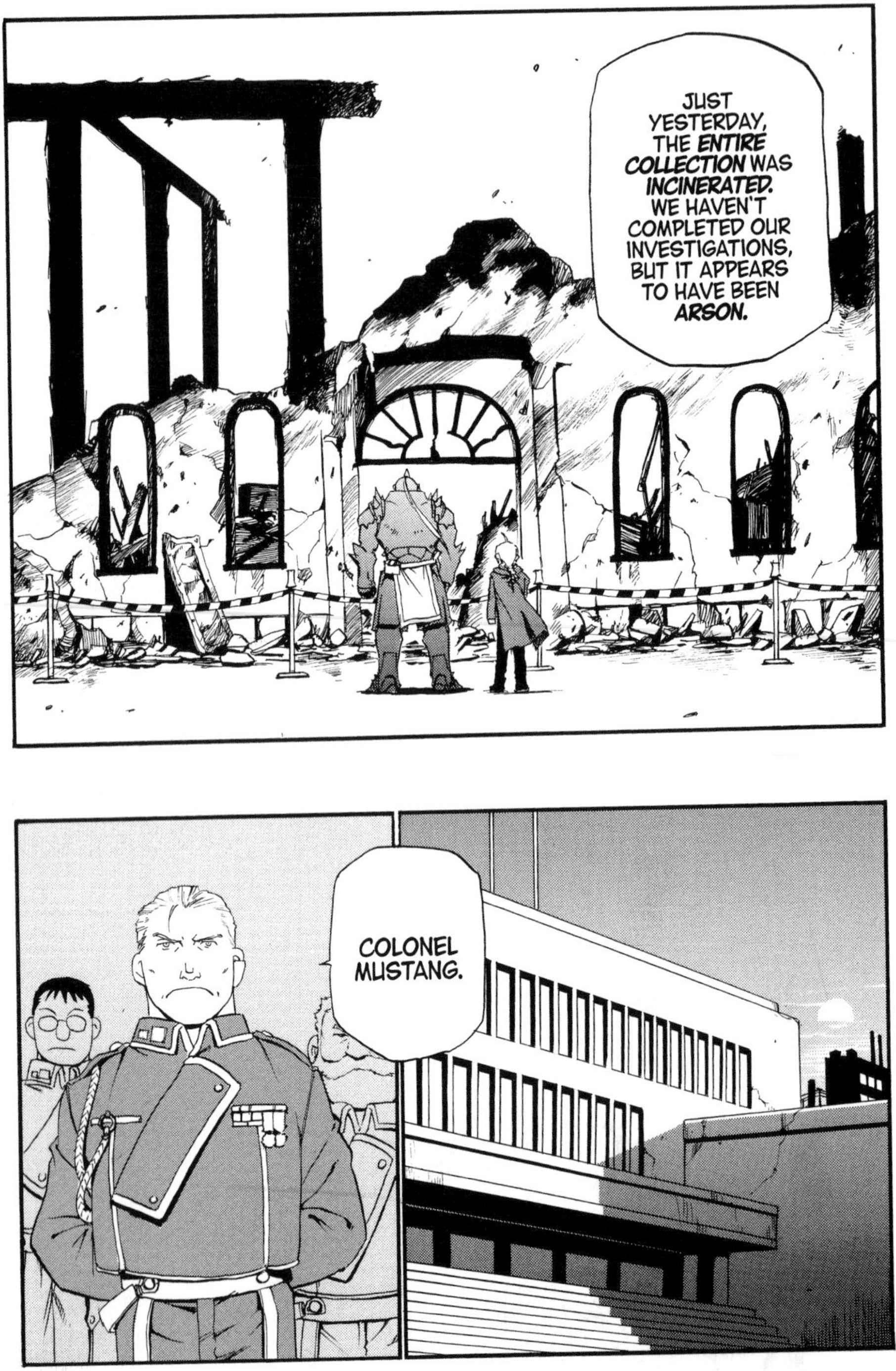
JUST YESTERDAY, THE ENTIRE COLLECTION WAS INCINERATED. WE HAVEN'T COMPLETED OUR INVESTIGATIONS, BUT IT APPEARS TO HAVE BEEN ARSON.
COLONEL MUSTANG.

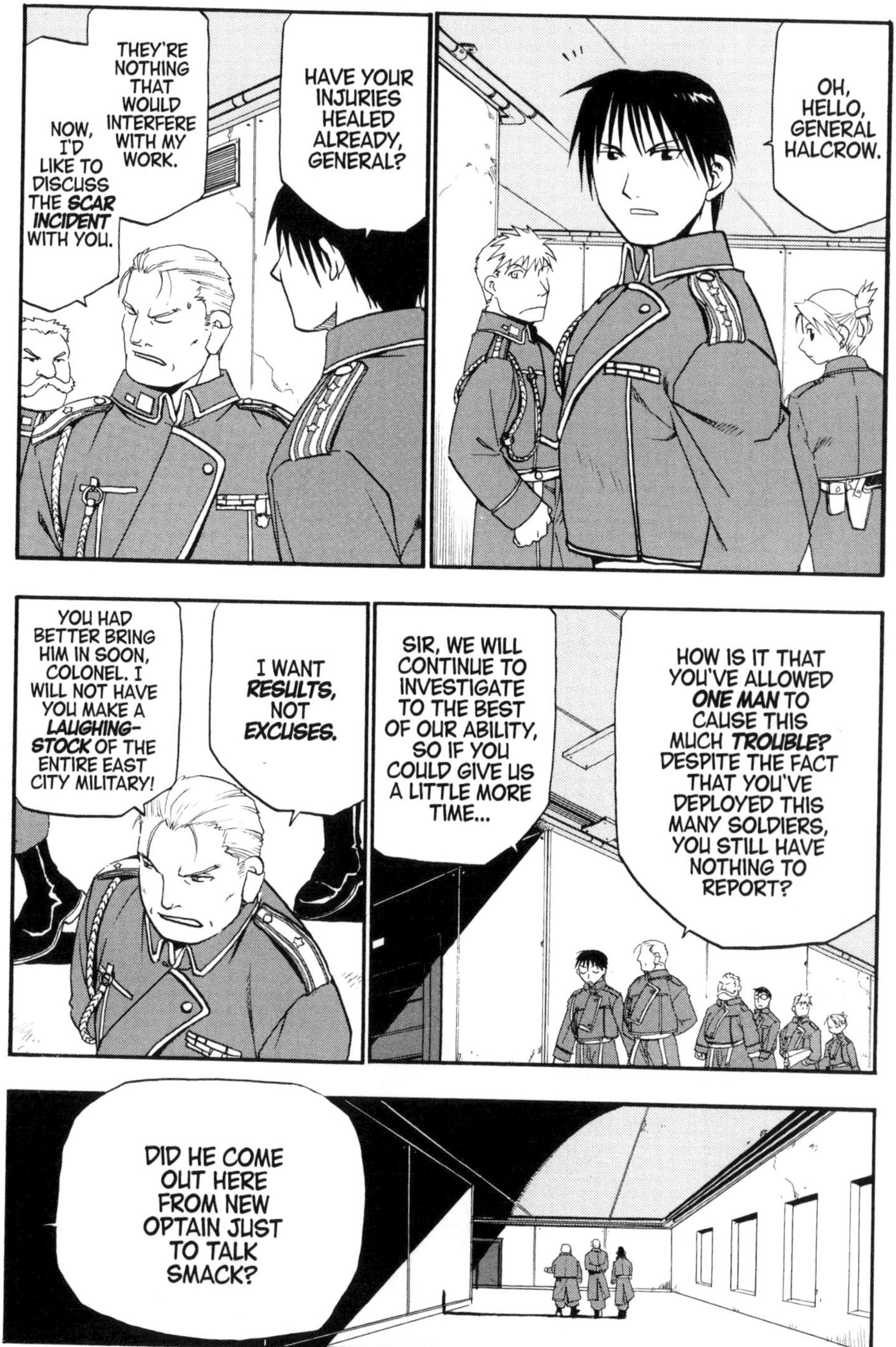
OH, HELLO, GENERAL HALCROW.
HAVE YOUR INJURIES HEALED ALREADY, GENERAL?
THEY'RE NOTHING THAT WOULD INTERFERE WITH MY WORK.
NOW, I'D LIKE TO DISCUSS THE SCAR INCIDENT WITH YOU.
HOW IS IT THAT YOU'VE ALLOWED ONE MAN TO CAUSE THIS MUCH TROUBLE? DESPITE THE FACT THAT YOU'VE DEPLOYED THIS MANY SOLDIERS, YOU STILL HAVE NOTHING TO REPORT?
SIR, WE WILL CONTINUE TO INVESTIGATE TO THE BEST OF OUR ABILITY, SO IF YOU COULD GIVE US A LITTLE MORE TIME...
I WANT RESULTS, NOT EXCUSES.
YOU HAD BETTER BRING HIM IN SOON, COLONEL. I WILL NOT HAVE YOU MAKE A LAUGHING-STOCK OF THE ENTIRE EAST CITY MILITARY!
DID HE COME OUT HERE FROM NEW OPTAIN JUST TO TALK SMACK?

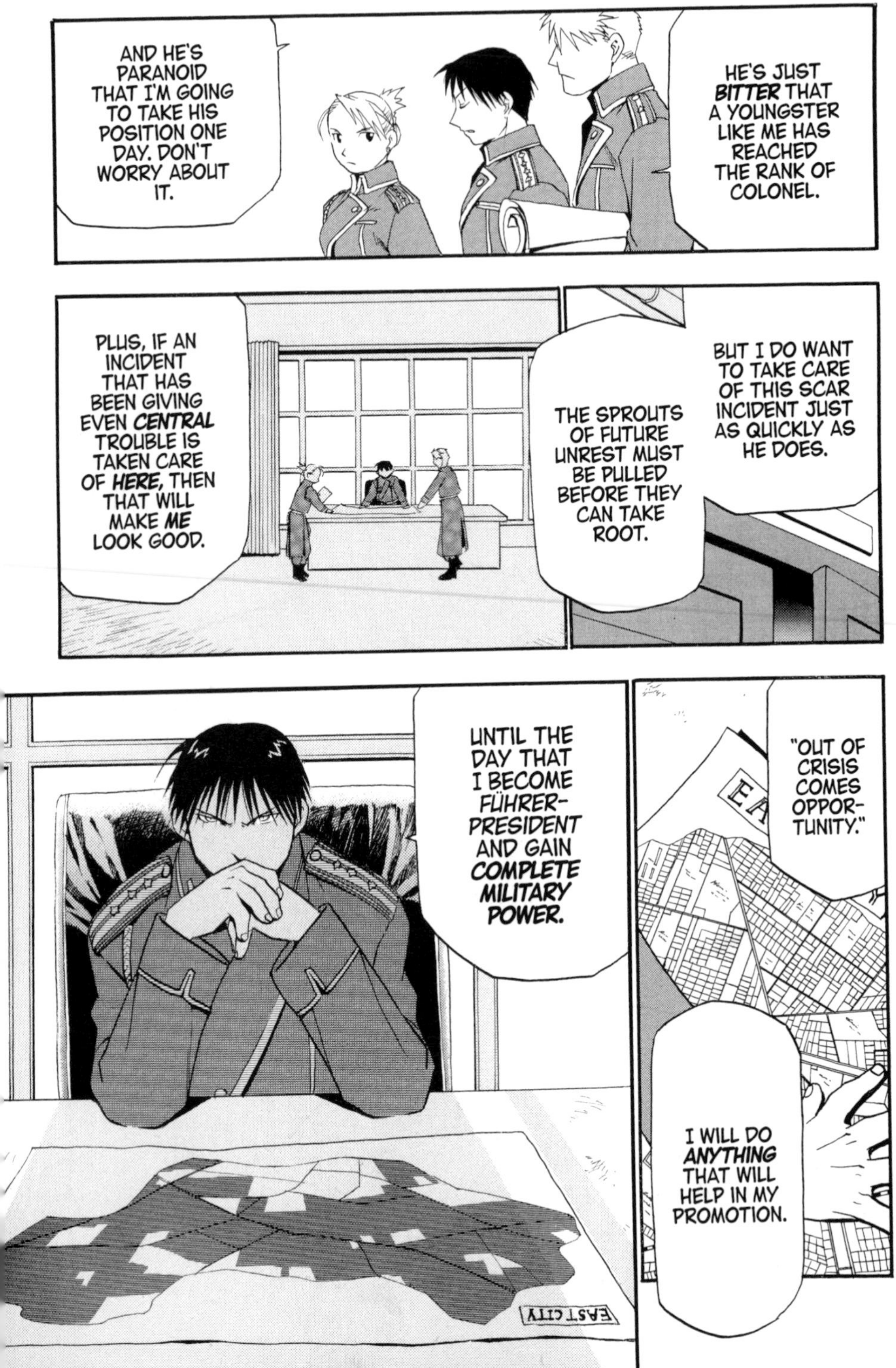
HE'S JUST BITTER THAT A YOUNGSTER LIKE ME HAS REACHED THE RANK OF COLONEL.
AND HE'S PARANOID THAT I'M GOING TO TAKE HIS POSITION ONE DAY. DON'T WORRY ABOUT IT.
BUT I DO WANT TO TAKE CARE OF THIS SCAR INCIDENT JUST AS QUICKLY AS HE DOES.
THE SPROUTS OF FUTURE UNREST MUST BE PULLED BEFORE THEY CAN TAKE ROOT.
PLUS, IF AN INCIDENT THAT HAS BEEN GIVING EVEN CENTRAL TROUBLE IS TAKEN CARE OF HERE, THEN THAT WILL MAKE ME LOOK GOOD.
"OUT OF CRISIS COMES OPPORTUNITY."
I WILL DO ANYTHING THAT WILL HELP IN MY PROMOTION.
UNTIL THE DAY THAT I BECOME FÜHRER-PRESIDENT AND GAIN COMPLETE MILITARY POWER.
EAST CITY

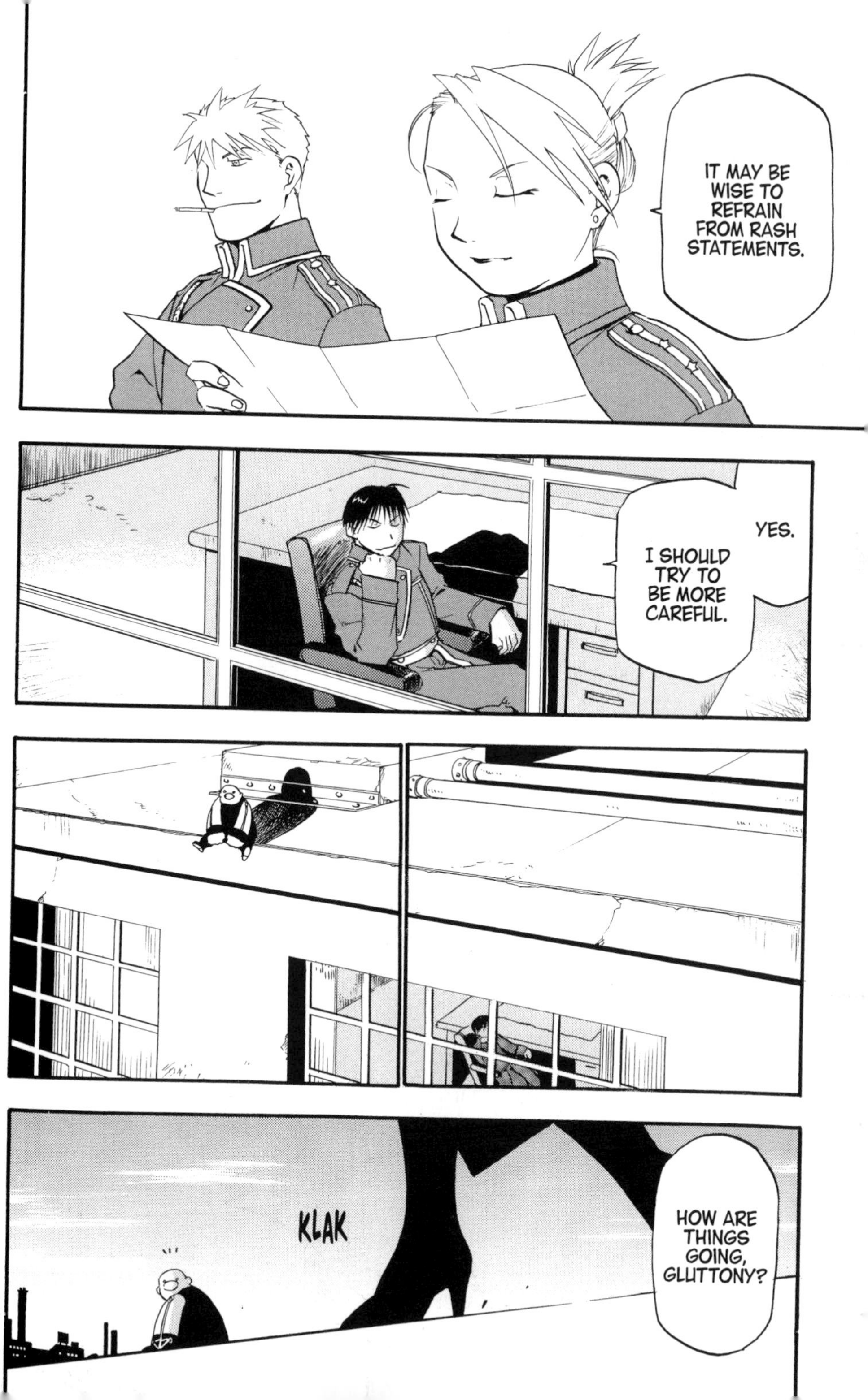
IT MAY BE WISE TO REFRAIN FROM RASH STATEMENTS.
YES.
I SHOULD TRY TO BE MORE CAREFUL.
KLAK
HOW ARE THINGS GOING, GLUTTONY?

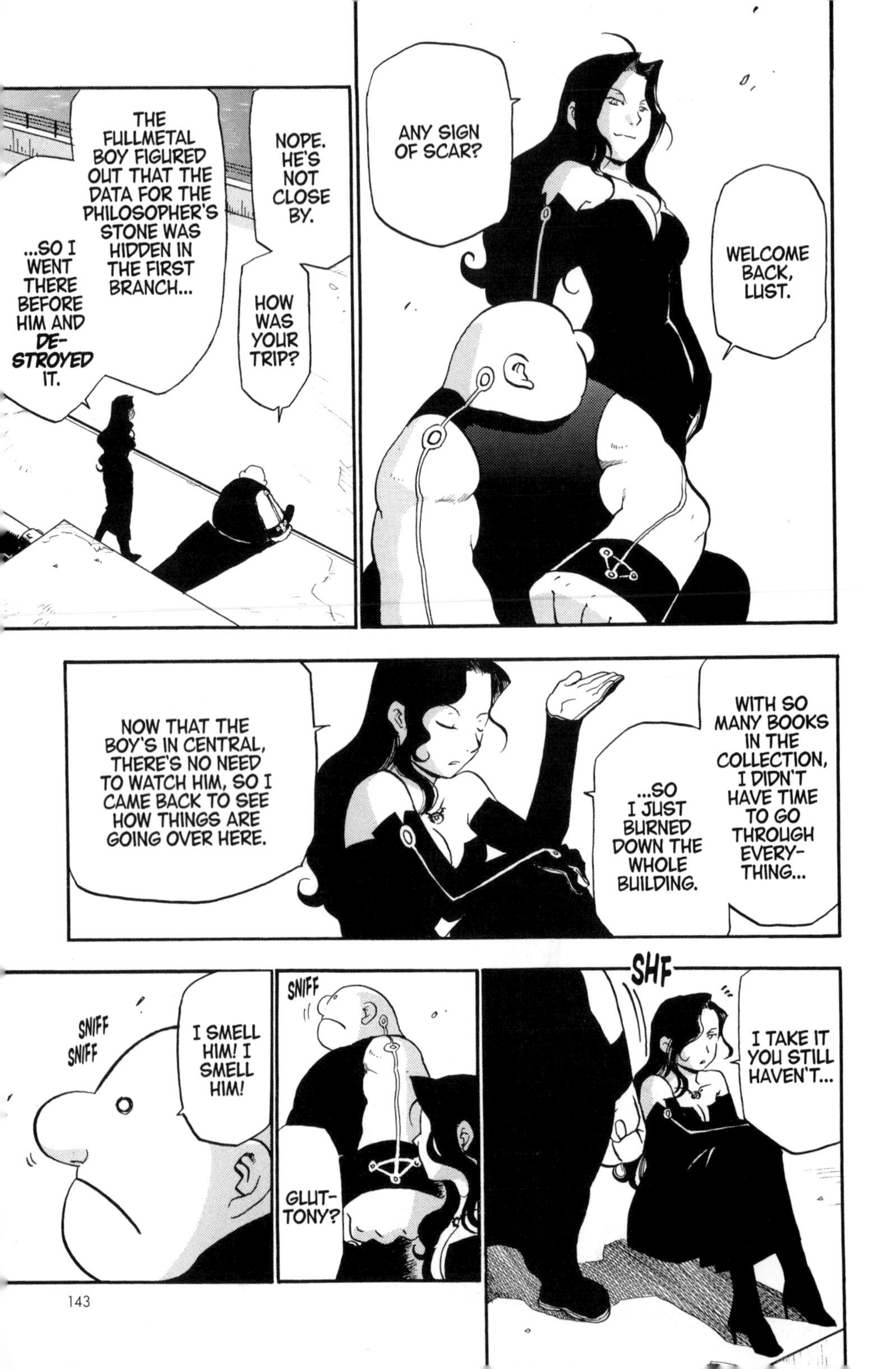
WELCOME BACK, LUST.
ANY SIGN OF SCAR?
NOPE. HE'S NOT CLOSE BY.
HOW WAS YOUR TRIP?
THE FULLMETAL BOY FIGURED OUT THAT THE DATA FOR THE PHILOSOPHER'S STONE WAS HIDDEN IN THE FIRST BRANCH...
...SO I WENT THERE BEFORE HIM AND DESTROYED IT.
WITH SO MANY BOOKS IN THE COLLECTION, I DIDN'T HAVE TIME TO GO THROUGH EVERYTHING...
...SO I JUST BURNED DOWN THE WHOLE BUILDING.
NOW THAT THE BOY'S IN CENTRAL, THERE'S NO NEED TO WATCH HIM, SO I CAME BACK TO SEE HOW THINGS ARE GOING OVER HERE.
SHF
I TAKE IT YOU STILL HAVEN'T...
SNIFF
GLUTTONY?
I SMELL HIM! I SMELL HIM!
SNIFF SNIFF

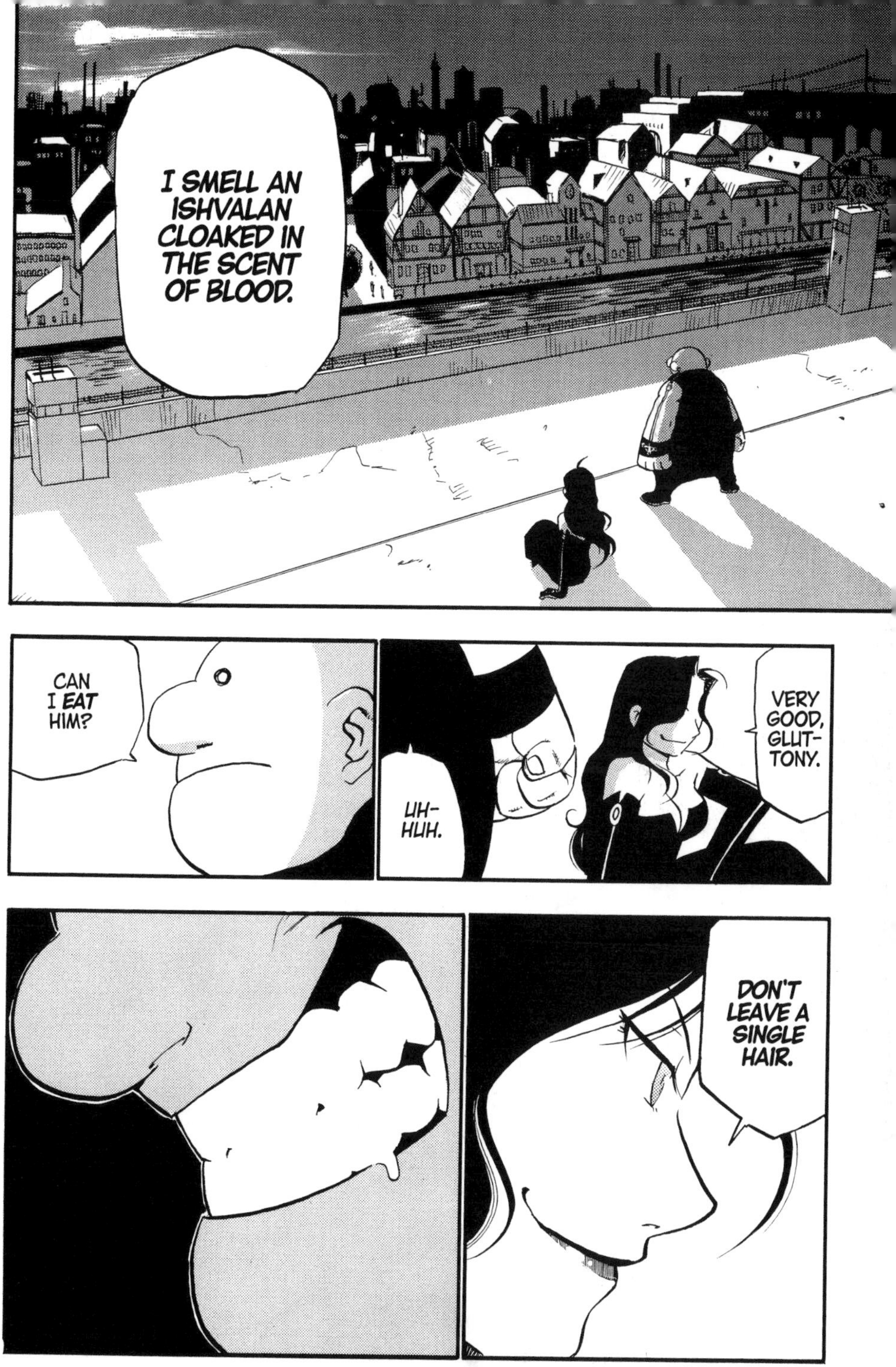
I SMELL AN ISHVALAN CLOAKED IN THE SCENT OF BLOOD.
VERY GOOD, GLUTTONY.
UH-HUH.
CAN I EAT HIM?
DON'T LEAVE A SINGLE HAIR.

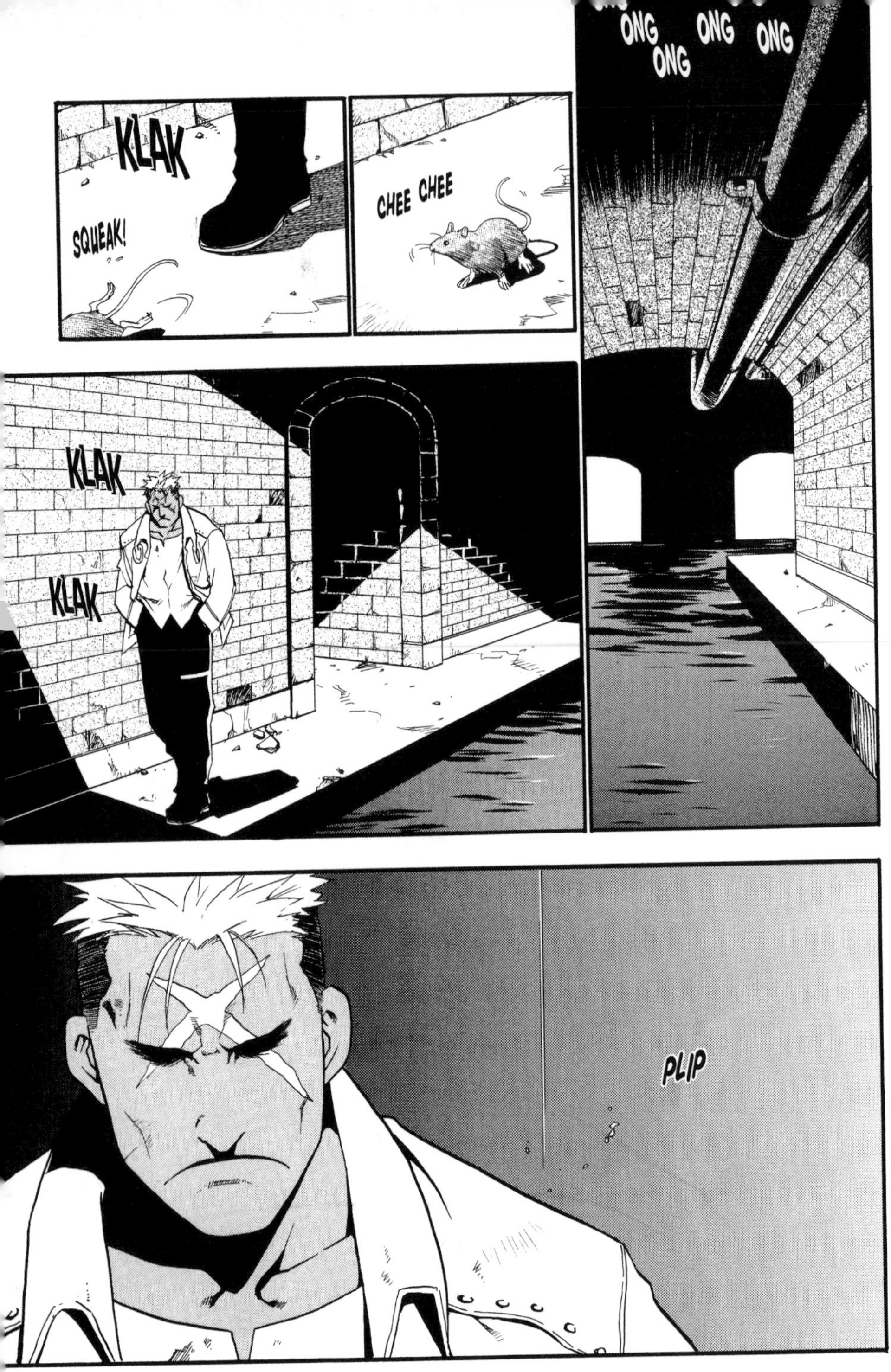
ONG
ONG
ONG
ONG
ONG
CHEE CHEE
KLAK
SQUEAK!
KLAK
KLAK
PLIP

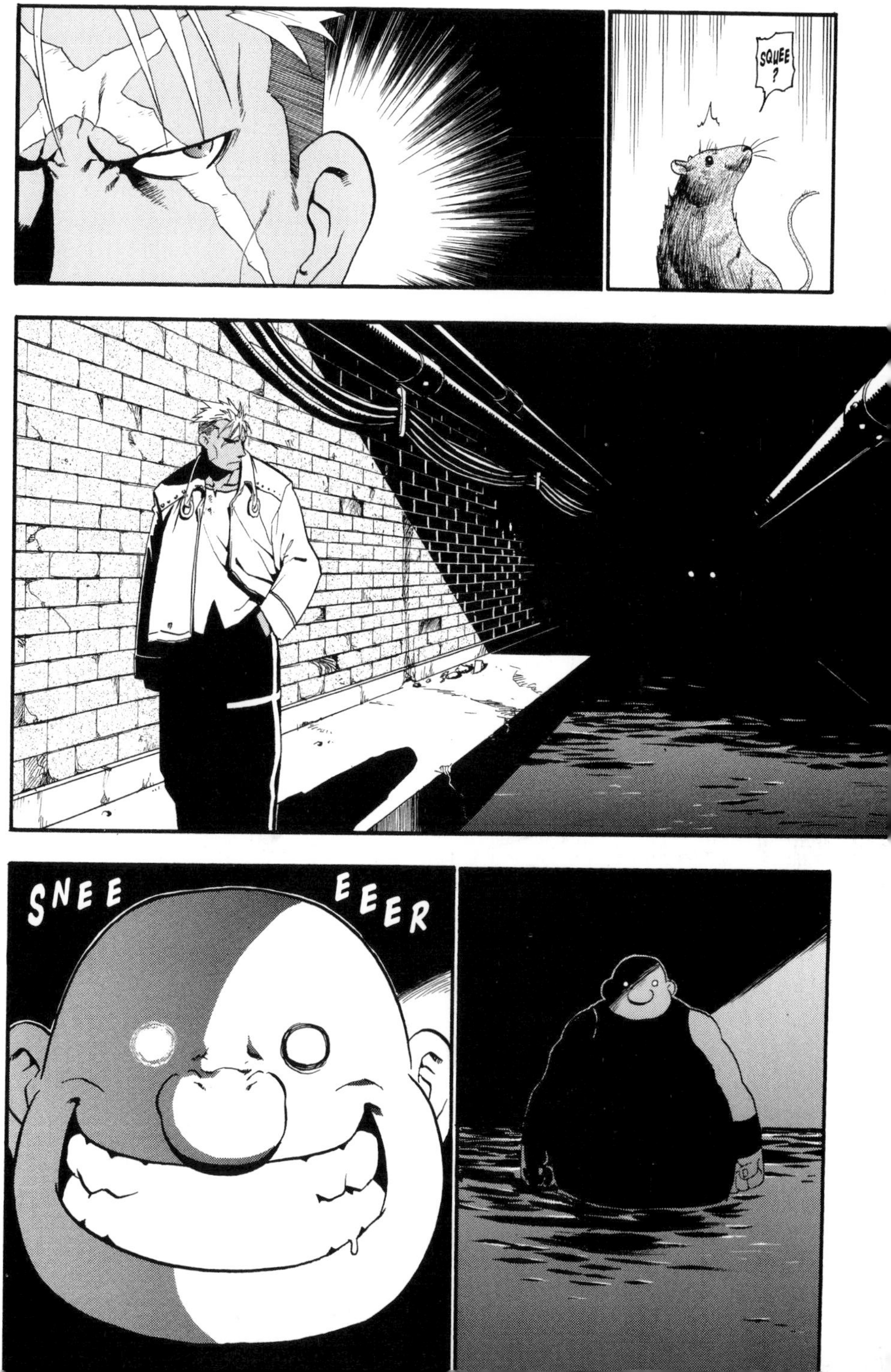
SQUEE ?
SNEE EEER

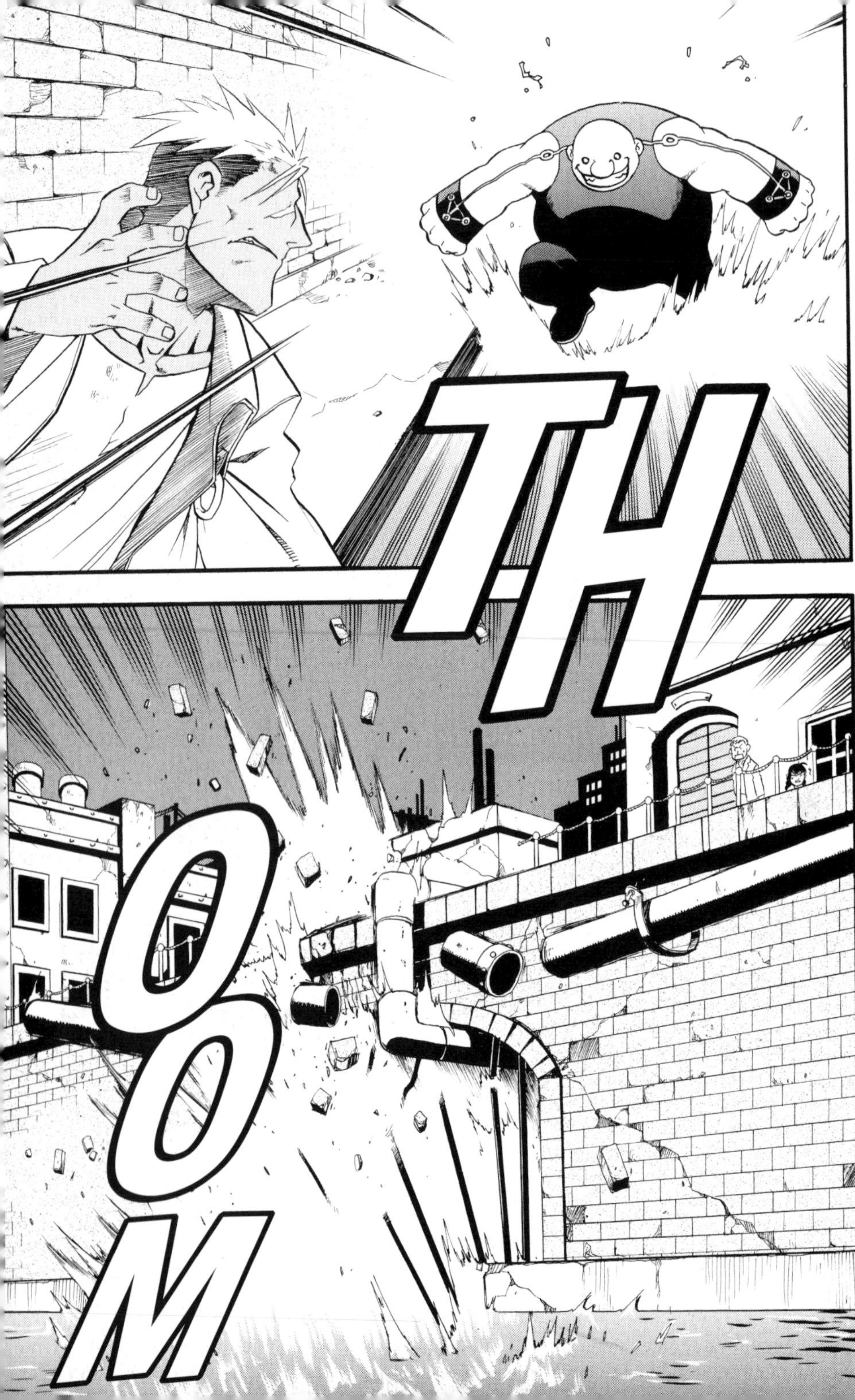

THOOM

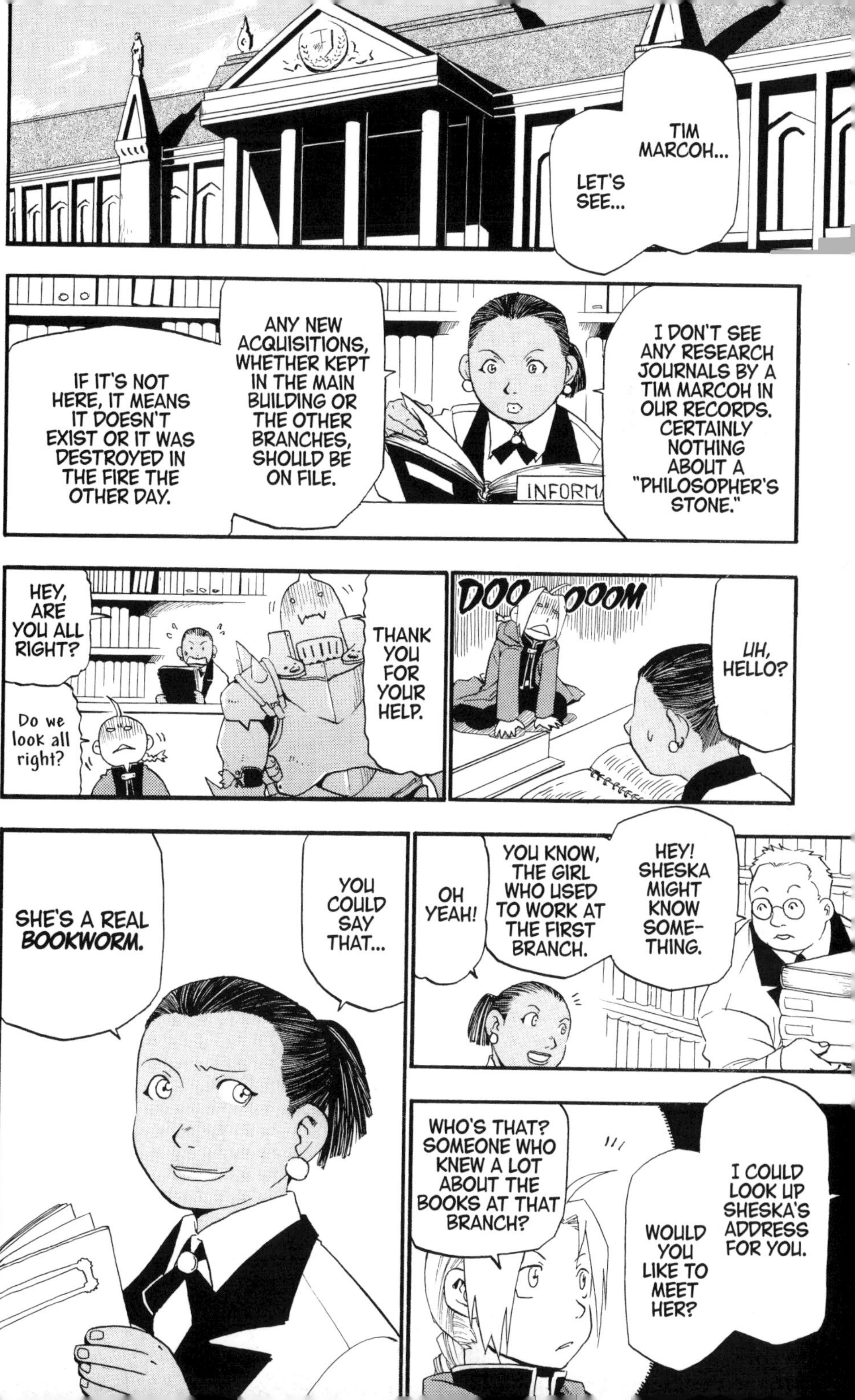
TIM MARCOH...
LET'S SEE...
I DON'T SEE ANY RESEARCH JOURNALS BY A TIM MARCOH IN OUR RECORDS. CERTAINLY NOTHING ABOUT A "PHILOSOPHER'S STONE."
ANY NEW ACQUISITIONS, WHETHER KEPT IN THE MAIN BUILDING OR THE OTHER BRANCHES, SHOULD BE ON FILE.
IF IT'S NOT HERE, IT MEANS IT DOESN'T EXIST OR IT WAS DESTROYED IN THE FIRE THE OTHER DAY.
INFORMA
DOOOOOM
UH, HELLO?
THANK YOU FOR YOUR HELP.
HEY, ARE YOU ALL RIGHT?
Do we look all right?
HEY! SHESKA MIGHT KNOW SOME-THING.
YOU KNOW, THE GIRL WHO USED TO WORK AT THE FIRST BRANCH.
OH YEAH!
I COULD LOOK UP SHESKA'S ADDRESS FOR YOU.
WOULD YOU LIKE TO MEET HER?
WHO'S THAT? SOMEONE WHO KNEW A LOT ABOUT THE BOOKS AT THAT BRANCH?
YOU COULD SAY THAT...
SHE'S A REAL BOOKWORM.

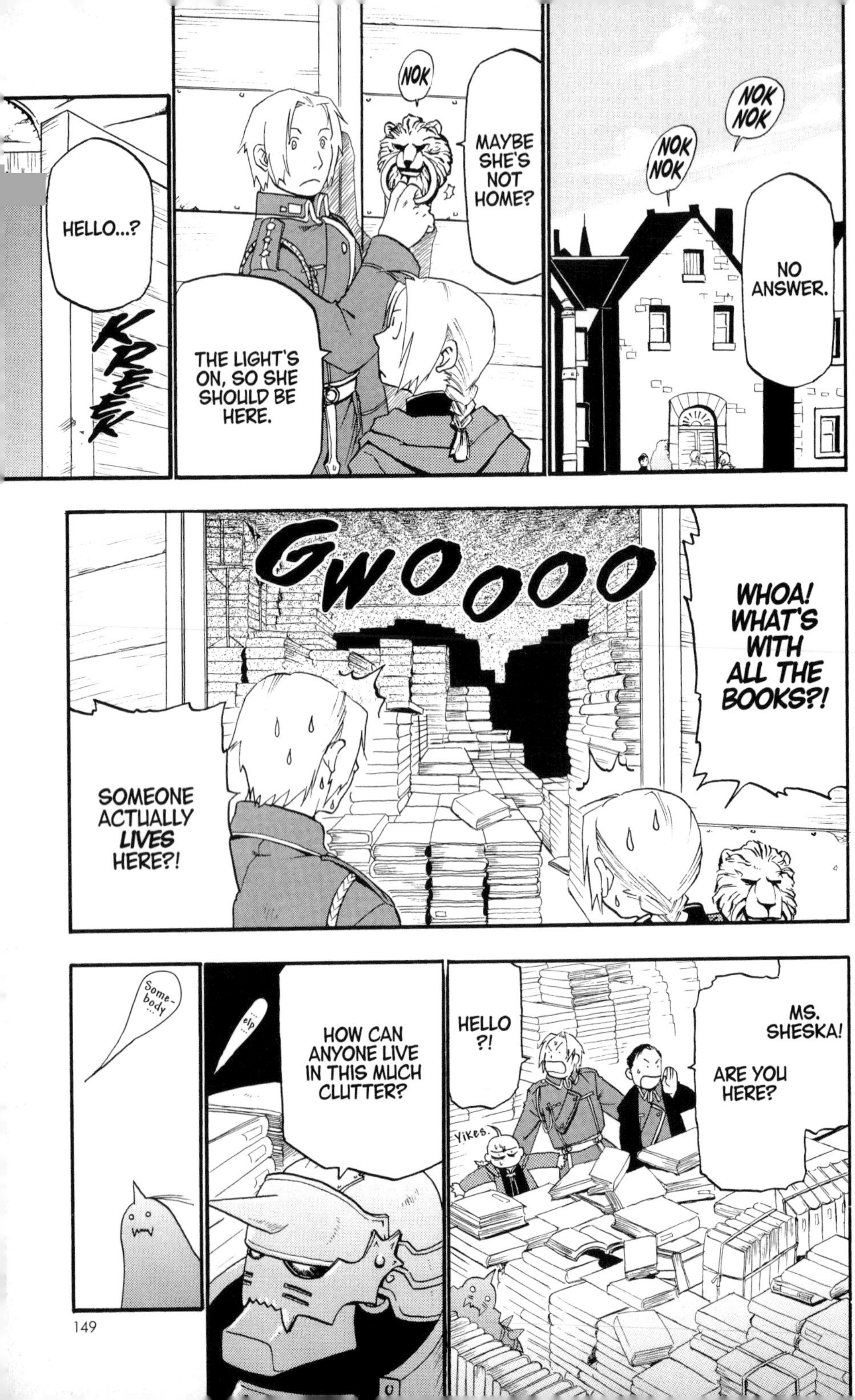
NOK NOK
NOK NOK
NO ANSWER.
NOK
MAYBE SHE'S NOT HOME?
THE LIGHT'S ON, SO SHE SHOULD BE HERE.
HELLO...?
KREEK
GWOOOO
WHOA! WHAT'S WITH ALL THE BOOKS?!
SOMEONE ACTUALLY LIVES HERE?!
MS. SHESKA!
ARE YOU HERE?
HELLO?!
Yikes.
HOW CAN ANYONE LIVE IN THIS MUCH CLUTTER?
...elp...
Somebody...

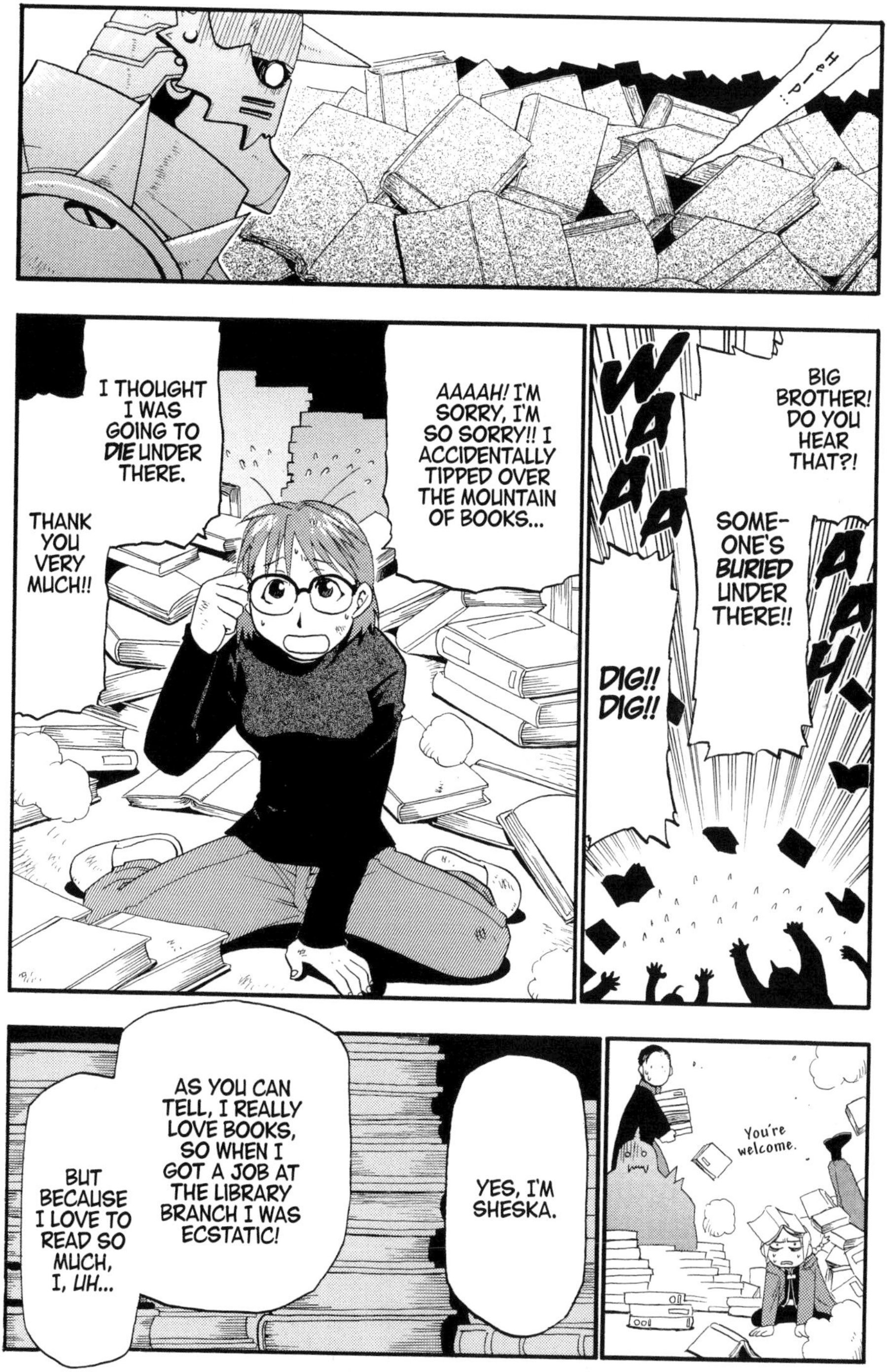
Help...
BIG BROTHER! DO YOU HEAR THAT?!
WAAAAAAAH
SOME-ONE'S BURIED UNDER THERE!!
DIG!! DIG!!
AAAAH! I'M SORRY, I'M SO SORRY!! I ACCIDENTALLY TIPPED OVER THE MOUNTAIN OF BOOKS...
I THOUGHT I WAS GOING TO DIE UNDER THERE.
THANK YOU VERY MUCH!!
You're welcome.
YES, I'M SHESKA.
AS YOU CAN TELL, I REALLY LOVE BOOKS, SO WHEN I GOT A JOB AT THE LIBRARY BRANCH I WAS ECSTATIC!
BUT BECAUSE I LOVE TO READ SO MUCH, I, UH...

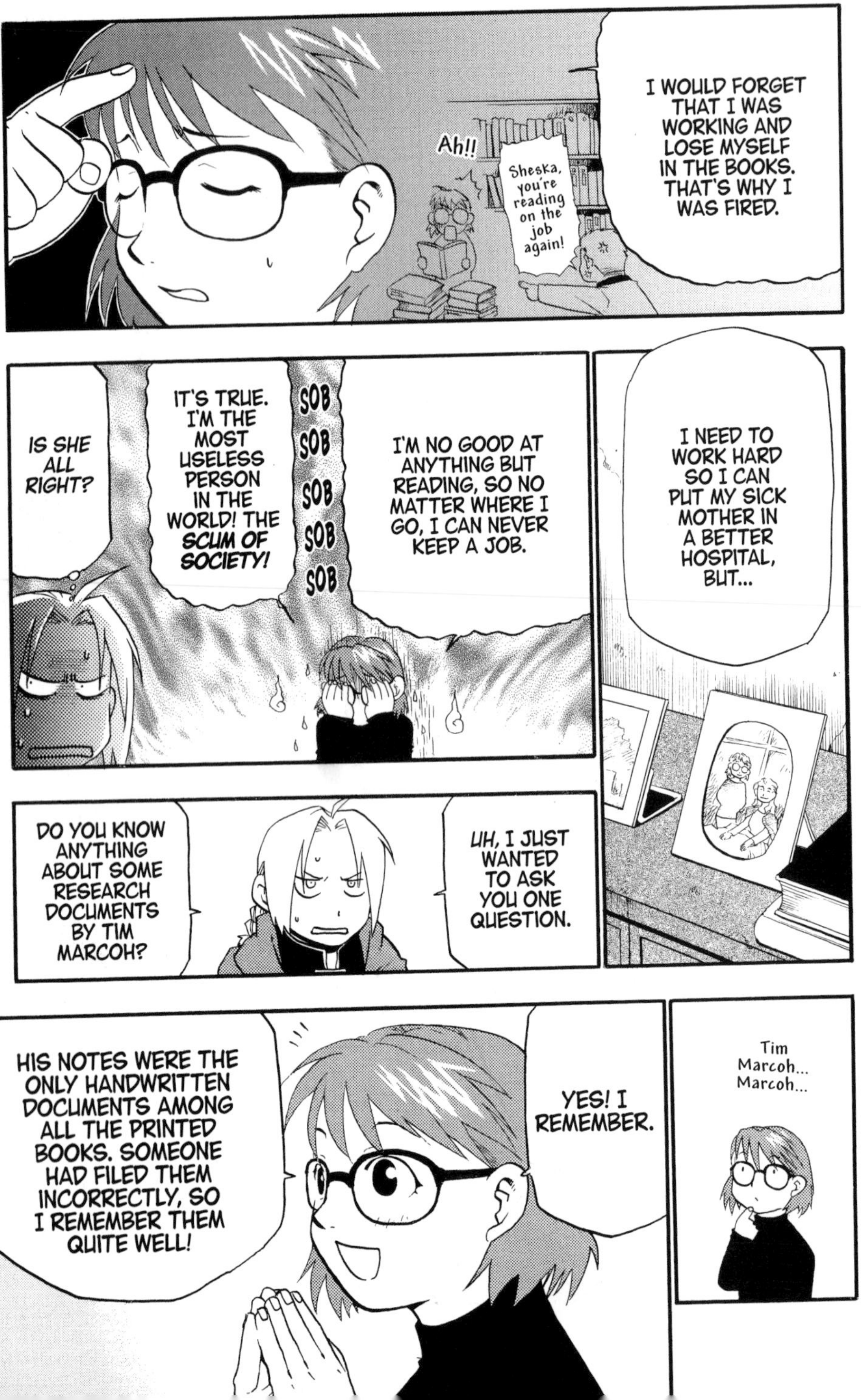
I WOULD FORGET THAT I WAS WORKING AND LOSE MYSELF IN THE BOOKS. THAT'S WHY I WAS FIRED.
Sheska, you're reading on the job again!
Ah!!
I NEED TO WORK HARD SO I CAN PUT MY SICK MOTHER IN A BETTER HOSPITAL, BUT...
I'M NO GOOD AT ANYTHING BUT READING, SO NO MATTER WHERE I GO, I CAN NEVER KEEP A JOB.
SOB SOB SOB SOB SOB
IT'S TRUE. I'M THE MOST USELESS PERSON IN THE WORLD! THE SCUM OF SOCIETY!
IS SHE ALL RIGHT?
UH, I JUST WANTED TO ASK YOU ONE QUESTION.
DO YOU KNOW ANYTHING ABOUT SOME RESEARCH DOCUMENTS BY TIM MARCOH?
Tim Marcoh... Marcoh...
YES! I REMEMBER.
HIS NOTES WERE THE ONLY HANDWRITTEN DOCUMENTS AMONG ALL THE PRINTED BOOKS. SOMEONE HAD FILED THEM INCORRECTLY, SO I REMEMBER THEM QUITE WELL!

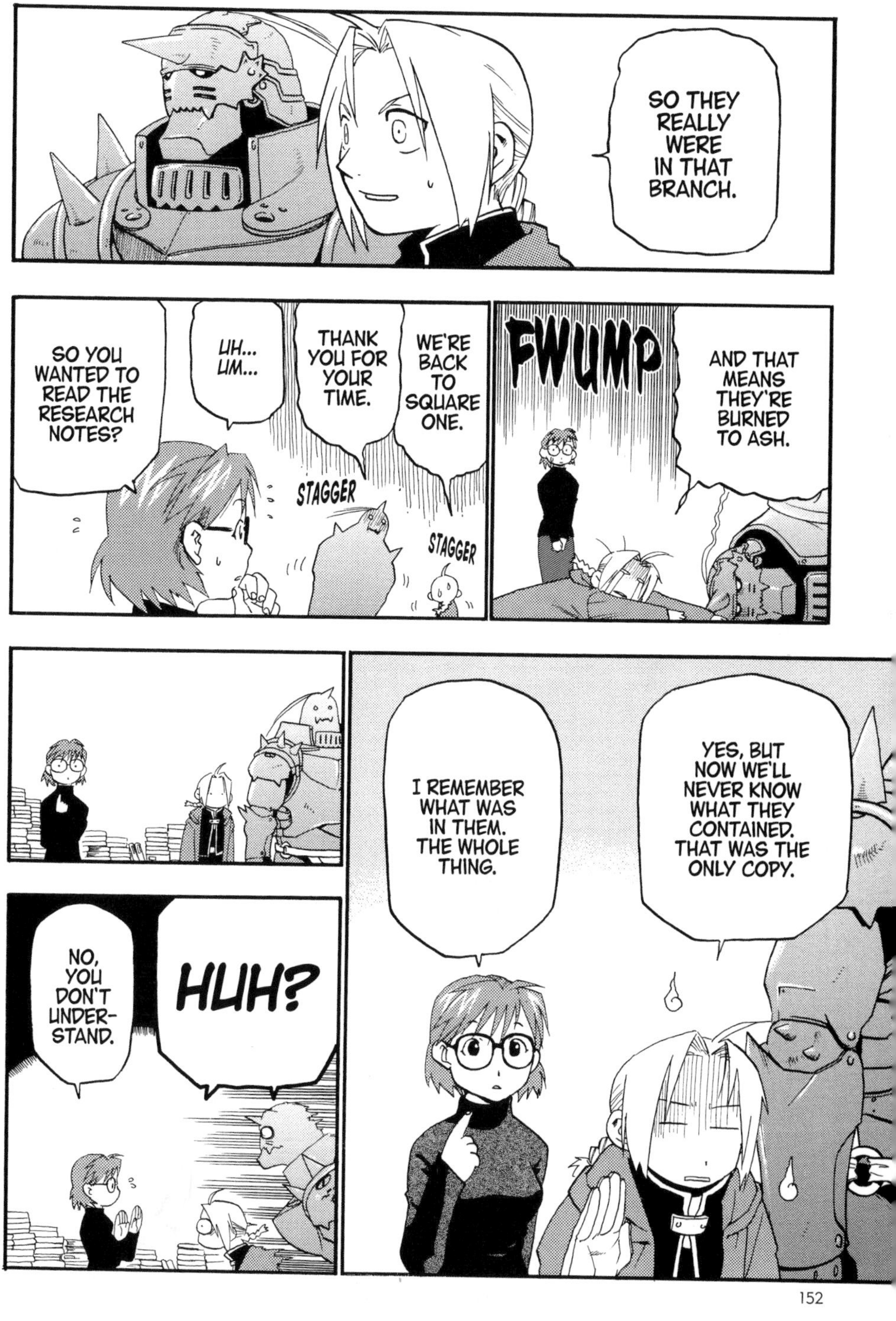
SO THEY REALLY WERE IN THAT BRANCH.
AND THAT MEANS THEY'RE BURNED TO ASH.
FWUMP
WE'RE BACK TO SQUARE ONE.
THANK YOU FOR YOUR TIME.
STAGGER
STAGGER
UH... UM...
SO YOU WANTED TO READ THE RESEARCH NOTES?
YES, BUT NOW WE'LL NEVER KNOW WHAT THEY CONTAINED. THAT WAS THE ONLY COPY.
I REMEMBER WHAT WAS IN THEM. THE WHOLE THING.
HUH?
NO, YOU DON'T UNDER-STAND.

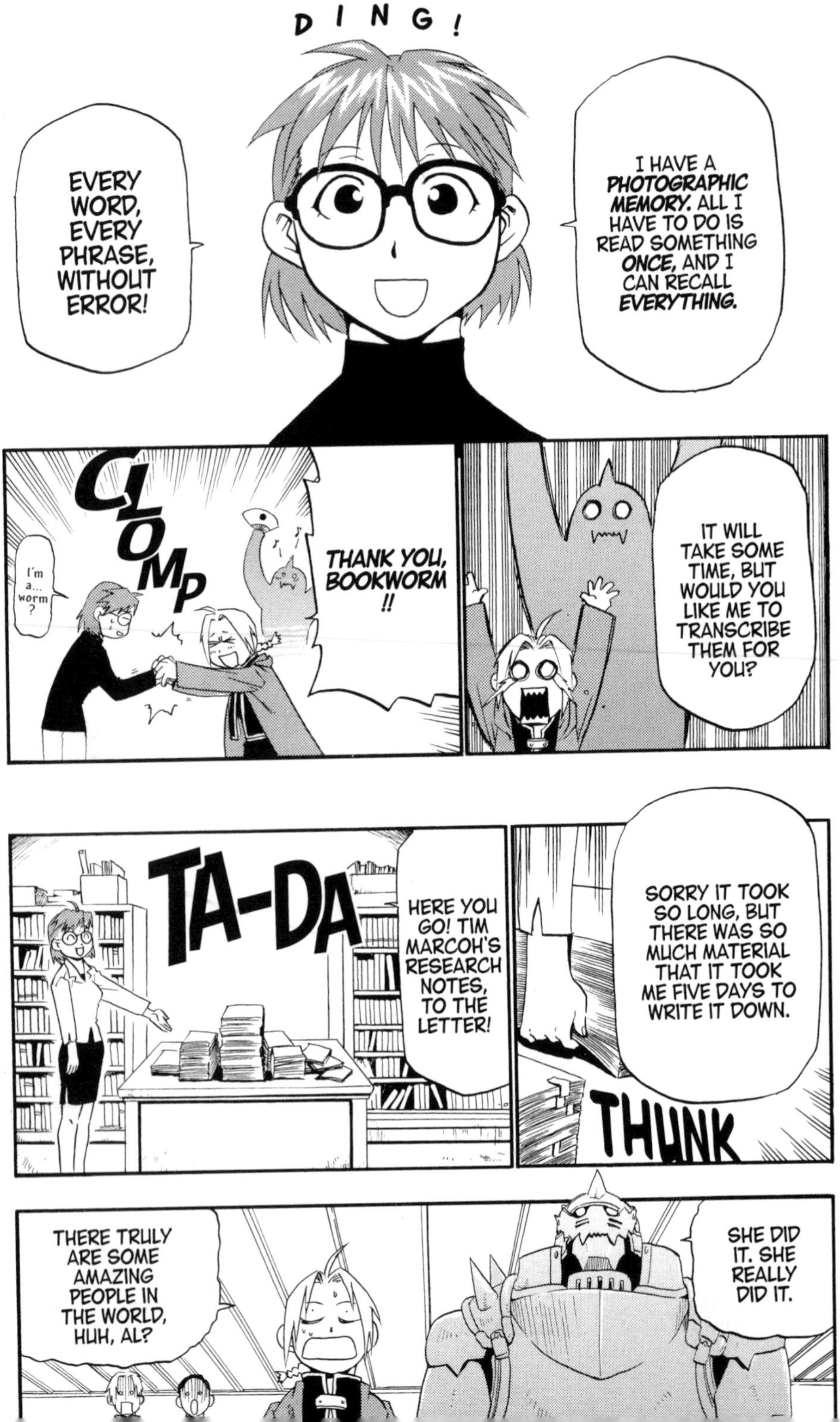
DING!
I HAVE A PHOTOGRAPHIC MEMORY. ALL I HAVE TO DO IS READ SOMETHING ONCE, AND I CAN RECALL EVERYTHING.
EVERY WORD, EVERY PHRASE, WITHOUT ERROR!
IT WILL TAKE SOME TIME, BUT WOULD YOU LIKE ME TO TRANSCRIBE THEM FOR YOU?
THANK YOU, BOOKWORM !!
CLOMP
I'm a... worm?
SORRY IT TOOK SO LONG, BUT THERE WAS SO MUCH MATERIAL THAT IT TOOK ME FIVE DAYS TO WRITE IT DOWN.
THUNK
HERE YOU GO! TIM MARCOH'S RESEARCH NOTES, TO THE LETTER!
TA-DA
SHE DID IT. SHE REALLY DID IT.
THERE TRULY ARE SOME AMAZING PEOPLE IN THE WORLD, HUH, AL?

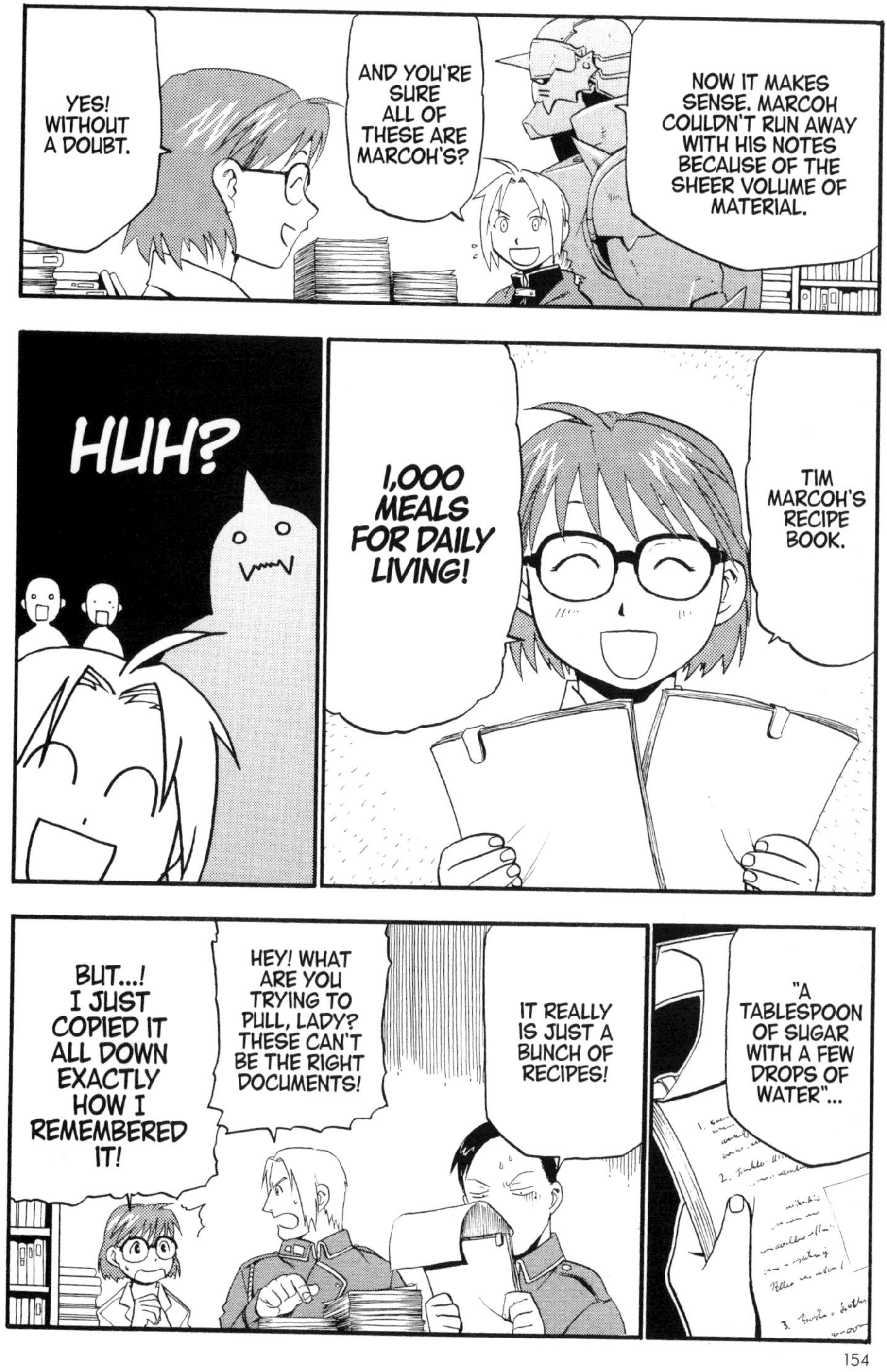
NOW IT MAKES SENSE. MARCOH COULDN'T RUN AWAY WITH HIS NOTES BECAUSE OF THE SHEER VOLUME OF MATERIAL.
AND YOU'RE SURE ALL OF THESE ARE MARCOH'S?
YES! WITHOUT A DOUBT.
TIM MARCOH'S RECIPE BOOK.
1,000 MEALS FOR DAILY LIVING!
HUH?
"A TABLESPOON OF SUGAR WITH A FEW DROPS OF WATER"...
IT REALLY IS JUST A BUNCH OF RECIPES!
HEY! WHAT ARE YOU TRYING TO PULL, LADY? THESE CAN'T BE THE RIGHT DOCUMENTS!
BUT...! I JUST COPIED IT ALL DOWN EXACTLY HOW I REMEMBERED IT!

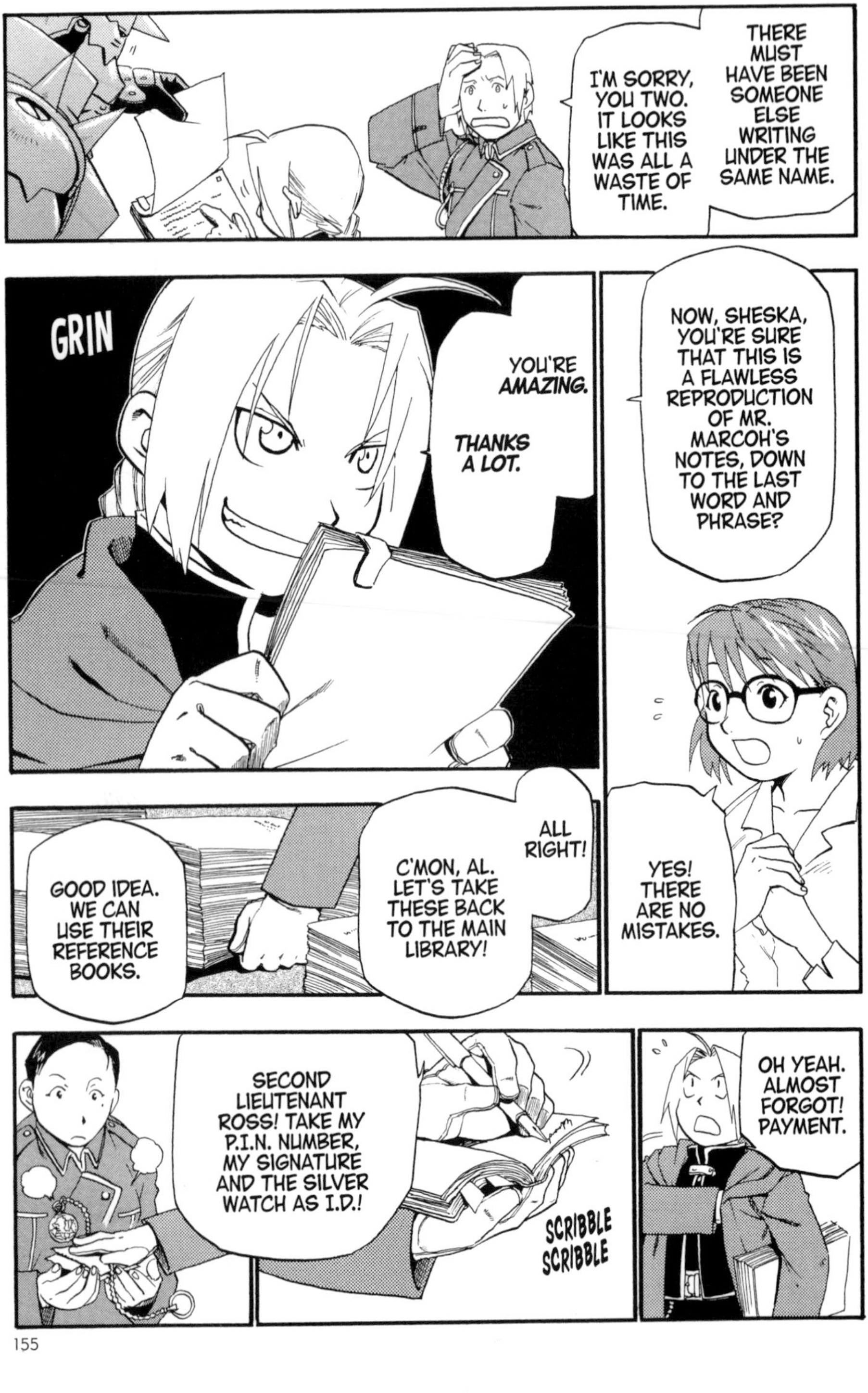
THERE MUST HAVE BEEN SOMEONE ELSE WRITING UNDER THE SAME NAME.
I'M SORRY, YOU TWO. IT LOOKS LIKE THIS WAS ALL A WASTE OF TIME.
NOW, SHESKA, YOU'RE SURE THAT THIS IS A FLAWLESS REPRODUCTION OF MR. MARCOH'S NOTES, DOWN TO THE LAST WORD AND PHRASE?
YES! THERE ARE NO MISTAKES.
YOU'RE AMAZING.
THANKS A LOT.
GRIN
ALL RIGHT!
C'MON, AL. LET'S TAKE THESE BACK TO THE MAIN LIBRARY!
GOOD IDEA. WE CAN USE THEIR REFERENCE BOOKS.
OH YEAH. ALMOST FORGOT! PAYMENT.
SECOND LIEUTENANT ROSS! TAKE MY P.I.N. NUMBER, MY SIGNATURE AND THE SILVER WATCH AS I.D.!
SCRIBBLE SCRIBBLE

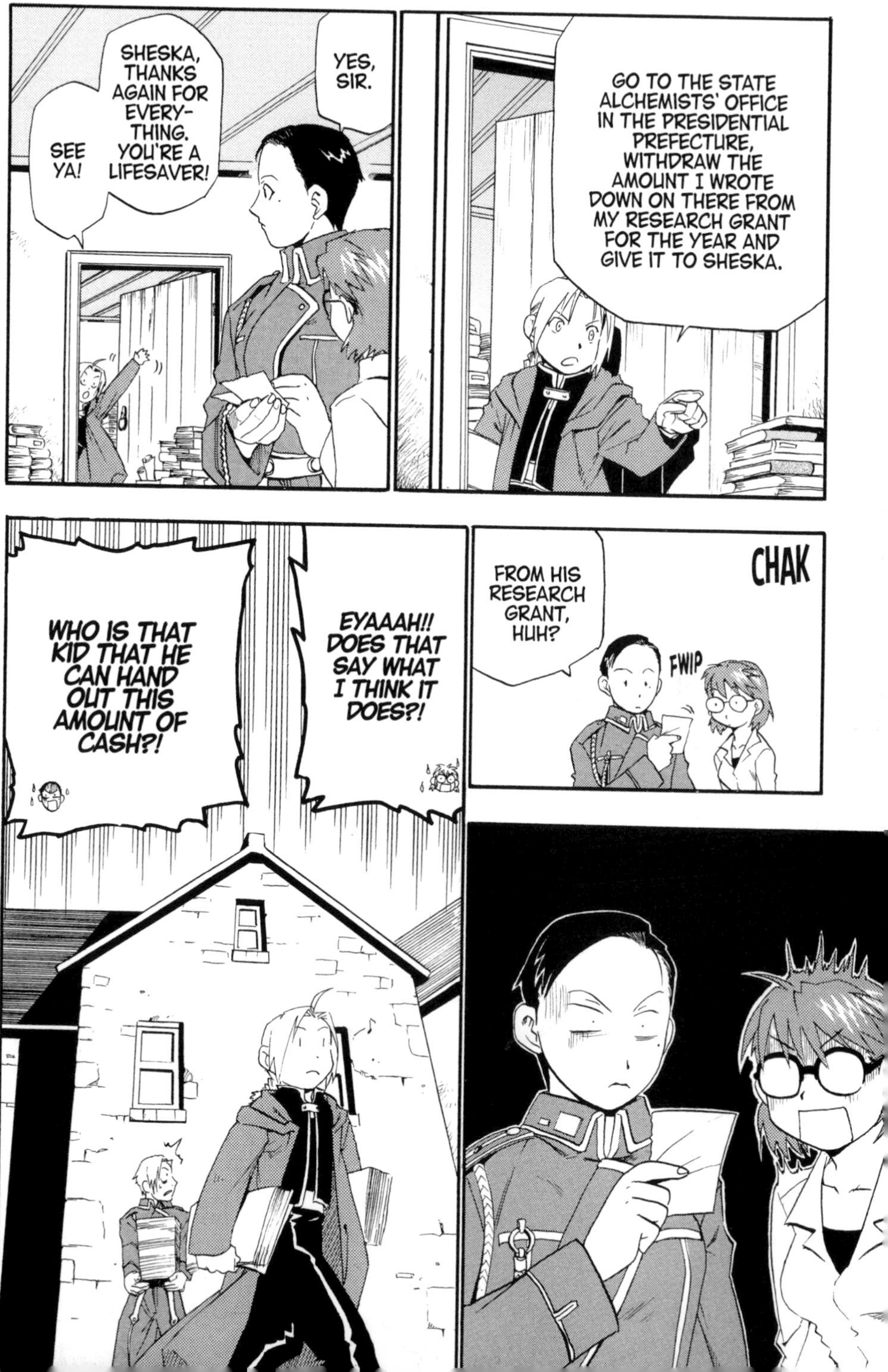
GO TO THE STATE ALCHEMISTS' OFFICE IN THE PRESIDENTIAL PREFECTURE, WITHDRAW THE AMOUNT I WROTE DOWN ON THERE FROM MY RESEARCH GRANT FOR THE YEAR AND GIVE IT TO SHESKA.
YES, SIR.
SHESKA, THANKS AGAIN FOR EVERY-THING. YOU'RE A LIFESAVER!
SEE YA!
CHAK
FROM HIS RESEARCH GRANT, HUH?
FWIP
EYAAAH!! DOES THAT SAY WHAT I THINK IT DOES?!
WHO IS THAT KID THAT HE CAN HAND OUT THIS AMOUNT OF CASH?!

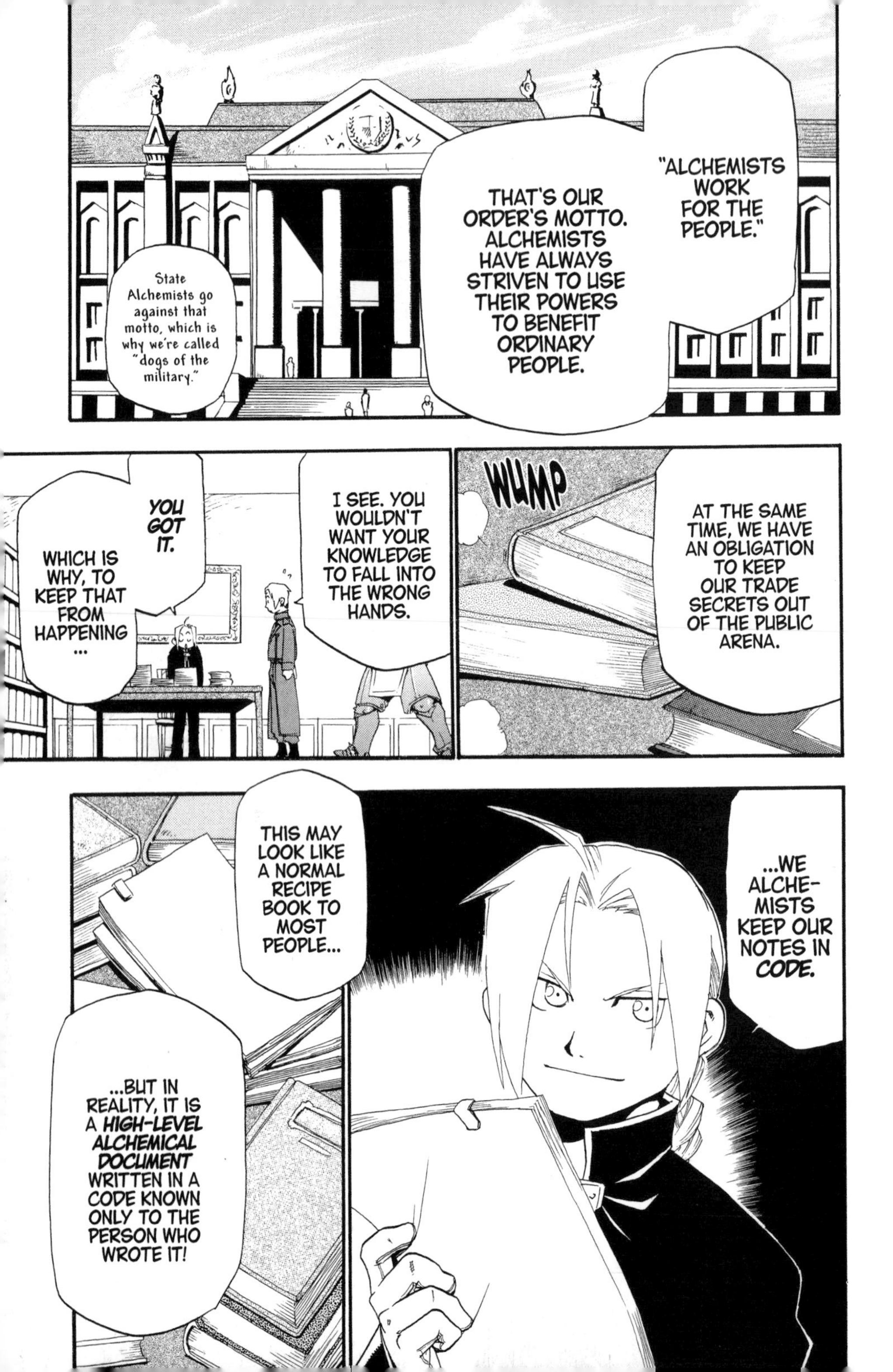
"ALCHEMISTS WORK FOR THE PEOPLE."
THAT'S OUR ORDER'S MOTTO. ALCHEMISTS HAVE ALWAYS STRIVEN TO USE THEIR POWERS TO BENEFIT ORDINARY PEOPLE.
State Alchemists go against that motto, which is why we're called "dogs of the military."
WUMP
AT THE SAME TIME, WE HAVE AN OBLIGATION TO KEEP OUR TRADE SECRETS OUT OF THE PUBLIC ARENA.
I SEE. YOU WOULDN'T WANT YOUR KNOWLEDGE TO FALL INTO THE WRONG HANDS.
YOU GOT IT.
WHICH IS WHY, TO KEEP THAT FROM HAPPENING...
...WE ALCHEMISTS KEEP OUR NOTES IN CODE.
THIS MAY LOOK LIKE A NORMAL RECIPE BOOK TO MOST PEOPLE...
...BUT IN REALITY, IT IS A HIGH-LEVEL ALCHEMICAL DOCUMENT WRITTEN IN A CODE KNOWN ONLY TO THE PERSON WHO WROTE IT!

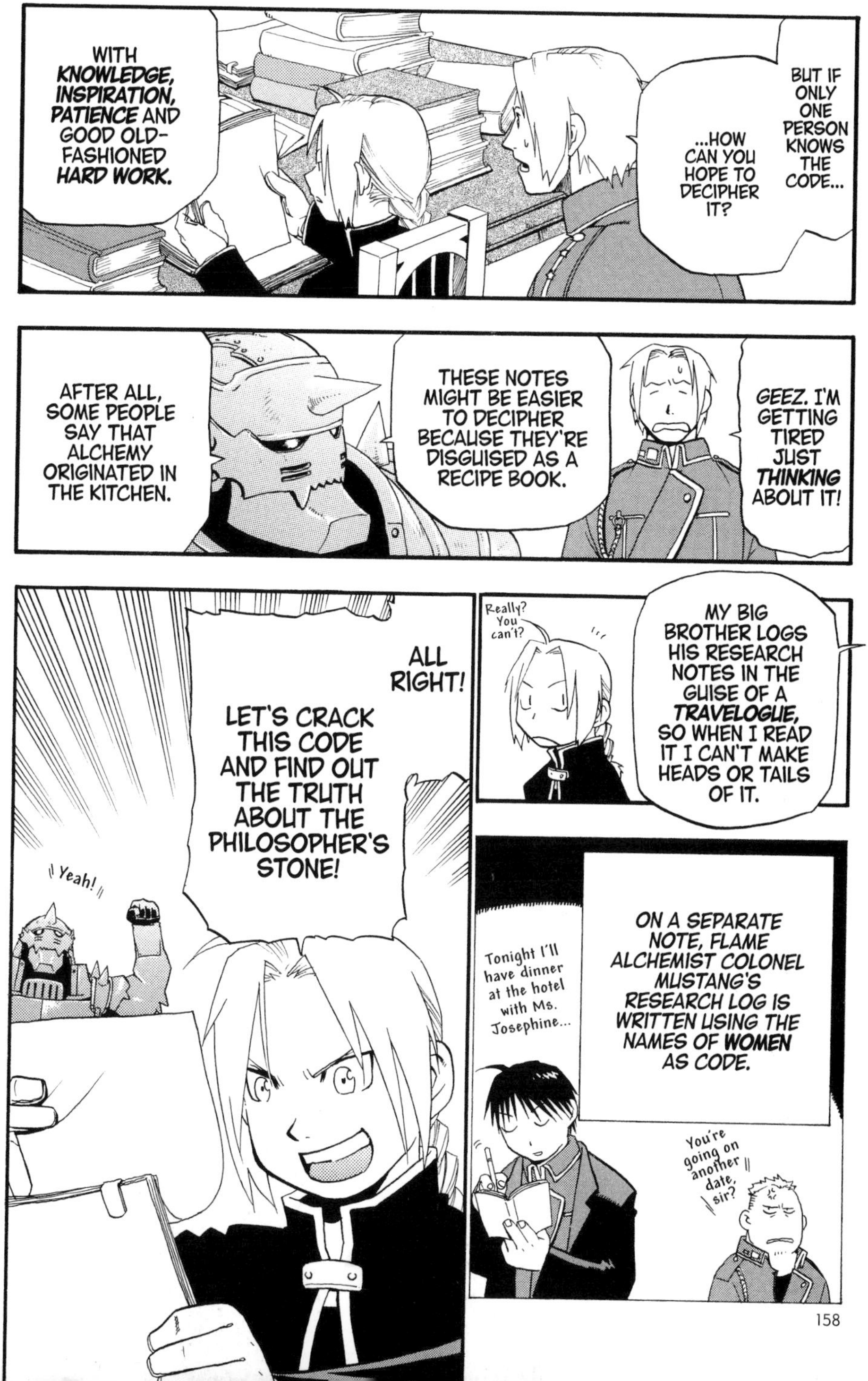
BUT IF ONLY ONE PERSON KNOWS THE CODE...
...HOW CAN YOU HOPE TO DECIPHER IT?
WITH KNOWLEDGE, INSPIRATION, PATIENCE AND GOOD OLD-FASHIONED HARD WORK.
GEEZ. I'M GETTING TIRED JUST THINKING ABOUT IT!
THESE NOTES MIGHT BE EASIER TO DECIPHER BECAUSE THEY'RE DISGUISED AS A RECIPE BOOK.
AFTER ALL, SOME PEOPLE SAY THAT ALCHEMY ORIGINATED IN THE KITCHEN.
MY BIG BROTHER LOGS HIS RESEARCH NOTES IN THE GUISE OF A TRAVELOGUE, SO WHEN I READ IT I CAN'T MAKE HEADS OR TAILS OF IT.
Really? You can't?
ON A SEPARATE NOTE, FLAME ALCHEMIST COLONEL MUSTANG'S RESEARCH LOG IS WRITTEN USING THE NAMES OF WOMEN AS CODE.
Tonight I'll have dinner at the hotel with Ms. Josephine...
You're going on another date, sir?
ALL RIGHT!
LET'S CRACK THIS CODE AND FIND OUT THE TRUTH ABOUT THE PHILOSOPHER'S STONE!
Yeah!

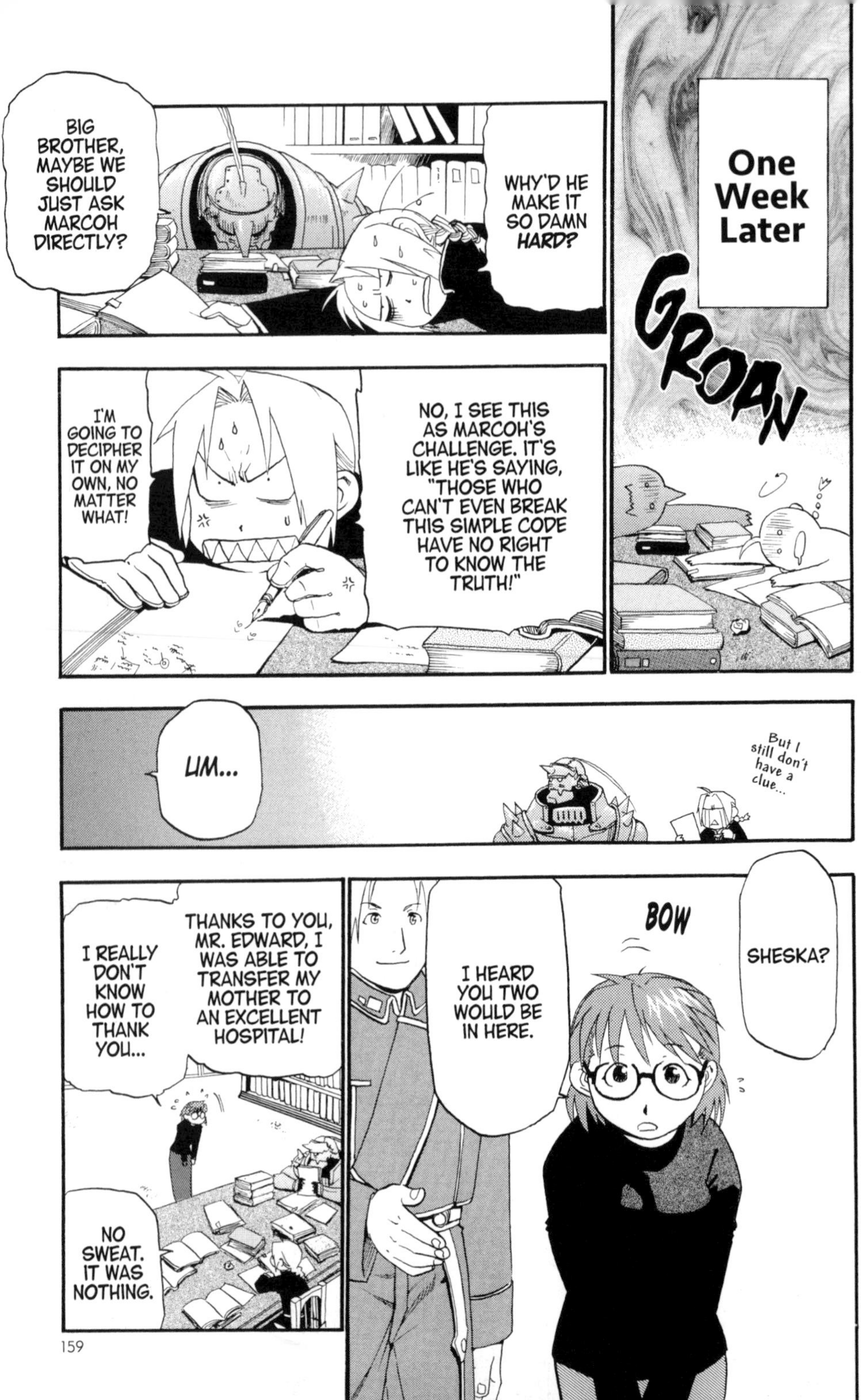
One Week Later
GROAN
WHY'D HE MAKE IT SO DAMN HARD?
BIG BROTHER, MAYBE WE SHOULD JUST ASK MARCOH DIRECTLY?
NO, I SEE THIS AS MARCOH'S CHALLENGE. IT'S LIKE HE'S SAYING, "THOSE WHO CAN'T EVEN BREAK THIS SIMPLE CODE HAVE NO RIGHT TO KNOW THE TRUTH!"
I'M GOING TO DECIPHER IT ON MY OWN, NO MATTER WHAT!
But I still don't have a clue...
UM...
SHESKA?
BOW
I HEARD YOU TWO WOULD BE IN HERE.
THANKS TO YOU, MR. EDWARD, I WAS ABLE TO TRANSFER MY MOTHER TO AN EXCELLENT HOSPITAL!
I REALLY DON'T KNOW HOW TO THANK YOU...
NO SWEAT. IT WAS NOTHING.

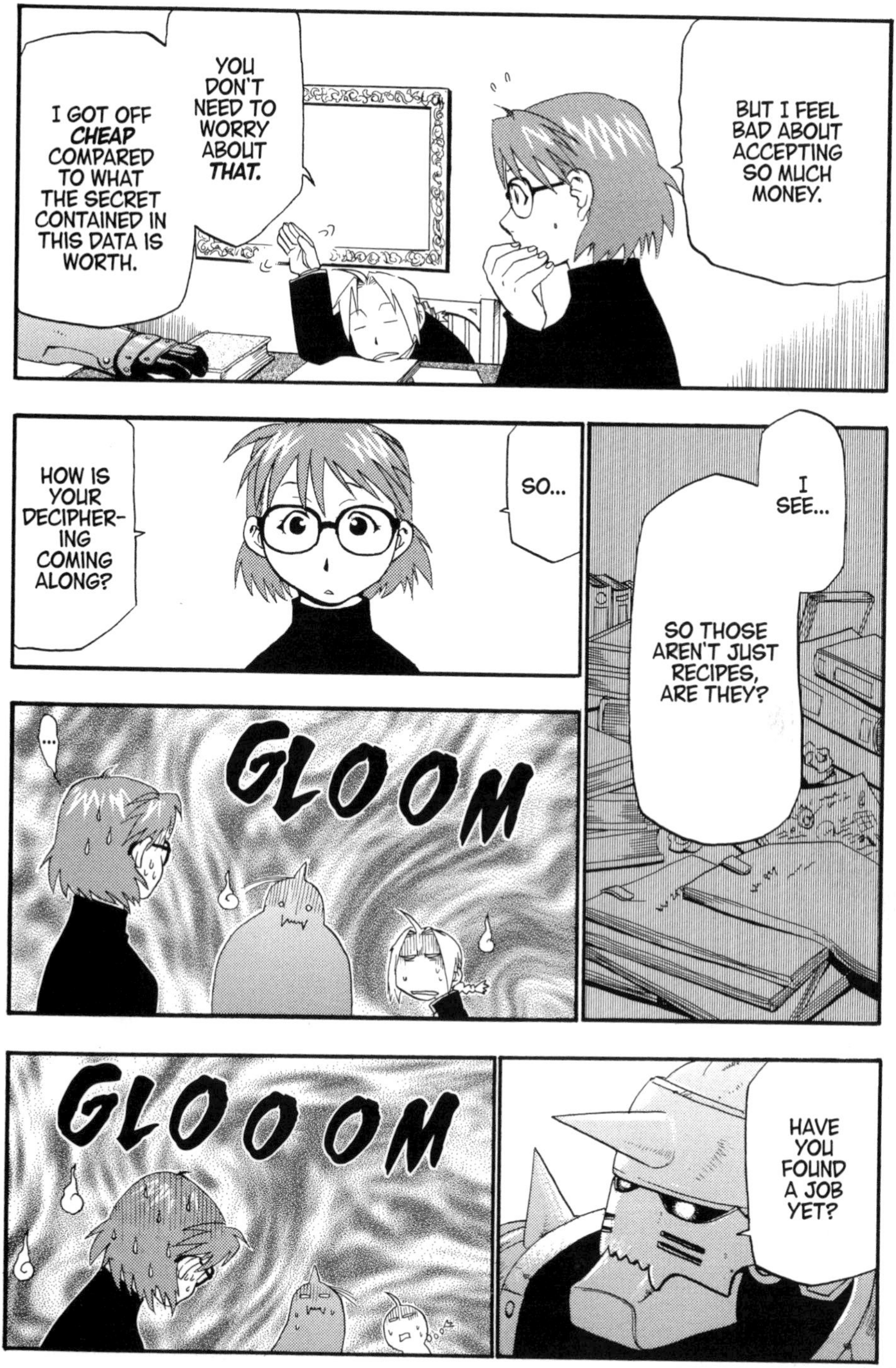
BUT I FEEL BAD ABOUT ACCEPTING SO MUCH MONEY.
YOU DON'T NEED TO WORRY ABOUT **THAT.**
I GOT OFF **CHEAP** COMPARED TO WHAT THE SECRET CONTAINED IN THIS DATA IS WORTH.
I SEE...
SO THOSE AREN'T JUST RECIPES, ARE THEY?
SO...
HOW IS YOUR DECIPHER-ING COMING ALONG?
GLOOM
...
HAVE YOU FOUND A JOB YET?
GLOOOOM

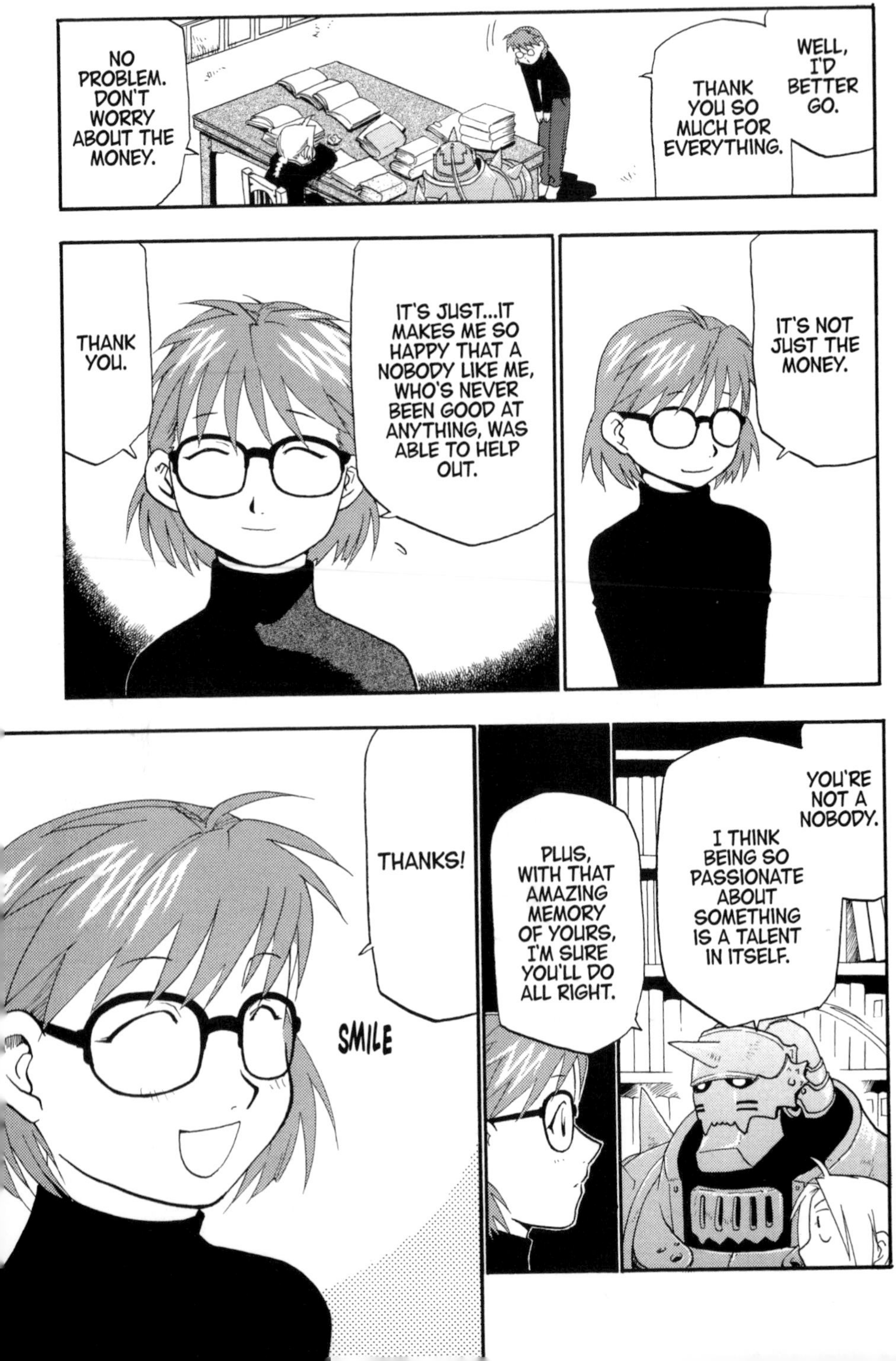

WELL, I'D BETTER GO.
THANK YOU SO MUCH FOR EVERYTHING.
NO PROBLEM. DON'T WORRY ABOUT THE MONEY.
IT'S NOT JUST THE MONEY.
IT'S JUST...IT MAKES ME SO HAPPY THAT A NOBODY LIKE ME, WHO'S NEVER BEEN GOOD AT ANYTHING, WAS ABLE TO HELP OUT.
THANK YOU.
YOU'RE NOT A NOBODY.
I THINK BEING SO PASSIONATE ABOUT SOMETHING IS A TALENT IN ITSELF.
PLUS, WITH THAT AMAZING MEMORY OF YOURS, I'M SURE YOU'LL DO ALL RIGHT.
THANKS!
SMILE

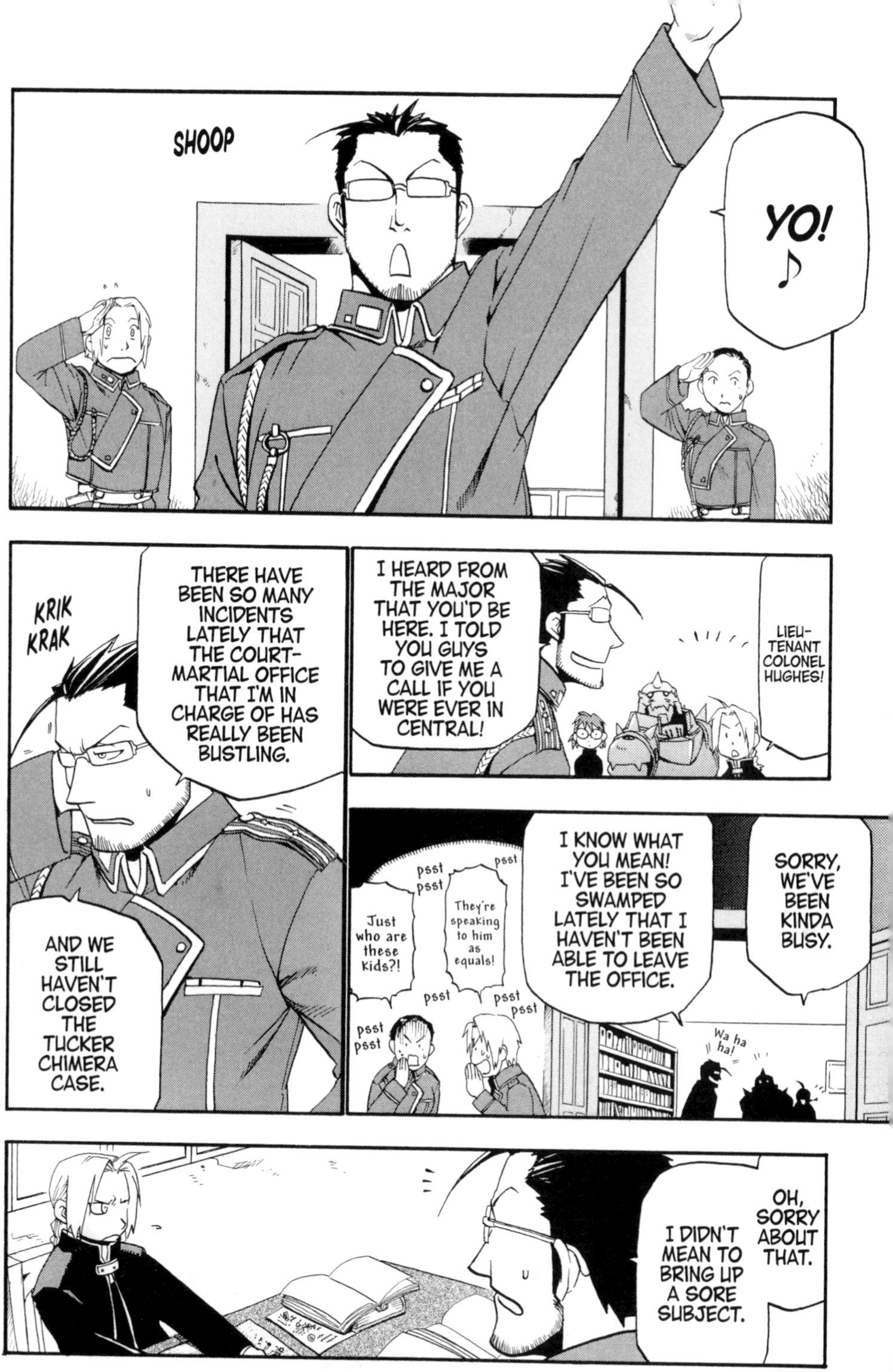
YO! ♪
SHOOP
LIEU-TENANT COLONEL HUGHES!
I HEARD FROM THE MAJOR THAT YOU'D BE HERE. I TOLD YOU GUYS TO GIVE ME A CALL IF YOU WERE EVER IN CENTRAL!
SORRY, WE'VE BEEN KINDA BUSY.
I KNOW WHAT YOU MEAN! I'VE BEEN SO SWAMPED LATELY THAT I HAVEN'T BEEN ABLE TO LEAVE THE OFFICE.
psst psst
They're speaking to him as equals!
Just who are these kids?!
psst psst
psst
psst psst
Wa ha ha!
THERE HAVE BEEN SO MANY INCIDENTS LATELY THAT THE COURT-MARTIAL OFFICE THAT I'M IN CHARGE OF HAS REALLY BEEN BUSTLING.
KRIK KRAK
AND WE STILL HAVEN'T CLOSED THE TUCKER CHIMERA CASE.
OH, SORRY ABOUT THAT.
I DIDN'T MEAN TO BRING UP A SORE SUBJECT.

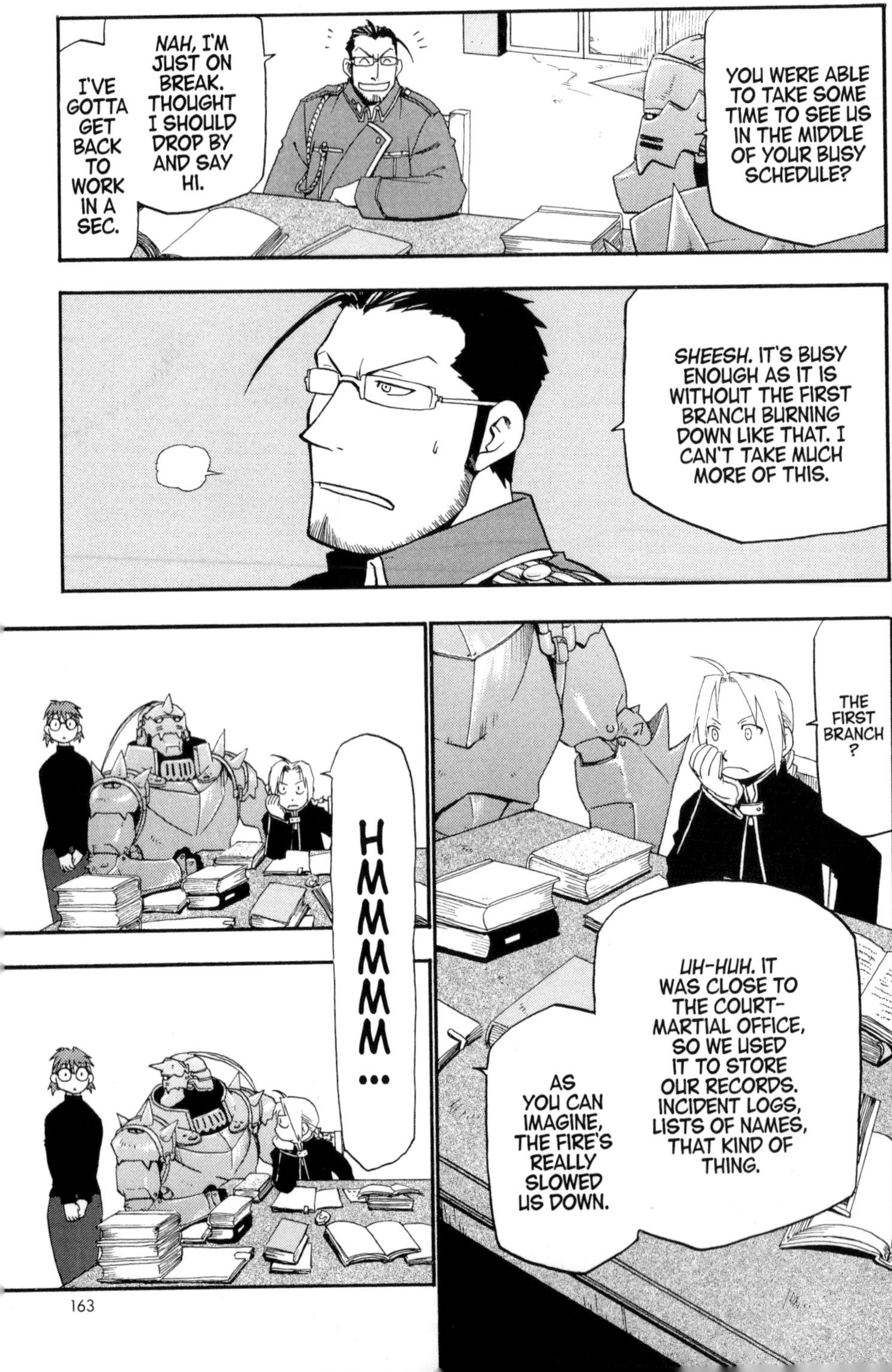
YOU WERE ABLE TO TAKE SOME TIME TO SEE US IN THE MIDDLE OF YOUR BUSY SCHEDULE?
NAH, I'M JUST ON BREAK. THOUGHT I SHOULD DROP BY AND SAY HI.
I'VE GOTTA GET BACK TO WORK IN A SEC.
SHEESH. IT'S BUSY ENOUGH AS IT IS WITHOUT THE FIRST BRANCH BURNING DOWN LIKE THAT. I CAN'T TAKE MUCH MORE OF THIS.
THE FIRST BRANCH?
UH-HUH. IT WAS CLOSE TO THE COURT-MARTIAL OFFICE, SO WE USED IT TO STORE OUR RECORDS. INCIDENT LOGS, LISTS OF NAMES, THAT KIND OF THING.
AS YOU CAN IMAGINE, THE FIRE'S REALLY SLOWED US DOWN.
HMMMMM...

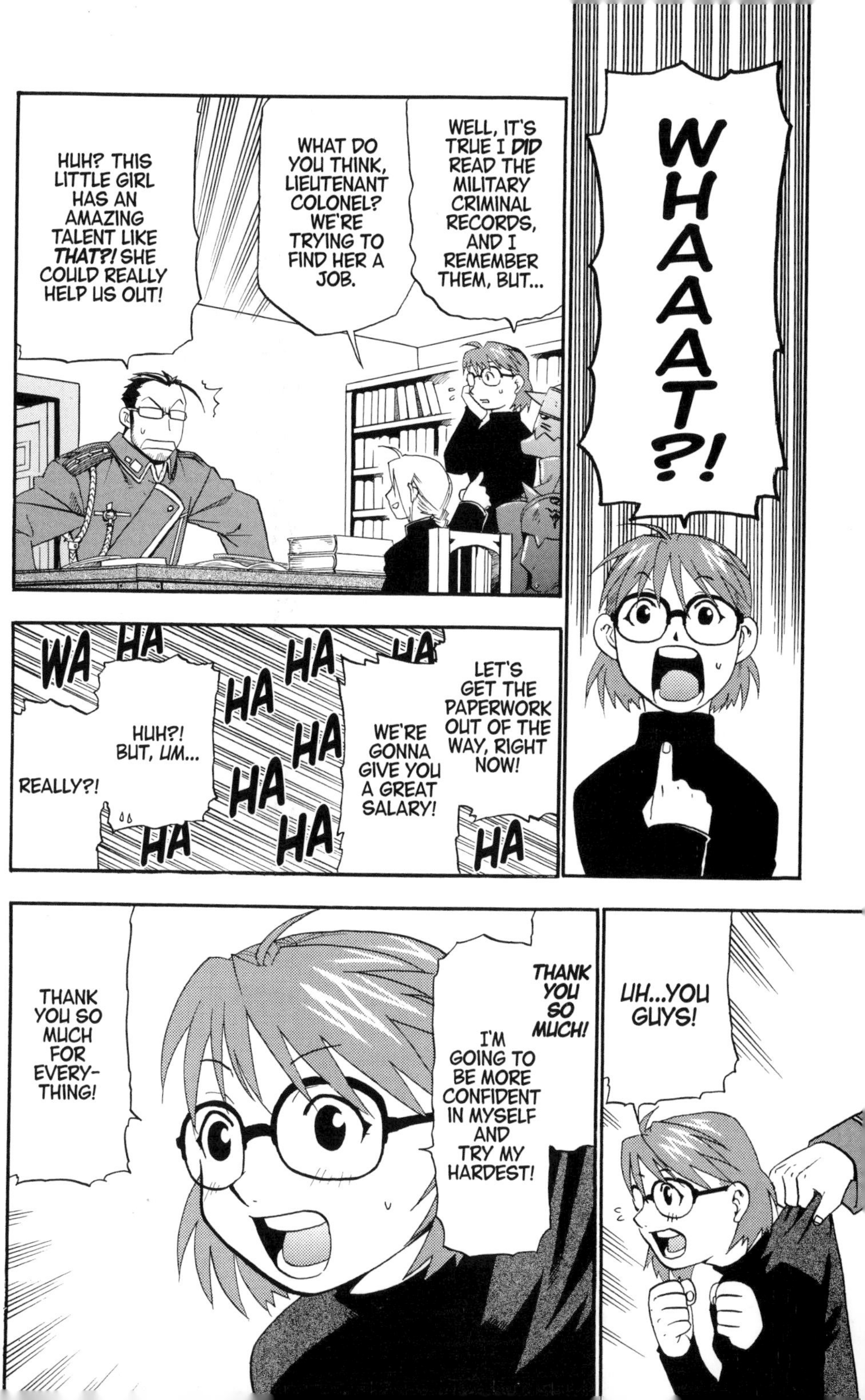
WHAAAT?!
WELL, IT'S TRUE I DID READ THE MILITARY CRIMINAL RECORDS, AND I REMEMBER THEM, BUT...
WHAT DO YOU THINK, LIEUTENANT COLONEL? WE'RE TRYING TO FIND HER A JOB.
HUH? THIS LITTLE GIRL HAS AN AMAZING TALENT LIKE THAT?! SHE COULD REALLY HELP US OUT!
LET'S GET THE PAPERWORK OUT OF THE WAY, RIGHT NOW!
WE'RE GONNA GIVE YOU A GREAT SALARY!
HUH?! BUT, UM...
REALLY?!
WA HA HA HA HA HA HA HA HA HA HA
UH...YOU GUYS!
THANK YOU SO MUCH!
I'M GOING TO BE MORE CONFIDENT IN MYSELF AND TRY MY HARDEST!
THANK YOU SO MUCH FOR EVERY-THING!

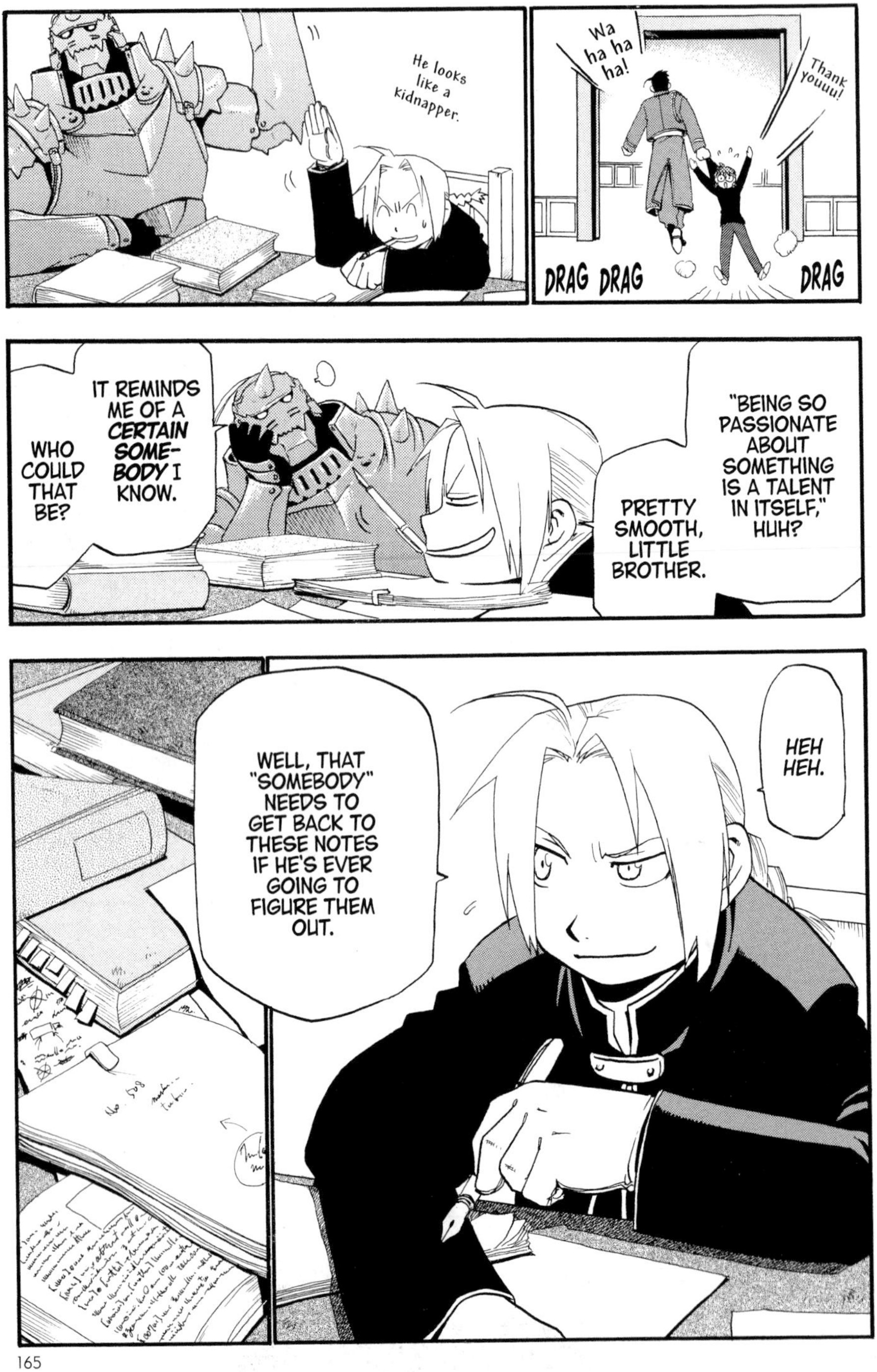

Thank youuu!
Wa ha ha ha!
DRAG
DRAG DRAG
He looks like a kidnapper.
"BEING SO PASSIONATE ABOUT SOMETHING IS A TALENT IN ITSELF," HUH?
PRETTY SMOOTH, LITTLE BROTHER.
IT REMINDS ME OF A CERTAIN SOMEBODY I KNOW.
WHO COULD THAT BE?
HEH HEH.
WELL, THAT "SOMEBODY" NEEDS TO GET BACK TO THESE NOTES IF HE'S EVER GOING TO FIGURE THEM OUT.

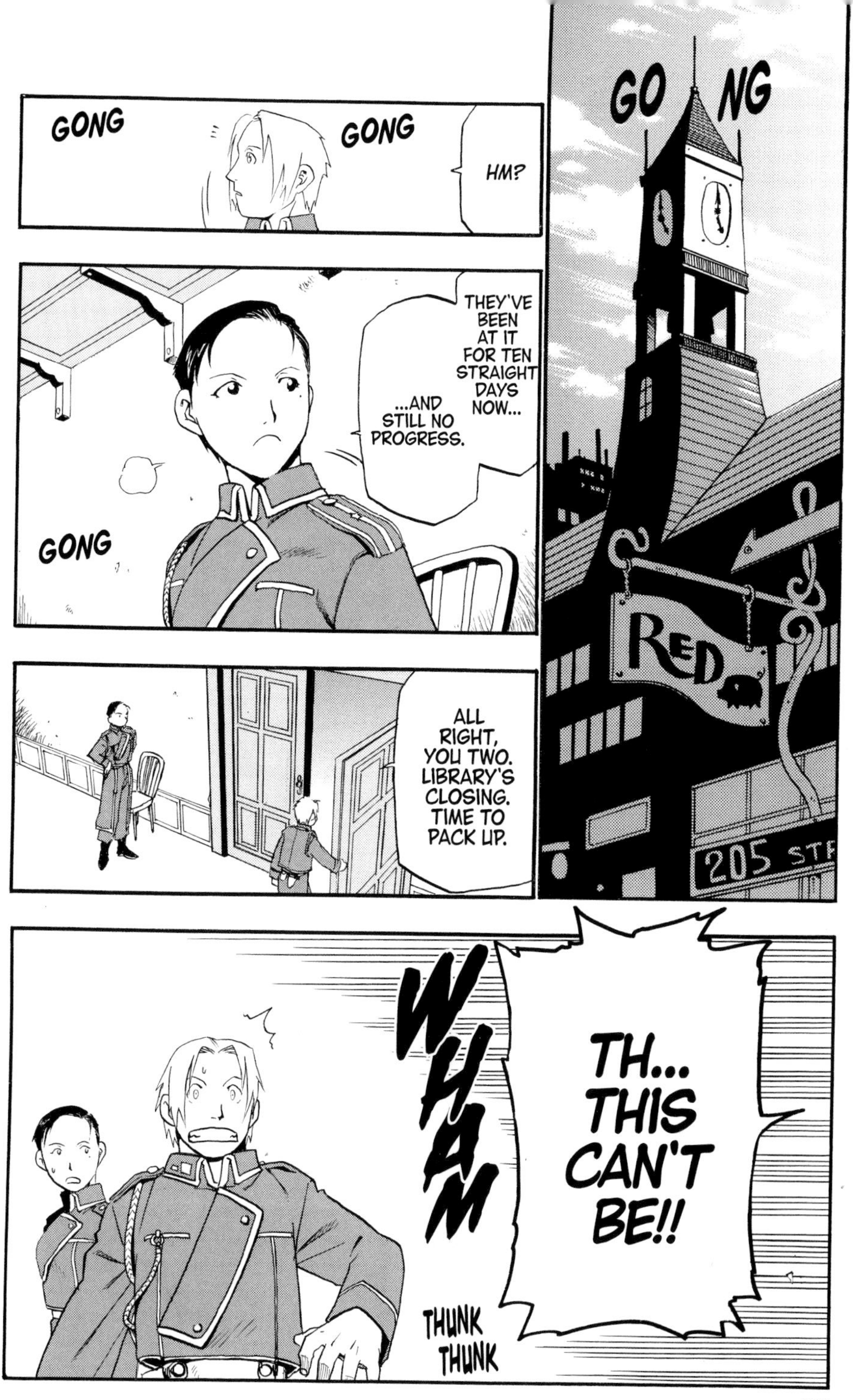
GO NG
RED
205
GONG
GONG
HM?
THEY'VE BEEN AT IT FOR TEN STRAIGHT DAYS NOW...
...AND STILL NO PROGRESS.
GONG
ALL RIGHT, YOU TWO. LIBRARY'S CLOSING. TIME TO PACK UP.
TH... THIS CAN'T BE!!
WHAM
THUNK THUNK

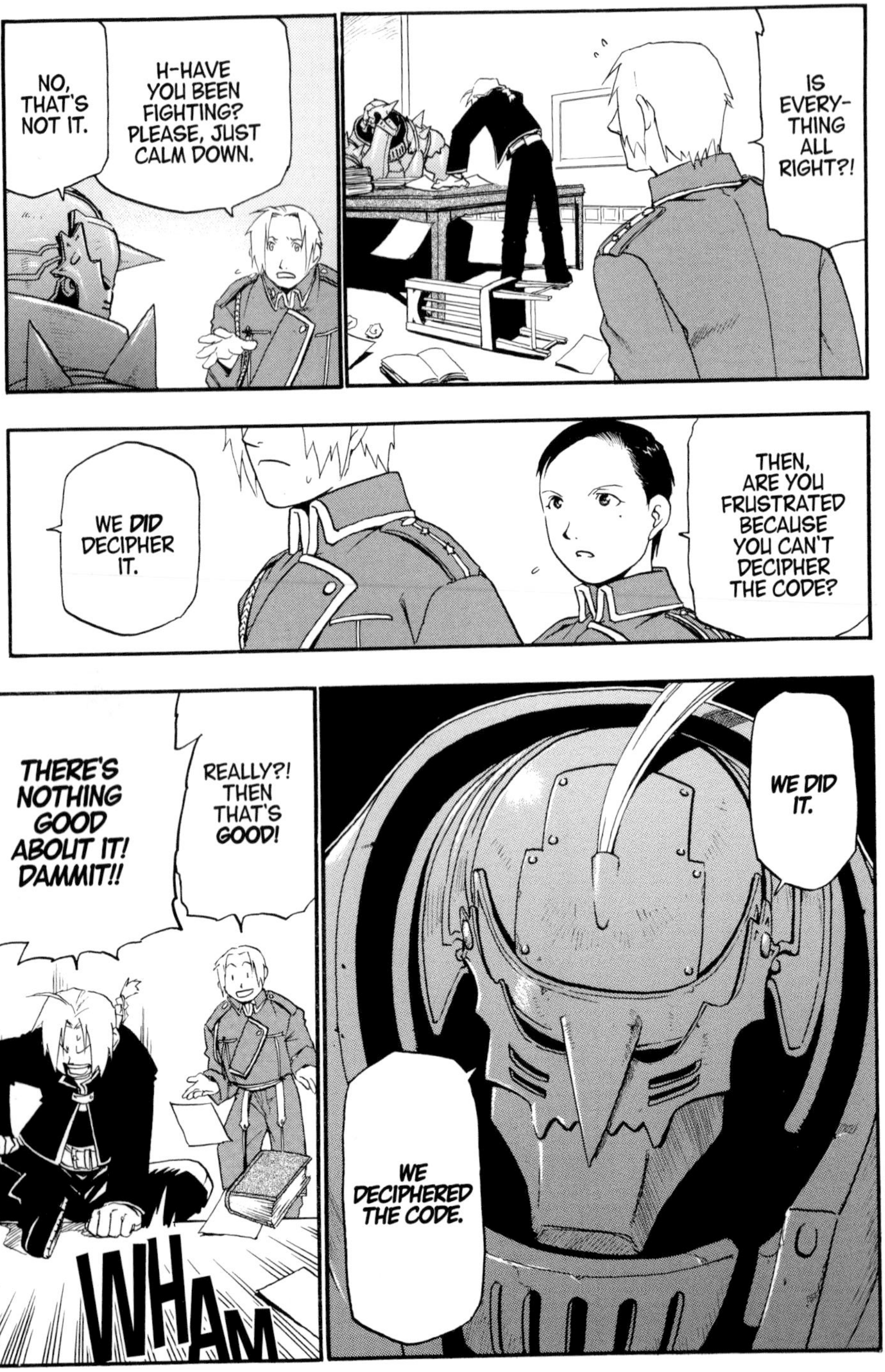
IS EVERYTHING ALL RIGHT?!
H-HAVE YOU BEEN FIGHTING? PLEASE, JUST CALM DOWN.
NO, THAT'S NOT IT.
THEN, ARE YOU FRUSTRATED BECAUSE YOU CAN'T DECIPHER THE CODE?
WE DID DECIPHER IT.
WE DID IT.
WE DECIPHERED THE CODE.
REALLY?! THEN THAT'S GOOD!
THERE'S NOTHING GOOD ABOUT IT! DAMMIT!!
WHAM

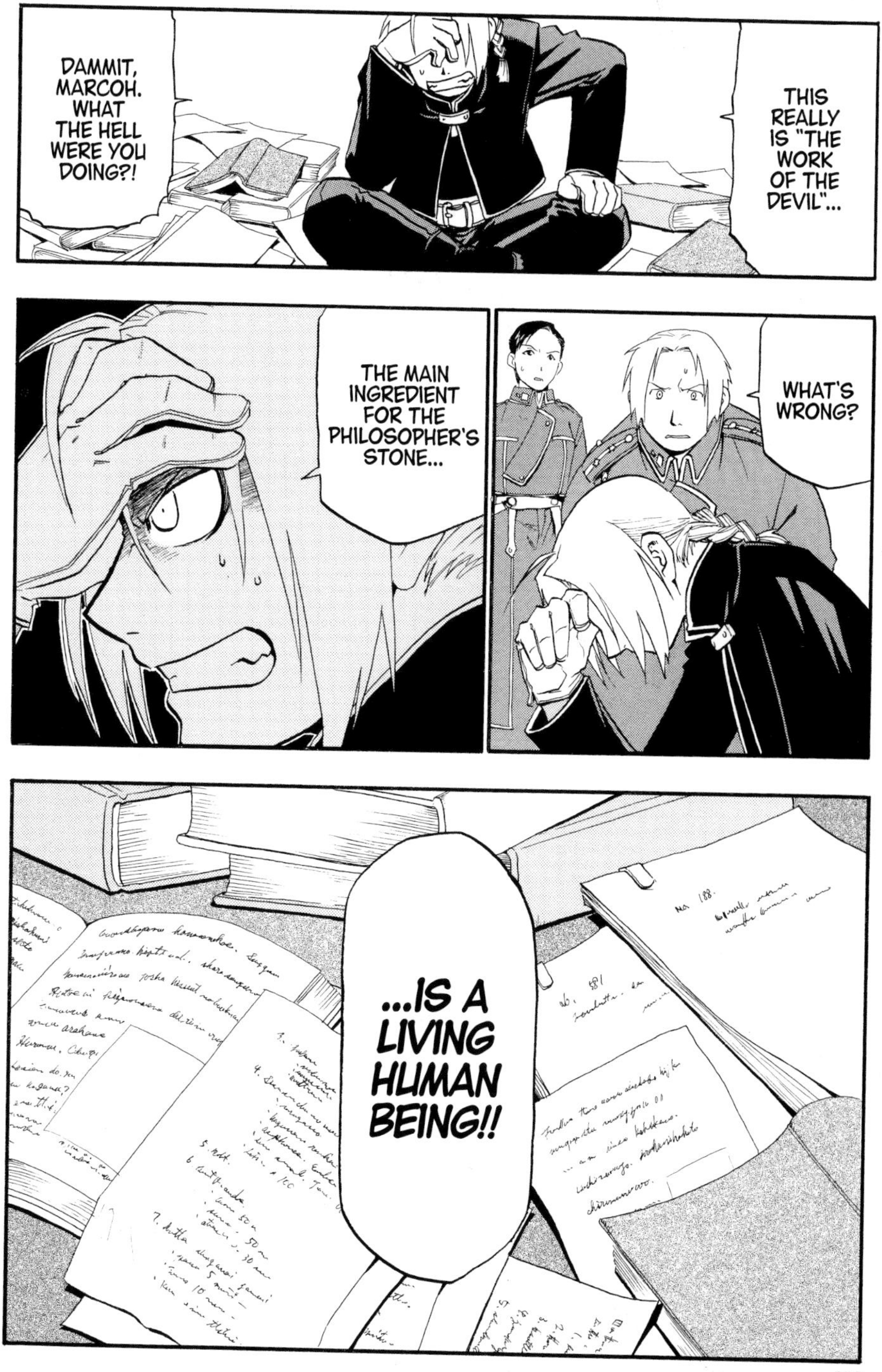
THIS REALLY IS "THE WORK OF THE DEVIL"...
DAMMIT, MARCOH. WHAT THE HELL WERE YOU DOING?!
WHAT'S WRONG?
THE MAIN INGREDIENT FOR THE PHILOSOPHER'S STONE...
...IS A LIVING HUMAN BEING!!

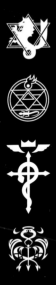

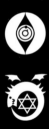

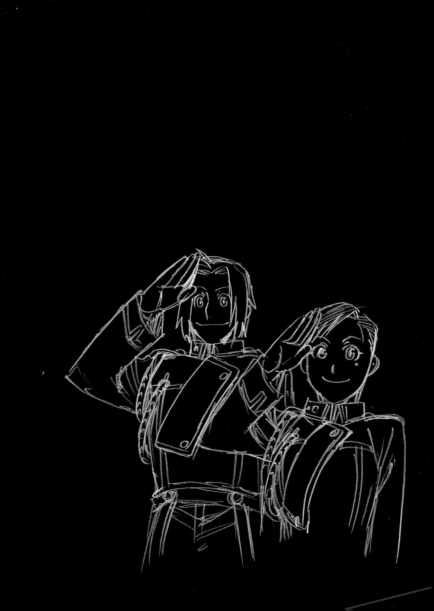

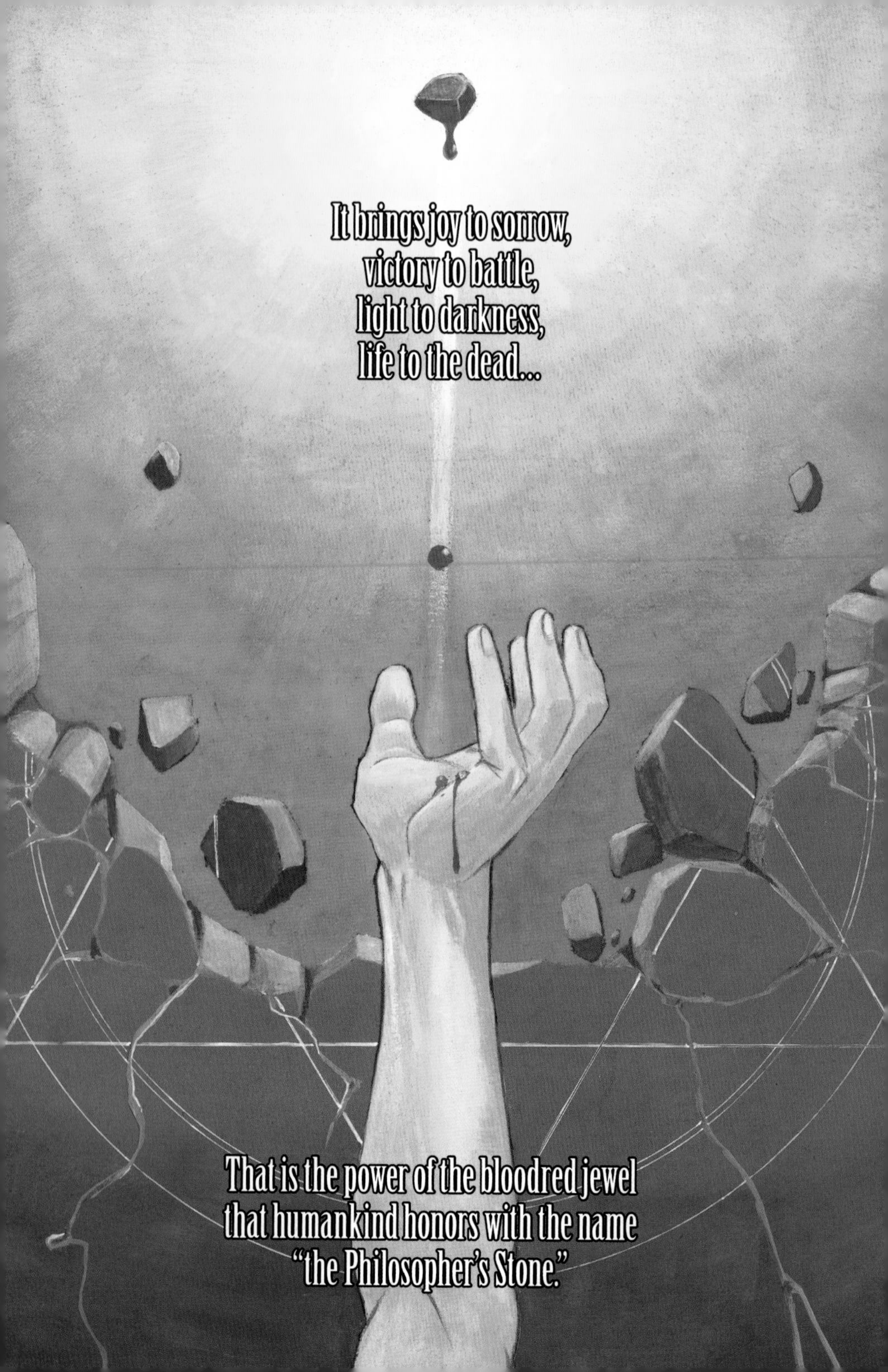
It brings joy to sorrow,
victory to battle,
light to darkness,
life to the dead...
That is the power of the bloodred jewel
that humankind honors with the name
"the Philosopher's Stone."

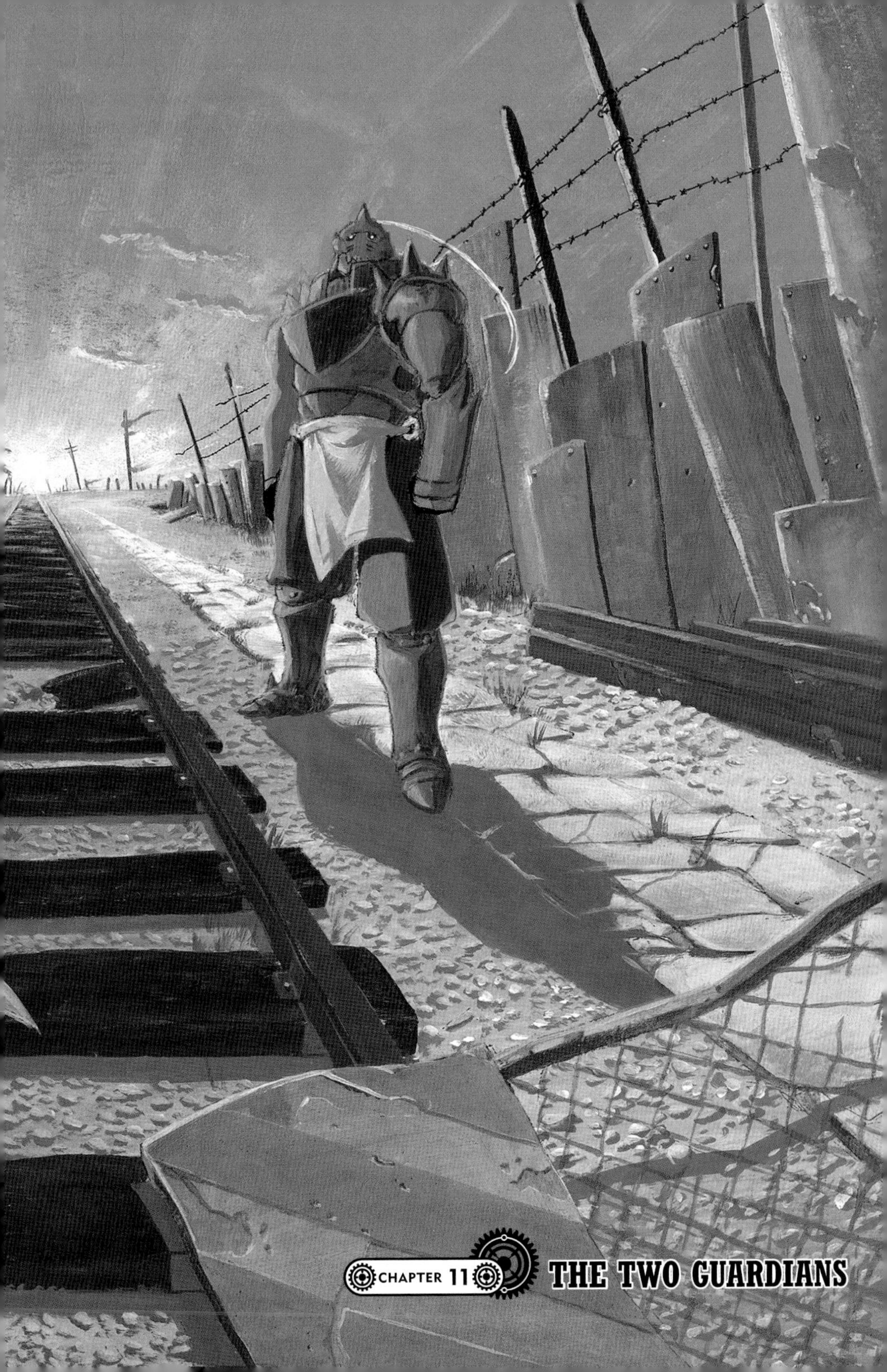
CHAPTER 11
THE TWO GUARDIANS

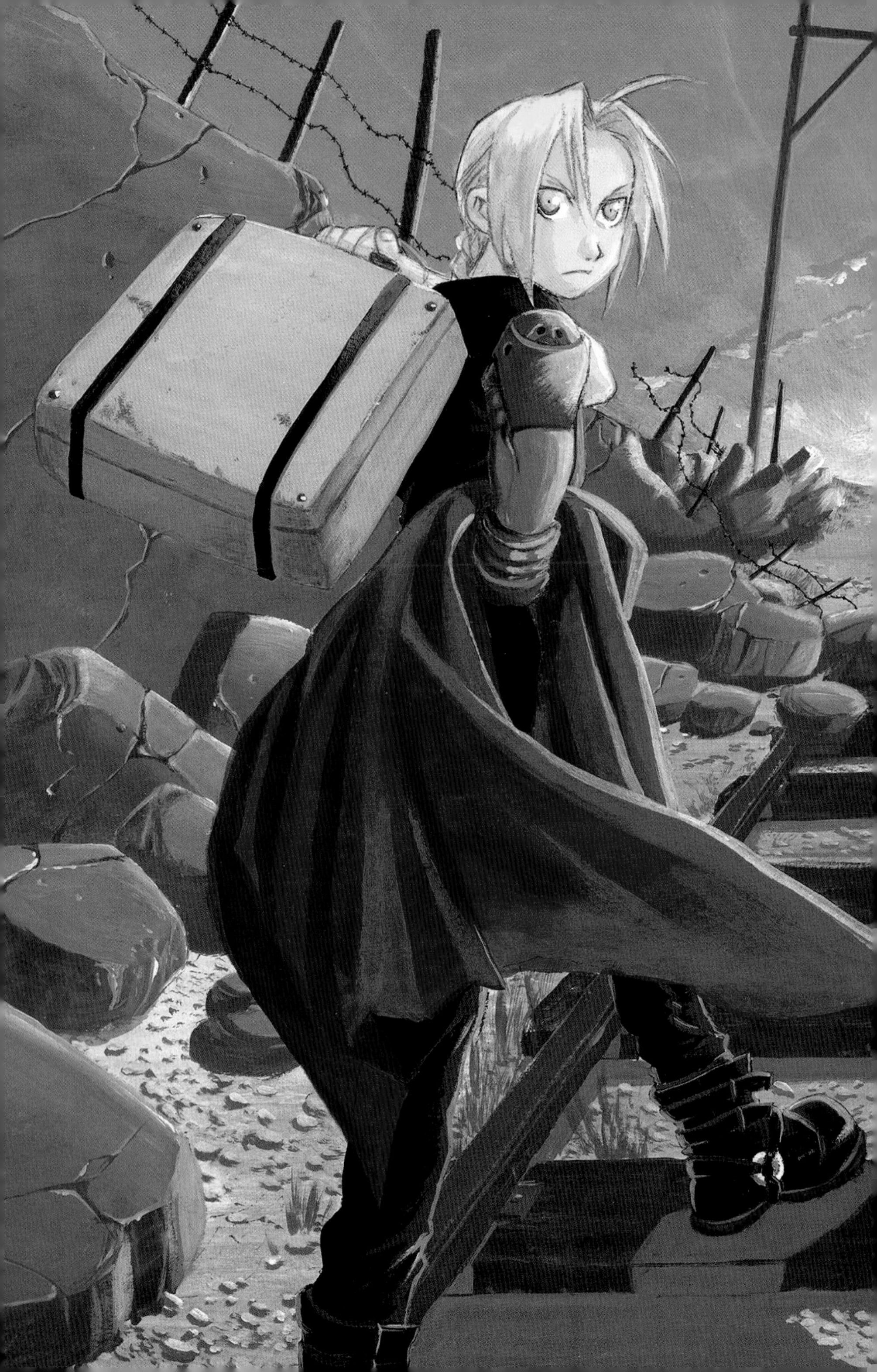

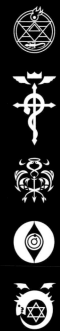

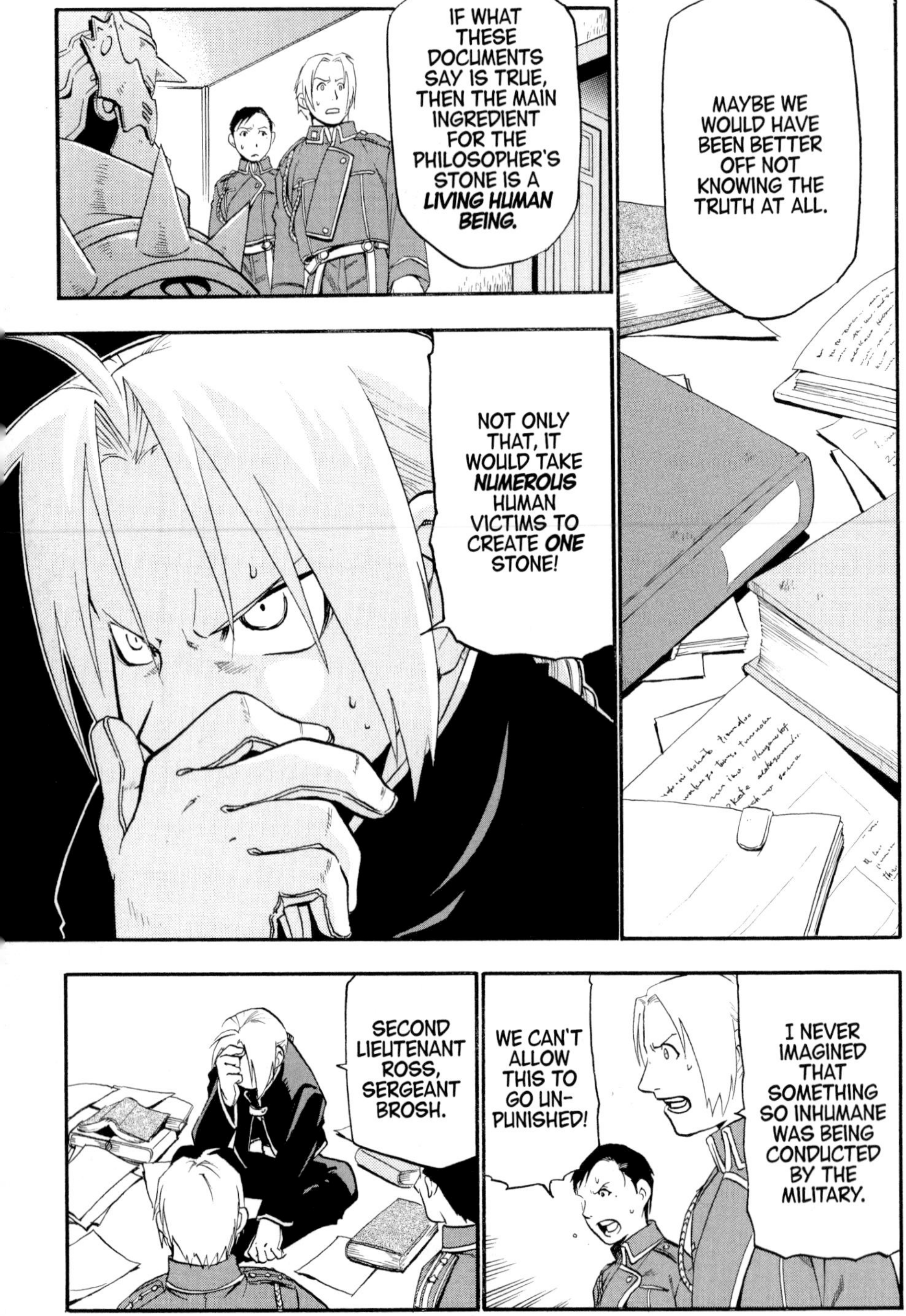
MAYBE WE WOULD HAVE BEEN BETTER OFF NOT KNOWING THE TRUTH AT ALL.
IF WHAT THESE DOCUMENTS SAY IS TRUE, THEN THE MAIN INGREDIENT FOR THE PHILOSOPHER'S STONE IS A **LIVING HUMAN BEING.**
NOT ONLY THAT, IT WOULD TAKE **NUMEROUS** HUMAN VICTIMS TO CREATE **ONE** STONE!
I NEVER IMAGINED THAT SOMETHING SO INHUMANE WAS BEING CONDUCTED BY THE MILITARY.
WE CAN'T ALLOW THIS TO GO UN-PUNISHED!
SECOND LIEUTENANT ROSS, SERGEANT BROSH.

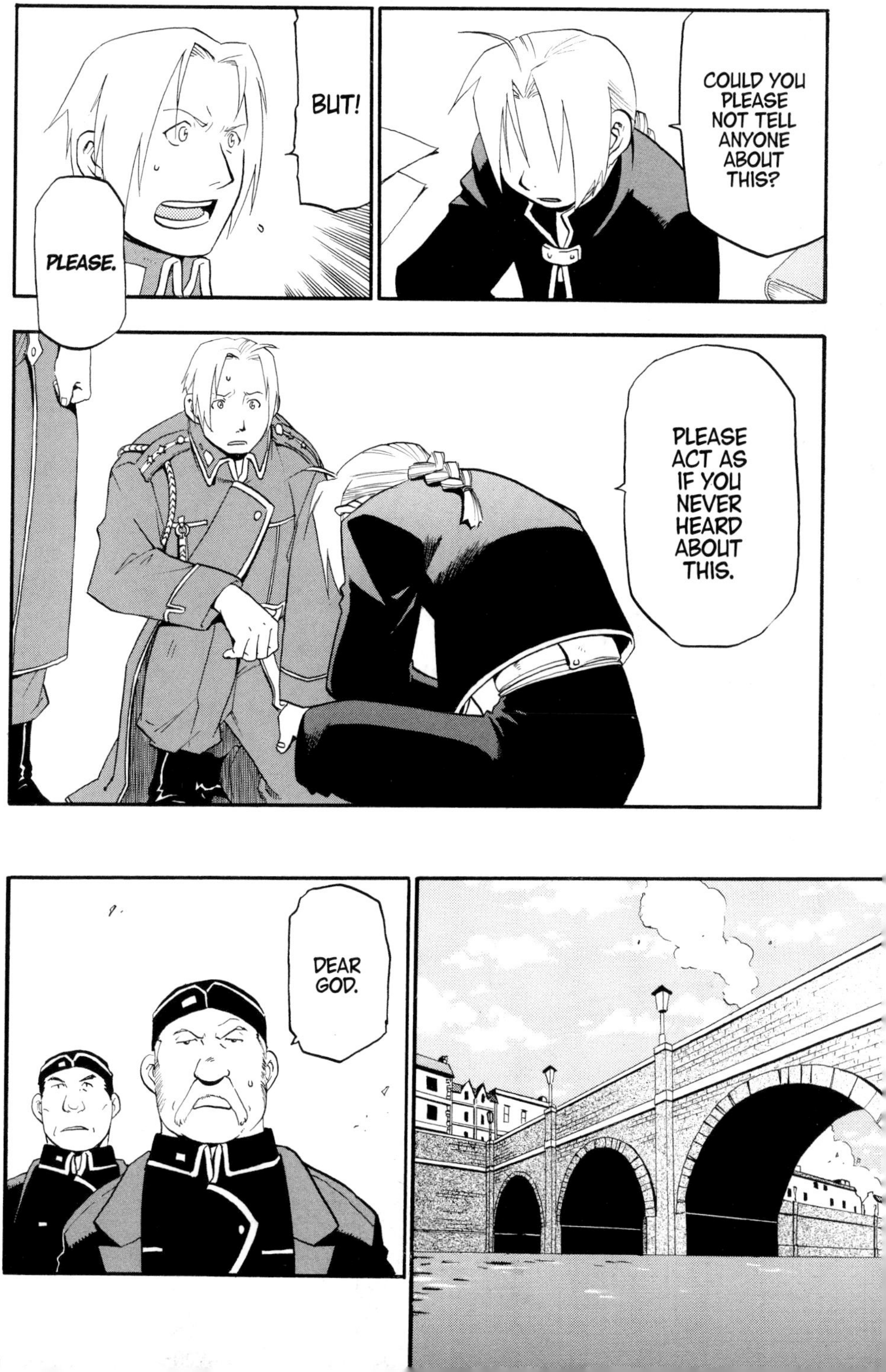
COULD YOU PLEASE NOT TELL ANYONE ABOUT THIS?
BUT!
PLEASE.
PLEASE ACT AS IF YOU NEVER HEARD ABOUT THIS.
DEAR GOD.

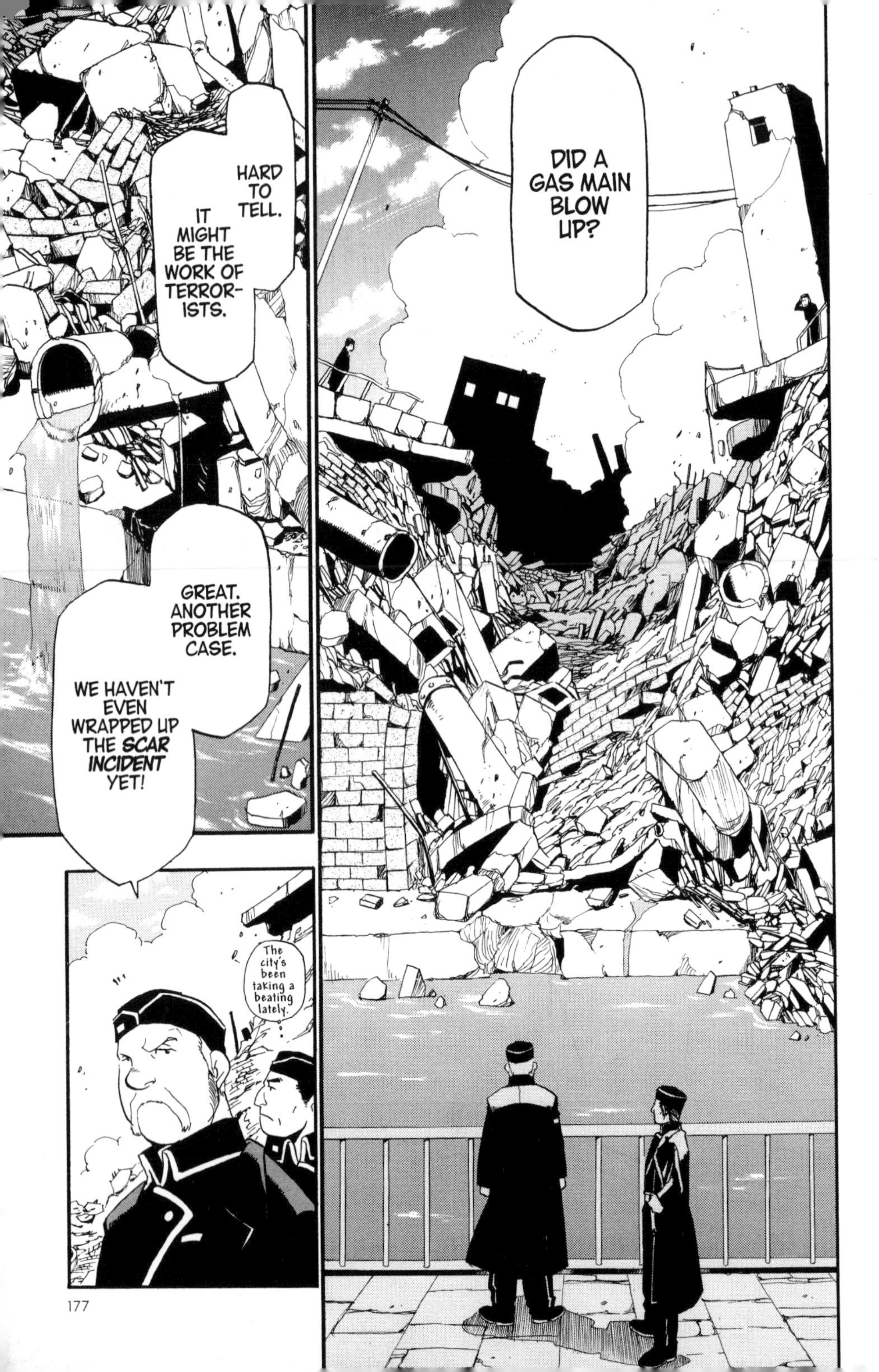
DID A GAS MAIN BLOW UP?
HARD TO TELL.
IT MIGHT BE THE WORK OF TERRORISTS.
GREAT. ANOTHER PROBLEM CASE.
WE HAVEN'T EVEN WRAPPED UP THE **SCAR INCIDENT** YET!
The city's been taking a beating lately.

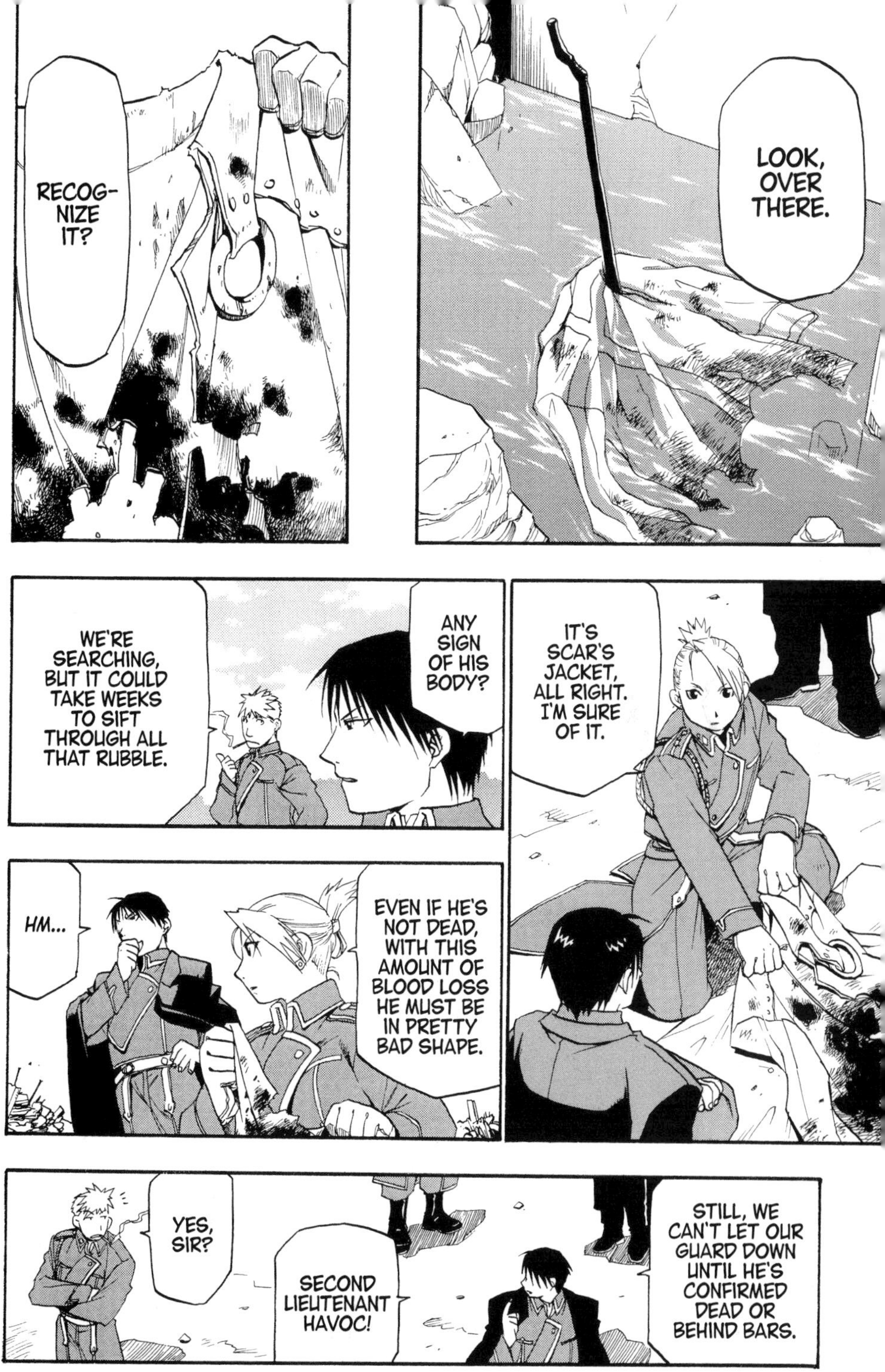
LOOK, OVER THERE.
RECOG-NIZE IT?
IT'S SCAR'S JACKET, ALL RIGHT. I'M SURE OF IT.
ANY SIGN OF HIS BODY?
WE'RE SEARCHING, BUT IT COULD TAKE WEEKS TO SIFT THROUGH ALL THAT RUBBLE.
EVEN IF HE'S NOT DEAD, WITH THIS AMOUNT OF BLOOD LOSS HE MUST BE IN PRETTY BAD SHAPE.
HM...
STILL, WE CAN'T LET OUR GUARD DOWN UNTIL HE'S CONFIRMED DEAD OR BEHIND BARS.
SECOND LIEUTENANT HAVOC!
YES, SIR?

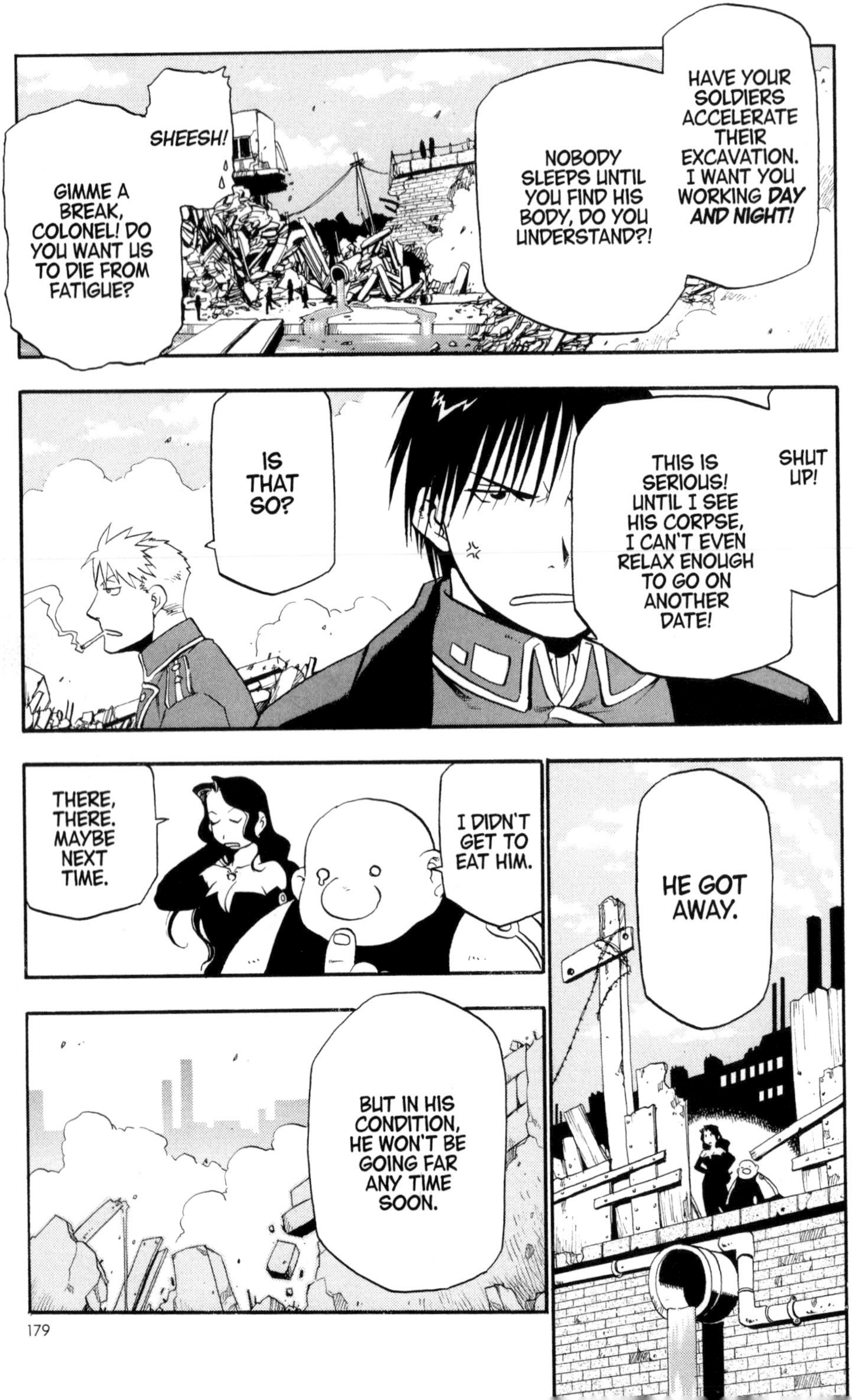

HAVE YOUR SOLDIERS ACCELERATE THEIR EXCAVATION. I WANT YOU WORKING **DAY AND NIGHT!**
NOBODY SLEEPS UNTIL YOU FIND HIS BODY, DO YOU UNDERSTAND?!
SHEESH!
GIMME A BREAK, COLONEL! DO YOU WANT US TO DIE FROM FATIGUE?
SHUT UP!
THIS IS SERIOUS! UNTIL I SEE HIS CORPSE, I CAN'T EVEN RELAX ENOUGH TO GO ON ANOTHER DATE!
IS THAT SO?
HE GOT AWAY.
I DIDN'T GET TO EAT HIM.
THERE, THERE. MAYBE NEXT TIME.
BUT IN HIS CONDITION, HE WON'T BE GOING FAR ANY TIME SOON.

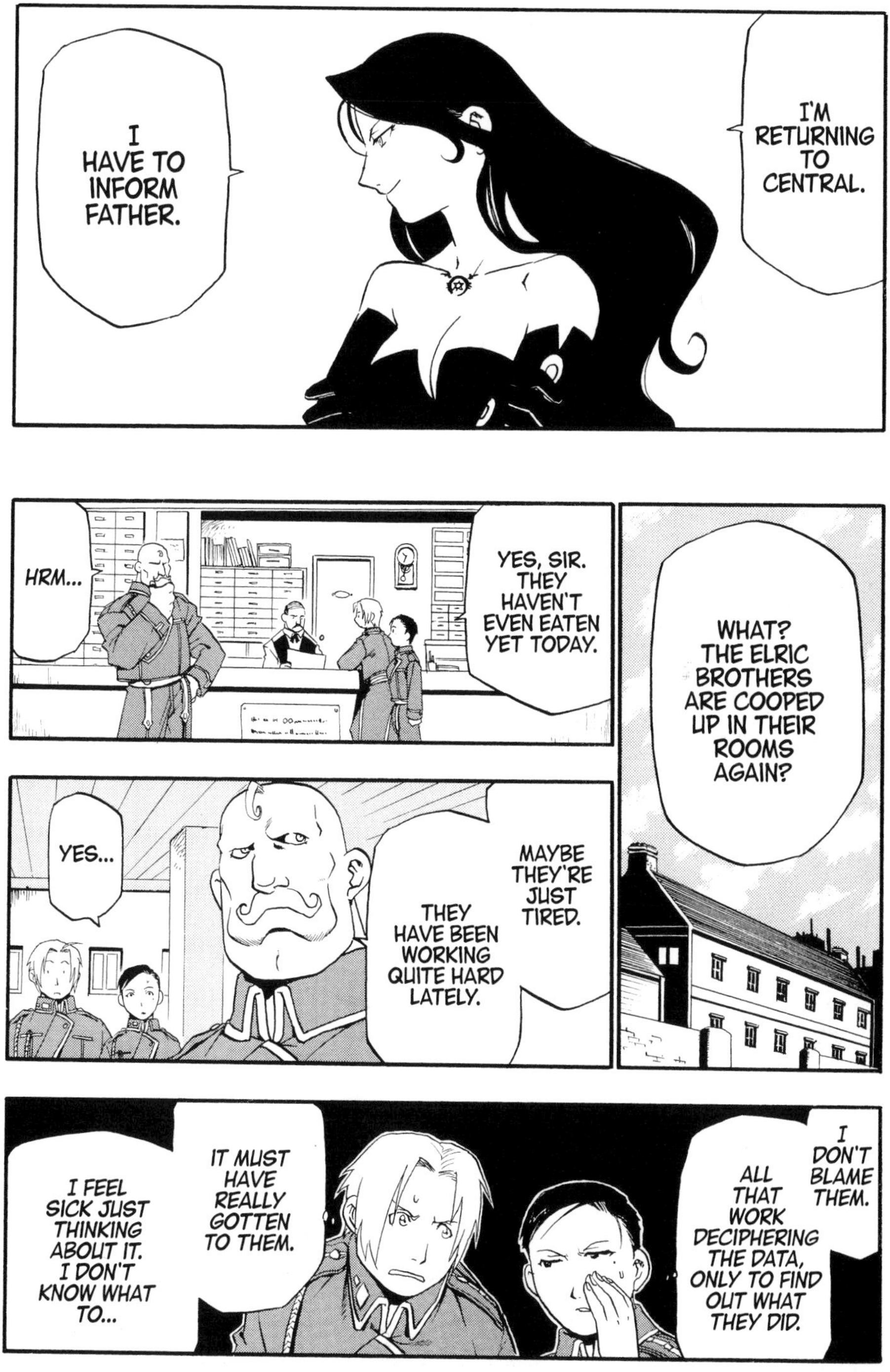
I'M RETURNING TO CENTRAL.
I HAVE TO INFORM FATHER.
WHAT? THE ELRIC BROTHERS ARE COOPED UP IN THEIR ROOMS AGAIN?
YES, SIR. THEY HAVEN'T EVEN EATEN YET TODAY.
HRM...
MAYBE THEY'RE JUST TIRED.
THEY HAVE BEEN WORKING QUITE HARD LATELY.
YES...
I DON'T BLAME THEM.
ALL THAT WORK DECIPHERING THE DATA, ONLY TO FIND OUT WHAT THEY DID.
IT MUST HAVE REALLY GOTTEN TO THEM.
I FEEL SICK JUST THINKING ABOUT IT. I DON'T KNOW WHAT TO...

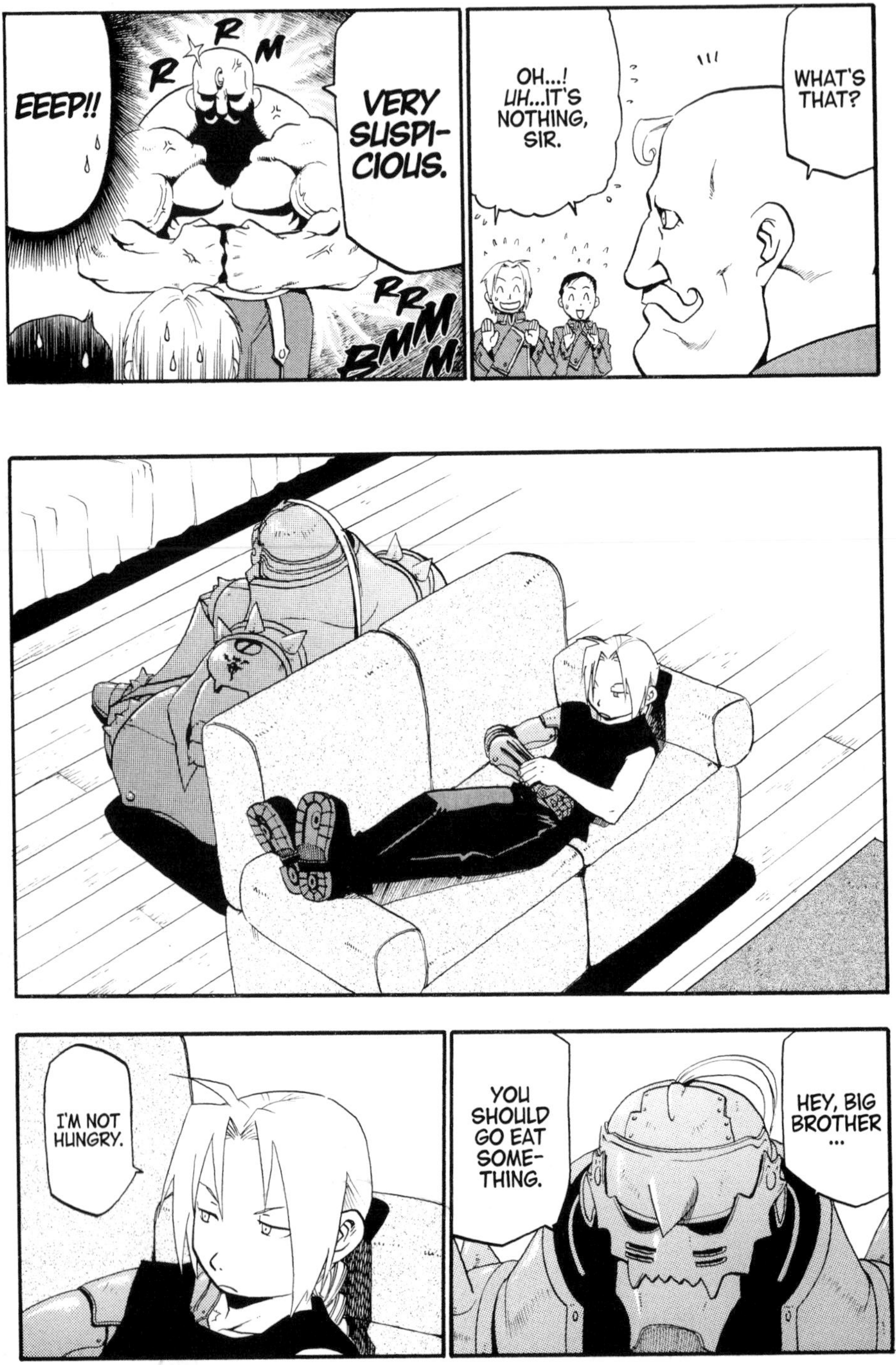
WHAT'S THAT?
OH...! UH...IT'S NOTHING, SIR.
VERY SUSPICIOUS.
RRM
EEEP!!
RRM BMMM
HEY, BIG BROTHER ...
YOU SHOULD GO EAT SOMETHING.
I'M NOT HUNGRY.

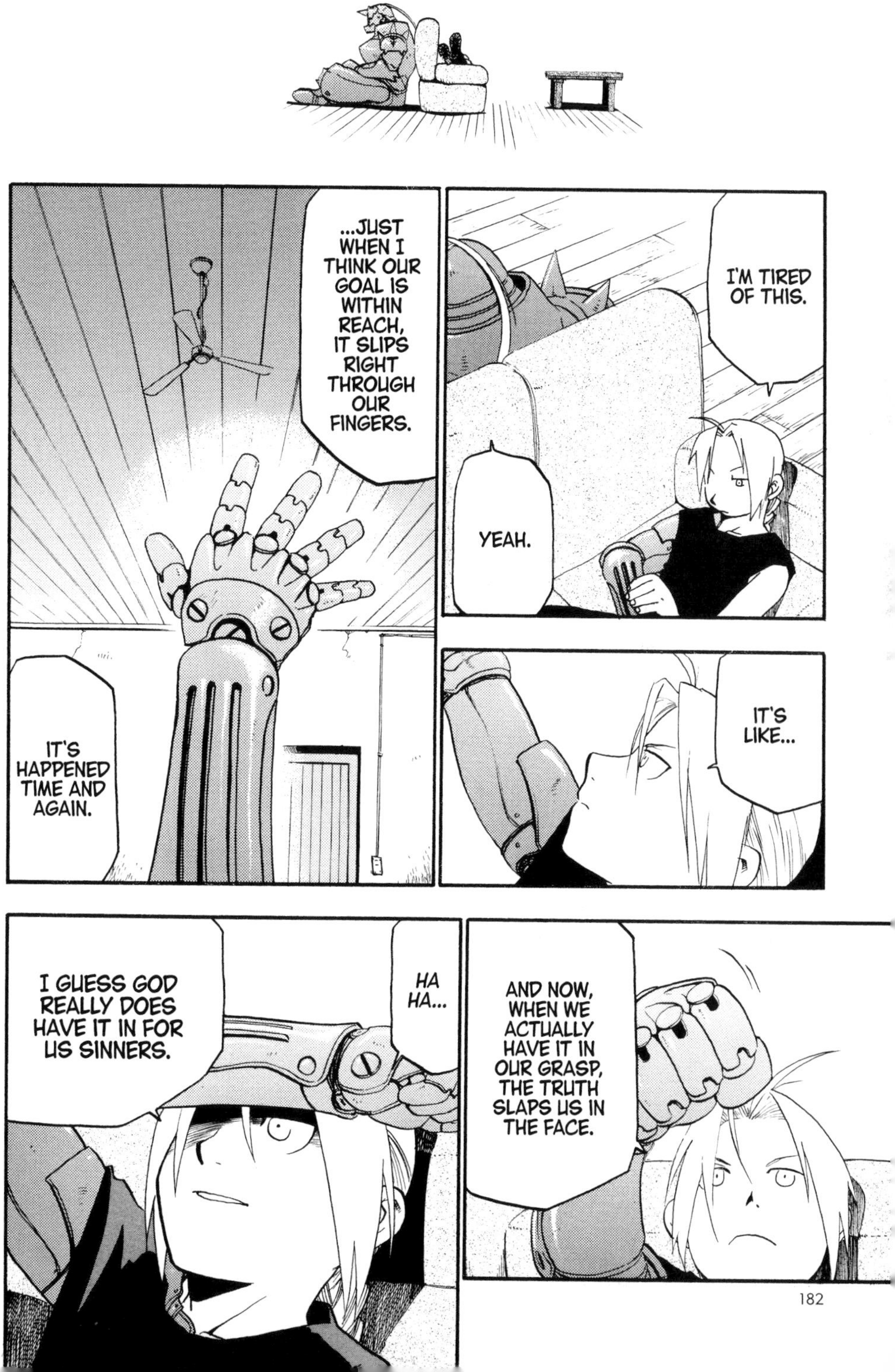
I'M TIRED OF THIS.
YEAH.
IT'S LIKE...
...JUST WHEN I THINK OUR GOAL IS WITHIN REACH, IT SLIPS RIGHT THROUGH OUR FINGERS.
IT'S HAPPENED TIME AND AGAIN.
AND NOW, WHEN WE ACTUALLY HAVE IT IN OUR GRASP, THE TRUTH SLAPS US IN THE FACE.
HA HA...
I GUESS GOD REALLY DOES HAVE IT IN FOR US SINNERS.

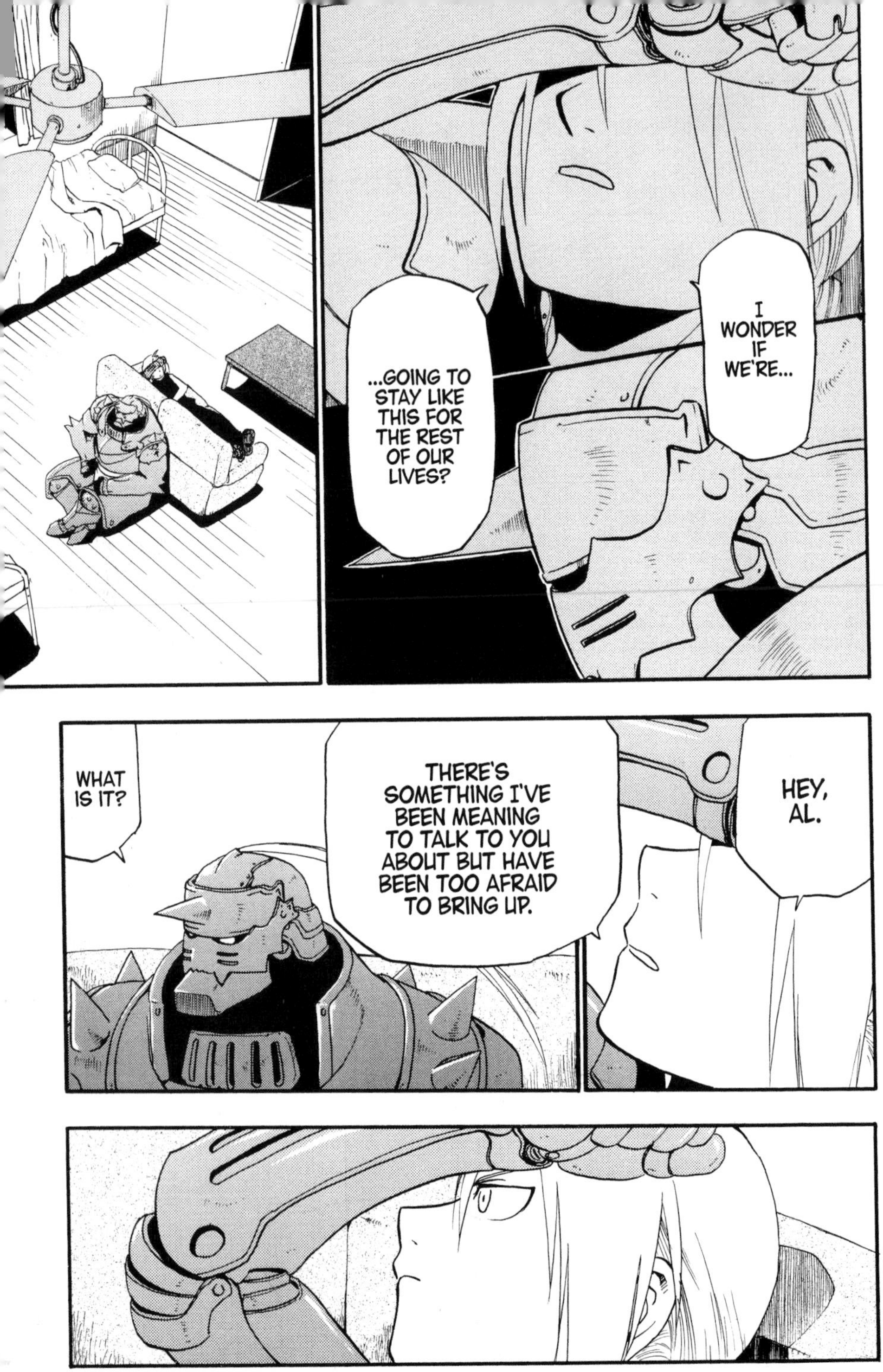
I WONDER IF WE'RE...
...GOING TO STAY LIKE THIS FOR THE REST OF OUR LIVES?
HEY, AL.
THERE'S SOMETHING I'VE BEEN MEANING TO TALK TO YOU ABOUT BUT HAVE BEEN TOO AFRAID TO BRING UP.
WHAT IS IT?

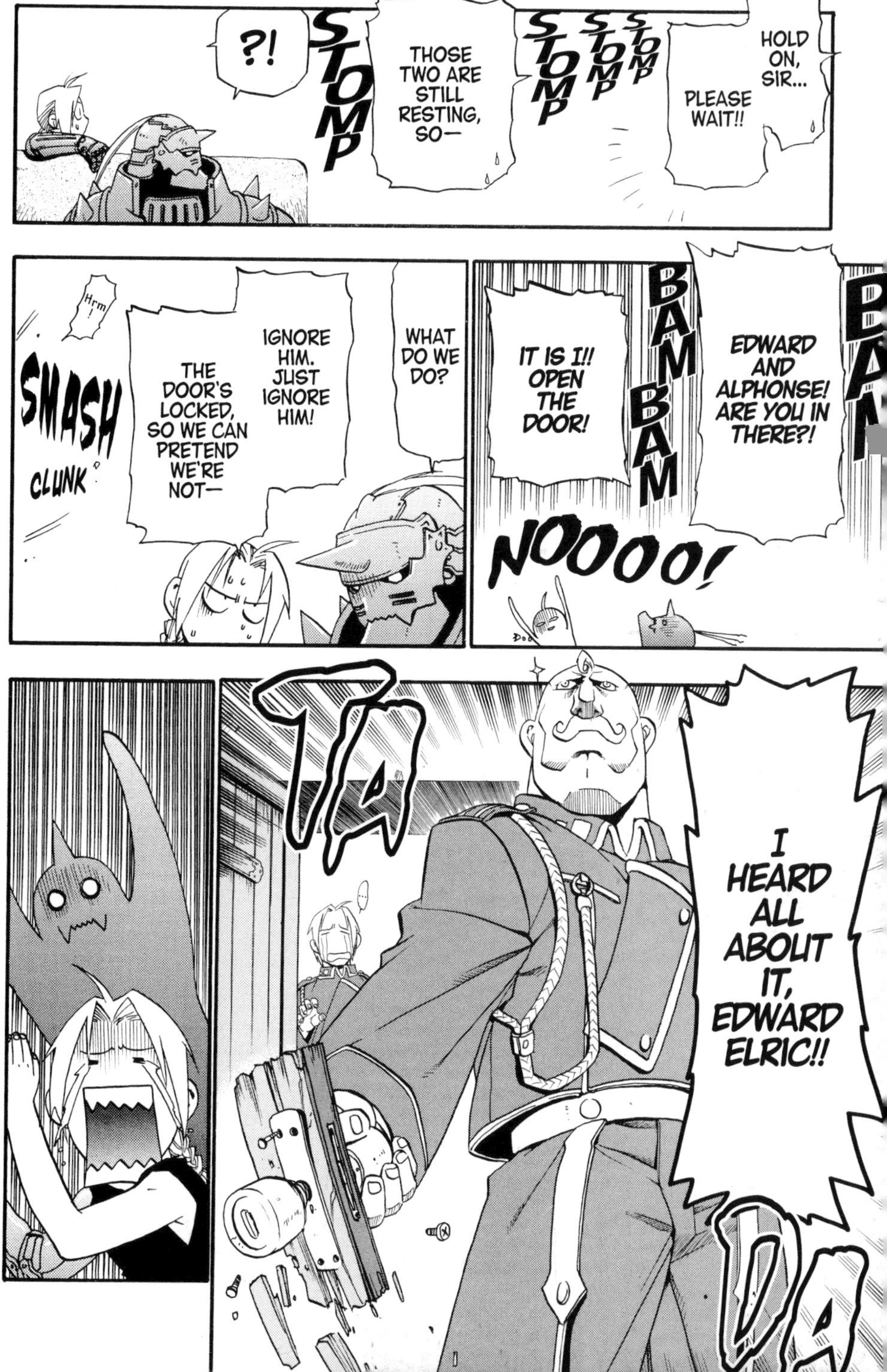
HOLD ON, SIR...
PLEASE WAIT!!
STOMP
STOMP
STOMP
THOSE TWO ARE STILL RESTING, SO—
STOMP
?!
BAM
EDWARD AND ALPHONSE! ARE YOU IN THERE?!
BAM
BAM
IT IS I!! OPEN THE DOOR!
NOOOOO!
WHAT DO WE DO?
IGNORE HIM. JUST IGNORE HIM!
THE DOOR'S LOCKED, SO WE CAN PRETEND WE'RE NOT—
Hrm!
SMASH
CLUNK
TA
I HEARD ALL ABOUT IT, EDWARD ELRIC!!
DA

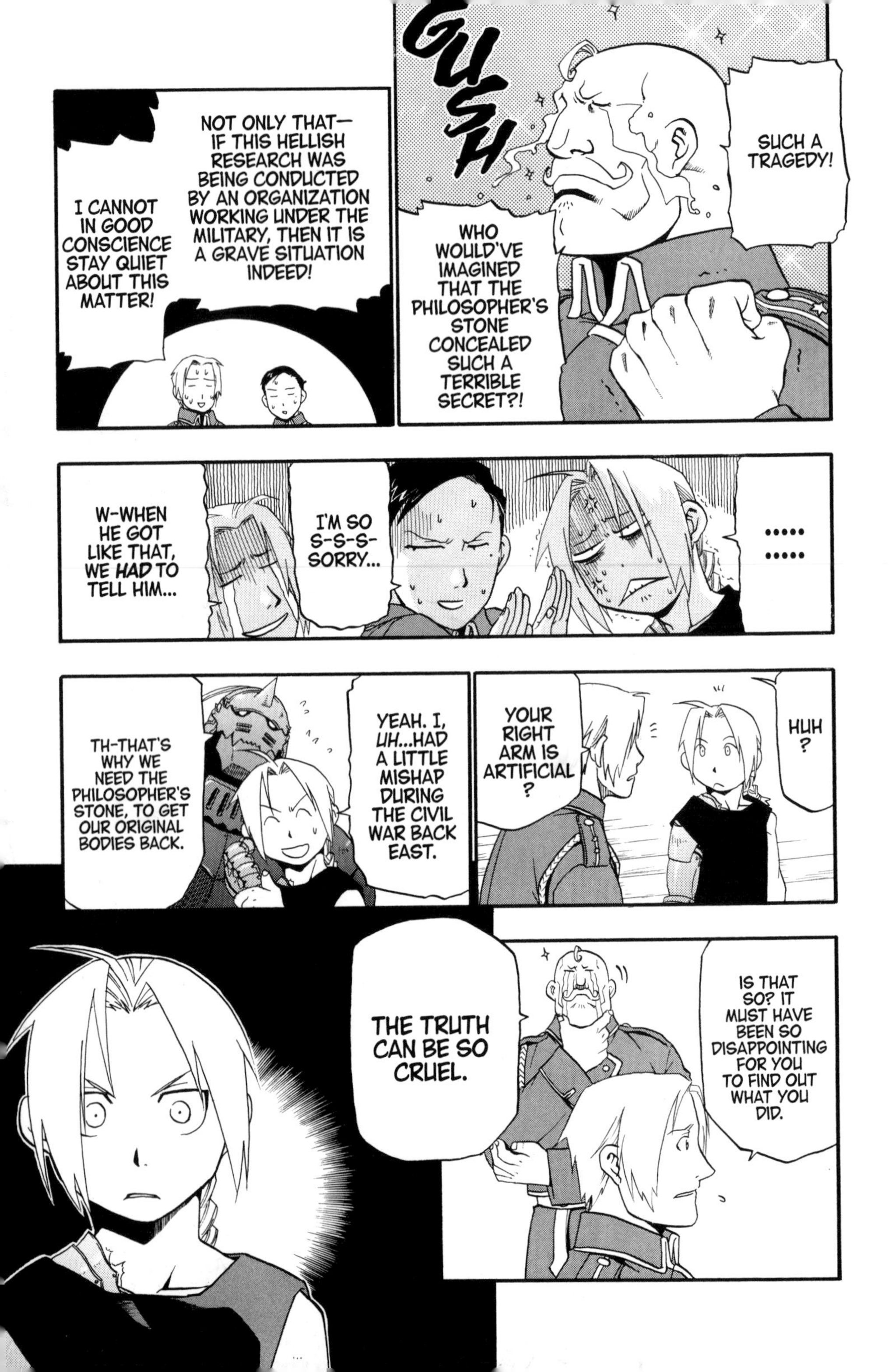
GUSH
SUCH A TRAGEDY!
WHO WOULD'VE IMAGINED THAT THE PHILOSOPHER'S STONE CONCEALED SUCH A TERRIBLE SECRET?!
NOT ONLY THAT— IF THIS HELLISH RESEARCH WAS BEING CONDUCTED BY AN ORGANIZATION WORKING UNDER THE MILITARY, THEN IT IS A GRAVE SITUATION INDEED!
I CANNOT IN GOOD CONSCIENCE STAY QUIET ABOUT THIS MATTER!
....
I'M SO S-S-S-SORRY...
W-WHEN HE GOT LIKE THAT, WE **HAD** TO TELL HIM...
HUH?
YOUR RIGHT ARM IS ARTIFICIAL?
YEAH. I, UH...HAD A LITTLE MISHAP DURING THE CIVIL WAR BACK EAST.
TH-THAT'S WHY WE NEED THE PHILOSOPHER'S STONE, TO GET OUR ORIGINAL BODIES BACK.
IS THAT SO? IT MUST HAVE BEEN SO DISAPPOINTING FOR YOU TO FIND OUT WHAT YOU DID.
THE TRUTH CAN BE SO CRUEL.

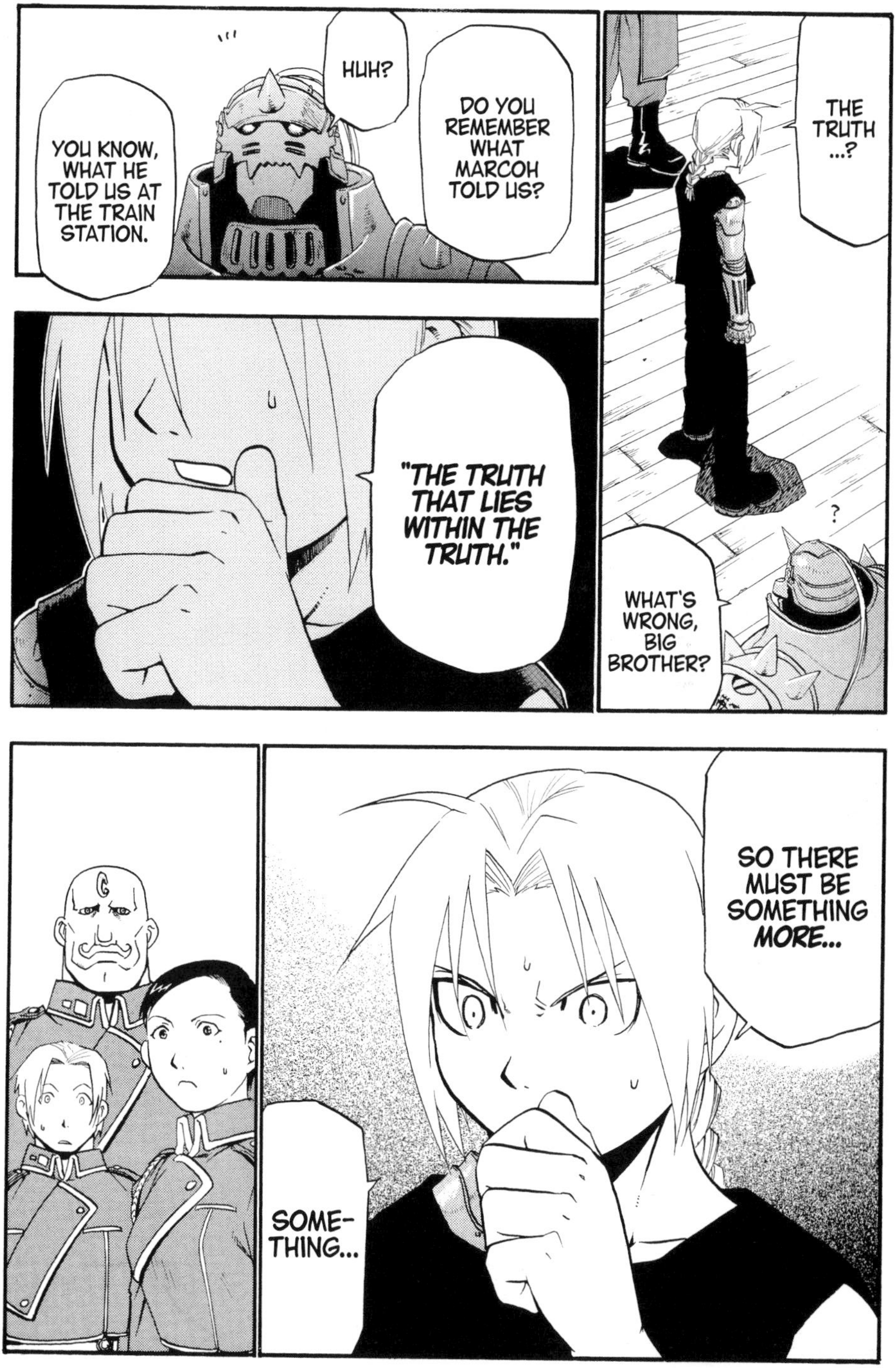
THE TRUTH ...?
WHAT'S WRONG, BIG BROTHER?
HUH?
DO YOU REMEMBER WHAT MARCOH TOLD US?
YOU KNOW, WHAT HE TOLD US AT THE TRAIN STATION.
"THE TRUTH THAT LIES WITHIN THE TRUTH."
SO THERE MUST BE SOMETHING MORE...
SOME-THING...

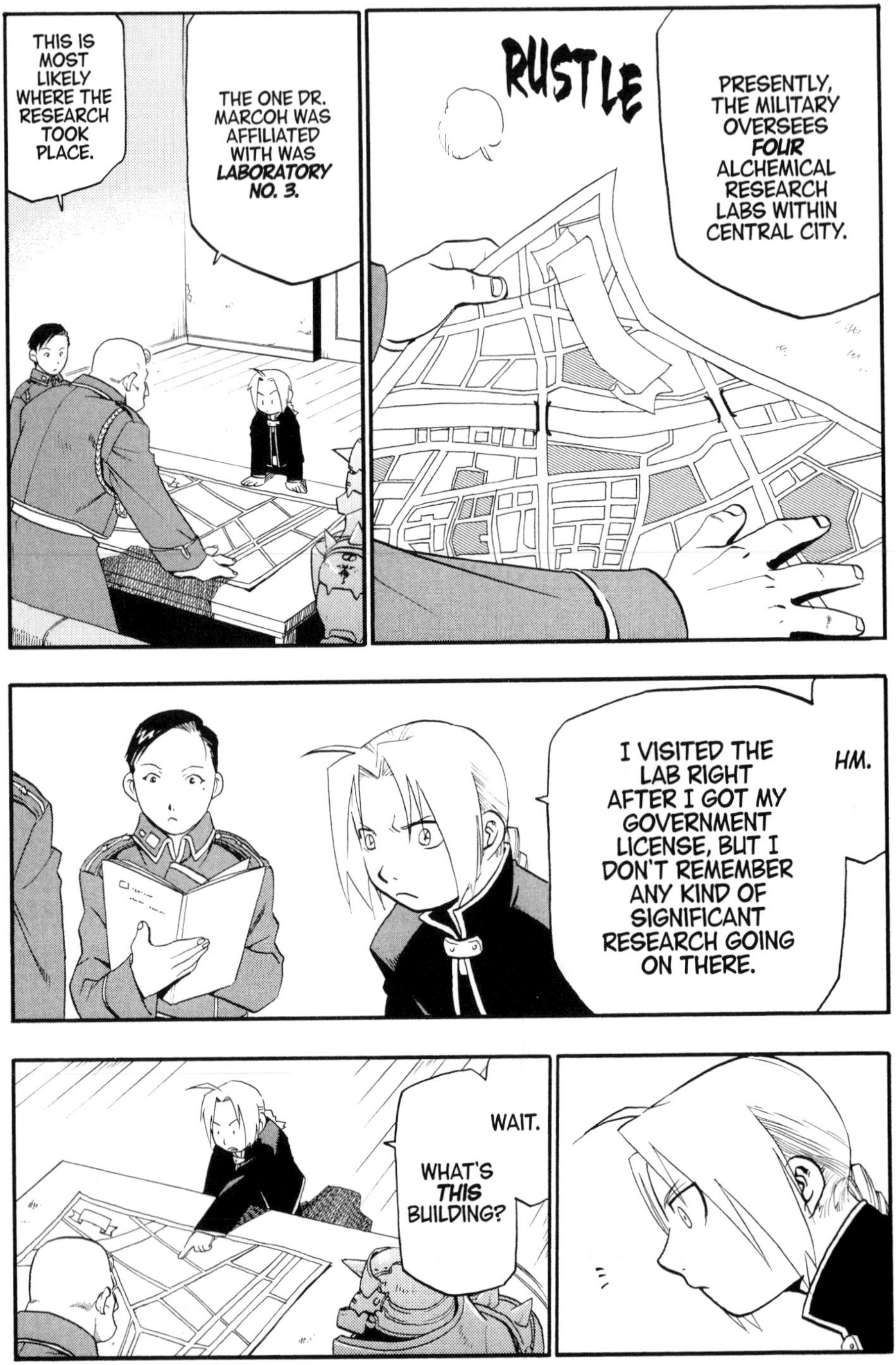
RUSTLE
PRESENTLY, THE MILITARY OVERSEES **FOUR** ALCHEMICAL RESEARCH LABS WITHIN CENTRAL CITY.
THE ONE DR. MARCOH WAS AFFILIATED WITH WAS ***LABORATORY NO. 3.***
THIS IS MOST LIKELY WHERE THE RESEARCH TOOK PLACE.
HM.
I VISITED THE LAB RIGHT AFTER I GOT MY GOVERNMENT LICENSE, BUT I DON'T REMEMBER ANY KIND OF SIGNIFICANT RESEARCH GOING ON THERE.
WAIT.
WHAT'S ***THIS*** BUILDING?

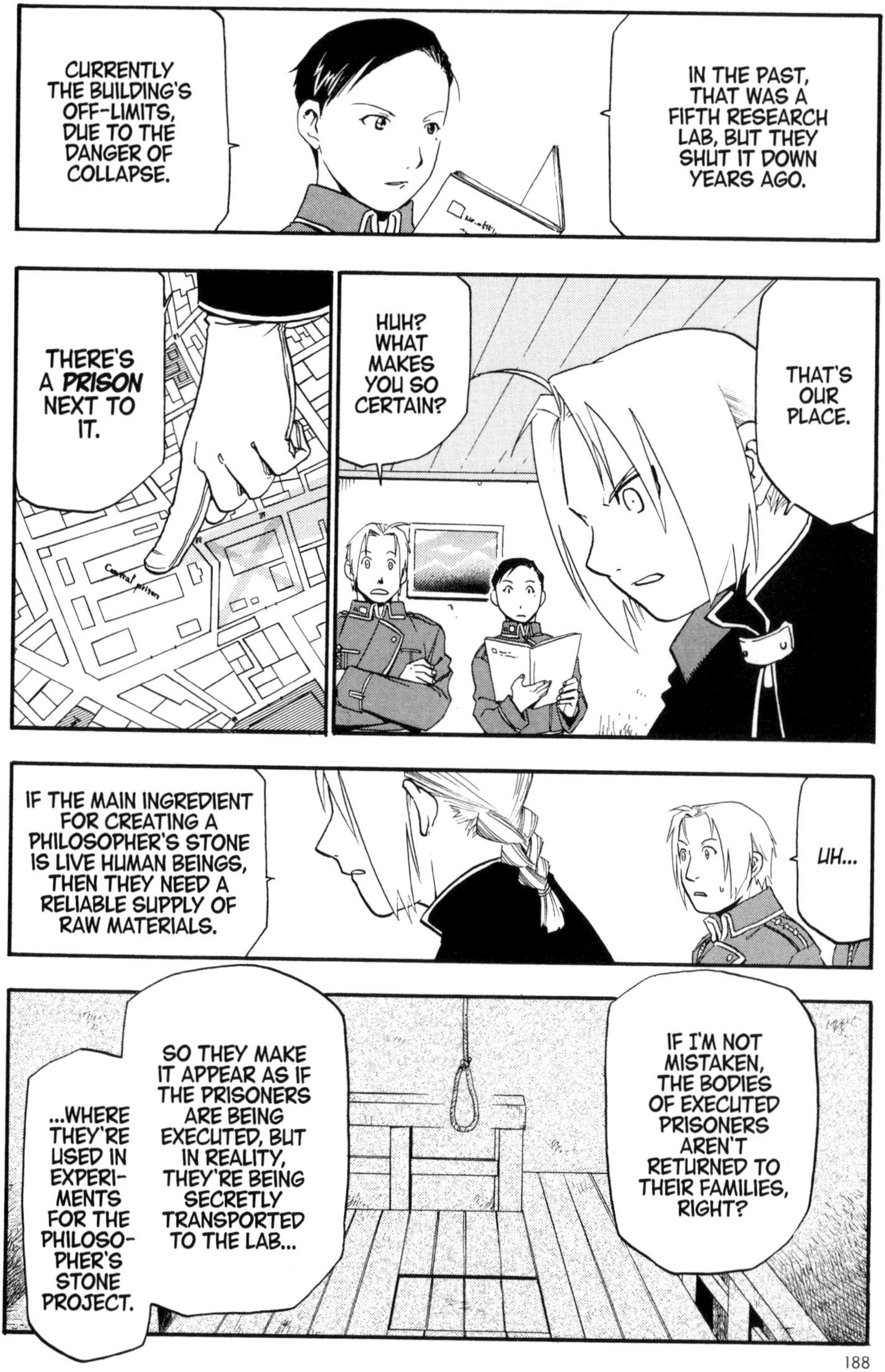
IN THE PAST, THAT WAS A FIFTH RESEARCH LAB, BUT THEY SHUT IT DOWN YEARS AGO.
CURRENTLY THE BUILDING'S OFF-LIMITS, DUE TO THE DANGER OF COLLAPSE.
THAT'S OUR PLACE.
HUH? WHAT MAKES YOU SO CERTAIN?
THERE'S A **PRISON** NEXT TO IT.
Central prison
UH...
IF THE MAIN INGREDIENT FOR CREATING A PHILOSOPHER'S STONE IS LIVE HUMAN BEINGS, THEN THEY NEED A RELIABLE SUPPLY OF RAW MATERIALS.
IF I'M NOT MISTAKEN, THE BODIES OF EXECUTED PRISONERS AREN'T RETURNED TO THEIR FAMILIES, RIGHT?
SO THEY MAKE IT APPEAR AS IF THE PRISONERS ARE BEING EXECUTED, BUT IN REALITY, THEY'RE BEING SECRETLY TRANSPORTED TO THE LAB...
...WHERE THEY'RE USED IN EXPERIMENTS FOR THE PHILOSOPHER'S STONE PROJECT.

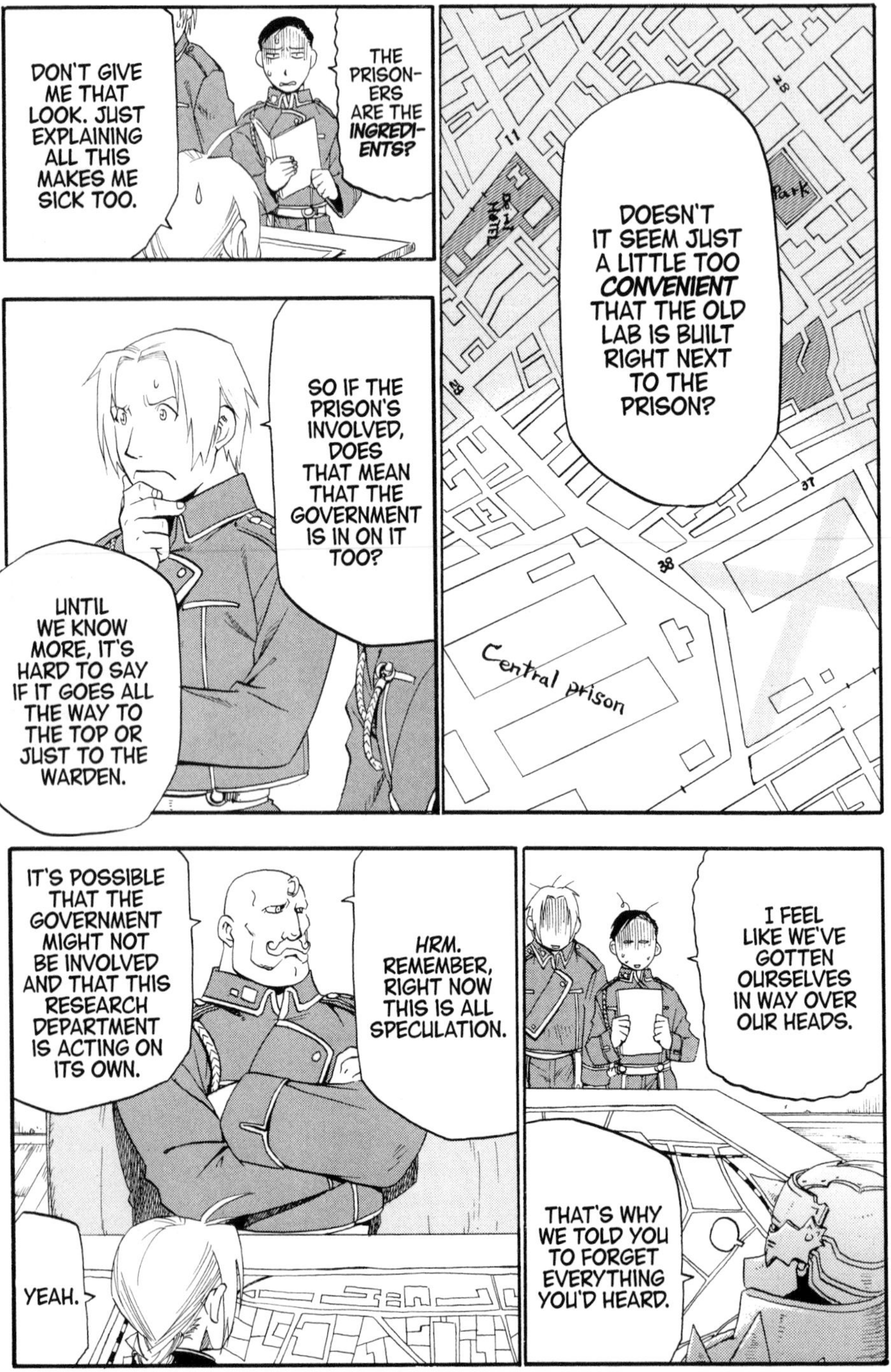

DOESN'T IT SEEM JUST A LITTLE TOO **CONVENIENT** THAT THE OLD LAB IS BUILT RIGHT NEXT TO THE PRISON?
28
11
Park
29
37
38
Central prison
THE PRISONERS ARE THE ***INGREDIENTS?***
DON'T GIVE ME THAT LOOK. JUST EXPLAINING ALL THIS MAKES ME SICK TOO.
SO IF THE PRISON'S INVOLVED, DOES THAT MEAN THAT THE GOVERNMENT IS IN ON IT TOO?
UNTIL WE KNOW MORE, IT'S HARD TO SAY IF IT GOES ALL THE WAY TO THE TOP OR JUST TO THE WARDEN.
I FEEL LIKE WE'VE GOTTEN OURSELVES IN WAY OVER OUR HEADS.
THAT'S WHY WE TOLD YOU TO FORGET EVERYTHING YOU'D HEARD.
HRM. REMEMBER, RIGHT NOW THIS IS ALL SPECULATION.
IT'S POSSIBLE THAT THE GOVERNMENT MIGHT NOT BE INVOLVED AND THAT THIS RESEARCH DEPARTMENT IS ACTING ON ITS OWN.
YEAH.

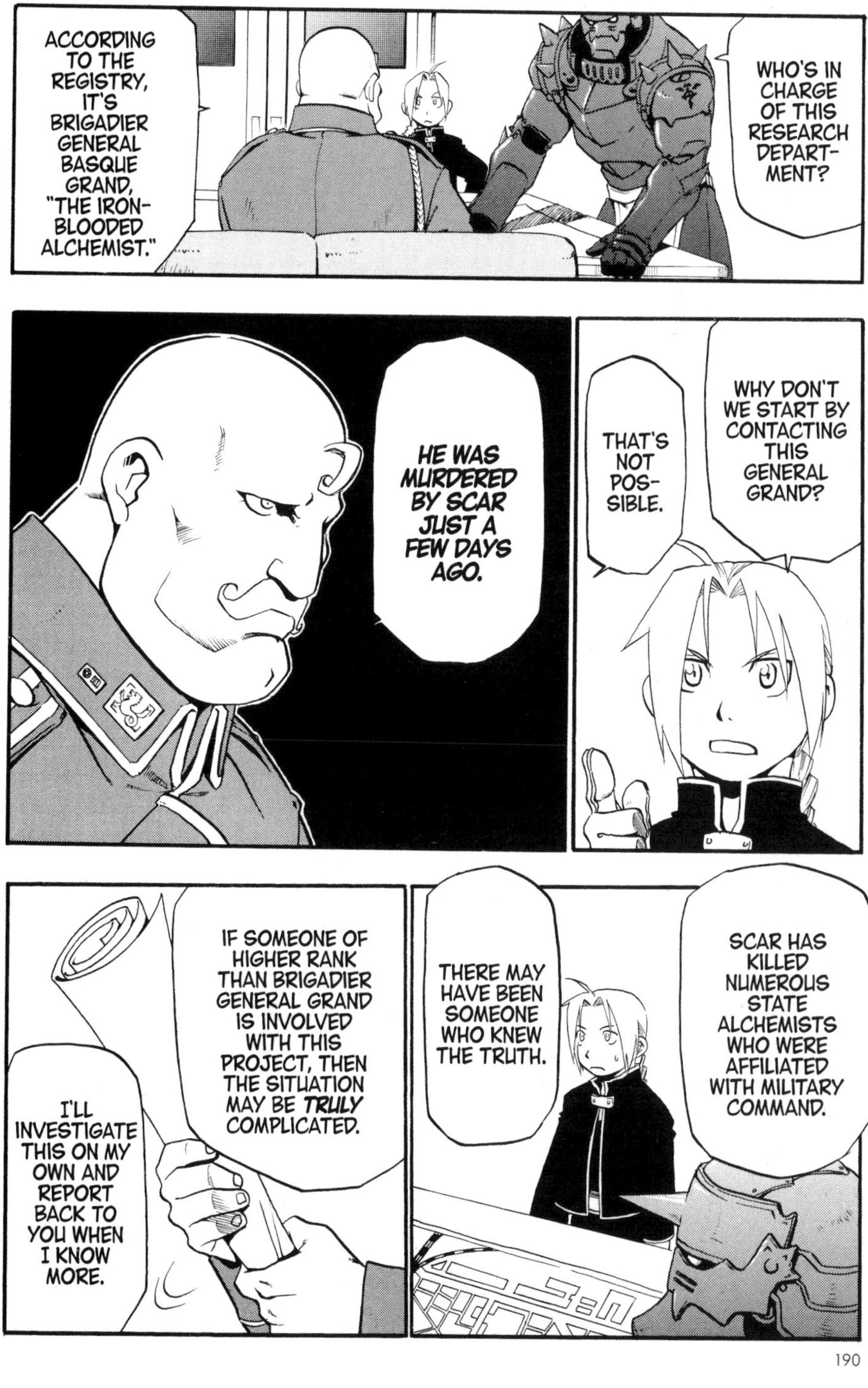

WHO'S IN CHARGE OF THIS RESEARCH DEPART-MENT?
ACCORDING TO THE REGISTRY, IT'S BRIGADIER GENERAL BASQUE GRAND, "THE IRON-BLOODED ALCHEMIST."
WHY DON'T WE START BY CONTACTING THIS GENERAL GRAND?
THAT'S NOT POS-SIBLE.
HE WAS MURDERED BY SCAR JUST A FEW DAYS AGO.
SCAR HAS KILLED NUMEROUS STATE ALCHEMISTS WHO WERE AFFILIATED WITH MILITARY COMMAND.
THERE MAY HAVE BEEN SOMEONE WHO KNEW THE TRUTH.
IF SOMEONE OF HIGHER RANK THAN BRIGADIER GENERAL GRAND IS INVOLVED WITH THIS PROJECT, THEN THE SITUATION MAY BE *TRULY* COMPLICATED.
I'LL INVESTIGATE THIS ON MY OWN AND REPORT BACK TO YOU WHEN I KNOW MORE.

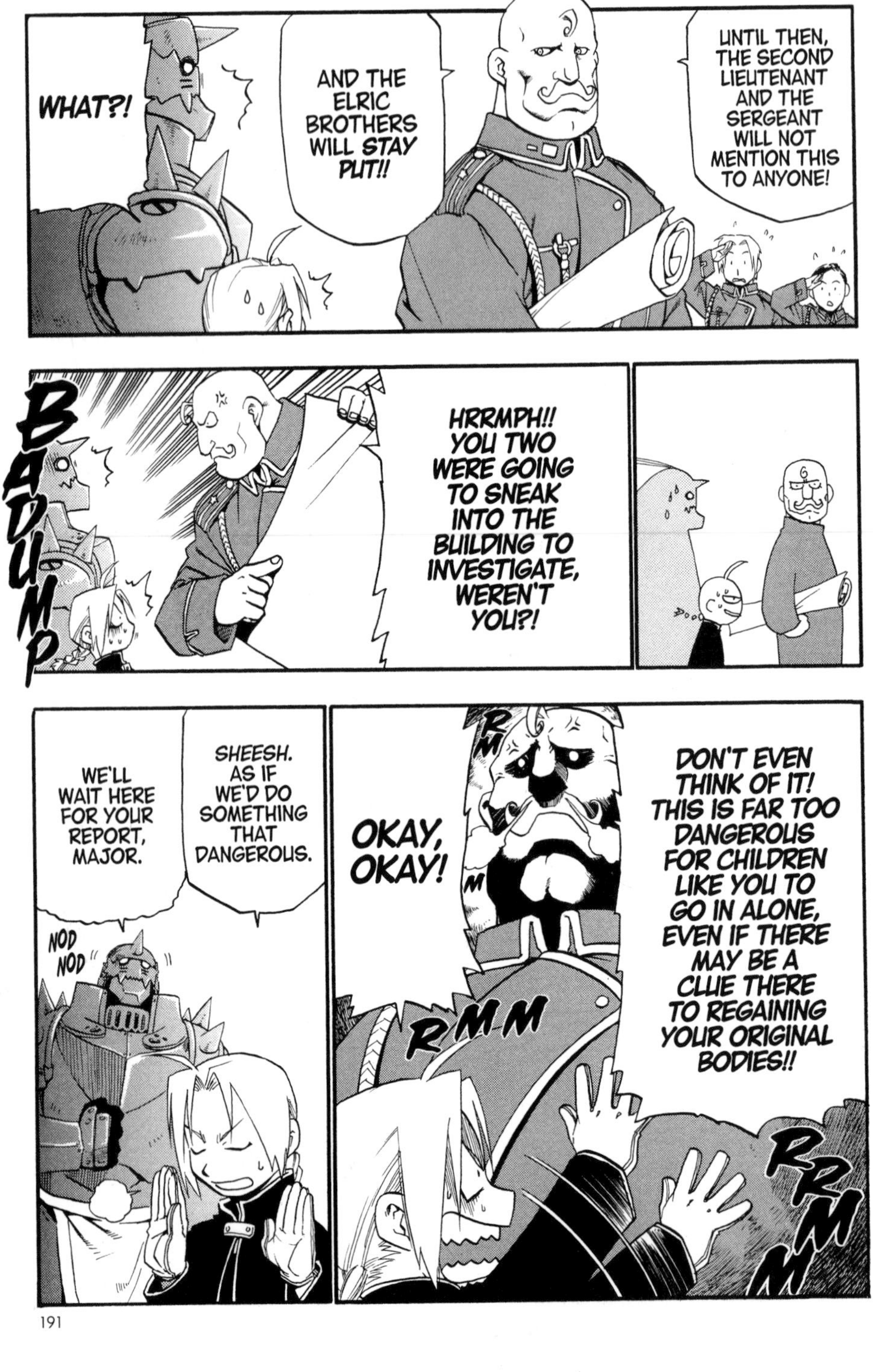
UNTIL THEN, THE SECOND LIEUTENANT AND THE SERGEANT WILL NOT MENTION THIS TO ANYONE!
AND THE ELRIC BROTHERS WILL STAY PUT!!
WHAT?!
HRRMPH!! YOU TWO WERE GOING TO SNEAK INTO THE BUILDING TO INVESTIGATE, WEREN'T YOU?!
BADUMP
DON'T EVEN THINK OF IT! THIS IS FAR TOO DANGEROUS FOR CHILDREN LIKE YOU TO GO IN ALONE, EVEN IF THERE MAY BE A CLUE THERE TO REGAINING YOUR ORIGINAL BODIES!!
RMM
RMM
RRMM
OKAY, OKAY!
SHEESH. AS IF WE'D DO SOMETHING THAT DANGEROUS.
WE'LL WAIT HERE FOR YOUR REPORT, MAJOR.
NOD NOD

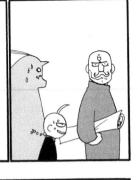

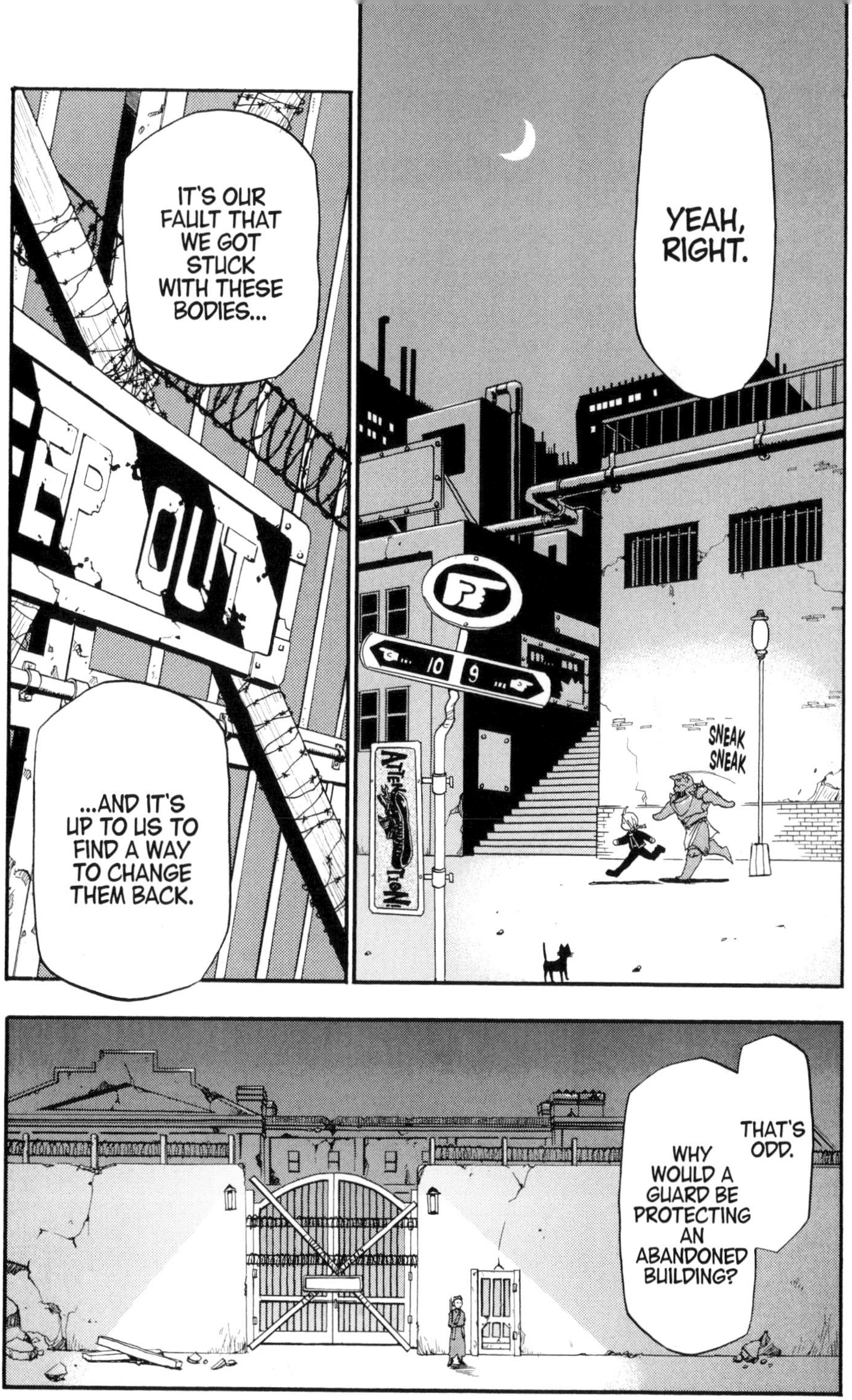
YEAH, RIGHT.
SNEAK SNEAK
IT'S OUR FAULT THAT WE GOT STUCK WITH THESE BODIES...
...AND IT'S UP TO US TO FIND A WAY TO CHANGE THEM BACK.
THAT'S ODD.
WHY WOULD A GUARD BE PROTECTING AN ABANDONED BUILDING?

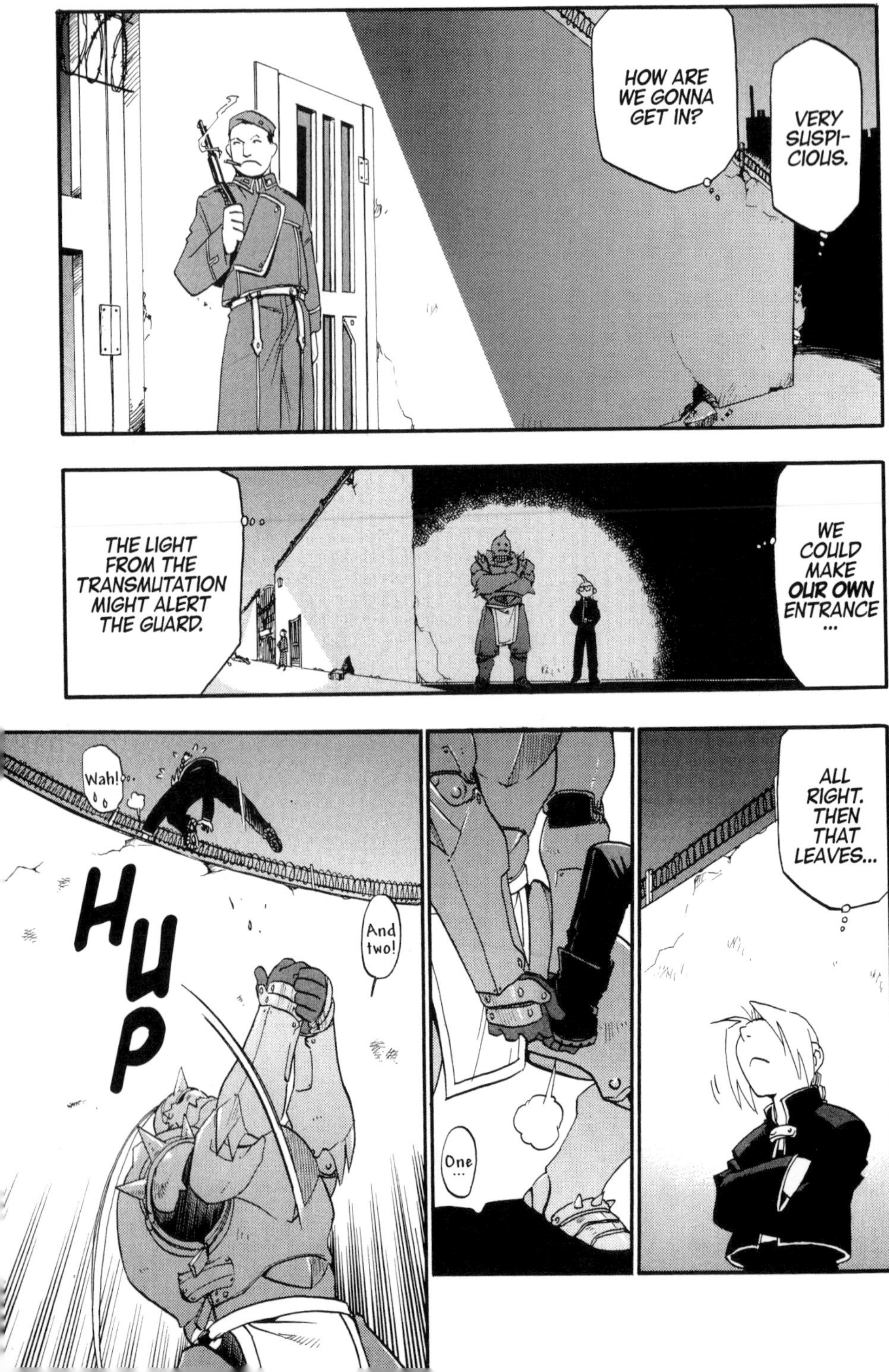

VERY SUSPICIOUS.
HOW ARE WE GONNA GET IN?
WE COULD MAKE **OUR OWN** ENTRANCE...
THE LIGHT FROM THE TRANSMUTATION MIGHT ALERT THE GUARD.
ALL RIGHT. THEN THAT LEAVES...
One...
And two!
HUP
Wah!

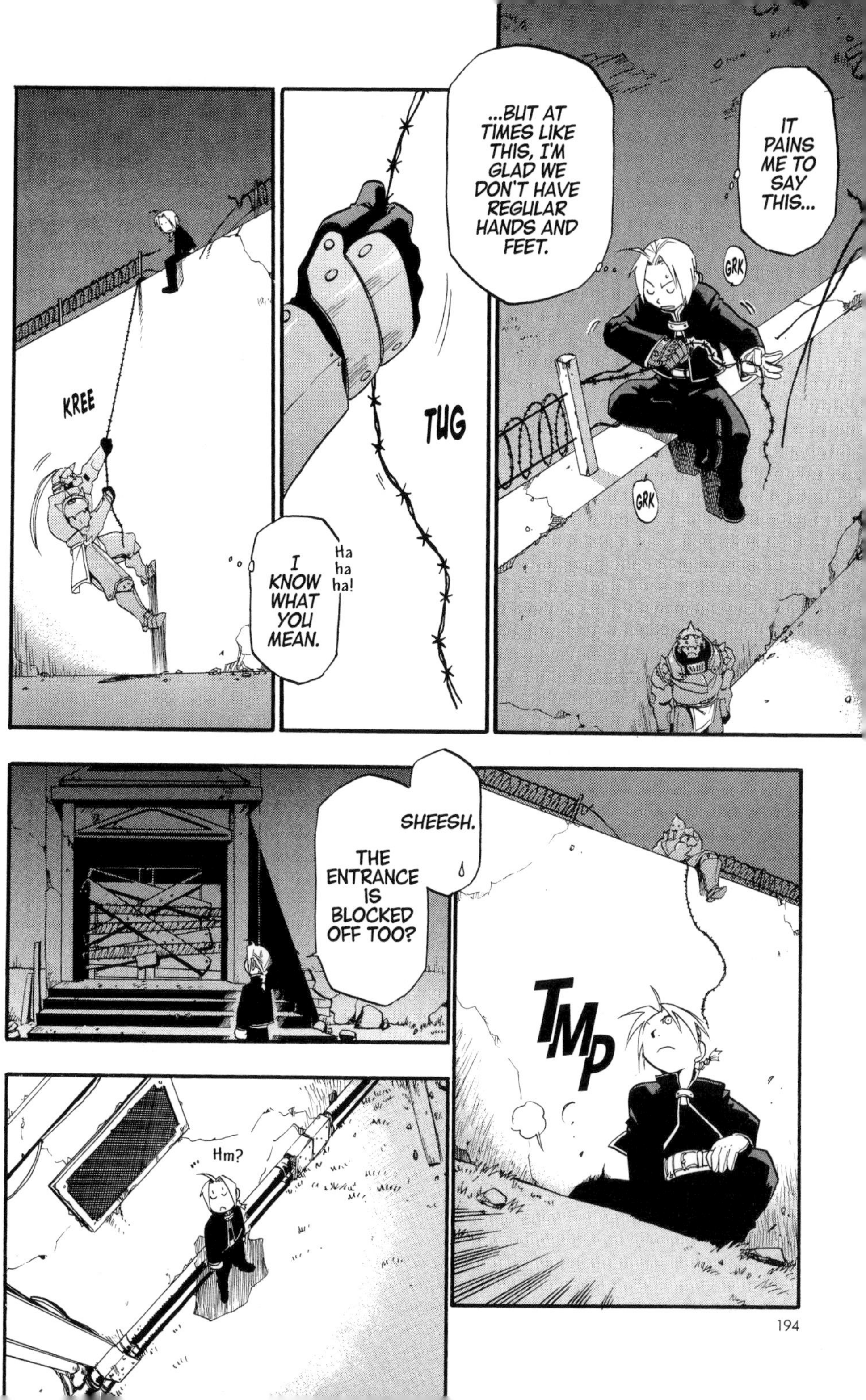
IT PAINS ME TO SAY THIS...
...BUT AT TIMES LIKE THIS, I'M GLAD WE DON'T HAVE REGULAR HANDS AND FEET.
GRK
GRK
TUG
Ha ha ha!
I KNOW WHAT YOU MEAN.
KREE
TMP
SHEESH.
THE ENTRANCE IS BLOCKED OFF TOO?
Hm?

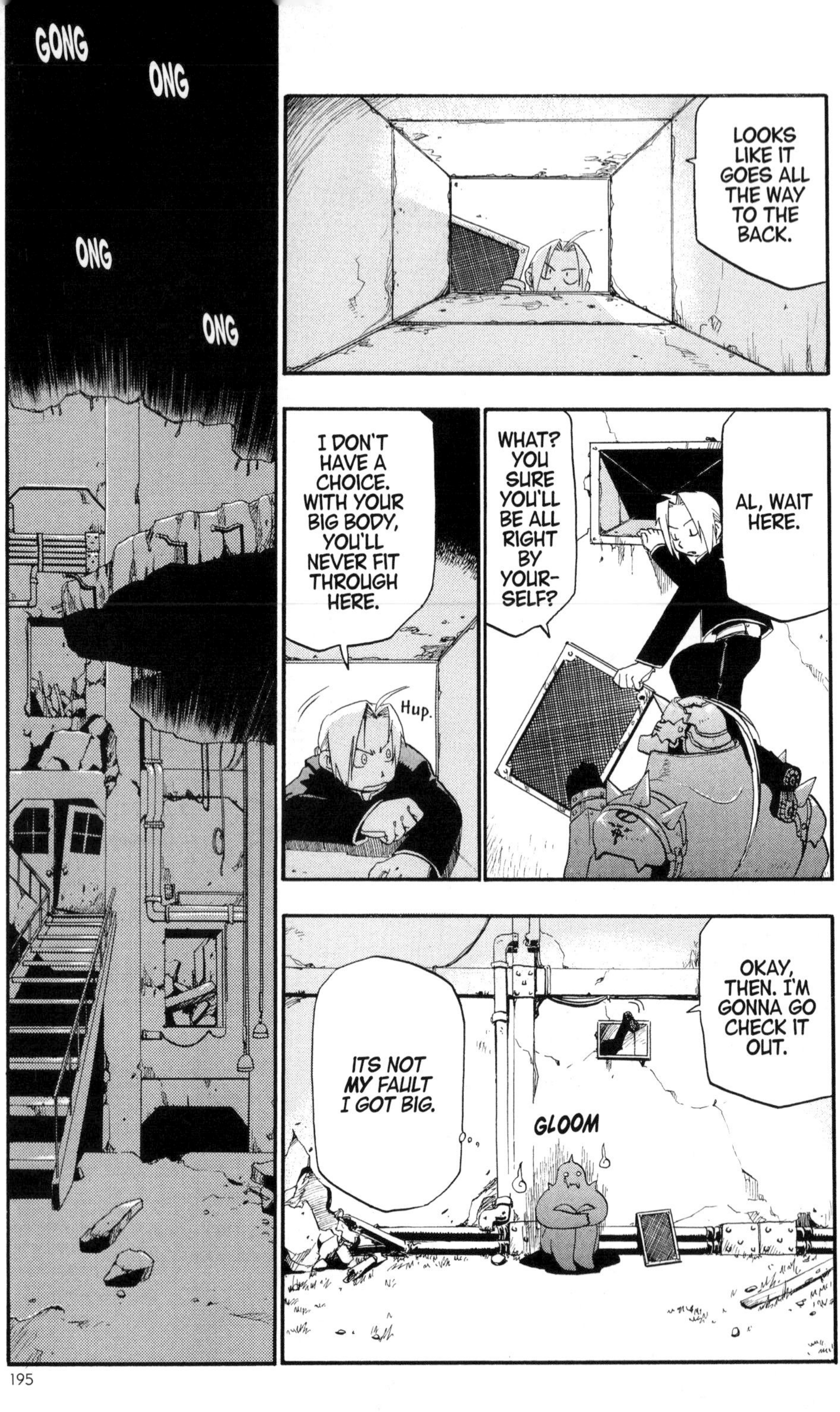
LOOKS LIKE IT GOES ALL THE WAY TO THE BACK.
AL, WAIT HERE.
WHAT? YOU SURE YOU'LL BE ALL RIGHT BY YOURSELF?
I DON'T HAVE A CHOICE. WITH YOUR BIG BODY, YOU'LL NEVER FIT THROUGH HERE.
Hup.
OKAY, THEN. I'M GONNA GO CHECK IT OUT.
GLOOM
ITS NOT MY FAULT I GOT BIG.
GONG
ONG
ONG
ONG

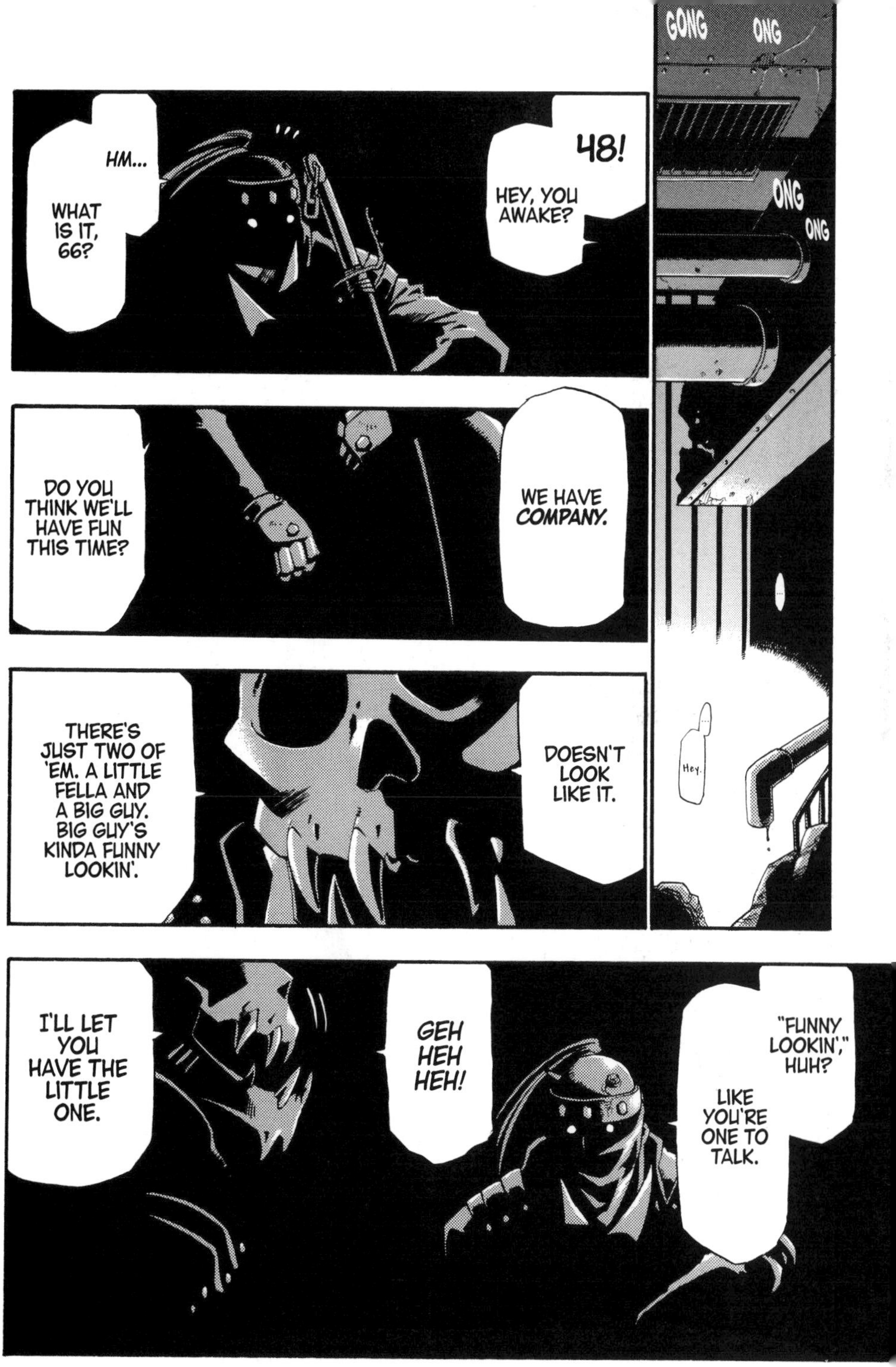
GONG
ONG
ONG
ONG
...
...
Hey.
48!
HEY, YOU AWAKE?
HM...
WHAT IS IT, 66?
WE HAVE COMPANY.
DO YOU THINK WE'LL HAVE FUN THIS TIME?
DOESN'T LOOK LIKE IT.
THERE'S JUST TWO OF 'EM. A LITTLE FELLA AND A BIG GUY. BIG GUY'S KINDA FUNNY LOOKIN'.
"FUNNY LOOKIN'," HUH?
LIKE YOU'RE ONE TO TALK.
GEH HEH HEH!
I'LL LET YOU HAVE THE LITTLE ONE.

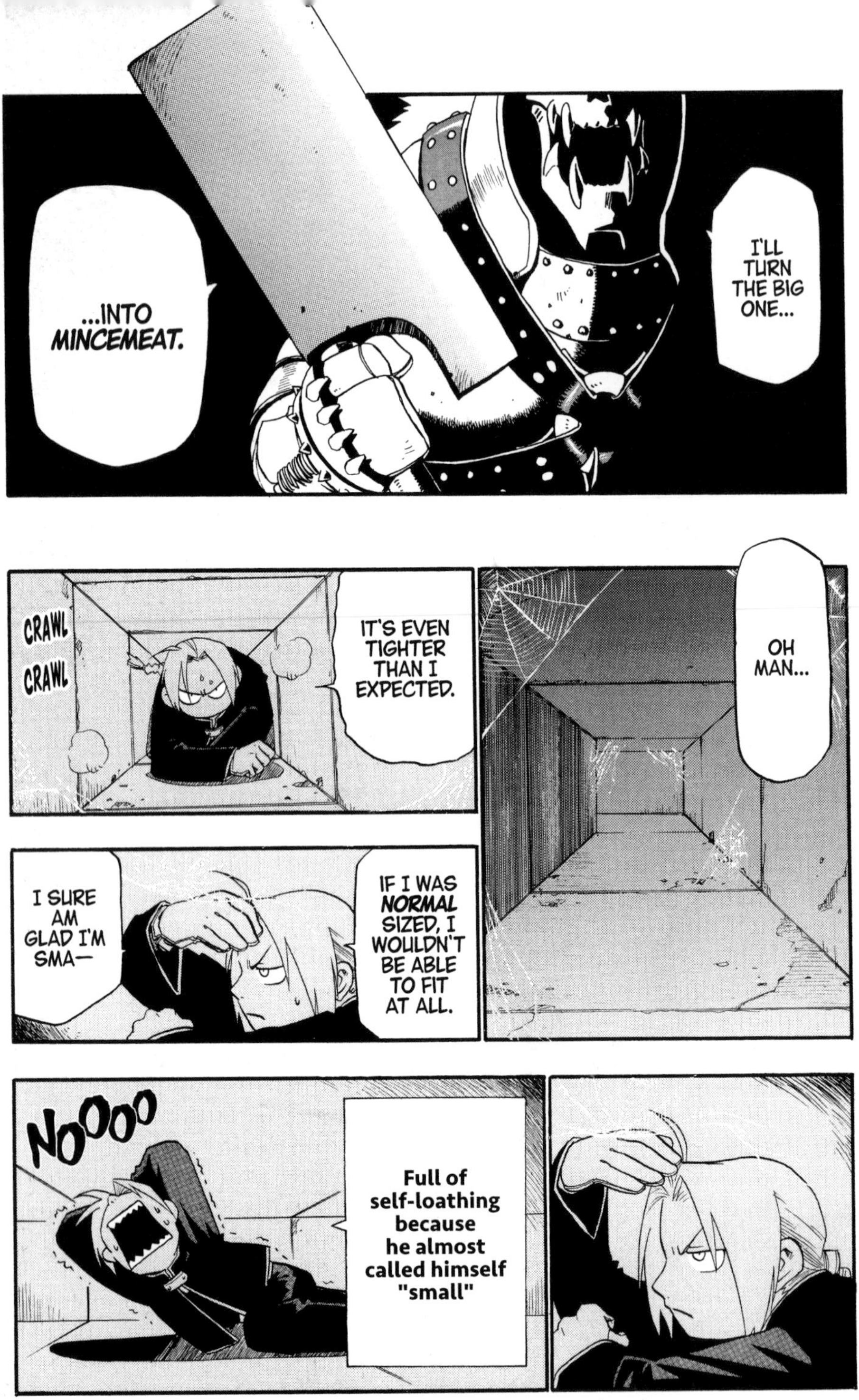
I'LL TURN THE BIG ONE...
...INTO MINCEMEAT.
OH MAN...
CRAWL CRAWL
IT'S EVEN TIGHTER THAN I EXPECTED.
IF I WAS NORMAL SIZED, I WOULDN'T BE ABLE TO FIT AT ALL.
I SURE AM GLAD I'M SMA—
Full of self-loathing because he almost called himself "small"
NOOOO

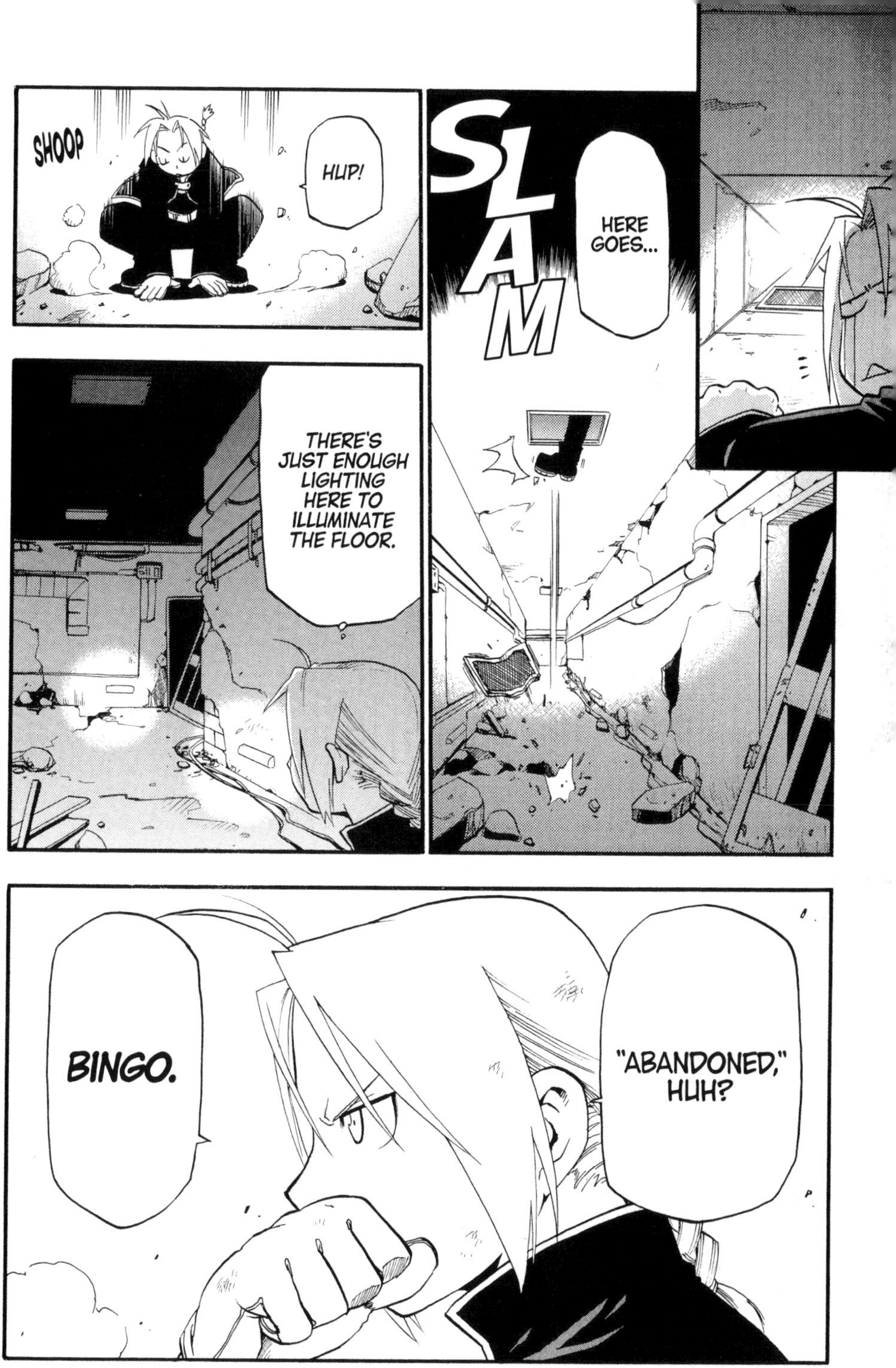
HERE GOES...
SLAM
SHOOP
HUP!
THERE'S JUST ENOUGH LIGHTING HERE TO ILLUMINATE THE FLOOR.
"ABANDONED," HUH?
BINGO.

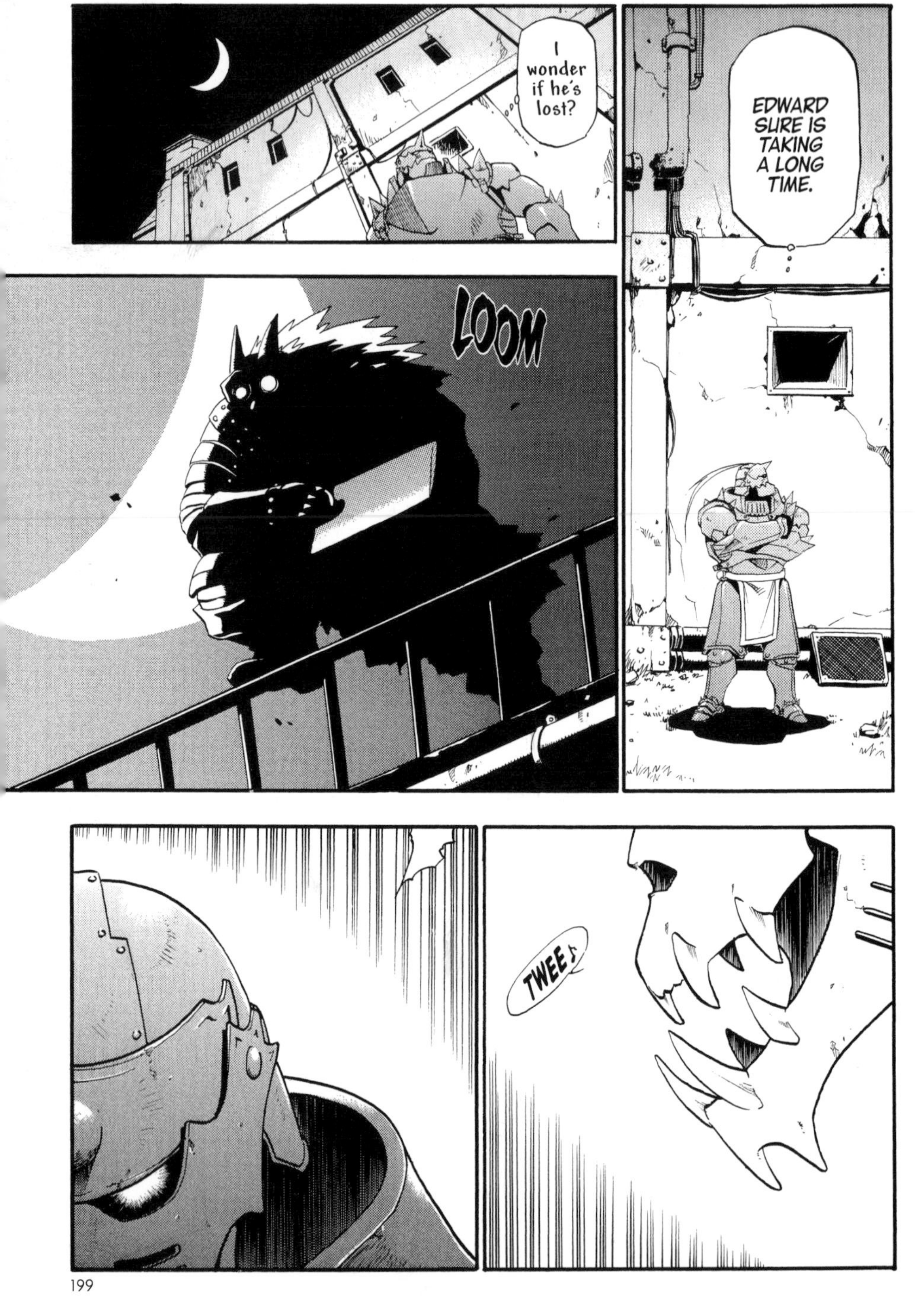
EDWARD SURE IS TAKING A LONG TIME.
I wonder if he's lost?
LOOM
TWEE♪

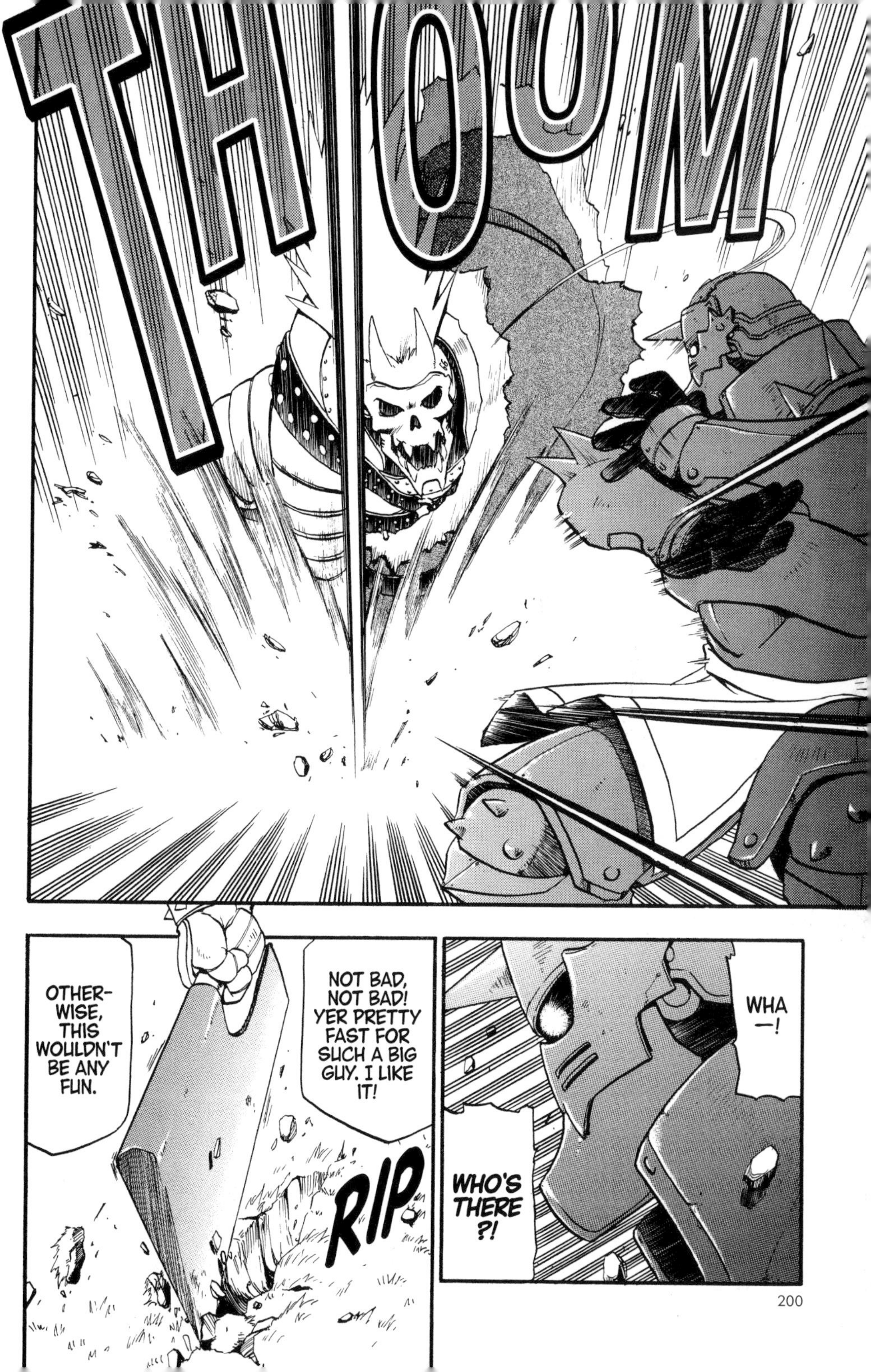
THOOM
WHA —!
WHO'S THERE ?!
NOT BAD, NOT BAD! YER PRETTY FAST FOR SUCH A BIG GUY. I LIKE IT!
OTHER-WISE, THIS WOULDN'T BE ANY FUN.
RIP

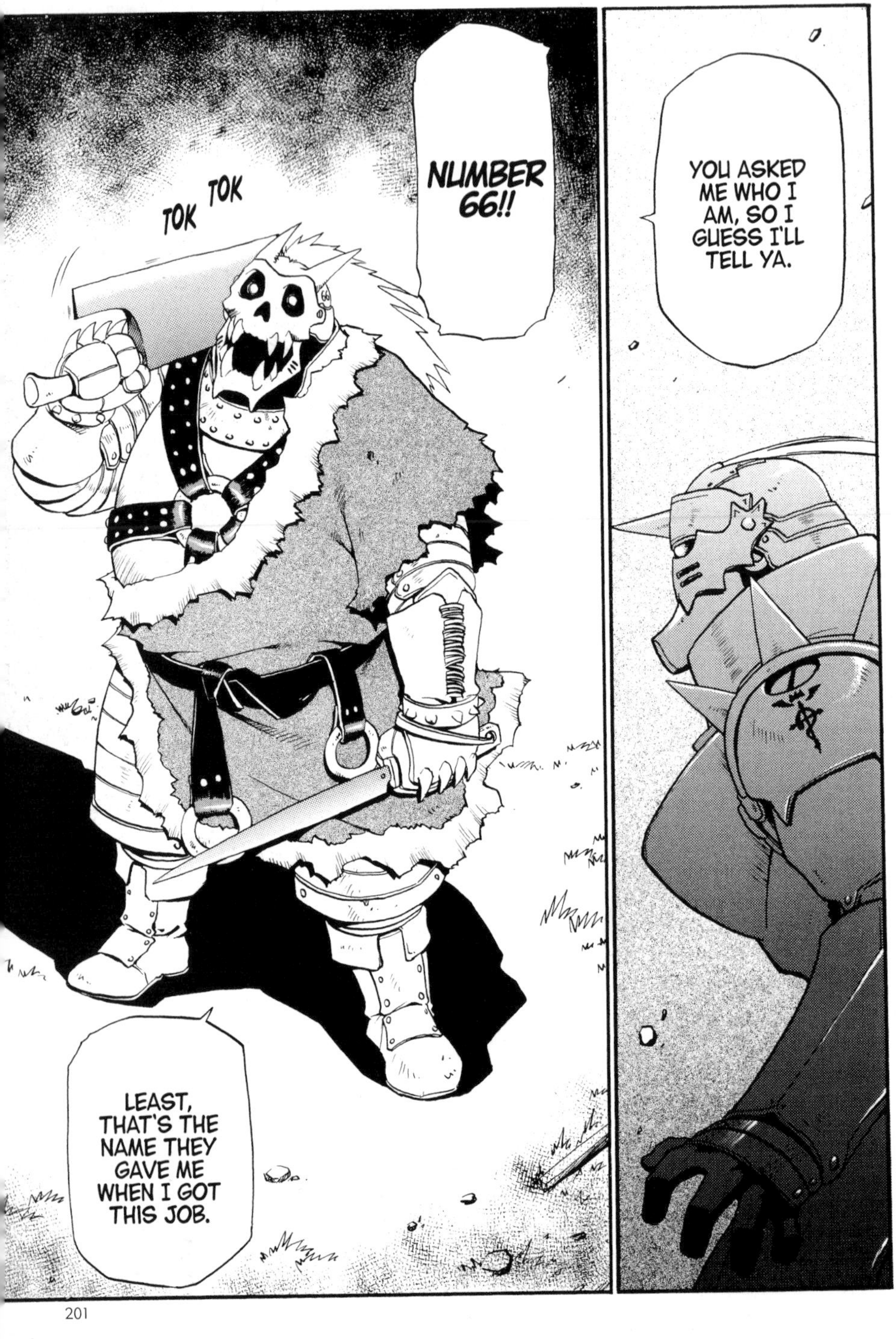
YOU ASKED ME WHO I AM, SO I GUESS I'LL TELL YA.
NUMBER 66!!
TOK TOK
LEAST, THAT'S THE NAME THEY GAVE ME WHEN I GOT THIS JOB.

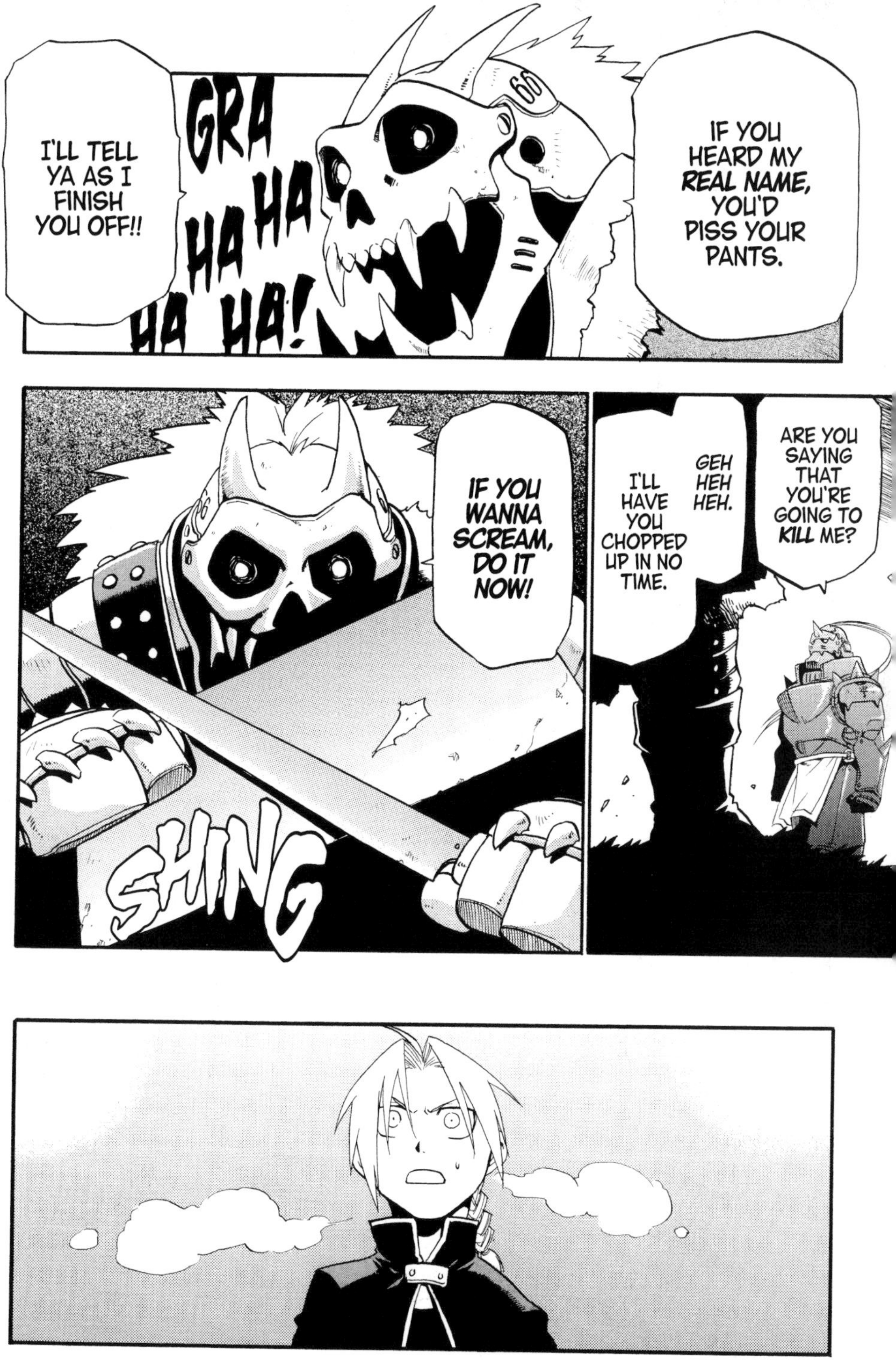
IF YOU HEARD MY REAL NAME, YOU'D PISS YOUR PANTS.
GRA HA HA HA HA!
I'LL TELL YA AS I FINISH YOU OFF!!
ARE YOU SAYING THAT YOU'RE GOING TO KILL ME?
GEH HEH HEH.
I'LL HAVE YOU CHOPPED UP IN NO TIME.
IF YOU WANNA SCREAM, DO IT NOW!
SHING

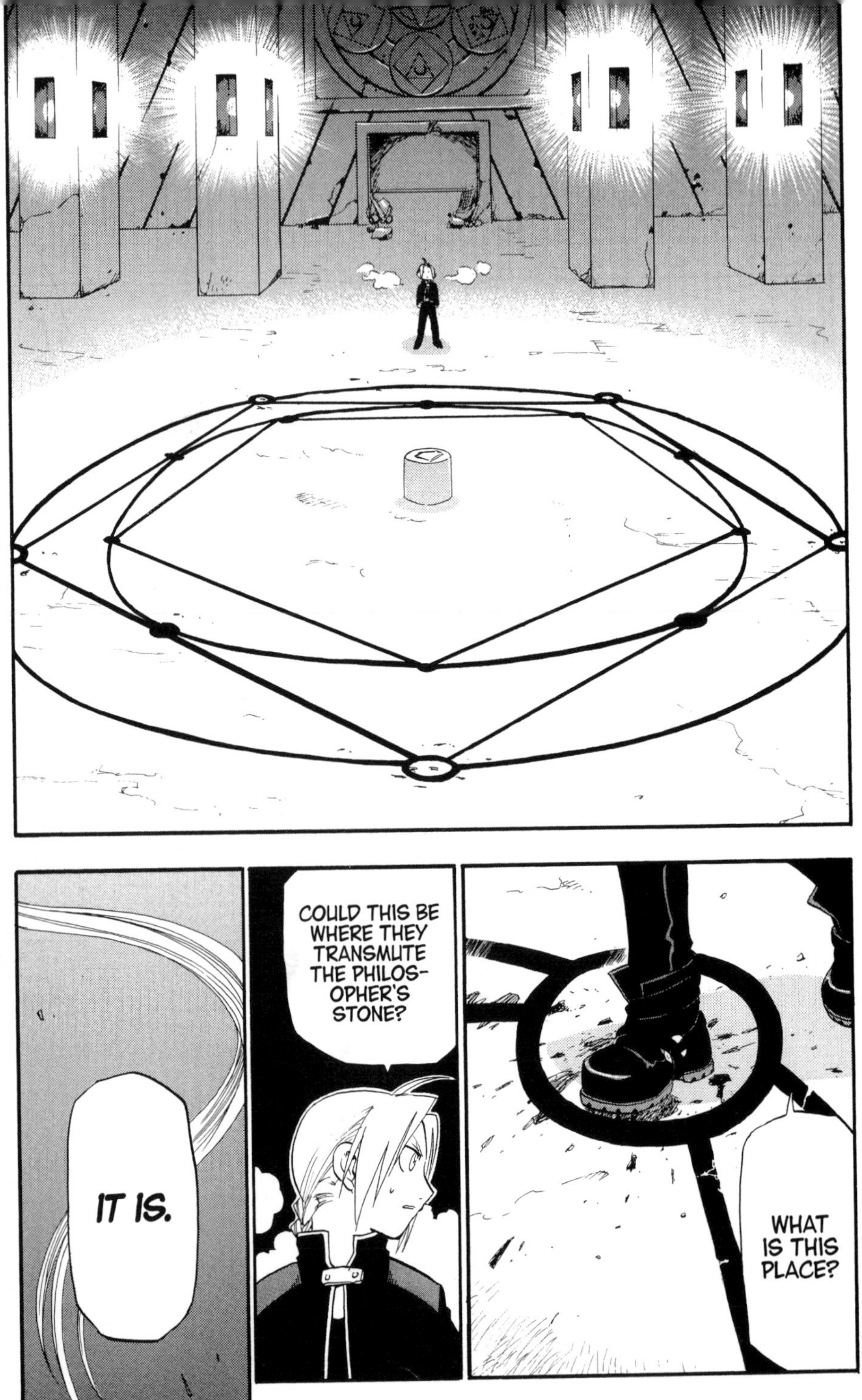
WHAT IS THIS PLACE?
COULD THIS BE WHERE THEY TRANSMUTE THE PHILOS-OPHER'S STONE?
IT IS.

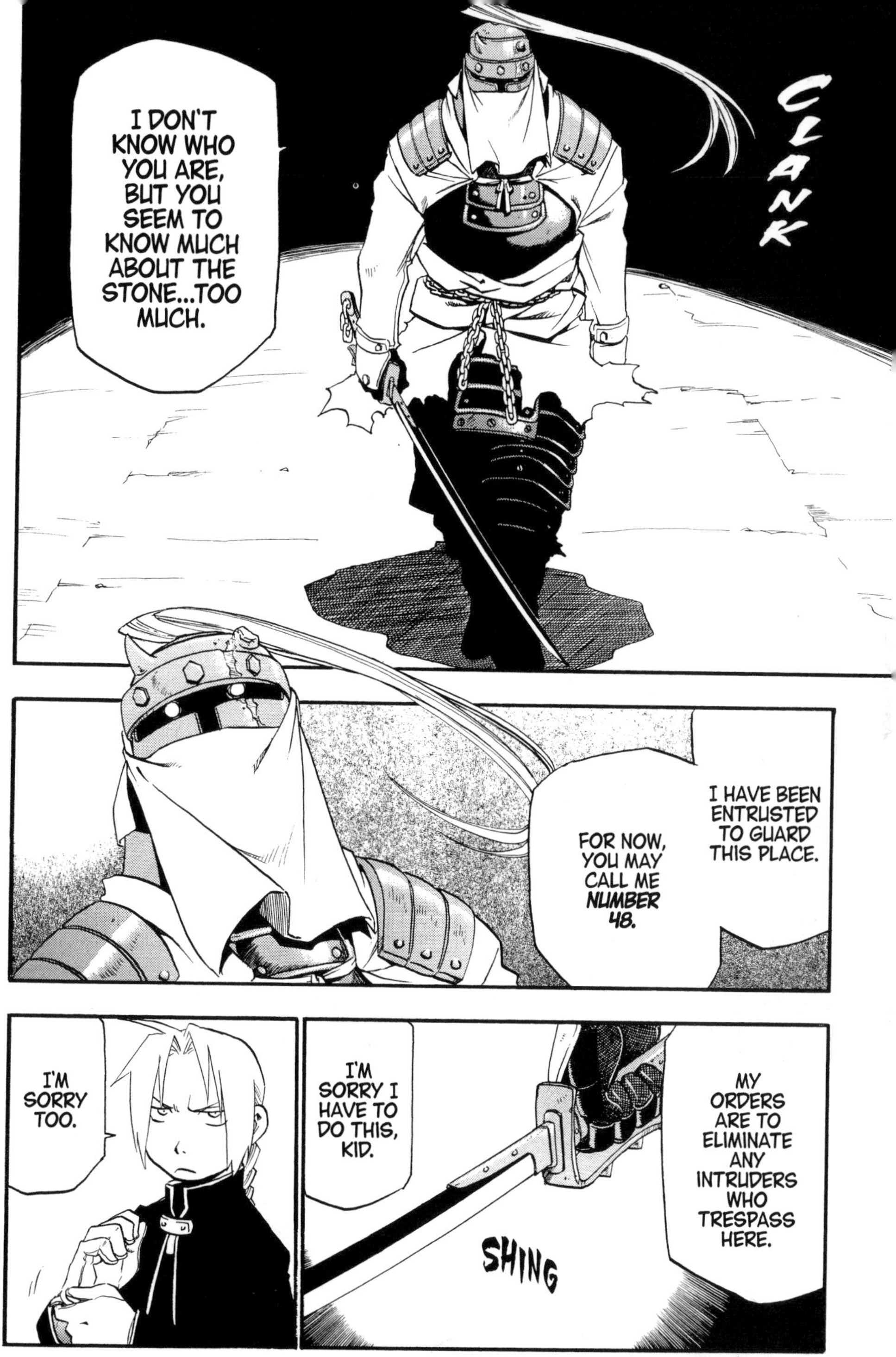
CLANK
I DON'T KNOW WHO YOU ARE, BUT YOU SEEM TO KNOW MUCH ABOUT THE STONE...TOO MUCH.
I HAVE BEEN ENTRUSTED TO GUARD THIS PLACE.
FOR NOW, YOU MAY CALL ME **NUMBER 48.**
MY ORDERS ARE TO ELIMINATE ANY INTRUDERS WHO TRESPASS HERE.
I'M SORRY I HAVE TO DO THIS, KID.
SHING
I'M SORRY TOO.

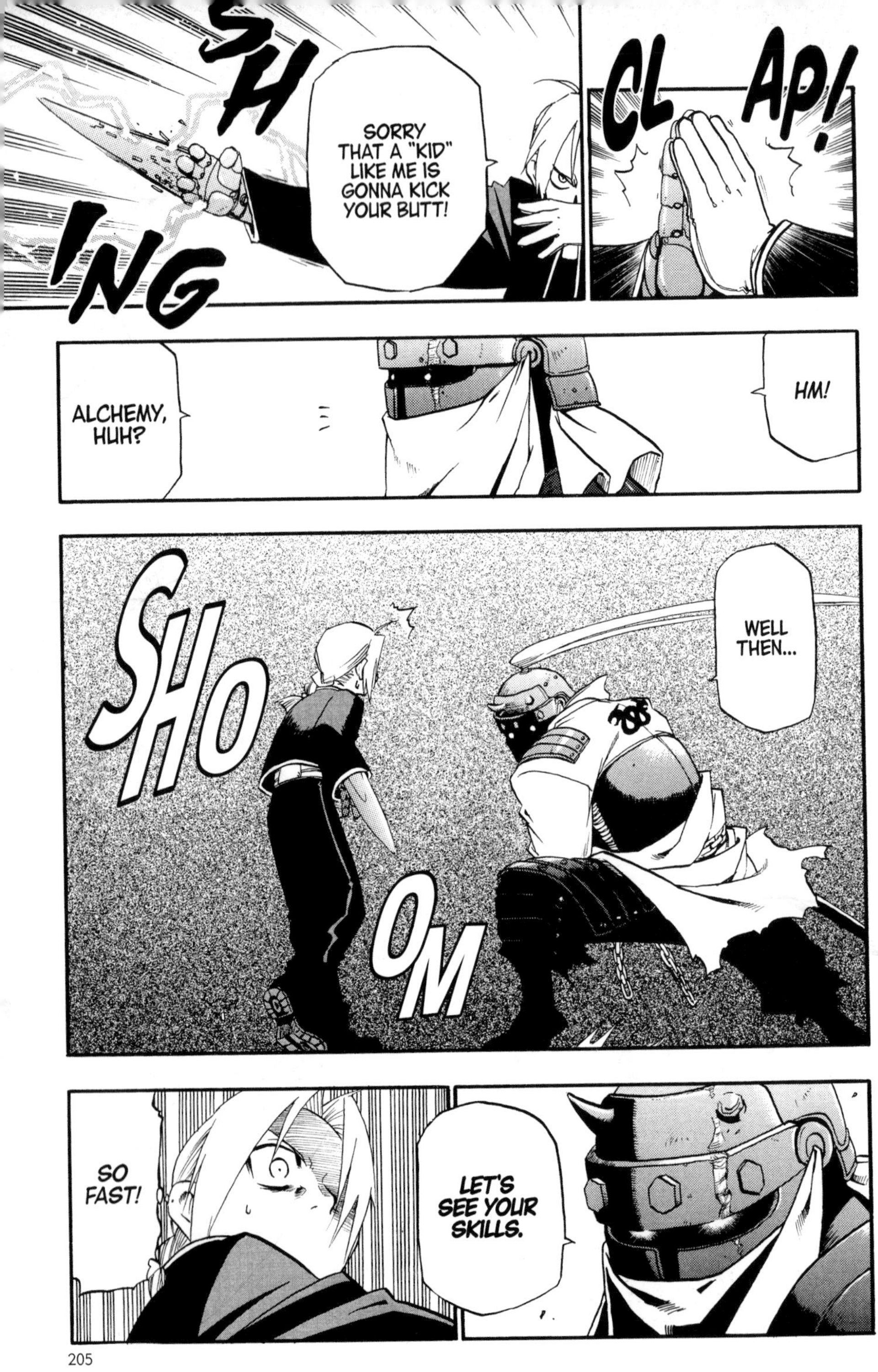
CLAP!
SHING
SORRY THAT A "KID" LIKE ME IS GONNA KICK YOUR BUTT!
HM!
ALCHEMY, HUH?
WELL THEN...
SHOOM
LET'S SEE YOUR SKILLS.
SO FAST!

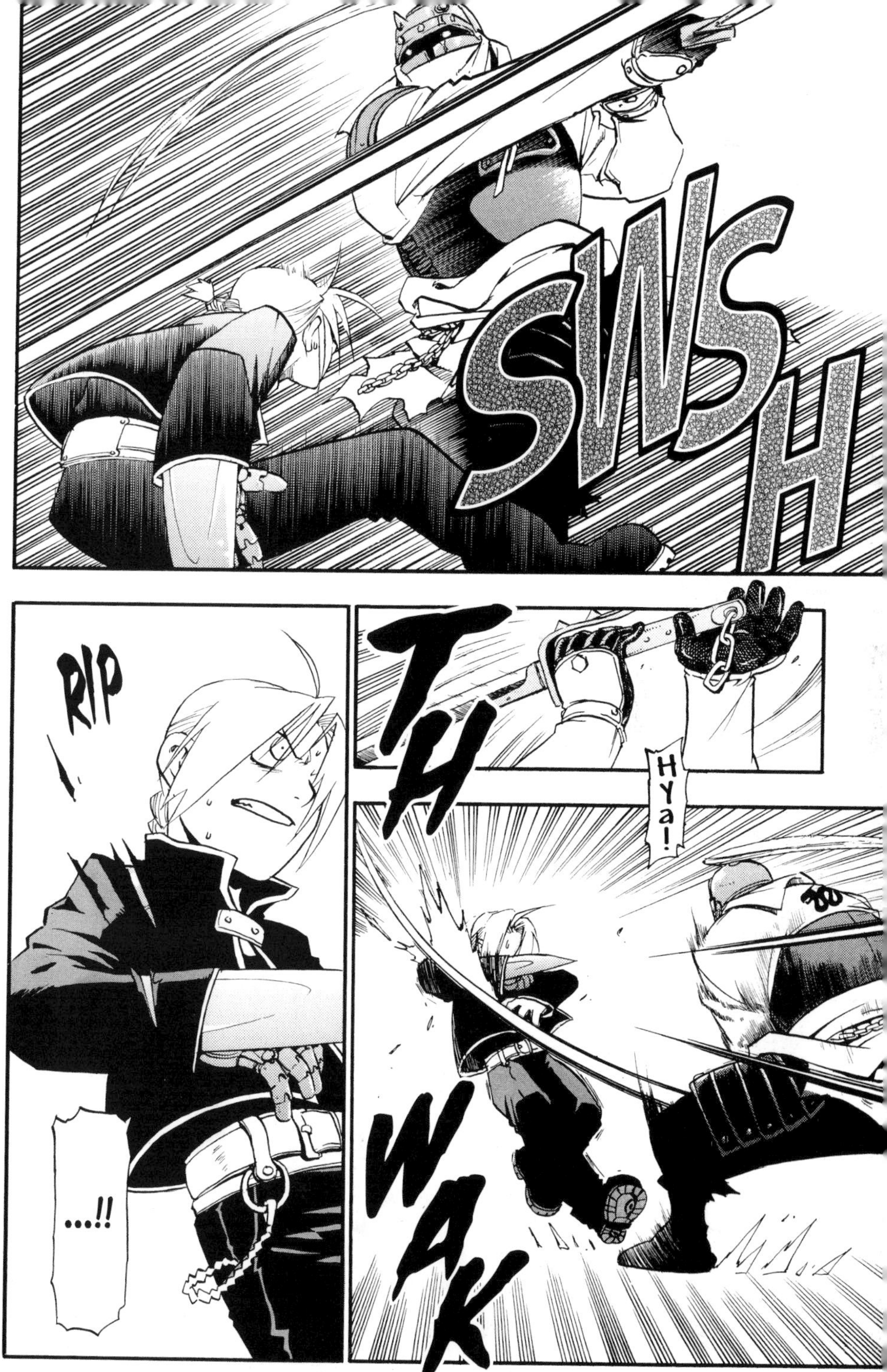
SWSH
HYa!
THWAK
RIP
...!!

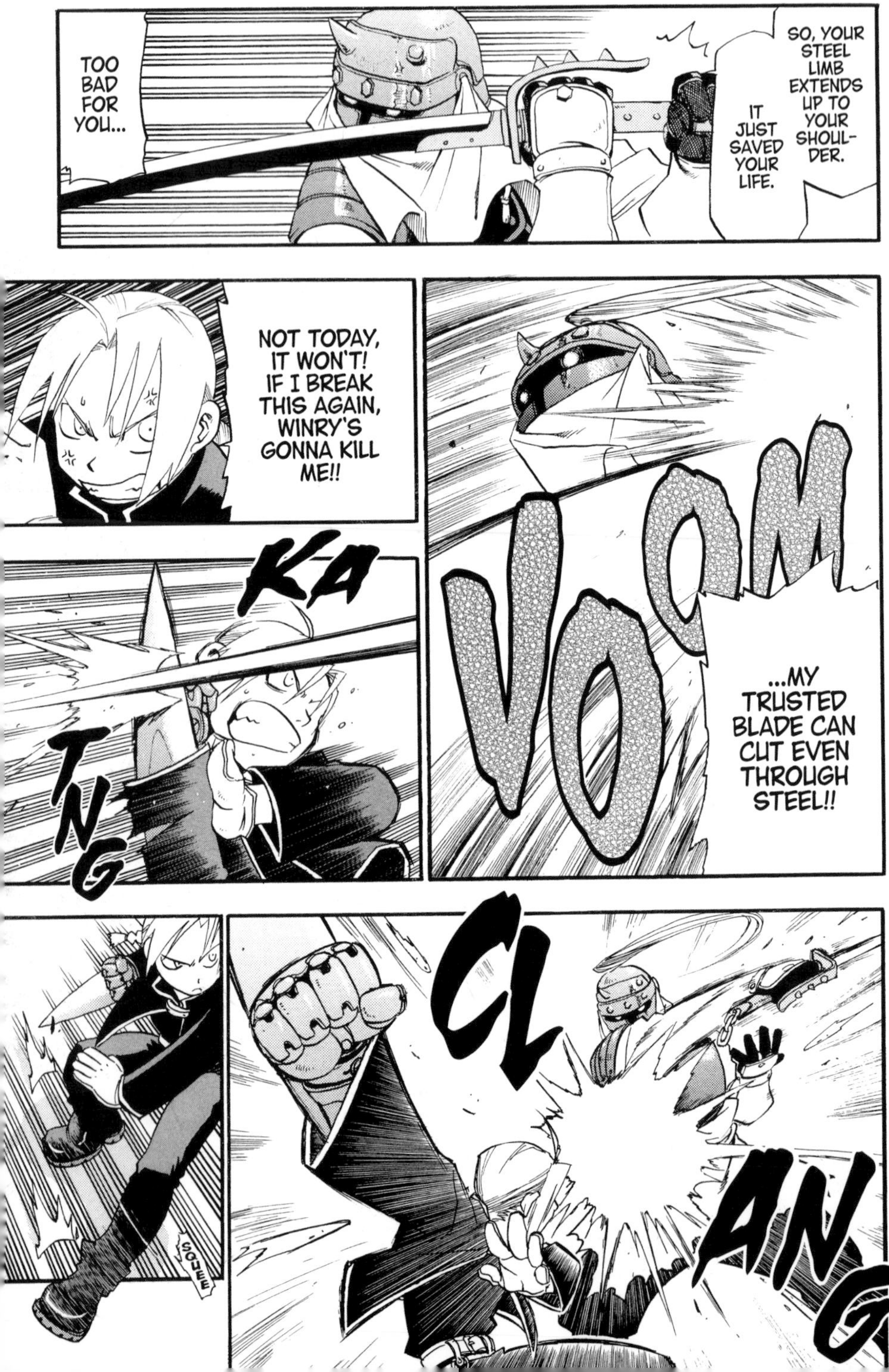
SO, YOUR STEEL LIMB EXTENDS UP TO YOUR SHOULDER.
IT JUST SAVED YOUR LIFE.
TOO BAD FOR YOU...
VOOOM
...MY TRUSTED BLADE CAN CUT EVEN THROUGH STEEL!!
NOT TODAY, IT WON'T! IF I BREAK THIS AGAIN, WINRY'S GONNA KILL ME!!
KA
TNG
CLANG
SQUEEE

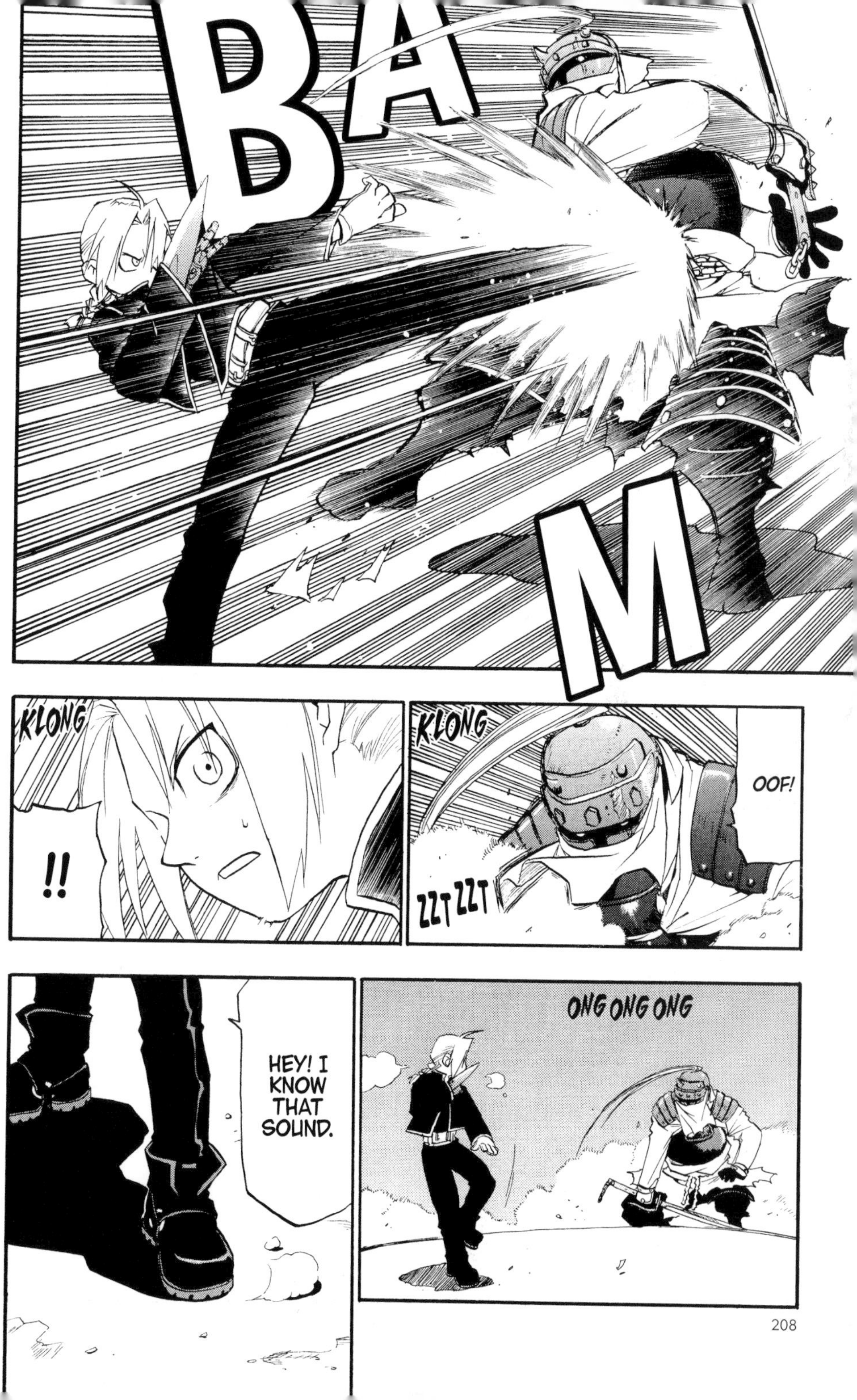
BA
M
KLONG
OOF!
ZZT ZZT
KLONG
!!
ONG ONG ONG
HEY! I KNOW THAT SOUND.

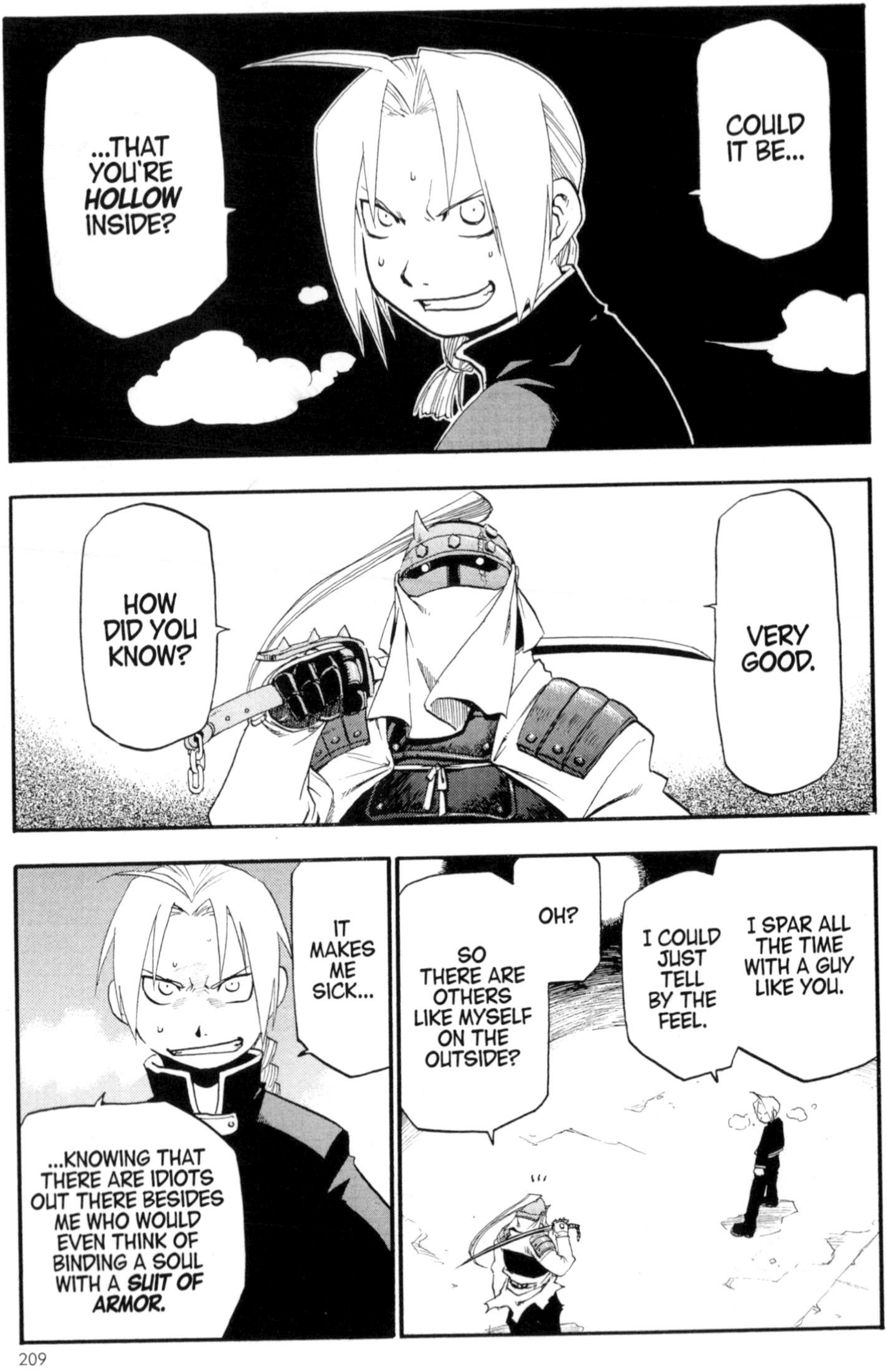
COULD IT BE...
...THAT YOU'RE HOLLOW INSIDE?
VERY GOOD.
HOW DID YOU KNOW?
I SPAR ALL THE TIME WITH A GUY LIKE YOU.
I COULD JUST TELL BY THE FEEL.
OH?
SO THERE ARE OTHERS LIKE MYSELF ON THE OUTSIDE?
IT MAKES ME SICK...
...KNOWING THAT THERE ARE IDIOTS OUT THERE BESIDES ME WHO WOULD EVEN THINK OF BINDING A SOUL WITH A SUIT OF ARMOR.

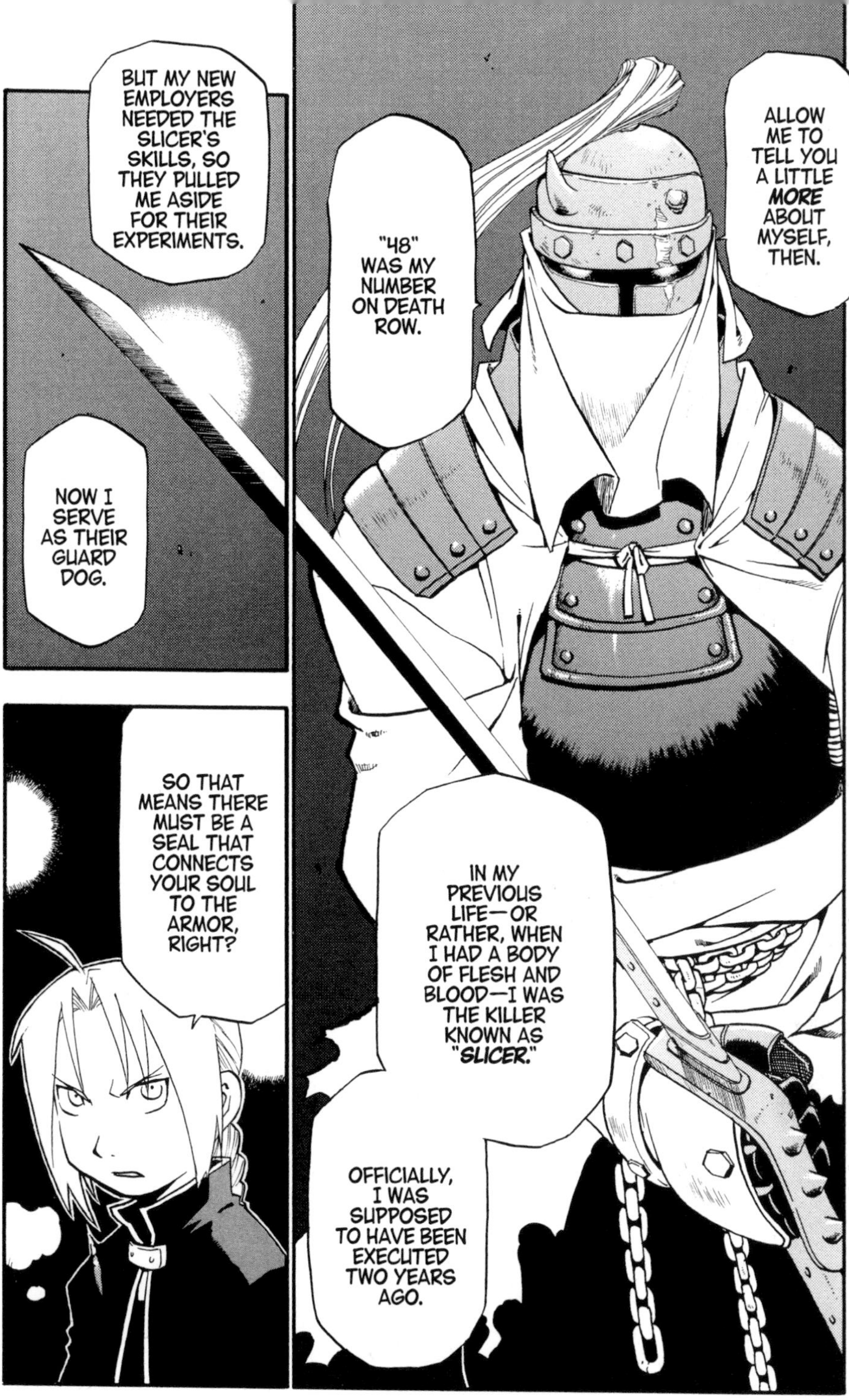
ALLOW ME TO TELL YOU A LITTLE MORE ABOUT MYSELF, THEN.
"48" WAS MY NUMBER ON DEATH ROW.
IN MY PREVIOUS LIFE—OR RATHER, WHEN I HAD A BODY OF FLESH AND BLOOD—I WAS THE KILLER KNOWN AS "SLICER."
OFFICIALLY, I WAS SUPPOSED TO HAVE BEEN EXECUTED TWO YEARS AGO.
BUT MY NEW EMPLOYERS NEEDED THE SLICER'S SKILLS, SO THEY PULLED ME ASIDE FOR THEIR EXPERIMENTS.
NOW I SERVE AS THEIR GUARD DOG.
SO THAT MEANS THERE MUST BE A SEAL THAT CONNECTS YOUR SOUL TO THE ARMOR, RIGHT?

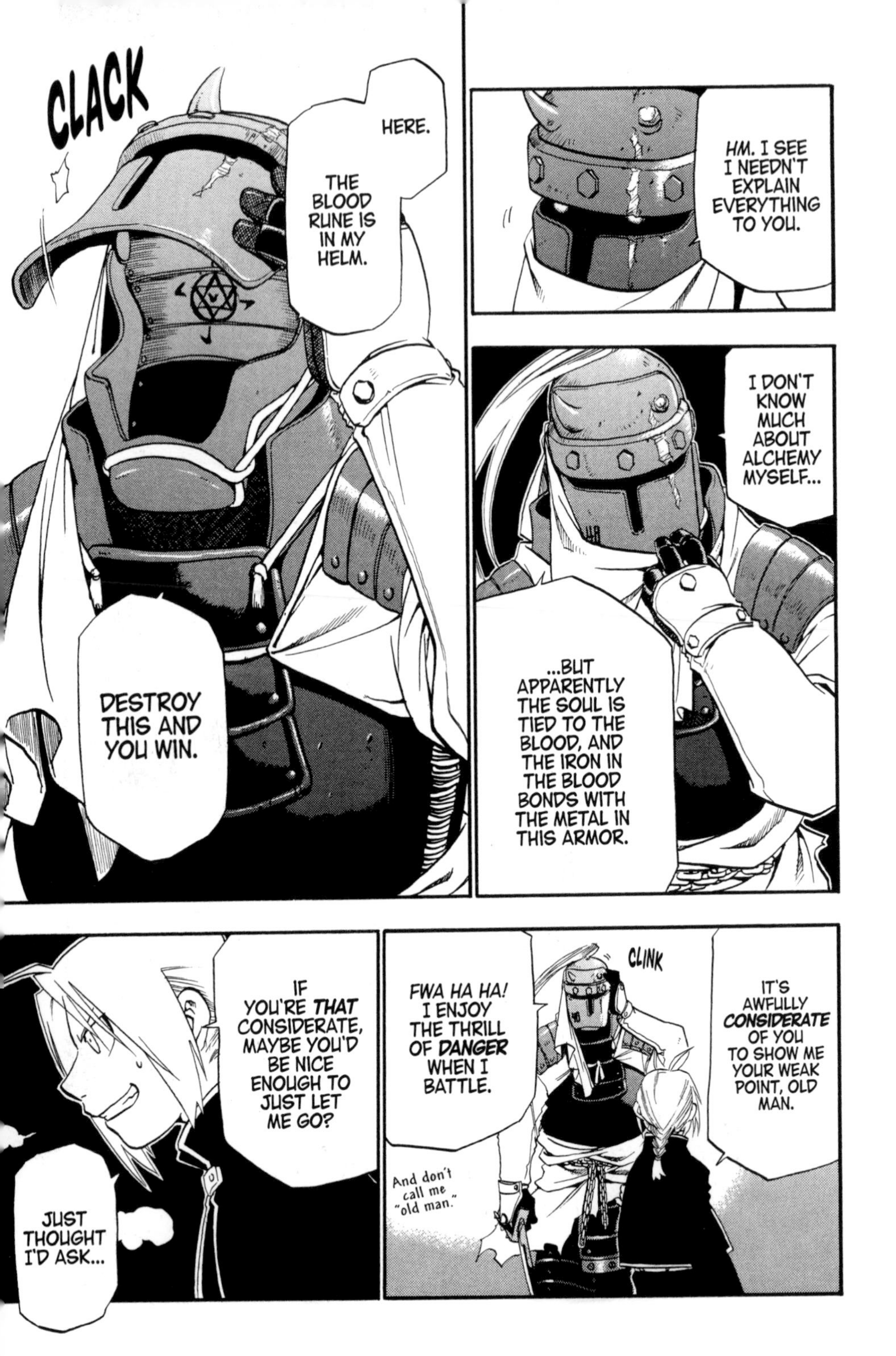
HM. I SEE I NEEDN'T EXPLAIN EVERYTHING TO YOU.
I DON'T KNOW MUCH ABOUT ALCHEMY MYSELF...
...BUT APPARENTLY THE SOUL IS TIED TO THE BLOOD, AND THE IRON IN THE BLOOD BONDS WITH THE METAL IN THIS ARMOR.
CLACK
HERE.
THE BLOOD RUNE IS IN MY HELM.
DESTROY THIS AND YOU WIN.
CLINK
IT'S AWFULLY **CONSIDERATE** OF YOU TO SHOW ME YOUR WEAK POINT, OLD MAN.
FWA HA HA! I ENJOY THE THRILL OF **DANGER** WHEN I BATTLE.
And don't call me "old man."
IF YOU'RE **THAT** CONSIDERATE, MAYBE YOU'D BE NICE ENOUGH TO JUST LET ME GO?
JUST THOUGHT I'D ASK...

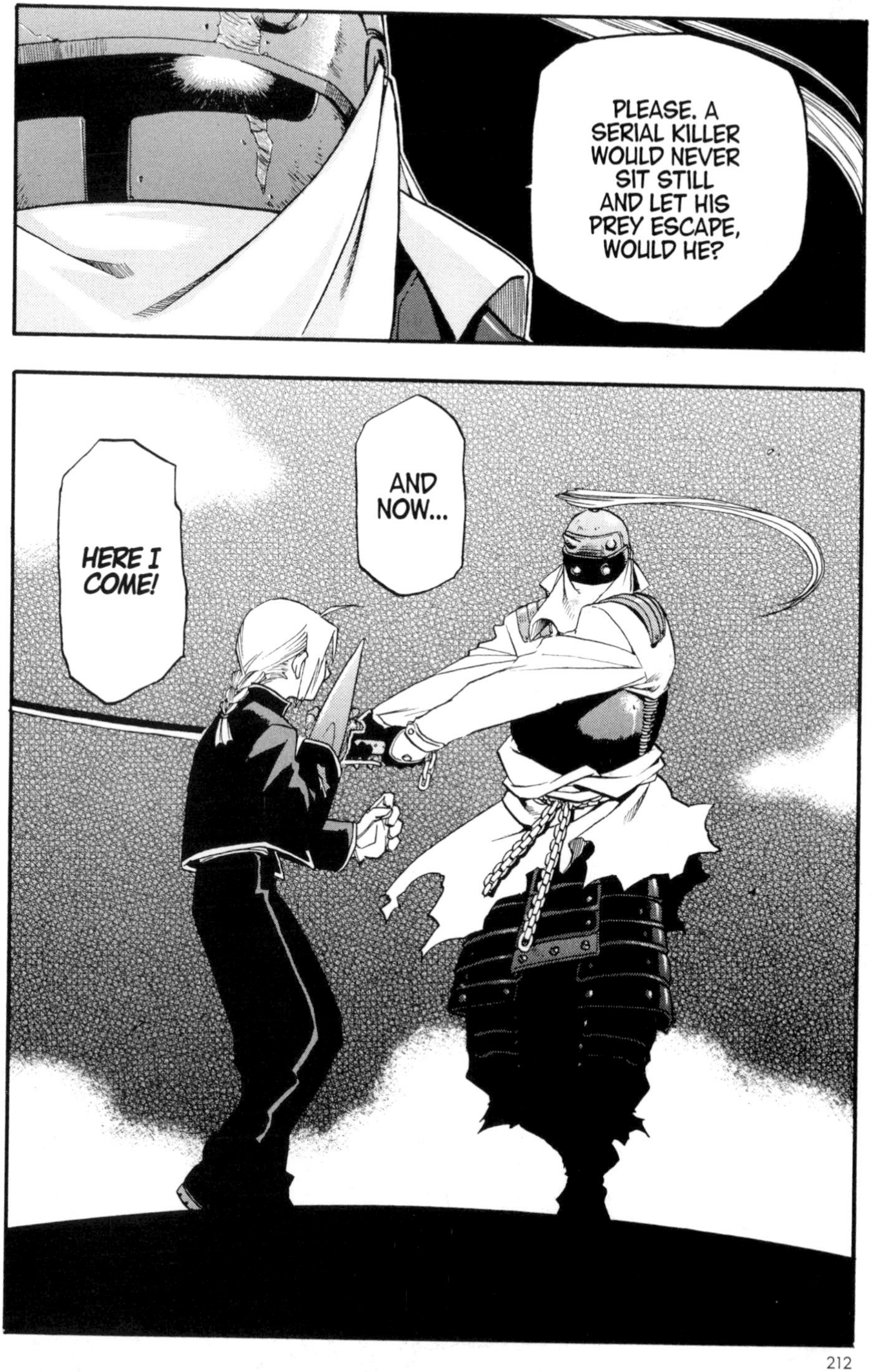
PLEASE. A SERIAL KILLER WOULD NEVER SIT STILL AND LET HIS PREY ESCAPE, WOULD HE?
AND NOW...
HERE I COME!

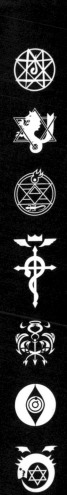

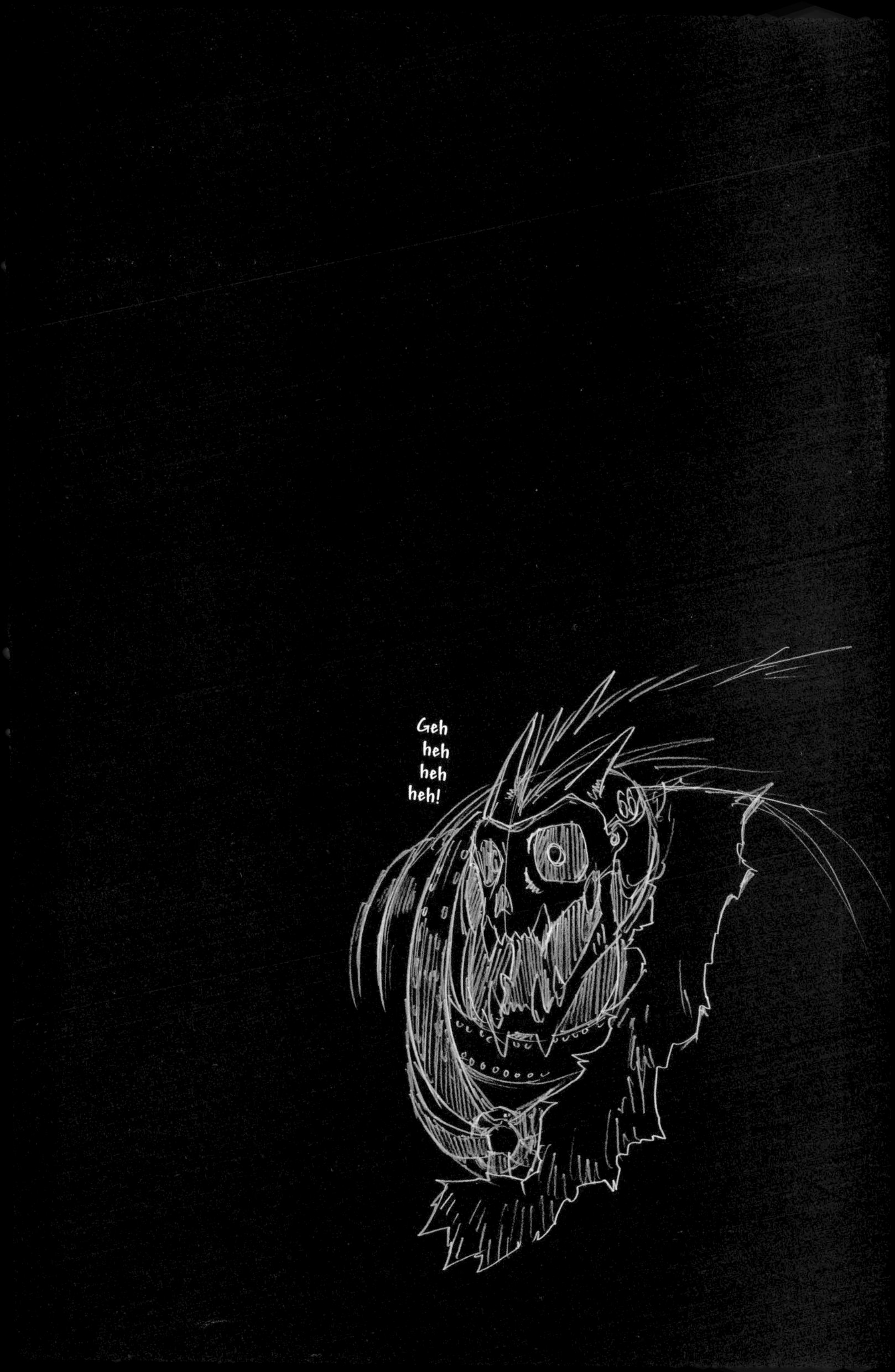
Geh heh heh heh!

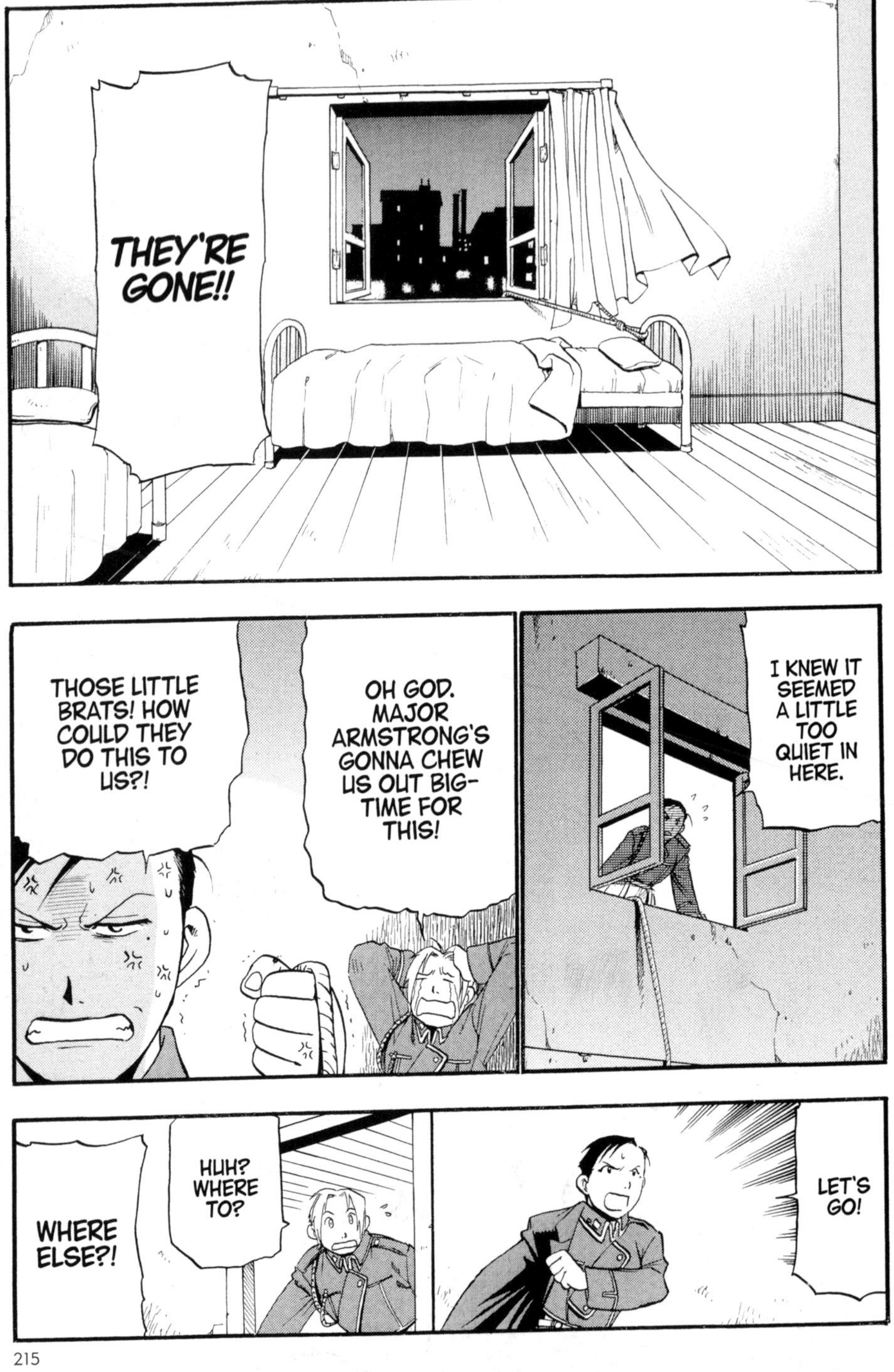
THEY'RE GONE!!
I KNEW IT SEEMED A LITTLE TOO QUIET IN HERE.
OH GOD. MAJOR ARMSTRONG'S GONNA CHEW US OUT BIG-TIME FOR THIS!
THOSE LITTLE BRATS! HOW COULD THEY DO THIS TO US?!
LET'S GO!
HUH? WHERE TO?
WHERE ELSE?!

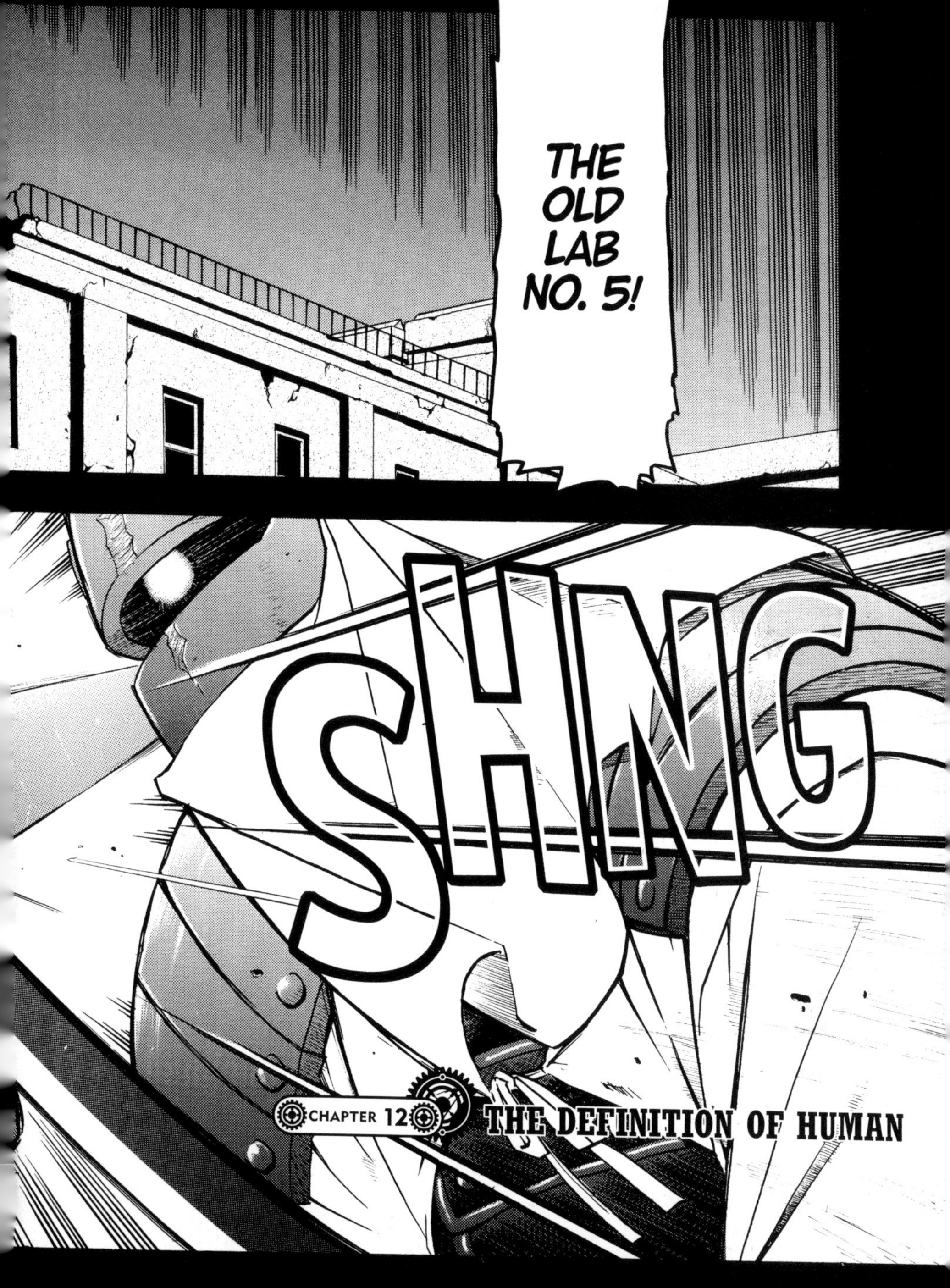
THE OLD LAB NO. 5!
SHNG
CHAPTER 12
THE DEFINITION OF HUMAN

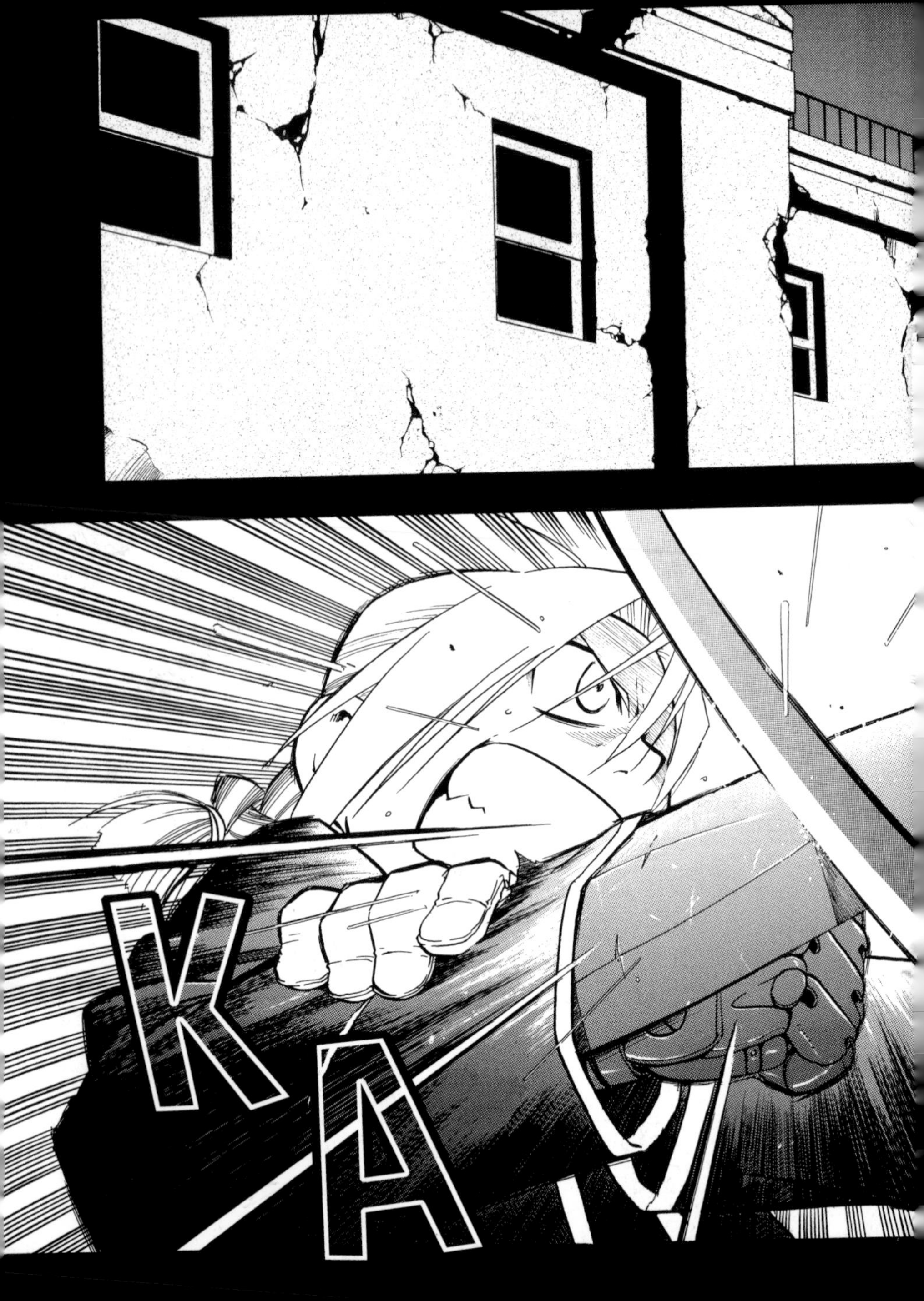
KA

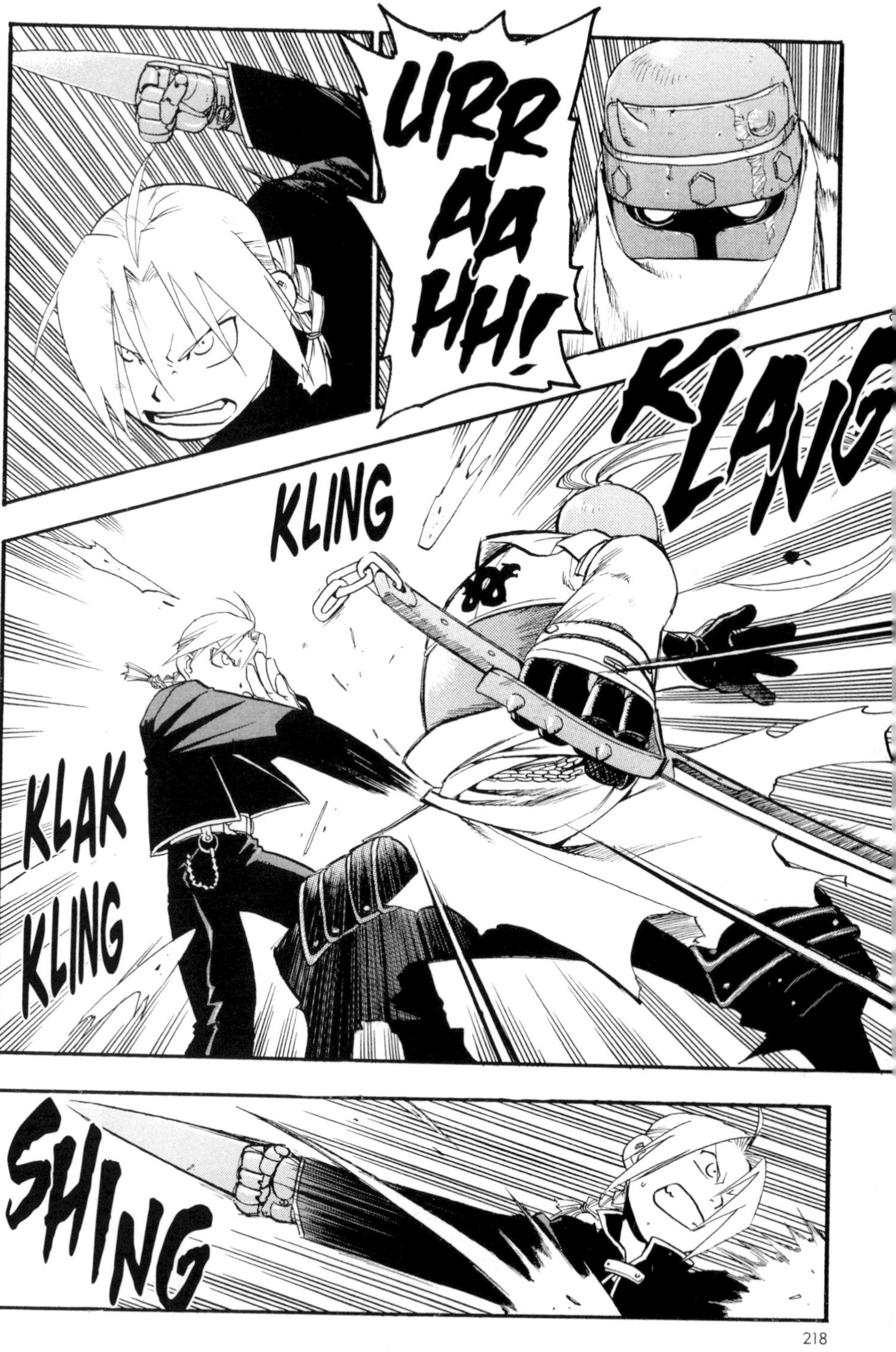
URR AA HH!
KLANG
KLING
KLAK KLING
SHING

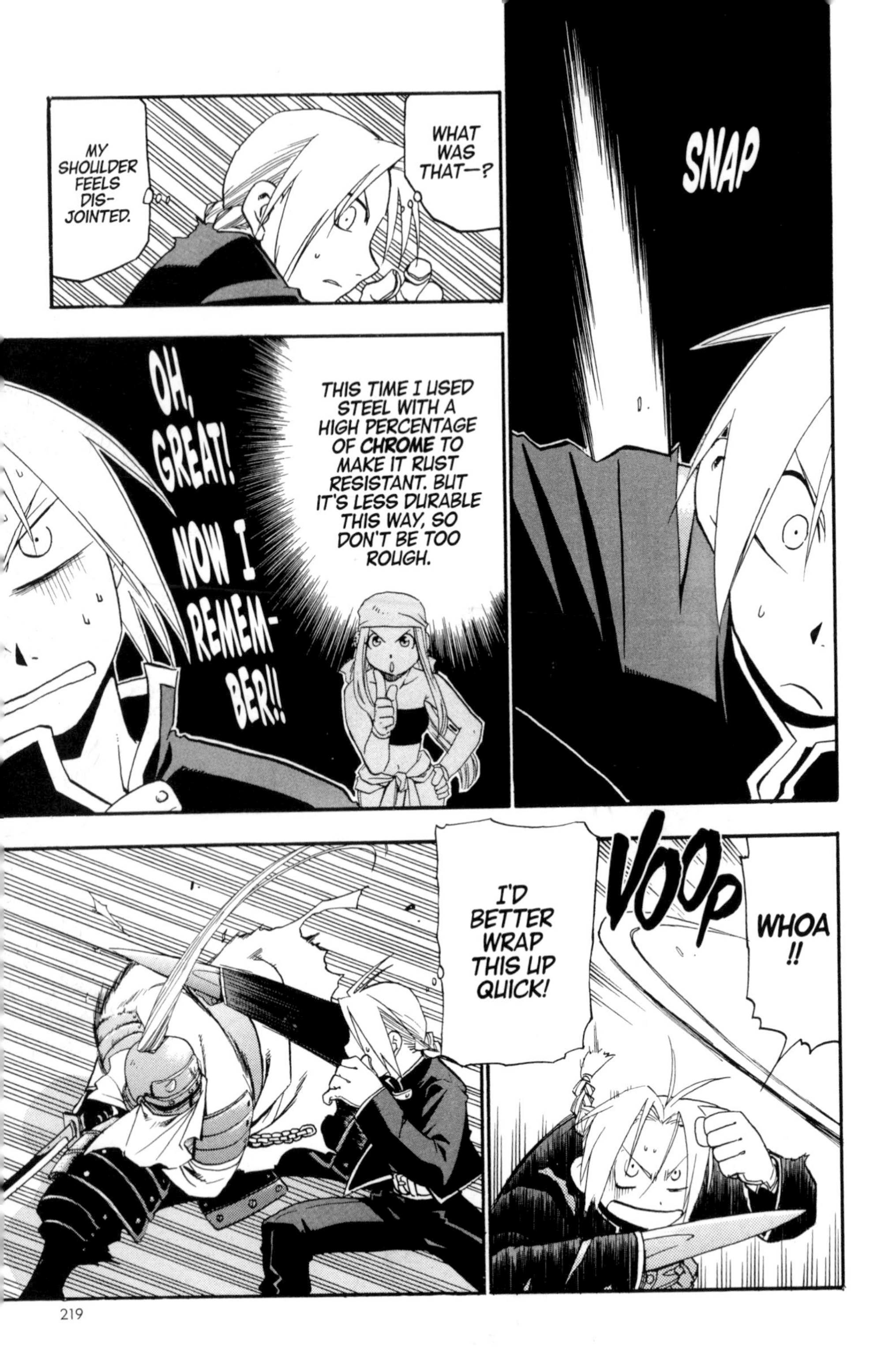
SNAP
WHAT WAS THAT—?
MY SHOULDER FEELS DIS-JOINTED.
THIS TIME I USED STEEL WITH A HIGH PERCENTAGE OF **CHROME** TO MAKE IT RUST RESISTANT. BUT IT'S LESS DURABLE THIS WAY, SO DON'T BE TOO ROUGH.
OH, GREAT! NOW I REMEM-BER!!
VOOP
WHOA !!
I'D BETTER WRAP THIS UP QUICK!

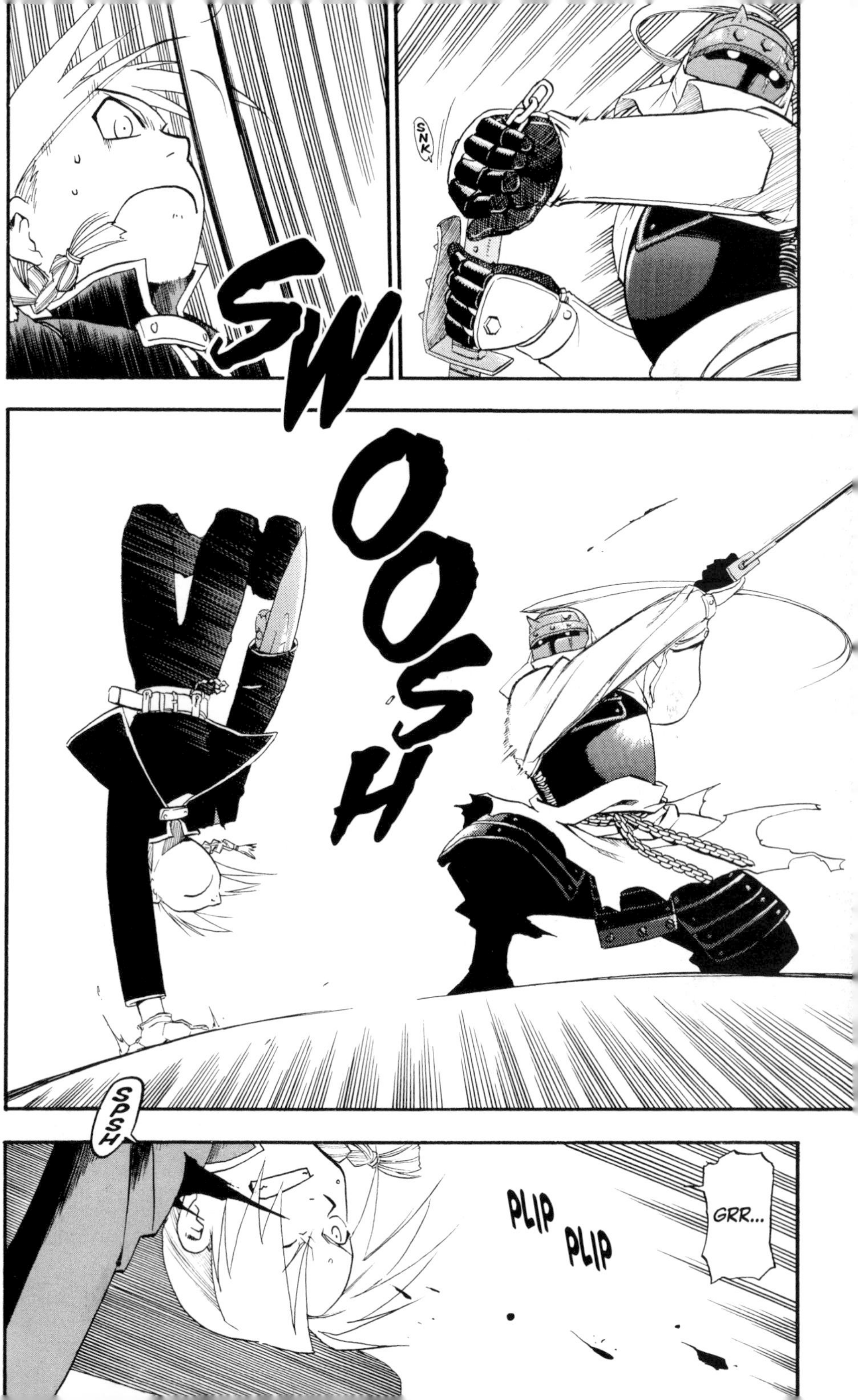
SNK
SWOOSH
SPSH
GRR...
PLIP
PLIP

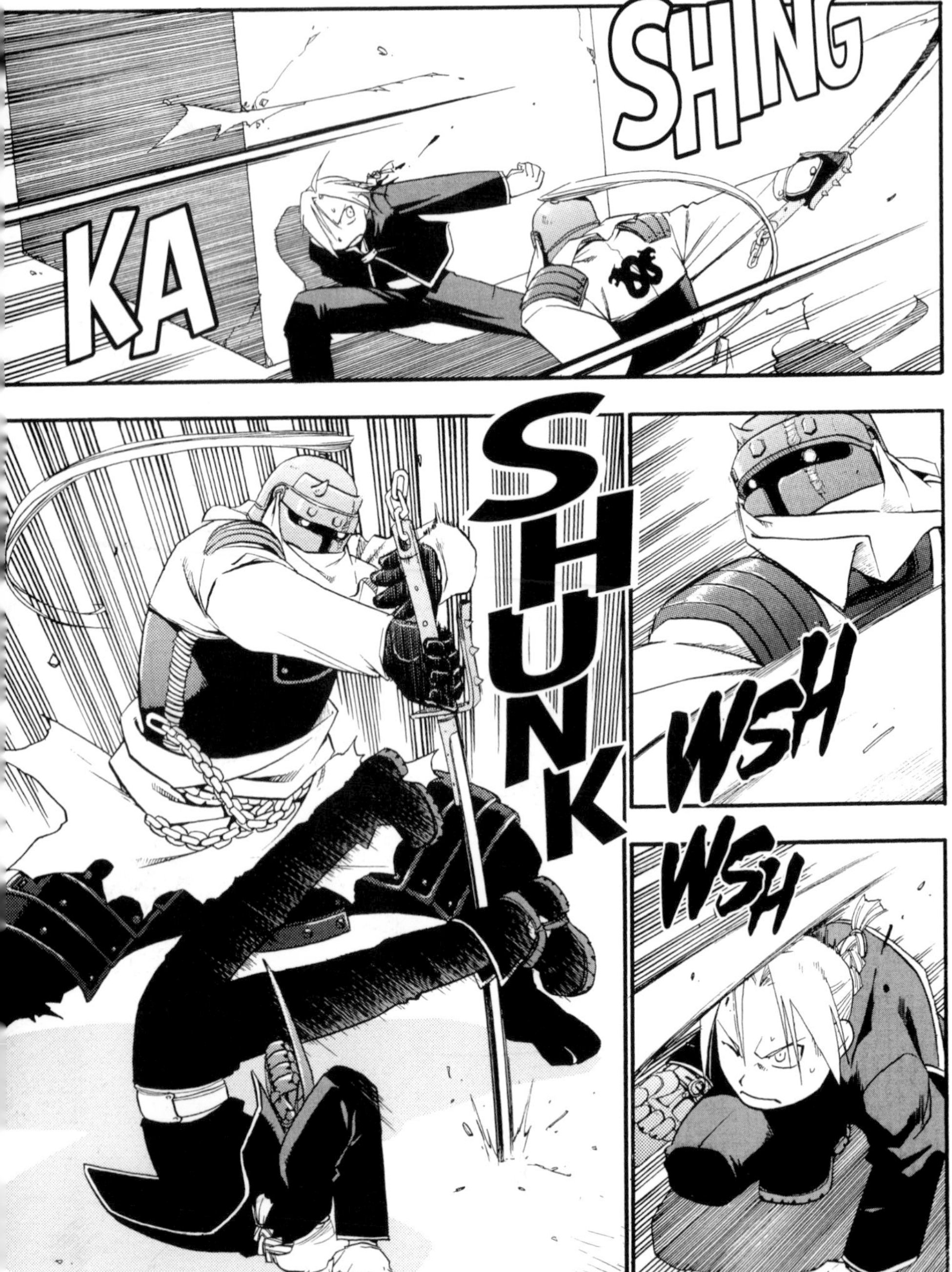
SHING
KA
WSH
WSH
SHUNK

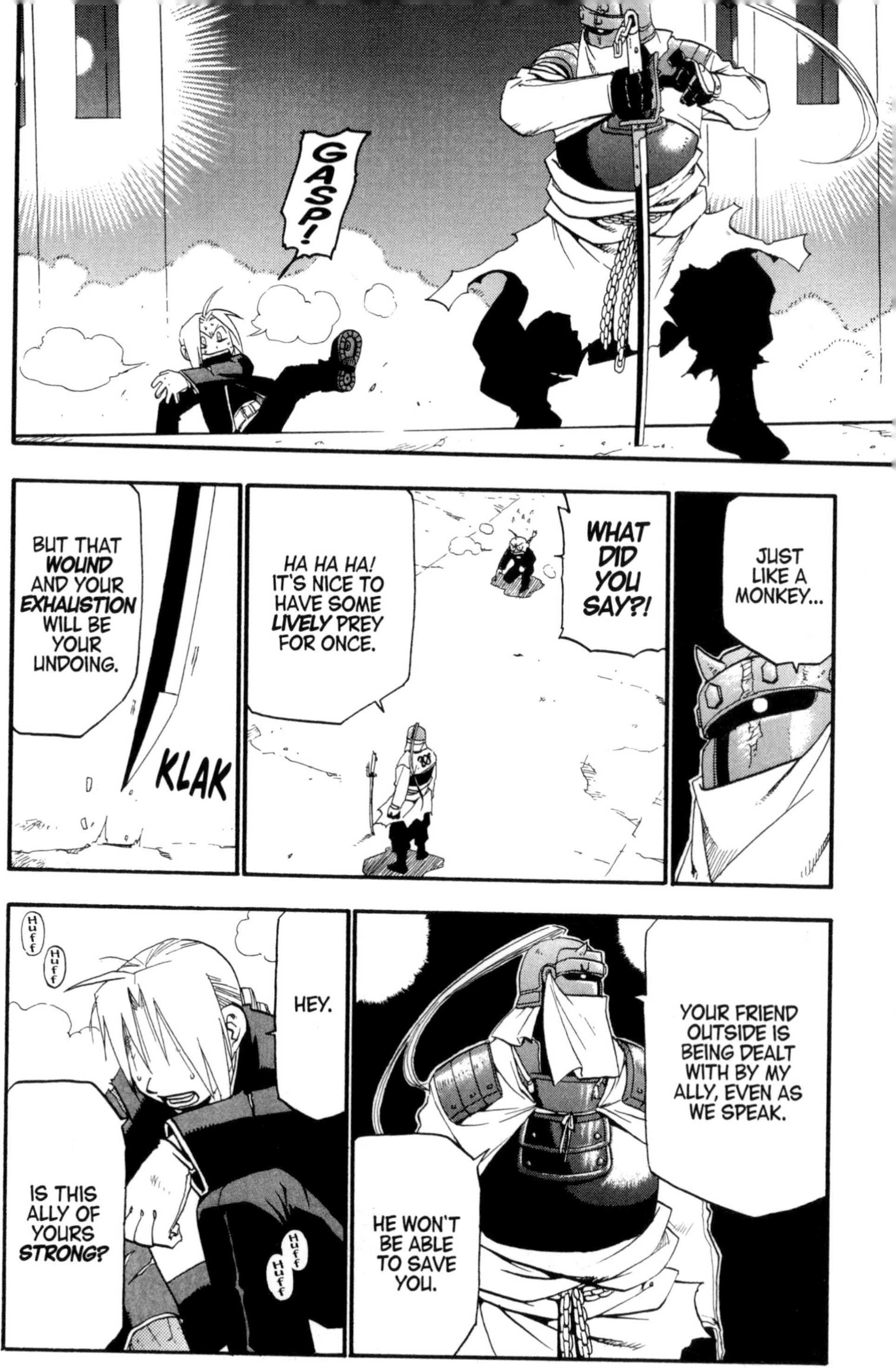
GASP!
JUST LIKE A MONKEY...
WHAT DID YOU SAY?!
HA HA HA! IT'S NICE TO HAVE SOME LIVELY PREY FOR ONCE.
BUT THAT WOUND AND YOUR EXHAUSTION WILL BE YOUR UNDOING.
KLAK
YOUR FRIEND OUTSIDE IS BEING DEALT WITH BY MY ALLY, EVEN AS WE SPEAK.
HE WON'T BE ABLE TO SAVE YOU.
Huff
Huff
HEY.
IS THIS ALLY OF YOURS STRONG?
Huff
Huff

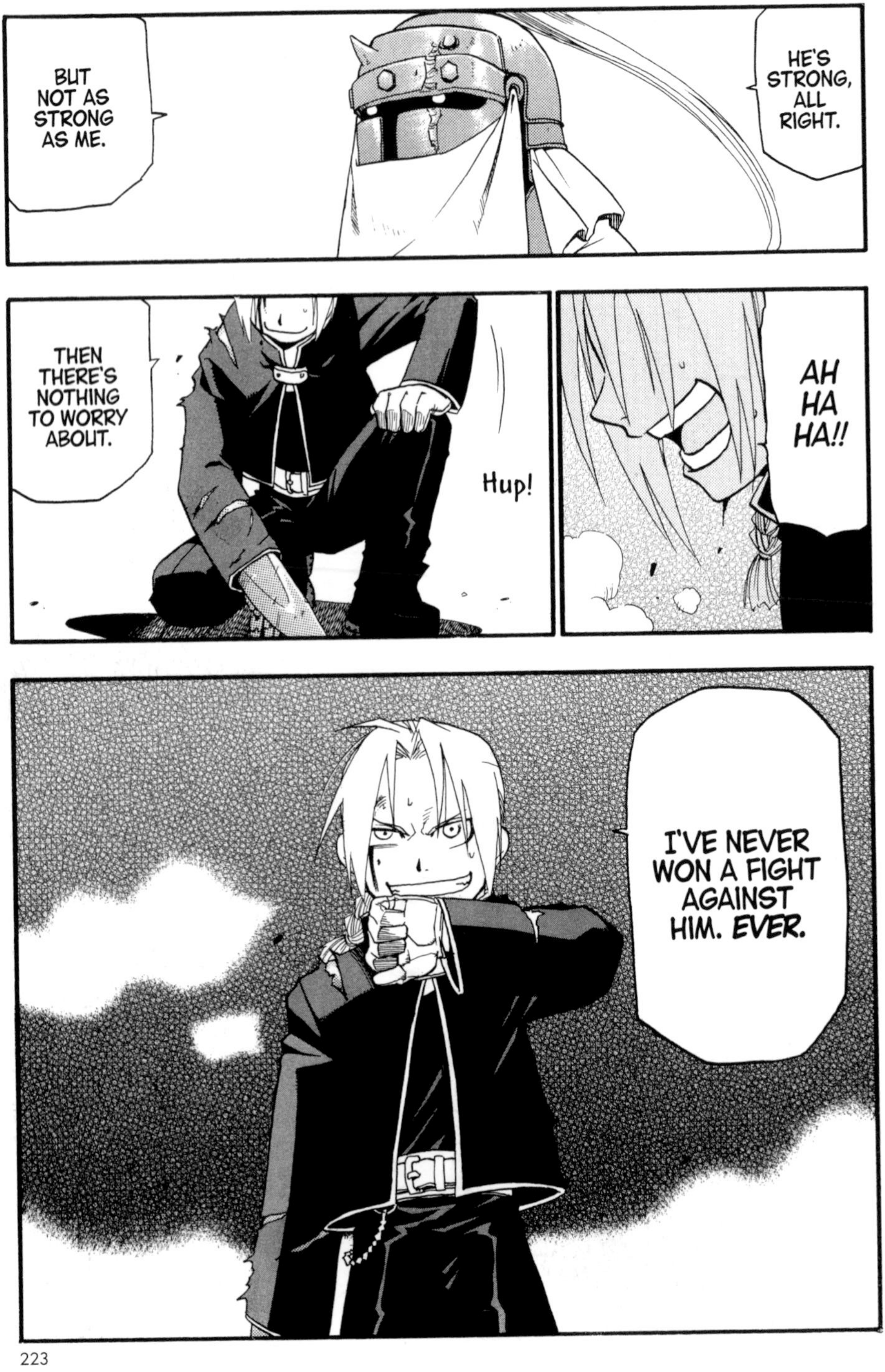
HE'S STRONG, ALL RIGHT.
BUT NOT AS STRONG AS ME.
AH HA HA!!
THEN THERE'S NOTHING TO WORRY ABOUT.
Hup!
I'VE NEVER WON A FIGHT AGAINST HIM. EVER.

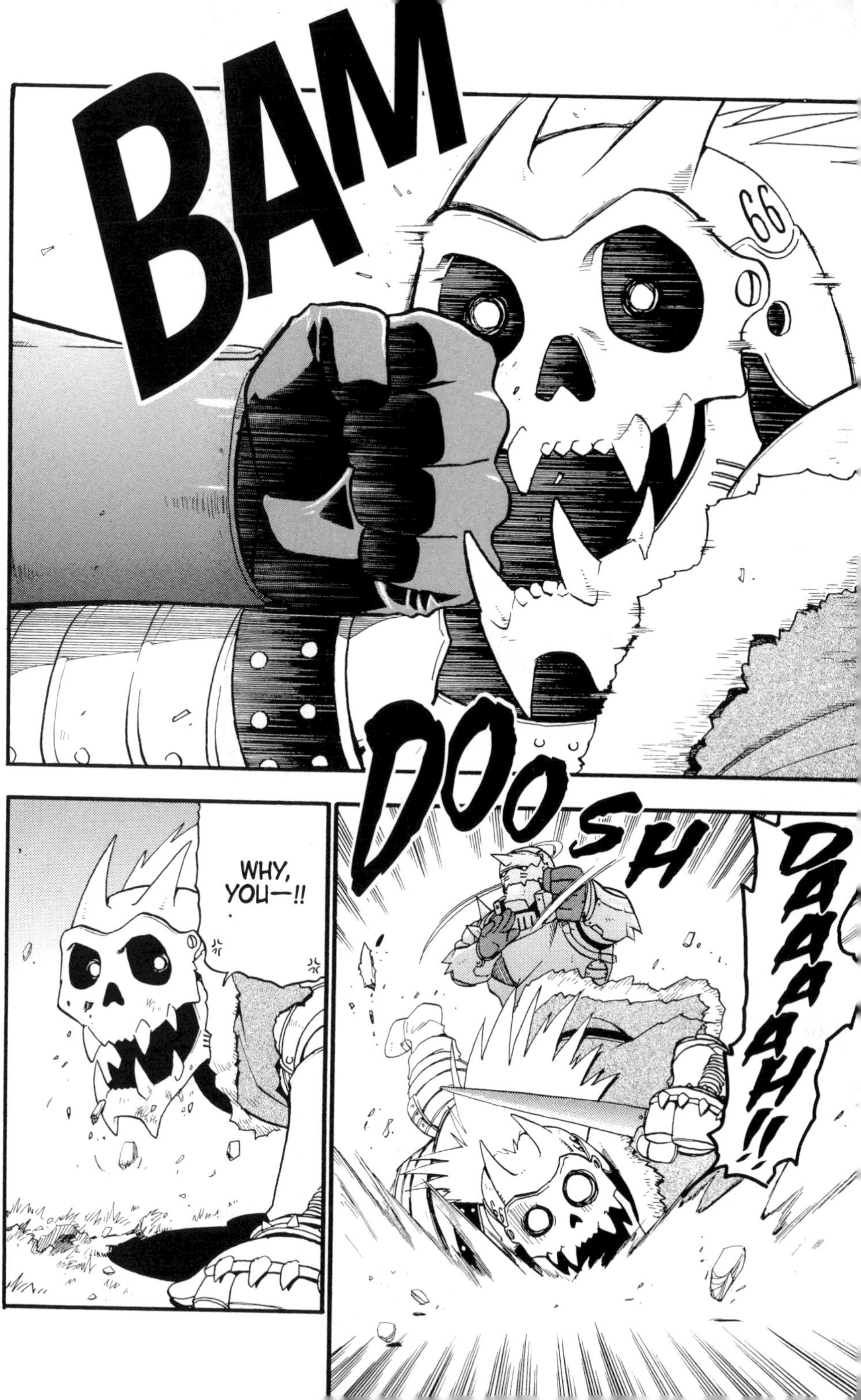
BAM
DOOSH
DAAAAAH!!
WHY, YOU—!!

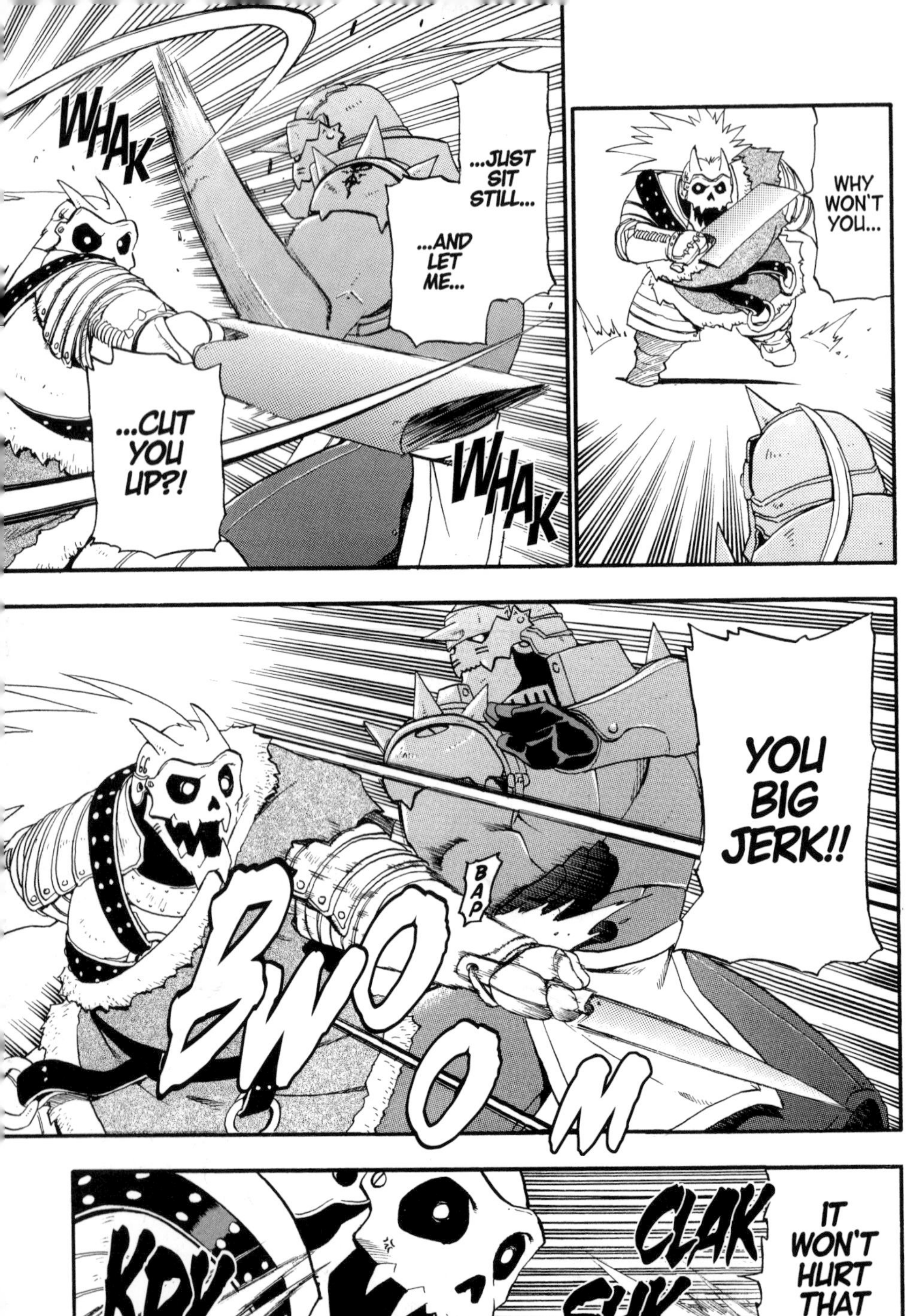
WHY WON'T YOU...
...JUST SIT STILL...
...AND LET ME...
...CUT YOU UP?!
WHAK
WHAK
YOU BIG JERK!!
BAP
BWOOM
IT WON'T HURT THAT BAD!!
CLAK
SHK
KRK

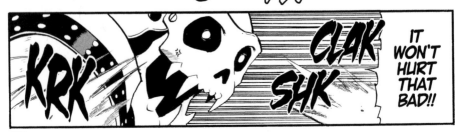

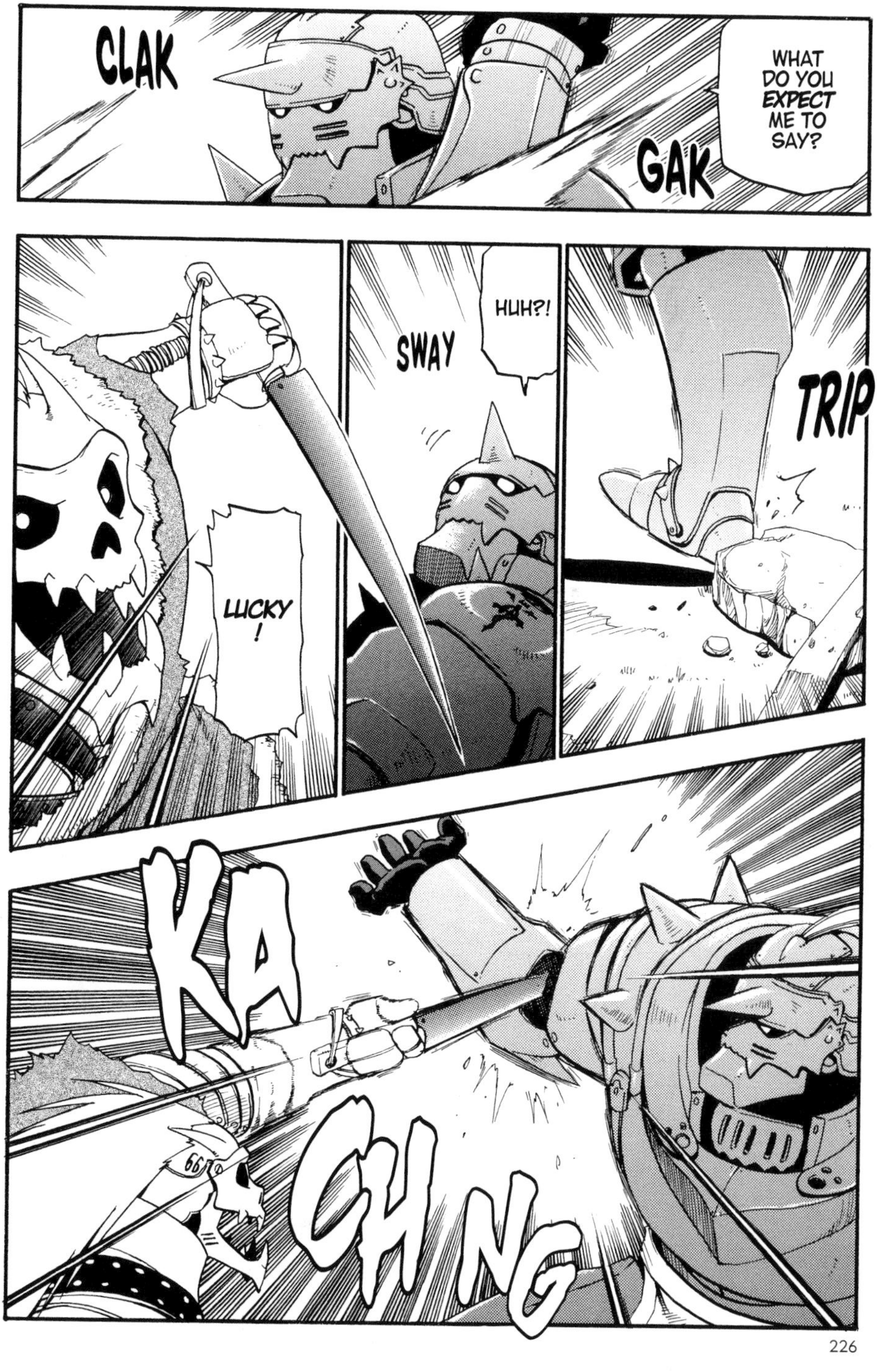
WHAT DO YOU EXPECT ME TO SAY?
CLAK
GAK
TRIP
HUH?!
SWAY
LUCKY!
KA CHING

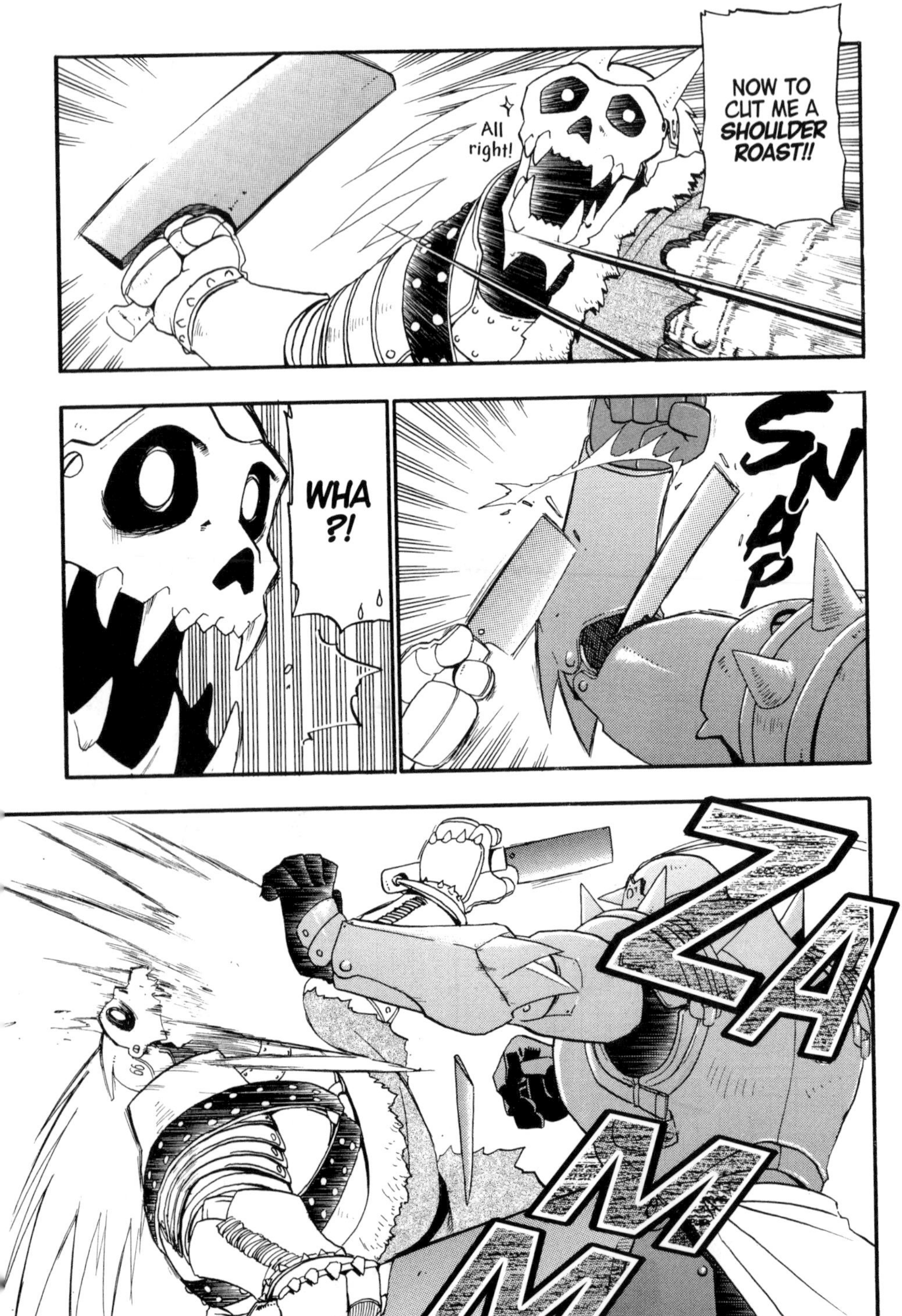
NOW TO CUT ME A SHOULDER ROAST!!
All right!
SNAP
WHA ?!
ZAMMM

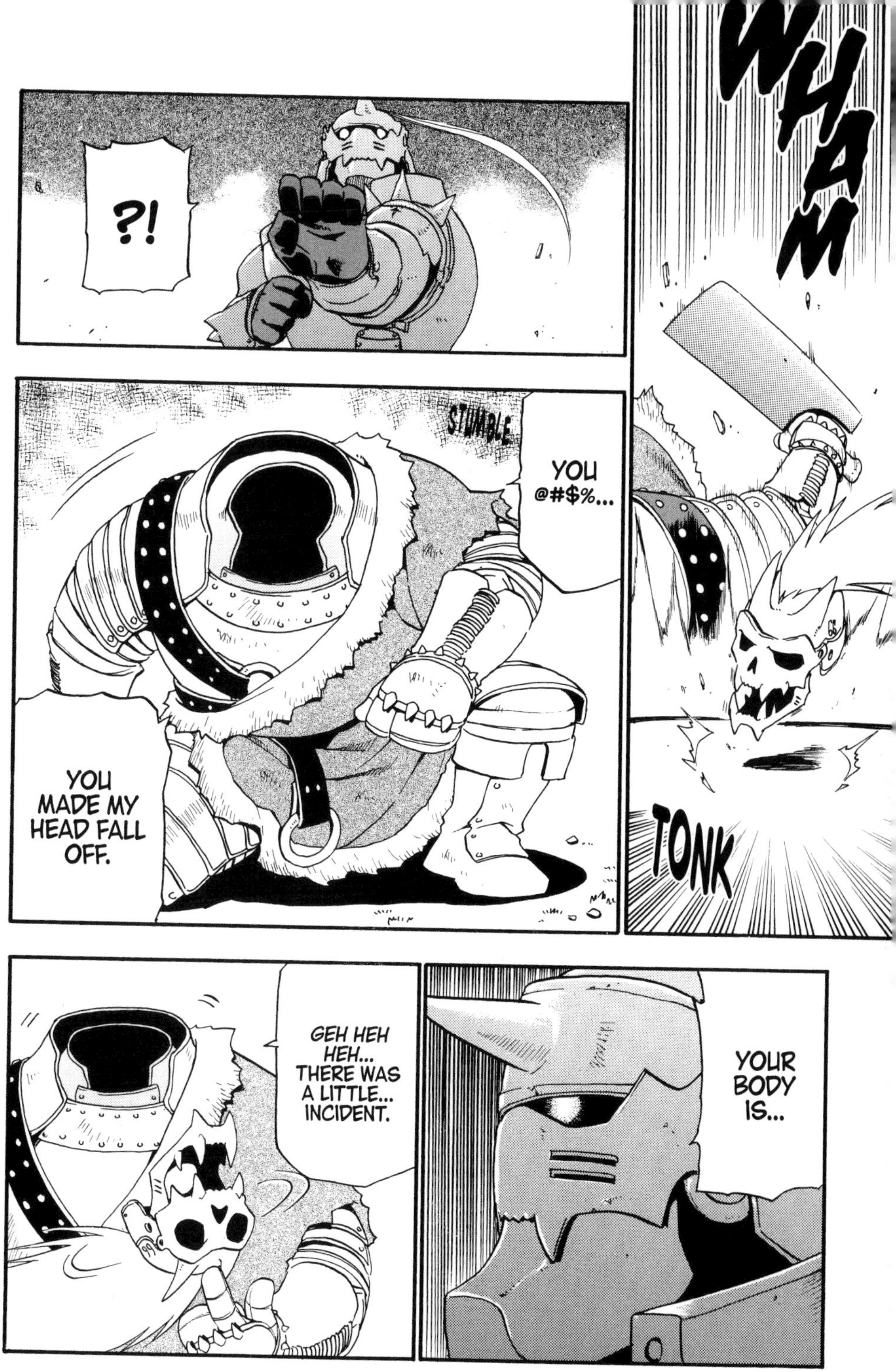
WHAM
TONK
?!
STUMBLE
YOU @#$%...
YOU MADE MY HEAD FALL OFF.
YOUR BODY IS...
GEH HEH HEH... THERE WAS A LITTLE... INCIDENT.

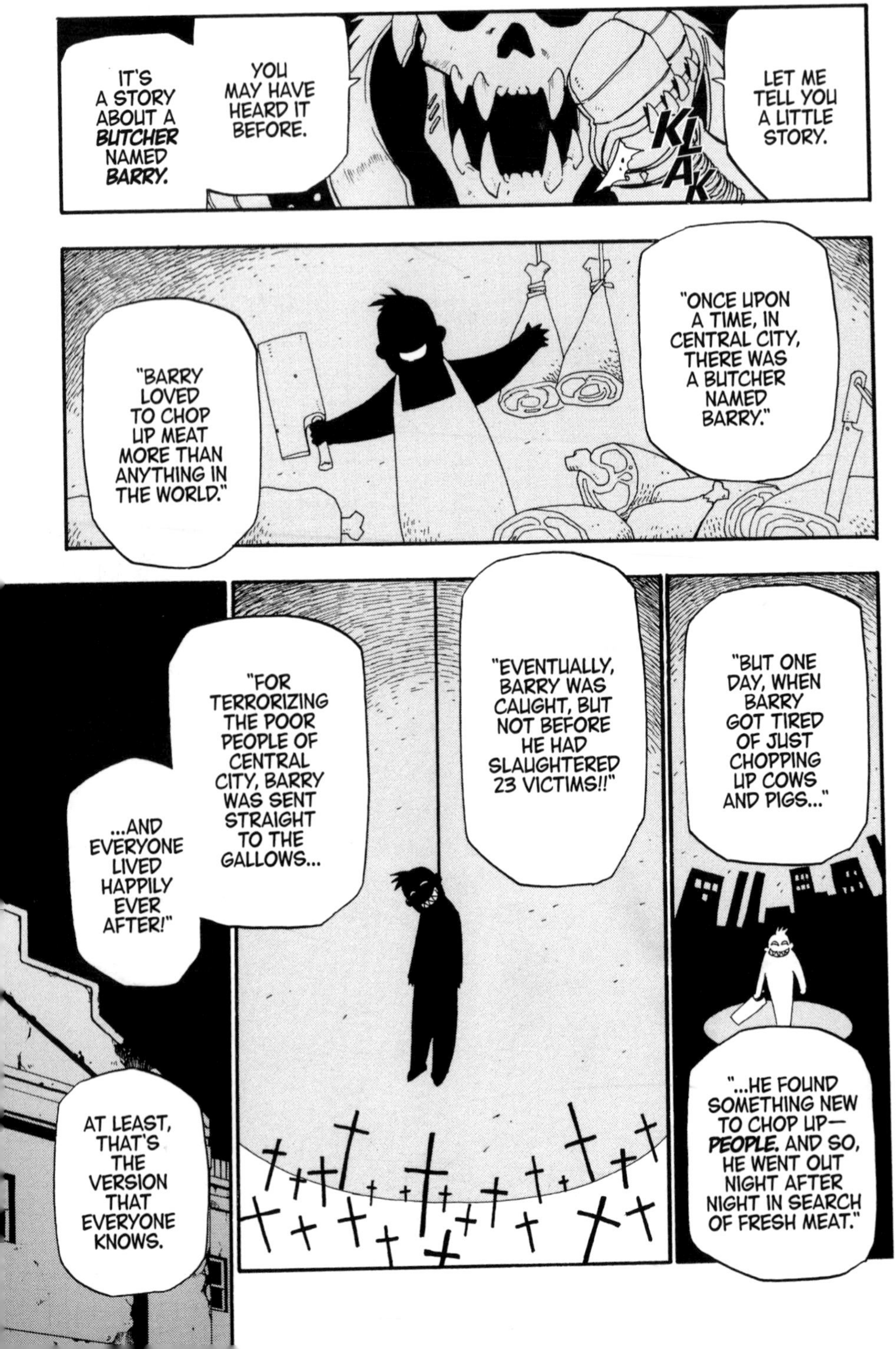
LET ME TELL YOU A LITTLE STORY.
KLAK
YOU MAY HAVE HEARD IT BEFORE.
IT'S A STORY ABOUT A BUTCHER NAMED BARRY.
"ONCE UPON A TIME, IN CENTRAL CITY, THERE WAS A BUTCHER NAMED BARRY."
"BARRY LOVED TO CHOP UP MEAT MORE THAN ANYTHING IN THE WORLD."
"BUT ONE DAY, WHEN BARRY GOT TIRED OF JUST CHOPPING UP COWS AND PIGS..."
"...HE FOUND SOMETHING NEW TO CHOP UP—PEOPLE. AND SO, HE WENT OUT NIGHT AFTER NIGHT IN SEARCH OF FRESH MEAT."
"EVENTUALLY, BARRY WAS CAUGHT, BUT NOT BEFORE HE HAD SLAUGHTERED 23 VICTIMS!!"
"FOR TERRORIZING THE POOR PEOPLE OF CENTRAL CITY, BARRY WAS SENT STRAIGHT TO THE GALLOWS...
...AND EVERYONE LIVED HAPPILY EVER AFTER!"
AT LEAST, THAT'S THE VERSION THAT EVERYONE KNOWS.

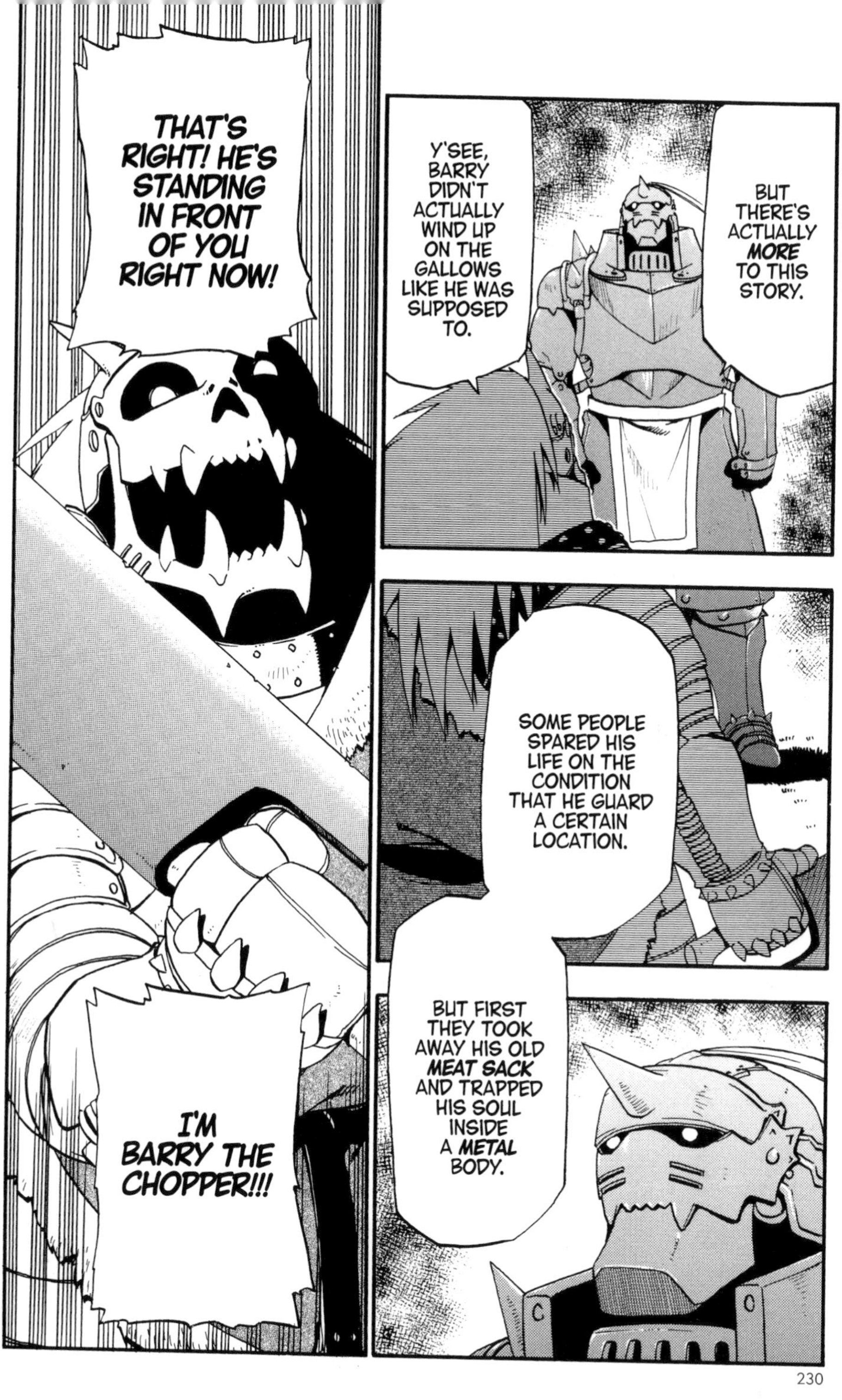
BUT THERE'S ACTUALLY MORE TO THIS STORY.
Y'SEE, BARRY DIDN'T ACTUALLY WIND UP ON THE GALLOWS LIKE HE WAS SUPPOSED TO.
SOME PEOPLE SPARED HIS LIFE ON THE CONDITION THAT HE GUARD A CERTAIN LOCATION.
BUT FIRST THEY TOOK AWAY HIS OLD MEAT SACK AND TRAPPED HIS SOUL INSIDE A METAL BODY.
THAT'S RIGHT! HE'S STANDING IN FRONT OF YOU RIGHT NOW!
I'M BARRY THE CHOPPER!!!

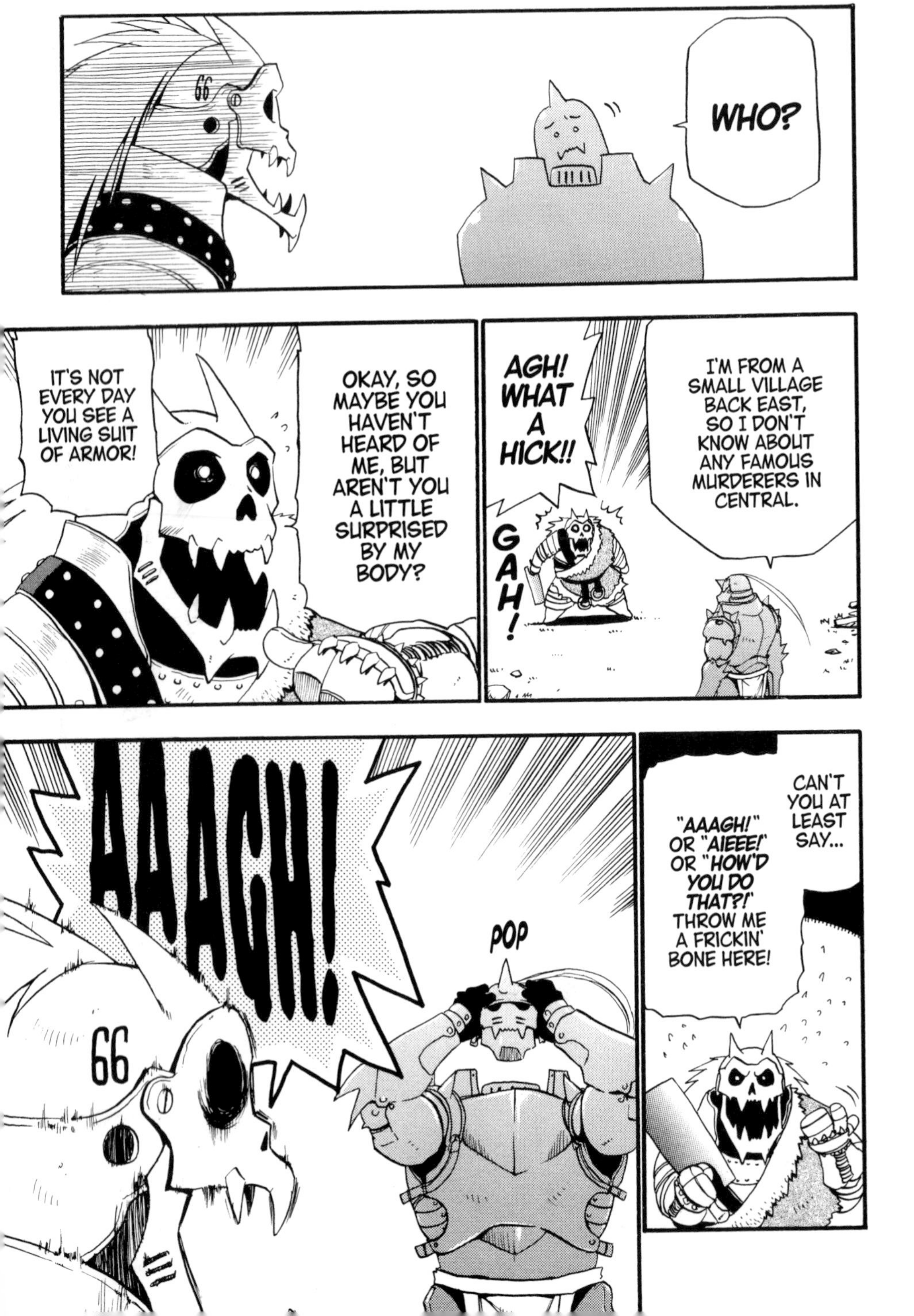
WHO?
66
I'M FROM A SMALL VILLAGE BACK EAST, SO I DON'T KNOW ABOUT ANY FAMOUS MURDERERS IN CENTRAL.
AGH! WHAT A HICK!!
GAH!
OKAY, SO MAYBE YOU HAVEN'T HEARD OF ME, BUT AREN'T YOU A LITTLE SURPRISED BY MY BODY?
IT'S NOT EVERY DAY YOU SEE A LIVING SUIT OF ARMOR!
CAN'T YOU AT LEAST SAY...
"AAAGH!" OR "AIEEE!" OR "HOW'D YOU DO THAT?!" THROW ME A FRICKIN' BONE HERE!
POP
AAAGH!
66

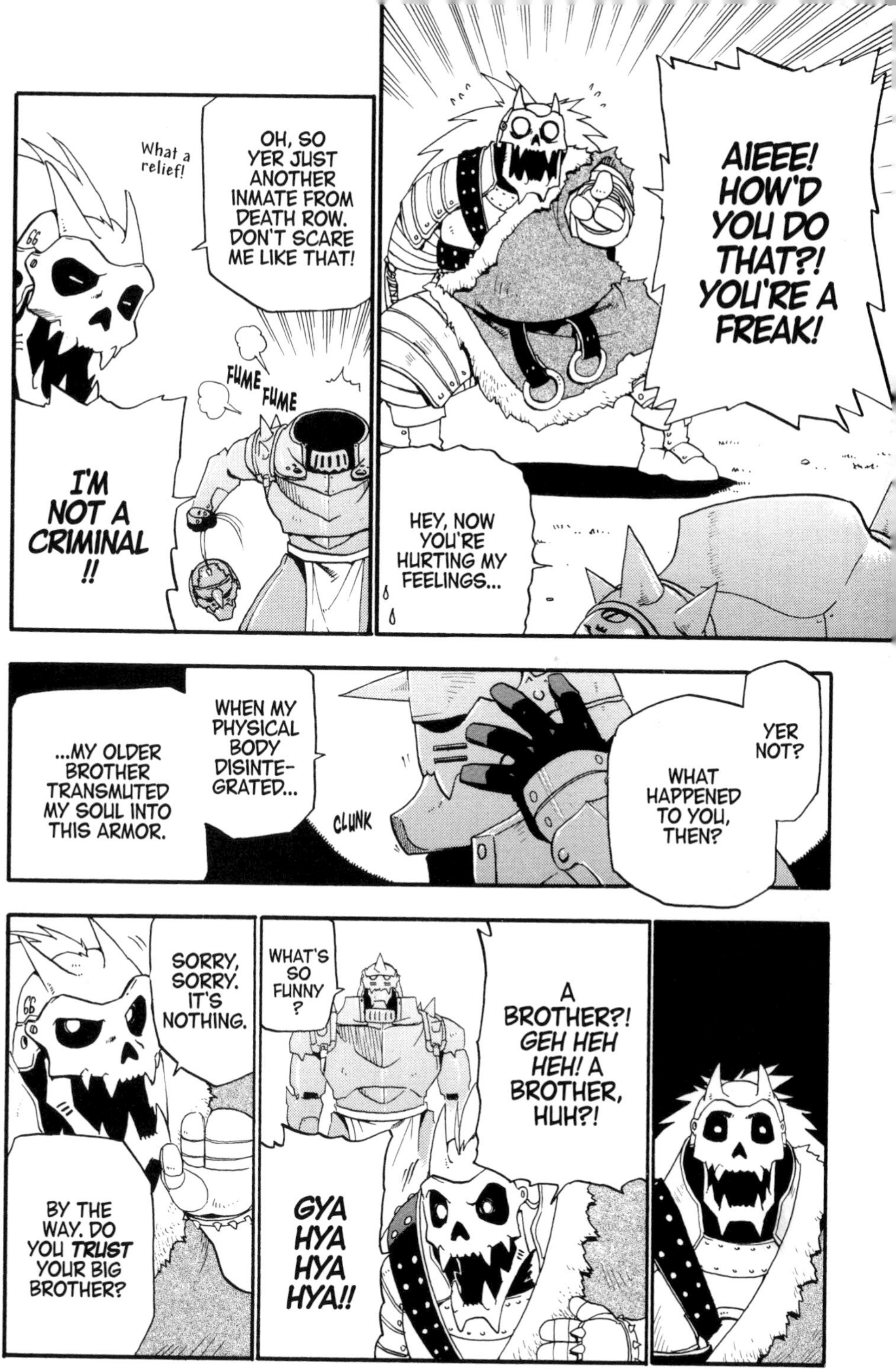
AIEEE! HOW'D YOU DO THAT?! YOU'RE A FREAK!
HEY, NOW YOU'RE HURTING MY FEELINGS...
OH, SO YER JUST ANOTHER INMATE FROM DEATH ROW. DON'T SCARE ME LIKE THAT!
What a relief!
FUME FUME
I'M NOT A CRIMINAL!!
YER NOT?
WHAT HAPPENED TO YOU, THEN?
CLUNK
WHEN MY PHYSICAL BODY DISINTEGRATED...
...MY OLDER BROTHER TRANSMUTED MY SOUL INTO THIS ARMOR.
A BROTHER?! GEH HEH HEH! A BROTHER, HUH?!
WHAT'S SO FUNNY?
GYA HYA HYA HYA!!
SORRY, SORRY. IT'S NOTHING.
BY THE WAY. DO YOU TRUST YOUR BIG BROTHER?

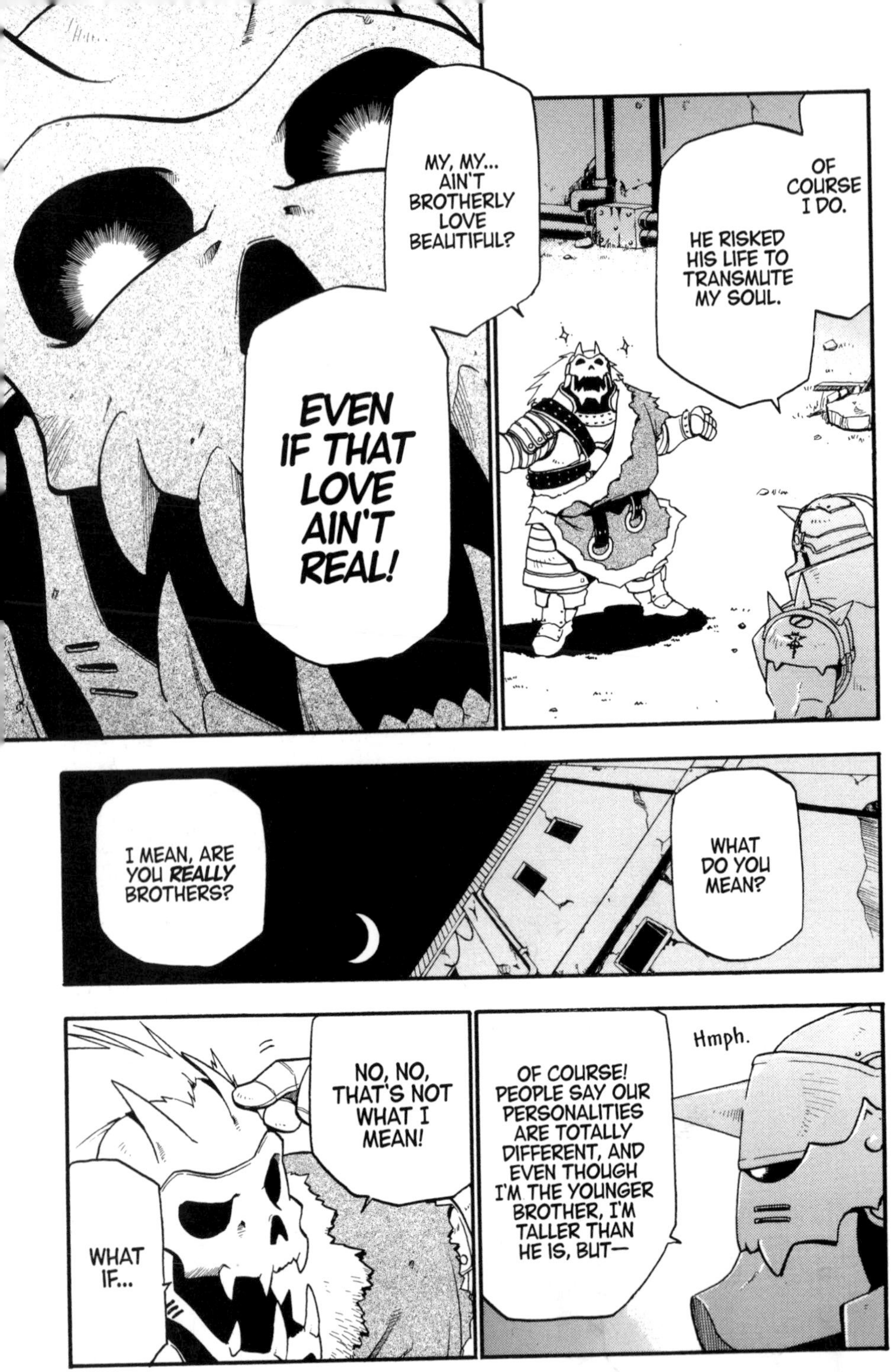
OF COURSE I DO.
HE RISKED HIS LIFE TO TRANSMUTE MY SOUL.
MY, MY... AIN'T BROTHERLY LOVE BEAUTIFUL?
EVEN IF THAT LOVE AIN'T REAL!
WHAT DO YOU MEAN?
I MEAN, ARE YOU *REALLY* BROTHERS?
Hmph.
OF COURSE! PEOPLE SAY OUR PERSONALITIES ARE TOTALLY DIFFERENT, AND EVEN THOUGH I'M THE YOUNGER BROTHER, I'M TALLER THAN HE IS, BUT—
NO, NO, THAT'S NOT WHAT I MEAN!
WHAT IF...

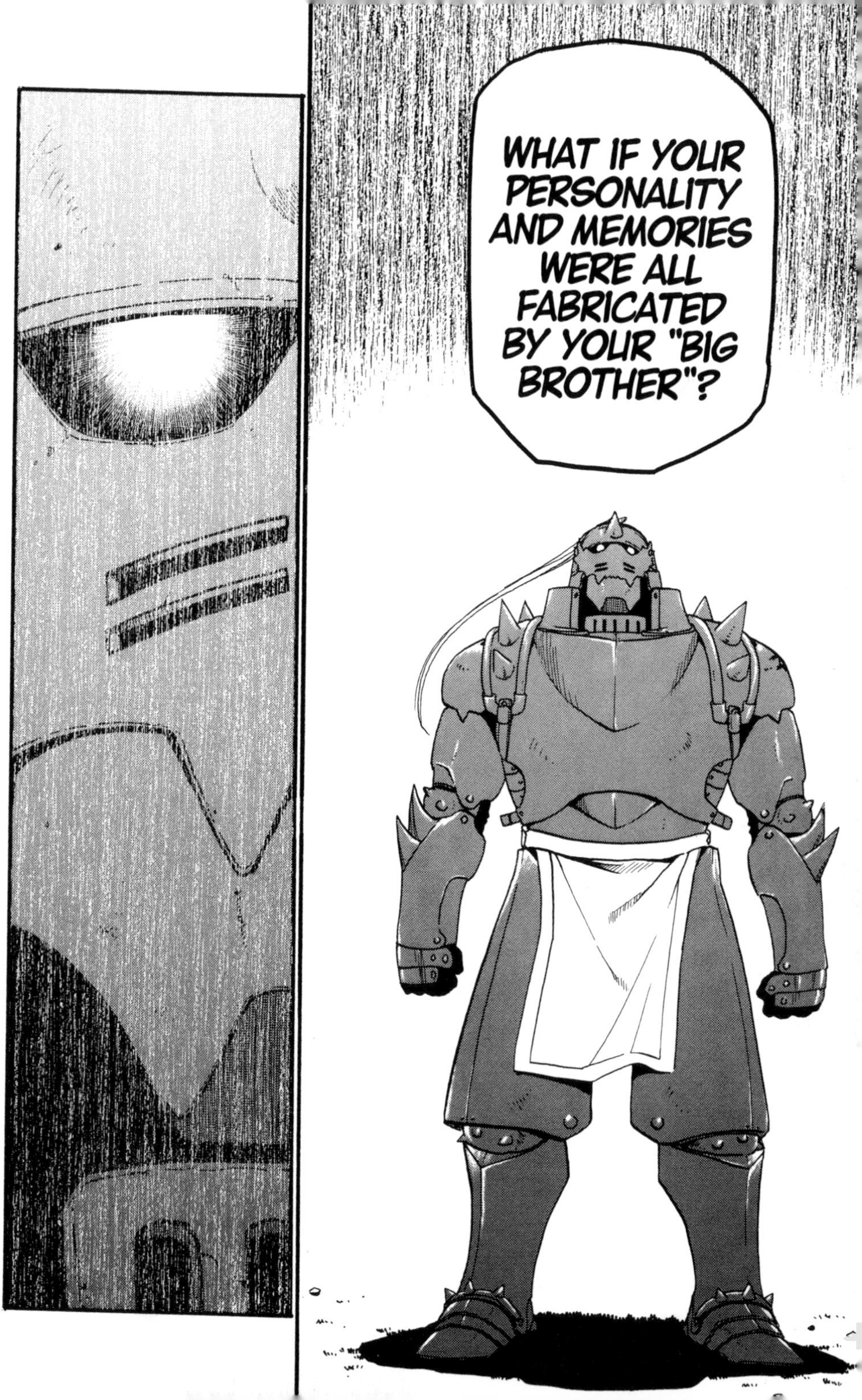
WHAT IF YOUR PERSONALITY AND MEMORIES WERE ALL FABRICATED BY YOUR "BIG BROTHER"?

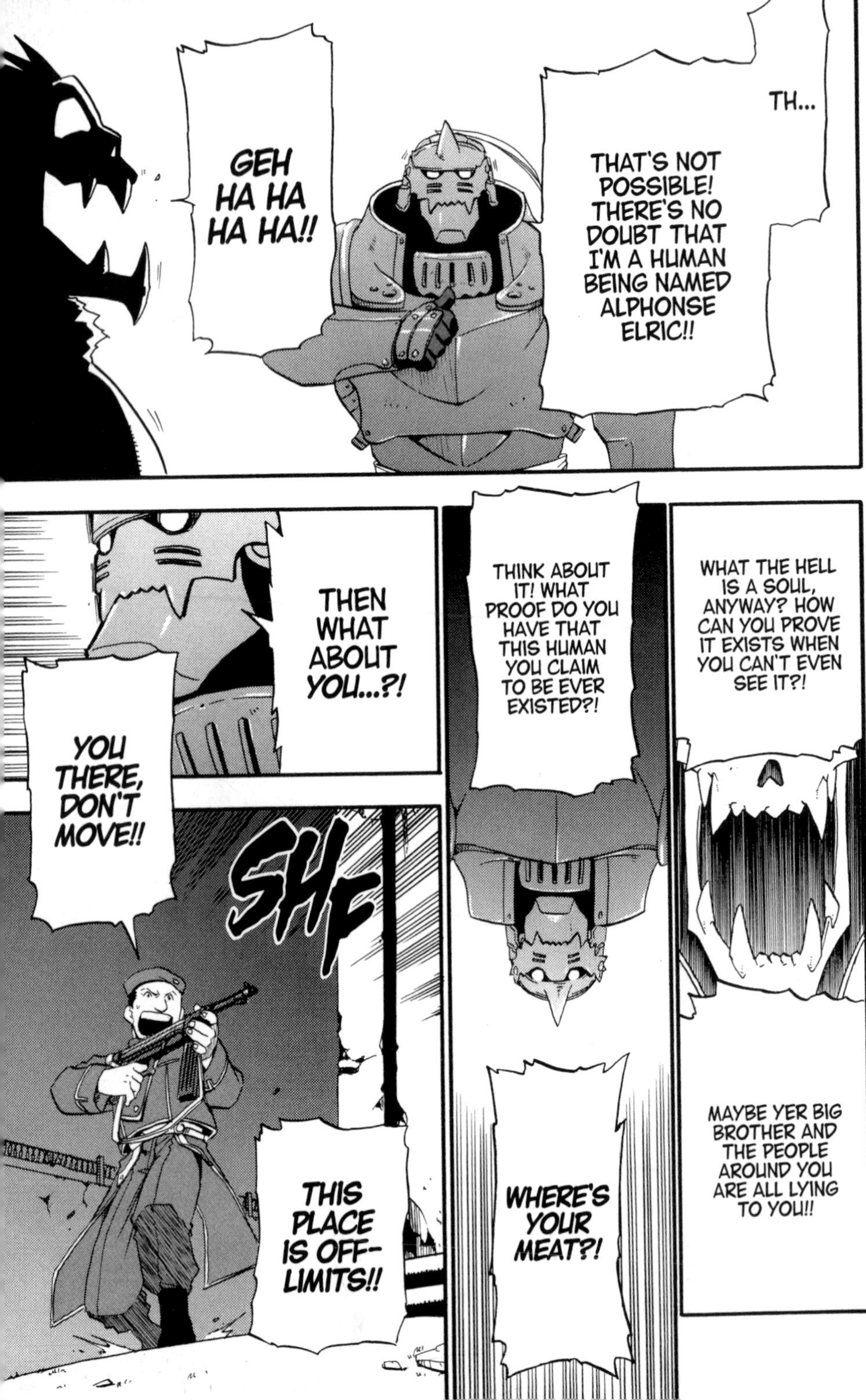
TH...
THAT'S NOT POSSIBLE! THERE'S NO DOUBT THAT I'M A HUMAN BEING NAMED ALPHONSE ELRIC!!
GEH HA HA HA HA!!
WHAT THE HELL IS A SOUL, ANYWAY? HOW CAN YOU PROVE IT EXISTS WHEN YOU CAN'T EVEN SEE IT?!
MAYBE YER BIG BROTHER AND THE PEOPLE AROUND YOU ARE ALL LYING TO YOU!!
THINK ABOUT IT! WHAT PROOF DO YOU HAVE THAT THIS HUMAN YOU CLAIM TO BE EVER EXISTED?!
WHERE'S YOUR MEAT?!
THEN WHAT ABOUT YOU...?!
YOU THERE, DON'T MOVE!!
SHF
THIS PLACE IS OFF-LIMITS!!

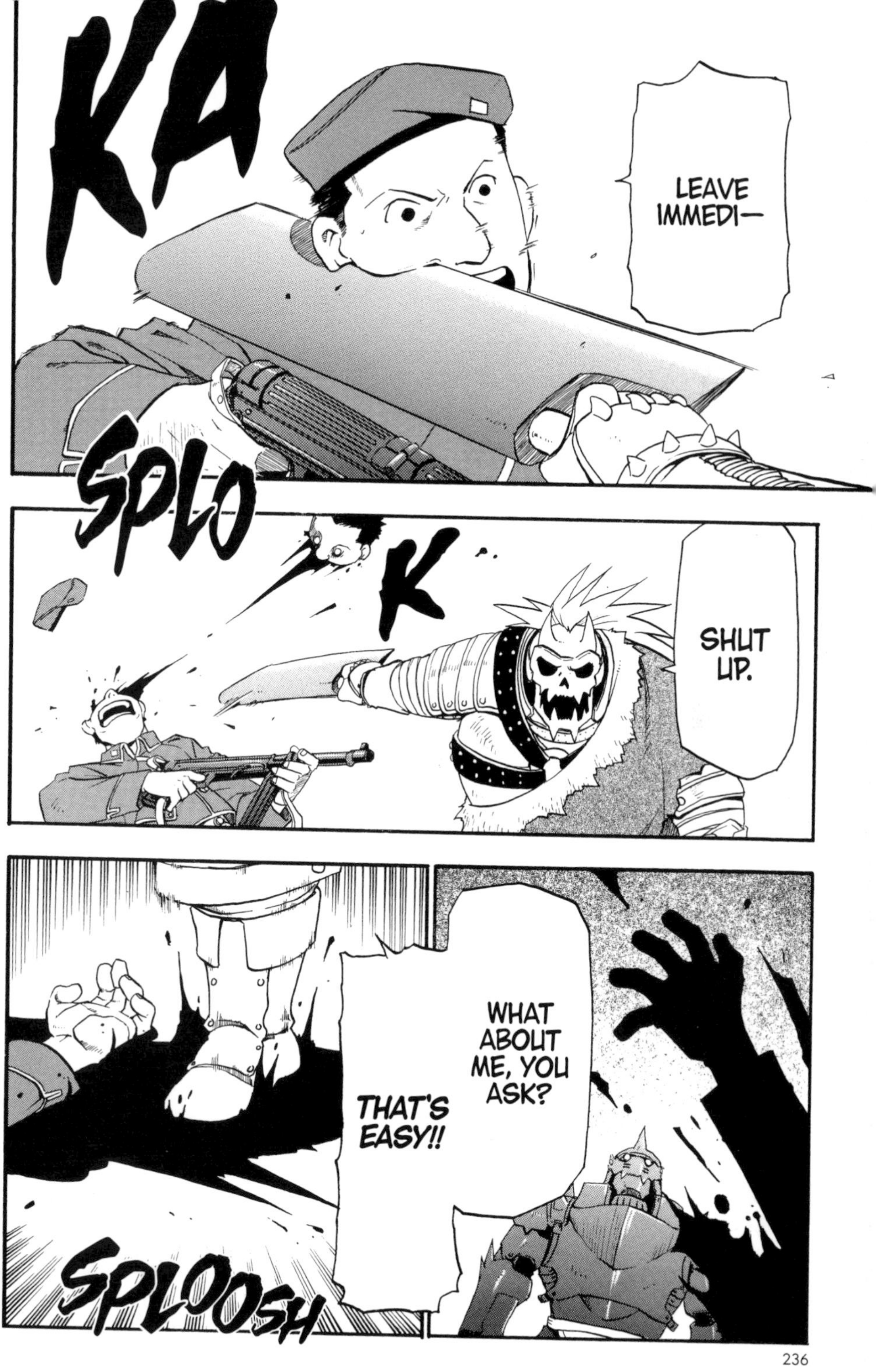

LEAVE IMMEDI—
KA
SHUT UP.
SPLOK
WHAT ABOUT ME, YOU ASK?
THAT'S EASY!!
SPLOOSH

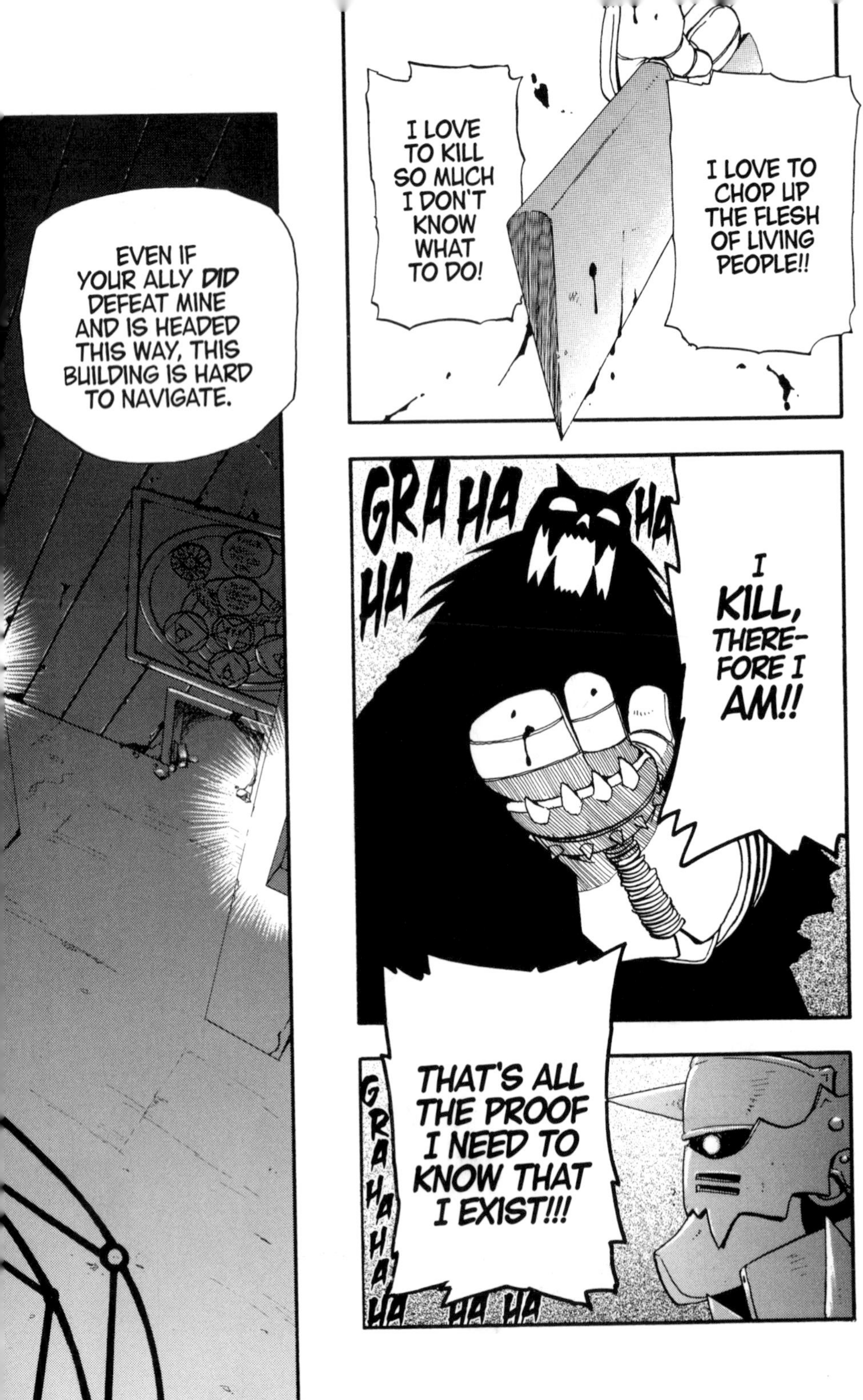
I LOVE TO CHOP UP THE FLESH OF LIVING PEOPLE!!
I LOVE TO KILL SO MUCH I DON'T KNOW WHAT TO DO!
GRAHAHA HA HA
I KILL, THEREFORE I AM!!
THAT'S ALL THE PROOF I NEED TO KNOW THAT I EXIST!!!
GRAHAHAHAHA HA HA
EVEN IF YOUR ALLY DID DEFEAT MINE AND IS HEADED THIS WAY, THIS BUILDING IS HARD TO NAVIGATE.

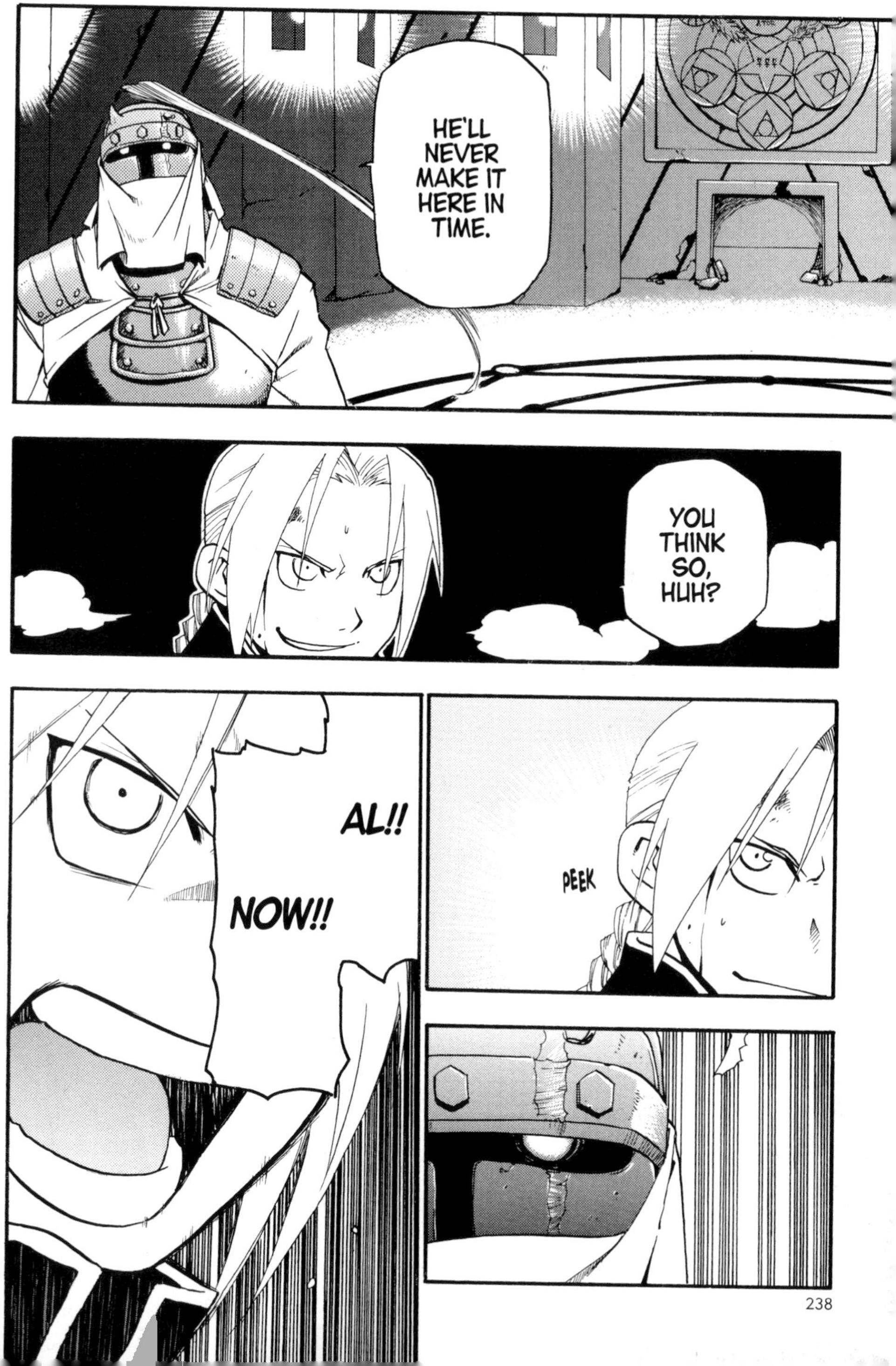
HE'LL NEVER MAKE IT HERE IN TIME.
YOU THINK SO, HUH?
PEEK
AL!!
NOW!!

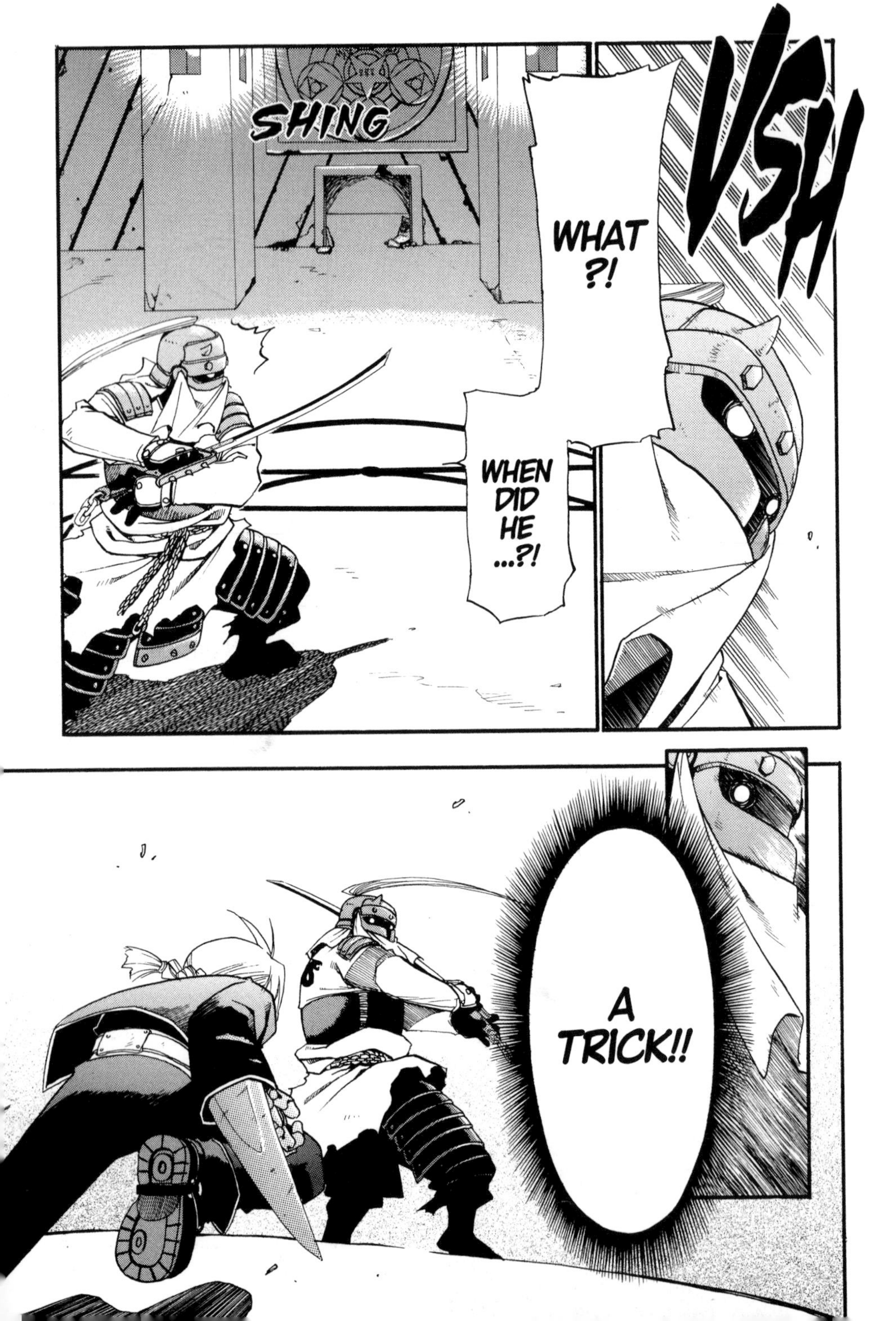
VSSH
WHAT?!
WHEN DID HE ...?!
SHING
A TRICK!!

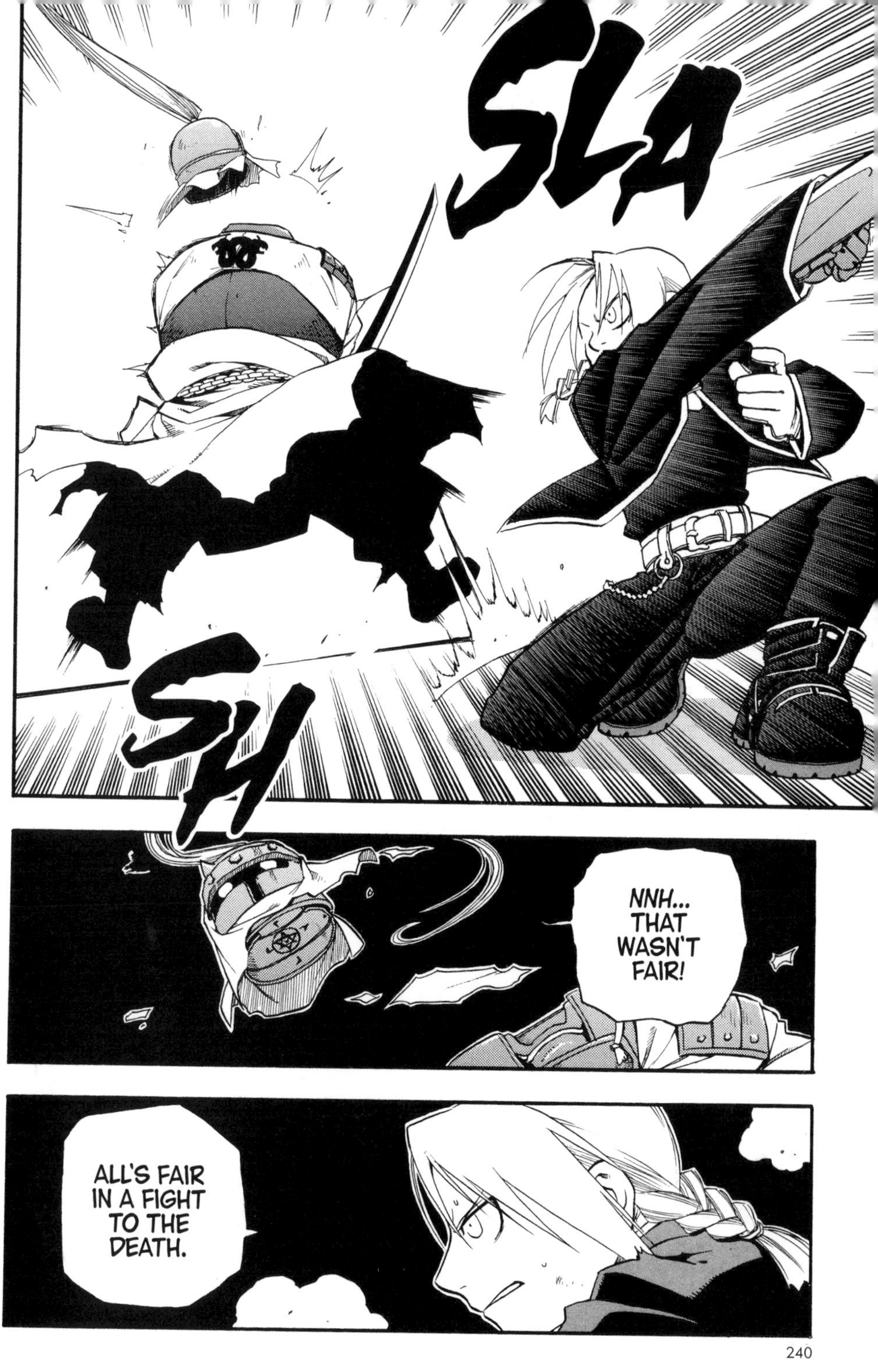
SLA
SH
NNH... THAT WASN'T FAIR!
ALL'S FAIR IN A FIGHT TO THE DEATH.

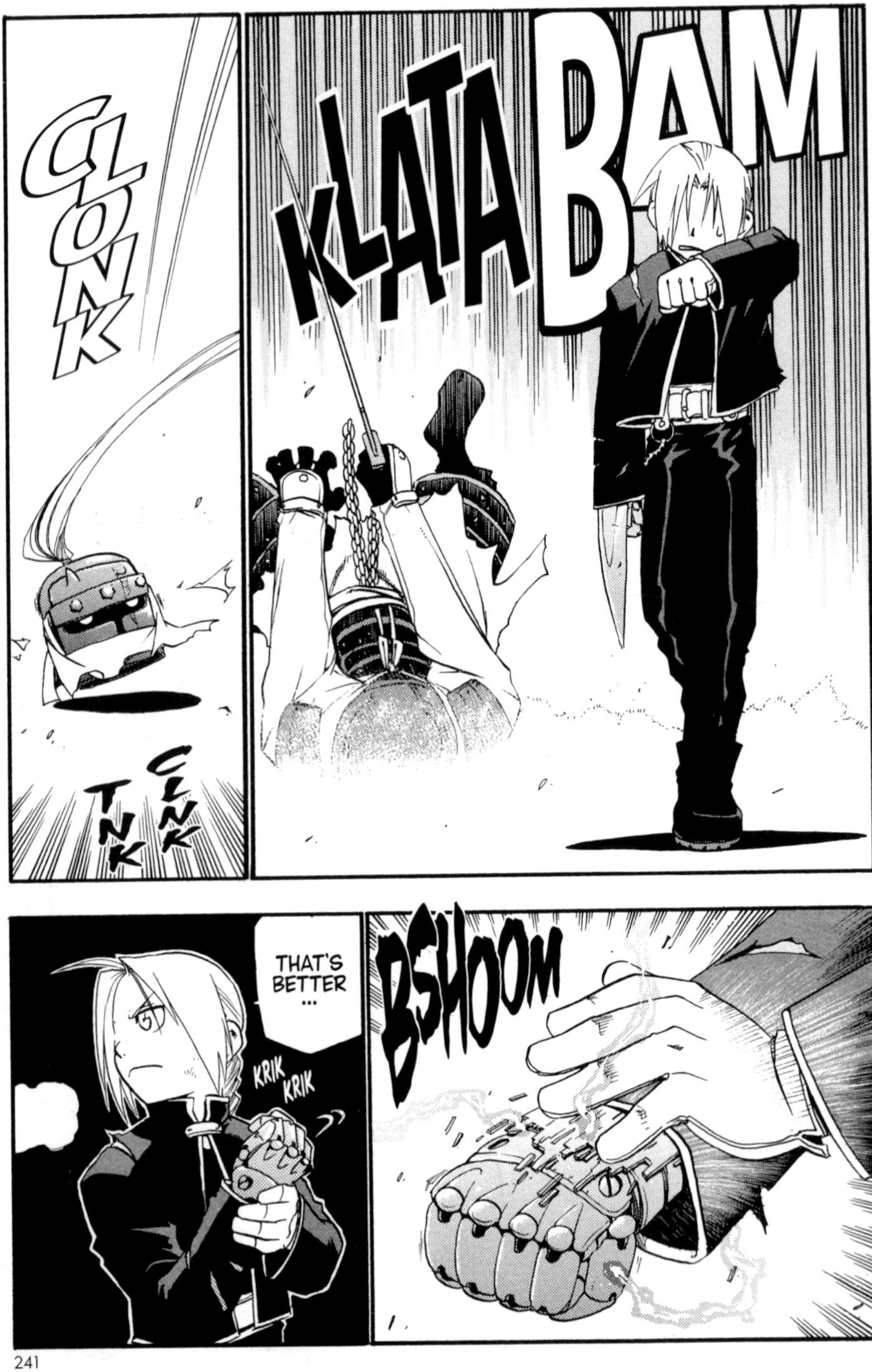
KLATABAM
CLONK
CLNK
TNK
BSHOOM
THAT'S BETTER ...
KRIK KRIK

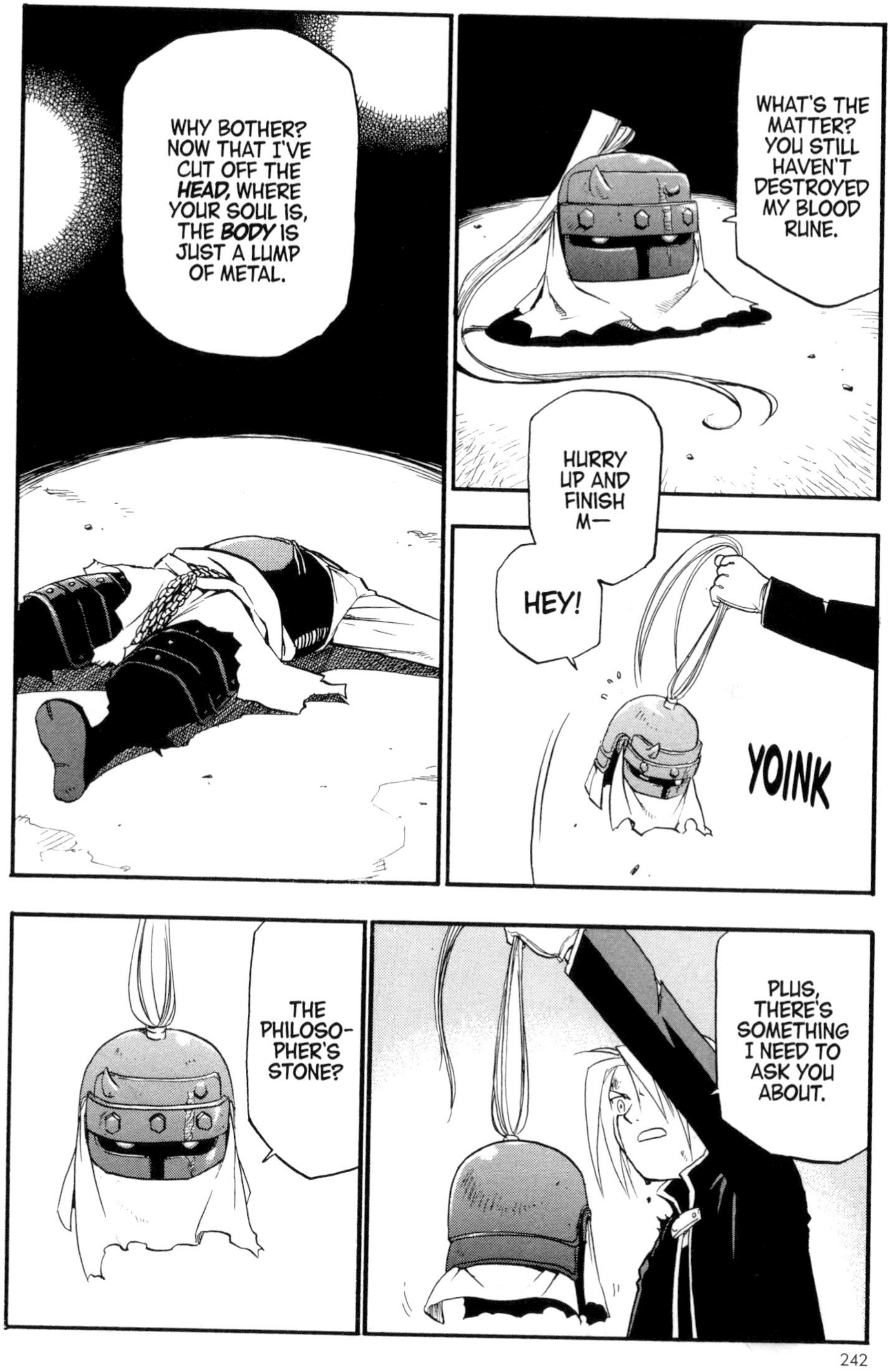
WHAT'S THE MATTER? YOU STILL HAVEN'T DESTROYED MY BLOOD RUNE.
HURRY UP AND FINISH M—
HEY!
YOINK
WHY BOTHER? NOW THAT I'VE CUT OFF THE HEAD, WHERE YOUR SOUL IS, THE BODY IS JUST A LUMP OF METAL.
PLUS, THERE'S SOMETHING I NEED TO ASK YOU ABOUT.
THE PHILOSO-PHER'S STONE?

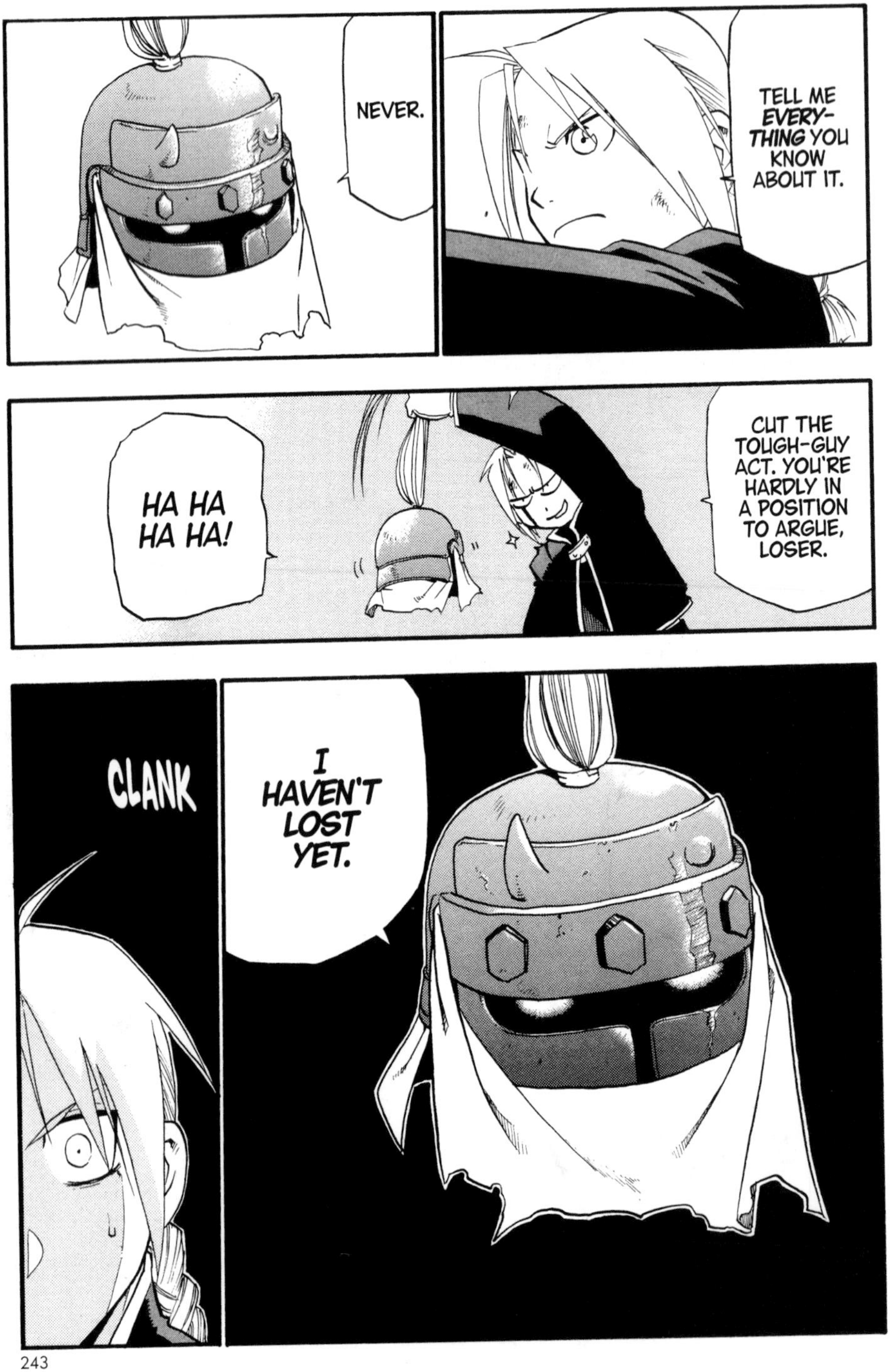
TELL ME EVERY-THING YOU KNOW ABOUT IT.
NEVER.
CUT THE TOUGH-GUY ACT. YOU'RE HARDLY IN A POSITION TO ARGUE, LOSER.
HA HA HA HA!
I HAVEN'T LOST YET.
CLANK

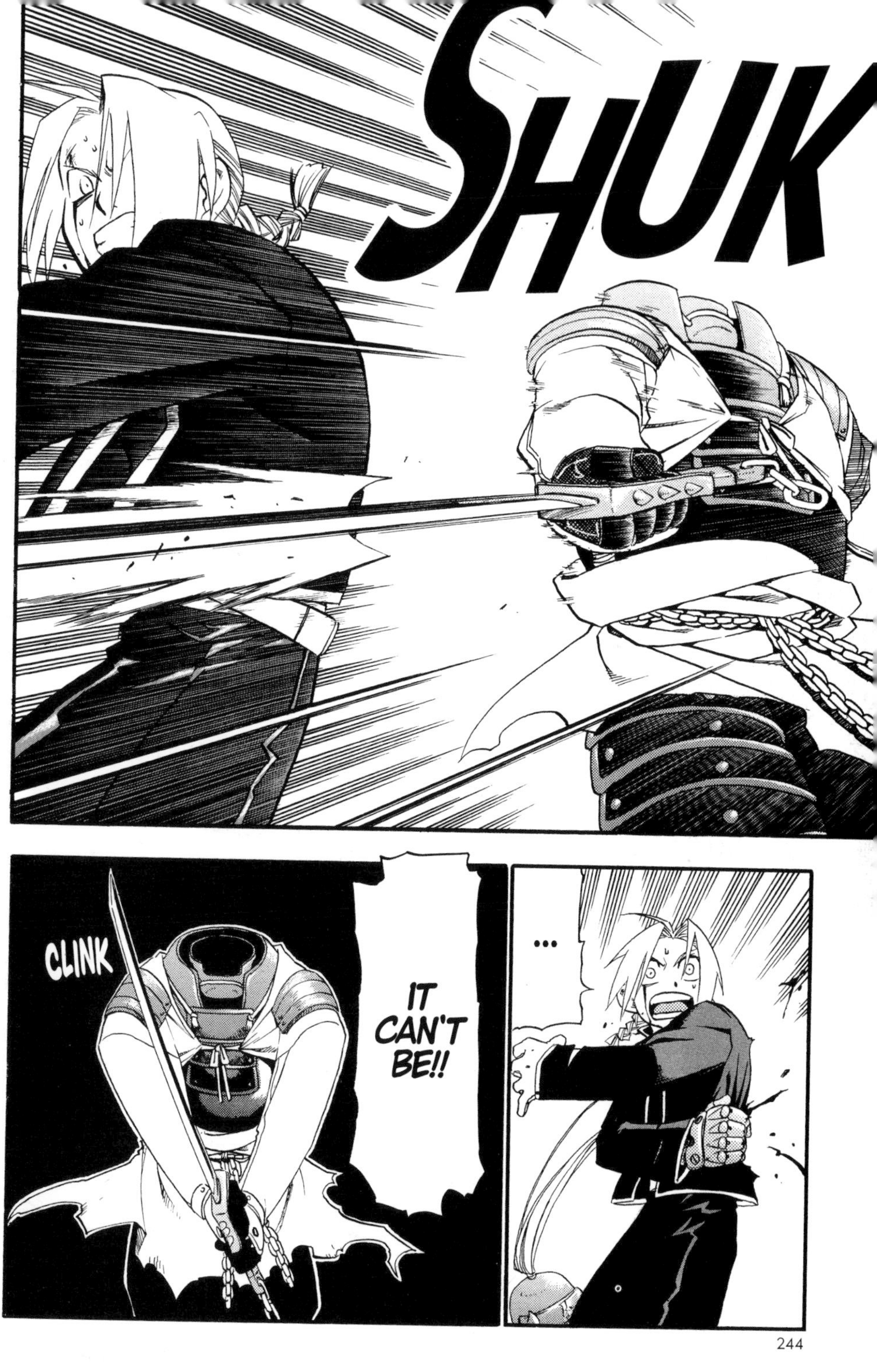
SHUK
...
IT CAN'T BE!!
CLINK

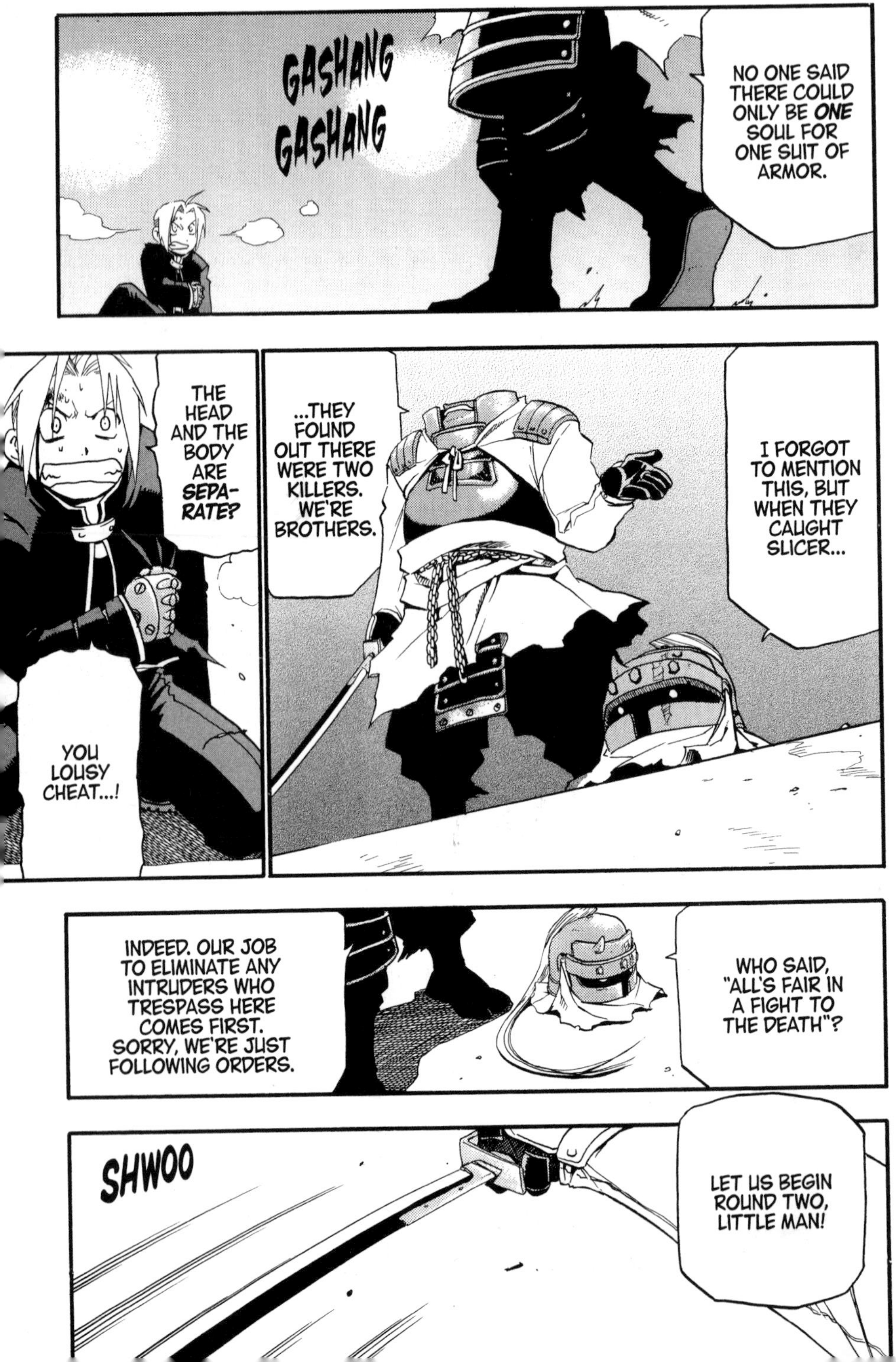
NO ONE SAID THERE COULD ONLY BE ONE SOUL FOR ONE SUIT OF ARMOR.
GASHANG GASHANG
I FORGOT TO MENTION THIS, BUT WHEN THEY CAUGHT SLICER...
...THEY FOUND OUT THERE WERE TWO KILLERS. WE'RE BROTHERS.
THE HEAD AND THE BODY ARE SEPARATE?
YOU LOUSY CHEAT...!
WHO SAID, "ALL'S FAIR IN A FIGHT TO THE DEATH"?
INDEED. OUR JOB TO ELIMINATE ANY INTRUDERS WHO TRESPASS HERE COMES FIRST. SORRY, WE'RE JUST FOLLOWING ORDERS.
LET US BEGIN ROUND TWO, LITTLE MAN!
SHWOO

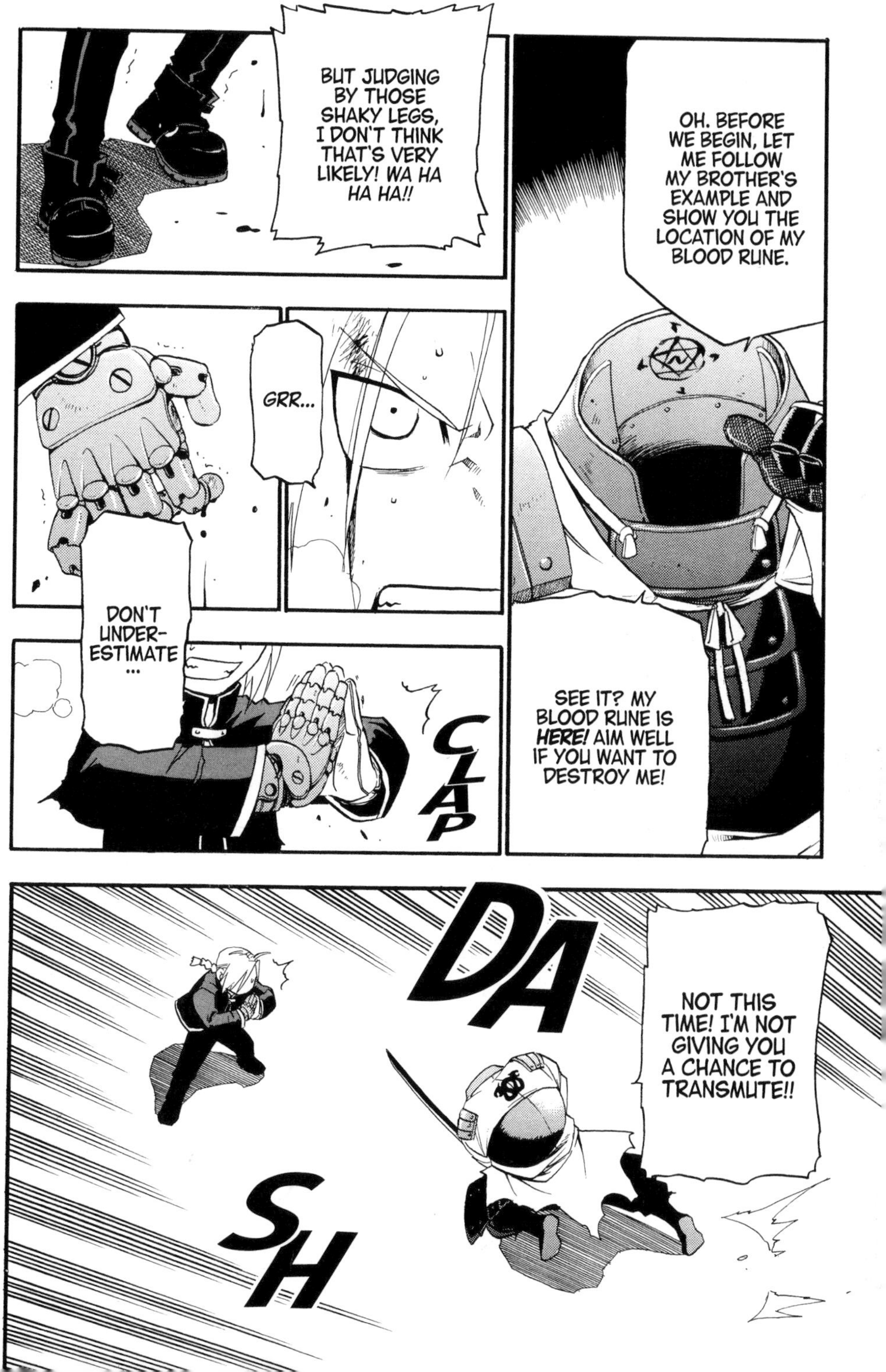

OH. BEFORE WE BEGIN, LET ME FOLLOW MY BROTHER'S EXAMPLE AND SHOW YOU THE LOCATION OF MY BLOOD RUNE.
SEE IT? MY BLOOD RUNE IS ***HERE!*** AIM WELL IF YOU WANT TO DESTROY ME!
BUT JUDGING BY THOSE SHAKY LEGS, I DON'T THINK THAT'S VERY LIKELY! WA HA HA HA!!
GRR...
DON'T UNDER-ESTIMATE ...
CLAP
NOT THIS TIME! I'M NOT GIVING YOU A CHANCE TO TRANSMUTE!!
DA
SH

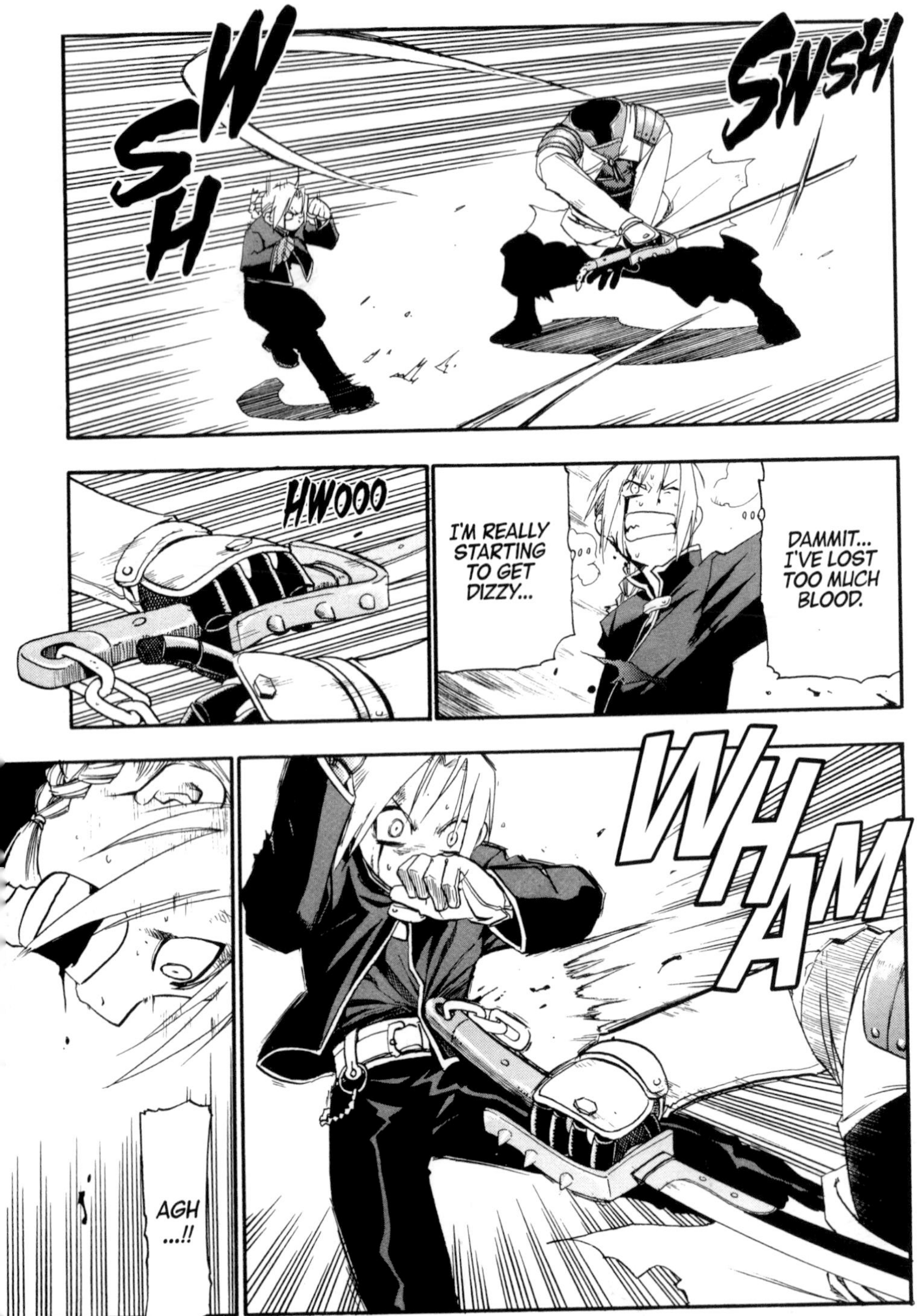
SWSH
SWSH
DAMMIT... I'VE LOST TOO MUCH BLOOD.
I'M REALLY STARTING TO GET DIZZY...
HWOOO
WHAM
AGH ...!!

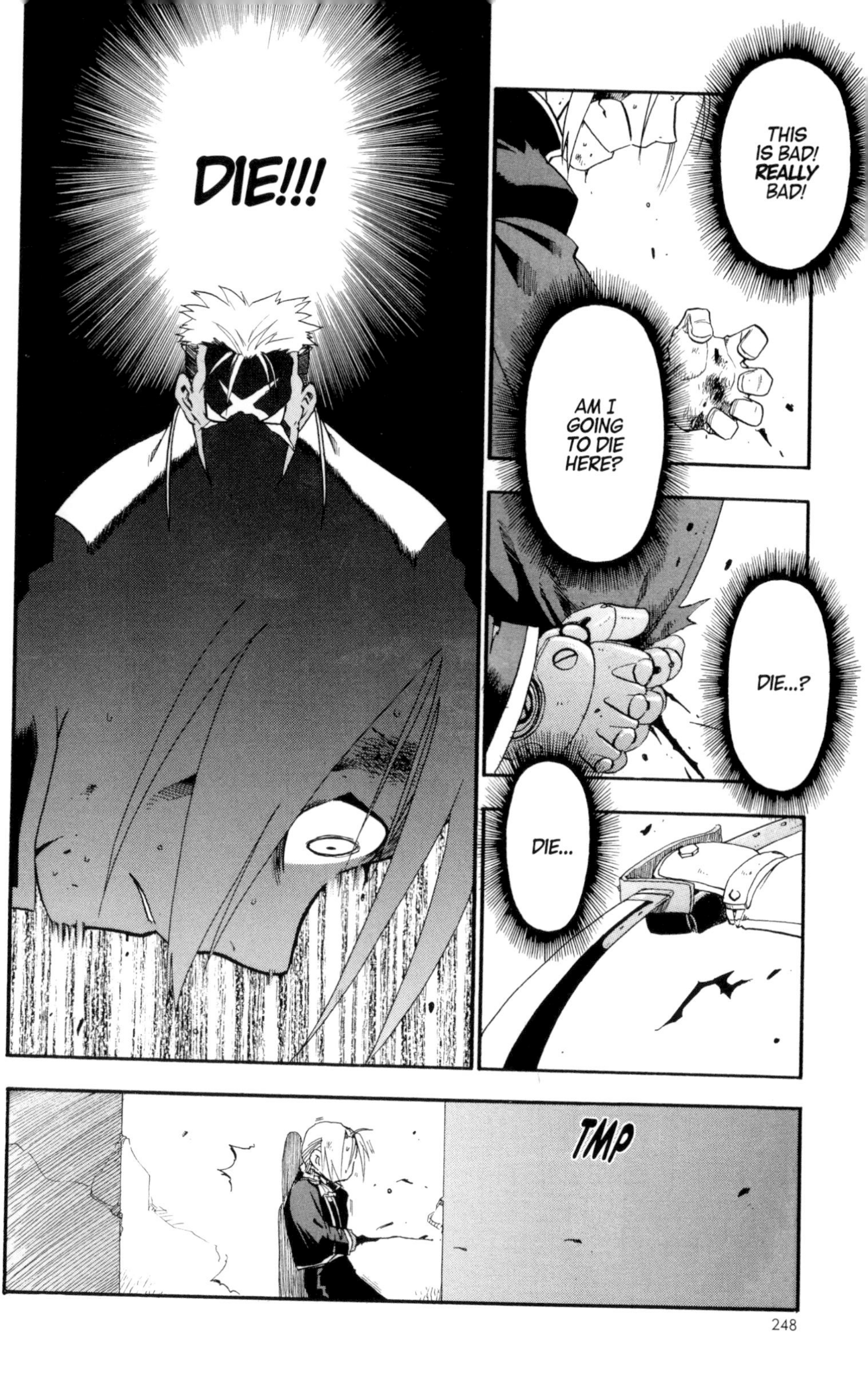
THIS IS BAD! REALLY BAD!
AM I GOING TO DIE HERE?
DIE...?
DIE...
DIE!!!
TMP

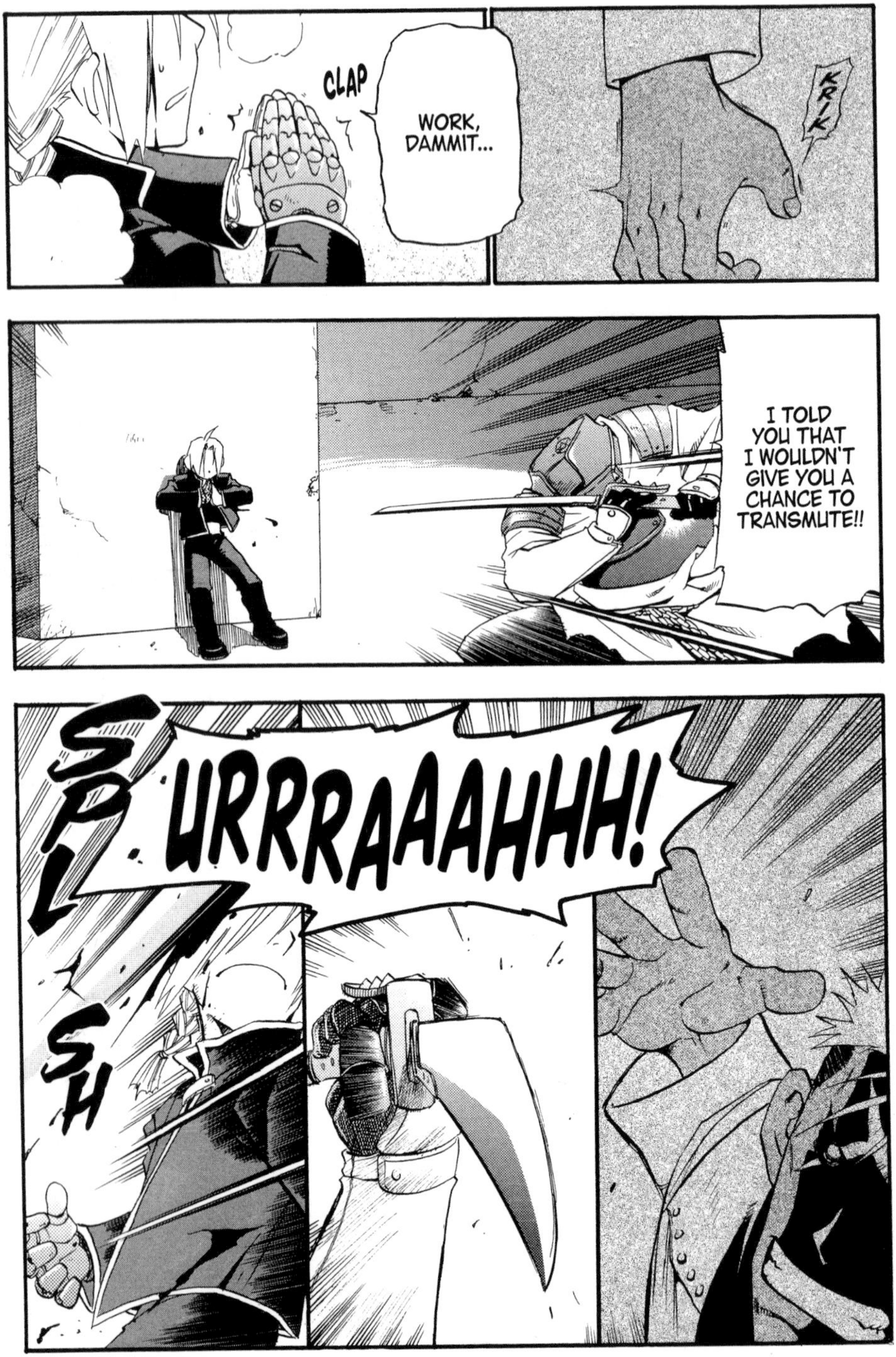
KRIK
CLAP
WORK, DAMMIT...
I TOLD YOU THAT I WOULDN'T GIVE YOU A CHANCE TO TRANSMUTE!!
URRRAAAHHH!
SPLSH

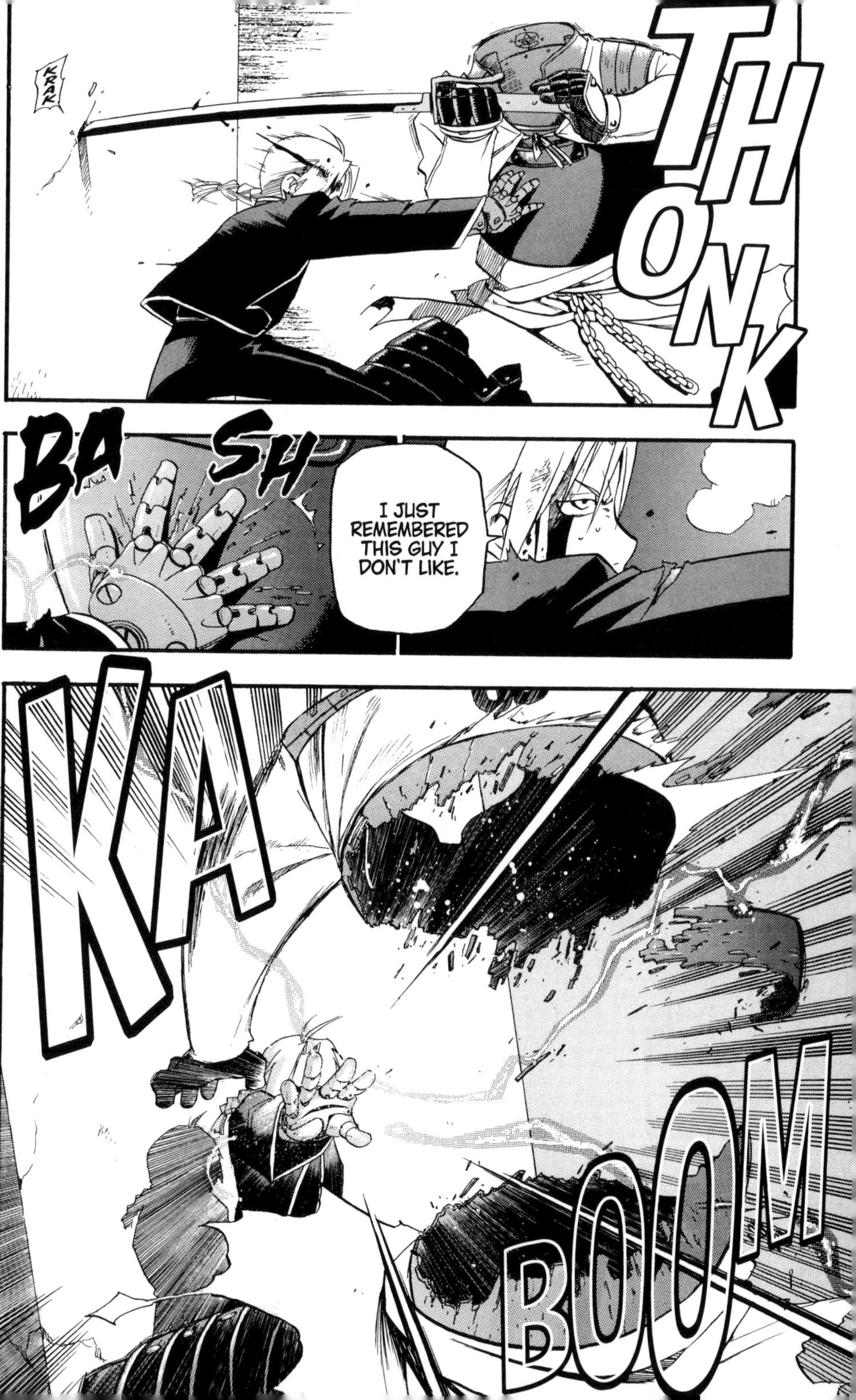
THONK
KRAK
I JUST REMEMBERED THIS GUY I DON'T LIKE.
BASH
KABOOM

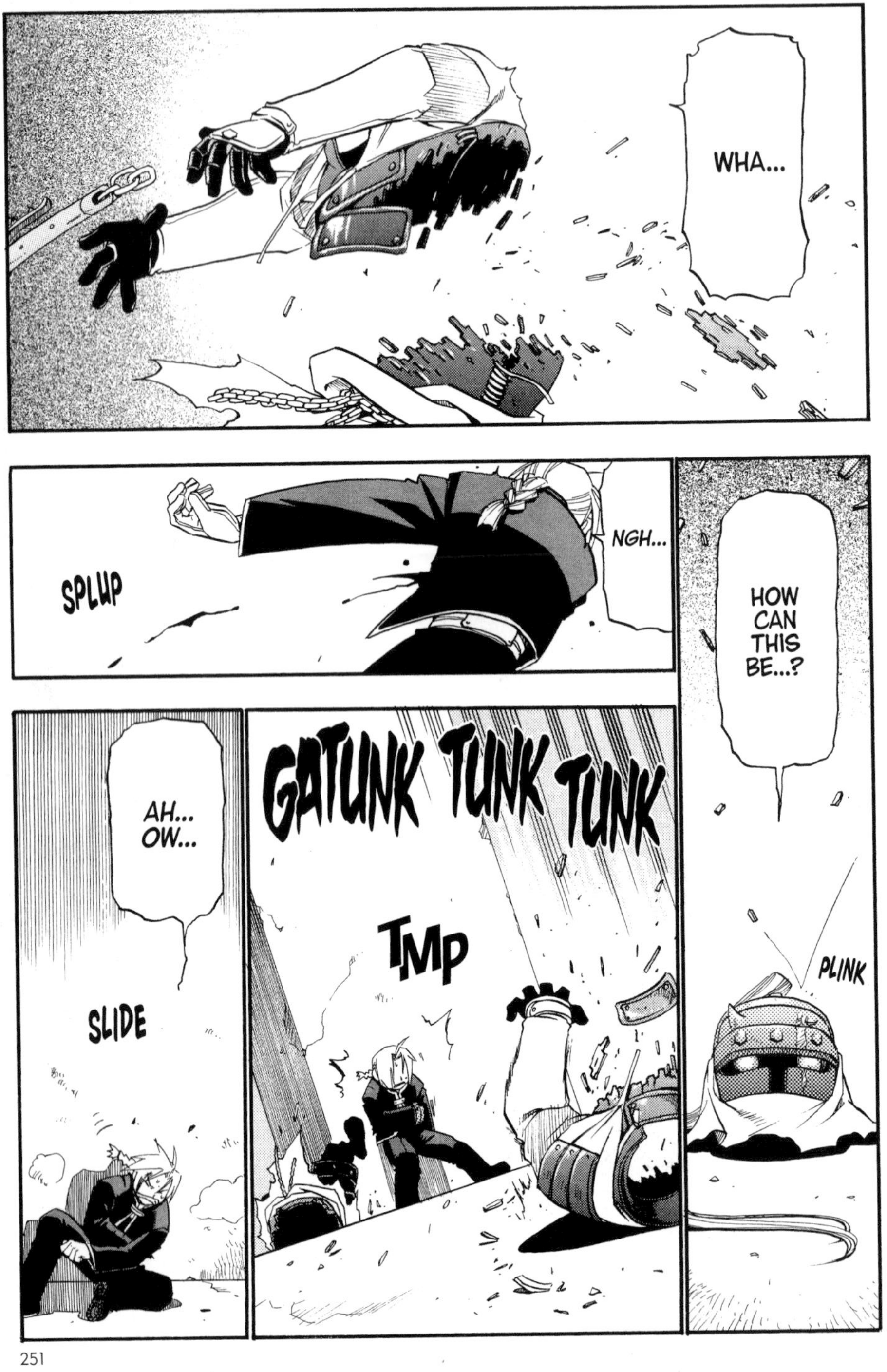
WHA...
HOW CAN THIS BE...?
PLINK
NGH...
SPLUP
GATUNK TUNK TUNK
TMP
AH... OW...
SLIDE

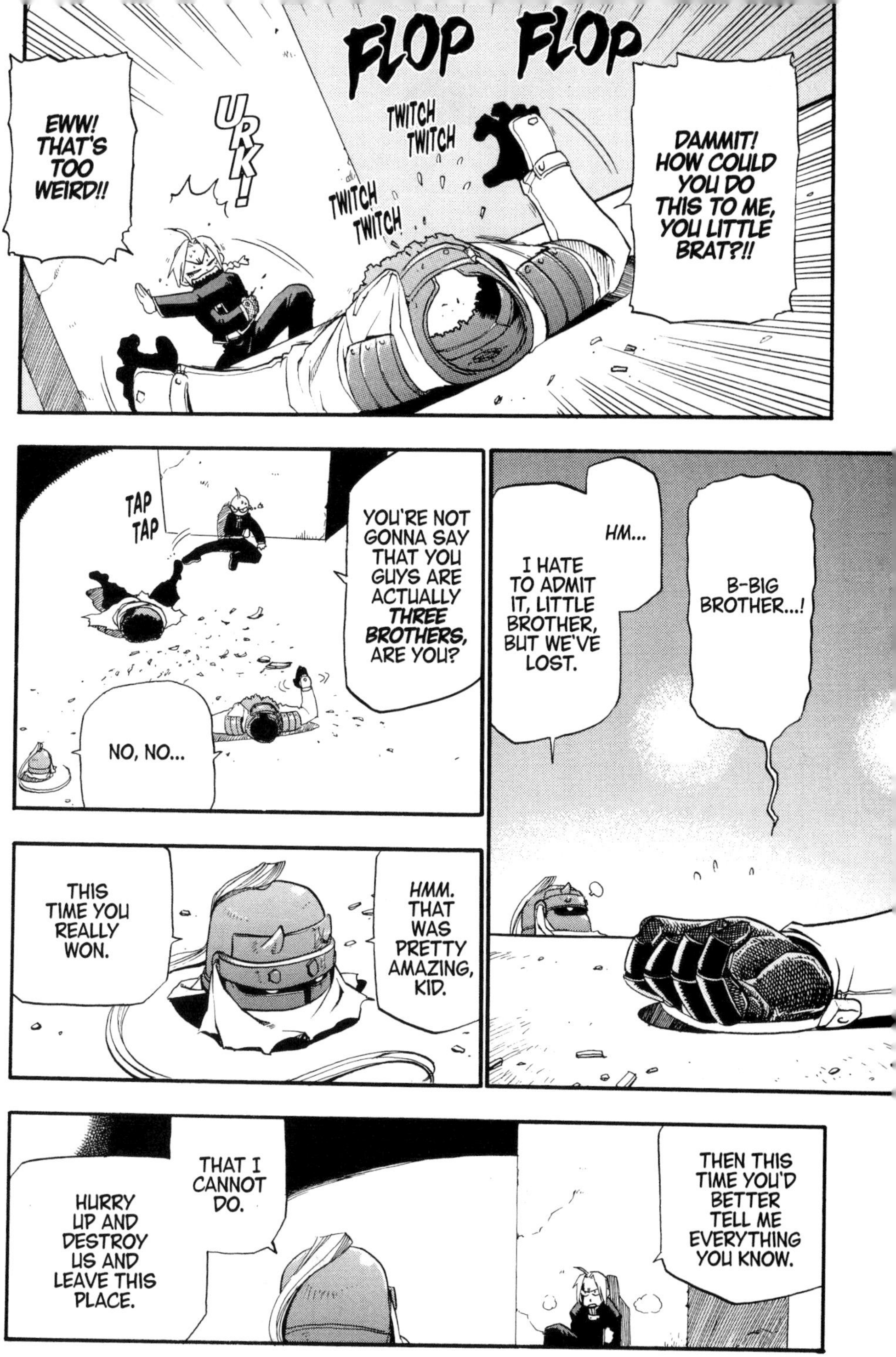
DAMMIT! HOW COULD YOU DO THIS TO ME, YOU LITTLE BRAT?!!
FLOP FLOP
TWITCH TWITCH
TWITCH TWITCH
URK!
EWW! THAT'S TOO WEIRD!!
B-BIG BROTHER...!
HM...
I HATE TO ADMIT IT, LITTLE BROTHER, BUT WE'VE LOST.
YOU'RE NOT GONNA SAY THAT YOU GUYS ARE ACTUALLY *THREE BROTHERS*, ARE YOU?
TAP TAP
NO, NO...
HMM. THAT WAS PRETTY AMAZING, KID.
THIS TIME YOU REALLY WON.
THEN THIS TIME YOU'D BETTER TELL ME EVERYTHING YOU KNOW.
THAT I CANNOT DO.
HURRY UP AND DESTROY US AND LEAVE THIS PLACE.

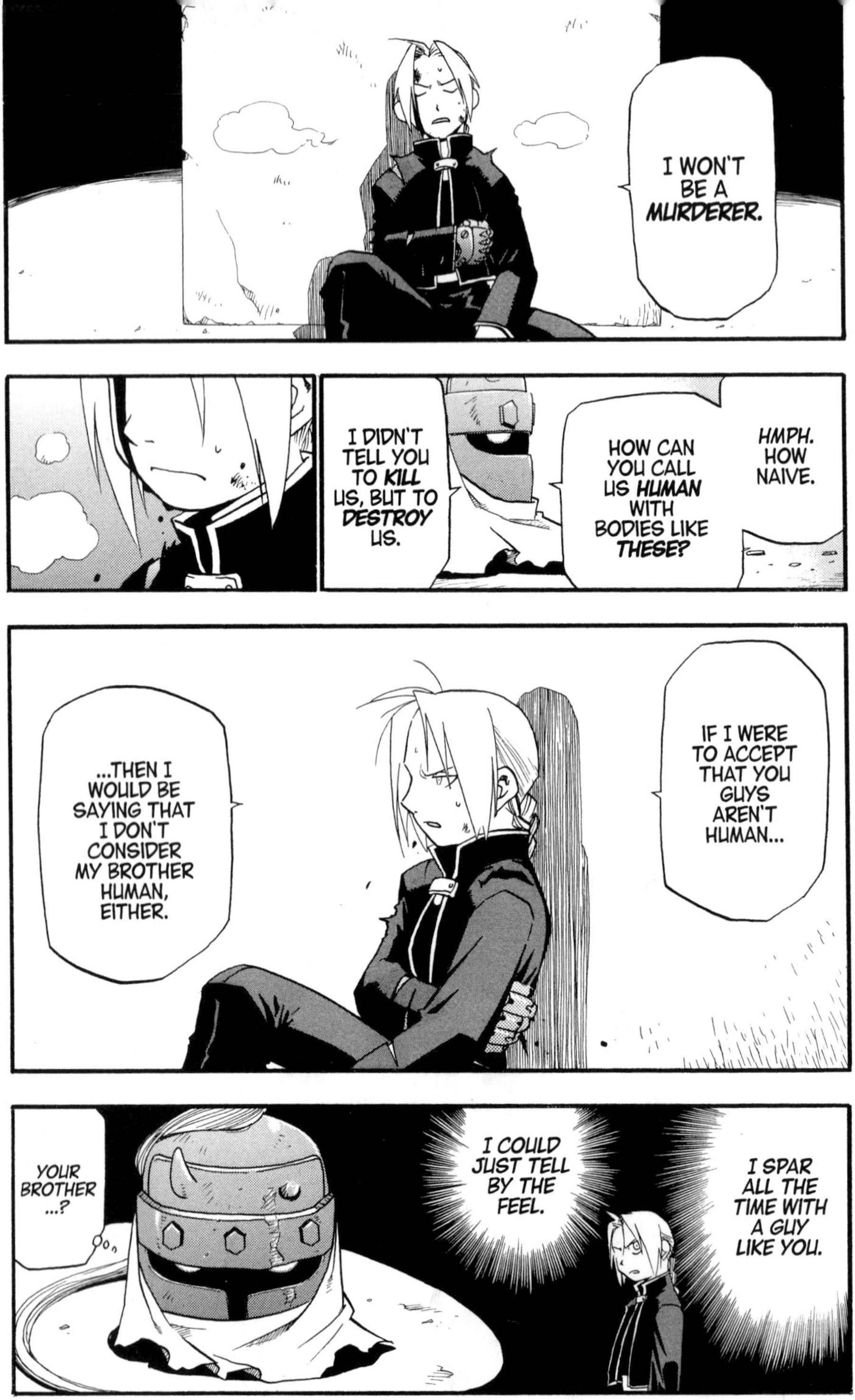
I WON'T BE A MURDERER.
HMPH. HOW NAIVE.
HOW CAN YOU CALL US HUMAN WITH BODIES LIKE THESE?
I DIDN'T TELL YOU TO KILL US, BUT TO DESTROY US.
IF I WERE TO ACCEPT THAT YOU GUYS AREN'T HUMAN...
...THEN I WOULD BE SAYING THAT I DON'T CONSIDER MY BROTHER HUMAN, EITHER.
I SPAR ALL THE TIME WITH A GUY LIKE YOU.
I COULD JUST TELL BY THE FEEL.
YOUR BROTHER ...?

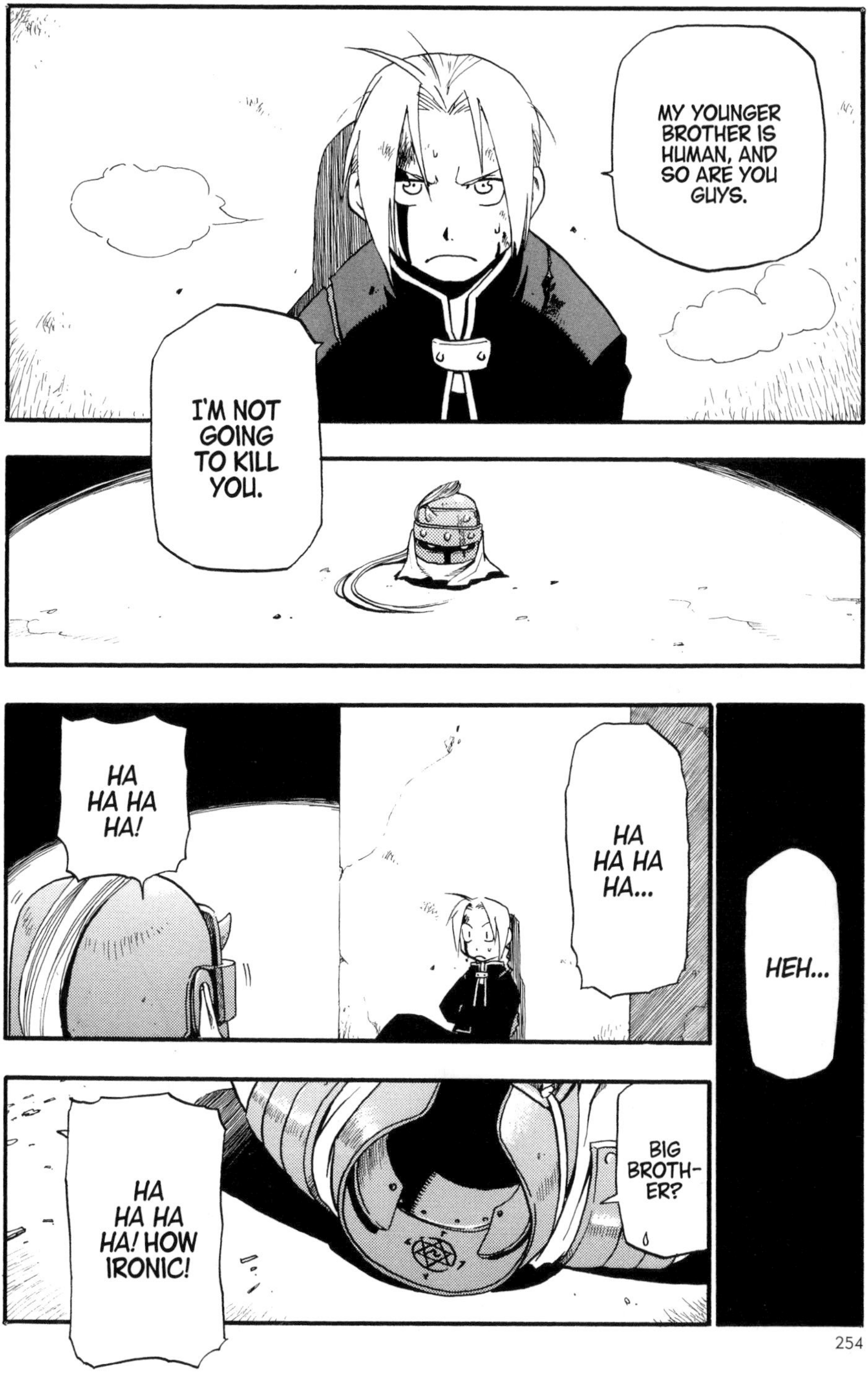
MY YOUNGER BROTHER IS HUMAN, AND SO ARE YOU GUYS.
I'M NOT GOING TO KILL YOU.
HEH...
HA HA HA HA...
HA HA HA HA!
BIG BROTH-ER?
HA HA HA HA! HOW IRONIC!

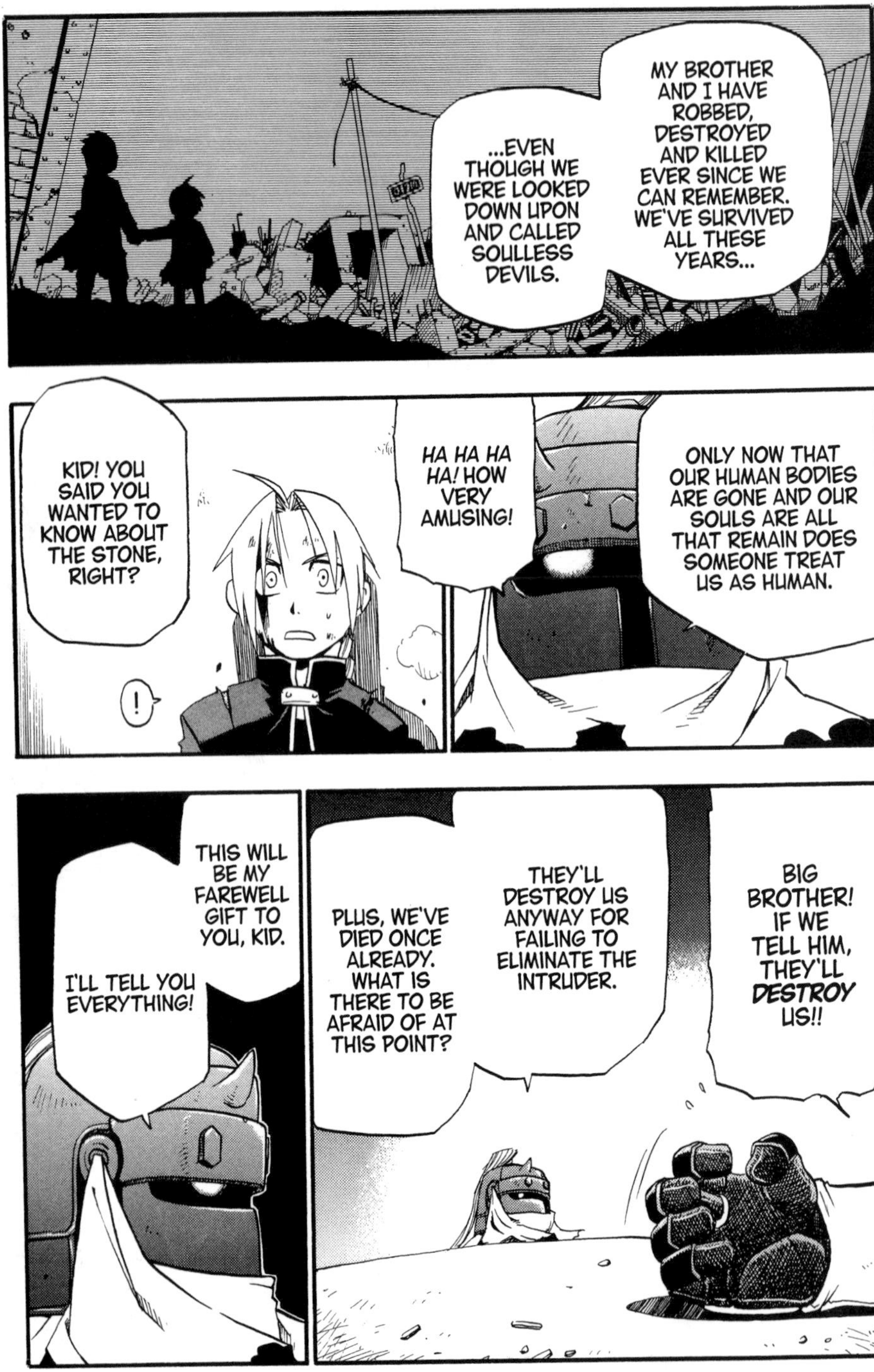
MY BROTHER AND I HAVE ROBBED, DESTROYED AND KILLED EVER SINCE WE CAN REMEMBER. WE'VE SURVIVED ALL THESE YEARS...
...EVEN THOUGH WE WERE LOOKED DOWN UPON AND CALLED SOULLESS DEVILS.
ONLY NOW THAT OUR HUMAN BODIES ARE GONE AND OUR SOULS ARE ALL THAT REMAIN DOES SOMEONE TREAT US AS HUMAN.
HA HA HA HA! HOW VERY AMUSING!
KID! YOU SAID YOU WANTED TO KNOW ABOUT THE STONE, RIGHT?
!
BIG BROTHER! IF WE TELL HIM, THEY'LL **DESTROY** US!!
THEY'LL DESTROY US ANYWAY FOR FAILING TO ELIMINATE THE INTRUDER.
PLUS, WE'VE DIED ONCE ALREADY. WHAT IS THERE TO BE AFRAID OF AT THIS POINT?
THIS WILL BE MY FAREWELL GIFT TO YOU, KID.
I'LL TELL YOU EVERYTHING!

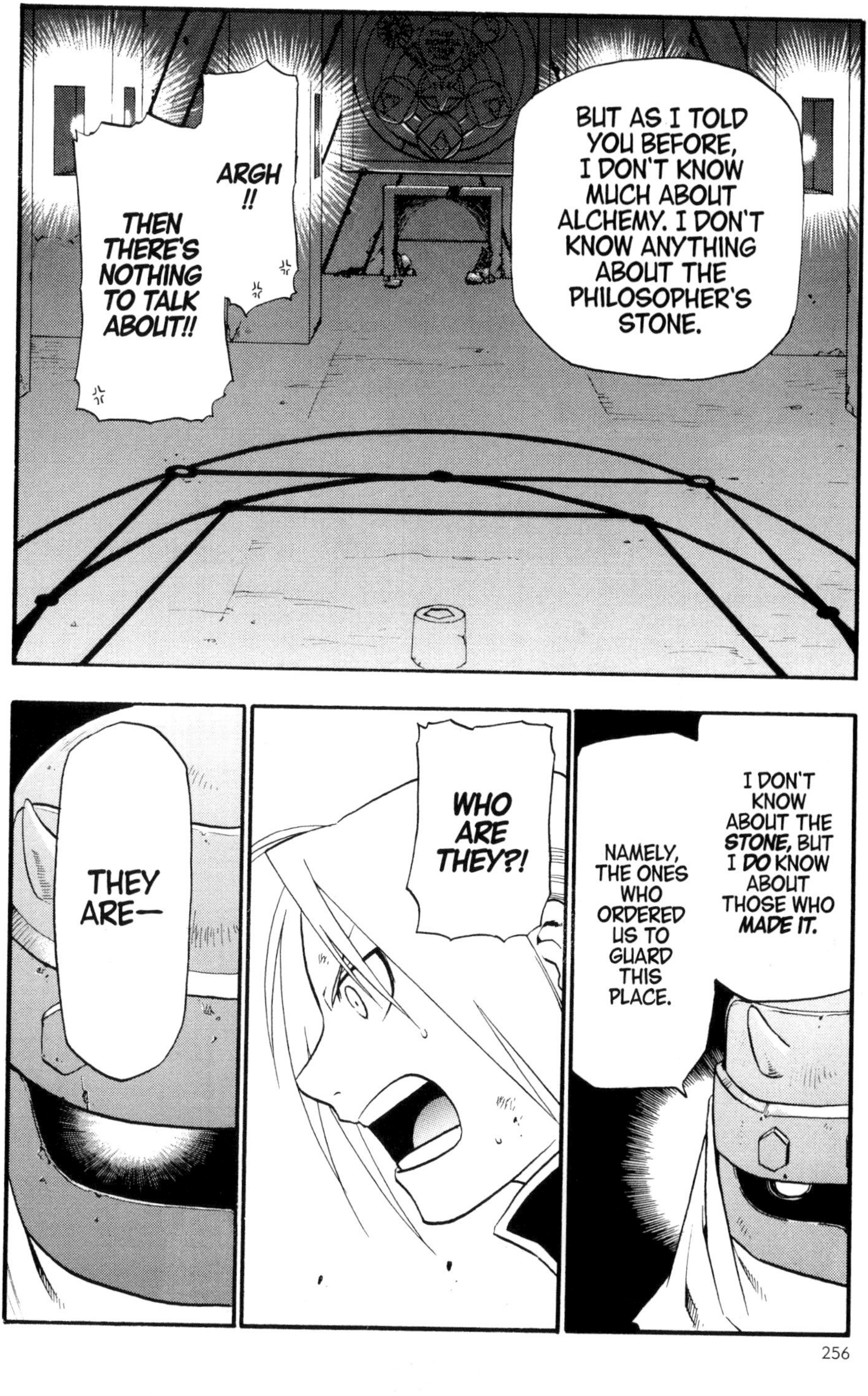
BUT AS I TOLD YOU BEFORE, I DON'T KNOW MUCH ABOUT ALCHEMY. I DON'T KNOW ANYTHING ABOUT THE PHILOSOPHER'S STONE.
ARGH!!
THEN THERE'S NOTHING TO TALK ABOUT!!
I DON'T KNOW ABOUT THE STONE, BUT I DO KNOW ABOUT THOSE WHO MADE IT.
NAMELY, THE ONES WHO ORDERED US TO GUARD THIS PLACE.
WHO ARE THEY?!
THEY ARE—

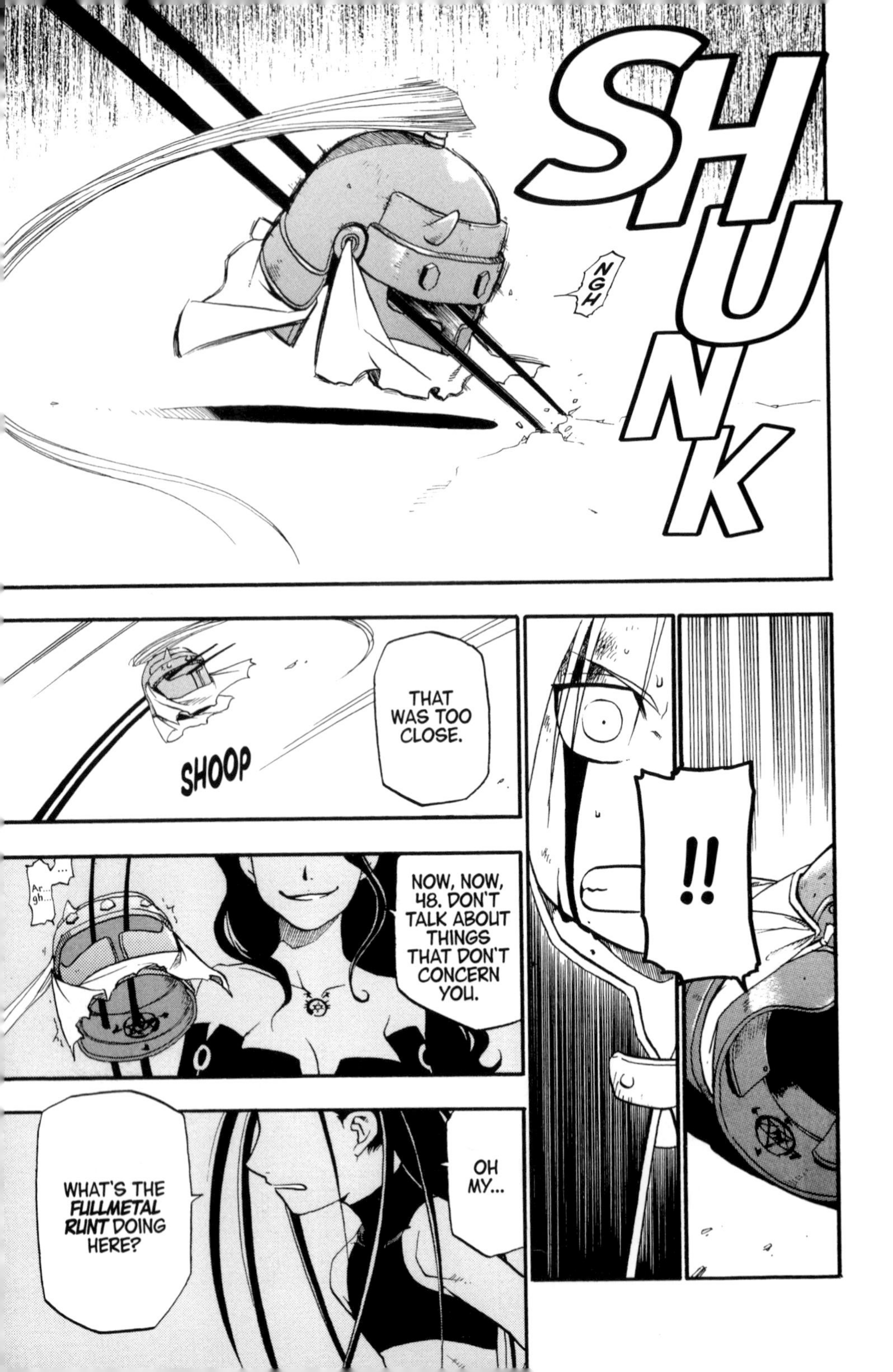
SHUNK
NGH
!!
THAT WAS TOO CLOSE.
SHOOP
NOW, NOW, 48. DON'T TALK ABOUT THINGS THAT DON'T CONCERN YOU.
... Ar... gh...
OH MY...
WHAT'S THE **FULLMETAL RUNT** DOING HERE?

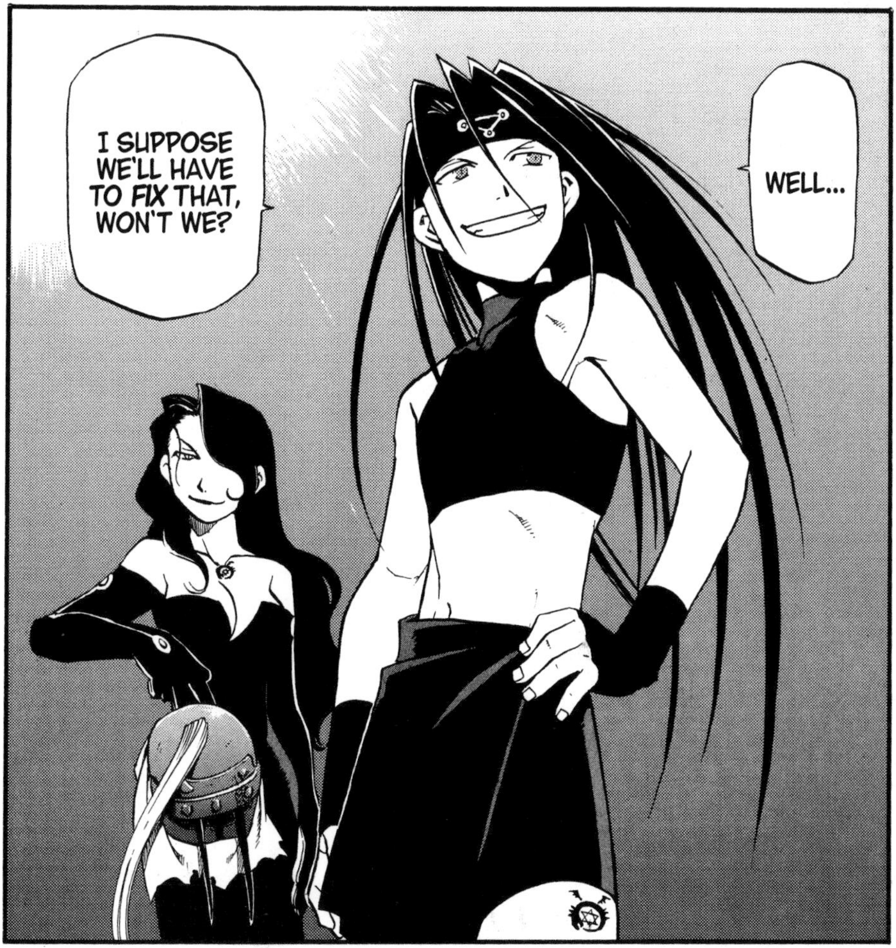
WELL...
I SUPPOSE WE'LL HAVE TO *FIX* THAT, WON'T WE?

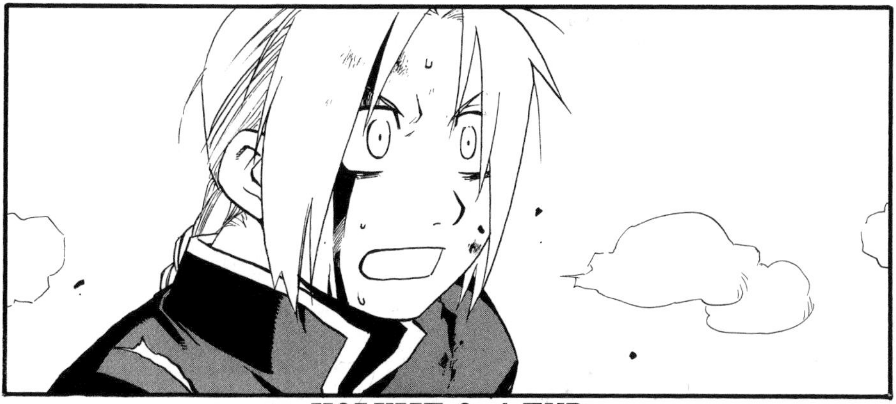

VOLUME 2 / END

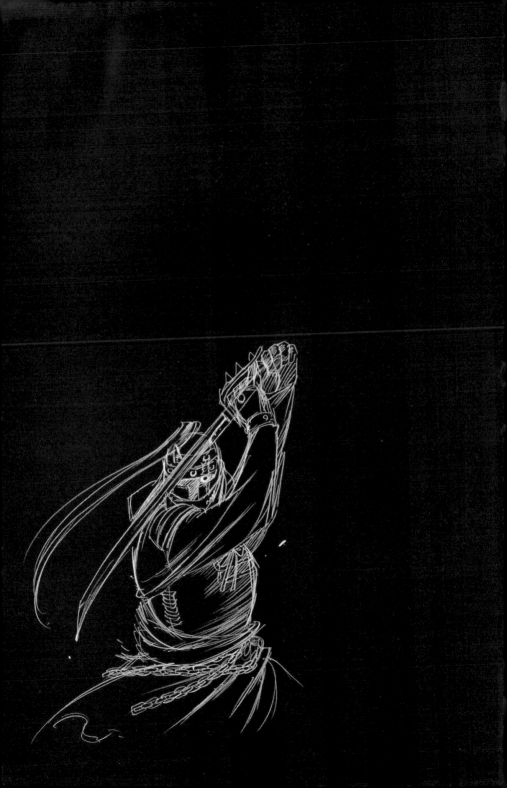

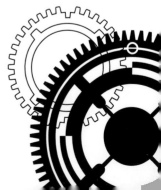

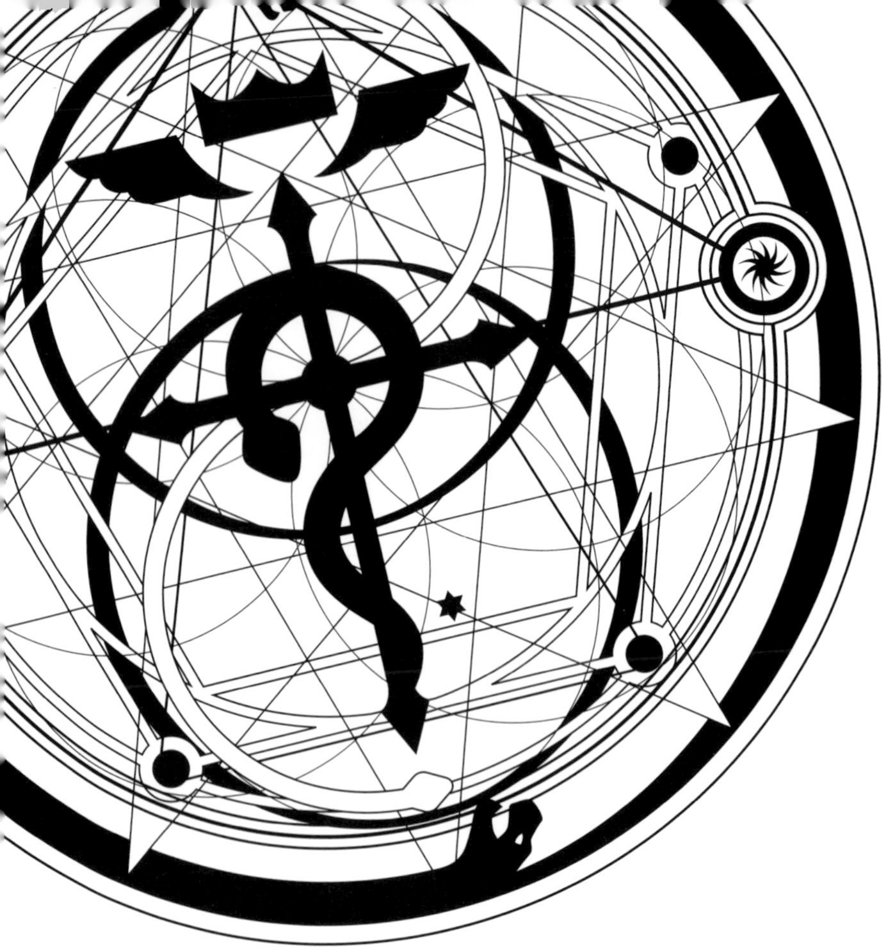

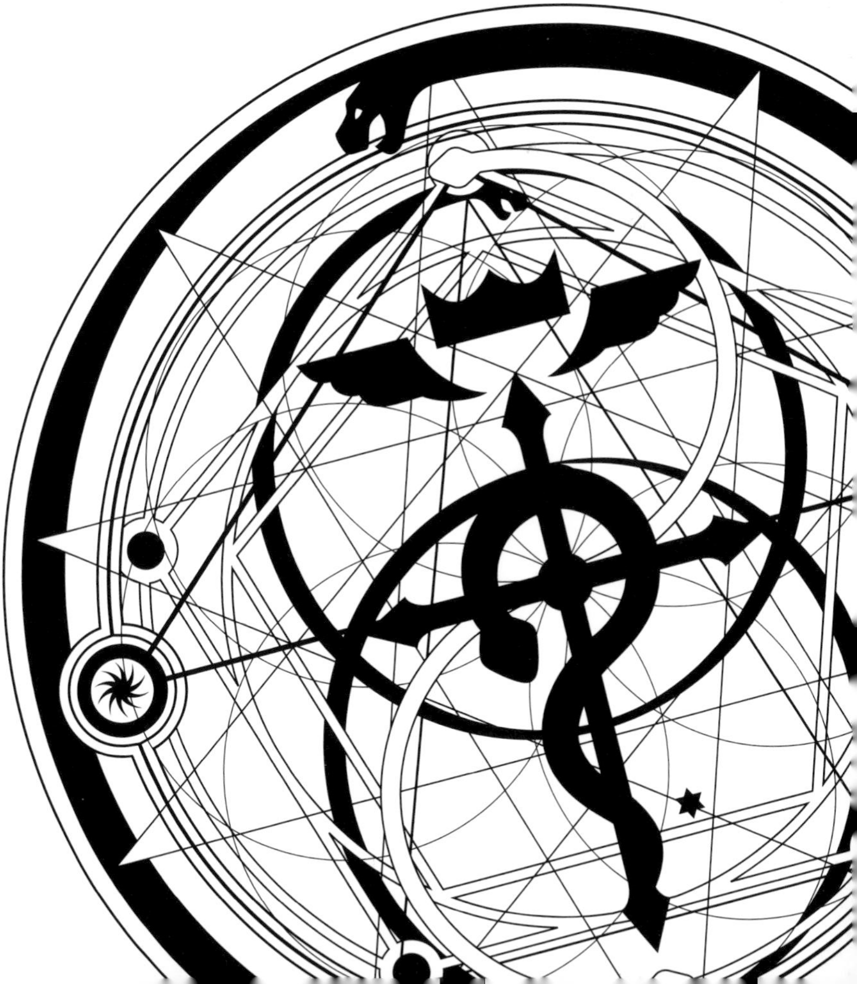

FULLMETAL ALCHEMIST

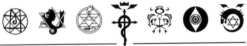

CONCEPT SKETCHES

02

Al draft 1
I wrote a note to myself about
"equivalent exchange."

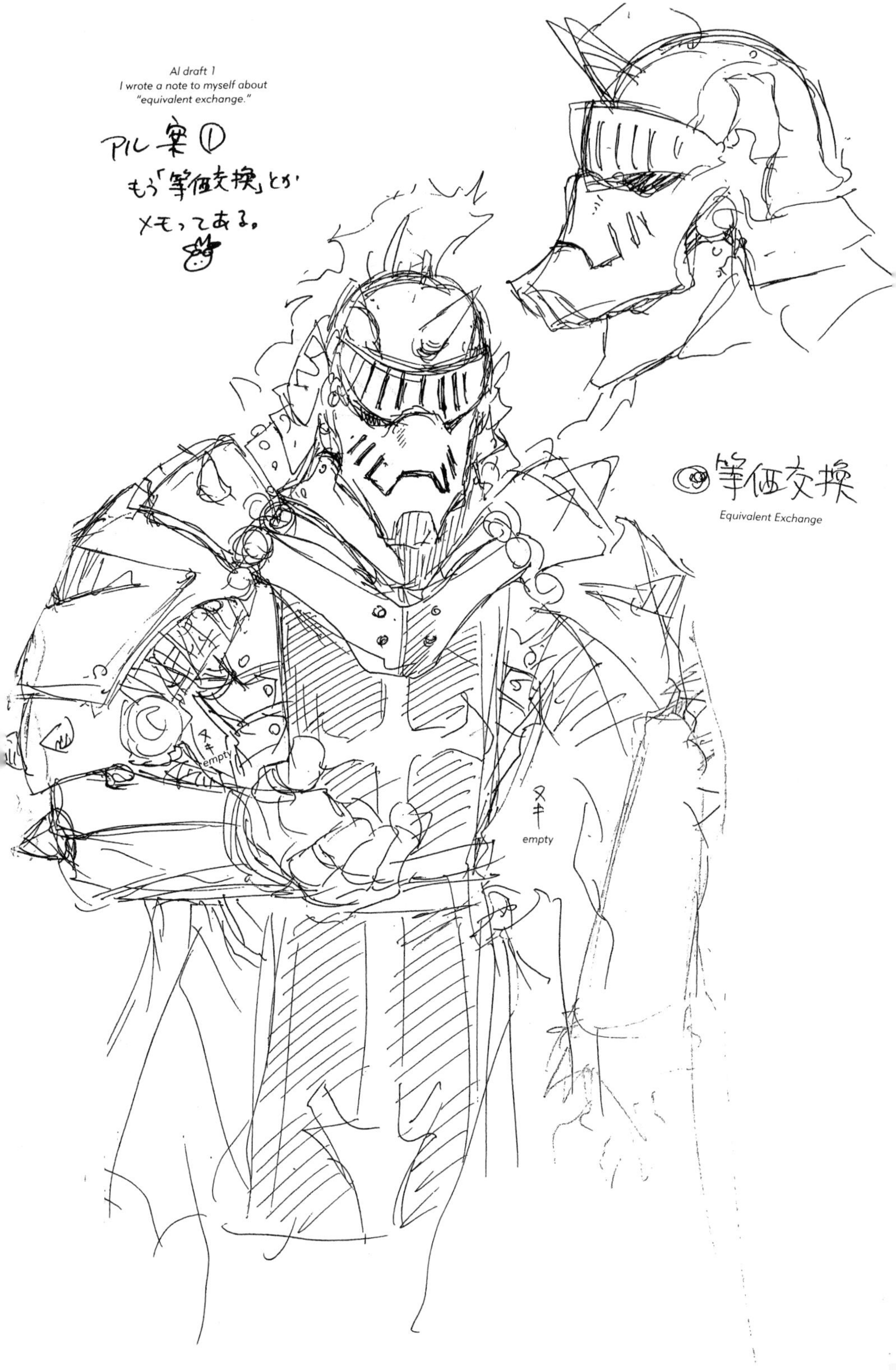
アル案①
もう「等価交換」とか
メモってある。
◎等価交換
メ
キ
メ
キ

Equivalent Exchange

empty

empty

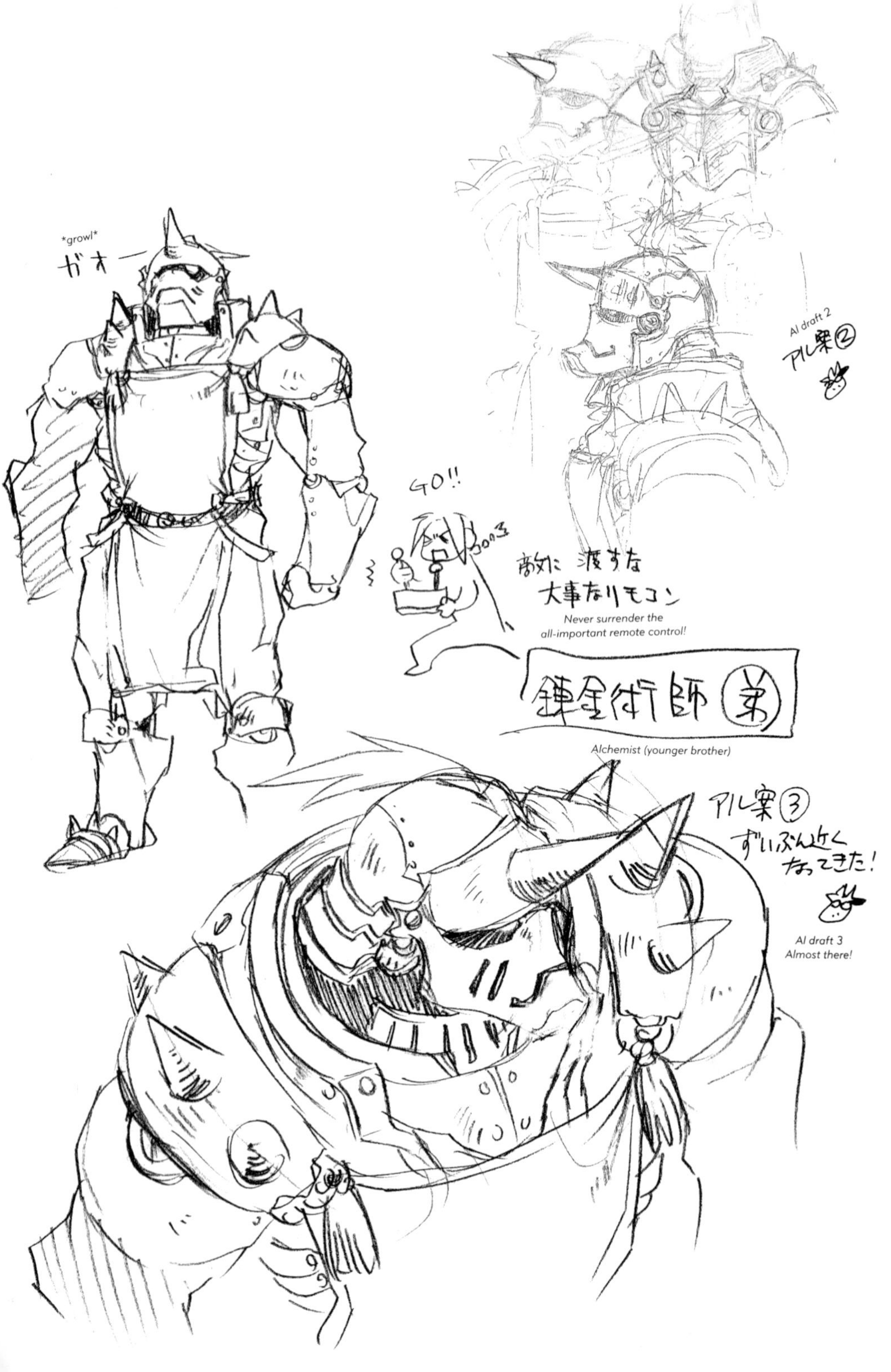
Al draft 2
アル案②
growl
ガオー
GO!!
敵に 渡すな
大事なリモコン
Never surrender the
all-important remote control!
錬金術師 (弟)
Alchemist (younger brother)
アル案③
ずいぶん近く
なってきた!
Al draft 3
Almost there!

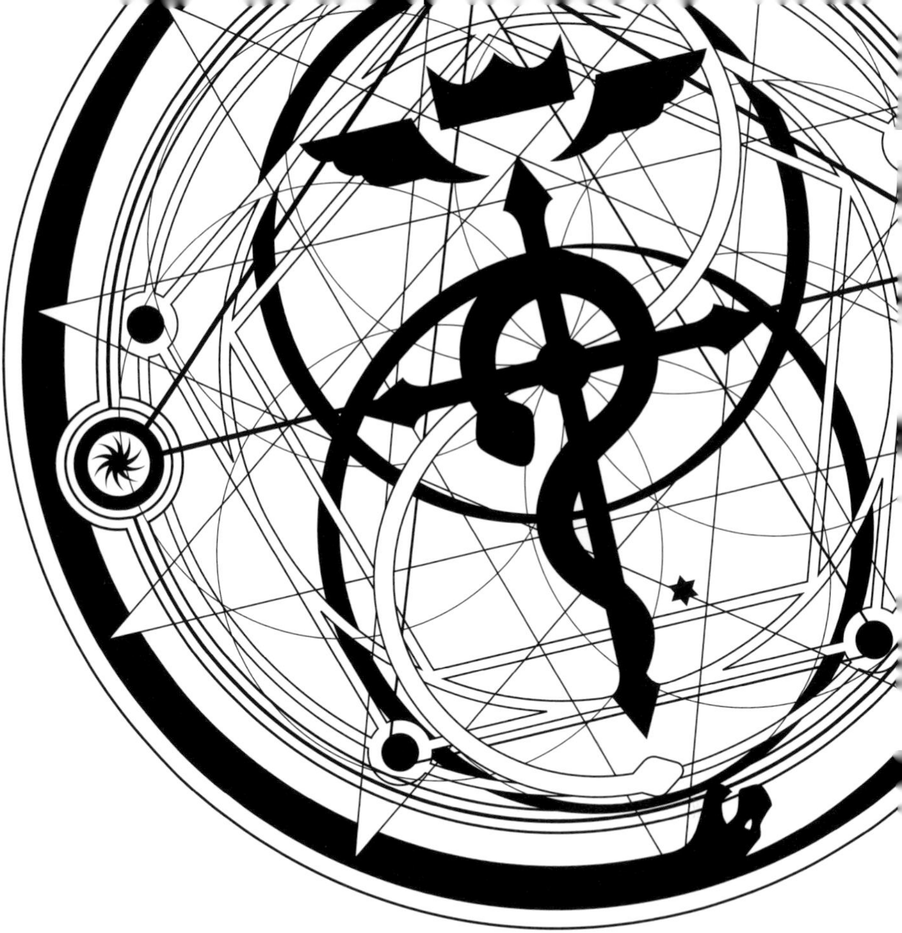

ABOUT THE AUTHOR

Born in Hokkaido, Japan, Hiromu Arakawa first attracted attention in 1999 with her award-winning manga *Stray Dog*. Her series *Fullmetal Alchemist* was serialized from 2001 to 2010 with a story that spanned 27 volumes and became an international critical and commercial success, receiving both the Shogakukan Manga Award and Seiun Award and selling over 70 million copies worldwide. *Fullmetal Alchemist* has been adapted into anime twice, first as *Fullmetal Alchemist* in 2003 and again as *Fullmetal Alchemist: Brotherhood* in 2009. The series has also inspired numerous films, video games and novels.

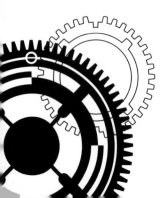

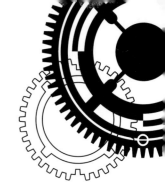

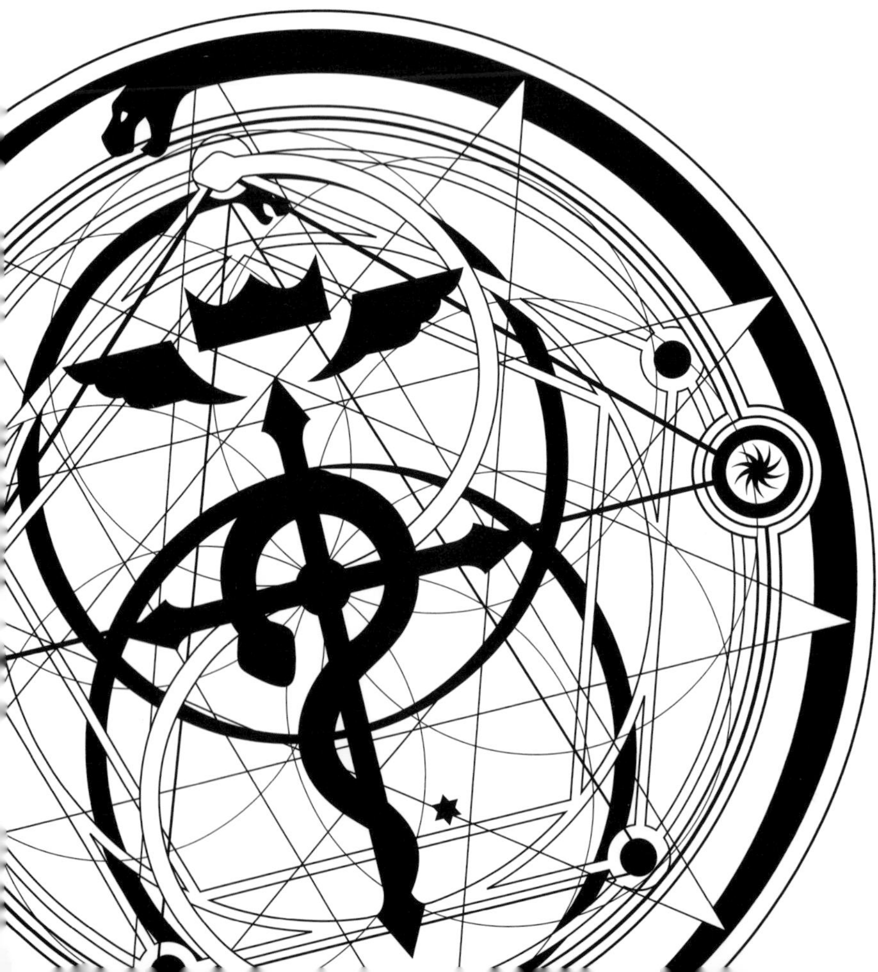

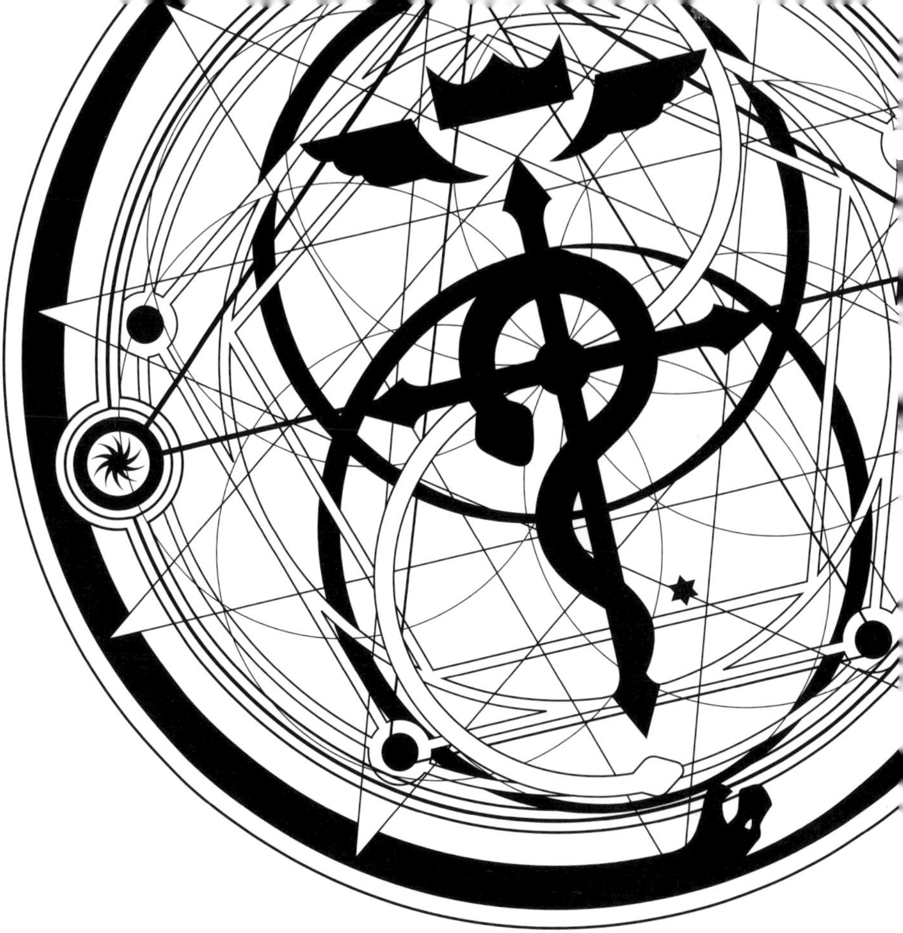

FULLMETAL EDITION

FULLMETAL ALCHEMIST

VOLUME 02

Story and Art by HIROMU ARAKAWA

Translation: AKIRA WATANABE
English Adaptation: JAKE FORBES, EGAN LOO
VIZ Media Edition Editor: JASON THOMPSON
Touch-Up Art & Lettering: STEVE DUTRO
Design: ADAM GRANO
Editor: HOPE DONOVAN

FULLMETAL ALCHEMIST KANZENBAN vol. 2
© 2011 Hiromu Arakawa/SQUARE ENIX CO., LTD.
First published in Japan in 2011 by SQUARE ENIX CO., LTD.
English translation rights arranged with SQUARE ENIX CO.,
LTD. and VIZ Media, LLC

Printed in Canada

Published by VIZ Media, LLC
P.O. Box 77010
San Francisco, CA 94107

10 9 8 7 6 5 4 3 2 1
First printing, August 2018

viz.com

This is the last page.

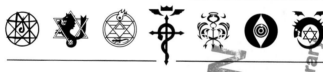

Fullmetal Alchemist reads right to left.

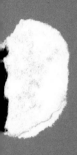